Arms Control & Disarmament

The War/Peace Bibliography Series

RICHARD DEAN BURNS, EDITOR

This Series has been developed in cooperation with the Center for the Study of Armament and Disarmament, California State University, Los Angeles.

Arms Control and Disarmament:

A Bibliography

Richard Dean Burns

ABC-Clio, Inc.

Santa Barbara, California

Oxford, England

Library of Congress Cataloging in Publication Data

Burns, Richard Dean.
    Arms control and disarmament.

    (The War/peace bibliography series; no. 6)
    Includes index.
    1. Atomic weapons and disarmament—Bibliography.
2. Disarmament—Bibliography. 3. Arms control—
Bibliography. I. Title.
Z6464.D6B87 [JX1974.7] 016.327′174 77-24931
ISBN 0-87436-245-8

American Bibliographical Center—Clio Press
2040 Alameda Padre Serra
Santa Barbara, California 93103

European Bibliographical Center—Clio Press
Woodside House, Hinksey Hill
Oxford OX1 5BE, England

Manufactured in the United States of America.

About the War/Peace Bibliography Series

WITH THIS BIBLIOGRAPHICAL series, the Center for the Study of Armament and Disarmament, California State University, Los Angeles, seeks to promote a wider understanding of martial violence and the alternatives to its employment. The Center, which was formed by concerned faculty and students in 1962–1963, has as its primary objective the stimulation of intelligent discussion of war/peace issues. More precisely, the Center has undertaken two essential functions: (1) to collect and catalogue materials bearing on war/peace issues; and (2) to aid faculty, students, and the public in their individual and collective probing of the historical, political, economic, philosophical, technical, and psychological facets of these fundamental problems.

This bibliographical series is, obviously, one tool with which we may more effectively approach our task. Each issue in this series is intended to provide a comprehensive "working," rather than definitive, bibliography on a relatively narrow theme within the spectrum of war/peace studies. While we hope this series will prove to be a useful tool, we also solicit your comments regarding its format, contents, and topics.

RICHARD DEAN BURNS
SERIES EDITOR

Contents

PART ONE: VIEWS, OVERVIEWS, & THEORY

CHAPTER ONE

CHAPTER TWO

CHAPTER THREE

Historical Surveys & Contemporary Views   43

CHAPTER FOUR

League of Nations & United Nations   69

CHAPTER FIVE

Special Issues:
Inspection, Verification & Supervision   89

CHAPTER SIX

Special Issues: Economic Consequences
of Disarmament, Negotiations, Science & Technology,
Bureaucratic Politics & the Military-Industrial Complex,
& Legal & Psychological Dimensions 109

PART TWO: ACCORDS, PROPOSALS & TREATIES

CHAPTER SEVEN

Limitation of Weapons & Personnel 139

x   *Contents*

CHAPTER TEN

Regulating & Outlawing Weapons & War 253

CHAPTER ELEVEN

Controlling Arms Manufacture & Traffic 295

CHAPTER TWELVE

CHAPTER THIRTEEN

Acknowledgments

OVER THE YEARS many, many people have contributed their time and energy to the development of the bibliographical files of the Center for the Study of Armament and Disarmament—the basic source from which this volume was drawn. I wish to thank these students, colleagues, and friends for their support of the Center and its projects, including the compilation of this bibliography. Special acknowledgment must go to Thomas A. Meeker, who assisted in the formative stages, and to Arthur Gillingham, who hunted down many an errant citation. Josie Juarez and Marge Gilbert, who typed the final manuscript, deserve special recognition, for without their efforts this project could not have been completed. Paulette Wamego, who copy edited the manuscript for the publisher, stoutly maintained standards of accuracy and detail for which I am most grateful. And finally I wish to acknowledge my gratitude to my wife, Frances R. Burns, for moral support that made it possible for me to continue with a most trying task and for the final helping hand in preparing the index.

I am aware, of course, that as the compiler I alone am responsible for the selection of materials and organization of this volume, and for those errors that have inevitably crept into it.

RICHARD DEAN BURNS

Introduction

LATE IN THE autumn of 1969, the United Nations General Assembly solemnly proclaimed the 1970s to be the "Decade of Disarmament." Its resolution called upon the governments of the world "to make every effort to achieve a constructive solution of the problem of general and complete disarmament." The signing of the Strategic Arms Limitation Treaties (SALT) in Moscow on May 26, 1972, by President Nixon and Secretary General Brezhnev gave many people hope that the United Nations dream might be possible.

Yet SALT, and the numerous other arms control measures negotiated since 1946, have not been universally approved. The late 1950s and early 1960s witnessed a heated debate between people who favored negotiating controls on weapons and those who flatly rejected that idea. American critics challenged efforts to ban nuclear tests and to limit armaments as dangerous and illusory on the basis that Communists agreed to those measures only as a means of weakening the West. Those Americans who defended the post-1946 arms control efforts argued that these charges were extreme and unreasonable because this nation's powerful strategic deterrence system would be affected only minimally by these measures and because the agreements represented a necessary, cautious, step-by-step process designed to achieve a stable, less menacing world.

By the early 1970s, this debate shifted dramatically. Where the debate had pitted arms controllers and disarmers against those who opposed any reduction of our military efforts, differences now appeared *between arms controllers and disarmers*. While one can overemphasize this latest rift, it is nevertheless significant and fundamental. The arms controllers, to put it simply, believe that the most realistic path to a more peaceful world lies in the use of limited, step-by-step measures to enhance the current deterrence system. Consequently, they tend to give higher priority to seeking means which will stabilize the strategic military balance than to seeking means for arms reductions.

The disarmers wish to reduce the importance of the deterrence system itself. They argue that partial arms control measures, at best, provide only short-term, piecemeal benefits and ignore the unprecedented peril posed by the vast numbers of weapons of mass destruction. Even though the disarmers have supported partial measures, they believe that such efforts are largely "cosmetic" in effect and conceal the lack of essential progress (or even attention) to the main goal—international disarmament.

This controversy may baffle some observers who will, understandably, wonder what the terms "arms control" and "disarmament" mean.

As a descriptive term, "disarmament" has presented semantic problems since coming into vogue during the 19th century and, particularly, since its widespread use in the decades immediately after World War I. While purists might employ "disarmament" in the literal sense—the total elimination of armaments— most diplomats and writers did not. "Disarmament does not mean the disbanding of the whole nor even the greater part of the armed forces of the world," Philip J. Noel-Baker explained in 1926. "It means, rather, the reduction, the modest but, we hope, not negligible reduction, of those forces, and their limitation by a general international treaty. . . ." He goes on, in this same book, entitled *Disarmament*, to discuss the outlawing of chemical-biological weapons, the prohibition of aerial bombardment of cities, and the regulation of the international sales of arms and munitions. The term has been similarly used in the post–World War II era by some commentators and agencies. The United Nations and its subsidiary organizations, according to one of its officials, have been using "disarmament" as "a generic term covering all measures relating to the field—from small steps to reduce tensions or build confidence, through regulation of armaments or arms control, up to general and complete disarmament."

The post–World War II academic specialists who linked the technology of nuclear weaponry to the politics of the Cold War chose, in the early 1950s, to substitute "arms control" for "disarmament." The latter term not only lacked precision of definition, as these professionals saw it, but it tended to carry a tone of utopianism. Moreover, these new experts believed that "arms control" better described the new military-diplomatic relationship. Thomas C. Schelling and Morton H. Halperin in their classic *Strategy and Arms Control* (1961) defined "arms control" as a concept which recognized that "our military relation with potential enemies is not one of pure conflict and opposition, but involves strong elements of mutual interest in the avoidance of a war that neither side wants, in minimizing the costs and risks of the arms competition, and in curtailing the scope and violence of war in the event it occurs."

While both "disarmament" and "arms control" have become umbrella terms encompassing a wide variety of techniques or measures, the latter term is by far the more abstract. The arms controllers have preferred an "open definition" which provides operational flexibility. Yet the very inclusiveness of the open definition sacrifices precision and endangers its generic *raison d'être*—arms control verges on being indistinguishable, for example, from "conflict management."

In developing this bibliography I have accepted generally a broad definition of arms control and disarmament. Additionally, I have sought to apply this definition to historical examples of arms control and disarmament. This historical review suggests that one may distinguish at least six general categories of arms control and disarmament techniques. These arbitrary classifications, which form the structural design of Part Two, are:

1. Limitation and reduction of weapons and personnel—such as Rome's limiting Carthage's forces in the Treaty of Zama (201 B.C.), Napoleon's restrictions on the Prussian army (1808), the naval limitation treaties of the 1920s and 1930s, and the SALT treaties (1972);

2. Demilitarization, denuclearization and neutralization—such as the Athenian-Persia

pact (c. 448 B.C.), excluding warships from the Aegean Sea, the Rush-Bagot Agreement (1817), excluding warships from Great Lakes, the Austrian State Treaty (1955), declaring Austria a permanent neutral, and the Latin America Denuclearization Treaty (1967);

3. Regulating and outlawing weapons and war—such as the Rome-Carthage treaty (201 B.C.), prohibiting Carthage from possessing war elephants, the Lateran Council (1139), outlawing use of crossbows against fellow Christians, the Hague treaties (1899, 1907), restricting use of poison gas and bombing, the submarine protocols of the 1930s, and the Geneva Protocol (1925) and Bacteriological Weapons Convention (1972), prohibiting chemical-bacteriological (CB) warfare;

4. Controlling arms manufacture and traffic—such as the Israel-Philistine arrangement (1100 B.C.), which prevented Israel's possession of iron-tipped spears and swords, the China arms embargo (1919), restricting arms trade with warring factions, the League efforts at regulating international arms traffic (1919, 1925), the U.N. embargo of arms to South Africa (1963), and the Nonproliferation Treaty (1968);

5. Rules of war — such as the Peace and Truce of God (989–1450), which defined "noncombatants" and prohibited combat on certain days, the Declaration of St. Petersburg (1868), prohibiting "dum-dum" bullets and defining the basis of laws of war, the Hague treaties (1899, 1907), formally establishing rules of combat, and the Roerich Pact (1935) and the Hague Convention (1954), protecting cultural treasures;

6. Stabilizing the international environment—such as the numerous treaties regarding the Turkish Straits (1805–1936), stabilizing the eastern Mediterranean, the Nuclear Test Ban Treaty (1963), reducing radiation in the environment, the "hot line" pacts (1963, 1971), improving communication between U.S. and U.S.S.R. to reduce the chance of accidental war, and the Weather Modification Proposal (1972–), protecting the environment.

Obviously, these categories are not exclusive, for the outlawing of weapons has the same effect as limiting them and a treaty which prohibits the placing of weapons of mass destruction in outer space (1967) also is an example of demilitarization of a geographical area. Some treaties also incorporate several different arms control techniques within a single document: the Treaty of Versailles (1919), for example, limited German weapons and military personnel, outlawed possession of specific weapons, and demilitarized certain areas. Despite these qualifications, the value of such categories is that they help provide a clearer perspective of how arms control devices have been developed.

The historical methods of achieving arms control and disarmament may be divided into three broad categories, each of which is subdivided into two additional categories. There are, then, six general methods by which arms control and disarmament objectives may be achieved:

Retributive Measures

Extermination is an ancient and drastic means of ensuring no future warlike response from one's opponent and is most clearly dramatized by Rome's destruction of Carthage in 150 B.C.

Imposition usually results when the victors force arms limitation measures on their vanquished foes; two examples are the terms imposed upon Carthage (201 B.C.) and upon Germany at Versailles (1919).

Unilateral Measures

Unilateral neglect (often confused with the succeeding method) refers to a nation's failure to provide for an adequate defense; examples include the U.S.'s "unilateral" disarmament after the Civil War (1866) and Britain and the U.S.'s self-imposed reduction after World War I.

Unilateral decision is a consciously decided policy of self-imposed military restrictions or limitations. The Peace and Truce of God and the outlawing of the crossbow during the Middle Ages are two examples; other examples include Japan's post–World War II constitution (Art. 9) and Austria's treaty (1955), both restricting armaments to "defensive" purposes.

Reciprocal Measures

Bilateral negotiation is a traditional means by which two nations seek mutually acceptable solutions to problems created by armaments. The Anglo-French Naval Pact (1787), the Rush-Bagot Agreement (1817), the Anglo-German Naval Agreement (1935), and the SALT treaties represent but a few such settlements.

Multilateral negotiation is the most common twentieth century approach, since military-political problems are at least regional, if not global, and thus involve the vital interests of several states; also the range of weapons and their destructive capacities tend to support a multinational approach. The Hague treaties (1899, 1907), the Washington Naval Treaty (1922), the test ban accord (1963), and the Nonproliferation Treaty (1968) are demonstrative of this method.

During the decades following both world wars the major powers almost constantly engaged in some form of negotiations over the problems of weaponry. In many instances, discussions have been multilateral undertakings under the auspices of the League of Nations and, later, the United Nations. (Chapter 4 contains citations to general accounts and documentary collections relating to these efforts.)

There are, of course, many other dimensions and issues to arms control and disarmament. Of these various issues, two questions have been frequently asked: first, what factors have prompted agreements on arms control and disarmament? and, second, what risks and dangers, hopes and expectations do past agreements suggest for future accords?

The initial question really consists of two parts: where in the policy-making process does the idea of developing these provisions originate? and, what were the factors motivating the designing of such provisions? In many instances, nations have deliberately initiated proposals as high priority policies with specific, clearly perceived, arms control and disarmament objectives. The motivation for launching these negotiations is not always easy to identify, nor is it often singular. Political reasons for making disarmament a high priority objective would include concern for external factors—such as the aggravation of outstanding international issues by new tensions produced by escalating weaponry or an arms race becoming itself an international political issue—and for internal factors—such as a powerful "peace sentiment" which

requires recognition. In either instance, a nation's espousing of disarmament could be undertaken for propaganda purposes with little real expectation of tangible results; two examples of this might be the Soviet Union's pressing for "general and complete disarmament" during the early days of the Cold War, and the U.S.'s undertaking the negotiations for a "mutual-balanced force reduction" (MBFR) during the late 1960s and 1970s.

Similarly, it has been argued that several post-1945 arms control measures have been negotiated because they were popular and they restricted weaponry nobody wanted anyway. The outer space treaty (1967), the seabed accord (1971), and the bacteriological warfare pact (1972) have been labelled "cosmetic" agreements by disarmers.

Where serious efforts to obtain a limitation of strategic weapons is involved, probably the most basic reason behind these national policies is economic—these weapons systems are becoming too costly. This does not necessarily mean that national resources are unable to bear the expenditures, but rather that if the building of armaments is to be given continued primacy among national priorities, then other, perhaps more desired, domestic programs would have to be curtailed or government revenues, i.e., taxes, greatly increased. The financial costs involved in past navy building competitions often was the most significant factor in bringing about limitation agreements; this would certainly appear to have been true with the Rush-Bagot accord (1817), the Argentine-Chile protocol (1902), and the numerous naval pacts of the 1920s and 1930s. It is, seemingly, a major factor pressing the current SALT negotiations.

In other instances, arms control proposals have been advanced, during the course of negotiations dealing with complex political issues, as distinct elements of a broad compromise. In these cases, arms control measures usually have been developed without much forethought as low-level policy alternatives. Generally the measures involved have been of limited importance to basic national military postures and, often, these compromises have involved some form of demilitarized zones. Examples of this process can be found in the negotiations of the Russo-Finnish treaty (1920), the Spitsbergen pact (1920), the Korean armistice (1953), and the Geneva protocols on Indochina (1954).

The idea of employing demilitarization provisions apparently originated as a device of diplomacy in each of these cases; that is, the introduction of arms control concepts during the negotiations developed from the necessity for diplomatic innovation. In none of these instances, it should be noted, were immediate, vital, national security issues affected.

The second question, relating to the dangers and risks of arms control and disarmament measures, must be approached from both contemporary and historical assessments. Contemporary observers are usually governed by their own personal commitments: the more enthusiastic supporters seem to underestimate the dangers and risks, while opponents dourly overestimate them. This point can be illustrated by looking at the opponents to the London naval treaty (1930):

> *Frederick Hale (before the U.S. Senate):* "The British by the terms of this treaty have us hamstrung and hog-tied and there will keep us as long as limitations of armaments are the order of the day."
> *Winston Churchill (before the House of Commons):* "I am astonished that any Admiralty board of naval officers could have been found to accept responsibility for such a hamstringing stipulation."
> *T. Inukai (before the Japanese Diet):* [The Government has] "betrayed the country by entering into an agreement at the London Conference inadequate for Japan's needs."

A similar list of favorable comments could be presented; no doubt the contemporary observers were swayed by their assumptions about defense needs and by the particular criteria each selected.

Even though the history of arms control and disarmament is little known or understood, there seem to be certain factors which stand out in the several published "episodic" studies. These accounts show that arms control and disarmament agreements rarely have been the cause of hostilities; on the contrary, the record suggests that often these pacts have eased tensions, at least for a period of time, between potential belligerents. Authoritarian governments appear to have honored reciprocal arms control agreements as often as popularly based governments. Evidently, the key to successful contracts is mutual self-interest: when this mutuality persists the agreements continue to function, when this mutuality disintegrates so does the effectiveness of the agreement.

Yet even when such pacts have been long honored, there does not appear to be a corresponding advance in national moral consciousness. For example, even though the Geneva "poison gas" protocol was generally upheld by the major belligerents during World War II (even by the United States, which was not a party to the protocol), these same nations failed to transfer this enlightenment to other weapons of equal destructiveness. Consequently, President Roosevelt rather pretentiously refused to consider the use of gas against Japanese-held islands while he allowed "area" bombing to proceed against German cities, and President Truman routinely sanctioned the fire-bombing of Tokyo and the atomic bombing of Hiroshima and Nagasaki. In these instances, the dynamics of weapons technology outstripped the intentions of arms control principles and accords. If total control of weapons and war-making must be a gradual, step-by-step process, as contemporary arms control specialists insist, then obviously there must not be any pause between steps under the illusion that individual pacts can provide a momentum or "spirit" of their own.

All in all, the results of arms control efforts have been, historically, as one would expect—quite mixed. Some attempts have stood out as uncritically successful, some have proven dismal failures, and still others have fallen somewhere in between. The Rush-Bagot understanding (1817) and the Karlstadt convention (1905) are examples of successful efforts; while the submarine protocol (1936) and the Indochina protocols (1954) rank among the failures. The majority of efforts toward arms control and disarmament should be listed somewhere between complete success and gross failure.

By design and nature, arms control (and even literal disarmament) mechanisms are not ends in themselves, nor should they be so considered. These mechanisms, both formal and informal, seek to accomplish two purposes: to reduce the likelihood of war; and, if that fails, to diminish the violence in any war that takes place. It is clear, by definition and by historical experience, that these mechanisms can greatly assist in the construction of a stable, peaceful international community, but that arms control and disarmament agreements cannot, by themselves, solve the political, economic, social, and moral problems that lie at the heart of the world's ills.

That this is true seems borne out by the interwar experiences of arms limitation. Philip Noel-Baker argues (with considerable validity in my opinion) that the naval treaties of the 1920s and 1930s were technically nearly perfect. The major problem was that these arms control devices could not, by themselves, surmount the vast political and economic differences which gradually arose in Europe and Asia.

An arms control and disarmament treaty possesses most of the same characteristics of any political agreement between nations: its construction is only in part an act of prophecy, essentially its function is to register the best interests of the signatory nations in terms of contemporary reality. To argue otherwise would be to dismiss the treaty-making function entirely. A treaty is like an extremely tender seedling: it may begin life in apparent good health, but it requires constant attention, much cultivation, occasional grafting for new vitality, and even then it may die because of genetic weaknesses or because of the neighbor's dog.

If Justice Oliver Wendell Holmes' oft-quoted dictum—that a page of history is worth a volume of logic—is valid, then past arms control and disarmament negotiations and treaties have much to tell us. But if the past can be enlightening, it may also be deceiving. Many historians like to argue that societies which fail to study their past are destined to relive their mistakes; yet contemporary history suggests also that those societies which have evolved rigid formulas from past experiences—such as Munich—may be subjected to even more serious consequences. In other words, one would be well advised to ponder Mark Twain's note of caution: "We should be careful to get out of an experience only the wisdom that is in it—and stop there; lest we be like the cat that sits down on a hot stove lid. She will never sit down on a hot stove lid again—and that is well; but also she will never sit down on a cold one anymore."

Few historians would (or should) argue that the past can provide ready answers to current issues. What history can do is assist in drafting the *proper questions* we should address to contemporary problems. Here are a few such questions that have occurred to me after years of reviewing past arms control and disarmament activities.

1. How do we define arms control and disarmament?
   a. By what techniques has arms control been employed?
   b. By what means or methods has it been achieved?
2. What motivates nations to seek arms control accords—economic, security, or ideological factors?
3. What are reasonable objectives for arms control? Is parity essential? or possible?
4. What are the risks and dangers associated with entering into an arms control agreement?

a. How realistic is it to negotiate with authoritarian governments?

b. How essential are verification and control procedures? What kinds are best? or reasonable?

5. To what extent have past arms control agreements "worked"?

a. What expectations should we have for the future?

b. How is success or failure measured? Is simple duration adequate?

The pages that follow list a wide variety of sources which relate to these and other questions. It is my hope that this bibliography—culled from the extensive files of the Center for the Study of Armament and Disarmament at California State University, Los Angeles—will assist you in your search for answers.

Part One

VIEWS, OVERVIEWS, & THEORY

One

Research Resources & AC&D Organizations

THE PURPOSE OF this chapter is threefold: 1) to suggest tools for updating this bibliography and for additional research, 2) to list "simulation" studies dealing with arms control and disarmament (AC&D) and other essays relating to AC&D research, and 3) to collect materials concerning the activities of a selected few AC&D organizations. The studies and research reports of each organization are scattered below according to their subject topics; however, they have been collected by organization in the index.

Current books and essays on arms control and disarmament issues may be located in various ways. *Arms Control Today* (1970–), a monthly publication of the Washington, D.C.-based Arms Control Association, carries an excellent, increasingly comprehensive list of current items. The indexes to periodicals and newspapers listed below are also extremely valuable tools. Military journals are indexed by the *Air University Library Index to Military Periodicals;* "political science" publications are indexed in *ABC Pol Sci* and the *International Bibliography of Political Science;* and popular magazines are indexed by the *Reader's Guide*

and the *Social Science and Humanities Index.* Appended to the U.S. Arms Control and Disarmament Agency's (ACDA) annual *Documents on Disarmament* is a list of the year's appropriate government publications.

Contemporary AC&D materials are collected in two excellent annual series. The Stockholm International Peace Research Institute's (SIPRI) *Yearbook of World Armament and Disarmament* (1968/69–) provides interpretive essays and documents, while the ACDA's *Documents on Disarmament* (1960–) reveals national policies and views. The best single volume of AC&D documents is T. N. Dupuy and G. M. Hammerman's *A Documentary History of Arms Control and Disarmament* (1973).

Sources of contemporary military data and statistics are several. The London-based Institute for Strategic Studies publishes two annuals that are especially valuable: *The Military Balance* (1962–) and *The Strategic Balance* (1967–). The League of Nations published an annual *Armament Yearbook* (1925–1940), which provides a historical reference. Among the many other annuals not listed below, include

Jane's Fighting Ships and *Brassey's* yearly estimates. Data on military sales and transfers are listed in Chapter 11, Controlling Arms Manufacture & Traffic, below.

Auxiliary research materials may be found by consulting John Brown Mason's *Research Resources*, 2 vols. (1968, 1971) and Frederick Holler's *The Information Sources of Political Science* (1975). Helen Poulton's *The Historian's Handbook* (1972) is valuable for locating historical sources.

Bibliographical Resources

GENERAL GUIDES

1 *ABC POL SCI: Advance Bibliography of Contents: Political Science and Government.* Santa Barbara, Ca.: ABC-Clio, 1969–.

2 *America: History and Life.* Santa Barbara, Ca.: ABC-Clio, 1963–.

3 *Current Thought on Peace and War: A Semi-Annual Digest of Literature and Research in Progress on the Problems of World Order and Conflict.* Durham, N.C., 1960–.

4 Holler, Frederick. *The Information Sources of Political Science.* 5 vols. Santa Barbara, Ca.: ABC-Clio, 1975.

5 *International Bibliography of Political Science.* Oxford: Basil Blackwell, 1950-.

6 *International Conciliation: A Catalogue of Publications, 1924–1967.* New York: Carnegie Endowment for International Peace, 1971.

7 Mason, John Brown, comp. *Research Resources: Annotated Guide to the Social Sciences.* Vol. 1: *International Relations and Recent History: Indexes, Abstracts and Periodicals.* Vol. 2: *Official Publications: U.S. Government, United Nations International Organizations, and Statistical Sources.* Santa Barbara, Ca.: ABC-Clio, 1968, 1971.

8 *Peace Research Abstracts.* Oakville, Ont.: Canadian Peace Research Institute, 1964–.

9 Poulton, Helen J. *The Historian's Handbook: A Descriptive Guide to Reference Works.* Norman: Univ. of Oklahoma Press, 1972.

10 *Public Affairs Information Service Bulletin.* New York: Public Affairs Information Service, 1951–.

11 *Reader's Guide to Periodical Literature.* New York: H. W. Wilson, 1905–.

12 Winchell, Constance M. *Guide to Reference Books.* 8th ed. Chicago: American Library Assoc., 1967. [Supplements, 1968, 1970.]

13 Zawodny, J. K. *Guide to the Study of International Relations.* San Francisco: Chandler, 1966.

ARMS CONTROL & DISARMAMENT

Bibliographies which deal with a specific aspect of arms control and disarmament, such as the SALT talks, will be listed under that subject entry.

14 Clemens, Walter C., Jr., comp. *Soviet Disarmament Policy, 1917–1963: An Annotated Bibliography of Soviet and Western Sources.* Stanford: Stanford Univ. Press, 1965.

15 Collart, Yves. *Disarmament: A Study Guide and Bibliography on the Efforts of the United Nations.* The Hague: Nijhoff, 1958.

16 Cook, Blanche Wiesen. *Bibliography on Peace Research in History.* Santa Barbara, Ca.: ABC–Clio, 1969.

17 Coward, H. Roberts. *A Selected Bibliography on Arms Control and Related Problems.* Cambridge: M.I.T., Center for International Studies, 1963.

18 *Disarmament and Arms Control: Selected Readings.* New York: Foreign Policy Assoc., 1961.

19 Fischer, George. *Soviet Disarmament Policy: A Survey of Recent Sources.* Cambridge: M.I.T., Center for International Studies, 1961.

20 Gray, Charles; Leslie B. Gray; and Glen W. Gregory. *A Bibliography of Peace Research: Indexed by Key Words.* Eugene, Ore.: General Research Analysis Methods, 1968.

21 Green, Henrietta H. *Disarmament and Peace: A Selected, Annotated Bibliography.* Baltimore: Johns Hopkins Univ., Operations Research Office, 1960.

22 Harrison, Stanley L. *Arms Control: Selected Bibliography: Some Recent Writings on Disarmament, Arms Control, and the Spread of Nuclear Weapons.* Washington, D.C.: Weapons Systems Evaluation Group, 1962.

23 Hellman, Florence S. *Disarmament, with Special Reference to Naval Limitation: A Bibliographical List.* Washington, D.C.: Library of Congress, Division of Bibliography, 1929.

24 Jack, Homer A. *A Bibliography on Disarmament: A Classified Listing of 271 Volumes.* New York: World Conference of Religion & Peace, 1972.

25 League of Nations. *Annotated Bibliography on Disarmament and Military Questions.* Geneva, 1931.

26 Matthews, Mary Alice. *Disarmament and Security: Selected List of Recent Books, Pamphlets and Periodical Articles.* Washington, D.C.: Carnegie Endowment for International Peace, 1931.

27 Pickus, Robert, and Robert Woito. *To End War: An Introduction to the Ideas, Organizations and Current Books.* New York: Harper & Row, 1970.

28 U.N. Atomic Energy Commission. *An International Bibliography on Atomic Energy: Political, Economic, and Social Aspects.* 2 vols. AEC/INF/7 rev. 2. New York, 1949, 1951.

29 U.N. Dag Hammarskjöld Library. *Disarmament: A Selected Bibliography, 1962–1967.* New York: Columbia University Press, 1967.

30 U.S. Arms Control & Disarmament Agency. *A Brief Bibliography: Arms Control, and Disarmament.* ACDA Pub. 22. Washington, D.C.: G.P.O., 1964.

31 U.S. Department of the Air Force. Air Force Academy Library. *Arms Control.* Special Bibliographies Series, no. 20. Colorado Springs: Air Force Academy, Feb. 1962.

32 U.S. Department of the Army. Army Library. *Disarmament: A Bibliographic Record, 1916–1960.* Washington, D.C.: G.P.O., 1960.

33 ———. *U.S. Security, Arms Control, and Disarmament, 1960–1961.* Harry Moskowitz and Jack Roberts, eds. Washington, D.C.: G.P.O., 1961.

34 ———. *U.S. Security, Arms Control, and Disarmament, 1961–1965.* Harry Moskowitz and Jack Roberts, eds. Washington, D.C.: G.P.O., 1965.

35 U.S. Department of State. Disarmament Administration. *Disarmament, Arms Control and National Security: A Basic Bibliography.* Washington, D.C.: G.P.O., 1961.

36 U.S. Library of Congress. Division of Bibliography. *The League of Nations and Disarmament: A Bibliographical List.* Washington, D.C.: G.P.O., 1929.

37 ———. General References and Bibliography Division. *Arms Control and Disarmament: A Quarterly Bibliography.* Washington, D.C.: G.P.O., 1964–1973.

38 ———. Legislative Reference Service. *Controlling the Further Development of Nuclear Weapons: A Collection of Excerpts and a Bibliography.* Washington, D.C.: G.P.O., 1958, pt. 4, pp. 51–54.

39 "Bibliography on Arms Control and Disarmament." *Intercom* 5 (Feb.–Mar. 1963): 61–72.

40 Coward, H. Roberts. "Bibliography on Arms Control and Related Problems." *Summer Study on Arms Control, Collected Papers.*

Boston: American Academy of Arts & Sciences, 1961, pp. 441–59.

41 "Disarmament—A Bibliography." *Survival* 2 (Jan.–Feb. 1960): 38–40.

42 "Disarmament: A Guide to Understanding the Problem." *Intercom* 10 (Jan.–Feb. 1968): 31–80.

43 Dougherty, James E. "Disarmament Debate: A Review of Current Literature." *Orbis* 5 (Fall 1961): 342–59; 5 (Winter 1962): 489–511.

44 Jensen, Lloyd. "Disarmament and Arms Control: Some of the Recent Literature." *Background* 6 (Winter 1963): 41–47.

45 Oboler, Eli M. "World Disarmament: A Selected Reading List." *Choice* 6 (July–Aug. 1969): 630–32.

46 [Pax Bibliography]. *Peace* 3 (Spring–Summer 1967): 3–38.

47 "Some References on Disarmament and Security." *International Affairs* [London] 10 (Sept. 1931): 666–83.

48 Wolk, Herman S. "The Growing Bookshelf on Arms and Arms Control." *Air Force and Space Digest* 47 (Jan. 1964): 76–77 ff.

49 Wright, Christopher. "Selected Critical Bibliography on Disarmament." *Daedalus* 89 (Fall 1960): 1055–70.

MILITARY POLICY & STATISTICS

50 Burt, Richard, and Geoffrey Kemp, eds. *Congressional Hearings on American Defense Policy, 1947–1971: An Annotated Bibliography.* Lawrence: Univ. Press of Kansas, 1974.

51 Corbin, Doris. *Publications of the Social Science Department, 1963–1970.* Santa Monica, Ca.: Rand, 1971.

52 Gilson, Charles M., and Bill Sweetman. "Military Aircraft of the World." *Flight International* (Mar. 6, 1976): 549–606.

53 Greenwood, John, ed. *American Defense Policy Since 1945: A Preliminary Bibliography.* Lawrence: Univ. Press of Kansas, 1973.

54 *Jane's Weapons Systems, 1971–1972.* 3d ed. R. T. Pretty and D. H. Archer, eds. New York: McGraw-Hill, 1971.

55 Larson, Arthur D. *National Security Affairs: A Guide to Information Sources.* Detroit: Gale, 1973.

56 League of Nations. *Armament Year-Book.* Geneva, 1925–1939.

57 Luttwak, Edward. *A Dictionary of Modern War.* New York: Harper & Row, 1971.

58 MacGuire, Michael. "Western and Soviet Naval Building Programs, 1965–1976." *Survival* 18 (Sept.–Oct. 1976): 204–09.

59 *The Military Balance.* London: International Institute for Strategic Studies, 1962–.

60 Millett, Allan R., and B. Franklin Cooling III, comps. *Doctoral Dissertations in Military Affairs: A Bibliography.* Manhattan: Kansas State Univ. Library, 1972.

61 Parrish, Michael. *Soviet Armed Forces: Books in English, 1950–1967.* Stanford, Ca.: Hoover Institution Press, 1970.

62 "Second Annual Soviet Aerospace Almanac." *Air Force Magazine* 59 (Mar. 1976): 37–120.

63 Sloutzki, Nokhim M. *The World Armaments Race, 1919–1939.* Geneva: Geneva Research Centre, 1941.

64 *The Strategic Survey.* London: International Institute for Strategic Studies, 1967–.

65 U.S. Arms Control & Disarmament Agency. *World Military Expenditures.* Washington, D.C.: G.P.O., 1966/67–.

66 U.S. Department of the Army. *Nuclear Weapons and the Atlantic Alliance: A Bibliographic Survey.* DA Pamphlet 20–66. Washington, D.C.: G.P.O., 1965.

67 ———. *Nuclear Weapons and NATO: Analytical Survey of Literature.* DA Pamphlet 50–1. Washington, D.C.: G.P.O., 1975.

68 U.S. Senate. Committee on Government Operations. Subcommittee on National Security Staffing and Operations. *Administration of National Security: A Bibliography.* Washington, D.C.: G.P.O., 1963.

INDEXES

69 *Air University Library Index to Military Periodicals.* Maxwell Air Force Base, Ala.: Air Univ. Library, 1949–.

70 *Social Science and Humanities Index.* New York: H. W. Wilson, 1913–. [Formerly *International Index to Periodicals.*]

71 *The Christian Science Monitor Index.* Corvallis, Ore.: Helen M. Cropsey, 1969–.

72 *The New York Times Index.* New York: New York Times Co., 1913–. [Monthly and annual accumulations.]

73 *The Times [London]: Index to the Times.* London: The Times, 1906–. [Monthly and annual accumulations.]

74 *The Wall Street Journal Index.* New York: Dow Jones, 1958–.

PERIODICALS & JOURNALS

75 *Current Digest of the Soviet Press.* New York: Joint Committee on Slavic Studies, 1949–.

76 *Foreign Affairs.* New York: Council on Foreign Relations, 1922–.

77 *Foreign Policy.* New York: National Affairs, Inc., 1970–.

78 *International Affairs: A Monthly Journal of Political Analysis.* Moscow: Izvestia Printing Office, 1955–.

79 *International Security.* Cambridge: Harvard Univ., Program for Science and International Affairs, 1976–.

80 League of Nations. *Official Journal.* Geneva, 1920–1940.

81 *Peking Review: A Magazine of Chinese News and Views.* Peking: People's Republic of China, 1958–.

82 *Polish Perspectives: A Monthly Review.* Warsaw: Polish Institute of International Affairs, 1957–.

83 *Review of International Affairs.* Belgrade: Federation of Yugoslav Journalists, 1950–.

84 *U.N. Monthly Chronicle.* New York: United Nations, 1964–. [Preceded by *U.N. Weekly Bulletin.* New York: United Nations, 1945–1953; *U.N. Review.* New York: United Nations, 1954–1963.]

85 *U.S. Department of State Bulletin.* Washington, D.C.: G.P.O., 1939–.

86 *Arms Control Today: Current Events in Arms Control and Disarmament.* Washington, D.C.: Arms Control Assoc., 1974–.

87 *Bulletin of the Atomic Scientists: A Magazine of Science and Public Affairs.* Chicago: Univ. of Chicago Press, 1945–.

88 *Bulletin of Peace Proposals.* Oslo: Universitetsforlaget, for International Peace Research Assoc., Groningen, 1970–.

89 *Defense Monitor.* Washington, D.C.: Center for Defense Information, 1972–.

90 *Disarmament.* Paris: World Veterans Federation, 1964–.

91 *Disarmament: News & Views.* New York: Council on Religion & International Affairs, 1972–.

92 *Disarmament and Arms Control: An International Quarterly Journal.* London: Pergamon Press, 1963–1965.

93 *Facts on File: A Weekly News Guide with Cumulative Index.* New York: Person's Index, 1940–.

94 *Instant Research on Peace and Violence.* Tampere, Finland: Tampere Peace Research Institute, 1970–.

95 *International Conciliation.* New York: Carnegie Endowment for International Peace, 1907–.

96 *Journal of Conflict Resolution: A Quarterly for Research Related to War and Peace.* Ann Arbor: Center for Conflict Resolution, 1957–. [A 12-year author index appears in 12 (Dec. 1968): 533–50.]

97 *Journal of Peace Research.* Oslo: Universitetsforlaget, for International Peace Research Assoc., Groningen, 1964–.

98 *Orbis: A Quarterly Journal of World Affairs.* Philadelphia: Foreign Policy Research Institute, 1957–. [See editorial section, "Reflections on the Quarter."]

99 *Peace Research: A Monthly Journal of Original Research on the Problems of War.* Oakville, Ont.: Canadian Peace Research Institute, 1969–.

100 Peace Research Society (International). *Papers.* Philadelphia: Peace Research Society, 1964–.

101 *Pugwash Newsletter.* London: Continuing Committee of the Pugwash Conferences on Science & World Affairs, 1963–.

102 *Survival.* London: International Institute for Strategic Studies, 1959–.

103 *Vital Speeches of the Day.* Pelham, N.Y.: City News Publishing Co., 1934–.

104 *War/Peace Report.* New York: War/Peace Report, 1961–1971.

105 World Peace Council. *Bulletin of the World Council of Peace.* Vienna: Secretariat of the World Council of Peace, 1954–.

DOCUMENTARY COLLECTIONS

106 *Cumulative Subject Index to the Monthly Catalog of United States Government Publications, 1900–1971.* 14 vols. Washington, D.C.: Carrollton Press, 1972.

107 U.N. Dag Hammarskjöld Library. *United Nations Documents Index.* New York: United Nations, 1950–.

Foreign Relations

108 *Documents on American Foreign Relations.* New York: Harper & Row, 1951–.

109 Royal Institute of International Affairs. *Documents on International Affairs, 1928–.* London: Oxford Univ. Press, 1929–.

110 Schlesinger, Arthur M., Jr., ed. *Dynamics of World Power: Documentary History of U.S. Foreign Policy, 1945–1973.* 5 vols. New York: Chelsea House, McGraw-Hill, 1973.

111 Siegler, Heinrich von, ed. *Dokumentation zur Abruestung und Sicherheit von 1943 bis 1959.* Bad Godesberg: Siegler, 1960.

112 U.S. Department of State. *American Foreign Policy: Current Documents.* Washington, D.C.: G.P.O., 1956–1967.

113 ———. *American Foreign Policy, 1950–1955: Basic Documents.* Washington, D.C.: G.P.O., 1957.

114 ———. *Foreign Relations of the United States: Diplomatic Papers.* Washington, D.C.: G.P.O., 1862–.

115 U.S. Senate. Committee on Foreign Relations. *A Decade of American Foreign Policy: Basic Documents, 1941–1949.* Washington, D.C.: G.P.O., 1950.

Arms Control & Disarmament

116 Dupuy, Trevor N., and Gay M. Hammerman, eds. *A Documentary History of Arms Control and Disarmament.* New York: Bowker, 1973.

117 Heurlin, Bertel, comp. *Nedrustning* [Disarmament]. Copenhagen: Gyldendal, 1970.

118 National Lawyers Guild. *A Summary of Disarmament Documents 1945–1962.* San Francisco, 1963.

119 U.S. Arms Control & Disarmament Agency. *Documents on Disarmament.* Washington, D.C.: G.P.O., 1960–. [This annual edition succeeds U.S. Department of State. *Documents on Disarmament, 1945–1959.* 2 vols. Washington, D.C.: G.P.O., 1960.]

120 U.S. Senate. Committee on Foreign Relations. Subcommittee on Disarmament. *Disarmament and Security: A Collection of Documents, 1919–1955.* Washington, D.C.: G.P.O., 1956.

121 World Council of Peace. *Documents and Papers on Disarmament, 1945–1955: Official Statements Pertaining to Disarmament Negotiations between the Great Powers.* Vienna, 1956.

YEARBOOKS

122 *The Annual Register of World Events.* London: Longmans, Green, 1758–.

123 Council on Foreign Relations. *Political Handbook and Atlas of the World: Governments and Inter-governmental Organizations.* New York, 1927–.

124 *Keesing's Contemporary Archives.* Bristol: Keesing's Publications, 1931–. [Weekly.]

125 London Institute of World Affairs. *Year Book of World Affairs.* London: Stevens & Sons, 1947–.

126 *The New International Year Book: A Compendium of the World's Progress for the Year.* New York: Funk & Wagnalls, 1932–.

127   Royal Institute of International Affairs. *Survey of International Affairs.* London: Oxford Univ. Press, 1925–.

128   *SIPRI Yearbook of World Armament and Disarmament.* Stockholm: Stockholm International Peace Research Institute, 1968–69–.

129   *Statesman's Year-Book: Statistical and Historical Annual of the States of the World.* New York: Macmillan, 1864–.

130   U.N. Department of Public Information. *Yearbook of the United Nations.* New York, 1947–.

Lexicons

131   "Arms Control: A Special Report." *Business Week* (Mar. 18, 1961): 54–93.

132   "A Brief Dictionary of Peace and War." *Reconciliation Quarterly* (Sept. 1972): 14–58.

133   Brooke, Sen. Edward. "The Lexicon of Arms Control Literature." *Congressional Record* 120 (Jan. 29, 1974): S631–33.

134   Institute for Defense Analyses. *Lexicon of Terms Relevant to National Security Studies on Arms Control, Annex I (including an appendix) of Proceedings of the Seminar on Deterrence and Arms Control. July 25–27, 1960.* IDA. AA P–1. Washington, D.C., 1960.

135   Lambert, Robert W. *Glossary of Arms Control and Disarmament Terms.* ACDA Research Report 67–2. Washington, D.C.: G.P.O., 1967.

136   U.S. Arms Control & Disarmament Agency. *SALT Lexicon.* ACDA Pub. 71. Washington, D.C.: G.P.O., 1974.

Treaties

137   Beilenson, Laurence W. *The Treaty Trap.* New York: Public Affairs Press, 1969.

138   Jacobs, F. G. "Varieties of Approach to Treaty Interpretation—with Special Reference to the Draft Convention on the Law of Treaties before the Vienna Diplomatic Conference." *International and Comparative Law Quarterly* 18 (Apr. 1969): 318–46.

139   Jessup, Philip C. "The United States and Treaties for the Avoidance of War." *International Conciliation*, no. 239 (Apr. 1928).

140   Kearney, R. D., and R. E. Dalton. "The Treaty on Treaties." *American Journal of International Law* 64 (Mar. 1970): 495–561.

141   MacCloskey, Brig. Gen. Monro. *Pacts for Peace.* New York: Richard Rosen Press, 1967.

142   Nahlik, S. E. "Grounds of Invalidity and Termination of Treaties." *American Journal of International Law* 65 (Oct. 1971): 736–56.

143   Rosenne, Shabtai. *The Law of Treaties: A Guide to the Legislative History of the Vienna Convention.* Leiden: Sijthoff, 1970.

144   Sprudzs, Adolf. *Treaty Sources in Legal and Political Research: Tools, Techniques, and Problems—The Conventional and the New.* International Studies, no. 3. Tucson: Univ. of Arizona, Institute of Government Research, 1971.

145   Toscano, M. *History of Treaties and International Politics.* Rev. ed. Baltimore: Johns Hopkins Press, 1966.

146   Zemanek, Karl, ed. *Agreements of International Organizations and the Vienna Convention on the Law of Treaties.* Vienna: Springer Verlag, 1971.

Treaty Texts

147   Harvard Univ. Law School Library. *Index to Multilateral Treaties: A Chronological List of Multiparty International Agreements from the Sixteenth Century through 1963, with Citations to their Text.* V. Mostecky, ed. Cambridge, 1965.

148   Israel, Fred L., ed. *Major Peace Treaties of Modern History: 1648–1967.* 4 vols. New York: Chelsea House, 1967.

149   Keesing's Publications. *Treaties and Alliances of the World: An International Survey Covering Treaties in Force and Communities of States.* New York: Scribner's, 1968.

150   League of Nations. *Treaty Series.* 205 vols. London: Harrison, 1920–1946.

151   Myers, Denys Peter. *Manual of Collections of Treaties and of Collections Relating to*

Treaties. Cambridge: Harvard Univ. Press, 1922.

152 Shapiro, Leonard, ed. *Soviet Treaty Series.* 2 vols. Washington, D.C.: Georgetown Univ. Press, 1950, 1955.

153 U.N. *Treaty Series.* New York, 1946–.

154 U.S. Arms Control & Disarmament Agency. *Arms Control and Disarmament Agreements: Texts and History of Negotiations.* Washington, D.C.: G.P.O., 1975.

155 U.S. Department of the Air Force. *Treaties Governing Land Warfare.* AFP 110–1–3. Washington, D.C.: G.P.O., July 21, 1958.

156 U.S. Department of State. Office of Legal Advisor. *A List of Treaties and Other International Agreements in Force on January 1, 1970.* Washington, D.C.: G.P.O., 1970.

157 U.S. House. Committee on Foreign Affairs. *Collective Defense Treaties, with Maps, Texts of Treaties, a Chronology, Status of Forces Agreements, and Comparative Chart.* Prepared by Helen Mattas. Rev. ed. Washington, D.C.: G.P.O., 1969.

GUIDES TO FILMS & SONGS

158 Denisoff, R. Serge. *Songs of Protest, War and Peace: A Bibliography and Discography.* Rev. ed. Santa Barbara, Ca.: ABC–Clio, 1973.

159 Dougall, Lucy. *War, Peace Film Guide.* Rev. ed. Chicago: World Without War Publications, 1973.

160 *The Count Down: A Study of World Disarmament.* United Nations. Released by NET Film Service, 1958. [Motion picture.]

161 *Defense and Disarmament.* New York Times, Office of Educational Activities, 1957. [Filmstrip.]

162 *For Lasting Peace.* United Nations, Department of Public Information, 1952. [Filmstrip.]

163 *Modern Arms and Free Men.* March of Time, 1950. [Motion picture.]

164 *Personal Diplomacy at the Summit.* Current Affairs Films, 1960. [Filmstrip.]

165 *A Sane Nuclear Policy.* WQED. Released by NET Film Service, 1960. [Motion picture.]

166 *Teller-Pauling Debate: Fallout and Disarmament.* KQED. Released by NET Film Service, 1958. [Motion picture.]

167 *War and Peace.* Palmer Films. Released by NET Film Service, 1954. [Motion picture.]

168 *We Seek Peace.* Board of World Peace of the Methodist Church, 1954. [Filmstrip.]

AC&D Simulation & Research

169 Bonham, G. Matthew. "Simulating International Disarmament Negotiations." *Journal of Conflict Resolution* 15:9 (1971): 299–316.

170 Davis, Robert H. "Arms Control Simulation: The Search for an Acceptable Method." *Journal of Conflict Resolution* 7:3 (1963): 590–602.

171 ——, et al. *A Game for Studying the Problems of Arms Control.* Santa Monica, Ca.: Systems Development, 1962.

172 ——. *Arms Control Simulation.* TM–L–633. Santa Monica, Ca.: Systems Development, 1961.

173 Kalman, Peter J. "Application of a Theorem by Scarf on Cooperative Solutions to N-Person Games to Problems of Disarmament." *Journal of Political Economy* 79 (Nov.–Dec. 1971): 1388–96.

174 *Simulation and Games: An International Journal of Theory, Design, and Research.* Beverly Hills, Ca.: Sage, 1970–.

175 Aaron, Lt. Col. Harold R. "Arms Control Research in the Department of Defense." *Journal of Arms Control* 1:3 (1963): 261–63.

176 Barnet, Richard J. "Research on Disarmament." *Background* 6 (Winter 1963): 3–15.

177 Bohn, Lewis C. *On Motives for Disarmament Research.* Santa Monica, Ca.: Rand, Oct. 1959.

178 Buckingham, William A., Jr. "Client-Oriented Social Research: How Could Social and Behavioral Scientists Contribute to the U.S. Arms Control & Disarmament Agency?" Ph.D. diss., Ohio State Univ., 1974.

179 Feld, Bernard T., et al. *A Program of Research on the Technical Problems of Arms Control.* Boston: American Academy of Arts & Sciences, 1960.

180 Goriainov, Makar, and Igor S. Glagolev. "Notes on Conducting Research on Peace and Disarmament Conducted in the USSR." *International Social Science Journal* 17:3 (1965): 417–19.

181 Janowitz, Morris. "Sociological Research on Arms Control." *American Sociologist* 6 (June 1971): 23–30.

182 Kaliadin, A. N. "Problems of Disarmament Research." *Journal of Peace Research* 9:3 (1972): 237–45.

183 Klineberg, Rosemary. *Studies on Information and Arms Control.* Washington, D.C.: Institute for Defense Analyses, 1963.

184 Knorr, Klaus E. "Contributions of United States Industry to Arms Control Research." *Journal of Conflict Resolution* 7:3 (1963): 484–90.

185 Kumar, M. "Recent Advances in Research on Disarmament." *International Studies* 3 (1962): 335–48.

186 Millett, Allan R. "Arms Control and Research on Military Institutions." *Armed Forces and Society* 2 (Fall 1974): 61–78.

187 Scoville, Herbert, Jr., and Thomas A. Halsted. "Arms Control." *Annual Report of Carnegie Endowment for International Peace.* Washington, D.C.: Carnegie Endowment for International Peace, 1974, pp. 25–30.

188 Teeple, John B. "Recent Arms Control Research in Europe." *Bulletin of the Atomic Scientists* 21 (Oct. 1965): 37–39.

189 U.K. Foreign & Commonwealth Office. *International Repertory of Institutions Specializing in Research in Peace and Disarmament.* Reports and Papers in the Social Sciences, no. 23. London: H.M.S.O., 1966.

Organizations & Agencies

Arms Control & Disarmament Agency (USA)

190 "The Arms Control Agency: It's Small, Short of Cash, But Growing in Influence." *Space/Aeronautics* 50 (Sept. 1968): 26 ff.

191 "Arms Control and Disarmament Agency Problems." *Defense Monitor* 3 (Aug. 1974): 8–11.

192 Barnet, Richard J. "The United States Arms Control and Disarmament Agency." *Disarmament and Arms Control* 3 (Spring 1965): 50–62.

193 Carter, Luther. "Arms Control Agency: Fred Ikle, New Captain of a Disabled Ship." *Science* (May 11, 1973): 570–72.

194 Clarke, Duncan L. "Arms Control and Disarmament Agency: Effective?" *Foreign Service Journal* 52 (Dec. 1975): 12–14 ff.

195 ———. "Nixon Installs a 'Peace Cabinet'— But Where is the Peace Agency?" *War/Peace Report* 13 (Mar.–Apr. 1973): 27–29.

196 ———. "Role of Military Officers in the U.S. Arms Control and Disarmament Agency." *Military Review* 54 (Dec. 1974): 47–53.

197 ———. "Ups and Downs of Arms Control." *Bulletin of the Atomic Scientists* 30 (Sept. 1974): 44–49.

198 Dickson, Paul. "The Disarmers: A Look at the ACDA." *Vista* 8 (July–Aug. 1972): 38–52.

199 "Executive Order 11044: Interagency Coordination of Arms Control and Disarmament Matters, August 20, 1962." *Documents on Disarmament, 1962.* Washington, D.C.: G.P.O., 1963, II: 788–91.

200 Foster, William C. "The United States Arms Control and Disarmament Agency." *Disarmament and Arms Control* 1 (Autumn 1963): 111–17.

201 Greenberg, Daniel S. "Arms Agency: Executive Order Gives It a Boost at a Time When Its Prestige is Sagging." *Science* (Sept. 7, 1962): 738–39.

202 ———. "Disarmament Agency: It Gives Quest for Peace and Institutional Standing." *Science* (Sept. 22, 1961): 24–25.

203 ———. "Disarmament Agency: It Has Suddenly Stepped Into Public View." *Science* (Feb. 16, 1962): 518.

204 ———. "Disarmament Agency: It Is Off to a Slow Start." *Science* (Dec. 8, 1961): 1870–71.

205 Herzfeld, Norma K. "Disarmament Inches Ahead." *Commonweal* (Sept. 3, 1965): 631–35.

206 Herzog, Arthur. "Waiting for G.C.D." *War/Peace Report* 5 (Apr. 1965): 3–7.

207 Humphrey, Sen. Hubert H. "Arms Control and Disarmament Act of 1974." *Congressional Record* 121 (Mar. 12, 1975): S3778–80.

208 Kastenmeier, Rep. Robert W. "United States Machinery for Disarmament." In Seymour Melman, ed., *Disarmament: Its Politics and Economics*. Boston: American Academy of Arts & Sciences, 1962, pp. 177–92.

209 Lall, Betty Goetz. "Government Sponsored Research for Disarmament." *Bulletin of the Atomic Scientists* 21 (Feb. 1965): 44–46.

210 Langer, Elinor. "ACDA: Criticism of Arms Agency Increases, but Congress Grows Friendly and Outlook Brightens." *Science* (July 19, 1963): 255–56.

211 ———. "New Science Head for Disarmament Agency." *Science* (Nov. 22, 1963): 1045.

212 Martin, Laurence W. "Disarmament: An Agency In Search of a Policy." *Reporter* (July 4, 1963): 22–26.

213 Nordness, Nedville E. "ACDA: The First Year of Research." *Bulletin of the Atomic Scientists* 19 (Jan. 1963): 36.

214 Ruggieri, Nicholas. "The Man [William C. Foster] Who Made Arms Control 'Respectable.'" *Foreign Service Journal* 48 (Feb. 1971): 15–17.

215 Schneider, Barry R. "Arms Restraint: Too Weak a Voice." *Defense Monitor* 3 (Aug. 1974): 5–6.

216 Timberlake, Clare H. "Planning of U.S. Arms Policy." In James E. Dougherty and John F. Lehman, Jr., eds., *The Prospects for Arms Control*. New York: MacFadden-Bartell, 1965, pp. 145–51.

217 Zablocki, Rep. Clement J. "Proposed ACDA Legislation." *Congressional Record* 121 (Jan. 16, 1975): H162–63.

Origins

218 "Arms Control: Last Chance?" *Newsweek* (Mar. 20, 1961): 35–36.

219 Cavers, David F. "The Challenge of Planning Arms Controls." *Foreign Affairs* 34 (Oct. 1955): 50–66.

220 "Congress Urged to OK Disarmament Agency." *Business Week* (Aug. 26, 1961): 30–31.

221 Humphrey, Sen. Hubert H. "Government Organization for Arms Control." *Daedalus* 89 (Fall 1960): 967–83.

222 ———. "Government Organization for Arms Control." In Donald G. Brennan, ed., *Arms Control, Disarmament, and National Security*. New York: Braziller, 1961, pp. 391–403.

223 [Kennedy, Pres. John F.]. "President Kennedy Sends Congress Draft Bill to Establish U.S. Disarmament Agency for World Peace and Security." *U.S. Department of State Bulletin* (July 17, 1961): 99–106.

224 [———, and John J. McCloy]. "Letters from the Presidential Adviser on Disarmament Matters to President Kennedy: Recommendations for a United States Disarmament Agency for World Peace and Security, June 23, 1961." *Documents on Disarmament, 1961*. Washington, D.C.: G.P.O., 1962, pp. 197–98.

225 National Planning Assoc. *1970 Without Arms Control*. Planning Pamphlet 104. Washington, D.C., 1958.

226 ———. *Strengthening the Government for Arms Control*. Planning Pamphlet 109. Washington, D.C., 1960. [Reprinted by the U.S. Senate, 86th Cong., 2d Sess., as Sen. Doc. 123, August 1960.]

227 Smith, Frederic Walton. "Organization of the Government for Disarmament." M.A. thesis, American Univ., 1962.

228 U.S. House. Committee on Foreign Affairs. "Disarmament or Disaster." *Congressional Record* 108 (Oct. 2, 1962): H21795–97.

229 ———. Hearings: *To Establish a United States Arms Control Agency*. 87th Cong., 1st Sess., Aug. 24, 25, 28; Sept. 7, 1961.

230 ———. Report: *To Establish a United States Arms Control Agency*. Report no. 1165. 87th Cong., 1st Sess., 1961.

231 U.S. Senate. Committee on Foreign Relations. Hearings: *Disarmament Agency*. 87th Cong., 1st Sess., Aug. 14–16, 1961.

232 U.S. Senate. Office of the Adviser to the President on Disarmament. *Report on S.2180 Creating a United States Disarmament*

Agency for World Peace and Security. Washington, D.C.: G.P.O., 1961.

233   *United States Statutes at Large.* 87th Cong., 1st Sess. Washington, D.C.: G.P.O., 1961, pp. 631–39. [Public Law 87–297, Sept. 26, 1961.]

Stassen Group, 1955–1958

234   Adams, Sherman. *Firsthand Report: The Story of the Eisenhower Administration.* New York: Popular Library, 1962, pp. 314–26.

235   "Childe Harold and Disarmament." *Nation* (Mar. 16, 1957): 225.

236   Collins, Frederick W. "The Purging of Stassen." *Nation* (Mar. 15, 1958): 221–23.

237   Eisenhower, Pres. Dwight D. "Special Assistant to the President for Developing Disarmament Policy." *U.S. Department of State Bulletin* (Apr. 4, 1955): 556–57.

238   Frye, William R. "Mr. Stassen's Burglar Alarm." *Reporter* (Sept. 22, 1955): 14–19.

239   Inglis, David R. "Arms Control Efforts Buried In State." *Bulletin of the Atomic Scientists* 13 (May 1957): 74–75.

240   ———. "The Stassen Appointment: Turning Point in Disarmament Thinking?" *Bulletin of the Atomic Scientists* 11 (June 1955): 216.

241   "Peace Secretary Explains His Job." *Nation's Business* 43 (Jan. 1955): 96–97.

242   Roberts, Chalmers M. "The Hopes and Obstinacy of Harold Stassen." *Reporter* (Sept. 5, 1957): 25–29.

243   Stassen, Harold E. "Developing U.S. Policy on Disarmament." *U.S. Department of State Bulletin* (May 16, 1955): 801–05.

244   ———. "Disarmament and the President's Geneva Proposal." *U.S. Department of State Bulletin* (Oct. 31, 1955): 703–11.

Congress, Agency & AC&D Impact Statements

245   "Arms Control: Impact Statements Called a 'Farce' and a 'Mockery'." *Science* (Oct. 1, 1976): 36–37.

246   "Arms Control Impact Statements Declassified [texts]." *Arms Control Today* 6 (Oct. 1976): 5–7.

247   Berdes, George. "Congress' New Leverage." *Center Magazine* 9 (July–Aug. 1976): 76–80.

248   Boffery, Philip M. "Arms Control Agency: New Law Seeks to End Its Period of 'Eclipse.' " *Science* (Dec. 26, 1975): 1275–78.

249   Harrington, Rep. Michael J. "Building Arms Control into the National Security Process." *Arms Control Today* 5 (Feb. 1975): 4–5.

250   Humphrey, Sen. Hubert. "Arms Control and Disarmament Impact Statement." *Congressional Record* 122 (Aug. 9, 1976): S13935–37.

251   Lall, Betty Goetz. "Arms Control Impact Statements: A New Approach to Slowing the Arms Race?" *Arms Control Today* 6 (July–Aug. 1976): 1–5.

252   "Senate Committee Rejects Arms Control Impact Statements." *Defense & Space Business Daily* (Sept. 27, 1976): 141–42.

Reports & Reviews

253   U.S. Arms Control & Disarmament Agency. *Annual Report to Congress* [1961–]. Washington, D.C.: G.P.O., 1962–. [Reprinted in annual issue of *Documents on Disarmament, 1961–.* Washington, D.C.: G.P.O., 1962–.]

254   U.S. House. Committee on Armed Services. Hearings & Report: *Review of Arms Control and Disarmament Activities.* 93d Cong., 2d Sess., 1974.

255   U.S. House. Committee on Foreign Affairs. Hearings: *To Amend the Arms Control and Disarmament Act.* 2 pts. 88th Cong., 1st Sess., 1963.

256   ———. Hearings: *To Amend Further the Arms Control and Disarmament Act.* 89th Cong., 1st Sess., Jan. 26, 27, 1965.

257   ———. Hearings: *Arms Control and Disarmament Act Amendments, 1968.* 90th Cong., 2d Sess., Feb. 1–20, 1968.

258   ———. Hearings: *Arms Control and Disarmament Act Amendments, 1970.* 91st Cong., 2d Sess., Feb. 26, 1970.

259   ———. Hearings: *Arms Control and Disarmament Act Amendment.* 92d Cong., 2d Sess., Mar. 9, 1972.

260 ———. Hearings: *Arms Control and Disarmament Amendment*. 93d Cong., 2d Sess., 1974.

261 ———. Hearings: *Arms Control and Disarmament Act Amendments*. 94th Cong., 1st Sess., 1975.

262 ———. Subcommittee on National Security Policy and Scientific Development. Staff Study: *Review of Arms Control Legislation and Organization*. Washington, D.C.: G.P.O., Sept. 1974.

263 U.S. Senate. Committee on Foreign Relations. Hearings: *Review of Operations of the Arms Control and Disarmament Agency*. 87th Cong., 2d Sess., Mar. 8, 1962.

264 ———. Hearings: *To Amend the Arms Control and Disarmament Act*. 88th Cong., 1st Sess., 1963.

265 ———. Hearings: *To Amend the Arms Control and Disarmament Act*. 89th Cong., 1st Sess., Feb. 22, 23, 1965.

266 ———. Hearings: *Arms Control and Disarmament Act Amendment, 1968*. 90th Cong., 2d Sess., Mar. 9, 1968.

267 ———. Hearings: *Arms Control and Disarmament Act Amendment, 1970*. 91st Cong., 2d Sess., Mar. 23, 1970.

268 ———. Hearings: *Arms Control and Disarmament Act Amendment, 1972*. 92d Cong., 2d Sess., Mar. 16, 1972.

269 ———. Hearings: *Arms Control and Disarmament Act Amendment, 1974*. 93d Cong., 2d Sess., Mar. 5, 7, 1974.

PEACE SECRETARY/DEPARTMENT OF PEACE

270 Eddy, J. "Department of Peace Called for at National Conference." *Christian Century* (May 16, 1973): 578–79.

271 Hartke, Sen. Vance. "The Case for Establishing a Department of Peace." *War/Peace Report* 9 (May 1969): 7–9.

272 ———. "The Peace Department." *Playboy* (May 1970): 135–36, 230–32.

273 Schuman, Fredrick L. *Why a Department of Peace?* Beverly Hills, Ca.: Another Mother for Peace, 1969.

274 "Senator Vance Hartke's Proposal for Department of Peace." *Commonweal* (Feb. 21, 1969): 631–32.

275 U.S. House. Committee on Foreign Affairs. Hearings: *To Create a Department of Peace*. 79th Cong., 1st Sess., Nov. 8, 1945.

276 U.S. Senate. "Senate Bill 4019: Introduction of Bill Establishing a Department of Peace by Vance Hartke." *Congressional Record* 114 (Sept. 11, 1968): S26350–58.

277 ———. "Senate Bill 953: Introduction of a Bill Establishing a Department of Peace by Vance Hartke." *Congressional Record* 115 (Feb. 7, 1969): S3151–57.

278 Waskow, Arthur I. *Toward a Peacemakers Academy: A Proposal for a First Step Toward a United Nations Transnational Peacemaking Force*. The Hague: W. Junk, 1967.

PUGWASH MOVEMENT

Summaries of resolutions and themes of annual conferences can usually be found in the *Bulletin of the Atomic Scientists;* check index for other listings.

Historical Perspectives

279 La, Betty Goetz. "Pugwash: Progress and Prospects." *War/Peace Report* 6 (Nov. 1966): 6–7.

280 Malecki, Ignacy. "Twelve Years of Pugwash." *Polish Perspectives* 12 (Oct. 1969): 24–31.

281 Malek, Ivan. "A Report on the Pugwash Movement." *Gandhi Marg* 9 (July 1965): 236–39.

282 Mann, George. "Lab Coat Diplomacy: The Hazards of Ignorant Objectivity." *Georgia Review* 25:2 (1971): 159–81.

283 Rabinowitch, Eugene. "The Pugwash Conference—Pugwash History and Outlook." *Bulletin of the Atomic Scientists* 13 (Sept. 1957): 243–48.

284 Rotblat, Joseph. *Pugwash: The First Ten Years*. New York: Humanities Press, 1967.

285 ———. *Science and World Affairs: History of the Pugwash Conferences*. London: Dawsons, 1962.

286 ———. *Scientists in the Quest For Peace: A History of the Pugwash Conferences.* Cambridge: M.I.T. Press, 1972.

287 Russell, Lord Bertrand. "The Early History of the Pugwash Movement." In Seymour Melman, ed., *Disarmament: Its Politics and Economics.* Boston: American Academy of Arts & Sciences, 1962, pp. 18–31.

288 Schwartz, Leonard E. "Perspective on Pugwash." *International Affairs* [London] 43 (July 1967): 498–515.

Contemporaneous Assessments

289 Barnes, H. J. "Pugwash Fights Atrophy." *Science News* (Oct. 7, 1967): 350–51.

290 Cahn, Anne H. "A Student's View of Pugwash." *Bulletin of the Atomic Scientists* 27 (Apr. 1971): 36–37.

291 Coughlin, William J. "The Pugwash Conference." *Missiles and Rockets* (Dec. 6, 1965): 46.

292 "Disarmament and Arms Limitation: Pugwash Assessment." *Bulletin of the Atomic Scientists* 27 (Mar. 1971): 20–23.

293 Doty, Paul. "Community of Science and the Search for Peace." *Science* (Sept. 10, 1971): 998-1002.

294 Feld, Bernard T. "Scientists as Diplomats: What is Pugwash Anyway?" *Nation* (Nov. 6, 1972): 431–35.

295 ———. "The 21st Pugwash Conference on Science and World Affairs." *Science* (Dec. 10, 1971): 1150 ff.

296 Lapter, Karol. "Pugwash and Peace." *Polish Perspectives* 10 (Jan. 1967): 42–48.

297 McDaniel, G. C. "Pugwash Movement: Science's Conscience?" *Christian Century* (Oct. 14, 1970): 1232–34.

298 *Proceedings of the Twentieth Pugwash Conference on Science and World Affairs: Peace and International Cooperation: A Programme for the Seventies.* London: Taylor & Francis, 1970.

299 "Pugwash In Good Shape." *Nature* [London] (Sept. 21, 1968): 1205–06.

300 "Pugwash: Raison d'etre." *Bulletin of the Atomic Scientists* 28 (Feb. 1972): 22–29.

301 Rabinowitch, Eugene. "After Pugwash—The Soviet Reaction." *Bulletin of the Atomic Scientists* 13 (Nov. 1957): 314–15.

302 ———. "On the SOCHI Conference." *Bulletin of the Atomic Scientists* 26 (Apr. 1970): 18–20.

303 Rich, Alexander. "Science and Survival: The Pugwash Conference at Sochi, U.S.S.R." *Science* (Dec. 12, 1969): 1445–46.

304 Sohn, Louis B. "Pugwash on Disarmament." *Nation* (Jan. 14, 1961): 25–27.

305 Thirring, Hans. "Comments on Pugwash: From the West—Perils from War." *Bulletin of the Atomic Scientists* 14 (Mar. 1958): 121–22.

306 Topchiev, A. V. "Comments on Pugwash: From the East—To Prevent Atomic War." *Bulletin of the Atomic Scientists* 14 (Mar. 1958): 118–20.

307 U.S. Senate. Committee on the Judiciary. Subcommittee to Investigate the Administration of the Internal Security Laws. Report: *The Pugwash Conferences: A Staff Analysis.* 87th Cong., 1st Sess., 1961.

STOCKHOLM INTERNATIONAL PEACE RESEARCH INSTITUTE (SIPRI)

SIPRI publications are listed in the index.

308 Barnaby, Frank. "Peace Research and SIPRI." *Nature* [London] (Dec. 14, 1973): 397–400.

309 ———. "Peace Research: The Study of Armaments and Disarmament." *Ethics in Science & Medicine* 2 (1975): 25–42.

310 Greenberg, Daniel S. "Peace Research: SIPRI, in Sweden, is Making a Role for Itself." *Science* (Dec. 27, 1968): 1465–66.

311 Hawkes, Nigel. "Peace Research Institute Losing Old Staff, Pondering Role." *Science* (Oct. 20, 1972): 286–88.

312 SIPRI. *Report of Activities.* Stockholm, 1968–. [Annually.]

Two

Introduction to AC&D Issues

THE METHODS, OBJECTIVES, and risks of arms control and disarmament are not easily defined. Arguments are frequent between those who support these ideas and those who do not; also, there is considerable argument between arms controllers and disarmers themselves over proper courses of action. The books and essays listed here seek to define the general nature and purpose of arms control and disarmament, and the relationship of these ideas with other fundamental issues, such as national security, military strategy, and world peace. These writings, consequently, focus on the abstract and theoretical aspects of arms control and disarmament.

In arms control, the "state of the art" may be briefly traced through two collections of essays, printed in *Daedalus*, written fifteen years apart. Donald G. Brennan, in *Arms Control, Disarmament, and National Security* (1961), summarized the ideas of arms controllers in 1960; this has been subsequently updated in F. A. Long and G. W. Rathjens, eds., *Arms, Defense Policy and Arms Control* (1976). Two other recent books also provide insight into the mechanics of arms control: D. V.

Edwards' *Arms Control in International Politics* (1969) and R. M. Lawrence's *Arms Control and Disarmament* (1973).

Disarmament as the national policy, more correctly defined as weapons reduction, fell from favor with the rise of the arms controllers in the early 1960s. The essays listed here survey the disarmers' anguish and optimism, as well as criticism of their approach. Marion H. McVitty's *Preface to Disarmament: An Appraisal of Recent Proposals* (1970) analyzes the failure of American-Soviet proposals for general and complete disarmament.

Some disarmers have favored a unilateral approach to the problems of war and arms races. This extreme technique is favorably examined by April Carter in a series of essays entitled *Unilateral Disarmament: Its Theory and Policy* (1965). Another idea, unilateral initiatives, has been suggested in Amitai Etzioni's *The Hard Way to Peace: A New Strategy* (1962), which also offers a critique of the extremist approach.

The uneasy harmony between arms controllers and disarmers began to be disrupted in the 1970s, when the latter became disillusioned with the failure of negotiations to call for reductions as well as limitations of military forces. The essays by Frank Barnaby, "False Promises of Disarmament," in *New Scientist* (1970) and by Bernard T. Feld, "The Sorry History of Arms Control," in *Bulletin of the Atomic Scientists* (1970) have spearheaded the criticism of arms controllers and their policies.

An excellent annual summary of the world's weapons dilemma can be found in the Stockholm International Peace Research Institute's (SIPRI) *Yearbook of World Armament and Disarmament* (1968/69–). SIPRI's director, Frank Barnaby, and Ronald Huisken have condensed much of the institute's findings in their *Arms Uncontrolled* (1975), an excellent survey of today's arms control and disarmament issues.

Survey of AC&D Issues

313 "Arms, Defense Policy, and Arms Control." *Daedalus* 104 (Summer 1975): 1–214. [Entire issue.]

314 "Arms Control." *Daedalus* 89 (Fall 1960): 647–1070. [Special issue.]

315 Barker, Charles A., ed. *Problems of World Disarmament: A Series of Lectures Delivered at the Johns Hopkins University.* Boston: Houghton Mifflin, 1963.

316 Barnaby, Frank, and Ronald Huisken. *Arms Uncontrolled.* Cambridge: Harvard Univ. Press, 1975.

317 Barnet, Richard J., and Richard A. Falk, eds. *Security in Disarmament.* Princeton: Princeton Univ. Press, 1965.

318 Bernard, Stephen. "Some Political and Technical Implications of Disarmament." *World Politics* 8 (Oct. 1955): 71–90.

319 Brennan, Donald G., ed. *Arms Control, Disarmament, and National Security.* New York: Braziller, 1961. [Based on the special Fall 1960 issue of *Daedalus.*]

320 Burns, Arthur Lee. "Disarmament or the Balance of Terror?" *World Politics* 11 (Oct. 1959): 132–45.

321 Burns, Richard Dean, and Walter Fisher, eds. *Armament and Disarmament: A Continuing Dispute.* Belmont, Ca.: Wadsworth, 1964.

322 Burton, John W. *Peace Theory: Preconditions of Disarmament.* New York: Knopf, 1962.

323 Chamberlain, Neil W. *The West in a World Without War.* New York: McGraw-Hill, 1963.

324 Claude, Inis L. *Swords into Plowshares.* New York: Random House, 1956.

325 Clemens, Walter C., Jr., ed. *Toward a Strategy of Peace.* Chicago: Rand McNally, 1965.

326 Coste, Rene. *Dynamique de la Paix.* Paris: Journai Descleé, 1965.

328 Dean, Fred M. "The Bird's-eye View of Arms Control and Disarmament." *Air University Review* 17 (May–June 1966): 2–11.

329 "Disarmament and Arms Control." *International Conciliation*, no. 574 (Sept. 1969): 28–42.

330 Dougherty, James E. *How to Think About Arms Control and Disarmament.* New York: Crane, Russak, 1973.

331 ———, and John F. Lehman, Jr., eds. *Arms Control for the Late Sixties.* Princeton: Van Nostrand, 1967.

332 ———. *The Prospects for Arms Control.* New York: MacFadden-Bartell, 1965.

333 Edwards, David V. *Arms Control in International Politics.* New York: Holt, Rinehart & Winston, 1969.

334 Etzioni, Amitai, and Martin Weglinisky, eds. *War and Its Prevention*. New York: Harper & Row, 1970.

335 Falk, Richard A. "On Minimizing the Use of Nuclear Weapons: A Comparison of Revolutionary and Reformist Perspectives." *Minimizing the Use of Nuclear Weapons*. Monograph, no. 23. Princeton: Princeton Univ., Center of International Studies, Mar. 1966.

336 ———, and Saul H. Mendlovitz, eds. *The Strategy of World Order*. 4 vols. New York: World Law Fund, 1966.

337 Frisch, David H., ed. *Arms Reduction— Program and Issue*. New York: Twentieth Century Fund, 1961.

338 Hadley, Arthur Twining. *The Nation's Safety and Arms Control*. New York: Viking, 1961.

339 Henkin, Louis, ed. *Arms Control: Issues for the Public*. Englewood Cliffs, N.J.: Prentice-Hall, 1961.

340 Joliot-Curie, Frederic. *La Paix, le Désarmement et la Coopération Internationale*. Paris: Edition "Défense de la Paix," 1959.

341 Kahn, Herman, and Carl Dibble. "Criteria for Long-Range Nuclear Control Policies." *California Law Review* 55 (May 1967): 473–92.

342 Katz, Amrom H. "Good Disarmament—And Bad." *Air Force and Space Digest* 44 (May 1961): 48–55.

343 ———. "Some Things to Do and Some to Think." *Bulletin of the Atomic Scientists* 17 (Apr. 1961): 139–43.

344 Keyston, J. E. *The Nature of the Disarmament Problem*. Toronto: Canadian Institute of International Affairs, 1961.

345 Lawrence, Robert M. *Arms Control and Disarmament: Practice and Promise*. Minneapolis: Burgess, 1973.

346 ———. "The Political Realities of Disarmament." Ph.D. diss., Univ. of Kansas, 1962.

347 Lefever, Ernest W., ed. *Arms and Arms Control: A Symposium*. New York: Praeger, 1962.

348 Long, Franklin, and George W. Rathjens, eds. *Arms, Defense Policy and Arms Control*. New York: Norton, 1976.

349 Luard, Evan, ed. *First Steps to Disarmament: A New Approach to the Problems of Arms Reduction*. New York: Basic Books, 1965.

350 Melman, Seymour. *Disarmament: Its Politics and Economics*. Boston: American Academy of Arts & Sciences, 1962.

351 Midgaard, Knut. "Arms Races, Arms Control, and Disarmament." *Cooperation and Conflict* 5:1 (1970): 20–51.

352 Richter, Robert C. "Disarmament and Arms Control." *International Conciliation*, no. 579 (Sept. 1970): 31–43.

353 Scientific Group for Disarmament. *Problems of Disarmament*. Moscow: Institute of World Economics & International Relations, 1963.

354 Sheinin, Yuri. "Disarmament or Balance of Terror?" *International Affairs* [Moscow] 7 (Aug. 1961): 22–27.

355 Singer, J. David. *Deterrence, Arms Control, and Disarmament: Toward a Synthesis in National Security Policy*. Columbus: Ohio State Univ. Press, 1962.

356 Slomich, Sidney J. "Arms Control and Disarmament: The Great Evasion." *Bulletin of the Atomic Scientists* 24 (June 1968): 18–22.

357 Stone, Jeremy J. *Containing the Arms Race: Some Specific Proposals*. Cambridge: M.I.T. Press, 1966.

358 Strachey, John. *On the Prevention of War*. New York: St. Martin's Press, 1961.

359 Tondel, Lyman M., and Louis Henkin. *Disarmament: Background Papers and Proceedings of the Fourth Hammarskjöld Forum*. Dobbs Ferry, N.Y.: Oceana, 1964.

360 U.S. Arms Control & Disarmament Agency. *Arms Control and Disarmament*. ACDA Pub. 11. Washington, D.C.: G.P.O., 1963.

361 Van Slyck, Philip. *Peace: The Control of National Power: A Guide for the Concerned Citizen on Problems of Disarmament and Strengthening of the United Nations*. Boston: Beacon Press, 1963.

362 Wadsworth, James J. *The Price of Peace*. New York: Praeger, 1962.

363 Warburg, James P. *Disarmament: The Challenge of the Nineteen Sixties*. Garden City, N.Y.: Doubleday, 1961.

364 York, Herbert F., ed. *Arms Control: Readings from Scientific American.* San Francisco: W. H. Freeman, 1973.

365 Young, Elizabeth. *A Farewell to Arms Control?* London: Penguin, 1972.

366 Young, Wayland. *Existing Mechanisms of Arms Control.* London: Pergamon, 1966.

367 ———. *Strategy for Survival: First Steps in Nuclear Disarmament.* Baltimore: Penguin, 1959.

368 Zeidler, Frank P. *Armament or Disarmament?* New York: Lutheran Church in America, Board of Social Ministry, 1970.

POLITICAL DIMENSIONS

369 Allen, James S. "The Politics of Disarmament." In Herbert Aptheker, ed., *A Symposium: Disarmament and the American Economy.* New York: New Century Publishers, 1960, pp. 12–19.

370 Bloomfield, Lincoln P. "Arms Control & International Order." *International Organization* 23 (Summer 1969): 637–55.

371 Boulding, Kenneth E. "Arms Limitation and Integrative Activity as Elements in the Establishment of Stable Peace." In James E. Dougherty and John F. Lehman, Jr., eds., *Arms Control for the Late Sixties.* Princeton: Van Nostrand, 1967, pp. 237–46.

372 ———. "The University, Society, and Arms Control." *Journal of Conflict Resolution* 7:3 (1963): 458–63.

373 Buchan, Alastair. "Arms Nobody Wants to Control." *New Republic* (Nov. 6, 1965): 17–18.

374 Cooper, Spencer. "Disarmament and Trade Protection." *Socialist Review* 44 (Sept. 1929): 21–25.

375 Falk, Richard A. "Arms Control, Foreign Policy, and Global Reform." *Daedalus* 104 (Summer 1975): 35–52.

376 Fox, William T. R. "Political and Diplomatic Prerequisites of Arms Control." *Daedalus* 89 (Fall 1960): 1000–1014.

377 Goldman, Ralph M. "A Transactional Theory of Political Integration and Arms Control." *American Political Science Review* 63 (Sept. 1969): 719–33.

378 Griffiths, Franklyn. "Transnational Politics and Arms Control." *International Journal* 26 (Autumn 1971): 640–74.

379 Inglis, David R. "Transition to Disarmament." In Robert A. Goldwin, ed., *America Armed.* Chicago: Rand McNally, 1963, pp. 92–111.

380 Korovin, Eugene A. "Disarmament and Sovereignty." *International Affairs* [Moscow] 7 (Feb. 1961): 51–57.

381 Lall, Arthur S. "Territorial Disputes and Disarmament: Some General Propositions." *Disarmament* 9 (Mar. 1966): 6–10.

382 Levine, Robert A. "Arms Agreement: A Model of Stalemate." *Journal of Conflict Resolution* 6:4 (1962): 308–18.

383 London, Kurt L. "Disarmament and World Communism." In James E. Dougherty and John F. Lehman, Jr., eds., *The Prospects for Arms Control.* New York: MacFadden-Bartell, 1965, pp. 83–94.

384 Martin, Laurence W. "Political Settlements and Arms Control." *Current History* 42 (May 1962): 296–301.

385 North, Robert C. "Arms Control and the Dynamics of International Conflict." *Stanford Journal of International Studies* 7 (Spring 1972): 96–108.

386 Ramundo, Bernard A. "Peaceful Coexistence: Arms Control in the Building of Communism." *Wayne State Law Review* 12 (Spring 1966): 596 ff.

387 Rubinstein, Alvin Z. "Political Barriers to Disarmament." *Orbis* 9 (Spring 1965): 166–71.

388 Schwartz, Donald M. "Arms Control and Supra-Nationalism." *Bulletin of the Atomic Scientists* 27 (Apr. 1971): 38 ff.

389 Sheikh, Mujib A. "Disarmament and the Ideological Conflict." *Pakistan Horizon* 20:1 (1967): 48–52.

390 Shulman, Marshall D. "Arms Control in an International Context." *Daedalus* 104 (Summer 1975): 53–62.

391 Willot, Albert. "Political Strategy and Armaments Control." *NATO Review* 24 (Aug. 1976): 3–6.

392   Wilson, Eugene E. "Strategy of Disarmament." *Ordnance* 40 (Jan.–Feb. 1956): 589–91.

SECURITY

393   American Friends Service Committee. *Toward Security Through Disarmament: A Report.* Philadelphia, 1952.

394   Belovski, Dimce. "Security Through Disarmament." *Review of International Affairs* [Belgrade] (Oct. 5, 1968): 4–7.

395   Brennan, Donald G. "Some Fundamental Problems of Arms Control and National Security." *Orbis* 15 (Spring 1971): 218–31.

396   Brown, Harold. "Security Through Limitations." *Foreign Affairs* 47 (Apr. 1969): 422–32.

397   Cadogon, Alexander. "Disarmament and Security." *Annals of the American Academy of Political and Social Science* 252 (July 1947): 84–92. [Hereafter cited as *Annals of the Amer. Acad. of Pol. & Soc. Sci.*]

398   Claude, Inis L. "Peace and Security Through Disarmament: Disarmament as an Approach to Peace." In John C. Garnett, comp., *Theories of Peace and Security.* New York: St. Martin's Press, 1970, pp. 123–35.

399   Dougherty, James E. "Key to Security: Disarmament or Arms Stability?" *Orbis* 4 (Fall 1960): 261–83.

400   Fenwick, Charles G. "Organization for Mutual Security: The Condition Precedent to Disarmament." *Annals of the Amer. Acad. of Pol. & Soc. Sci.* 126 (July 1926): 154–57.

401   Foster, William C. "Risk and Security in the Age of Nuclear Weapons." *Journal of Conflict Resolution* 7:3 (1963): 326–32. [Also printed as ACDA Pub. 12, 1963.]

402   Hoijer, O. *La Sécurité Internationale et ses Modes de Réalisation.* Vol. 4: *Réduction des Armements.* Paris: Editions Internationales, 1930.

403   Kapur, Ashok. "Arms Control and Military Security." *Foreign Affairs Reports* 19 (Jan. 1970): 1–6.

404   King, James E., Jr. "Arms Control and United States Security." In Louis Henkin, ed., *Arms Control: Issues for the Public.* Englewood Cliffs, N.J.: Prentice-Hall, 1961, pp. 76–111.

405   Kintner, William R. "Arms Control and National Security: A Caveat." In James E. Dougherty and John F. Lehman, Jr., eds., *Arms Control for the Late Sixties.* Princeton: Van Nostrand, 1967, pp. 31–44.

406   Leghorn, Col. Richard S. "The Pursuit of Rational World-Security Arrangements." In Donald G. Brennan, ed., *Arms Control, Disarmament, and National Security.* New York: Braziller, 1961, pp. 407–22.

407   Nevins, Allan. "Arms and Security." *Current History* 40 (May 1934): 196–98.

408   Philip, André. *Sécurité et Désarmement.* Paris: Valois, 1932.

409   Powell, Craig. "Realistic Arms Control Can Enhance National Security." *Armed Forces Management* 13 (Dec. 1966): 46, 51, 54.

410   Robbins, George N. *Security By Disarmament.* London: Williams & Norgate, 1932.

411   Sohn, Louis B. "Security Through Disarmament." *Nation* (Feb. 25, 1961): 159.

412   Tabacovici, G. G. *Sécurité et Désarmement.* Paris: Pedone, 1932.

413   U.S. Arms Control & Disarmament Agency. *Arms Control and National Security.* 2d ed. Washington, D.C.: G.P.O., 1970.

PEACEKEEPING & WORLD GOVERNMENT

See also Chapter 5, Special Issues: Inspection, Verification & Supervision.

414   Bloomfield, Lincoln P. "Arms Control & International Order." *International Organization* 23 (Summer 1969): 637–55.

415   ———. "Arms Control and World Government." *World Politics* 14 (July 1962): 633–45.

416   Boyd, Andrew. "Disarmament and World Government." *World Affairs* [London] 125 (Summer 1962): 41–43.

417   Falk, Richard A. "Provision for Peaceful Change in a Disarming World." In Richard J. Barnet and Richard A. Falk, eds., *Security in Disarmament.* Princeton: Princeton Univ. Press, 1965, pp. 347–60.

418 Finkelstein, Lawrence S. *Defense, Disarmament and World Order.* Toronto: Canadian Institute of International Affairs, 1962.

419 Kintner, William R. "The Case Against International Control of Weapons." *Current History* 47 (Aug. 1964): 103–06, 116.

420 Krivchikova, Emiliia S. *Vooruzhennye Sily OON: Mezhdunarodnye Pravovye Voprosy* [U.N. armed forces: International law problems]. Moscow: Izd-vo Instituta Mezhdunarodnykh Otnoshenii, 1965.

421 Martin, Paul. "Peace-Keeping and Disarmament." *Disarmament* 6 (June 1965): 1–3.

422 Nash, Vernon. "The Case for International Control of Weapons." *Current History* 47 (Aug. 1964): 97–102, 115.

423 Wolfers, Arnold. "Disarmament, Peacekeeping and the National Interest." *The United States in a Disarmed World.* Baltimore: Johns Hopkins Press, 1966, pp. 3–32.

Arms Control

424 Art, Robert J. "Restructuring the Military-Industrial Complex: Arms Control in International Perspective." *Public Policy* 22 (Fall 1974): 423–59.

425 Barber, James A., Jr. "The Objectives of Arms Control." *Naval War College Review* 22 (Feb. 1970): 35–43.

426 Barrett, Raymond J. "The Hard Realities of Arms Controls." *Air Force Magazine* 55 (Feb. 1972): 47–49.

427 Bowie, Robert R. "Basic Requirements of Arms Control." In Donald G. Brennan, ed., *Arms Control, Disarmament, and National Security.* New York: Braziller, 1961, pp. 43–55.

428 Brennan, Donald G. "Setting and Goals of Arms Control." *Arms Control, Disarmament, and National Security.* New York: Braziller, 1961, pp. 19–42.

429 Brodie, Bernard. "On Objectives of Arms Control." *International Security* 1 (Summer 1976): 17–36.

430 Bull, Hedley. "Arms Control: A Stocktaking and Prospectus." *Problems of Modern Strategy.* New York: Praeger, 1970.

431 ———. "Arms Control and World Order." *International Security* 1 (Summer 1976): 3–16.

432 Cahn, Anne H., et al. "The Search for a New Handle on Arms Control." *Bulletin of the Atomic Scientists* 30 (Apr. 1974): 7.

433 Carroll, Kent J. "A Second Step Toward Arms Control." *Military Review* 47 (May 1967): 77–84.

434 Clemens, Walter C., Jr. "Arms Control as a Way to Peace." *World Affairs* [London] 135 (Winter 1972): 197–219.

435 Crane, Brian. "Arms Control: A New Approach to Disarmament." *Canadian Institute of International Affairs* 21 (Feb. 1962): 1–20.

436 Crane, Robert D. "Some Basic Strategies of Arms Control." In James E. Dougherty and John F. Lehman, Jr., eds., *The Prospects for Arms Control.* New York: MacFadden-Bartell, 1965, pp. 108–30.

437 Dowell, Frank H. "The Biological Basis of Arms Control." *Air University Review* 16 (Mar.–Apr. 1965): 64–67.

438 Ferguson, Allen R. "Mechanics of Some Limited Disarmament Measures." *American Economic Review, Papers and Proceedings* 51 (1961): 479–88.

439 Frye, William R. "Characteristics of Recent Arms-Control Proposals and Agreements." In Donald G. Brennan, ed., *Arms Control, Disarmament, and National Security.* New York: Braziller, 1961, pp. 68–87.

440 Giddings, Ralph L., Jr. "Arms Control: No Simple Answers." *U.S. Naval Institute Proceedings* 96 (Feb. 1970): 41–45.

441 Gomer, Robert. "Some Thoughts on Arms Control." *Bulletin of the Atomic Scientists* 17 (Apr. 1961): 133–37.

442 Gray, Colin S. "The Limits of Arms Control." *Air Force Magazine* 58 (Aug. 1975): 70–72.

443 Hassner, Pierre. "Faut-il Enterrer l'Arms Control?" *Etudes Internationales* 4 (Dec. 1973): 411–33.

444 Hosmer, Craig. "Semantics and Asymmetries [of Arms Control]." In James E. Dougherty and John F. Lehman, Jr., eds., *Arms Control for the Late Sixties.* Princeton: Van Nostrand, 1967, pp. 25–30.

445 Lal, Nand. "Arms Control: An Approach to Disarmament." *Indian Journal of Political Science* 30 (July–Sept. 1969): 277–90.

446 "The Partial Measures Approach to Disarmament." *U.N. Review* 4 (Dec. 1957): 4–9, 44, 45.

447 Perle, Richard N. "Arms Control Criteria." *Military Review* 50 (Oct. 1970): 82–93.

448 Pfaltzgraff, Robert L., Jr. "The Rationale for Superpower Arms Control." In William R. Kintner and Robert L. Pfaltzgraff, Jr., eds., *SALT: Implications for Arms Control in the 1970's*. Pittsburgh: Pittsburgh Univ. Press, 1973, pp. 3–20, 95–103.

449 ———, ed. *Contrasting Approaches to Strategic Arms Control*. Lexington, Mass.: D. C. Heath, 1974.

450 Posvar, Col. Wesley W. "The New Meaning of Arms Control." *Air Force Magazine* 46 (June 1963): 38–47.

451 Rathjens, George W. "Changing Perspectives on Arms Control." *Daedalus* 104 (Summer 1975): 201–14.

452 Roberts, Richard B., and Frank T. McClure. "Arms, Arms Control and Foreign Policy." *Journal of Arms Control* 1:3 (1963): 163–83.

453 Schelling, Thomas C. "A Framework for the Evaluation of Arms-Control Proposals." *Daedalus* 104 (Summer 1975): 187–200.

454 Smith, Ralph S. "Arms Control: A Pragmatic Approach to Shared Security." *Armed Forces Management* 15 (Feb. 1969): 17 ff.

455 Sohn, Louis B. "Problems of Arms Control." *Harvard Law Record* (Feb. 4, 1960): 11–13.

456 Wiesner, Jerome B. "A Strategy for Arms Control." *Saturday Review* (Mar. 4, 1967): 17–20.

MILITARY IMPLICATIONS

457 Amme, Carl H., Jr. "Arms Control Restraints and Military Policy." In James E. Dougherty and John F. Lehman, Jr., eds., *The Prospects for Arms Control*. New York: MacFadden-Bartell, 1965, pp. 204–13.

458 Brewer, Thomas L. "Military Officers and Arms Control: Personality Correlates of Attitudes." *Journal of Political & Military Sociology* 3 (Spring 1975): 15–25.

459 Coverdale, Col. Craig G., and Capt. David W. Owen. "Not Mutually Exclusive: The Soldier's Role in Arms Control." *Army* 25:8 (1975): 26–31.

460 Damien, George D. "Arming Through Disarmament." *Military Review* 51 (Mar. 1971): 30–38.

461 Inglis, David R. "Tactical Atomic Weapons and the Problem of Ultimate Controls in Disarmament Planning." *Bulletin of the Atomic Scientists* 8 (Mar. 1952): 79–84.

462 Kahn, Herman. "Arms Control and the Current Arms Environment." In James E. Dougherty and John F. Lehman, Jr., eds., *The Prospects for Arms Control*. New York: MacFadden-Bartell, 1965, pp. 33–49.

463 Kelly, George A. "Arms Control and the Military Establishment." *Military Review* 41 (Jan. 1961): 62–72.

464 Lall, Betty Goetz. "Disarmament Policy and the Pentagon." *Bulletin of the Atomic Scientists* 20 (Sept. 1964): 37–40.

465 Riva, Col. Daniel F. "The Attitude of Professional Military Officers Toward Arms Control and Disarmament." Ph.D. diss., Univ. of Missouri at Kansas City, 1967.

466 Ruggieri, Nicholas. "Arms Control and the Military Man." *Foreign Service Journal* 48 (Feb. 1971): 18–19, 54.

STRATEGY

467 Academy for Interscience Methodology. Museum of Science and Industry. *Maintenance of Strategic Models for Arms Control Analysis*. ACDA/WEC–213. Chicago, Feb. 1974. [Mimeograph.]

468 Averch, H. *Strategic Ambiguity, Asymmetry and Arms Control*. RM–3426–PR. Santa Monica, Ca.: Rand, 1963.

469 Bernal, J. D. "Disarmament and Limited Nuclear War." *New World Review* 26 (Jan. 1958): 30–37.

470 Bethe, Hans A. "Disarmament and Strategy." *Survival* 4 (Nov.–Dec. 1962): 267–76.

471   Bondurant, Joan V. "Paraguerilla Strategy: A New Concept in Arms Control." *Journal of Conflict Resolution* 7:3 (1963): 235–45.

472   Brown, Seyom. "Invulnerable Retaliatory Capability and Arms Control." *World Politics* 13 (July 1961): 518–43.

473   Coffey, Joseph I. "Strategic Superiority, Deterrence and Arms Control." *Orbis* 13 (Winter 1970): 991–1007.

474   ———. *Strategy, Strategic Forces and Arms Control.* Ann Arbor: Bendix Systems Division, 1964. [Reprinted in *Orbis* 9 (Spring 1965): 98–115.]

475   Dean, Arthur H. "Disarmament Negotiations and the Strategic Dialogue." In James E. Dougherty and John F. Lehman, Jr., eds., *The Prospects for Arms Control.* New York: MacFadden-Bartell, 1965, pp. 131–44.

476   Friedman, Peter, and Roger C. Wood. "Arms Control and Limited Strategic War." *Papers of the Michigan Academy of Science, Arts, and Letters* 51 (1966): 319–31.

477   Glick, Edward B., and Lewis A. Frank. "Arms Control and Defensive Systems." *Military Review* 48 (Feb. 1968): 31–38.

478   LeGhait, Edouard. *No Carte Blanche to Capricorn: The Folly of Nuclear War Strategy.* New York: Bookfield House, 1960.

479   McWethy, Capt. Robert D. "Arms Control and the Navy." *Naval Review* (1966): 154–71.

480   Pabsch, Wiegand. "Security and Arms Control: A View From NATO." *NATO Review* 24 (Feb. 1976): 8–12.

481   Phelps, John B. "Some Reflections on Counter-Force and Arms Control." *Journal of Arms Control* 1:2 (1963): 145–48.

482   Pugh, George E. "Restraints, Strategy and Arms Control." *Orbis* 7 (Summer 1963): 199–208.

483   Russett, Bruce M. "A Countercombatant Deterrent? Feasibility, Morality, and Arms Control." In Sam G. Sarkesian, ed., *The Military-Industrial Complex: A Reassessment.* Beverly Hills, Ca.: Sage, 1972, pp. 201–35.

484   Schelling, Thomas C., and Morton H. Halperin. *Strategy and Arms Control.* New York: Twentieth Century Fund, 1961.

485   Schilling, Warner R. "Weapons, Doctrine, and Arms Control: A Case from the Good Old Days." *Journal of Conflict Resolution* 7:3 (1963): 192–214.

486   Shubik, Martin. "On the Study of Disarmament and Escalation." *Journal of Conflict Resolution* 12:1 (1968): 83–101.

487   Smith, Maj. Gen. Dale O. "How Arms-Control Doctrine Can Affect U.S. Strategy." *Air Force and Space Digest* 45 (Dec. 1962): 71–73.

488   Taylor, Gen. Maxwell D. *Swords and Plowshares.* New York: Norton, 1972.

Disarmament

489   Abt, Clark C. "Disarmament as a Strategy." *Journal of Conflict Resolution* 7:3 (1963): 293–308.

490   Aptheker, Herbert. "The Ideology of Disarmament." In Herbert Aptheker, ed., *A Symposium: Disarmament and the American Economy.* New York: New Century Publishers, 1960, pp. 5–12.

491   Ballou, Cmdr. Sidney. "The Practicability of Disarmament." *U.S. Naval Institute Proceedings* 54 (Apr. 1928): 268–72.

492   Bliss, Gen. Tasker H. "What is Disarmament?" *Foreign Affairs* 4 (Apr. 1926): 353–68.

493   Bretnor, Reginald. "Disarmament: Deadend and Detour: Can Our Weaponry be Defused?" *Michigan Quarterly Review* 8 (Winter 1969): 33–42.

494   Bullard, R. L. "The Possibility of Disarmament by International Agreement." *Annals of the Amer. Acad. of Pol. & Soc. Sci.* 96 (July 1921): 49–52.

495   Burhop, E. H. S. "Nuclear Weapons and Disarmament." *Scientific World* 10:4 (1966): 17–20.

496   Byrd, Elbert M. "Toward a Policy of Arms Displacement." *Social Studies* 61 (Mar. 1970): 109–19.

497   Call, A. D. "Is Disarmament Possible?" *Annals of the Amer. Acad. of Pol. & Soc. Sci.* 120 (July 1925): 81–86.

498 Cavers, David F. "Disarmament as a Cumulative Process for Peace." In Seymour Melman, ed., *Disarmament: Its Politics and Economics.* Boston: American Academy of Arts & Sciences, 1962, pp. 32–47.

499 Clark, Grenville. "The Practical Prospects for Disarmament and Genuine Peace." *Proceedings of the American Philosophical Society* (Dec. 16, 1953): 645–51.

500 Colard, Daniel. *Le Désarmement.* Paris: Colin, 1972.

501 Coulthard, Robert O. "Disarmament—The World's Enigma." *Naval War College Review* 12 (Sept. 1960): 1–75.

502 Davis, Edgar B. "Disarmament: The Economic Basis of a Reconstructed World." *Academy of Political Sciences Proceedings* 9 (July 1921): 173–79, 503–09. [Hereafter cited as *Acad. of Pol. Sci. Proceedings.*]

503 Dienne, Jean. "The Peace Movement and the Struggle for Disarmament." *World Marxist Review* 3 (Sept. 1960): 2–9.

504 "Disarmament Is Not a Utopia." *World Marxist Review* 2 (Nov. 1959): 3–7.

505 Emelyanov, V. "Atomic Power and Disarmament." *Bulletin of the Atomic Scientists* 19 (Oct. 1963): 16–20.

506 "A Forum on Nuclear Disarmament." *Impact of Science on Society* 22 (July–Sept. 1972): 209–72.

507 Frye, William R. "Disarmament: A Modern Holy Grail?" *Foreign Policy Bulletin* (July 15, 1955): 161–62.

508 Galtung, Johan. "Two Approaches to Disarmament: The Legalist and the Structuralist." *Journal of Peace Research* 4:3 (1967): 161–95.

509 Gasteyger, Curt. "The Problems of International Disarmament." *Military Review* 46 (Jan. 1966): 23–29.

510 Genevey, Pierre. "Actualité de Désarmement." *Politique Etrangère* 32:2 (1967): 125–33.

511 Glagolev, Igor S. "Is Disarmament Practical?" *Bulletin of the Atomic Scientists* 18 (Sept. 1962): 11–13.

512 Green, Wade. *Disarmament: The Challenge of Civilization.* New York: Coward-McCann, 1966.

513 Jack, Homer A. "Toward Disarmament." *Current History* 64 (Mar. 1973): 42–50.

514 ———. "Toward Nuclear Disarmament." *Humanist* 21 (May–June 1961): 142–47.

515 Lipsky, Mortimer. *A Time for Hysteria: A Citizen's Guide to Disarmament.* New York: A. S. Barnes, 1969.

516 Madariaga, Salvador de. "Disarmament? The Problem Lies Deeper." *New York Times Magazine* (Oct. 11, 1959): 17, 71–75.

517 ———. "The Myth of Disarmament." *Combat Force Journal* 2 (Feb. 1952): 39–40.

518 Meyer, Peter. "Is Disarmament Possible?" *New Leader* (Oct. 1955): 8–10.

519 Miller, James C. "The Corporate Ideal and Postwar Disarmament." Ph.D. diss., Univ. of Washington, 1972.

520 Millis, Walter. "Disarmament: A Dissenting View." *New York Times Magazine* (July 28, 1957): 8 ff.

521 ———. "Essential Conditions of Disarmament." *Social Science* 33 (Oct. 1958): 226–33.

522 Paolucci, Capt. Dominic A. "The Realities of Arms Limitations." *U.S. Naval Institute Proceedings* 98 (May 1972): 178–89.

523 Pringle, Katherine. "New Approaches to Disarmament." *Editorial Research Reports* (Mar. 15, 1961): 1–18.

524 Rabinowitch, Eugene. "About Disarmament." *Bulletin of the Atomic Scientists* 13 (Oct. 1957): 277–82.

525 Reves, Emery. "Why Waste Time Discussing Disarmament?" *Look* (Mar. 28, 1961): 67–72.

526 Riva, Col. Daniel F. "Disarmament: Hope or Hoax?" *Military Review* 44 (Aug. 1964): 26–28.

527 Saundby, Air Marshal Sir Robert. "Problems of Disarmament." *Military Review* 36 (Mar. 1956): 89–95.

528 Schelling, Thomas C. "Perspective on Disarmament." *Disarmament* 9 (Mar. 1966): 11–13.

529 Senghaas, Dieter. "Armament Dynamics and Disarmament." *Instant Research on Peace and Violence* 6:1–2 (1976): 3–17.

530 Sheinin, Yuri. "A Soviet Scientist Looks at Disarmament." *Bulletin of the Atomic Scientists* 20 (Jan. 1964): 19–22.

531 Singh, Ram. "Duplicity About Disarmament." *Radical Humanist* 35 (May 1972): 39–41.

532 Sohn, Louis B. "Basic Problem of Disarmament." *Notre Dame Lawyer* 41 (Dec. 1965): 133–51.

533 Sokol, Anthony E. "Disarmament—Is it Possible?" *U.S. Naval Institute Proceedings* 87 (Apr. 1961): 57–64.

534 "Some Concrete Strategies in the Field of Disarmament." *Instant Research on Peace and Violence* 1:4 (1972): 228–44.

535 Spingarn, Jerome H. *Is Disarmament Possible?* New York: Public Affairs Committee, 1956.

536 Szilard, Leo. "Disarmament and the Problem of Peace." *Bulletin of the Atomic Scientists* 11 (Oct. 1955): 297–307.

537 Talensky, Gen. Nikolai A. "The Technical Problems of Disarmament." *International Affairs* [Moscow] 7 (Mar. 1961): 60–63.

538 Vandenhove, V. M. "General Disarmament, Not 'Balance of Terror.'" *World Marxist Review* 5 (Apr. 1962): 89–91.

539 Walsh, T. J. "The Urge for Disarmament." *Annals of the Amer. Acad. of Pol. & Soc. Sci.* 96 (July 1921): 45–48.

540 Waskow, Arthur I. "Alternative Models of a Disarmed World." *Disarmament and Arms Control* 2 (Winter 1963–64): 59–74.

541 ———. "Historiography and the Disarmed World: A Problem in the Study of an Unprecedented Future." *Diogenes* [Montreal] 48 (Winter 1964): 139–46.

542 Willot, Albert. "Essai sur le Désarmement Nucléaire." *Chronique de Politique Etrangère* 21 (Sept. 1968): 557–627.

543 *World Without Arms, World Without Wars.* 2 vols. Moscow: Foreign Languages Publishing House, 1960.

544 Wright, Quincy. "Conditions for Successful Disarmament." *Journal of Conflict Resolution* 7:3 (1963): 286–92.

545 Young, Wayland. "Disarmament: Proposals and Concessions." *Survival* 4 (May–June 1962): 127–29, 136.

GENERAL & COMPLETE DISARMAMENT (GCD)

For U.S.-U.S.S.R. negotiations on GCD in the 1960s, see Chapter 7, Limitation of Weapons & Personnel.

546 Arkadyev, Nikolai N. *General and Complete Disarmament: The Road to Peace.* Moscow: Foreign Languages Publishing House, 1962.

547 Arzumanjan, A. A. "Comprehensive Disarmament." *Bulletin of the Atomic Scientists* 17 (Apr. 1961): 127–30.

548 Barclay, C. N. "Total Disarmament." *Army Quarterly* 74 (Jan. 1960): 185–90.

549 Bogdanov, Oleg V. *Vseobshchee i Polnoe Razoruzhenie.* Moscow: Izd-vo Instituta Mezhdunarodnykh Otnoshenii, 1964.

550 Bolte, Charles Guy. *The Price of Peace: A Plan for Disarmament.* Boston: Beacon Press, 1956.

551 Cohen, Benjamin V. "U.S. Charts Course Toward Comprehensive, Coordinated Disarmament Program." *U.S. Department of State Bulletin* (Nov. 12, 1952): 752–55.

552 Egov, S., and S. Datlin. "General and Complete Disarmament—A Crucial Question. . . ." *Kommunist* 12 (Aug. 1960): 100–110.

553 Feld, Bernard T. "The Geneva Negotiations on General and Complete Disarmament." In Seymour Melman, ed., *Disarmament: Its Politics and Economics.* Boston: American Academy of Arts & Sciences, 1962, pp. 7–17.

554 Fisher, Adrian S. "United States Presents Views on the Question of General and Complete Disarmament." *U.S. Department of State Bulletin* (Jan. 15, 1968): 97–100.

555 Griffiths, Franklyn. "Proposals of Total Disarmament in Soviet Foreign Policy, 1927–1932 and 1959–1960." Certificate essay, Columbia Univ., Russian Institute, 1962.

556 Herzog, Arthur. "Waiting for G.C.D." *War/Peace Report* 5 (Apr. 1965): 3–7.

557 Hook, Sidney. "The Political Aspects of General and Complete Disarmament." In James E. Dougherty and John F. Lehman, Jr., eds., *The Prospects for Arms Control.* New York: MacFadden-Bartell, 1965, pp. 153–63.

558 Katz, Amrom H. "The Technical Aspects of General and Complete Disarmament." In James E. Dougherty and John F. Lehman, Jr., eds., *The Prospects for Arms Control.* New York: MacFadden-Bartell, 1965, pp. 58–82.

559 Khrushchev, Nikita S. *General and Complete Disarmament—Guarantee of Peace and Security for All People.* New York: Crosscurrents Press, 1962. [Address, July 10, 1962.]

560 ———. "Soviet Proposals for Complete Disarmament." *Current History* 37 (Nov. 1959): 299–303.

561 Kirillin, V. A. "The Road to General and Complete Disarmament." *Disarmament and Arms Control* 2 (Winter 1963–64): 10–15.

562 Knorr, Klaus E. "Supranational vs. International Models for General and Complete Disarmament." In Richard J. Barnet and Richard A. Falk, eds., *Security in Disarmament.* Princeton: Princeton Univ. Press, 1965, pp. 384–400.

563 Krieger, David. "Toward a World Disarmament Community." *Bulletin of Peace Proposals* 4:2 (1973): 183–92.

564 Leonard, James F. "U.S. Reviews Position on General and Complete Disarmament." *U.S. Department of State Bulletin* (Aug. 17, 1970): 198–203.

565 Levine, Robert A. "Disarmament and Arms Control." *New Leader* (Feb. 19, 1962): 15–18.

566 Lister, Charles E. "The Folklore of General Disarmament." *International Affairs* [London] 39 (Apr. 1963): 427–42.

567 MacDonald, Michael, et al. *Some Thoughts on the Balance of Power Under General and Complete Disarmament.* Menlo Park, Ca.: Stanford Research Institute, 1961.

568 MacLean, D. A. "World Disarmament: A Moral View." *American Journal of Economics and Sociology* 4 (Oct. 1944): 1–8.

569 McVitty, Marion H. *Preface to Disarmament: An Appraisal of Recent Proposals.* Washington, D.C.: Public Affairs Press, 1970.

570 Roberts, Adam. "Is General and Complete Disarmament Dead?" *War/Peace Report* 13 (Feb. 1973): 16–19.

571 Strausz-Hupé, Robert. "The Disarmament Delusion." *U.S. Naval Institute Proceedings* 86 (Feb. 1960): 41–47.

572 Thomas, Norman. "Toward Total Disarmament." *Dissent* 7 (Spring 1960): 163–66.

573 Vavra, S. "The Problem of General and Complete Disarmament Following the XV Session of the General Assembly of the United Nations." *Review of Contemporary Literature* 8 (1961): 127–44.

574 Wiesner, Jerome B. "Hope for God?" *Bulletin of the Atomic Scientists* 24 (Jan. 1968): 10–15.

575 Willot, Albert. *Le Désarmement Général et Complet: Une Approche.* Brussels: Université Libre de Bruxelles, Editions de l'Institut de Sociologie, 1965.

DISARMAMENT & DETERRENCE

576 Buchan, Alastair. "The Deterrent and Disarmament." *Journal of the Royal United Services Institution* 106 (May 1961): 182–94.

577 "Defense and Disarmament." *American Economic Review* 53 (May 1963): 413–45.

578 Ferguson, Allen R. *Disarmament and Deterrence.* P–2553. Santa Monica, Ca.: Rand, 1962.

579 Schelling, Thomas C. "The Role of Deterrence in Total Disarmament." *Foreign Affairs* 40 (Apr. 1962): 392–406.

580 Singer, J. David. "From Deterrence to Disarmament." *International Journal* 16 (Autumn 1961): 307–26.

UNILATERAL DISARMAMENT

581 Abt, Clark C., et al. *Theoretical Aspects of Unilateral Arms Control.* Bedford, Mass.: Raytheon, 1963.

582 Becker, Benjamin M. "The Myth of Arms Control and Disarmament." *Bulletin of the Atomic Scientists* 27 (Apr. 1971): 5–8, 45–48.

583 Bottome, Edgar M. "Limiting Nuclear Arms: Can the U.S. Take Unilateral Steps?" *Current* 130 (June 1971): 60–63.

584 Carter, April, ed. *Unilateral Disarmament:*

Its Theory and Policy from Different International Perspectives. London: Housemans, 1965.

585   Casper, Barry M., and John B. Phelps. *Unilateral Arms Control: A Survey.* Washington, D.C.: Institute for Defense Analyses, 1963.

586   Cohen, Benjamin V. "Case Against Unilateral Disarmament." *U.S. Department of State Bulletin* (June 30, 1952): 1029–31.

587   Etzioni, Amitai. "Unilateralism—A Hopeless Hope." *The Hard Way to Peace: A New Strategy.* New York: Collier Books, 1962, pp. 60–83.

588   "Fifteen Years in Hell is Enough." *Christian Century* (Aug. 3, 1960): 891–92.

589   Fromm, Erich. "The Case for Unilateral Disarmament." In Donald G. Brennan, ed., *Arms Control, Disarmament, and National Security.* New York: Braziller, 1961, pp. 187–97.

590   Halperin, Morton H. "Three Roads to Unilateralism." *New Leader* (Aug. 20, 1962): 12–15.

591   Kieselhosst, D. C. "Unilateral Disarmament: An Analysis and Justification." Ph.D. diss., Univ. of Minnesota, 1969.

592   Marris, Robin. "The Consequences of Unilateralism: The World of Polaris." *Socialist Commentary* (Sept. 1960): 2–6.

593   Olson, Theodore M. "The Movement of Non-Violent Direct Action for Unilateral Disarmament: What Is It and What It Mean for the Church?" Ph.D. diss., Drew Univ., 1962.

594   Sharp, Gene. "A Radical Approach to Peace and Security: National Defense Without Armaments." *War/Peace Report* 10 (Apr. 1970): 3–10.

595   Sibley, Mulford Q. "Unilateral Disarmament." In Robert A. Goldwin, ed., *America Armed*, Chicago: Rand McNally, 1963, pp. 112–40.

596   ———. "What About Unilateral Disarmament?" *Liberation* 1 (Nov. 1956): 17–19.

597   Teller, Edward. "A Unilateral Disarmament Step?" *Current* 129 (June 1970): 63 ff.

598   Toynbee, Philip. *The Fearful Choice: A Debate on Nuclear Policy.* Detroit: Wayne State Univ. Press, 1959.

Denmark

599   Andersen, C. A. "Disarmament in Denmark." *Labour Monthly* 11 (Nov. 1929): 327–28.

600   Arneson, Ben A. "Denmark Votes to Disarm." *Christian Century* (Oct. 9, 1929): 1244–45.

601   Bellquist, Eric C. "Possible Effects of Danish Disarmament." *American Scandinavian Review* 19 (May 1931): 299–300.

602   Hart, Joseph K. "Will Denmark Disarm?" *Survey* (Oct. 1, 1925): 25–29.

603   Jorgensen, Bent B. *Socialdemokratiets Syn Paa Forsvaret: Med Saerligt Henblik paa Perioden 1929–35.* Diss., Univ. of Copenhagen, 1970.

604   Moritzen, Julius. "Disarmament in Denmark." *Nation* (Dec. 9, 1925): 655–56.

605   Wieslander, H. *I Nedrustingens Tecken.* Lund: Gleerup, 1966.

606   Wuorinen, John H. "Denmark's Disarmament Program." *Current History* 31 (Oct. 1929): 182–83.

Great Britain (CND)

607   Boulton, David. *Voices From the Crowd Against the H Bomb.* London: P. Owen, 1964.

608   Brook, G. "Unilateralism and the Campaign for Nuclear Disarmament." *Contemporary Issues* 12 (Sept. 1964): 52–56.

609   Bull, Hedley. "The Many Sides of British Unilateralism." *Reporter* (Mar. 16, 1961): 35–37.

610   Catlin, George E. G. "On Unilateralism." *Contemporary Review* 199 (Jan. 1961): 1–6.

611   DeWeerd, Harvey A. "British Unilateralism: A Critical View." *Yale Review* 51 (Summer 1962): 574–88.

612   Driver, Christopher. *The Disarmers.* London: Hodder & Stoughton, 1964.

613   Duff, Peggy. "CND: 1958–1965." *Left, Left, Left: A Personal Account of Six Protest Campaigns, 1945–1965.* London: Allison & Busby, 1971, pp. 113–257.

614   Gaitskell, Hugh. "The Case Against Unilateralism." *New Leader* (Nov. 14, 1960): 9–11.

615 King-Hall, Stephen. *Defense in the Nuclear Age.* New York: Harper, 1957.

616 Lomas, Charles W., and Michael Taylor, comps. *The Rhetoric of the British Peace Movement.* New York: Random House, 1971.

617 Marquand, David. "England, the Bomb, the Marchers." *Commentary* 29 (May 1960): 380–86.

618 Maxwell, Andrew. "The Anti-Bomb Movement in Britain." *Contemporary Issues* 12 (Jan. 1963): 48–88.

619 ———. "The Campaign for Nuclear Disarmament in Britain." *Contemporary Issues* 9 (Oct.–Nov. 1958): 201–21.

620 Myers, Frank E. "British Peace Politics: The Campaign for Nuclear Disarmament and the Committee of 100, 1957–1962." Ph.D. diss., Columbia Univ., 1965.

621 Parkin, Frank. *Middle Class Radicalism: The Social Bases of the British Campaign for Nuclear Disarmament.* New York: Praeger, 1968.

622 Russell, Lord Bertrand. "The Case for British Nuclear Disarmament." *Bulletin of the Atomic Scientists* 18 (Mar. 1962): 6–10.

623 ———. *Common Sense and Nuclear Warfare.* New York: Simon & Schuster, 1959.

624 ———. *Has Man a Future?* New York: Simon & Schuster, 1962.

Unilateral Initiatives

625 Etzioni, Amitai. *The Hard Way to Peace: A New Strategy.* New York: Collier Books, 1962.

626 Foster, Richard B. *U.S. Unilateral Arms Control Measures and the Setting for Negotiations.* Menlo Park, Ca.: Stanford Research Institute, 1961.

627 ———. "Unilateral Arms Control Measures and Disarmament Negotiations." *Orbis* 6 (Summer 1962): 258–80.

628 Horowitz, Irving L. "Unilateral Initiatives: A Strategy in Search of a Theory." *Diogenes* [Montreal] 50 (Summer 1965): 112–27.

629 Huddle, Franklin P. "Military Aspects of Independent Initiative in Arms Control." *Journal of Conflict Resolution* 7:3 (1963): 272–83.

630 Levine, Robert A. "Unilateral Initiatives: A Cynic's View." *Bulletin of the Atomic Scientists* 19 (June 1963): 22–25.

631 Osgood, Charles E. *An Alternative to War or Surrender.* Urbana: Univ. of Illinois Press, 1962.

632 ———. "A Case for Graduated Unilateral Disengagement." *Bulletin of the Atomic Scientists* 16 (Apr. 1960): 127–31.

633 Sibley, Mulford Q. *Unilateral Initiatives and Disarmament.* Philadelphia: American Friends Service Committee, 1964.

634 Thee, Marek. "Disarmament Through Unilateral Initiatives." *Bulletin of Peace Proposals* 5:4 (1974): 381–84.

Budgetary Limitations

See also Chapter 4, Disarmament Conference, 1932–34, Conference Documents, League of Nations, National Defence Expenditures Commission.

635 Glagolev, Igor S. "The Reduction of Military Expenditures." *Disarmament and Arms Control* 2 (Summer 1964): 310–16.

636 Perillier, Louis. *De la Limitation des Armements par la Méthode Budgétaire.* Paris: Rousseau, 1932.

637 Symington, Sen. Stuart. "A Plan for Economic Disarmament." *Congressional Record* 101 (Mar. 2, 1955): S1953–58.

638 "U.S. Presents Initiative in Disarmament Committee on Limitation of Military Expenditures." *U.S. Department of State Bulletin* (Aug. 25, 1975): 282–85.

639 Vayrynen, Raimo. "Cutting Down Military Budgets: Some Perspectives." *Instant Research on Peace and Violence* 6:1–2 (1976): 72–80.

Arms Control vs. Disarmament

640 Barnaby, Frank. "False Promises of Disarmament." *New Scientist* (Aug. 6, 1970): 278–79.

641 ———. *Nuclear Disarmament or Nuclear War?* Stockholm: SIPRI, 1975.

642 Feld, Bernard T. "The Charade of Piecemeal Arms Limitations." *Bulletin of the Atomic Scientists* 31 (Jan. 1975): 8–15.

643 ———. "Doves of the World, Unite." *New Scientist* (Dec. 26, 1974): 910–15.

644 ———. "The Sorry History of Arms Control." *Bulletin of the Atomic Scientists* 26 (Sept. 1970): 22–26.

645 Finch, Edward R. "Arms Control is Not Disarmament." *International Lawyer* 4 (July 1970): 465–71.

646 Foster, William C. "Arms Control vs. 'Idealism.'" *Vista* 5 (May–June 1970): 80–81.

647 Inglis, David R. "The Sweet Voice of Reason." *Bulletin of the Atomic Scientists* 30 (Sept. 1974): 50–51.

648 Kinsella, Kevin J. "Disarmament: The Current State of the Fraud." *Science Journal* 6 (Nov. 1970): 40–44.

649 Melman, Seymour. "How Not to Disarm: The 'Arms Control' Doctrine." In Henry M. Christman, ed., *Peace and Arms: Reports from the Nation*. New York: Sheed & Ward, 1964.

650 Singer, J. David, and Anatol Rapoport. "The Armers and the Disarmers: Is Debate Possible?" *Nation* (Mar. 2, 1963): 174–77.

651 Thee, Marek. "Crisis in Arms Control." *Bulletin of Peace Proposals* 7:2 (1976): 99–102.

652 York, Herbert F. "The Dangers of Partial Disarmament." *Current* 133 (Oct. 1971): 41–44.

653 ———. "A Little Arms Control Can be a Dangerous Thing." *War/Peace Report* 11 (Aug.–Sept. 1971): 3–7.

654 Young, Wayland, and Elizabeth Young. "Disarmament vs. Arms Control: A Discussion of Criteria." *Commentary* 32 (Aug. 1961): 124–34.

AC&D Debates & Public Opinion

655 "Arms Control vs. the Right Wing." *War/Peace Report* 3 (Apr. 1963): 7.

656 Donoho, William T. "Arms Control, Disarmament and the American Public." *War/Peace Report* 3 (Apr. 1963): 3–5.

657 Ershine, Hazel G. "The Polls: Defense, Peace and Space." *Public Opinion Quarterly* 25 (Fall 1961): 478–89.

658 Greenewalt, Crawford H. "Mr. K's 'Stark Illusion': The Notion that U.S. Business Resists Disarmament is Revealed as Most Fanciful of Khrushchev's Inventions." *Better Living* 14 (Nov.–Dec. 1960): 28–30.

659 Hanson, Joseph O., Jr. "Public Understanding of Disarmament." *Journal of Conflict Resolution* 7:3 (1963): 469–73.

660 Herzog, Arthur. *The War-Peace Establishment*. New York: Harper & Row, 1965.

661 Hoffman, Fredrik. "Arms Debates—A 'Positional' Interpretation." *Journal of Peace Research* 7:3 (1970): 219–29.

662 Jeffries, Vincent. "Political Generations and the Acceptance or Rejection of Nuclear Warfare." *Journal of Social Issues* 30:3 (1974): 119–36.

663 Knecht, Marcel. "Public Opinion and Disarmament." *Annals of the Amer. Acad. of Pol. & Soc. Sci.* 144 (July 1929): 148–50.

664 Levine, Robert A. *The Arms Debate*. Cambridge: Harvard Univ. Press, 1963.

665 ———. "Facts and Morals in the Arms Debate." *World Politics* 14 (Jan. 1962): 239–58.

666 Merritt, Richard L., and Ellen B. Pirro. *Press Attitudes on Arms Control in Four Countries, 1946–1963*. New Haven: Yale Univ., Political Science Research Library, 1966.

667 Miller, Robert M. "The Attitudes of the Major Protestant Churches in America Toward War and Peace, 1919–1929." *Historian* 19:1 (Nov. 1957): 13–38.

668 Nathan, James A., and James K. Oliver. "Public Opinion and U.S. Security Policy." *Armed Forces and Society* 2 (Fall 1975): 46–62.

669 Paarberg, Rob. "Forgetting About the Unthinkable." *Foreign Policy*, no. 10 (Spring 1973): 132–40.

670 Pomerance, Josephine W. "Public Opinion and Disarmament." *Bulletin of the Atomic Scientists* 17 (Apr. 1961): 149–52.

671 Price, Charles C. "Political Action for a Livable World." *Bulletin of the Atomic Scientists* 30 (Apr. 1974): 43 ff.

672 Relyea, Harold C. "Hawk's Nest: The American Security Council." *Nation* (Jan. 24, 1972): 113–16.

673 Sebald, Hans, and Rudolfo N. Gallegos. "Voices of War and Peace—What Do They Know?" *Pacific Sociological Review* 14 (Oct. 1971): 487–510.

674 Van Cleave, William R. "The Nuclear Weapons Debate." *U.S. Naval Institute Proceedings* 92 (May 1966): 27–38.

675 Wilson, Andrew. "Public Opinion and Disarmament." *Disarmament* 11 (Sept. 1966): 8–10.

Advocates

676 Badurina, Berislav. "Disarmament: Today's Imperative." *Review of International Affairs* [Belgrade] (Dec. 1970): 3–5.

677 Barnaby, Frank. "Megatonomania 1973." *New Scientist* (Apr. 26, 1973): 202–204, 207–208.

678 Barnet, Richard J. "Why Not Disarmament?" *Commonweal* (Oct. 14, 1960): 62–64.

679 Cousins, Norman. *In Place of Folly.* New York: Washington Square Press, 1962.

680 Davis, Jerome. "Total Disarmament is Not an Impossible Ideal." *Gandhi Marg* 43 (July 1967): 224–31.

681 Evgen'ev, I. "Disarmament—The Surest Way to a Durable Peace." *Kommunist* 15 (Oct. 1959): 103–09.

682 Ferry, W. H. "Peace Through Disarmament." *Progressive* 25 (May 1961): 22–26.

683 Lall, Arthur S. "On the Agenda of Mankind: Disarmament." *Columbia University Forum* 9 (Spring 1966): 32–37.

684 Limpus, Lowell. *Disarm!* New York: Freedom Press, 1960.

685 Lvov, M. "Disarmament—Both Necessary and Possible." *New Times* [Moscow] 45 (Nov. 1971): 15–18.

686 MacBride, Seán. "Peace: The Desperate Imperative of Humanity." *Bulletin of Peace Proposals* 6:1 (1975): 70–76.

687 Melman, Seymour. "To Make Disarmament Real." *Current History* 42 (May 1962): 302–05.

688 Millis, Walter. "A Demilitarized World and How to Get There." *Saturday Review* (Sept. 12, 1964): 18–23, 30–32.

689 Moch, Jules S. *Human Folly: To Disarm or Perish?* Trans. by Edward Huans. London: Gollancz, 1955.

690 ———. "Jules Moch on Disarmament." *Reporter* (Dec. 15, 1955): 23–26.

691 Pauling, Linus C. *No More War!* New York: Dodd, Mead, 1962.

692 Russell, Lord Bertrand. "The Importance of Disarmament." *International Affairs* [Moscow] 7 (Jan. 1961): 83–85.

693 Schweitzer, Albert. *Peace or Atomic War?* New York: Henry Holt, 1958.

694 Swomley, John M., Jr. "The Case for Disarmament." *Progressive* 24 (Apr. 1960): 35–38.

Opponents

695 Allen, Gary. "Disarmament: They're Promoting the Peace of the Grave." *American Opinion* 13 (June 1970): 1–18.

696 Burnham, James. "The Disarmament Industry." *National Review* (July 13, 1957): 59.

697 Courtney, Kent, and Phoebe Courtney. *Disarmament: A Blueprint for Surrender.* New Orleans: Conservative Society of America, 1963.

698 Denvignes, Gen. Joseph Cyrille Magdelaine. *La Farce du Désarmement.* Paris: Tallandier, 1930.

699 "Disarmament Capitulation." *National Defender* (May 1962): 1–8.

700 Evans, Medford. "The Atomic Disarmament Trap." *National Review* (Nov. 26, 1955): 13–15.

701 Fuller, Gen. J. F. C. "Disarmament and Delusion." *Current History* 36 (Sept. 1932): 649–54.

702 Greaves, Lt. Col. Fielding L. "Peace in Our Time—Fact or Fable?" *Military Review* 42 (Dec. 1962): 55–58.

703 Hargreaves, Maj. Reginald. "The Haunted Quest." *U.S. Naval Institute Proceedings* 79 (Mar. 1953): 256–65.

704 Hickmott, J. R. "Disarmament Means Danger." *Contemporary Review* 211 (Oct. 1967): 169–71.

705 Kaplan, Morton A. "The Case Against Disarmament." *New Leader* (Sept. 4–11, 1961): 12–16.

706 Morris, Robert. *Disarmament: Weapon of Conquest.* New York: Bookmailer, 1963.

707 ———. "Merger is the Goal." *Daughters of the American Revolution Magazine* 98 (Oct. 1964): 824–27, 846–47.

708 Nickerson, Hoffman. "Disarmament, Policy and Politics." *Can We Limit War?* 1933. Reprint. Port Washington, N.Y.: Kennikat, 1973, pp. 144–71.

709 Possony, Stefan T. "No Peace Without Arms." *Review of Politics* 6 (Apr. 1944): 216–27.

710 Roddis, Sara Jones. "Disarmament or Surrender." *National Defender* (Aug.–Sept. 1962): 1–6.

711 Schlafly, Phyllis, and Chester Ward. *The Gravediggers.* Alton, Ill.: Pere Marquette Press, 1964.

712 Smith, Maj. Gen. Dale O. "Dangers of Disarmament." *American Mercury* 85 (Sept. 1957): 91–96.

713 Tansill, Charles Callan. "The President [J. F. K.] . . . Up With Which We Will Not Put." *American Opinion* 10 (Nov. 1967): 31–38.

714 Teller, Edward. "Disarmament is a Lost Cause." *New Leader* (Mar. 19, 1958): 12–14.

715 U.S. House. Committee on Un-American Activities. *Report on the Communist "Peace" Offensive: A Campaign to Disarm and Defeat the United States.* Report no. 378. Washington, D.C.: G.P.O., 1951.

Three

Historical Surveys & Contemporary Views

CONTEMPORARY OBSERVATIONS AND aspirations, together with historical assessments, make up a considerable portion of the writings on arms control and disarmament (AC&D). This chapter brings together a list of those books and essays which deal generally and broadly with actual proposals and developments, as opposed to the entries listed in the previous chapter which deal with more abstract ideas and issues. These entries also are supplementary to subsequent chapters which focus on specific AC&D techniques, negotiations, and agreements.

An adequate history of arms control and disarmament remains to be written. There exist, however, a number of informative surveys. Gunji Hosono's *International Disarmament* (1926), while dated, provides an interesting overview, as does Henry W. Forbes' *The Strategy of Disarmament* (1962). These accounts may be profitably supplemented with Merze Tate's *The Disarmament Illusion* (1942) and *The United States and Armaments* (1948).

Since international negotiations on arms control and disarmament reached full stride during the 1920s and 1930s, most historical accounts focus on these decades. Among those which outline most aspects of these efforts are: R. D. Burns and D. Urquidi, *Disarmament in Perspective, 1919–1941* (1968); W. E. Rappard, *The Quest for Peace Since the World War* (1940), P. J. Noel-Baker, *The Arms Race: A Programme for World Disarmament* (1960), and the numerous volumes by J. W. Wheeler-Bennett. Salvador de Madariaga's *Disarmament* (1929) is one of the more perceptive contemporary accounts.

The limitation of naval forces occupied the particular attention of oceanic powers during the interwar years. While accounts dealing with the specific proposals and treaties are listed in Chapter 7 below, the more general surveys are here. G. V. Fagan's essay, "F. D. R. and Naval Limitation," in *U.S. Naval Institute Proceedings* (1955), Stephen Roskill's *Naval Policy Between the Wars* (1969), which presents a British view, and G. E. Wheeler's *Prelude to Pearl Harbor* (1963), which gives an American one, provide fine overviews.

The two best post-1945 surveys of arms control and disarmament proposals and negotiations, without much analysis, are Keesing's

Disarmament: Negotiations and Treaties, 1946–1971 (1972) and the United Nations' *The United Nations and Disarmament, 1945–1970* (1970). These may be updated by use of the SIPRI *Yearbook of World Armament and Disarmament*, which since 1968/69 has provided an excellent annual summary and analysis of events. Additionally, Hedley Bull's *The Control of the Arms Race* (1965) and J. W. Spanier and J. L. Nogee's *The Politics of Disarmament* (1962) are informative analyses of events. The early postwar negotiations are well drawn in Bernhard G. Bechhoefer's *Postwar Negotiations for Arms Control* (1961); for more specialized accounts, see Chapter 7, Baruch Plan (1946).

Chronologies

716 Congressional Quarterly Service. *History of Disarmament in the Postwar Years: A Comprehensive Chronology of International Negotiations, Events, and Organizations.* Washington, D.C., 1964.

717 Coward, H. Roberts. *Arms Control Measures Applicable to Regions: A Chronology and Checklist.* Cambridge: M.I.T., Center for International Studies, 1963.

718 U.S. Department of State. Bureau of Intelligence Research. *Soviet Disarmament Proposals, 1946–1958.* Washington, D.C.: G.P.O., 1959.

719 ———. *A Chronology of the Development of United States Disarmament Policy, 1953–1960.* Washington, D.C.: G.P.O., 1961. [Research Project no. 502, March, 1961, a revision and extension of Research Project no. 433.]

720 U.S. House. Committee on International Relations. *Chronologies of Major Developments in Selected Areas of International Relations.* Washington, D.C.: G.P.O., 1974–, Arms Control section. [Annual cumulative editions.]

721 U.S. Senate. Committee on Foreign Relations. *Disarmament: A Selected Chronology, January 1, 1918–March 19, 1956* [Staff Study, no. 2]. 84th Cong., 2d Sess., 1956.

General Surveys

722 Ansberry, William F. *Arms Control and Disarmament: Success or Failure?* Berkeley, Ca.: McCutchan, 1969.

723 Clemens, Walter C., Jr. "Nicholas II to SALT II: Continuity and Change in East-West Diplomacy." *International Affairs* [London] 49 (July 1973): 385–401.

724 ———. *The Superpowers and Arms Control: From Cold War to Interdependence.* Lexington, Mass.: D.C. Heath, 1973.

725 Craig, Gordon A., and Peter Paret. "The Control of International Violence: Some Historical Notes." *Stanford Journal of International Studies* 7 (Spring 1972): 1–21.

726 Falk, Stanley L. "Disarmament in Historical Perspective." *Military Review* 44 (Dec. 1964): 36–48.

727 Ferrell, Robert H. "Disarmament Conferences: Ballets at the Brink." *American Heritage* 22 (Feb. 1971): 5–7, 96, 98–100.

728 Forbes, Henry W. *The Strategy of Disarmament.* Washington, D.C.: Public Affairs Press, 1962.

729 Frase, Robert W. "Disarmament in Perspective." *Current History* 34 (Oct. 1957): 227–32.

730 Kaaitsman, Viktor M. *Sovetskii Soiuz, Razoruzhenie, Mir, Sobytiia i Fakty, 1917–1962.* Moscow: Izd-vo Instituta Mezhdunarodnykh Otnoshenii, 1962.

731 Luce, Clare Boothe. ["History of Attempts to Achieve Disarmament"]. *McCall's* (Nov. 1966): 34, 155.

732 Noel-Baker, Philip J. *The Arms Race: A Programme for World Disarmament.* New York: Oceana, 1960.

733 Perkins, Dexter. "Peace and Armament." *Virginia Quarterly Review* 34 (Autumn 1960): 497–516.

734 Smith, H. A. "The Problem of Disarmament in the Light of History." *International Affairs* [London] 10 (Sept. 1931): 600–621.

735 Stone, I. F. "A Century of Futility." *New York Review of Books* (Apr. 9, 1970): 30–33.

736 Tarr, Cedric W., Jr. "Conventional Weapons Control." *Current History* 47 (July 1964): 25–30.

737 Tate, Merze. *The United States and Armaments.* Cambridge: Harvard Univ. Press, 1948.

Historical Issues to 1914

738 Appleton, Lewis. *Fifty Years Historic Record of the Progress of Disarmament, 1849–1899.* London, 1900.

739 *Arms Limitation Plans for Europe Before 1914. [On the Reduction of Continental Armies: A Proposal* by Adolf Fischhof. *A Propos du Désarmement* by Augustin Hamon. *The Limitation of Armaments, and Limitation of Naval and Military Expenditure* by Paul Henri Benjamin Bastuat, Baron d'Estournelles de Constant.] New York: Garland, 1972.

740 Berthrong, Merrill G. "Disarmament in European Diplomacy 1816–1870." Ph.D. diss., Univ. of Pennsylvania, 1958.

741 Boardman, George Dana. *Disarmament of Nations: Or, Mankind One Body.* 4th ed. Philadelphia: Howard M. Jenkins, 1899.

742 Coulet, Robert. *La Limitation des Armements.* Paris: Librairie Générale de Droit et de Jurisprudence, 1910.

743 d'Estournelles de Constant, Paul Henri Benjamin Bastuat, Baron, *A French Plea for Limitation of Naval Expenses.* Boston: American Peace Society, 1906.

744 Dubois, Georges. *Des Charges de la Paix Armée et de la Limitation des Armements.* Caen: E. Laurier, 1909.

745 Hosono, Gunji. *International Disarmament.* New York: Columbia Univ., 1926. [Also published as *Histoire du Désarmement.* Paris: Pedone, 1930.]

746 Kuehl, Warren. "The World-Federation League: A Neglected Chapter in the History of a Movement." *World Affairs Quarterly* 31 (Jan. 1960): 349–64.

747 Picard, Rene. *La Question de la Limitation des Armements de Nos Jours.* Paris: Jouve, 1911.

748 Richards, Alfred B. *Cobden and His Pamphlet Considered: In a Letter to Richard Cobden.* 3d ed. London: Baily Brothers, 1853.

749 Tate, Merze. *The Disarmament Illusion: The Movement for a Limitation of Armaments to 1907.* New York: Macmillan, 1942.

750 Trueblood, Benjamin F. "The Case for Limitation of Armaments." *American Journal of International Law* 2 (Oct. 1908): 758 ff. [Reprinted in B. F. Trueblood, *The Development of the Peace Idea and Other Essays.* Boston: World Peace Foundation, 1932.]

751 Webster, Sir Charles K. "Disarmament Proposals in 1816." *Contemporary Review* 127 (Nov. 1922): 621–27.

752 Wehberg, Hans. *The Limitation of Armaments: A Collection of the Projects Proposed for the Solution of the Problem.* Washington, D.C.: Carnegie Endowment for International Peace, 1921.

Historical Issues, Interwar Years

753 Bowen, Adelphia Dane. "The Disarmament Movement, 1918–1935." Ph.D. diss., Columbia Univ., 1956.

754 Burns, Richard Dean, and Donald Urquidi. *Disarmament in Perspective: An Analysis of Selected Disarmament and Arms Control*

Agreements Between World Wars, 1919–1939. 4 vols. ACDA Report RS–55, Washington, D.C.: G.P.O., 1968.

755 Enock, Arthur G. *The Problems of Armaments: A Book for Every Citizen of Every Country.* New York: Macmillan, 1923.

756 Fanshawe, Maurice. *World Disarmament.* No. 294. London: League of Nations Union, 1931.

757 "General Survey of Disarmament Problem." *European Economic and Political Survey* (Apr. 30, 1927): 510–37; (May 15, 1927): 550–66.

758 Haestier, Richard Emile. *Guilt-Edged Insecurity: The Peace Farce Played by the World's Diplomatists.* London: Jarrolds, 1932.

759 Heald, Stephen. *Memorandum on the Progress of Disarmament, 1919–1932.* London: Royal Institute of International Affairs, 1932.

760 Johnsen, Julia E. *Disarmament.* New York: H. W. Wilson, 1930.

761 Jouhaux, Leon. *Le Désarmement.* Paris: F. Alcan, 1927.

762 Kirchhoff, Hermann. *Real Disarmament.* London: P. S. King & Sons, 1932.

763 Lefebure, Maj. Victor. *Common Sense about Disarmament.* London: Gollancz, 1932.

763a ———. *Scientific Disarmament.* New York: Macmillan, 1931.

764 Lyons, Jacques. *Les Problèmes du Désarmement.* Paris: Balvin, 1931.

765 Madariaga, Salvador de. *Disarmament.* New York: Coward-McCann, 1929.

766 Malik, Charles. *Disarmament.* New York: Coward-McCann, 1929.

767 Martin, Charles. *Disarmament and the Inter-Parliamentary Union.* Lausanne: Payot, 1931.

768 Myers, Denys P. *World Disarmament: Its Problems and Prospects.* Boston: World Peace Foundation, 1932.

769 Newbold, John. *Democracy, Debts and Disarmament.* London: Methuen, 1933.

770 Nickerson, Hoffman. *Can We Limit War?* New York: Frederick A. Stokes, 1934.

771 Niemeyer, Theodore, ed. *Handbuch des Abrüstungs Problems.* Berlin: W. Rotschild, 1928.

772 Noel-Baker, Philip J. *Disarmament.* London: Hogarth Press, 1926.

773 Ottik, Georges. *La Société des Nations et le Désarmement.* Geneva: Editions de l'Annuaire de la Société des Nations, 1932.

774 Rappard, William E. *The Quest for Peace Since the World War.* Cambridge: Harvard Univ. Press, 1940.

775 Reeley, Mary K., comp. *Selected Articles on Disarmament.* New York: H. W. Wilson, 1921.

776 Smith, Rennie. *General Disarmament or War?* London: Allen & Unwin, 1927.

777 Tuttle, Florence. *Alternatives to War.* New York: Harper, 1931.

778 Wheeler-Bennett, John W. *Information on the Reduction of Armaments.* London: Allen & Unwin, 1925.

779 ———. *Disarmament and Security Since Locarno, 1925–1931.* New York: Macmillan, 1932.

780 ———. *The Pipe Dream of Peace: The Story of the Collapse of Disarmament.* New York: Morrow, 1935.

781 ———, and F. E. Langermann. *Information on the Problem in Security, 1917–1926.* London: Allen & Unwin, 1927.

782 Williams, Benjamin H. *The United States and Disarmament.* New York: McGraw-Hill, 1931.

783 Wilson, Hugh R., Jr. *Disarmament and the Cold War in the Thirties.* New York: Vantage Press, 1963.

784 Brailsford, Henry N. "Disarmament." *Olives of Endless Age.* New York: Harper, 1928, pp. 370–88.

785 Chatfield, Charles. "Disarmament and the Devil Theories." *For Peace and Justice: Pacifism in America, 1914–1941.* Knoxville: Univ. of Tennessee Press, 1971, pp. 143–67.

786 "Disarmament Deadlock." *Foreign Policy Association Information Service* (Nov. 23, 1928): 381–96.

787 Dulles, Allen W. "Disarmament Puzzle." *Foreign Affairs* 9 (July 1931): 605–16.

788 ———. "Some Misconceptions About Disarmament." *Foreign Affairs* 5 (Apr. 1927): 413–26.

789 Khvostov, V. "Disarmament Negotiations: History of the Problem." *International Affairs* [Moscow] 7 (Jan. 1961): 92–97; 7 (Feb. 1961): 60–67.

790 Pratt, Adm. William V. "Disarmament and the National Defense." *U.S. Naval Institute Proceedings* 55 (Sept. 1929): 751–64.

790a Rogers, Lindsay. "The Struggle for Disarmament." *Current History* 35 (Feb. 1932): 629–37.

791 Schuman, Fredrick L. "The Wasted Decades: 1899–1939." *Current History* 46 (June 1964): 326–30.

792 Shotwell, James T. "An Academic Criticism of Disarmament Policies." *Proceedings of the Georgia University Institute of Public Affairs*, pt. 1 (1935): 28–41.

NAVAL LIMITATION—CONTEMPORANEOUS ASSESSMENTS

793 Anderson, Capt. Walter S. "Limitation of Naval Armaments." *U.S. Naval Institute Proceedings* 52 (Mar. 1926): 427–43.

794 Bywater, Hector C. "The Dismal Prospects for Limiting Armaments." *Atlantic Monthly* (Nov. 1924): 672–80.

795 ———. "French Naval Policy and Its Reactions." *Atlantic Monthly* (May 1925): 688–98.

796 Estienny, Paul. *Problème de la Limitation et de la Réduction des Armements Navals, 1921–1931.* Toulouse: Andrau & Laport, 1931.

797 Frothingham, Thomas G. "Power Behind Naval Disarmament." *Independent* (May 5, 1928): 422–24.

798 Gerould, James T. "British Attitude on Disarmament and Seapower." *Current History* 27 (Jan. 1928): 792–97.

799 ———. "Freedom of the Seas the Crux of Disarmament." *Current History* 29 (Feb. 1929): 721–32.

800 Harris, Henry W. *Naval Disarmament.* London: Allen & Unwin, 1930.

801 Kerguezec, Gustave de. "French Naval Aims." *Foreign Affairs* 4 (Apr. 1926): 369–82.

802 Knox, Dudley W. "Recent Developments in Limitation of Naval Armaments." *U.S. Naval Institute Proceedings* 52 (Oct. 1926): 1985–92.

803 Latimer, Hugh. *Naval Disarmament: A Brief Record from the Washington Conference to Date.* London: Royal Institute of International Affairs, 1930.

804 Maggi, Cecil A. "The Attitude of Certain American Newspapers on Anglo-American Naval Disarmament." M.A. thesis, Columbia Univ., 1930.

805 "National Defense and the Limiting of Naval Armaments." *Congressional Digest* 4 (Jan. 1925): 118–36.

806 Pratt, Adm. William V. "The Limitation of Armament: The Naval Viewpoint." *Annals of the Amer. Acad. of Pol. & Soc. Sci.* 126 (July 1926): 57–65.

807 ———. "Our Naval Policy." *U.S. Naval Institute Proceedings* 58 (July 1932): 953–70.

808 Richmond, Adm. Sir Herbert W. *Economy and Naval Security: A Plea for the Examination of the Problem of the Reduction in the Cost of Naval Armaments on the Lines of Strategy and Policy.* London: Benn, 1931.

809 Shillock, John C., Jr. "The Post-war Movements to Reduce Naval Armaments." *International Conciliation*, no. 245 (Dec. 1928): 569–656.

810 Smith-Hutton, H. H. "Naval Limitations." *U.S. Naval Institute Proceedings* 63 (Apr. 1937): 463–76.

811 Standley, Adm. William H., and R. A. Collins. "Should the United States Navy Be Built up to Treaty Strength?" *Congressional Digest* 13 (Apr. 1934): 120–22.

812 Talbot, Melvin F. "Navies and National Policies." *Yale Review* 27 (Dec. 1937–38): 333–47.

NAVAL LIMITATION—HISTORICAL ASSESSMENTS

813 Andrade, Ernest, Jr. "United States Naval

Policy in the Disarmament Era, 1921–1937." Ph.D. diss., Michigan State Univ., 1966.

814 Burns, Richard Dean, and Donald Urquidi. *Disarmament in Perspective, 1919–1941.* Vol. 3: *Limitation of Sea Power.* Washington, D.C., G.P.O., 1968.

815 Fagan, George V. "Anglo-American Naval Relations, 1927–1937." Ph.D. diss., Univ. of Pennsylvania, 1954.

816 ———. "F. D. R. and Naval Limitation." *U.S. Naval Institute Proceedings* 81 (Apr. 1955): 411–18.

817 Johnson, William S. "Naval Diplomacy and the Failure of Balanced Security in the Far East, 1921–1935." *Naval War College Review* 24 (Feb. 1972): 67–88.

818 Mets, Lt. Col. David R. "A Case Study in Arms Control: Naval Limitation Before Pearl Harbor and Post-war Arms Control Theory." Ph.D. diss., Univ. of Denver, 1972.

819 Roskill, Stephen. *Naval Policy Between the Wars: The Period of Anglo-American Antagonism, 1919–1929.* New York: Walker, 1969.

820 Rudoff, Robin M. "The Influence of the German Navy on the British Search for Naval Arms Control, 1928–1935." Ph.D. diss., Tulane Univ., 1964.

821 Solontsov, Z. M. "Iz Istorii Bor'by SShA za Gospodstvo na More." *Novaia i Noveishaia Istoriia* [U.S.S.R.] 2:2 (1958): 62–82.

822 Wheeler, Gerald E. "Isolated Japan: Anglo-American Diplomatic Cooperation, 1927–1936." *Pacific Historical Review* 30 (Feb. 1961): 165–78.

823 ———. *Prelude to Pearl Harbor: The United States Navy and the Far East, 1921–1931.* Columbia: Univ. of Missouri Press, 1963.

NATIONAL POLICIES & VIEWS

National policies and views relating to specific issues or negotiations can be found among the historical surveys above or under League of Nations, below, or under the various agreements, treaties, and conferences cited in Part Two.

824 Borchard, Edwin M. "A Limitation of Armaments?" *Yale Review* 15 (June 1926): 625–44.

825 Dennis, Alfred L. P. "The Protocol, Security, and Disarmament." *North American Review* 221 (June 1925): 665–79.

826 Dulles, Allen W. "Disarmament in the Atomic Age." *Foreign Affairs* 26 (Jan. 1947): 204–16.

827 Fiske, Adm. Bradley A. "The Possibilities of Disarmament." *Annals of the Amer. Acad. of Pol. & Soc. Sci.* 120 (July 1925): 77–80.

828 Gardiner, William H. "The Reduction of Armaments." *North American Review* 223 (June 1926): 216–33.

829 Gordon, Linley V. "Disarmament: Often Talked About, but Not Yet Achieved." *Review of Reviews* 80 (Aug. 1929): 73–74.

830 Hale, W. B. "Limitation of Armaments." *American Bar Association Journal* 18 (Mar. 1932): 195–204.

831 Harley, J. E. "Achievements and Problems in the Limitation of Armaments." *Southwestern Political and Social Science Quarterly* 8 (Sept. 1927): 179–88.

832 Harris, Henry W. "Will Disarmament Come?" *Contemporary Review* 133 (May 1928): 572–79.

833 Hicks, F. C. "Curtailment of Armaments." *Annals of the Amer. Acad. of Pol. & Soc. Sci.* 96 (July 1921): 56–62.

834 Howe, Walter B. "Pacifism Termed Handicap to Armament Limitation." *U.S. Daily* (Oct. 29, 1929): 2109–11.

835 Lenroot, Sen. I. L. "Disarmament and the Present Outlook for Peace." *Annals of the Amer. Acad. of Pol. & Soc. Sci.* 126 (July 1926): 142–45.

836 MacKay, R. A. "The Politics of Disarmament." *Dalhousie Review* 11 (Jan. 1932): 473–84.

837 Magruder, Adm. Thomas P. "Can Disarmament Abolish War?" *Annals of the Amer. Acad. of Pol. & Soc. Sci.* 138 (July 1928): 170–72.

838 ———, et al. "Significance of Growing World Armaments." *Annals of the Amer. Acad. of Pol. & Soc. Sci.* 144 (July 1929): 137–50.

839 Mitchell, Gen. William. "Some Considerations Regarding a Limitation of Armaments." *Annals of the Amer. Acad. of Pol. & Soc. Sci.* 120 (July 1925): 87–89.

840   Mondel, Rep. Frank W. "Limitation of Arma-
      ments by International Agreement." *Annals
      of the Amer. Acad. of Pol. & Soc. Sci.* 96
      (July 1921): 53–55.

841   Montluc, P. "La Question du Désarmement."
      Revue de Droit International (July–Sept.
      1921): 268–81.

842   Rathbone, Henry R. "The Road to Disarma-
      ment." *Annals of the Amer. Acad. of Pol. &
      Soc. Sci.* 138 (July 1928): 166–69.

843   Réquin, Gen. E. "Disarmament the Next
      Problem: Can we Limit Armaments?" *Living
      Age* 335 (Nov. 1928): 213–16.

844   Rogers, John J. "The Reduction of Arma-
      ments." *Annals of the Amer. Acad. of Pol. &
      Soc. Sci.* 96 (July 1921): 62–67.

845   Scammell, J. M. "Policies and the New Ar-
      mament Competition." *North American Re-
      view* 218 (Oct. 1923): 448–54.

846   Shotwell, James T. "Disarmament Alone No
      Guarantee of Peace." *Current History* 30
      (Sept. 1929): 1024–29.

847   ———. "Political and Technical Aspects of
      Disarmament." *Annals of the Amer. Acad. of
      Pol. & Soc. Sci.* 126 (July 1926): 79–82.

848   ———. "A Practical Plan for Disarmament:
      Draft Treaty of Disarmament and Security."
      International Conciliation, no. 201 (Aug.
      1924): 1–67.

849   Slayden, Rep. James L. "Disarmament and
      International Courts Prerequisite to a World
      Peace." *Annals of the Amer. Acad. of Pol. &
      Soc. Sci.* 72 (July 1917): 92–99.

850   Smiddy, T. A. "Possibility of Disarmament."
      *Annals of the Amer. Acad. of Pol. & Soc.
      Sci.* 120 (July 1925): 67–68.

851   Taft, Henry W. "Disarmament." *Annals of the
      Amer. Acad. of Pol. & Soc. Sci.* 138 (July
      1928): 154–56.

852   Thomas, Norman. "Armaments and Peace."
      *Annals of the Amer. Acad. of Pol. & Soc.
      Sci.* 144 (July 1929): 140–42.

853   Wright, Quincy. *Limitation of Armament.*
      New York: Institute of International Educa-
      tion, 1921.

FRANCE

854   Aubert, Louis. "Security: Key to French Pol-
      icy." *Foreign Affairs* 11 (Oct. 1932): 122–36.

855   Blum, Leon. *Peace and Disarmament.* Trans.
      by A. Werth. London: J. Cape, 1932.

856   Cot, Pierre. "Disarmament and French Public
      Opinion." *Political Quarterly* 2 (July 1931):
      367–77.

857   Doukas, K. A. "Armaments and the French
      Experiment." *American Political Science
      Review* 33 (Apr. 1939): 279–91.

858   La Bruyère, René. "France's New Army and
      Navy." *Current History* 24 (Apr. 1926):
      21–26.

859   Le Chartier, G. "French Policy and Disarma-
      ment." *Acad. of Pol. Sci. Proceedings* 12
      (July 1926): 35–40.

860   Marković, Lazar. *Le Désarmement et la
      Politique de Belgrade.* Paris: Société
      Générale d'Imprimerie, 1931.

861   Minart, Jacques. *Le Drame du Désarmement
      Français (Ses Aspects Politiques et Tech-
      niques): La Revanche Allemande* [1918–
      1939]. Paris: La NEF de Paris, 1959.

862   Niessel, Henri. "L'Armée Française et le Dé-
      sarmement." *Revue de France* 12 (Jan. 1932):
      342–66.

863   Schmidt, Wilhelm. "Frankreich Sabotiert die
      Abrüstung." *Schriften des Deutschen In-
      stituts für Aussenpolitische Forschung* 17
      (1940): 7–58.

864   Toledano, A. D. *Ce qu'il Faut Savoir sur le
      Désarmement.* Paris: Pedone, 1932.

GERMANY

For additional German views on arms control, see
Chapter 9 under Versailles Treaty (1919).

865   Baldwin, F. F. "German View of the Present
      Situation." *Outlook* (Feb. 20, 1924): 300–302.

866   Child, S. "What Germany Is Doing." *Outlook*
      (Mar. 28, 1923): 569.

867   Curtius, Julius. "The Fundamentals of Ger-
      man Disarmament Policy." In Richard K. B.

Schmidt and Adolf Grabowsky, eds., *The Problems of Disarmament.* Berlin: Carl Haymanns Verlag, 1933.

868 "German General on Disarmament." *Literary Digest* (Dec. 8, 1928): 18–19.

869 Groener, Gen. Wilhelm. "Die Abrüstungsbestimmungen von Versailles und die Deutsche Innere Politik." *Zeitschrift für Politik* 21 (Mar. 1932): 763–68.

870 Jones, Julian A., III. "Germany and the Disarmament Question, 1919–1933." Ph.D. diss., Fletcher School of Law & Diplomacy, 1967.

871 Meinck, Gerhard. *Hitler und die Deutsche Abrüstung, 1933–1937.* Wiesbaden: Franz Steiner Verlag, 1959.

872 Oertzen, Karl L. von. *Abrüstung oder Kriegvorbereitung.* Berlin: Zentralverlag, 1931.

873 Réquin, Gen. E. "The Armaments and Military Power of Germany." *Foreign Affairs* 11 (Jan. 1933): 230–44.

874 Richter, Rolf. "Der Abrüstungsgedanke in Theorie und Praxis und die Deutsche Politik [1920–1929]." *Wehrwissenschaftliche Rundschau* 18 (Aug. 1968): 442–66.

875 Schmidt, Richard K. B., and Adolf Grabowsky, eds. *The Problems of Disarmament.* Berlin: Carl Haymanns Verlag, 1933. [Special English-language supplement to *Zeitschrift für Politik*.]

876 Schwendemann, Karl. *Abrüstung und Sicherheit.* 2 vols. Berlin: Weidmann, 1933, 1936.

877 ———. "Deutschlands Weg in der Abrüstungsfrage." *Zeitschrift für Politik* 23 (Jan. 1934): 7–32.

Great Britain

878 Arnold-Forster, William. "English Politics and Disarmament." *Political Quarterly* 3 (Oct.–Dec. 1932): 365–80.

879 *Britain and World Peace: An Account of the National Government's Efforts to Promote Disarmament and to Ensure World Peace.* London: Burrup, Mathieson, 1935.

880 Carlton, David. "Disarmament With Guarantees: Lord Cecil, 1922–1927." *Disarmament and Arms Control* 3 (Autumn 1965): 143–64.

881 ———. *MacDonald Versus Henderson: The Foreign Policy of the Second Labour Government.* London: Macmillan, 1970.

882 Cecil, Viscount Robert. *A Letter to an M.P. on Disarmament.* London: Hogarth Press, 1931.

883 ———. "Political Foundations of Disarmament." *Round Table* 21 (Sept. 1931): 713–37.

884 Chaput, Rolland A. *Disarmament in British Foreign Policy.* London: Allen & Unwin, 1935.

885 Crosby, Gerda R. *Disarmament and Peace in British Politics, 1914–1919.* Cambridge: Harvard Univ. Press, 1957.

886 Cushendun, Lord. "Disarmament." *International Affairs* [London] 7 (Mar. 1928): 77–93.

887 Dalton, Hugh. *Towards the Peace of Nations.* London: Routledge, 1928.

888 Glasgow, George. "Great Britain and Disarmament." *Contemporary Review* 135 (Apr. 1929): 516–19.

889 Harris, Henry W. "British Policy and Disarmament." *Acad. of Pol. Sci. Proceedings* 12 (July 1926): 27–34.

890 Henderson, Arthur. *Labour's Peace Policy: Arbitration, Security, Disarmament.* London: Labour Party, 1934.

891 MacDonald, J. Ramsay. "League Must Solve Problem of Disarmament." *Commercial and Financial Chronicle* (Sept. 7, 1929): 1524–26.

892 Marcosson, F. "New Road to Disarmament: Interview with R. MacDonald." *Saturday Evening Post* (Aug. 3, 1929): 21.

893 Ponsonby, Arthur. "Disarmament by Example." *Contemporary Review* 132 (Dec. 1927): 687–93.

894 Smith, Rennie. "Labor and Disarmament." *Standard* 16 (Feb. 1930): 175–79.

Italy

895 Albanese, T. *Sicurezza—Disarmo.* Rome: Anonima Romana Editoriale, 1930.

896 Ellery, E. "Italy and Disarmament." *Current History* 26 (Apr. 1927): 115–16.

897 Gatto, R. L. *Disarmo e Difesa.* Milan: Corbaccio, 1925.

JAPAN

As with Italy, Japan's major interest in disarmament policies centered on the limitation of naval forces, see naval treaties below.

898 Crowley, James B. *Japan's Quest for Autonomy: National Security and Foreign Policy, 1921–1938.* Princeton: Princeton Univ. Press, 1966.

899 Ishii, Viscount Kikujiro. *Diplomatic Commentaries.* Trans. by W. R. Langdon. Baltimore: Johns Hopkins Press, 1936.

900 Kennedy, M. D. "Japanese Fighting Forces and Disarmament." *Some Aspects of Japan and Her Defense Forces.* London: Kegan Paul, Trench, Trubner, 1928.

901 Ono, Giichi. *War and Armament Expenditures of Japan.* New York: Oxford Univ. Press, 1922.

902 Takeuchi, Tatsuji. *War and Diplomacy in the Japanese Empire.* New York: Doubleday, Doran, 1935.

903 Tanin, O., and E. Yohan. *Militarism and Fascism in Japan.* London: Martin Lawrence, 1935.

SOVIET UNION

904 "The Battle for Disarmament: Documentary Survey . . . [Interwar Years]." *New Times* [Moscow] 27 (July 4, 1962): 4–8; 28 (July 8, 1962): 5–8; 29 (July 18, 1962): 6–9.

905 Bessonov, F. "The U.S.S.R. and Disarmament." *Parizhskii Vestnik* (Feb. 14, 1926). [Translated in *European Economic and Political Survey* (Apr. 17, 1926): 6–13.]

906 Charques, R. D. *The Soviets and the Next War: The Present Case for Disarmament.* London: Martin Secker, 1932.

907 Clemens, Walter C., Jr. "Lenin on Disarmament." *Slavic Review* 23 (Sept. 1964): 504–25.

908 ———. "Origins of the Soviet Campaign for Disarmament: The Soviet Position on Peace, Security, and Revolution at the Genoa, Moscow, and Lausanne Conferences, 1922–1923." Ph.D. diss., Columbia Univ., 1961.

909 Combe, E. "Les Soviets et le Désarmement." *Neue Schweizer Rundschau* 21 (Jan. 1928): 67–70.

910 Efremoff, Jean. "L'Armee Rouge et le Désarmement." *L'Esprit International* [Paris] (Apr. 1, 1932): 249–61.

911 Khaitsman, Viktor M. *SSSR i Problema Razoruzheniia (Mezhdu Pervoi i Vtoroi Mirovymi).* Moscow: Izd-vo Akademii Nauk SSSR, 1959.

912 ——— [Khoytsman]. *The USSR Disarmament Peace, 1917–1962.* Moscow: Institute of International Relations Publishing House, 1962.

913 Korovine, Eugene A. "L'U.R.S.S. et la Problème du Désarmement." *Revue de Droit International des Sciences Diplomatiques et Politiques* 4 (Oct. 1928): 319–28.

914 ———. "The U.S.S.R. and Disarmament." *International Conciliation*, no. 292 (Sept. 1933): 293–354.

915 Lambert, Robert W. *Soviet Disarmament Policy, 1922–1931.* ACDA Research Report 64–2. Washington, D.C.: ACDA, 1964.

916 Lawrence, London M. *The Soviet Union and Peace.* London: Martin Lawrence, 1929.

917 Lenin, N. "Disarmament." *Collection from the Social Democrat* (Dec. 1916). [Translated for *Labour Monthly* 12 (Aug. 1930): 451–60.]

918 "Litvinov on Disarmament." *Soviet Union Review* 7 (June 1929): 90–96.

919 [Litvinov, M.]. *Soviet's Fight for Disarmament.* London: Martin Lawrence, 1932.

920 *L'U.R.S.S. et le Désarmement.* 2d ed. Geneva: Bureau Permanente de L'Entente Internationale Contre La IIIᵉ Internationale, 1932.

921 "Program of the All-Russian Communist Party." In Jan F. Triska, ed., *Soviet Communism: Programs and Rules.* San Francisco: Chandler, 1962, pp. 130–53. [8th Cong., Mar. 18–23, 1919.]

922 Salvin, Maria. "Soviet Policy Toward Disarmament." *International Conciliation*, no. 428 (Feb. 1947): 42–117.

923 Slobin, Norval L. "Soviet Disarmament Proposals, 1917–1935." Ph.D. diss., Univ. of Chicago, 1942.

924 "The Soviet Union and Disarmament." *Communist Review* 3 (Aug. 1931): 309–22.

UNITED STATES

925 Allen, Gen. Henry. "Possibility of Disarmament: Necessity for United States Cooperation." *Annals of the Amer. Acad. of Pol. & Soc. Sci.* 120 (July 1925): 65–66.

926 Bullard, Arthur. "America and the Problem of Disarmament." *American Diplomacy in the Modern World.* Philadelphia: Univ. of Pennsylvania Press, 1928, pp. 90–127.

927 Burns, Richard Dean, and Donald Urquidi. "Woodrow Wilson and Disarmament: Ideas vs. Realities." *Aerospace Historian* 18 (Winter 1971): 186–94.

928 Coolidge, Pres. Calvin. "Promoting Peace Through Limitation of Armaments." *Ladies' Home Journal* (May 1929): 3–4.

929 Coudenhove-Kalergi, Richard N. "Open Letter to President Hoover: Military or Economic Security." *Living Age* 336 (June 1929): 274–76.

930 Davis, Norman H. "The Disarmament Problem." *Foreign Affairs* 13 (Apr. 1933): supplement i–x.

931 "Disarmament: What America Thinks." *Saturday Review* (Aug. 10, 1929): 150.

932 Gerould, James T. "America's Reduction Proposals Revitalize Disarmament Discussion: With Text of H. S. Gibson's Speech." *Current History* 30 (June 1929): 483–89.

933 ———. "Disarmament Proposals Making Little Headway." *Current History* 28 (Aug. 1928): 841–42.

934 Hegedus, Ronald de. "Urges American Bankers to Refuse Loans to Countries Which Are Not Disarming." *Commercial and Financial Chronicle* (Apr. 7, 1928): 2079.

935 [Hoover, Pres. Herbert C.]. "Big Disarmament Fight Looms in Washington." *Literary Digest* (Aug. 10, 1929): 5–6.

936 ———. "Hoover's Bid for Real Disarmament." *Literary Digest* (June 15, 1929): 10–11.

937 ———. "President Hoover Moves: Case for Disarmament." *Nation* [London] (Apr. 27, 1929): 98–100.

938 Hudson, Manley O. "America's Relation to World Peace." *Problems of Peace.* Geneva Institute of International Relations, Series 3. London: Oxford Univ. Press, 1929.

939 Irvin, Thomas C. "Norman H. Davis and the Quest for Arms Control, 1931–1938." Ph.D. diss., Ohio State Univ., 1963.

940 McDonald, James G. "President Hoover's Opportunity." *Annals of the Amer. Acad. of Pol. & Soc. Sci.* 144 (July 1929): 146–47.

941 Madariaga, Salvador de. "Disarmament: American Plan." *Atlantic Monthly* (Apr. 1929): 525–38.

942 Miller, David Hunter. "The Relation of America to Disarmament." *Annals of the Amer. Acad. of Pol. & Soc. Sci.* 126 (July 1926): 22–26.

943 Shotwell, James T., et al. "Disarmament and American Foreign Policy." *International Conciliation*, no. 220 (May 1926): 1–46.

944 "Should America Disarm? A Debate: Kirby Page, Bradley A. Fiske." *Forum* 81 (Feb. 1929): 70–74, 75–77.

945 Winkler, Fred H. "The War Department and Disarmament, 1926–1935." *Historian* 28 (May 1966): 426–46.

Contemporary Issues, Since 1945

The two best overviews on AC&D negotiations and events, without much commentary, are *Disarmament: Negotiations and Treaties* (1972) and the U.N.'s *The United Nations and Disarmament* (1970), listed below.

946 Barnet, Richard J. *Who Wants Disarmament?* Boston: Beacon Press, 1960.

947 Bechhoefer, Bernhard G. *Postwar Negotiations for Arms Control.* Washington, D.C.: Brookings Institution, 1961.

948 Biorklund, Elis. *International Atomic Policy During a Decade: An Historical-Political Investigation into the Problem of Atomic Weapons during the Period 1945–1955.* London: Allen & Unwin, 1956.

949 Bull, Hedley. *The Control of the Arms Race: Disarmament and Arms Control in the Missile Age.* 2d ed. New York: Praeger, 1965.

950 *Disarmament: Negotiations and Treaties, 1946–1971.* Keesing's Research Report no. 7. New York: Scribner's, 1972.

951 Forndran, Erhard A. G. *Rüstungskontrolle: Friedenssicherung zwischen Abschreckung.* Dusseldorf: Bertelsmann Universitätsverlag, 1970.

952 Morray, Joseph P. *From Yalta to Disarmament: Cold War Debate.* New York: Monthly Review Press, 1961.

953 Nogee, Joseph L. *The Diplomacy of Disarmament.* New York: Carnegie Endowment for International Peace, 1960.

954 Nutting, Anthony. *Disarmament: An Outline of the Negotiations.* London: Oxford Univ. Press, 1959.

955 Roberts, Chalmers M. *The Nuclear Years: The Arms Race and Arms Control, 1945–1970.* New York: Praeger, 1970.

956 Spanier, John W., and Joseph L. Nogee. *The Politics of Disarmament: A Study in Soviet-American Gamesmanship.* New York: Praeger, 1962.

957 U.N. Disarmament Affairs Division. *The United Nations and Disarmament, 1945–1970.* New York, 1970.

958 Viskov, Sergei I. *Za Mir bez Oruzhiia, za Mir bez Voin: Vneshniaia Politika SSSR, 1956–1963 gg.* Moscow: Mysl', 1964.

959 Volle, Herman, and Claus-Jurgen Duisberg. *Problem der Internationalen Abrüstung: Die Bemuhungen der Vereinten Nationen um Internationale Abrüstung und Sicherheit, 1945–1961.* Frankfurt: A. Metzner Verlag, 1964.

960 Zorin, V. A., ed. *Bor'ba Sovetskogo Soiuza za Razoruzhenie, 1946–1960.* Moscow: Izd-vo Instituta Mezhdunarodnykh Otnoshenii, 1961.

961 Bechhoefer, Bernhard G. "The Disarmament Deadlock: 1946–1955." *Current History* 42 (May 1962): 257–266, 280.

962 Benesch, Gustav. "Der Stand der Nuklearrustung nach 25 Jahren." *Aussenpolitik* 21 (July 1970): 416–30.

963 Burns, E. L. M. "Disarmament and Military Policy." *International Journal* 26 (Winter 1971): 619–34.

964 Chayes, Abram. "Nuclear Arms Control After the Cold War." *Daedalus* 104 (Summer 1975): 15–34.

965 Dickinson, William B., Jr. "Struggle for Disarmament." *Editorial Research Reports* (Feb. 25, 1960): 139–56.

966 Dougherty, James E. "The Status of the Arms Negotiations." *Orbis* 9 (Spring 1965): 49–97.

967 Epstein, William. *Disarmament: Twenty-Five Years of Effort.* Toronto: Canadian Institute of International Affairs, 1971.

968 Fischer, Georges. "Chronique du Désarmement." *Annuaire Français de Droit International* 17 (1971): 85–130.

969 Frye, William R. "The Quest for Disarmament Since World War II." In Louis Henkin, ed., *Arms Control: Issues for the Public.* Englewood Cliffs, N.J.: Prentice-Hall, 1961, pp. 18–48.

970 Hayden, Eric W. "Soviet-American Arms Negotiations, 1960–1968: A Prelude for SALT." *Naval War College Review* 24 (Jan. 1972): 65–82.

971 Jensen, Lloyd. "Postwar Disarmament Negotiations." *Current History* 46 (June 1964): 336–40.

972 Long, Franklin A. "Arms Control from the Perspective of the Nineteen-Seventies." *Daedalus* 104 (Summer 1975): 1–14.

973 McCloy, John J. "Balance Sheet on Disarmament." *Foreign Affairs* 40 (Apr. 1962): 339–59.

974 McVitty, Marion H. "Disarmament Negotiations: 1956–1962." *Social Education* 26 (Nov. 1962): 384–89, 396.

975 Mets, Lt. Col. David R. "Arms Control Since Hiroshima." *U.S. Naval Institute Proceedings* 99 (Dec. 1973): 18–26.

976 Mezerik, Avrahm G., ed. *Disarmament: Postwar Through 1957 including Satellites and Missiles.* New York: International Review Service, 1957.

977 Nanes, A. S. "Disarmament in the Last Seven Years." *Current History* 42 (May 1962): 267–74.

978 "On Past Disarmament Experiences and Some Basic Disarmament Issues [1945–1970s]." *Instant Research on Peace and Violence* 1:4 (1972): 208–27.

979 Randle, Robert F. "Arms Control Within a Changing Political Context." *International Journal* 26 (Autumn 1971): 735–52.

980 Ranger, Robin. "Arms Control Negotiations: Progress and Prospects." *Canadian Defense Quarterly* 4 (Winter 1974): 16–25.

981 Shaffer, Helen B. "Nuclear Balance of Terror: Twenty-five Years After Alamogordo." *Editorial Research Reports* (July 1970): 485–506.

982 Stone, I. F. "Theater of Delusion." *New York Review of Books* (Apr. 23, 1970): 15–16, 18–24.

983 Thompson, Carol L. "A History of Disarmament Proposals." *Current History* 36 (Jan. 1959): 38–41.

984 Watson, Lorna. "History of Disarmament Negotiations." *Peace Research Reviews* 1 (Apr. 1967): 1–107.

985 Wilcox, Francis O. *The Search for Disarmament.* Dept. of State Pub. 6398, General Foreign Policy Series 112. Washington, D.C.: G.P.O., 1956.

986 Women Strike for Peace. *The Story of Disarmament, 1945–1962.* Washington, D.C., 1962.

PROSPECTS FOR 1970s

987 Barnaby, Frank. "Disarmament Prospects in the 70's." *Humanist* [London] 85 (Sept. 1970): 262–64.

988 Burns, Richard Dean. "Arms Control and Disarmament: What Prospects for United States Policies in the 1970's?" *Vital Issues* 22 (Apr. 1973): 1–4.

989 Carter, Barry. "What Next in Arms Control?" *Orbis* 17 (Spring 1973): 176–96.

990 Dougherty, James E. "Arms Control in the 1970's." *Orbis* 15 (Spring 1971): 194–217.

991 Gerber, William. "Prospects for Arms Control." *Editorial Research Reports* (Apr. 9, 1969): 269–86.

992 Ignatieff, George. "The Outlook for Disarmament in the Coming Decade." *External Affairs* [Canada] 22 (Dec. 1970): 425–33.

993 Wiesner, Jerome B. "Arms Control: Current Prospects and Problems." *Bulletin of the Atomic Scientists* 26 (May 1970): 6–8, 38–39.

NATIONAL POLICIES & VIEWS

994 Barnet, Richard J. "The Current Disarmament Impasse." In James E. Dougherty and John F. Lehman, Jr., eds., *Arms Control for the Late Sixties.* Princeton: Van Nostrand, 1967, pp. 9–24.

995 Bethe, Hans A. "Disarmament Problems." *Bulletin of the Atomic Scientists* 26 (June 1970): 99–102.

996 Blackett, P. M. S. *Atomic Weapons and East-West Relations.* London: Cambridge Univ. Press, 1956.

997 ———. "Steps Toward Disarmament." *Scientific American* 206 (Apr. 1962): 45–53.

998 Blechman, Barry M. *Controlling Naval Armaments: Prospects and Possibilities.* Washington, D.C.: Brookings Institution, 1975.

999 Boyd, Andrew. "Of Arms and Men: A Report on Current Efforts Toward International Arms Control." *Vista* 4 (May–June 1969): 52–57.

1000 Buzzard, Adm. Anthony W. "Overall Western Policy and Plan for Disarmament." *Army Quarterly* [Great Britain] 86 (1963): 85–95.

1001 Cavers, David F. "The Arms Stalemate Ends." *Bulletin of the Atomic Scientists* 11 (Jan. 1955): 9–12.

1002 ———. "A Fresh Outlook on Disarmament." *Reporter* (July 8, 1952): 22–24.

1003 Chalfont, Lord Arthur G. J. "Controlling the Weapons of Mass Destruction." *Round Table* 61 (Jan. 1971): 33–41.

1004 Chamberlain, William H. "Disarmament: Hope or Trap?" *Modern Age* 5 (Summer 1961): 231–37.

1005 DeWeerd, Harvey A. "The Case for Weapons Limitation." *Army* 7:2 (1957): 23–27.

1006 ———. *Disarmament Failure and Weapons Limitations.* Report P–898. Santa Monica, Ca.: Rand, 1956.

1007 "Disarmament: The Fiction and Fact." *Newsweek* (May 20, 1957): 46–47.

1008 "Disarmament and Coexistence." *Current History* 42 (May 1962): 257–305.

1009 Eaton, Cyrus. "Disarmament and Soviet-American Relations." *International Affairs* [Moscow] 7 (Feb. 1961): 51–57.

1010 Frye, William R. "Disarmament: Atoms into Plowshares?" *Foreign Policy Association Headline Series* (Sept. 20, 1955).

1011 Herzfeld, Norma K. "Disarmament: Not Now." *Commonweal* (Dec. 23, 1966): 341–43.

1012 Hudson, Richard. "What Chances for Disarmament Progress?" *War/Peace Report* 2 (Apr. 1962): 3–5.

1013 Leghorn, Col. Richard S. "How the Arms Race Can Be Checked." *Reporter* (Mar. 6, 1958): 16–20.

1014 Levine, Robert A. "Breaking the Arms Stalemate." *Bulletin of the Atomic Scientists* 18 (June 1962): 8–11.

1015 Martin, Laurence W. "Cold War and Weapons Control." *Current History* 47 (July 1964): 1–5, 50.

1016 Matteson, Robert E. "The Disarmament Dilemma." *Orbis* 2 (Fall 1958): 285–299.

1017 Piterskii, N. "Some Problems of a Disarmed World." *Disarmament and Arms Control* 2 (Autumn 1964): 405–21.

1018 Schmidt, Petrus J. "Regulation, Limitation and Balanced Reduction of All Armed Forces and Armaments." *Acad. of Pol. Sci. Proceedings* 25 (Jan. 1953): 67–76.

1019 Schuman, Fredrick L. "The Impasse of Disarmament." *Current History* 41 (Nov. 1961): 267–72, 298.

1020 "Should the Development of Nuclear Weapons Be Prohibited by International Agreement?" *Congressional Digest* 37 (Oct. 1958): 225–56.

1021 Simons, Howard. "World-Wide Capabilities for Production and Control of Nuclear Weapons." *Daedalus* 88 (Summer 1959): 385–409.

1022 Topchiev, A. V. "Disarmament and the International Tension." *Bulletin of the Atomic Scientists* 14 (Dec. 1958): 405–08.

1023 Wiesner, Jerome B. "Comprehensive Arms-Limitations Systems." In Donald G. Brennan, ed., *Arms Control, Disarmament, and National Security*. New York: Braziller, 1961, pp. 198–233.

1024 Wittig, Peter. *Die Kontrolle der Atomaren Rustungen*. Cologne: Heymann, 1967.

1025 Wu Yuan-li. *Arms Control Arrangements for the Far East*. Stanford, Ca.: Hoover Institution Press, 1967.

UNITED STATES

1026 Bechhoefer, Bernhard G. "American Policies and Disarmament." In Stephen D. Kertesz, ed., *American Diplomacy in a New Era*. Notre Dame: Univ. of Notre Dame Press, 1961, pp. 83–143.

1027 Bernstein, Barton J. "The Quest for Security: American Foreign Policy and International Control of Atomic Energy, 1942–1946." *Journal of American History* 60 (Mar. 1974): 1003–44.

1028 Bowie, Robert R. "Arms Control and United States Foreign Policy." In Louis Henkin, ed., *Arms Control: Issues for the Public*. Englewood Cliffs, N.J.: Prentice-Hall, 1961, pp. 49–75.

1029 Brower, Michael. "Nuclear Strategy of the Kennedy Administration." *Bulletin of the Atomic Scientists* 18 (Oct. 1962): 34–41.

1030 Christman, Henry M. *Peace and Arms: Reports from the Nation*. New York: Sheed & Ward, 1964.

1031 Clark, Sen. Joseph S. "The Diplomacy of Peace." In James E. Dougherty and John F. Lehman, Jr., eds., *Arms Control for the Late Sixties*. Princeton: Van Nostrand, 1967, pp. 17–24.

1032 Cook, Fred J. "Coming Politics of Disarmament." *Nation* (Feb. 16, 1963): 131–35.

1033 DeWeerd, Harvey A. *United States Policies on Disarmament, 1946–1955—A Critique*. Report P–825. Santa Monica, Ca.: Rand, Mar. 1956.

1034 Drukman, Mason. "America's New Disarmament Policy." *New University Thought* 2 (Spring 1962): 52–65.

1035 Epstein, Carl P. "U.S. Policy Concerning Nuclear Control, 1950–1960." Ph.D. diss., American Univ., 1964.

1036 Fedder, Edwin H. "Would U.S. Senate Ratify a Disarmament Treaty?" *War/Peace Report* 4 (June 1964): 14.

1037 Finletter, Thomas K. "Facing Disarmament."

Bulletin of the Atomic Scientists 13 (May 1957): 154–56.

1038   Fletcher, Andria. *Arms Control and the Nixon Doctrine.* Santa Monica, Ca.: Southern California Arms Control & Foreign Policy Seminar, Jan. 1972.

1039   Gardner, Richard N. *Blueprint for Peace: Being the Proposals of Prominent Americans to the White House Conference on International Cooperation.* New York: McGraw-Hill, 1966.

1040   Inglis, David R. "The H-bomb and Disarmament Prospects." *Bulletin of the Atomic Scientists* 10 (Feb. 1954): 41–45, 64.

1041   Johansen, Robert C. "The Politics of Arms Control: American Policy-Making and Negotiating in 1957." Ph.D. diss., Columbia Univ., 1968.

1042   Kaufmann, William W. "Disarmament and American Foreign Policy." *Foreign Policy Reports* (Sept. 1, 1950): 89–92.

1043   Margolis, Howard. "From New York to Washington: Talking About Disarmament." *Bulletin of the Atomic Scientists* 22 (Feb. 1966): 38–40.

1044   Matteson, Robert E. "Disarmament Prospects After Cuba." *Journal of Conflict Resolution* 7:3 (1963): 338–50.

1045   Murray, Thomas E. *Nuclear Policy for War and Peace.* New York: World, 1960.

1046   Sherman, M. E. "Nixon and Arms Control." *International Journal* 24 (Spring 1969): 327–38.

1047   Shulman, Marshall D. "Arms Control and Disarmament: A View From the U.S.A." *Annals of the Amer. Acad. of Pol. & Soc. Sci.* 414 (July 1974): 64–72.

1048   Spingarn, Jerome H. "Disarmament: The Washington Scene." *Bulletin of the Atomic Scientists* 14 (Nov. 1958): 385–87.

1049   Stone, Jeremy J. "Bomber Disarmament." *World Politics* 17 (Oct. 1964): 13–39.

1050   Taylor, Harold. "How Credible Are Our Professions of Peace?" *Progressive* 27 (Mar. 1963): 31–34.

1051   "United States Disarmament Policy— Charges and Answers." *Journal of Arms Control* 1:1 (1963): 82–88.

Domestic Views

1052   "Arms Control and the 1976 Presidential Election." *Arms Control Today* 6 (Oct. 1976): 1–5.

1053   Austin, Sen. Warren R. "World Confidence and the Reduction of Armed Forces: The American Objective." *U.S. Department of State Bulletin* (Oct. 24, 1948): 511–16.

1054   Beam, Jacob D. "Strengthening Peace Through Arms Control and Disarmament." *U.S. Department of State Bulletin* (Sept. 6, 1965): 398–400.

1055   Clark, Sen. Joseph S. "Senator Clark on the White House Conference." *Bulletin of the Atomic Scientists* 22 (Mar. 1966): 30–33.

1056   Cohen, Benjamin V. "Whither Disarmament?" *U.S. Department of State Bulletin* (Feb. 2, 1953): 172–76.

1057   Dulles, John Foster. "Disarmament and Peace." *U.S. Department of State Bulletin* (Aug. 12, 1957): 267–72.

1058   ———. "Dynamic Peace." *U.S. Department of State Bulletin* (May 6, 1957): 715–19.

1059   [Eisenhower, Pres. Dwight D.]. "Ike Talks About Peace, Disarmament, Red China." *U.S. News & World Report* (Aug. 12, 1955): 28–29.

1060   ———. *Peace With Justice.* New York: Columbia Univ. Press, 1961.

1061   ———. "Steps on the Road to Peace." *U.S. Department of State Bulletin* (Apr. 25, 1955): 681–85.

1062   Fisher, Adrian S. "U.S. Makes Proposals for Safeguards for Peaceful Nuclear Activities and for Bomber Destruction." *U.S. Department of State Bulletin* (Apr. 21, 1964): 641–45.

1063   Foster, William C. "Arms Control: An American Viewpoint." *Ecumenical Review* 19 (Apr. 1967): 143–45.

1064   ———. "Arms Control: Foundation Stone in the Ramparts We Watch." *U.S. Department of State Bulletin* (May 3, 1965): 659–64.

1065   ———. "Arms Control: A Serious Business." *U.S. Department of State Bulletin* (July 11, 1966): 50–55.

1066   ———. "Crossroads in Arms Control." *U.S. Department of State Bulletin* (Oct. 7, 1968): 366–68.

1067   ———. "National Strategy, Security, and Arms Control." *U.S. Department of State Bulletin* (Nov. 25, 1963): 824–29.

1068   ———. "New Directions in Arms Control and Disarmament." *Foreign Affairs* 43 (July 1965): 587–601.

1069   ———. "Prospects for Arms Control." *Foreign Affairs* 47 (Apr. 1969): 413–21.

1070   ———. "Roadblocks to Arms Control and Disarmament Negotiations." *U.S. Department of State Bulletin* (July 12, 1965): 77–84.

1071   Gross, Ernest A. "Disarmament as One of the Vital Conditions of Peace." *U.S. Department of State Bulletin* (Mar. 30, 1953): 476–79.

1072   Gullion, Edmund A. "Disarmament Issues and Prospects." *U.S. Department of State Bulletin* (May 1, 1961): 634–38.

1073   Herter, Christian A. "National Security with Arms Limitations." *U.S. Department of State Bulletin* (Mar. 7, 1960): 354–61.

1074   Holifield, Rep. Chet. "Disarmament, 1957." *Congressional Record* 103 (July 11, 1957): H10300–304.

1075   Humphrey, Sen. Hubert H. "Arms Control: A Balance Sheet." *Congressional Record* 119 (Dec. 3, 1973): S21694–96.

1076   ———. "Disarmament: Prospects for Progress." *War/Peace Report* 1 (Apr. 1961): 3.

1077   ———. "First Step Toward Disarmament." *Nation* (May 24, 1958): 468–70.

1078   ———. "What Hope for Disarmament?" *New York Times Magazine* (Jan. 5, 1958): 11 ff.

1079   Johnson, Pres. Lyndon B. "Arms Control and Disarmament: Some Sober Truths." *U.S. Department of State Bulletin* (June 14, 1965): 973–74.

1080   ———. "The Disarmament Agenda of Mankind." *U.S. Department of State Bulletin* (Aug. 5, 1968): 137–38.

1081   Kennedy, Pres. John F. "Disarmament *Can* Be Won." *Bulletin of the Atomic Scientists* 16 (June 1960): 217–19.

1082   ———. "The Strategy of Peace: Disarmament is the Goal." *Vital Speeches* (July 1, 1963): 558–61.

1083   ———. *Toward a Strategy of Peace.* ACDA Pub. 17. Washington, D.C.: G.P.O., 1963.

1084   Lodge, Henry Cabot, Jr. "The Question of Disarmament." *U.S. Department of State Bulletin* (Nov. 2, 1959): 615–20.

1085   ———, and James J. Wadsworth. "Two Approaches to Disarmament." *U.S. Department of State Bulletin* (Dec. 14, 1953): 829–38.

1086   [McCloy, John J.]. "Reports on U.S. Activities in Field of Disarmament and Arms Control." *U.S. Department of State Bulletin* (Nov. 6, 1961): 762–70.

1087   McNamara, Robert S. "Secretary McNamara Discusses Asian Affairs and Nuclear Arms Control. . . ." *U.S. Department of State Bulletin* (Aug. 29, 1966): 303–11.

1088   Nixon, Pres. Richard M. "Sound Limitations on Armaments Urged By President Nixon." *U.S. Department of State Bulletin* (Mar. 15, 1971): 310–11.

1089   ———. "Where Nixon Stands on Arms Control and Disarmament." *War/Peace Report* 8 (Dec. 1968): 10–13.

1090   [Osborn, Frederick H.] *Atomic Impasse, 1948: A Collection of Speeches.* Dept. of State Pub. 3272. Washington, D.C.: G.P.O., 1948.

1091   Patterson, Moorehead. *The Record on Disarmament.* Dept. of State Pub. 5581. Washington, D.C.: G.P.O., Sept. 1954.

1092   Rusk, Dean. "Disarmament and Arms Control." *U.S. Department of State Bulletin* (July 2, 1962): 3–7.

1093   Smith, Gerard C. "Arms Control to Improve American Security." *U.S. Department of State Bulletin* (Oct. 2, 1972): 378–81.

1094   Steele, Charles C. "A Balanced Approach to Disarmament." *U.S. Department of State Bulletin* (Nov. 18, 1963): 793–98.

1095   Stevenson, Adlai E. "United States Summarizes Position on Disarmament and Arms Control." *U.S. Department of State Bulletin* (May 17, 1965): 762–74.

1096   ———. "Working Toward a World Without War." *U.S. Department of State Bulletin* (Dec. 18, 1961): 1023–32.

1097   Truman, Pres. Harry S. "A Plan for Reducing Armaments." *U.S. Department of State Bulletin* (Nov. 19, 1951): 799–803.

1098   Wadsworth, James J. "Disarmament." *Vital Speeches* (Nov. 15, 1954): 841–44.

1099   ———. "The Most Urgent Step Toward Peace." *Redbook* (Aug. 1963): 54–55, 78–80.

1100   ———. "The Question of Disarmament." *U.S. Department of State Bulletin* (Nov. 14, 1960): 760–69.

1101   ———. "Soviet Misrepresentation of Western Position on Disarmament." *U.S. Department of State Bulletin* (Apr. 11, 1955): 627–28.

1102   Wilcox, Francis O. "Disarmament: The Problem and the Prospects." *U.S. Department of State Bulletin* (May 23, 1960): 820–26.

1103   Yost, Charles W. "U.S. Discusses Progress in Arms Control." *U.S. Department of State Bulletin* (Dec. 22, 1969): 600–606.

Documents

1104   U.S. Arms Control & Disarmament Agency. *Disarmament: The Continuing Search.* Washington, D.C.: G.P.O., 1962.

1105   U.S. Atomic Energy Commission. *In the Matter of J. Robert Oppenheimer: Transcript of Hearing Before Personnel Security Board, Washington, D.C., April 12, 1954 through May 6, 1954.* Washington, D.C.: G.P.O., 1954.

1106   U.S. Department of State. *Disarmament: The Intensified Effort, 1955–1958.* Pub. 7070. Washington, D.C.: G.P.O., 1960.

1107   ———. *Disarmament at a Glance.* Pub. 7058. Washington, D.C.: G.P.O., 1960.

1108   ———. *United States Efforts Toward Disarmament.* Conference Series 3, 89. Washington, D.C.: G.P.O., 1953.

1109   U.S. House. Committee on Foreign Affairs. *Questions and Answers on Arms Control and Disarmament.* Washington, D.C.: G.P.O., 1961.

1110   U.S. Library of Congress. Legislative Reference Service. *Armaments Policy in the Postwar World.* Bulletin no. 34. Washington, D.C.: G.P.O., 1945.

1111   U.S. Senate. Committee on Armed Services. Hearings: *Arms Control and Disarmament.* 87th Cong., 2d Sess., 1962.

1112   ———. Senate. Committee on Foreign Relations. Hearings: *Arms Control Implications of Current Defense Budget.* 92d Cong., 1st Sess., June 16–July 14, 1971.

1113   ———. Hearings: *Control and Reduction of Armaments.* 19 pts. 84th Cong., 2d Sess.–85th Cong., 2d Sess., Jan. 25, 1956–Apr. 17, 1958. [Humphrey Committee.]

1114   ———. Hearings: *Disarmament and Foreign Policy.* 2 pts. 86th Cong., 1st Sess., Jan. 28–Feb. 26, 1959.

1115   ———. Hearings: *Disarmament Developments, Spring 1960.* 86th Cong., 2d Sess., 1960.

1116   ———. Hearings: *United States and Disarmament Problems.* 90th Cong., 1st Sess., Feb.–Mar., 1967.

1117   ———. Report [with 10 Staff Studies]: *Control and Reduction of Armaments: Final Report of the Subcommittee on Disarmament.* Sen. Report no. 2501. 85th Cong., 2d Sess., 1958.

Soviet Union

1118   Barnet, Richard J. "The Soviet Attitude on Disarmament." *Problems of Communism* 10 (May–June 1961): 32–37.

1119   Baylis, John. "Soviet Policy on Disarmament and Arms Control." *Army Quarterly and Defense Journal* 103 (Oct. 1972): 72–80.

1120   Bechhoefer, Bernhard G. "The Soviet Attitude Toward Disarmament." *Current History* 44 (Oct. 1962): 193–99.

1121   Bloomfield, Lincoln P., et al. *Khrushchev and the Arms Race: Soviet Interests in Arms Control and Disarmament, 1954–1964.* Cambridge: M.I.T. Press, 1966.

1122   Bogdanov, Oleg V. "A Soviet View of Disarmament." *World Federalist* 9 (Jan. 1965): 14–16.

1123   Burhop, E. H. S. "The Soviet Peace Policy: For Detente and Disarmament." *New World Review* 40 (Fall 1970): 33–44.

1124 Burkemper, Raymond G. "Soviet Disarmament Policy: What Lies Ahead?" *Naval War College Review* 19 (Nov. 1967): 29–59.

1125 Caldwell, Lawrence T. "The Soviet Union and Arms Control." *Current History* 67 (Oct. 1974): 150–54, 178–80.

1126 Clemens, Walter C., Jr. "Ideology in Soviet Disarmament Policy." *Journal of Conflict Resolution* 8:3 (1964): 7–22.

1127 ———. "Shifts in Soviet Arms Control Posture." *Military Review* 51 (July 1971): 28–36.

1128 ———. "Soviet Disarmament Proposals and the Cadre-Territorial Army." *Orbis* 8 (Winter 1964): 778–99.

1129 ———. "Underlying Factors in Soviet Disarmament Policy: Problems of Systematic Analysis." *Papers of the Peace Research Society (International)* 6 (1966): 51–70.

1130 Coffey, Joseph I. "The Soviet View of a Disarmed World." *Journal of Conflict Resolution* 8:3 (1964): 1–6.

1131 Dallin, Alexander, et al. *The Soviet Union and Disarmament: An Appraisal of Soviet Attitudes and Intentions.* New York: Praeger, 1964.

1132 Dougherty, James E. "Soviet Disarmament Policy: Illusion and Reality." In E. L. Dulles and R. D. Crane, eds., *Detente: Cold War Strategies in Transition.* New York: Praeger, 1965, ch. 7.

1133 ———. "The Soviet Union and Arms Control." *Orbis* 17 (Fall 1973): 737–77.

1134 Eliot, George F. "The X-Factor in Arms Limitation." *Orbis* 2 (Fall 1958): 300–314.

1135 Garthoff, Raymond L. "What's Behind Soviet Disarmament." *Army Combat Forces Journal* 6 (Oct. 1955): 22–27.

1136 Griffiths, Franklyn. "Inner Tensions in the Soviet Approach to Disarmament." *International Journal* 22 (Autumn 1967): 593–617.

1137 Gross, Ernest A. "Soviet Attitude Toward the Disarmament Problem." *U.S. Department of State Bulletin* (Apr. 6, 1953): 503–06.

1138 Holloway, David. "Technology and Political Decision in Soviet Armaments Policy." *Journal of Peace Research* 11:4 (1974): 257–80.

1139 Hudson, Geoffrey F. "Soviet Fears of the West." *Current History* 42 (May 1962): 291–95, 309.

1140 Institute for Defense Analyses. *Future Soviet Interests in Arms Control.* 2 vols. ACDA Report. IR–151. Arlington, Va.: 1970.

1141 Karpov, Victor P. "Soviet Stand on Disarmament." *Journal of Conflict Resolution* 7:3 (1963): 333–37.

1142 Kenez, P., et al. *Soviet Arms Control Theory, 1958–1962.* Waltham, Mass.: Raytheon, 1962.

1143 Kennan, George F. "Arms Control and Soviet Aims." *New Leader* (Feb. 23, 1959): 5–6.

1144 Kolkowicz, Roman. "The Role of Disarmament in Soviet Policy: A Means or an End?" In James E. Dougherty and John F. Lehman, Jr., eds., *The Prospects for Arms Control.* New York: MacFadden-Bartell, 1965, pp. 95–104.

1145 ———; Matthew P. Gallagher; and Benjamin S. Lambeth. *The Soviet Union and Arms Control: A Superpower Dilemma.* Baltimore: Johns Hopkins Press, 1970.

1146 Larson, Thomas B. *Disarmament and Soviet Policy, 1964–1968.* Englewood Cliffs, N.J.: Prentice-Hall, 1969.

1147 MacKintosh, Malcolm, and Harry Willetts. "Arms Control and the Soviet National Interest." In Louis Henkin, ed., *Arms Control: Issues for the Public.* Englewood Cliffs, N.J.: Prentice-Hall, 1961, pp. 141–73.

1148 Osborn, Frederick H. "The USSR and the Atom." *International Organization* 5 (Aug. 1951): 480–98.

1149 Patterson, Moorehead. "Soviet Stand on Disarmament." *U.S. Department of State Bulletin* (Aug. 9, 1954): 213–14.

1150 Pitersky, N. "A Soviet View of a Disarmed World." In Walter C. Clemens, Jr., ed., *Toward a Strategy of Peace.* Chicago: Rand McNally, 1965, pp. 171–90.

1151 Ritvo, Herbert. "Internal Divisions on Disarmament in the USSR." In Seymour Melman, ed., *Disarmament: Its Politics and Economics.* Boston: American Academy of Arts & Sciences, 1962, pp. 212—37.

1152 Scanlan, James P. "Disarmament and the USSR." *Military Review* 50 (Mar. 1970): 29–42.

1153   Slusser, Robert M. "Disarmament in Soviet Foreign Policy." In Charles A. Barker, ed., *Problems of World Disarmament*. Boston: Houghton Mifflin, 1963, pp. 116–29.

1154   Sugg, Howard A. I. "Soviet Disarmament Theory Since 1959: An Analytical Study." Ph.D. diss., American Univ., 1967.

1155   Sullivan, Eugene P. "Soviet Disarmament Policy, 1968–1972." Ph.D. diss., Notre Dame Univ., 1974.

1156   Tatum, Lawrence B. "An Examination of Soviet Disarmament Policy with Emphasis Upon Principles of Disarmament Revealed Therein." Ph.D. diss., Syracuse Univ., 1961.

1157   U.S. Congress. Joint Committee on Atomic Energy. *Soviet Atomic Espionage*. Washington, D.C.: G.P.O., 1950.

1158   U.S. Senate. Committee on Foreign Relations. Staff Study: *Control and Reduction of Armaments: Attitudes of Soviet Leaders Toward Disarmament*. No. 8. 85th Cong., 1st Sess., 1957.

1159   Waterkamp, Rainer. "Wandlungen von Theorie und Praxis der Sowjetischen Abrüstungsstrategie, 1954–1965." *Modern Welt* 7:1 (1966): 71–105.

1160   Wolfe, Thomas W. "Khrushchev's Disarmament Strategy." *Orbis* 4 (Spring 1960): 13–27.

1161   ———. *Some Factors Bearing on Soviet Attitudes Toward Disarmament*. Report P–2766. Santa Monica, Ca.: Rand, 1963.

1162   ———. "Soviet Attitudes Towards Arms Control and Disarmament." *Temple Law Quarterly* 38 (Winter 1965): 123–32.

1163   ———. "The Soviet Union and Arms Control." In James E. Dougherty and John F. Lehman, Jr., eds., *Arms Control for the Late Sixties*. Princeton: Van Nostrand, 1967, pp. 121–42.

Domestic Views

1164   Alekseev, A. "Important Initiative for Disarmament." *International Affairs* [Moscow] 14 (Sept. 1968): 7–11.

1165   Alexandrov, V. "Western Zigzags on Disarmament." *International Affairs* [Moscow] 6 (Aug. 1960): 56–60.

1166   Andreyev, G. "Disarmament and the Inspirers of the Cold War." *International Affairs* [Moscow] 4 (June 1958): 8–14.

1167   ———. "Disarmament Talks: Truth and Fiction." *International Affairs* [Moscow] 7 (June 1961): 3–14.

1168   ———. "Two Lines in the Disarmament Talks." *International Affairs* [Moscow] 10 (Mar. 1964): 21–33.

1169   ———. "Who Is Stalling on Disarmament?" *International Affairs* [Moscow] 2 (Oct. 1956): 18–26.

1170   Arkadyev, Nikolai N. "An Artificial Deadlock." *International Affairs* [Moscow] 6 (Aug. 1960): 61–69.

1171   ———. "The Soviet Union and Disarmament." *New Times* [Moscow] 26 (June 1971): 18–19.

1172   Authors' Collective. *Militarism and Disarmament*. Moscow: State Political Press, 1963.

1173   Bogdanov, Oleg V. *Razoruzhenie-Garantiia Mira*. Moscow: Izd-vo Instituta Mezhdunarodnykh Otnoshenii, 1972.

1174   Brezhnev, Leonid. "Soviet Statement on Disarmament." *Current History* 61 (Oct. 1971): 240.

1175   Bulganin, N. A. *The Soviet Union on Disarmament*. London: Soviet News Pamphlet, no. 90, 1957.

1176   "Disarmament: Vital Problem of Our Time —Symposium." *International Affairs* [Moscow] 6 (Nov. 1960): 53–56.

1177   Grinyov, O. "Soviet Efforts for Disarmament." *International Affairs* [Moscow] 13 (Dec. 1967): 63–69.

1178   Gromov, L. "Our Idea of a World Without Arms." *International Affairs* [Moscow] 8 (July 1962): 49–64.

1179   Gromyko, Andrei. "Disarmament: The Soviet Position." *Survival* 5 (Jan.–Feb. 1963): 29 ff.

1180   Khrushchev, Nikita S. *Address by N. S. Khrushchev at World Congress for General Disarmament and Peace, July 10, 1962*. New York: Crosscurrents Press, 1962.

1181   ———. *Disarmament for Durable Peace and Friendship. . . .* Moscow: Foreign Languages Publishing House, 1960.

1182 ———. "Khrushchev Notes Breakup of Disarmament Talks." *Current Digest of the Soviet Press* (July 27, 1960): 17–20.

1183 ———. "Khrushchev's Press Conference on Disarmament, June 3, 1960." *Current Digest of the Soviet Press* (July 6, 1960): 3–8.

1184 Khvostov, V. "The Prospects for Disarmament." *International Affairs* [Moscow] 8 (Nov. 1962): 45–49.

1185 Kirylov, V. "The Post-war Disarmament Problem." *International Affairs* [Moscow] 5 (Sept. 1959): 13–18.

1186 Korovin, Eugene A. "Disarmament and the Problem of Combatting Aggression." *International Affairs* [Moscow] 6 (May 1960): 81–83.

1187 Kudriavtsev, Dmitrii I. *Bor'ba SSSR za Razoruzhenie Posle Vtoroi Mirovoi Voiny: Mezhdunarodnopravovoi Ocherk.* Moscow: Izd-vo Moskovskogo Universiteta, 1962.

1188 Lada, I. V. *Esli Mir Razoruzhitsia.* Moscow: Izd-vo Instituta Mezhdunarodnykh Otnoshenii, 1961.

1189 Leonidov, A. "Military Monopolies Against Disarmament." *Kommunist* 1 (Jan. 1960): 92–102.

1190 Morozov, Vasilii A. *Razoruzhenie i Problema Kapitalisticheskogo Rynka.* Moscow: Mysl', 1964.

1191 Sanakoyev, S. H. "Our Idea of a World Without Arms." *International Affairs* [Moscow] 8 (July 1962): 49–64.

1192 Shestov, V. "Disarmament Problems Today." *International Affairs* [Moscow] 11 (Nov. 1965): 53–58.

1193 ———. "The Main Disarmament Problem." *International Affairs* [Moscow] 16 (Oct. 1970): 35–38.

1194 ———. "Soviet Programme of Nuclear Disarmament." *International Affairs* [Moscow] 17 (Sept. 1971): 78–83.

1195 Shevchenko, A. "Disarmament: A Problem That Can Be Solved." *International Affairs* [Moscow] 17 (May 1971): 66–72.

1196 ———. "Some Lessons of the Disarmament Struggle." *International Affairs* [Moscow] 17 (Mar. 1971): 29–36.

1197 Slavianov, M. "Atomic and Conventional Arms." *International Affairs* [Moscow] 1 (Jan. 1955): 23–29.

1198 ———. "Who is Blocking Disarmament?" *International Affairs* [Moscow] 4 (Jan. 1958): 22–30.

1199 Talensky, Gen. Nikolai A. "Disarmament and Its Enemies." *International Affairs* [Moscow] 7 (Dec. 1961): 14–19.

1200 ———. "The Soviet Disarmament Programme and Its Critics." *International Affairs* [Moscow] 5 (Nov. 1959): 7–12.

1201 Viktorov, V. "The Soviet Disarmament Programme." *Soviet Military Review* 6 (June 1973): 56–58.

1202 ———. "The Soviet Union and Disarmament." *International Affairs* [Moscow] 2 (June 1956): 42–48.

1203 Yevgenyev, I. "The Nations Want Disarmament." *International Affairs* [Moscow] 4 (Aug. 1958): 18–22.

1204 ———, and P. Fyodorov. "The Way to Solve the Disarmament Problem." *International Affairs* [Moscow] 2 (July 1956): 17–25.

1205 Zorin, V. A. "Soviet Government Statement Concerning Disarmament Talks." *Soviet News* (Aug. 28, 1957): 149–54.

Documents

1206 Chernenko, K. U., comp. *Soviet Foreign Policy: Basic Acts and Documents of the Supreme Soviet of the U.S.S.R., 1956–1962.* Moscow: Foreign Languages Publishing House, 1962.

1207 *Disarmament: The Road to a World Without War: A Selection of Documents of the Soviet Government, 1958–1962.* London: Soviet News Pamphlet, 1962.

1208 *Materials of the Fifth Session of the U.S.S.R. Supreme Soviet Concerning Disarmament and Prohibition of Atomic and Hydrogen Weapons, July 16, 1956.* Moscow: Foreign Languages Publishing House, 1956.

1209 *The Soviet Stand on Disarmament: A Collection of Nineteen Basic Soviet Documents on General and Complete Disarmament, the Termination of Nuclear Weapons Tests, and* the *Relaxation of International Tensions.* New York: Crosscurrents Press, 1960.

PEOPLE'S REPUBLIC OF CHINA

1210 Barnett, A. Doak. "The Inclusion of Communist China in Arms Control Programs." In Donald G. Brennan, ed., *Arms Control, Disarmament, and National Security.* New York: Braziller, 1961, pp. 282–303.

1211 ———. "A Nuclear China and U.S. Arms Policy." *Foreign Affairs* 48 (Apr. 1970): 427–42.

1212 Bobrow, Davis B. "Chinese and American Interests in Arms Control." *Background* 9 (Aug. 1965): 91–110.

1213 "China, Nuclear Weapons and Disarmament: China States Its Position." *War/Peace Report* 5 (Jan. 1965): 3–5.

1214 Clough, Ralph N., et al. *The United States, China and Arms Control.* Washington, D.C.: Brookings Institution, 1975.

1215 Diao, Richard, and Donald Zagoria. *The Nature of Mainland Chinese Economic Structures, Leadership and Policy, 1949–1969, and Prospects for Arms Control and Disarmament.* 2 vols. ACDA Report E–124. Washington, D.C.: G.P.O., Feb. 1972.

1216 Friedman, Edward. "Now's Time to Talk With China." *Bulletin of the Atomic Scientists* 25 (June 1969): 10–11.

1217 Gelber, Harry G. "Nuclear Weapons in Chinese Strategy." *Problems of Communism* 20 (Nov.–Dec. 1971): 33–44.

1218 Halperin, Morton H., and Dwight H. Perkins. *Communist China and Arms Control.* New York: Praeger, 1965.

1219 Hinton, Harold C. "China's Attitude Toward Arms Control." In James E. Dougherty and John F. Lehman, Jr., eds., *Arms Control for the Late Sixties.* Princeton: Van Nostrand, 1967, pp. 115–20.

1220 Hsieh, Alice Langley. "China's Nuclear-Missile Programme Regional or Intercontinental?" *China Quarterly* 45 (Jan.–Mar. 1971): 85–99.

1221 ———. Two Major Powers and the Problem of Disarmament: The Position of Communist China." *Disarmament* 2 (June 1964): 11–13.

1222 Hudson, Geoffrey F. "Paper Tigers & Nuclear Teeth." *China Quarterly* 39 (July–Sept. 1969): 64–75.

1223 Kalicki, J. H. "China, America, and Arms Control." *World Today* 26 (Apr. 1970): 147–55.

1224 Kapur, Ashok. "China, Arms Control and Nuclear Weapons." *China Report* 5 (Nov.–Dec. 1969): 1–11.

1225 Lall, Arthur S. "Political Effects of the Chinese Bomb." *Bulletin of the Atomic Scientists* 20 (May 1964): 17–21.

1226 Lall, Betty Goetz. "On Disarmament Issues: Mainland China and U.S. Security." *Bulletin of the Atomic Scientists* 20 (Apr. 1964): 24–27.

1227 Lattimore, Owen. "The China Factor in the Arms Race." In Charles A. Barker, ed., *Problems of World Disarmament.* Boston: Houghton Mifflin, 1963, pp. 130–42.

1228 Lindsay, Lord. "Dialogue on Disarmament: The Case of China and the United States." *World Today* 19 (Dec. 1963): 523–32.

1229 Liu, Leo Y. "China as a Nuclear Power: Its Effects on Asia." *International Problems* [Israeli Institute of International Affairs] 10 (Dec. 1971): 56–70.

1230 ———. "China's Attitude Towards Her Nuclear Weapons." *China Report* 7 (May–June 1971): 34–42.

1231 Pollack, Jonathan D. "Chinese Attitudes Towards Nuclear Weapons, 1964–1969." *China Quarterly* 50 (Apr.–June 1972): 244–71.

1232 Robertson, Walter S. "Disarmament and the Chinese Communist Threat." *U.S. Department of State Bulletin* (Mar. 16, 1959): 375–78.

1233 Stanford Univ. Hoover Institution on War, Revolution, and Peace. *Arms Control Implications of Communist China's Domestic and Foreign Politics.* 3 vols. ACDA Report IR–53. Stanford, Ca.: Hoover Institution Press, 1967.

1234 U.S. Congress. Joint Committee on Atomic Energy. Hearings: *Impact of Chinese Communist Nuclear Weapons on United States National Security.* 90th Cong., 1st Sess., 1967.

1235   U.S. Senate. Committee on Government Operations. Report: *Negotiation and Statecraft: Chinese Comment on Strategic Policy and Arms Limitation.* 93d Cong., 2d Sess., 1974.

1236   Vesa, Unto. "The Development of Chinese Thinking on Disarmament." *Instant Research on Peace and Violence* 4:2 (1974): 53–78.

Official Position

1237   Chen Chu. "Expounds China's Principled Stand in Supporting 'Declaration of Indian Ocean as Peace Zone.'" *Survey of China Mainland Press* (Dec. 22, 1971): 116–18.

1238   ———. "Reaffirms China's Principled Stand on Complete Prohibition, Through Destruction of Nuclear Weapons." *Survey of China Mainland Press* (Dec. 21, 1971): 85–86.

1239   ———. "Reiterates China's Stand on Nuclear Disarmament at UN General Assembly First Committee Meeting." *Survey of China Mainland Press* (Dec. 22, 1971): 115–16.

1240   Chiao Kuan-hua. "Explains Chinese Government's Principled Stand." *Peking Review* (Dec. 3, 1971): 14–16.

1241   Ford, Anna. *A Record of Major Chinese Official Statements on Nuclear Arms Control.* Santa Monica, Ca.: California Arms Control & Foreign Policy Seminar, Aug. 1971.

1242   [People's Republic of China]. *People of the World Unite, For the Complete, Thorough, Total, and Resolute Prohibition and Destruction of Nuclear Weapons!* Peking: Foreign Language Press, 1963.

1243   ———. "Statement of the Chinese Government Advocating the Complete, Thorough, Total and Resolute Prohibiting and Destruction of Nuclear Weapons [and] Proposing a Conference of the Government Heads of All Countries of the World." *Peking Review* (Aug. 2, 1963): 7–8.

Sino-Soviet Dispute & AC&D

1244   Chiao Kuan-hua. "Soviet Disarmament Proposal is a Fraud." *Peking Review* (Nov. 17, 1972): 5–6.

1245   Clemens, Walter C., Jr. *The Arms Race and Sino-Soviet Relations.* Stanford, Ca.: Hoover Institution Press, 1968.

1246   ———. *Moscow and Arms Control: Evidence from the Sino-Soviet Dispute.* Cambridge: M.I.T., Center for International Studies, June 1965.

1247   ———. "The Sino-Soviet Dispute: Dogma and Dialectics on Disarmament." *International Affairs* [London] 41 (Apr. 1965): 204–22.

1248   Gusachenko, V. "Disarmament and the Manoeuvres of Peking." *New Times* [Moscow] 36 (Sept. 1972): 18–19.

1249   Halperin, Morton H. "Sino-Soviet Relations and Arms Control: An Introduction." *China Quarterly* 26 (Apr.–June 1966): 118–22.

1250   ———, ed. *Sino-Soviet Relations and Arms Control.* Cambridge: M.I.T. Press, 1967.

1251   "Neither Calumny nor Abuse Can Cover Up Deceitfulness of Soviet 'Disarmament' Proposals." *Peking Review* (Nov. 24, 1972): 10–11.

1252   Rubakov, V. "Peking and Disarmament." *New Times* [Moscow] 50 (Dec. 1971): 9–10.

1253   ———. "The People's Republic of China and the Disarmament Problem." *International Affairs* [Moscow] 18 (Sept. 1972): 26–32.

1254   "Sino-Soviet Relations and Arms Control." *China Quarterly* 26 (Apr.–June 1966): 118–70.

1255   Sonnenfeldt, Helmut. "The Chinese Factor in Soviet Disarmament Policy." *China Quarterly* 26 (Apr.–June 1966): 118–70.

1256   Zorin, V. A. "Disarmament Problems and Peking's Maneuvers." *Current Digest of the Soviet Press* (July 22, 1964): 11–12.

EUROPE

1257   Buchan, Alastair, and Philip Windsor. *Arms and Stability in Europe: A British-French-German Enquiry.* London: Chatto & Windus, 1963.

1258   Clemens, Walter C., Jr. "European Arms Control: How, What, and When?" *International Journal* 27 (Winter 1972): 45–72.

1259   Deutsch, Karl W. *Arms Control and the Atlantic Alliance: Europe Faces Coming Policy Decisions.* New York: Wiley, 1967.

1260   ———. *Arms Control and Disarmament Concepts in the European Political Environment.* ACDA Report IR–32. New Haven: Yale Univ. Press, 1966.

1261   ———. "Integration and Arms Control in the European Political Environment: A Summary Report." *American Political Science Review* 60 (June 1966): 354–65.

1262   *Disarmament in Europe.* Adelphi Papers, no. 10. London: Institute for Strategic Studies, June 1964.

1263   Freymond, Jacques. "European Views on Arms Control." In Louis Henkin, ed., *Arms Control: Issues for the Public.* Englewood Cliffs, N.J.: Prentice-Hall, 1961, pp. 174–200.

1264   Gearin, Cornelius. "The Military Aspects of Conflict Control in Central Europe." In Sam G. Sarkesian, ed., *The Military-Industrial Complex.* Beverly Hills, Ca.: Sage, 1972.

1265   Gorden, Morton, and Daniel Lerner. "The Setting for European Arms Controls: Political and Strategic Choices of European Elites." *Journal of Conflict Resolution* 9:4 (1965): 421–33.

1266   Gruenther, Gen. Alfred. "What Atomic Disarmament Means to NATO." *Vital Speeches* (Sept. 1, 1954): 676–79.

1267   Harrison, Stanley L. "Problems of Arms Control: United States Policy and the Defense of NATO." Ph.D. diss., American Univ., 1967.

1268   Irwin, Christopher. "Nuclear Aspects of West European Defense Integrations." *International Affairs* [London] 47 (Oct. 1971): 679–91.

1269   Krone, Robert M. "NATO Nuclear Policymaking." Ph.D. diss., Univ. of California, Los Angeles, 1972.

1270   Kuhn, Alfred G. "Active Disarmament Consultations in NATO." *NATO Letter* 18 (Mar. 1970): 20–23.

1271   ———. "NATO and Disarmament." *NATO Letter* 17 (Jan. 1969): 17–19.

1272   Merritt, Richard L., and Donald J. Puchala. "Western European Attitudes on Arms Control, Defense, and European Unity." In Karl W. Deutsch, *Arms Control in the European Environment.* New Haven: Yale Univ. Press, 1966. [Appendix 7.]

1273   Multan, W., and A. Towpik. "Die Westliche Abrüstungspolitik in Europa und Ihre Konsequenzen aus Ostlicher Sicht." *Europa-Archiv* (Apr. 10, 1974): 223 ff.

1274   Nutting, Anthony. "Disarmament, Europe, and Security." *International Affairs* [London] 36 (Jan. 1960): 1–16.

1275   Osgood, Robert E. "Can Arms Agreements Improve the Stability of the Atlantic Alliance?" In James E. Dougherty and John F. Lehman, Jr., eds., *The Prospects for Arms Control.* New York: MacFadden-Bartell, 1965, pp. 249–56.

1276   Parker, Elizabeth A. *East European Arms Control and Disarmament Proposals.* Research Paper P–482. Arlington, Va.: Institute for Defense Analyses, 1969.

1277   Planck, Charles R. "Arms Control, Disarmament, and Security in Europe: An Analysis of the Negotiations, 1955–1965." Ph.D. diss., Johns Hopkins Univ., 1968.

1278   Pugh, George E. "Arms Control Planning and NATO." In James E. Dougherty and John F. Lehman, Jr., eds., *The Prospects for Arms Control.* New York: MacFadden-Bartell, 1965, pp. 256–66.

1279   Romantecke, Leon. "The Atom and International Cooperation." *Polish Perspectives* 10 (Feb. 1967): 3–9.

1280   Russett, Bruce M., and Carolyn C. Cooper. *Arms Control in Europe: Proposals and Political Constraints.* Monograph Series 4:2. Denver: Univ. of Denver, 1967.

1281   Slessor, Sir John. "European Security and Disarmament after Geneva." *Air Power* 3 (Autumn 1955): 3–9.

1282   Spano, V. "What Disarmament Could Mean for Italy." *Bulletin of the World Council of Peace* [Vienna] (Jan. 15, 1960): 3–9.

1283   Strausz-Hupé, Robert. "Arms Control and the Atlantic Alliance." In James E. Dougherty and John F. Lehman, Jr., eds., *The Prospects for Arms Control.* New York: MacFadden-Bartell, 1965, pp. 242–48.

1284 U.S. Senate. Committee on Foreign Relations. *Handbook on Arms Control and Related Problems in Europe: Excerpts and Summaries of Official and Unofficial Proposals.* Washington, D.C.: G.P.O., 1959.

1285 Young, Wayland. "The Prospects for Arms Control in Europe." *Bulletin of the Atomic Scientists* 21 (Sept. 1965): 22–24.

FRANCE

1286 Geneste, Marc E. "A French View." In James E. Dougherty and John F. Lehman, Jr., eds., *Arms Control for the Late Sixties.* Princeton: Van Nostrand, 1967, pp. 45–51.

1287 ———. "A French View on Arms Control." *Military Review* 47 (Jan. 1967): 35–41.

1288 Mayer, R. L. "La France et le Désarmement." *Cahiers du Communisme* [Paris] 6 (Mar. 1960): 353–66.

1289 Mendl, Wolf. "French Attitudes on Disarmament." *Disarmament* 14 (June 1967): 13–17.

1290 Moch, Jules S. "Disarmament in 1966: Hopes and Facts." *Disarmament* 10 (June 1966): 7–10.

1291 Schwoebel, Jean. "Two Major Powers and the Problem of Disarmament: The Position of France." *Disarmament* 2 (June 1964): 7–9.

GREAT BRITAIN

1292 Butler, R. A. "Disarmament: A Time for Progress." *Vital Speeches* (Mar. 15, 1964): 331–36.

1293 Chalfont, Lord Arthur G. J. "Can We Make the World Drop the Bomb?" *Realites* (Sept. 1966): 34–37.

1294 Coleman, Herbert J. "British Government Planning 10-Year Cutback in Defense." *Aviation Week & Space Technology* (Dec. 9, 1974): 15.

1295 Dutt, R. Palme. "British Labour Movement and Nuclear Disarmament." *International Affairs* [Moscow] 6 (Dec. 1960): 51–57.

1296 ———. "Disarmament and Peace." *Labour Monthly* 42 (Feb. 1960): 49–63.

1297 Gowing, Margaret. *Independence and Deterrence: Britain Atomic Energy, 1945–1952.* New York: St. Martin's Press, 1975.

1298 Great Britain. British Information Service. *The Disarmament Question.* New York, 1956.

1299 Great Britain. Central Office of Information. *The Disarmament Question, 1945–1949.* London: H.M.S.O., 1950.

1300 ———. *The Disarmament Question, 1945–1953.* London: H.M.S.O., 1953.

1300A ———. *The Disarmament Question, 1954–1956.* London: H.M.S.O., 1957.

1301 Great Britain. Foreign Office. *Disarmament: The Path to Peace.* London: H.M.S.O., Apr. 1968.

1302 ———. *The Key to Disarmament.* London: H.M.S.O., 1964

1303 ———. *The Search for Disarmament: A Summary.* London: H.M.S.O., 1960.

1304 Healey, Denis. "The Only Reliable Way to Prevent Atomic War is to See Disarmament as a Weapon of Defense." *New Leader* (July 4–11, 1960): 6–7.

1305 "How to Disarm." *Economist* (Jan. 14, 1961): 109–11.

1306 Ormsby-Gore, David. "East-West Relations: Disarmament." *Vital Speeches* (Feb. 15, 1964): 286–88.

1307 Short, Renee. "Disarmament and the British People." *New Times* [Moscow] 48 (Nov. 1960): 18–19.

1308 Simpson, Mary M. "British Lords Debate Nuclear Disarmament." *Bulletin of the Atomic Scientists* 15 (June 1959): 260–65.

1309 Steele, J. A. "The Campaign for Nuclear Disarmament: Discusses the Most Active Mass Movement in the United Kingdom at the Present Time." *Queens Quarterly* 67 (Winter 1961): 547–56.

EAST GERMANY

1310 Klein, Peter. "Topical Issues of Disarmament." *German Foreign Policy* 9:2 (1970): 87–99.

1311 Kruger, Joachim. "The Struggle of the German Democratic Republic for Disarmament." *German Foreign Policy* 4:6 (1965): 430–38.

1312 *Was Bringt Die Abrüestung: Namhafte Wissenschaftler Geben Antwort.* Berlin: Dt. Friedensrat, 1961.

West Germany

1313 Brandt, Willy. "Limiting the Arms Race and Making Peace More Secure." *Peace: Writings and Speeches of the Nobel Peace Prize Winner 1971.* West Germany: Verlag Neue Gesellschaft, 1971.

1314 Braunthat, Gerard. "West German Trade Unions and Disarmament." *Political Science Quarterly* 73 (Mar. 1958): 82–99.

1315 Jansen, Thomas. *Abrüstung und Deutschland Frage: Die Abrüstungsfrage als Problem der Deutschen Aussenpolitik.* Mainz: Hase & Koehler Verlag, 1968.

1316 Mommsen, Wilhelm. *Deutsche Parteiprogramme: Eine Auswahl von Vormarz bis zur Gegenwart.* Munich: Isar Verlag, 1951.

1317 Richardson, James L. "Arms Control." *Germany and the Atlantic Alliance: The Interaction of Strategy and Politics.* Cambridge: Harvard Univ. Press, 1966, pp. 224–42.

1318 Schmidt, Helmut. "A German View." In James E. Dougherty and John F. Lehman, Jr., eds., *Arms Control for the Late Sixties.* Princeton: Van Nostrand, 1967, pp. 52–57.

Other Nations

Australia

1319 Australia. Department of External Affairs. "Arms Control and Disarmament." *Current Notes on International Affairs* 41 (May 1970): 253–66.

1320 ———. "Disarmament." *Current Notes on International Affairs* 29 (Mar. 1958): 139–49.

1321 ———. "Disarmament Negotiations, 1960–1961." *Current Notes on International Affairs* 32 (July 1961): 5–14.

1322 Menzies, D. "Disarmament." *Current Notes on International Affairs* 32 (Oct. 1961): 23–31.

Canada

1323 Arrol, Ian. "A New Canadian Policy for Defence." *World Federalist* 19 (Jan.–Mar. 1974): Canadian sec., p. C2.

1324 Canada. Department of External Affairs. "Arms Control and Disarmament." *Annual Report, 1970.* Ottawa: Information Canada, 1971, pp. 62–65.

1325 ———. *Report on Disarmament Discussions, 1957.* Ottawa: E. Cloutier, Queen's Printer, 1958.

1326 Davy, Grant R. "Canada's Role in the Disarmament Negotiations, 1946–1957." Ph.D. diss., Fletcher School of Law and Diplomacy, 1962.

1327 Laulicht, Jerome, and John Paul. "Issues of Peace and War: Canadian Attitudes on Disarmament and Defence Policy." *Social Problems* 11 (Summer 1963): 48–62.

1328 Lentner, Howard H. "Foreign Policy Decision-Making: The Case of Canada and Nuclear Weapons." *World Politics* 29 (Oct. 1976): 29–66.

1329 Preston, Richard A. "Can We Disarm?" *Behind the Headlines* [Canadian Institute of International Affairs] 17 (Jan. 1958): 1–16.

India

1330 "A Disarming View of Disarmament—India." *United Asia* 14 (Jan. 1962): 48–55.

1331 Ghatate, Narayan Madnav. "Disarmament in India's Foreign Policy, 1947–1965." Ph.D. diss., American Univ., 1966.

1332 Hellmann, Donald C., et al. *India and Japan: The Emerging Balance of Power in Asia and Opportunities for Arms Control, 1970–1975.* 4 vols. ACDA Report IR–170. New York: Columbia Univ., Apr. 1971.

1333 Jha, P. K. "India's Contribution Towards Disarmament." *Gandhi Marg* 12 (Apr. 1968): 206–12.

1334 Kasliwal, N. C. "Disarmament Priorities." *Indian Foreign Affairs* 8 (Aug. 1965): 15–16.

1335 Sullivan, Michael J., III. "Reorientation of Indian Arms Control Policy, 1969–1972." *Asian Survey* 13 (July 1973): 691–706.

Japan

1336   Haruhiko, Nishi. "Disarmament and the Great Powers: An Appeal From a Small Nation." *Japan Quarterly* 8 (Jan.–Mar. 1961): 14–24.

1337   Kishida, Junnosuke. "Ideas on Disarmament." *Japan Quarterly* 19 (Apr.–June 1972): 148–53.

1338   Poletayev, V. "Japanese Journalists Discuss Country's Disarmament." *International Affairs* [Moscow] 10 (Sept. 1964): 95–97.

Developing Nations

1339   Bassir, Olumbe. "Arms Control and the Developing Nations." *Arms Control and Disarmament* 1:1 (1968): 1–25.

1340   Cunningham, William J. *Arms Controls in Northeast Asia.* Washington, D.C.: Department of State, 1971–1972. [Case study prepared for the 14th session of the Senior Seminar in Foreign Policy.]

1341   Dolgopolov, Y. "Disarmament and the Newly Developing States." *International Affairs* [Moscow] 9 (Feb. 1963): 56–60.

1342   Doty, Paul. "The Role of the Smaller Powers." In Donald G. Brennan, ed., *Arms Control, Disarmament, and National Security.* New York: Braziller, 1961, pp. 304–16.

1343   Gude, Edward W., et al. *Arms Control in the Developing Areas.* Bedford, Mass.: Raytheon, 1963.

1344   Kadochenki, A. "Disarmament and Underdeveloped Countries." *International Affairs* [Moscow] 6 (July 1960): 31–35.

1345   Kemp, Geoffrey. "The Prospects for Arms Control in Latin America: The Strategic Dimensions." In Philippe C. Schmitter, ed., *Military Rule in Latin America.* Beverly Hills, Ca.: Sage, 1973.

1346   Khrushchev, Nikita S. *Disarmament and Colonial Freedom.* London: Lawrence & Wishart, 1961.

1347   Mezerik, Avrahm G. *Disarmament: Impact on Under-Developed Countries—Political, Social, Economic.* New York: International Review Service, 1961.

1348   M.I.T. Center for International Studies. *Regional Arms Control Arrangements for Developing Areas.* Report C/64–25. Cambridge, 1964.

1349   Nogee, Joseph L. "The Neutralist World and Disarmament Negotiations." *Annals of the Amer. Acad. of Pol. & Soc. Sci.* 362 (Nov. 1965): 71–80.

1350   Ouahrani, E. Abdelkader. "The Struggle for National Independence and Disarmament." *World Marxist Review* 5 (June 1962): 18–24.

1351   Redick, John R. "Regional Nuclear Arms Control in Latin America." *International Organization* 29 (Spring 1975): 415–45.

Four

League of Nations & United Nations

SINCE 1920, BOTH the League of Nations and the United Nations have played major roles in efforts to negotiate arms control and disarmament accords. As international organizations, these agencies have provided a rostrum from which new proposals could be put forward and a neutral arena in which delegates could explore various solutions to the problems of weapons and war. Thus, since the early sessions of the League, some international agency has provided the machinery to keep discussions about arms control and disarmament alive with widely varying degrees of success.

Although a goodly number of dissertations have been written about the arms control and disarmament activities of the League since 1945, no recent survey study has appeared. Consequently, the best overviews are found in W. E. Rappard, *The Quest for Peace Since the World War* (1940), cited in the previous chapter, J. T. Shotwell and M. Salvin, *Lessons on Security and Disarmament from the History of the League of Nations* (1949), and W. L. Mahaney, Jr., *The Soviet Union, the League of Nations, and Disarmament, 1917–1935* (1940).

Accounts of specific League undertakings are varied and uneven. Official records are listed below; these should be supplemented with the League's *Official Journal* (1920–1940), the appropriate volumes of the U.S. Department of State's *Foreign Relations of the United States: Diplomatic Papers* (1852–), and the Foreign and Commonwealth Office's *Documents on British Foreign Policy, 1919–1939* (1946–). The hopes and aspirations of the Preparatory Commission (1925–1931) are recounted in J. W. Wheeler-Bennett's accurate and reasoned *Disarmament and Security Since Locarno, 1925–1931* (1932). The failures of the Geneva Disarmament Conference (1932–1934) are well told in Wheeler-Bennett's fine contemporary supplement, *The Pipe Dream of Peace* (1935), while A. C. Temperley's *The Whispering Gallery of Europe* (1938) recounts the dismay of a British general turned diplomat. Additionally, there are several fine dissertations on the latter conference.

The United Nations has been a forum for the discussion of disarmament and has sponsored a number of commissions to study these ideas.

Ruth B. Russell's classic study, *A History of the United Nations Charter* (1958), reveals its early intentions. The United Nations' own overview, *The United Nations and Disarmament* (1945–1976), is indispensable in sorting out U.N. activities. Most of the other accounts concerning arms control and disarmament at the U.N. consist of articles, documents, and speeches; they are listed in the following pages.

The two longest-sitting commissions are the Eighteen-Nation Disarmament Commission (ENDC) and its successor, the Conference of the Committee on Disarmament (CCD), which has been meeting since 1962. The mimeographed verbatim minutes of these and other U.N. commissions have appeared, but complete sets are rare. The British documents are usually more readily available and easier to use.

Bibliographies

1352 Aufricht, Hans. *Guide to League of Nations Publications.* New York: Columbia Univ. Press, 1951.

1353 Carroll, Marie J. *Key to League of Nations Documents Placed on Public Sale.* 3 vols. Boston: World Peace Foundation, 1930–1934.

1354 Hass, Michael. *International Organization: An Interdisciplinary Bibliography.* Stanford, Ca.: Hoover Institution Press, 1971.

1355 Johnson, Harold S., and Baljit Singh. *International Organization: A Classified Bibliography.* East Lansing: Michigan State Univ., Asian Studies Center, 1969.

1356 Rubinstein, Alvin Z. "Selected Bibliography of Soviet Works on the United Nations, 1946–1959." *American Political Science Review* 54 (Dec. 1960): 985–91.

League of Nations

1357 "Arbitration, Security, and Reduction of Armaments." *League of Nations Monthly Summary* (May 15, 1929): 131–53.

1358 Cecil, Viscount Robert. "Disarmament and the League." *Way of Peace.* New York: John Day, 1928, pp. 211–32.

1359 Churchill, Winston. *Arms and the Covenant.* New York: Putnam's, 1938.

1360 Davis, Kathryn W. *The Soviets at Geneva: The U.S.S.R. at the League of Nations, 1919–1933.* Geneva: Librairie Kindig, 1934.

1361 De Lavallaz, P. *Essai sur le Désarmement et le Pacte de la Société des Nations.* Paris: Rousseau, 1926.

1362 Downing, Marvin L. "Hugh R. Wilson and American Relations With the League of Nations, 1927–1937." Ph.D. diss., Univ. of Oklahoma, 1970.

1363 Gardes, André. *Le Désarmement devant la Société des Nations.* Paris: Presses Modernes, 1929.

1364 Geinberg, G. A. *Le Problème du Désarmement devant la Société et en dehors d'Elle.* Paris: Presses Universitaires de France, 1930.

1365 Glasgow, George. "League and Disarmament." *Contemporary Review* 135 (May 1929): 653–57.

1366 ———. "Lord Cecil at Geneva." *Contemporary Review* 132 (June 1926): 781–85.

1367   ———. "Renewed Discussion on Disarmament." *Contemporary Review* 135 (June 1929): 787–92.

1368   Jones, Morgan. "Don't Despair of Disarmament: The League Can Still Lead the Way to Peace." *Labour* 4 (Feb. 1937): 138–39.

1369   League of Nations. "The Organization of Peace and Disarmament." *Ten Years of World Co-operation.* Geneva: Secretariat of the League of Nations, 1930, pp. 49–124.

1370   "League of Nations and Disarmament." *Editorial Research Reports* (Mar. 13, 1928):237–48.

1371   Mahaney, Wilbur Lee, Jr. "The Soviet Union, the League of Nations, and Disarmament, 1917–1935." Printed Ph.D. diss., Univ. of Pennsylvania, 1940.

1372   Notovich, F. *Mirovaya Politika Razoruzheniya Imperialistov Liga Natsii i SSSR.* Moscow: Moskovskii Rabochii, 1929.

1373   Scialoja, Vittorio. "Obstacles to Disarmament." *Foreign Affairs* 10 (Jan. 1932): 212–19.

1374   Scott, James Brown. "Disarmament Through International Organization." *Annals of the Amer. Acad. of Pol. & Soc. Sci.* 126 (July 1926): 146–50.

1375   Shatzky, Boris. "La Russie Sovietique et la Société des Nations." *Affaires Etrangères (Oct. 25, 1932): 535–57.*

1376   Shotwell, James T., and Maria Salvin. *Lessons on Security and Disarmament from the History of the League of Nations.* New York: King's Crown Press, 1949.

1377   Simonds, Frank H. "The Arms Limitation and the League." *Review of Reviews* 75 (Apr. 1927): 377–85.

1378   Temperley, Arthur Cecil. *The Whispering Gallery of Europe.* London: Collins, 1938.

1379   U.N. General Assembly. Sixth Session. Committee of Twelve. *The Organization and Scheme of Work of the League of Nations in the Matter of Disarmament.* . . . 3 pts. A/AC.503, A/AC.50/3/Corr.1. New York, 1951.

1380   Winkler, Fred H. "Disarmament and Security: The American Policy at Geneva, 1926–1935." *North Dakota Quarterly* 39:4 (1971): 21–33.

1381   ———. "The United States and the World Disarmament Conference, 1926–1935: A Study of the Formulation of Foreign Policy." Ph.D. diss., Northwestern Univ., 1957.

LEAGUE COVENANT

1382   Burns, Richard Dean, and Donald Urquidi. "The Peace Conference and General Disarmament [Art. 8]." *Disarmament In Perspective, 1919–1939.* 4 vols. Washington, D.C.: G.P.O., 1968, vol. 1, ch. 5.

1383   Miller, David Hunter. *The Drafting of the Covenant.* 2 vols. New York: Putnam's, 1928.

1384   Wilson, Florence. *The Origins of the League Covenant.* London: Hogarth Press, 1928.

DOCUMENTS

1385   League of Nations. Assembly. Third Committee. "Records of the 5th Assembly: Meetings of the Committees: Minutes of the 3d Committee." *Official Journal* 26 (1924). [Special supplement.]

1386   ———. "Records of the 8th Ordinary Session of the Assembly: Meetings of the Committees: Minutes of the 3d Committee." *Official Journal* 57 (1927): 1–84. [Special supplement.]

1387   ———. "Records of the 17th Ordinary Session of the Assembly: Meetings of the Committees: Minutes of the 3d Committee." *Official Journal* 158 (1936): 1–29. [Special supplement.]

1388   ———. *Reduction of Armaments: Report of the Third Committee to the Fourth Assembly.* A.111.1923.4. Geneva, 1923.

1389   League of Nations. Secretariat. Information Section. *League of Nations: Arbitration, Security and Reduction of Armaments: Documents and Proceedings of the Fifth Assembly.* Geneva, 1924.

1390   ———. *The League of Nations and Reduction of Armaments.* Geneva, 1923.

1391   ———. *The Reduction of Armaments and the Organization of Peace.* Geneva, 1928.

Permanent Advisory Commission

1392 League of Nations. Permanent Advisory Commission for Military, Naval and Air Questions. "[Report of] First Meeting." *Official Journal* 1 (Sept. 1920): 346–50.

1393 ———. "Permanent Organ of the Council for the Work of Disarmament: Report. . . ." *Official Journal* 7 (Feb. 1926): 119–20.

1394 ———. "Position of Members of the Permanent Advisory Commission Who Are Also Members of the Temporary Mixed Commission." *Official Journal* 4 (June 1923): 679.

1395 ———. "The Question of Armaments." *Official Journal* 2 (May 1921): 256–59.

1396 ———. "Reduction of Armaments." *Official Journal* 4 (Mar. 1923): 294–96.

1397 ———. "Report of the Commission to the Council . . ., 22 Oct. 1920." *Official Journal* 1 (Oct.–Nov. 1920): 37–45.

1398 ———. "Report. . . ." *Official Journal* 1 (Sept. 1920): 341–42.

1399 ———. "Report of the Permanent Advisory Commission for Military, Naval and Air Questions. . . . " *Official Journal* 5 (July 1924): 986–90.

1400 ———. "Report . . . on the Revision of the Rules of Procedures of the Permanent Advisory Commission for Military, Naval and Air Questions." *Official Journal* 5 (July 1924): 983–85.

1401 ———. "Sixteenth Session of the Permanent Advisory Commission for Military, Naval and Air Questions." *Official Journal* 6 (Feb. 1925): 226–28.

1402 ———. "Work of the Council Committee Relating to the Permanent Organ of the Council for Work of Disarmament." *Official Journal* 7 (Feb. 1926): 218–19.

Temporary Mixed Commission, 1920–1925

1403 League of Nations. Temporary Mixed Commission for the Reduction of Armament. "Exchange of Information: Report . . . Submitted to the Temporary Mixed Commission for the Reduction of Armament." *Official Journal* 4 (Aug. 1923): 1032–36.

1404 ———. "Fourth Session of the Temporary Mixed Commission on the Reduction of Armaments (July 3–7, 1922)." *Official Journal* 3 (Aug. 1922): 982–85.

1405 ———. "Limitation of Expenditure on Armaments." *Official Journal* 5 (Sept. 1924): 1179–84. [A circular letter.]

1406 ———. *Report of the Temporary Mixed Commission on Armaments.* A.81.1921. Geneva, Sept. 15, 1921.

1407 ———. "Report of the Temporary Mixed Commission for the Reduction of Armaments, Sept. 7, 1922." *International Conciliation*, no. 188 (July 1923): 1–150. [Reprinted as "The Reduction of Armaments."]

1408 ———. "Report of the Temporary Mixed Commission for the Reduction of Armaments, Sept. 30, 1924." *Official Journal* 5 (Oct. 1924): 1605–35.

1409 ———. "Work of the Temporary Mixed Commission." *Official Journal* 3 (Aug. 1922): 979–81.

1410 ———. "Work of the Temporary Mixed Commission for the Reduction of Armaments." *Official Journal* 4 (Apr. 1923): 426–30.

1411 ———. "Work of the Temporary Mixed Commission for the Reduction of Armaments." *Official Journal* 4 (July 1923): 719–20.

Coordination of PAC & TMC

1412 League of Nations. "Co-ordination of the Work of the Temporary Mixed Commission and the Permanent Advisory Commission for Military, Naval and Air Questions." *Official Journal* 5 (Apr. 1924): 728–30.

1413 ———. "Co-ordination of the Work of the Temporary Mixed Commission and the Permanent Advisory Commission." *Official Journal* 5 (Oct. 1924): 1379–80.

1414 ———. "First Session of the Co-ordination Commission: Report." *Official Journal* 6 (Apr. 1925): 443–45.

1415 ———. "Status of the Members of the Co-ordination Commission." *Official Journal* 6 (Feb. 1925): 130–31.

Preparatory Commission, 1925–1931

1416 "Deadlock In the Preparatory Commission." *Foreign Policy Association Information Service* (Nov. 23, 1928): 382–85.

1417 Dulles, Allen W. "Progress Toward Disarmament." *Foreign Affairs* 11 (Oct. 1932): 54–65.

1418 "Failure to Cut the World's Armies." *Literary Digest* (May 18, 1929): 11–12.

1419 [Great Britain. Delegation]. *Report of the British Representative to the Secretary of State for Foreign Affairs.* Cmd. 2888. London: H.M.S.O., 1927.

1420 "Human Nature and the Disarmament Plan." *Literary Digest* (June 29, 1929): 8–9.

1421 "Is Disarmament Possible? English and French Views. . . ." *Living Age* (May 1, 1928): 789–802.

1422 Knisley, Samuel D. "German Diplomacy and the Preparatory Commission for the Disarmament Conference, 1925–1930." Ph.D. diss., Univ. of North Carolina, 1972.

1423 Magruder, Adm. Thomas P. "Arbitration of Differences at Conference on Reduction of Armaments." *Annals of the Amer. Acad. of Pol. & Soc. Sci.* 144 (July 1929): 137–39.

1424 Miller, David Hunter. *Problems of Disarmament: Comments on the Geneva Questionnaire.* Pamphlet no. 37. New York: Foreign Policy Assoc., May 1926.

1425 Wheeler-Bennett, John W. *Disarmament and Security Since Locarno, 1925–1931.* New York: Macmillan, 1932.

1426 Woodward, David. "Limitation of Air Armaments." *Foreign Policy Association Information Service* (Oct. 29, 1930): 297–313.

1427 ———. "Limitation of Land Armaments." *Foreign Policy Association Information Service* (Apr. 2, 1930): 19–35.

SOVIET DISARMAMENT PROPOSAL, 1928

1428 Coates, W. P., comp. *U.S.S.R. and Disarmament: Discussion of Russia's Disarmament Proposals at Geneva, March 16–24, 1928: Convention for Partial Disarmament.* London: Anglo-Russian Parliamentary Committee, Aug. 1928.

1429 "Disarmament Dilemma: Russia and Great Britain at Geneva." *Commercial and Financial Chronicle* (Mar. 24, 1928): 1721–23.

1430 Fischer, Louis. "Shall the World Disarm?" *The Soviets in World Affairs.* 2 vols., 2d ed. Princeton: Princeton Univ. Press, 1951, II: 743–60.

1431 "Problem of Disarmament: Russia's Intervention." *Statist* (Mar. 24, 1928): 483–84.

1432 "Russia's Disarmament Proposals at Geneva." *Current History* 27 (Jan. 1928): 607–10.

1433 "The Russian Proposal." *Foreign Policy Association Information Service* (Nov. 23, 1928): 387–89.

1434 "The Soviet Disarmament Proposal at Geneva: Litvinov's Reply to Critics. . . ." *Soviet Union Review* 6 (May 1928): 66–86.

1435 "Soviet Union and General Disarmament." *Soviet Union Review* 6 (Jan. 1928): 2–5.

1436 Stone, Francis G. "The Soviets and Disarmament at Geneva." *Nineteenth Century and After* 103 (May 1928): 577–89.

DRAFT TREATY

1437 [Great Britain. Delegation]. *Despatch from Viscount Cecil of Chelmwood Enclosing the Report of the Preparatory Commission for the Disarmament Conference and the Disarmament Convention.* Cmd. 3757. London: H.M.S.O., 1931.

1438 Schwendemann, Karl. *Wirkliche oder Scheinbare Abrüstung? Der Konventionsentwurf der Vorbereitenden Abrüstungskommission.* Leipzig: R. Hofstetter, 1931. [*Disarmament, Real or Fictitious? The Draft of the Preparatory Disarmament Commission.* London: P. S. King & Sons, 1932.]

1439 Stone, William T. "The Draft Treaty for the World Disarmament Conference." *Foreign Policy Association Information Service* (Feb. 18, 1931): 471–88.

1440 "The Technical Aspects of the Draft Convention of the Preparatory Disarmament Commission." *Inter-Parliamentary Bulletin* 11 (Dec. 1931): 349–68.

1441 U.S. Department of State. *Report of the Preparatory Commission for the Disarmament Conference, and Draft Convention.* Conference Series 7. Washington, D.C.: G.P.O., 1931.

DOCUMENTS

1442 League of Nations. Assembly. Third Committee. *Reduction of Armaments: Arbitration, Security, Disarmament and the Work of the Preparatory Commission for the Disarmament Conference.* Geneva, 1927.

1443 League of Nations. Committee on Arbitration and Security. *Report of the Committee on Arbitration and Security on the Work of Its Third and Fourth Sessions.* 2 vols. Geneva, 1928–1930.

1444 League of Nations. Committee of Experts on Budgetary Questions. *Report to Sub-Commission B.* C.P.D./C.Q.B./35. Geneva, 1927.

1445 ———. *Report.* C.182.M.69.1931. IX. Geneva, 1931.

1446 League of Nations. Preparatory Commission for the Disarmament Conference. *Documents, 1–306.* 3 vols. Geneva, 1926–1931.

1447 ———. *Minutes.* 13 vols. 1st–6th Sess., May 18, 1926–Dec. 9, 1930.

1448 ———. Subcommission A. *Documents, 1–232.* Geneva, 1926.

1449 ———. Subcommission A. Air Commission. *Documents, 1–42.* Geneva, 1926.

1450 ———. *Record of Proceedings* 1st–3d Sess., June 22–Oct. 11, 1926.

1451 ———. Subcommission A. Military Committee. *Documents, 1–53.* Geneva, 1926.

1452 ———. *Record of Proceedings.* 1st–3d Sess., June 22–Oct. 23, 1926.

1453 ———. Subcommission A. Naval Committee. *Documents, 1–64.* Geneva, 1926.

1454 ———. Subcommission B. *Documents, 1–15.* Geneva, 1926–1927.

1455 ———. *Provisional Minutes.* 1st–4th Sess., May 26, 1926–Mar. 17, 1927.

Disarmament Conference, 1932–1934

1456 Alexander, Robert J. "The Disarmament Policy of the United States, 1933–1934." Ph.D. diss., Georgetown Univ., 1953.

1457 Alteras, Isaac. "The Geneva Disarmament Conference: The German Case." Ph.D. diss., City Univ. of New York, 1971.

1458 Arnold-Forster, William. *The Disarmament Conference.* London: National Peace Council, 1931.

1459 Clay, Kenneth. *Les Rapports Politiques: Franco-Allemande à la Conférence du Désarmement.* Geneva: Presses Zoniennes, 1939.

1460 Coulon, Pierre. *La Conférence du Désarmement.* Paris: Presses Modernes, 1934.

1461 Deboe, David C. "The United States and the Geneva Disarmament Conference, 1932–1934." Ph.D. diss., Tulane Univ., 1969.

1462 Deierhoi, Tyler. "The Conduct of German Policy at the Disarmament Conference of 1932." Ph.D. diss., Duke Univ., 1964.

1463 DeWolf, Francis C. *General Synopsis of Treaties of Arbitration, Conciliation, Judicial Settlement, Security and Disarmament Actually in Force Between Countries Invited to the Disarmament Conference.* Washington, D.C.: Carnegie Endowment for International Peace, 1933.

1464 Haskins, V. Lyle. "The Gleichberecht-Securite Issue at the World Disarmament Conference, 1932–1934." Ph.D. diss., Univ. of Oklahoma, 1973.

1465 Kyba, J. P. "British Attitudes Towards Disarmament and Rearmament, 1932–1935." Ph.D. diss., Univ. of London, 1967.

1466 Schwendemann, Karl. *Abrüstung und Sicherheit: Handbuch der Sicherheitsfrage und der Abrüstungskonferenz, mit einer Sammlung der Wichtigsten.* Leipzig: R. Hofstetter, 1933.

1467 Thompson, James H. "Great Britain and the World Disarmament Conference, 1932–1934." Ph.D. diss., Univ. of North Carolina, 1961.

1468 Wheeler-Bennett, John W. *The Pipe Dream of Peace: The Story of the Collapse of Disarmament.* New York: Morrow, 1935. [Also published as *The Disarmament Deadlock.* London: Routledge, 1934.]

1469 Arnold-Forster, William. "British Policy at the Disarmament Conference." *Political Quarterly* 3 (July 1932): 365–80.

1470 ———. "The First Stage in Disarmament: A Commentary on the Continuing Programme of the Conference." *Geneva Special Studies* 3:8 (1932).

1471 ———. "A Policy for the Disarmament Conference." *Political Quarterly* 2 (July 1931): 378–93.

1472 Benes, Edward. "Czechoslovakia and Disarmament." *Central European Observer* (Feb. 19, 1932): 115–17.

1473 Buell, Raymond L. "The Limitation of Armaments." *Institute of Politics: Report of the Round Tables and General Conference* (1932): 4–23.

1474 Cecil, Viscount Robert. "Facing the World Disarmament Conference." *Foreign Affairs* 10 (Oct. 1931): 13–22.

1475 ———, and Norman H. Davis. "Disarmament." *International Conciliation*, no. 285 (Dec. 1932): 1–74.

1476 Dickinson, Lord. "Is Disarmament Possible?" *Nineteenth Century and After* 112 (Sept. 1932): 272–78.

1477 Diest, Wilhelm. "Bruning, Herriot und die Abrüstungsgesprache von Bessinge, 1932." *Vierteljahrshefte für Zeitgeschichte* 5 (1957): 265–72.

1478 ———. "Schleicher und die Deutsche Abrüstungspolitik im Juni/Juli 1932." *Vierteljahrshefte für Zeitgeschichte* 7 (1959): 163–76.

1479 "Disarmament: The Background of the Conference. . . ." *Round Table* 23 (June 1932): 532–51.

1480 "Disarmament: The Naval Aspect." *Quarterly Review* 259 (Oct. 1932): 273–84.

1481 "The Disarmament Conference: A Critical Situation." *Bulletin of International News* (Oct. 12, 1933): 215–22.

1482 "The Disarmament Conference: The New Proposals." *Bulletin of International News* (Jan. 19, 1933): 435–41.

1483 "The Disarmament Conference: Opening of the Second Year." *Bulletin of International News* (Feb. 16, 1933): 493–501.

1484 Dovgalevsky, Valerian. "Soviet View of British Arms Plan." *Soviet Union Review* 11 (May 1933): 112–14.

1485 Dulles, Allen W. "Germany and the Crisis on Disarmament." *Foreign Affairs* 13 (Jan. 1934): 260–70.

1486 "The Foundations of Disarmament." *Round Table* 23 (Dec. 1932): 1–20.

1487 "Germany and the Disarmament Conference." *Bulletin of International News* (Oct. 26, 1933): 247–52.

1488 Gillies, William. "The Disarmament Conference: First Phase." *Labour Magazine* 11 (Aug.–Sept. 1932): 147–50.

1489 Glasgow, George. "Disarmament and Financial Recovery." *Queens Quarterly* 39 (Spring 1932): 12–28.

1490 ———. "Is Disarmament Possible?" *Contemporary Review* 182 (Dec. 1932): 369–75.

1491 Hamilton, Cicely. "The Herriot Plan." *Time and Tide* (Nov. 5, 1932): 1381–83.

1492 Jack, Ernst. "Disarmament." *World Affairs International* 3 (Oct. 1932): 45–73.

1493 Johnson, Albin E. "Myth of Disarmament." *Nation* (Mar. 13, 1929): 304–05.

1494 King-Hall, Stephen. "Now or Never." *Nineteenth Century and After* 112 (Nov. 1932): 513–24.

1495 Lippai, Z. *Behind the Scenes of the "Disarmament" Conference.* Moscow: Cooperative Publishing Society of Foreign Workers in the U.S.S.R., 1932.

1496 Martin, Kingsley. "The Disarmament Conference and the Russian Plan." *Political Quarterly* 5 (July 1934): 413–21.

1497 Metzsch, Horst von. "Die Behandlung der Wehrverbande auf der Abrüstungskonferenz." *Zeitschrift für Politik* 23 (1934): 106–20.

1498 ———. "Jahresbilanz der Abrüstungskonferenz." *Berliner Monatshefte* 11 (Feb. 1933): 107–28.

1499 Morgan, Laura P. *The Issues of the General Disarmament Conference: What Should Be the Position of the United States?* Washington, D.C.: National Council for Prevention of War, 1931.

1500 "Muddle, Muddle, Toil, and Trouble." *New Statesman and Nation* (Mar. 10, 1934): 332–33.

1501 Nevins, Allan. "Disarmament: A New Phase." *Current History* 39 (Nov. 1933): 199–203.

1502 ———. "Disarmament Deadlock." *Current History* 40 (June 1934): 320–23.

1503 Politis, Nicholas S., et al. "The Problem of Disarmament." *International Conciliation*, no. 298 (Mar. 1934): 59–80.

1504 Ponsonby, Arthur. *Disarmament: A Discussion*. London: Hogarth Press, 1932.

1505 Rheinbaben, Frhr. von. "Der Englische Abrüstungsplan in Deutsche Urteil." *Berliner Monatshefte* 11 (May 1933): 485–89.

1506 ———. "Genfer Abrüstungskonferenz—und Was Nun? Der Deutsche Kampf um Abrüstung und Gleichberechtigung." *Entscheidungen der Politik* 2 (1932): 5–70.

1507 Stone, William T. "The Disarmament Crisis, 1933." *Foreign Policy Reports* (Oct. 25, 1933): 186–96.

1508 ———. "The Disarmament Impasses." *Annals of the Amer. Acad. of Pol. & Soc. Sci.* 175 (Sept. 1934): 82–92.

1509 ———. "The World Disarmament Conference: First Stage, Feb. 2–Mar. 17, 1932." *Foreign Policy Reports* (May 11, 1932): 60–66.

1510 ———. "The World Disarmament Conference: Second Stage, Mar. 17, 1932–Jan. 11, 1933." *Foreign Policy Reports* (Jan. 18, 1933): 268–78.

1511 Twiss, W. L. O. "Disarmament with Special Reference to Asia." *Royal Central Asian Society Journal* 19 (July 1932): 447–58.

1512 White, Freda. "The Deadlock in Disarmament." *Nineteenth Century and After* 115 (May 1934): 485–98.

1513 Woods, Amy. "Oncoming World Disarmament." *World Unity* 11 (Feb. 1933): 325–33.

Issues: Limiting Aggressive Weapons

1514 Boggs, Marion W. *Attempts to Define and Limit "Aggressive" Armament in Diplomacy and Strategy*. Columbia: Univ. of Missouri Press, 1941.

1515 Fuller, Gen. J. F. C. "What is an Aggressive Weapon?" *English Review* 54 (Jan.–June 1932): 601–05.

1516 Liddell Hart, B. H. "Aggression and the Problem of Weapons." *English Review* 55 (July 1932): 71–78.

1517 Patch, Buell W. "Abolition of Aggressive Weapons." *Editorial Research Reports* (May 5, 1932): 307–24.

1518 Roosevelt, Pres. Franklin D. *Elimination of Weapons of Offensive Warfare*. House Doc. 36. Washington, D.C.: G.P.O., 1933.

Issues: Disarmament & Equality

1519 Ahlemann, Georg. *Das Heilige Nein*. Berlin: Elsner, 1934.

1520 Arnold-Forster, William. "Equality in Disarmament." *Labour Magazine* 11 (Oct. 1932): 243–46.

1521 Berdahl, Clarence A. "Disarmament and Equality." *Geneva Special Studies* 3:4 (1932): 1–16.

1522 Darcy, Paul. *L'Allemagne Toujours Armée*. Paris: Editions de Portique, 1933.

1523 Freund, Michael. *Von Versailles zur Wehrfreiheit*. Essen: Essener Verlagsanstalt, 1936.

1524 Great Britain. Foreign Office. *Declaration of the Policy of His Majesty's Government In The United Kingdom on Disarmament in Connexion with Germany's Claim to Equality of Rights*. Cmd. 4189. London: H.M.S.O., 1932.

1525 Rohde, Hans. *Franco-German Factors of Power: Comparative Studies of the Problems of Disarmament*. Berlin: Berliner Borsen Zeitung, 1932.

1526 Schilling, Karl. *Der Versailles Vertrag und die Abrüstung*. Berlin: Dummler, 1933.

1527 Schmidt, Richard K. B., and Adolf Grabowsky, eds. *Disarmament and Equal Rights: Facts and Problems Dealt with in the Negotiations on Disarmament and Equal Rights 1933–1934*. Berlin: Carl Haymanns Verlag, 1934.

1528 Schwendemann, Karl. *Gleiches Recht und Gleiche Sicherheit*. Berlin: Weidmannsche Buchhandlung, 1934.

PRELIMINARY DOCUMENTS

1529 League of Nations. *Disarmament: Preparations for the General Conference*. Geneva: Secretariat, Information Section, 1931.

1530 ———. *Particulars with Regard to the Position of Armaments in the Various Countries: Communications from the Governments . . ., 1–78*. Geneva, 1931–1932.

CONFERENCE DOCUMENTS

1531 League of Nations. Air Commission. *Documents, 1–71*. Geneva, 1932–1935.

1532 ———. *Records of the Conference for the Reduction and Limitation of Armaments. Series D, Vol. 3: Minutes of the Air Commission, Feb. 27–June 24, 1932*. Geneva, 1936.

1533 ———. *Report to the General Commission . . .* Conf. D. 123. Geneva, 1932.

1534 ———. Bureau. *Report Submitted to the Bureau on the Question of Supervision . . .* Conf. D. 140. Geneva, Oct. 12, 1932.

1535 ———. *Report Submitted to the Bureau on the Question of Air Forces*. Conf. D. 141. Geneva, Oct. 24, 1932.

1536 ———. *Report Submitted to the Bureau on the Prohibition of Chemical Warfare and Violations of the Prohibition to Use Chemical, Bacteriological and Incendiary Weapons*. Conf. D. 142. Geneva, Oct. 25, 1932.

1537 ———. *Second Report on the Question of Supervision, Approved by the Bureau on November 15, 1932*. Conf. D. 148. Geneva, Nov. 17, 1932.

1538 ———. Committee on Effectives. *Documents, 1–24*. Geneva, 1933–1934.

1539 ———. Committee on Miscellaneous Provisions. *Documents, 1–6*. Geneva, 1933–35.

1540 League of Nations. Committee on Guarantees of Execution. *Documents, 1–4*. Geneva, 1934.

1541 ———. Committee for the Regulation of the Trade in, and Private and State Manufacture of, Arms and Implements of War. *Progress Report to the General Commission*. Conf. D. 160. Geneva, 1933.

1542 ———. *Report to the General Commission. . . . Conf. D./C.G.171*. Geneva, 1934.

1543 ———. *Report on Progress of Work*. Conf. D. 145. Geneva, 1932.

1544 League of Nations. Conference for the Reduction and Limitation of Armaments, Geneva, 1932–. *Records of the Conference for the Reduction and Limitation of Armaments. Series A: Verbatim Records of Plenary Meetings*. Geneva, Feb. 2–July 23, 1932.

1545 ———. *Records of the Conference for the Reduction and Limitation of Armaments. Series B: Minutes of the General Commission*. 3 vols. Geneva, 1932–1936.

1546 ———. *Records of the Conference for the Reduction and Limitation of Armaments. Series C: Minutes of the Bureau*. Geneva, 1935–.

1547 League of Nations. Land Commission. *Documents, 1–46*. Geneva, 1932.

1548 ———. *Records of the Conference for the Reduction and Limitation of Armaments. Series D, Vol. 1: Minutes of the Land Commission, Feb. 27–June 6, 1932*. Geneva, 1935.

1549 ———. Land Commission. Committee of Experts. *Documents, 1–56*. Geneva, 1932.

1550 ———. Land Commission. Technical Committee. *Documents, 1–2*. Geneva, 1932.

1551 League of Nations. National Defence Expenditures Commission. *Records of the Conference for the Reduction and Limitation of Armaments. Series D, Vol. 4: Minutes of the National Defence Expenditures Commission, Feb. 27, 1932–June 3, 1933*. Geneva, 1935.

1552 ———. National Defence Expenditures Commission. Technical Committee. *Report of the Technical Committee. . . .* 2 vols. Conf. D. 158. Geneva, 1933.

1553 ———. Naval Commission. *Documents, 1–37*. Geneva, 1932.

1554 ———. *Records of the Conference for the*

Reduction and Limitation of Armaments. Series D, Vol. 2: *Minutes of the Naval Commission, Feb. 27–July 20, 1932.* Geneva, 1935.

1555 League of Nations. Political Commission. *Documents, 1–15.* Geneva, 1932–1933.

1556 ———. *Records of the Conference for the Reduction and Limitation of Armaments.* Series D, Vol. 5: *Minutes of the Political Commission, Feb. 27, 1932–Mar. 10, 1933.* Geneva, 1936.

1557 ———. Political Commission. Committee for Security Questions. *Documents, 1–12.* Geneva, 1933.

1558 League of Nations. Special Committee on Chemical and Bacteriological Weapons. *Documents, 1–38,* Geneva, 1932.

1559 ———. *Provisional Minutes.* 1st–26th Sess., Nov. 22–Dec. 13, 1932.

1560 ———. *Reply to the Questionnaire Submitted by the Bureau to the Special Committee.* Conf. D. 152. Geneva, 1932.

1561 League of Nations. Special Committee on Effectives. *Documents, 1–40.* Geneva, 1932–1933.

1562 ———. *Provisional Minutes.* 1st–25th Sess., Sept. 30, 1932–June 29, 1933.

1563 ———. Special Committee on Effectives. Colonial Committee. *Documents, 1–9.* Geneva, 1932.

1564 ———. Special Committee on Effectives. Technical Committee. *Documents, 1–123.* Geneva, 1932–1934.

1565 ———. *Provisional Minutes.* 1st–49th Sess., Apr. 25–June 12, 1933.

United Nations

RESEARCH RESOURCES

1566 U.N. Atomic Energy Commission. *An International Bibliography on Atomic Energy: Political, Economic, and Social Aspects.* 2 vols. AEC/INF/7 rev. 2. New York, 1949–1951.

1567 U.N. Department of Public Information. *Yearbook of the United Nations.* New York, 1947–.

1568 U.N. General Assembly. *Annual Report of the Secretary-General on the Work of the Organization.* New York, 1946–.

1569 *U.N. Monthly Chronicle.* New York: United Nations, 1964–. [Previously *U.N. Review.* New York: United Nations, 1954–1963.]

1570 Brainard, Alfred P. "The United Nations and the Question of Disarmament, 1950–1955." Ph.D. diss., Univ. of Washington, 1960.

1571 Edington, Robert Van. "Japan in the United Nations on the Issues of Nuclear Weapons." Ph.D. diss., Univ. of Washington, 1968.

1572 Goodrich, Leland M., and Anne P. Simons. *The United Nations and the Maintenance of International Peace and Security.* Washington, D.C.: Brookings Institution, 1955.

1573 Harrington, Charles W. *The Problem of Disarmament in the United Nations.* Geneva, 1950.

1574 Russell, Ruth B. *A History of the United Nations Charter: The Role of the United States, 1940–1945.* Washington, D.C.: Brookings Institution, 1958.

1575 U.N. Department of Public Information. *The United Nations and Disarmament, 1945–1965.* New York, 1967.

1576 ———. Department of Political and Security Council Affairs. *The United Nations and Disarmament, 1945–1970.* New York, 1970.

1577 ———. *The United Nations and Disarmament, 1970–1975.* New York, 1976.

1578 U.N. Secretary General (Thant). *Basic Problems of Disarmament: Reports.* E.70.I.17. New York, 1970.

1579 Bloomfield, Lincoln P. *The Politics of Arms Control: Troika, Veto, and International Institutions.* Special Studies Group, SM–3. Washington, D.C.: Institute for Defense Analyses, 1961.

1580 Cavers, David F. "Arms Control in the United Nations: A Decade of Disagreement." *Bulletin of the Atomic Scientists* 12 (Apr. 1956): 105–11.

1581 ———. "The Arms Stalemate Ends." *Bulletin of the Atomic Scientists* 11 (Jan. 1955): 9–12.

1582   Commission to Study the Organization of Peace. *Security and Disarmament Under the United Nations.* Report no. 5. New York, June 1947.

1583   Cooper, John S. "Major Problem of the United Nations: The Control and Reduction of Armaments." *U.S. Department of State Bulletin* (Dec. 25, 1950): 1023–26.

1584   Goldstein, Walter. "Disarmament, the U.N., and the Nuclear Club." *Correspondent* 34 (Spring–Summer 1965): 41–54.

1585   Green, Howard C. "The United Nations and Disarmament." *External Affairs* [Canada] 12 (Nov. 1960): 830–46.

1586   Izraelyan, V. "The United Nations and the Curbing of the Arms Race." *International Affairs* [Moscow] 22 (Mar. 1976): 62–64.

1587   Jack, Homer A. "The Confrontation at Geneva." *War/Peace Report* 4 (May 1964): 6–8.

1588   ———. "Disarmament at the U.N.: Discussions in Detente." *Bulletin of the Atomic Scientists* 20 (Feb. 1964): 33–36.

1589   ———. "The 1966 U.N. Disarmament Debate." *War/Peace Report* 6 (Dec. 1966): 12–14.

1590   ———. "U.N. Disarmament Resolutions." *Bulletin of the Atomic Scientists* 18 (Apr. 1962): 17.

1591   Klein, Peter. "The United Nations and the Problem of Disarmament." *German Foreign Policy* 9:6 (1970): 475–86.

1592   Kuhn, Alfred G. "Some Movement in Arms Control Field During First Year of U.N.'s Disarmament Decade." *NATO Letter* 19 (Mar.–Apr. 1971): 23–27.

1593   Kutakov, L. N. "The United Nations and Disarmament." *U.N. Monthly Chronicle* 7 (May 1970): 56–61.

1594   Lawson, R. C. "U.N.: Disarmament and Propaganda." *Current History* 22 (Apr. 1952): 216–20.

1595   Lilienthal, David E. "Unreality at Geneva." *Air Force and Space Digest* 46 (Apr. 1963): 114–15.

1596   Lipson, Leon. "Remarks and Discussion." *American Journal of International Law* 64 (Sept. 1970): 203–10.

1597   Lvov, M. "U.N.: Rostrum, Forum, Arena: Disarmament Problems at the 18th General Assembly." *International Affairs* [Moscow] 9 (Nov. 1963): 10–15.

1598   Margolis, Howard. "Arms Control and Disarmament: Notes on the Situation at Geneva." *Science* (Mar. 23, 1962): 1049–50.

1599   McVitty, Marion H. "The Role of the United Nations." *Current History* 46 (June 1964): 331–35.

1600   "The Nuclear Time Bomb: Report to U.N. Secretary General U Thant by the Task Force on Nuclear Arms Escalation." *Saturday Review* (Dec. 9, 1967): 16–19 ff.

1601   Ovinnikov, Richard S. "The USSR Position on Disarmament in the United Nations." *Annals of the Amer. Acad. of Pol. & Soc. Sci.* 414 (July 1974): 51–63.

1602   Skolnikoff, Eugene B. "Policy Note: An 'ACDA' for UN Policy." *International Organization* 27 (Winter 1973): 99–102.

1603   Steiniger, Peter A. "The Program of the United Nations for Strengthening International Security." *German Foreign Policy* 10:2 (1971): 393–400.

1604   Toynbee, Arnold J. "Disarmament After Geneva." *Collier's* (Jan. 20, 1956): 32–38.

1605   [U.N.]. "The Continuing Search for Disarmament." *U.N. Review* 5 (Dec. 1958): 6–14.

1606   ———. "Disarmament: Assembly Adopts Resolutions on Napalm, Chemical Weapons, Nuclear Tests, World Conference and Related Questions." *U.N. Monthly Chronicle* 11 (Jan. 1974): 32–37.

1607   ———. "Disarmament: The Continuing Quest for Agreement." *U.N. Review* 4 (May 1957): 6–11 ff.

1608   ———. "Efforts of the United Nations to Achieve Disarmament: Report on the Various Proposals Made During 1955." *U.N. Review* 3 (Jan. 1956): 40–47.

1609   U.N. Department of Public Information. *Disarmament: Imperative of Peace: Achievements of the United Nations.* New York, 1970.

1610   ———. *Disarmament: The United Nations Effort.* New York, 1956.

1611   ———. *Disarmament and the United Na-*

tions: *The "Partial-Measures" and Other Decisions of the General Assembly's Twelfth Session.* New York, 1958.

1612 ———. "Disarmament and United Nations Responsibility." *U.N. Review* 6 (June 1960): 6–7, 54.

1613 ———. *A Step Forward: Disarmament and the United Nations.* New York, 1955.

General Assembly

1614 Acheson, Dean G. "U.S., U.K. and France Place Disarmament Resolution Before the General Assembly." *U.S. Department of State Bulletin* (Dec. 3, 1951): 879–90.

1615 Alexeyev, A. "Disarmament Questions at the 26th UN General Assembly." *International Affairs* [Moscow] 18 (Apr. 1972): 11–15.

1616 Austin, Sen. Warren R. "Meeting of the General Assembly: U.S. Position on Regulation and Reduction of Armaments." *U.S. Department of State Bulletin* (Nov. 24, 1946): 934–35.

1617 ———. *World Confidence and the Reduction of Armed Forces: The American Objective.* Dept. of State Pub. 3319. Washington, D.C.: G.P.O., 1948.

1618 Boggs, Marion W. "Regulation and Reduction of Armaments: Action of the General Assembly." *U.S. Department of State Bulletin* (Feb. 23, 1947): 311–320, 333.

1619 Carnegie Endowment for International Peace. "Disarmament and Arms Control." *Issues Before the 21st General Assembly. International Conciliation,* pamphlet no. 559. New York, Sept. 1966.

1620 "Disarmament: Assembly Adopts Seven Resolutions." *U.N. Monthly Chronicle* 6 (Jan. 1969): 46–55.

1621 "A Disarmament Plan: Three Power Plan, Nov. 7, 1951: Soviet Counterproposal, Nov. 16, 1951: Revised Western Plan, Nov. 19, 1951." *Current History* 22 (Jan. 1952): 47–49.

1622 "Discussion of Tripartite Resolution on Disarmament." *U.S. Department of State Bulletin* (Jan. 7, 1952): 21–28.

1623 "Divergent Views on Disarmament Discussed." *U.S. Department of State Bulletin* (Jan. 7, 1952): 17–20.

1624 Frye, William R. "Disarmament Comes Back to the General Assembly." *Bulletin of the Atomic Scientists* 13 (Nov. 1957): 333–35.

1625 Ivekovic, M. "The Renewal of Disarmament Talks: Prospects at the 15th United Nations General Assembly." *Review of International Affairs* [Belgrade] (Oct. 5, 1960): 12–14.

1626 Jack, Homer A. "Disarmament in the 20th General Assembly." *Disarmament* 13 (Mar. 1967): 13–19.

1627 ———. "Disarmament at the U.N.: The Quiet Assembly." *Bulletin of the Atomic Scientists* 19 (Feb. 1963): 39–44.

1628 Jessup, Philip C. "General Assembly Established Subcommittee to Discuss Disarmament." *U.S. Department of State Bulletin* (Dec. 10, 1951): 953–58.

1629 Lodge, Henry Cabot, Jr. "General Assembly Action on Disarmament." *U.S. Department of State Bulletin* (Jan. 9, 1956): 55–61.

1630 ———. "U.N. General Assembly Adopts Western Proposal on Principles of Disarmament: Votes to Enlarge Commission." *U.S. Department of State Bulletin* (Dec. 16, 1957): 961–66.

1631 Martin, Joseph, Jr. "U.S. Reviews Progress on Disarmament Issues in 1973 Before U.N. General Assembly." *U.S. Department of State Bulletin* (Jan. 21, 1974): 64–70.

1632 Osborn, Frederick H. "General Assembly Considers Steps for Reduction of Armaments." *U.S. Department of State Bulletin* (Nov. 21, 1948): 630–33.

1633 Pechota, V. "The Disarmament Question Before the Fifteenth Session of the U.N. General Assembly." *Review of Contemporary Literature* 7 (1960): 126–34.

1634 U.S. Department of State. *Atomic Energy and Conventional Armaments: Selected Statements* [and] *United Nations Resolutions, Sept. 21–Dec. 12, 1948.* Pub. 3414. Washington, D.C.: G.P.O., 1949.

1635 ———. *International Control of Atomic Energy: Growth of a Policy.* Pub. 2702. Washington, D.C.: G.P.O., 1946.

1636 ———. *International Control of Atomic Energy: Policy at the Crossroads.* Pub. 3161. Washington, D.C.: G.P.O., 1948.

1637 ———. *A Report on the International Control of Atomic Energy.* Pub. 2498. Washington, D.C.: G.P.O., Mar. 16, 1946.

1638 U.S. Senate. Committee on Foreign Relations. Report: *United Nations Action on Disarmament: A Survey of the Debate and Resolutions of the 14th Session of the General Assembly.* 86th Cong., 2d Sess., 1960.

1639 [U.S.S.R.]. "Communication of the Soviet Government Regarding the Bilateral Soviet-American Negotiations on Disarmament. . . ." *International Affairs* [Moscow] 7 (Oct. 1961): 127–40.

1640 Yost, Charles W. "United States Reviews Major Disarmament Issues Facing U.N. General Assembly." *U.S. Department of State Bulletin* (Dec. 28, 1970): 803–07.

Security Council

1641 Boyd, Andrew. *Fifteen Men on a Powder Keg: A History of the U.N. Security Council.* New York: Stein & Day, 1971.

1642 "Disarmament Discussion Postponed: Security Council Agrees to United States Request for Deferment." *U.N. Weekly Bulletin* (Jan. 28, 1947): 54–59.

1643 "First Step Toward Disarmament: Early Action by Security Council Unanimously Recommended." *U.N. Weekly Bulletin* (Dec. 24, 1946): 4–10.

1644 "Security Council to Determine Data Required: Question Related to Disarmament Proposal." *U.N. Weekly Bulletin* (Dec. 24, 1946): 36–43.

ATOMIC ENERGY COMMISSION

See Part Two, Baruch Plan (1946).

1645 Shils, Edward. "The Failure of the UNAEC: An Interpretation." *University of Chicago Law Review* 15 (Summer 1948): 855–76.

1646 U.N. Atomic Energy Commission. *Official Records.* 1st–24th Meetings. Lake Success, N.Y., 1946–1949. [Supplements 1–3, 1946.]

1647 ———. *Official Supplement: Special Supplement, Report to the Security Council.* AEC. 18. Lake Success, N.Y., 1946.

1648 ———. *Official Records, Second Year: Special Supplement, Second Report to the Security Council, September 11, 1947.* AEC. 26. Lake Success, N.Y., 1947.

1649 ———. *Official Records, Third Year: Special Supplement, Third Report to the Security Council, May 17, 1948.* AEC. 31. Lake Success, N.Y., 1948.

1650 ———. *Official Records, Fourth Year: Special Supplement No. 1.* Lake Success, N.Y., 1949.

COMMISSION FOR CONVENTIONAL ARMAMENTS

1651 "Armaments Commission Begins Work." *U.N. Weekly Bulletin* (Apr. 1, 1947): 303–07.

1652 "Commission on 'Conventional' Armaments: New Body to Report to Security Council in Three Months." *U.N. Weekly Bulletin* (Feb. 25, 1947): 143–48.

1653 Ludlow, James M. *The Establishment of the Commission for Conventional Armaments.* Dept. of State Pub. 2823. Washington, D.C.: G.P.O., 1947. [Also printed in *U.S. Department of State Bulletin* (Apr. 27, 1947): 731–740, 743.]

1654 Nash, Frank. "U.S. Views on Control of Conventional Armaments." *U.S. Department of State Bulletin* (June 12, 1950): 957–58.

1655 U.N. Department of Political and Security Council Affairs. "The Commission for Conventional Armaments." *The United Nations and Disarmament, 1945–1970.* New York, 1970, pp. 25–34.

Disarmament Commission, 1952–1960

1656 Cohen, Benjamin V. "Retiring Deputy U.S. Representative on Disarmament Commission Reports to the President." *U.S. Department of State Bulletin* (Jan. 26, 1953): 142–54.

1657 ———. "U.S., U.K., and France Propose Plan to Limit Arms by Type and Quantity." *U.S. Department of State Bulletin* (Aug. 25, 1952): 290–93.

1658 ———. "U.S., U.K., and France Submit Proposals for Numerical Limitation of Armed Forces." *U.S. Department of State Bulletin* (June 9, 1952): 907–11.

1659 Inglis, David R. "UN Disarmament Commission Proceedings [Feb.–Nov. 1952]." *Bulletin of the Atomic Scientists* 8 (Nov. 1952): 271–74.

1660 [Lodge, Henry Cabot, Jr., and James J. Wadsworth.] "Continuing the U.N. Search for Agreement on Disarmament." *U.S. Department of State Bulletin* (July 30, 1956): 196–211.

1661 U.N. First Committee. Subcommittee 18. *Summary of Records.* A/C.1/SC.18/SR.1–10. 1st–10th Meetings, Dec. 3–8, 1951. [Mimeograph.]

1662 U.N. General Assembly. Sixth Session. Committee of Twelve. *Summary Records.* A/AC.50/SR.1–9. 1st–9th Meetings, Feb. 14, 1951–Sept. 28, 1951.

1663 U.S. Department of State. *The Record of Disarmament: Report of U.S. Deputy Representative to Disarmament Commission on London Meeting of Subcommittee of Five and on Disarmament Commission Meetings, July, 1954.* Pub. 5581. Washington, D.C.: G.P.O., 1954.

1664 ———. *United States Efforts Toward Disarmament: Report to the President by the Deputy U.S. Representative on the United Nations Disarmament Commission.* Pub. 4902. Washington, D.C.: G.P.O., 1953.

1665 U.N. Disarmament Commission. *Official Records.* 1st–70th Meetings, Feb. 4, 1952–1960.

1666 ———. *Official Records: Special Supplement No. 1, Second Report of the Disarmament Commission.* DC. 20. New York, 1954.

1667 ———. *Official Records: Supplement for January, February and March 1952.* New York, 1952. [Supplements for Apr.–June, July–Sept., Oct.–Dec. 1952; Jan.–Mar., Apr.–June, July–Sept., Oct.–Dec. 1953; Jan.–Mar., Apr.–June, July–Sept., Oct.–Dec. 1954; Jan.–Mar., Apr.–Dec. 1955; Jan.–Dec. 1956; Jan.–Dec. 1957; Jan.–Dec. 1958; Jan.–Dec. 1959; Jan.–Dec. 1960.]

FIVE-POWER SUBCOMMITTEE, 1954–1957

1668 Great Britain. Foreign Office. *Report of the* [United Nations] *Disarmament Talks.* Cmnd. 228. London: H.M.S.O., 1957.

1669 Patterson, Moorehead. "Results of London Talks on Disarmament . . ." *U.S. Department of State Bulletin* (Aug. 2, 1954): 171–83.

1670 Spingarn, Jerome H. "Five Months in London." *Bulletin of the Atomic Scientists* 13 (Spring 1957): 257–61.

1671 [U.N.]. "Determined Efforts to Seek Agreement on Disarmament." *U.N. Review* 3 (July 1956): 16–20.

1672 U.S. Department of State. "Four Western Powers Submit Eleven-point Disarmament Plan." *U.S. Department of State Bulletin* (Sept. 16, 1957): 451–55.

1673 ———. *The Record on Disarmament: Report of the Deputy U.S. Representative to the United Nations Disarmament Commission on London Meeting.* . . . International Organization & Conference Series 3, 102. Washington, D.C.: G.P.O., 1954.

1674 ———. *Struggle for Disarmament: The Record of Five Power Confidential Negotiations in London, May–June, 1954.* London: U.S. Information Service, 1955.

1675 ———. "U.N. Disarmament Commission Subcommission Documents." *U.S. Department of State Bulletin* (May 30, 1955): 892–905.

FIVE-POWER SUBCOMMITTEE—DOCUMENTS

1676 Great Britain. Foreign Office. *Report of the Proceedings of the Sub-Committee of the United Nations Disarmament Commission Held at Lancaster House, London, May 13–June 22, 1954.* Cmd. 9240. London: H.M.S.O., 1954.

1677 ———. *Report of the Proceedings of the Sub-Committee of the United Nations Disarmament Commission, 1955.* Cmd. 9636. London: H.M.S.O., 1955.

1678 ———. *Report of the Proceedings of the Sub-Committee of the United Nations Commission Held at Lancaster House, London, March 19–May 4, 1956.* Cmd. 9770. London: H.M.S.O., 1956.

1679 ———. *Report of the Proceedings of the Sub-Committee of the United Nations Disarmament Commission Held at Lancaster House, London, March 18–September 6, 1957.* Cmnd. 333. London: H.M.S.O., 1957.

1680 ———. *Verbatim Records of the Meetings of the Sub-Committee of the United Nations Disarmament Commission Held at Lancaster House, London, May 13–June 22, 1954.* Cmd. 9205. London: H.M.S.O., 1954.

1681 ———. *Verbatim Records of the Meetings of the Second Session of the Sub-Committee of the United Nations Disarmament Commission Held at Lancaster House, London, February 25–May 18, 1955.* Cmd. 9648–9650. London: H.M.S.O., 1956.

1682 ———. *Verbatim Records of the Meetings of the Second Session of the Sub-Committee of the United Nations Disarmament Commission Held at New York, June 1–October 7, 1955.* Cmd. 9651–9652. London: H.M.S.O., 1956.

1683 U.N. Disarmament Commission. Subcommittee of the Disarmament Commission. *Verbatim Records.* 2d–157th Meetings, May 13, 1954–Sept. 6, 1957. DC/SC.1/PV.2–157.

Ten-Nation Disarmament Committee, 1960

1684 Arkadyev, Nikolai N. "The Ten-Nation Talks: The Western Plan." *New Times* [Moscow] 13 (Mar. 1960): 14–17.

1685 Eaton, F. M. "U.S. Delegation to Conference on Disarmament Submits Report to Secretary Herter." *U.S. Department of State Bulletin* (Aug. 22, 1960): 267–74.

1686 Lahoda, T. "The Disarmament Problem and the Ten Nation Committee." *Review of Contemporary Literature* 7 (1960): 311–25.

1687 *New Proposals for Disarmament: Including Khrushchev, U.N. 10-Nation Group.* New York: International Review Service, 1959.

1688 Nogee, Joseph L. "Propaganda and Negotiation: The Case of the Ten-Nation Disarmament Committee." *Journal of Conflict Resolution* 7:3 (1963): 510–21.

1689 Speidel, Helm. "The Truth About Disarmament Talks." *NATO's Fifteen Nations* 5 (1960): 10–19.

1690 [U.N.]. "The Hopes of the World." *U.N. Review* 6 (Apr. 1960): 16–19.

1691 ———. "The Major Problem: Disarmament, Twelve Draft Resolutions Before First Committee." *U.N. Review* 7 (Dec. 1960): 6–9.

1692 ———. "Unanimous Agreement on Disarmament Forum: All Proposals Referred to New Ten-Nation Committee." *U.N. Review* 6 (Dec. 1959): 6–9.

1693 Wadsworth, James J. "Committee I Continues Discussion of Disarmament." *U.S. Department of State Bulletin* (Nov. 28, 1960): 836–41.

DOCUMENTS

1694 Great Britain. Foreign Office. *Verbatim Records of the Meetings of the Ten-Power Disarmament Committee Held at the Palais des Nations, Geneva, March 15–April 29, 1960 and June 7–June 27, 1960.* Cmnd. 1152. London: H.M.S.O., 1960.

1695 [U.S. Department of State]. "Ten-Nation Conference on Disarmament Terminated by Soviet Walkout (June 27, 1960). . . ." *U.S. Department of State Bulletin* (July 18, 1960): 88–93.

1696 ———. "U.S. Delegation to Conference on Disarmament Submits Report to Secretary Herter: Official Report of the U.S. Delegation to the Conference of the Ten-Nation Committee on Disarmament, Held at Geneva, March 15–June 28, 1960." *U.S. Department of State Bulletin* (Aug. 22, 1960): 267–74.

Eighteen-Nation Disarmament Commission & Conference of Committee on Disarmament, 1962–

1697 Ahmed, M. Samir. "The Role of the Neutrals in the Geneva Negotiations." *Disarmament and Arms Control* [London] 1 (Summer 1963): 25–32.

1698 Arkadev, Nikolai N. "Disarmament Committee: Ten Years." *New Times* Moscow 12 (Mar. 1972): 4–5.

1699   Blackett, P. M. S. "The First Real Chance for Disarmament." *Harper's* 226 (Jan. 1963): 25–32.

1700   ———. "The Real Road to Disarmament: The Military Background to the Geneva Talks." *New Statesman* (Mar. 2, 1962): 295–300.

1701   Bodnar, James S. *Report on the Debate in the United Nations Disarmament Committee, April 21–June 16, 1965.* Washington, D.C.: U.S. ACDA, 1965.

1702   [Canada. Department of External Affairs]. "Working to Stop the Arms Race." *External Affairs* [Canada] 23 (Jan. 1971): 12–16.

1703   "Conference of the Committee on Disarmament." *International Affairs* [Moscow] 18 (June 1972): 119–21.

1704   "Disarmament: Conference to Eighteen Nation Committee Reconvenes." *U.N. Monthly Chronicle* 6 (Apr. 1969): 51–52.

1705   Doty, L. L. "Collapse of Disarmament Conference Seen." *Aviation Week & Space Technology* (Aug. 31, 1964): 16–17.

1706   Einhorn, Clare. "Fifth Annual Round of Eighteen-Nation Committee on Disarmament." *German Foreign Policy* 5:6 (1966): 454–62.

1707   Forndran, Erhard A. G. *Probleme der Internationalen Abrüstung: Die Internationalen Bemühungen um Abrüstung und Kooperative Rüstungssteuerung, 1962–1968.* Frankfurt: A. Metzner, 1970.

1708   Foster, William C. "Conference of 18-Nation Disarmament Committee Reconvenes at Geneva." *U.S. Department of State Bulletin* (Aug. 23, 1965): 333–37.

1709   Gasteyger, Curt. "The Eighteen Nation Disarmament Conference." *Disarmament* 10 (June 1966): 16–20.

1710   ———. "The Eighteen Nation Disarmament Conference." *Disarmament* 12 (Dec. 1966): 16–20.

1711   ———. "The Eighteen Nation Disarmament Conference." *Disarmament* 16 (Dec. 1967): 26–30.

1712   ———. "The Geneva Disarmament Conference: Report on the Negotiations." *Disarmament* 8 (Dec. 1965): 5–13.

1713   ———, and James Knott. "The Geneva Disarmament Conference: Some Institutional Aspects." *Disarmament* 3 (Sept. 1964): 1–3.

1714   Gould, Loyal N. *The ENDC and the Press.* Stockholm: Amquist & Wilksell, 1969.

1715   Gromyko, Andrei. "On the Negotiations in Geneva." *Current Digest of the Soviet Press* (May 30, 1962): 10–13.

1716   Herbert, Hugo. "Die Konferenzen." *Revue Militaire Générale* 9 (Nov. 1970): 546–61.

1717   Jack, Homer A. "The 1965 Session of the United Nations Disarmament Commission." *Disarmament* 7 (Sept. 1965): 17–19.

1718   ———. "Seventeen Continue." *Bulletin of the Atomic Scientists* 20 (June 1964): 43–45.

1719   [Johnson, Pres. Lyndon B.]. "President Johnson Calls Upon Soviet Union for Concrete Actions to Promote Peace." *U.S. Department of State Bulletin* (Feb. 3, 1964): 157–63.

1720   Keys, Donald F. "Meanwhile, Back in the Disarmament Committee. . . ." *War/Peace Report* 10 (Aug.–Sept. 1970): 8–9, 16.

1721   Lall, Arthur S. *Negotiating Disarmament: The Eighteen Nation Disarmament Conference: The First Two Years, 1962–1964.* Ithaca, N.Y.: Cornell Univ., Center for International Studies, 1964.

1722   Lang, Daniel. "Letter From Geneva." *New Yorker* (June 25, 1966): 108–110 ff.

1723   ———. "Letter from Geneva." *New Yorker* (Aug. 5, 1967): 70 ff.

1724   Neidle, Alan F. "Peace-Keeping and Disarmament: A Report of the Discussion at the Conference of the Eighteen-Nation Committee on Disarmament." *American Journal of International Law* 57 (Jan. 1963): 46–72.

1725   Rusk, Dean. "U.S. Proposes Patterns for Future Work of Disarmament Conference." *U.S. Department of State Bulletin* (Apr. 16, 1962): 618–24.

1726   Schacky, Erwin F. von. "Aktuelle Probleme der Abrüstungsverhandlungen: Die Ausgangslage für die Diesjährige Tagung der Konferenz des Abrüstungsauschusses in Genf." *Europa-Archiv* (Mar. 10, 1971): 171–82.

1727   Schulze, Rep. Richard T. "Conference of the Committee on Disarmament." *Congressional Record* 122 (July 21, 1976): E3976–77.

1728 Shestov, V. "Disarmament Committee Resumes Work." *International Affairs* [Moscow] 16 (Apr. 1970): 103.

1729 ———. "Geneva After the Recess." *International Affairs* [Moscow] 10 (Aug. 1964): 16–20.

1730 Shington, Derrick. "How the Press Covers the Geneva Negotiations." *Disarmament and Arms Control* 2 (Autumn 1964): 441–48.

1731 Smith, Gerard C. "The Conference of the Committee on Disarmament: Opportunities for Achievement." *U.S. Department of State Bulletin* (Mar. 16, 1970): 354–58.

1732 Sullivan, Michael J., III. "Conference at the Crossroads: Future Prospects of the Committee on Disarmament." *International Organization* 29 (Spring 1975): 393–413.

1733 Tait, Richard M. "In Defence of the Big Conference." *Disarmament and Arms Control* 2 (Summer 1964): 331–41.

1734 Tozzoli, Gian Paolo. "Geneva Negotiations as a Constituent Assembly." *Disarmament and Arms Control* 2 (Spring 1964): 126–35.

1735 [U.N.]. "Disarmament: Commission Adopts Resolutions." *U.N. Monthly Chronicle* 2 (July 1965): 17–31.

1736 [U.S. Department of State]. "Eighteen-Nation Disarmament Committee Recesses 1964 Session." *U.S. Department of State Bulletin* (Oct. 12, 1964): 524–27.

1737 ———. "A Summary of Developments at the Conference of the 18-Nation Committee of Disarmament, Geneva, March 14–June 15, 1962." *U.S. Department of State Bulletin* (July 23, 1962): 154–59.

1738 Verona, Sergiu. "The Geneva Disarmament Conference: Some Considerations." *Instant Research on Peace and Violence* 6:1–2 (1976): 62–71.

1739 Wallau, Theodor. "Die Aufgaben des Genfer Abrüstungsauschusses im Jahre 1972." *Europa-Archiv* (Apr. 10, 1972): 249–56.

1740 "Who is Frustrating Hopes at Geneva?" *International Affairs* [Moscow] 8 (June 1962): 3–7.

1741 "World Forum on Disarmament." *International Affairs* [Moscow] 11 (July 1965): 53–56.

DOCUMENTS

1742 Great Britain. Foreign Affairs. *Documents: Establishment* [of 18-Nation Committee]. Cmnd. 1694. London: H.M.S.O., Apr. 1962.

1743 ———. *Further Documents Relating to the Conference of the 18-Nation Committee on Disarmament.* (Mar. 14–June 15, 1962), Cmnd. 1792. London: H.M.S.O., July 1962.

1744 ———. *Further Documents. . . .* (July 16–Sept. 8, 1962) Cmnd. 1857. London: H.M.S.O., Nov. 1962.

1745 ———. *Further Documents. . . .* (Nov. 26–Dec. 20, 1962) Cmnd. 1958. London: H.M.S.O., Mar. 1963.

1746 ———. *Further Documents. . . .* (Feb. 12–June 21, 1963) Cmnd. 2184. London: H.M.S.O., Dec. 1963.

1747 ———. *Further Documents. . . .* (July 30–Aug. 29, 1963) Cmnd. 2353. London: H.M.S.O., May 1964.

1748 ———. *Further Documents. . . .* (Jan. 21–Apr. 28, 1964) Cmnd. 2486. London: H.M.S.O., Nov. 1964.

1749 ———. *Further Documents. . . .* (June 9–Sept. 17, 1964) Cmnd. 2595. London: H.M.S.O., Apr. 1965.

1750 ———. *Further Documents. . . .* (Disarmament Negotiations, 1965) Cmnd. 3020. London: H.M.S.O., July 1966.

1751 ———. *Further Documents. . . .* (Jan. 27–May 10, 1966) Cmnd. 3120. London: H.M.S.O., Dec. 1966.

1752 ———. *Further Documents. . . .* (June 14–Aug. 25, 1966) Cmnd. 3346. London: H.M.S.O., Aug. 1967.

1753 ———. *Further Documents. . . .* (Feb. 21–Dec. 18, 1967) Cmnd. 3767. London: H.M.S.O., Oct. 1968.

1754 ———. *Further Documents. . . .* (Jan. 18–June 19, 1968) Cmnd. 3940. London: H.M.S.O., 1969.

1755 ———. *Further Documents. . . .* (July 16–Dec. 20, 1968) Cmnd. 4141. London: H.M.S.O., Sept. 1969.

1756 ———. *Further Documents. . . .* (Mar. 18–Oct. 1969) Cmnd. 4399. London: H.M.S.O., 1970.

1757   ———. *Further Documents. . . .* (Disarmament Negotiations, 1970) Cmnd. 4725. London: H.M.S.O., Aug. 1971.

1758   ———. *Further Documents. . . .* (Disarmament Negotiations, 1971) Cmnd. 5011. London: H.M.S.O., 1972.

1759   ———. *Further Documents. . . .* (Disarmament Negotiations, 1972) Cmnd. 5344. London: H.M.S.O., 1973.

1760   U.N. General Assembly. Eighteen-Nation Committee on Disarmament. *Documents, ENDC/1–.* Geneva, Mar. 1962–.

1761   ———. *Final Verbatim Record, ENDC/ PV.1–.* Geneva, Mar. 14, 1962–. [Indexes issued irregularly by U.S. Delegation to the Conference of the Eighteen-Nation Committee on Disarmament.]

Five

Special Issues: Inspection, Verification & Supervision

FOR THE PAST five decades one of the most vexing problems of arms control and disarmament deliberations has been inspection, verification, and supervision of armaments. Throughout the past half-century, the demand for supervision and control has stemmed from a single, consistent fear, that an aggressive government might ignore its pledge to reduce or keep within prescribed limits its military forces, and thus treacherously gain a significant advantage over nations keeping their bargain.

The terms "supervision" and "control" are often used interchangeably without distortion. They refer to broad functions necessary to carry out an arms control or disarmament agreement. "Inspection" and "verification" also are frequently employed interchangeably; yet many specialists define the latter as the process of determining compliance with an agreement, and the former as *one* method. In this bibliography the specialists' definitions have been altered somewhat; however, I believe the following classifications are clear and useful.

While attention was focused on these issues during the lengthy interwar disarmament negotiations, it did not approach the emphasis given them in later decades. The best description of these interwar inspection and supervision debates and activities are in my essays, "Supervision, Control and Inspection of Armament: 1919–1941 Perspective," *Orbis* (1971) and "International Arms Inspection Policies Between World Wars, 1919–1934," *Historian* (1969).

During the post-1945 discussions between the United States and the Soviet Union over arms control and disarmament proposals, inspection, verification, and control became serious points of contention. There are several good essays describing these postwar arguments; however, for the novice, R. J. Barnet and R. A. Falk's *Security in Disarmament* (1965) and Seymour Melman's *Inspection for Disarmament* (1958) provide fine introductions. The legal aspects of these issues are discussed by D. S. Aronowitz in *Legal Aspects of Arms Control Verification in the United States* (1965), Louis Henkin in *Arms Control and Inspection in American Law* (1958), and by H. J. Berman and P. B. Maggs in *Disarmament Inspection Under Soviet Law* (1967). It has been said that the U.S. Arms Control and Disarmament Agency has spent more time and money studying these problems than any other single issue, therefore, one could profitably examine their published reports.

Many questions have been raised concerning compliance and/or evasion of treaty terms. Claims have been made that cheating has taken place in the past and questions raised about how violations should be dealt with in the future. David W. Wainhouse's *International Peace Observation* (1966) examines cer-

tain historical episodes; however, items relating to specific treaties have been generally placed in the chapter with the treaties themselves. The index will be a valuable aid in bringing these items together.

Finally, the issue of nuclear theft has raised considerable concern. These are summarized in R. A. Leachman and P. Althoff's *Preventing Nuclear Theft: Guidelines for Industry and Government* (1972) and M. Willrich and T. B. Taylor's *Nuclear Theft: Risks and Safeguards* (1974).

General Overview

1762 U.S. Atomic Energy Commission. *Safeguards Dictionary*. Washington, D.C.: G.P.O., 1971.

1763 ———. *Safeguards and Nuclear Materials Management: An Annotated Bibliography of Selected Literature*. Washington, D.C.: G.P.O., 1969.

HISTORICAL ASSESSMENTS TO 1945

1764 Burns, Richard Dean. "International Arms Inspection Policies Between World Wars, 1919–1934." *Historian* 31 (Aug. 1969): 583–603.

1765 ———. "Origins of the United States' Inspection Policy: 1926–1946." *Disarmament and Arms Control* 2 (Spring 1964): 157–69.

1766 ———. "Supervision, Control and Inspection of Armament: 1919–1941 Perspective." *Orbis* 15 (Fall 1971): 943–52.

1767 League of Nations. Conference for the Reduction and Limitation of Armaments. "Report Submitted to the Bureau on the Question of Supervision. . . ." *Conference Documents*. Vol. 2. Conf. D. 140–Conf. D/Bureau 22. Geneva, 1932.

1768 ———. "Second Report on the Question of Supervision [Nov. 15, 1932]." *Conference Documents*. Vol. 2. Conf. D. 148–Conf. D/Bureau 36(i). Geneva, 1932.

1769 ———. "Third Report on the Question of Supervision [Dec. 7, 1932]." *Conference Documents*. Vol. 2. Conf. D. 148–Conf. D/Bureau 39. Geneva, 1932.

1770 Patch, Buell W. "International Inspection: Inspection as an Enforcement Instrument, Inspection and Armament Control, 1919–1933: New Proposal for International Inspection." *Editorial Research Reports* (Dec. 6, 1946): 837–59.

1771 "United States Government's Views on Report of League Commission Concerning International Supervision of Agreements Limiting Armaments." *Commercial and Financial Chronicle* (May 7, 1927): 2697–99.

CONTEMPORARY VIEWS, SINCE 1945

1772 Anders, Allison. "Inspectorate: Another True But Wierd Tale." *American Opinion* 8 (May 1965): 73 ff.

1773   Bailey, Terrell W. "Inspection and Control of Nuclear Armaments in a Nation-State System: United States-Russian Disarmament Negotiations, 1945–1962." Ph.D. diss., Univ. of Florida, 1963.

1774   Barnet, Richard J. "Inspection: Shadow and Substance." In Richard J. Barnet and Richard A. Falk, eds., *Security in Disarmament*. Princeton: Princeton Univ. Press, 1965, pp. 15–36.

1775   Bloomfield, Lincoln P. "The Politics of Administering Disarmament." *Disarmament and Arms Control* 1 (Autumn 1963): 118–32.

1776   Bowie, Robert R. "Basic Requirements of Arms Control." *Daedalus* 89 (Fall 1960): 708–22.

1777   Brennan, Donald G. "The Role of Inspection in Arms Control." *Summer Study on Arms Control, 1960: Collected Papers*. Boston: American Academy of Arts & Sciences, 1961, pp. 247–52.

1778   Cavers, David F. "Atomic Controls in Disarmament Planning." *Bulletin of the Atomic Scientists* 8 (Mar. 1952): 84–87.

1779   Deutsch, Karl W. "Communications, Arms Inspection and National Security." In Quincy Wright et al., eds., *Preventing World War III*. New York: Simon & Schuster, 1962, pp. 62–73.

1780   Dougherty, James E. "Nuclear Weapons Control." *Current History* 47 (July 1964): 31–38, 52.

1781   Falk, Richard A. "Inspection, Trust, and Security During Disarmament." In Richard J. Barnet and Richard A. Falk, eds., *Security in Disarmament*. Princeton: Princeton Univ. Press, 1965, pp. 37–49.

1782   ———. "The Limitations of Inspection for Drastic Disarmament." In Richard J. Barnet and Richard A. Falk, eds., *Security in Disarmament*. Princeton: Princeton Univ. Press, 1965, pp. 226–39.

1783   Finkelstein, Lawrence S. "Arms Inspection." *International Conciliation*, no. 540 (Nov. 1962): 1–89.

1784   Hahn, Walter F. *Internal Motives for Soviet Secrecy*. Research Paper P-31, Study Phoenix Paper 5. Washington, D.C.: Institute for Defense Analyses, June 1963.

1785   Hawkes, Russell. "Public Will Be Unwilling to Buy Costly Arms Inspection System." *Missiles and Rockets* (July 13, 1964): 22.

1786   Jacob, Philip E. "The Disarmament Consensus: Toward Balanced and Phased Disarmament: The Problem of Control." *International Organization* 14 (Spring 1960): 233–60.

1787   Jones, Joseph M. "Can Atomic Energy Be Controlled?" *Harper's* 192 (May 1946): 425–31.

1788   Kaplan, Morton A. "The Fantasy of Disarmament: Continuing the Arms Race in the Absence of Foolproof Inspection Will Prevent War Rather than Cause It." *New Leader* (Mar. 2, 1959): 6–8.

1789   Kissinger, Henry A. "Controls, Inspection and Limited War." *Reporter* (June 13, 1957): 14–19.

1790   Lall, Betty Goetz. "Perspectives on Inspection for Arms Control." *Bulletin of the Atomic Scientists* 21 (Mar. 1965): 51–53.

1791   Laurence, William L. "On Inspection and Control." *The Hell Bomb*. New York: Knopf, 1951, pp. 149–98.

1792   Lodge, Henry Cabot, Jr. "Inspection as a Key to Disarmament." *U.S. Department of State Bulletin* (Sept. 12, 1955): 438–40.

1793   Maguire, Bassett, Jr. "Disarmament: A Captive Inspectorate." *Journal of Arms Control* 1:3 (1963): 149–51.

1794   Mayer, R. L. "Le Controle: Cooperation ou Espionnage?" *Cahiers du Communisme* [Paris] 6 (June 1960): 938–48.

1795   McNaughton, Gen. A. G. L. "National and International Control of Atomic Energy." *International Journal* 3 (Winter 1947–1948): 11–23.

1796   Morgenstern, Oskar. "Goal: An Armed, Inspected, Open World." *Fortune* 62 (July 1960): 93–95, 219–27.

1797   Murphy, Charles J. V. "Nuclear Inspection: A Near Miss." *Fortune* 59 (Mar. 1959): 122–25.

1798   Neyer, Joseph. "Is Atomic-Fission Control a Problem in Organizational Techniques?" *Ethics* 57 (July 1947): 289–96.

1799   Osborn, Frederick. "The Search for Atomic

Control." *Atlantic Monthly* (Apr. 1948): 48–50.

1800   Rich, Alexander, and John R. Platt. "How to Keep the Peace in a Disarmed World." *Bulletin of the Atomic Scientists* 22 (Apr. 1966): 14–19.

1801   Simons, Howard. "World-Wide Capabilities for Production and Control of Nuclear Weapons." *Daedalus* 88 (Summer 1959): 385–409.

1802   Stone, William T. "Controlled Disarmament." *Editorial Research Reports* (July 11, 1955): 459–76.

1803   Teller, Edward. "The Feasibility of Arms Control and the Principle of Openness." In Donald G. Brennan, ed., *Arms Control, Disarmament, and National Security.* New York: Braziller, 1961, pp. 122–37.

1804   Waskow, Arthur I. *Keeping the World Disarmed.* Santa Barbara, Ca.: Center for the Study of Democratic Institutions, 1965.

LEGAL ASPECTS

1805   Aronowitz, Dennis S. *Legal Aspects of Arms Control Verification in the United States.* Dobbs Ferry, N.Y.: Oceana, 1965.

1806   Bathhurst, M. E. "Legal Aspects of the International Control of Atomic Energy." *British Yearbook of International Law,* no. 24 (1947): 1–32.

1807   Berman, Harold J., and Peter B. Maggs. *Disarmament Inspection Under Soviet Law.* Dobbs Ferry, N.Y.: Oceana, 1967.

1808   Henkin, Louis. *Arms Control and Inspection in American Law.* New York: Columbia Univ. Press, 1958.

1809   ———. "Arms Inspection and the Constitution." *Bulletin of the Atomic Scientists* 15 (May 1959): 192–97.

1810   ———. "Arms Inspection and the Constitution." *Hastings Law Journal* 11 (Feb. 1960): 267–84.

1811   Partan, Daniel G. "Individual Responsibility Under a Disarmament Agreement in American Law." *Minnesota Law Review* 49 (Apr. 1965): 889–955.

1812   Rodgers, Rear Adm. William L. "Can Courts and Tribunals Maintain Peace?" *Annals of the Amer. Acad. of Pol. & Soc. Sci.* 120 (July 1925): 69–76.

1813   Sorahan, Joseph R. "Reconnaissance Satellites: Legal Characterization and Possible Utilization for Peacekeeping." *McGill Law Journal* 13:3 (1967): 458–93.

1814   Stein, Eric. "Impact of New Weapons Technology on International Law: Selected Aspects." *Recueil des Cours* [The Hague] 133, pts. 7–8 (1971): 233–387.

1815   Zile, Zigurds L.; Robert Sharlet; and Jean C. Love. *The Soviet Legal System and Arms Inspection: A Case Study in Policy Implementation.* New York: Praeger, 1972. [Based on Research Report ACDA–GC–83, 1967.]

Inspection & Verification

1816   Bechhoefer, Bernhard G. "Weapons Control." *Proceedings of the American Society of International Law* (1958): 236–42.

1817   Billik, B. H., and H. L. Roth. "On the Logical Establishment of Global Surveillance and Communication Nets." *Journal of Astronautical Sciences* 12 (Fall 1965): 88–99.

1818   Bloomfield, Lincoln P., and Louis Henkin. "Inspection and the Problem of Access." In Richard J. Barnet and Richard A. Falk, eds., *Security in Disarmament.* Princeton: Princeton Univ. Press, 1965, pp. 107–22.

1819   Brennan, Donald G. "The Detection of High-Altitude Missile Tests." In Seymour Melman, ed., *Inspection for Disarmament.* New York: Columbia Univ. Press, 1958, pp. 171–84.

1820   ———; D. E. Dustin; and H. G. Weiss. *The Use of Radar for Monitoring International Agreements on Missile and Space Flights.* Report no. 36G–0046. Lexington, Mass.: M.I.T., Lincoln Laboratory, 1960.

1821   Dresher, Melvin. *A Sampling Inspection Problem in Arms Control Agreements: A Game-Theoretic Analysis.* RM–2972–ARPA. Santa Monica, Ca.: Rand, Feb. 1962.

1822   Feld, Bernard T. "Inspection Techniques of Arms Control." In Donald G. Brennan, ed., *Arms Control, Disarmament, and National Security.* New York: Braziller, 1961, pp. 317–32.

1823 Finkelstein, Lawrence S. "The Uses of Reciprocal Inspection." In Seymour Melman, ed., *Disarmament: Its Politics and Economics*. Boston: American Academy of Arts & Sciences, 1962, pp. 82–98.

1824 Melman, Seymour. "Disarmament Inspection: Its Cost and Efficiency." *Disarmament* 6 (June 1965): 11–13.

1825 ———. "How Can Inspection Be Made to Work?" *Bulletin of the Atomic Scientists* 14 (Sept. 1958): 270–72.

1826 ———. "The Political Implications of Inspection for Disarmament." *Journal of International Affairs* 13:1 (1959): 34–46.

1827 ———, ed. *Inspection for Disarmament.* New York: Columbia Univ. Press, 1958.

1828 Nutting, Anthony. "Proposals on Disarmament: Basic Requirements for Effective Control and Inspection." *Vital Speeches* (Oct. 1, 1955): 1509–12.

1829 Orear, Jay. "A New Approach to Inspection." *Bulletin of the Atomic Scientists* 17 (Mar. 1961): 107–10.

1830 O'Sullivan, Thomas C. "Disadvantages of Reliable Inspection." *Bulletin of the Atomic Scientists* 19 (Mar. 1963): 18–19.

1831 Packman, Martin. "Inspection for Disarmament." *Editorial Research Reports* (June 11, 1957): 423–40.

1832 Penrose, Lionel S. "Radiation, Public Health and Inspection for Disarmament." In Seymour Melman, ed., *Inspection for Disarmament*. New York: Columbia Univ. Press, 1958, pp. 100–108.

1833 Pilisuk, Marc. "Timing and Integrity of Inspection in Arms Reduction Games." *Papers of the Peace Research Society* (International) 5 (1966): 99–108.

1834 Rodberg, Leonard S. "Graduated Access Inspection." *Journal of Arms Control* 1:2 (1963): 139–44.

1835 ———. "The Rationale of Inspection." In Seymour Melman, ed., *Disarmament: Its Politics and Economics*. Boston: American Academy of Arts & Sciences, 1962, pp. 68–81.

1836 Scoville, Herbert, Jr. "The Technology of Surveillance." *Society* 12 (1975): 58–63.

1837 Singer, J. David. "Disarmament and the Fallibility of Inspection." *Political Research: Organization and Design (PROD)* 2 (Nov. 1958): 22–24.

1838 ———. "Inspection and Protection in Arms Reduction." *Journal of Arms Control* 1:1 (1963): 56–72.

1839 U.S. Arms Control & Disarmament Agency. *Advanced Technology for Arms Control Inspection*. ACDA Report ST–105. Vol. 5. Los Angeles: North American Aviation, 1967.

1840 ———. *Analysis of Requirements for Automation of Data Processing for Inspection Field Tests*. ACDA Report WEC–29. New York: Burroughs, 1964.

1841 ———. *Design of Field Test of Inspection in Production of Strategic Delivery Vehicles*. ACDA Report WEC–18. Ann Arbor: Bendix, 1964.

1842 Vance, Robert T. "Inspection: Essential Element of Arms Control and Disarmament." Ph.D. diss., George Washington Univ., 1965.

1843 Vost, Peter. "Wenn der Revisor Kommt . . . [When the inspector comes . . .]." *Europaische Begegnung* 10 (Jan. 1970): 6–9.

INSPECTION TECHNIQUES

1844 Avallone, Eugene A. "Inspection for Disarmament: High Precision Gyroscopes and Accelerometers." In Seymour Melman, ed., *Inspection for Disarmament*. New York: Columbia Univ. Press, 1958, pp. 130–33.

1845 Barten, John H. "Inspection of Technology." *Disarmament and Arms Control* 3 (Spring 1965): 41–49.

1846 Boley, Bruno A. "Critical Aspects of Air Frame Design and Production." In Seymour Melman, ed., *Inspection for Disarmament*. New York: Columbia Univ. Press, 1958, pp. 139–46.

1847 Burlage, Henry, Jr. "Amenability of the Air-Borne Propulsion Systems Industry to Production Inspection." In Seymour Melman, ed., *Inspection for Disarmament*. New York: Columbia Univ. Press, 1958, pp. 147–57.

1848 Derman, Cyrus, and Morton Klein. "On the Feasibility of Using a Multiple Linear Regression Model for Verifying a Declared Inventory." In Seymour Melman, ed., *Inspection for Disarmament*. New York: Columbia Univ. Press, 1958, pp. 220–24.

1849 Feld, Bernard T., et al. *The Technical Problems of Arms Control*. New York: Institute for International Order, 1960.

1850 Katz, Amrom H. "Feasibility and Palatability of Disarmament: Some Technical Aspects." *Disarmament* 7 (Sept. 1965): 1–6.

1851 Kolcum, Edward H. "Operational Russian Satellites Scan U.S." *Aviation Week & Space Technology* (Feb. 22, 1965): 22.

1852 Linde, Hans A. "Verification Requirements for a Production Cutoff of Weapons-Grade Fissionable Material." In Richard J. Barnet and Richard A. Falk, eds., *Security in Disarmament*. Princeton: Princeton Univ. Press, 1965, pp. 69–79.

1853 Marsel, Charles J. "Technical Memorandum on the Feasibility of Inspection of Certain Aspects of Long-Range Missile Propellants." In Seymour Melman, ed., *Inspection for Disarmament*. New York: Columbia Univ. Press, 1958, pp. 158–70.

1854 Phelps, John B. "Some Problems of Missile Production Inspection." In David H. Frisch, ed., *Arms Reduction: Program and Issues*. New York: Twentieth Century Fund, 1961, pp. 104–22.

Zonal Approach

1855 Abt, Clark C. "Progressive Zonal Inspection of Disarmament." *Disarmament and Arms Control* 2 (Winter 1963–64): 90–95.

1856 Inglis, David R. "The Region-By-Region System of Inspection and Disarmament." *Journal of Conflict Resolution* 9:2 (1965): 187–99.

1857 Sohn, Louis B. "Progressive Zonal Inspection: Basic Issues." In Seymour Melman, ed., *Disarmament: Its Politics and Economics*. Boston: American Academy of Arts & Sciences, 1962, pp. 121–33.

1858 ———. "Zonal Inspection." *Disarmament and Arms Control* 2 (Spring 1964): 204–07.

1859 U.S. Arms Control & Disarmament Agency. *Progressive Inspection for Disarmament:* *The Concept of Progressive Zonal Inspection.* ACDA Pub. 13. Washington, D.C.: G.P.O., 1963.

1860 Wheeler, Gershon J. "Inspection in a Nuclear-Free Zone." *Journal of Conflict Resolution* 7:3 (1963): 394–97.

On-Site Technique

1861 Holst, Johan J. "Fixed Control Posts and European Stability." *Disarmament and Arms Control* 2 (Summer 1964): 262–98.

1862 Ulrich, R. R. *Fiber Optic Seals: A Portable System for Field Use in International Safeguards and Arms Control Applications.* Washington, D.C.: Harry Diamond Laboratories for U.S. ACDA, Oct. 1971.

1863 Willot, Albert. *Désarmement: Les Postes d'Observation.* Brussels: Editions de l'Institut de Sociologie de l'Université Libre de Bruxelles, 1968.

1864 Windsor, Philip. "Observation Posts." In Evan Luard, ed., *First Steps to Disarmament*. New York: Basic Books, 1965.

Aerial Surveillance

1865 Brandenberger, Arthur J. "What Can Photos Tell Us." *International Science and Technology* 69 (Sept. 1967): 56–62, 65–66.

1866 Brown, Neville. "Reconnaissance from Space." *World Today* 27 (Feb. 1971): 68–76.

1867 Butz, J. S. "New Vistas in Reconnaissance from Space." *Air Force and Space Digest* 51 (Mar. 1968): 46–56.

1868 Chevallier, Raymond. "Role du Renseignement Aerien en Temps de Paix." *Forces Aeriennes Françaises* 20 (Nov. 1965): 540–46.

1869 Cornelius, George. "Air Reconnaissance— Great Silent Weapon." *U.S. Naval Institute Proceedings* 85 (July 1959): 35–42.

1870 Davies, Merton E., and Bruce C. Murray. "Inspection of Earth from Orbit." *The View from Space: Photographic Exploration of the Planets.* New York: Columbia Univ. Press, 1971, pp. 9–33.

1871 "Detection of ICBM's Key in MOL Approval." *Aviation Week & Space Technology* (Sept. 27, 1965): 26–27.

1872   Galloway, Alec. "A Decade of U.S. Reconnaissance Satellites." *Interavia* 27:4 (1972): 376–80.

1873   Greenwood, Ted. "Reconnaissance and Arms Control." *Scientific American* 228 (Feb. 1973): 14–25.

1874   ———. *Reconnaissance, Surveillance and Arms Control.* Adelphi Paper, no. 88. London: International Institute for Strategic Studies, 1972.

1875   Jasani, Bhupendra. "Verification Using Reconnaissance Satellites." *SIPRI Yearbook of World Armament and Disarmament.* New York: Humanities Press, 1973, pp. 60–101.

1876   Jensen, Neils. *Optical and Photographic Reconnaissance Systems.* New York: Wiley, 1968.

1877   Katz, Amrom H. "Observation Satellites: Problems and Prospects." *Astronautics* 5 (Apr. 1960): 26–29 ff; 5 (June 1960): 26–29 ff; 5 (July 1960): 28–29 ff; 5 (Aug. 1960): 30 ff; 5 (Sept. 1960): 32–33 ff; 5 (Oct. 1960): 36–37 ff.

1878   Klass, Philip J. "Anti-Soviet Laser Use Suspected." *Aviation Week & Space Technology* (Dec. 8, 1975): 12–16.

1879   ———. "Keeping the Nuclear Peace: Spies in the Sky." *New York Times Magazine* (Sept. 3, 1972): 6–7, 31–32, 35–36.

1880   ———. *Secret Sentries in Space.* New York: Random House, 1971.

1881   Latour, Charles. "Ocean Surveillance from the Sky." *NATO's Fifteen Nations* 19 (Oct.–Nov. 1974): 34–43.

1882   Levison, Walter J. "Capabilities and Limitations of Aerial Inspection." In Seymour Melman, ed., *Inspection for Disarmament.* New York: Columbia Univ. Press, 1958, pp. 59–74.

1883   Moore, Otis C. "No Hiding Place in Space." *Air Force Magazine* 57 (Aug. 1974): 43–48.

1884   Ossenbeck, Frederick J., and Patricia C. Kroeck, eds. *Open Space and Peace: A Symposium on Effects of Observation.* Stanford, Ca.: Hoover Institution Press, 1964.

1885   Perry, G. E. "Cosmos Observation." *Flight International* (July 1, 1971): 29–32.

1886   ———. "The Cosmos Programme." *Flight International* (Dec. 26, 1968): 1077–79.

1887   ———. "The Cosmos Programme." *Flight International* (May 8, 1969): 773–76.

1888   ———. "Reconnaissance Aspects of 8-day Cosmos Satellites." *Spaceflight* 10 (June 1968): 204–06.

1889   Possony, Stefan T. "Open Skies, Arms Control, and Peace." *Air Force and Space Digest* 47 (Mar. 1964): 71–72.

1890   Pursglove, S. David. "Electronics Expands Vision of Sky Spies." *Electronic Design* (Oct. 11, 1965): 26–33.

1891   Rochlin, Robert S. "Observation Satellites for Arms Control Inspection." *Journal of Arms Control* 1:3 (1963): 224–27.

1892   "Snoopy's Brothers." *Nature* [London] (June 7, 1969): 909–10.

1893   "Soviets Resume Satellite Intercept Tests." *Aviation Week & Space Technology* (Feb. 23, 1976): 20.

1894   "Spies in Space: They Make an Open Book of Russia." *U.S. News & World Report* (Sept. 9, 1968): 69–72.

1895   "The Spy Race in the Sky." *U.S. News & World Report* (Oct. 12, 1970): 24–26.

1896   Strother, Robert. "Space Cameras on Peace Patrol." *Reader's Digest* (Jan. 1962): 107–11.

1897   Taubenfeld, Howard J. "Surveillance from Space: The American Case for Peace Keeping and Self-Defense." *Air Force and Space Digest* 46 (Oct. 1963): 54 ff.

1898   Taylor, John W. R., and David Monday. *Spies in the Sky.* New York: Scribner's, 1972.

1899   Vayrynen, Raimo. "Military Uses of Satellite Communication." *Instant Research on Peace and Violence* 2:1 (1973): 44–49.

1900   White, Peter T. "The Camera Keeps Watch on the World." *New York Times Magazine* (Apr. 3, 1966): 26 ff.

Ike's "Open Skies" Plan

1901   Dulles, John Foster. "Foreign Ministers Conclude Conference at Geneva." *U.S. Department of State Bulletin* (Nov. 28, 1955): 872–87.

1902   [Eisenhower, Pres. Dwight D.]. "Ike's Plan

for Arms Inspection." *U.S. News & World Report* (July 29, 1955): 82.

1903   Leghorn, Col. Richard S. "How Aerial Inspection Would Work." *U.S. News & World Report* (Jan. 28, 1955): 79–94.

1904   ———. "How Aerial Inspection Would Work." *U.S. News & World Report* (July 29, 1955): 83.

1905   ———. "U.S. Can Photograph Russia from the Air Now." *U.S. News & World Report* (Aug. 5, 1955): 70–75.

1906   "Open Skies and the Atlantic Alliance: A Critical Examination." *British Survey Main Series* (Sept. 1957): 18–24.

1907   Quigg, Philip W. "Open Skies and Open Space." *Foreign Affairs* 38 (Oct. 1958): 95–106.

1908   U.S. Department of State. *The Geneva Conference of Heads of Government, July 18–23.* Pub. 6046. Washington, D.C.: G.P.O., 1955.

1909   ———. *The Geneva Meeting of Foreign Ministers, October 27, 1955 to November 16, 1955.* Pub. 6156. Washington, D.C.: G.P.O., 1955.

1910   "U.S. Informs Russia: Arms-Inspection Plan Could Start at Once." *U.S. News & World Report* (Sept. 9, 1955): 104–06.

1911   U.S. White House Disarmament Staff. *Fact Sheet on Aerial Inspection.* Disarmament Background Series, no. M–9. Washington, D.C.: G.P.O., 1957.

1912   Young, Raymond W. "The Aerial Inspection Plan and Air Space Sovereignty." *George Washington Law Review* 24 (Apr. 1956): 565–89.

Social & Psychological Approaches

1913   Bohn, Lewis C. *Knowledge Detection: A Non-Physical Inspection Method for Arms Control.* Bedminster, N.J.: Lockheed Systems Research Center, Jan. 1961.

1914   ———. "Non-Physical Inspection Techniques." In Donald G. Brennan, ed., *Arms Control, Disarmament, and National Security.* New York: Braziller, 1961, pp. 347–64; and in Quincy Wright et al., eds., *Preventing World War III.* New York: Simon & Schuster, 1962, pp. 20–39.

1915   ———. *Psychological Inspection.* Rand R–P–1917. Santa Monica, Ca.: Rand, 1960.

1916   Evan, William M. "An International Public Opinion Poll on Disarmament and 'Inspection by the People': A Study of Attitudes Toward Supranationalism." In Seymour Melman, ed., *Inspection for Disarmament.* New York: Columbia Univ. Press, 1958: 231–50.

1917   Galtung, Johan. "Popular Inspection of Disarmament Processes." *Cooperation and Conflict* 2:3–4 (1967): 121–38.

1918   Gerard, Ralph. "To Prevent Another World War: Truth Detection." *Journal of Conflict Resolution* 5:2 (1961): 212–18.

1919   McNeil, Elton B. "Psychological Inspection." *Journal of Arms Control* 1:2 (1963): 124–38.

1920   Melman, Seymour. "Inspection by the People." In Quincy Wright et al., eds., *Preventing World War III.* New York: Simon & Schuster, 1962, pp. 40–51.

1921   Milburn, Thomas W., et al. *Non-Physical Inspection Techniques.* Boston: American Academy of Arts & Sciences, 1961.

1922   O'Sullivan, Thomas C. "Social Inspection." *Journal of Conflict Resolution* 7:3 (1963): 370–78.

1923   Pool, Ithiel de Sola. "Public Opinion and the Control of Armaments." *Daedalus* 89 (Fall 1960): 984–99.

1924   Portnoy, Barry M. "Arms Control Procedure: Inspection by the People—A Reevaluation and a Proposal." *Cornell International Law Journal* 4 (Summer 1971): 153–65.

1925   U.S. Arms Control and Disarmament Agency. *Studies of the Social and Psychological Aspects of Verification, Inspection and International Assurance.* 5 vols. ACDA Report E–104. Lafayette, Ind.: Purdue Univ., School of Industrial Administration, 1968–1969.

VERIFICATION PROCEDURES

1926   Austin, Sen. Warren R. "United States Urges System of Verification in Control of International Armaments." *U.S. Department of State Bulletin* (Oct. 31, 1949): 649–51.

1927   Institute for Defense Analyses. *Verification and Response in Disarmament Agreements.* 2 vols. Washington, D.C.: G.P.O., 1962. [Woods Hole Summer Study, prepared for ACDA. Excerpts appear in *Bulletin of the Atomic Scientists* 19 (Apr. 1963): 44–48; Richard J. Barnet and Richard A. Falk, eds., *Security in Disarmament.* Princeton: Princeton Univ. Press, 1965.]

1928   Lall, Betty Goetz. "Information in Arms Control Verification." *Bulletin of the Atomic Scientists* 20 (Oct. 1964): 43–45.

1929   Phelps, John B. "Information and Arms Control." *Summer Study on Arms Control, 1960: Collected Papers.* Boston: American Academy of Arts & Sciences, 1961: 253–60. [Also in *Journal of Arms Control* 1:1 (1963): 44–45.]

1930   Piggott, Francis J. C. "Verification: Intelligence or Inspection?" *Disarmament* 6 (June 1965): 18–20.

1931   Scoville, Herbert, Jr. "Verification of Nuclear Arms Limitations: An Analysis." *Bulletin of the Atomic Scientists* 26 (Oct. 1970): 6–12.

1932   Soloman, Herbert. "Use of Sampling in Disarmament Inspection." In Seymour Melman, ed., *Inspection for Disarmament.* New York: Columbia Univ. Press, 1958, pp. 225–30.

1933   Timberlake, Clare H. "U.S. Outlines Verification Measures to Assure Compliance with Proposed Freeze of Strategic Nuclear Vehicles." *U.S. Department of State Bulletin* (Sept. 21, 1964): 413–17.

1934   [U.N.]. "Proposals to Disclose and Verify Arms, Forces." *U.N. Weekly Bulletin* (June 1, 1952): 448–51.

1935   U.S. Arms Control & Disarmament Agency. *Verification: the Critical Element of Arms Control.* Pub. 85. Washington, D.C.: G.P.O., Mar. 1976.

1936   ———. *Verification Requirements for Restrictions on Strategic Delivery Vehicles.* 2 vols. ACDA Report ST-6. Ann Arbor: Bendix, 1963.

1937   "U.S. Proposals for Progressive and Continuing Disclosure and Verification of Armed Forces and Armaments." *U.S. Department of State Bulletin* (Apr. 14, 1952): 586–89.

1938   "Verification of the Destruction of Rockets and Bombers." *Disarmament and Arms Control* 1 (Autumn 1963): 189–92.

1939   Wainhouse, David W., et al. *Arms Control Agreements: Design for Verification and Organization.* Baltimore: Johns Hopkins Press, 1968.

1940   Wright, Michael. *Disarm and Verify: An Explanation of the Central Difficulties and of National Policies.* New York: Praeger, 1964.

1941   Young, Wayland. "Verification." *Disarmament and Arms Control* 2 (Summer 1964): 342–52.

National Means

1942   Crangle, Robert D. "Spying, the CIA and the New Technology." *Ripon Forum* 6 (Feb. 1970): 7–14.

1943   Deutsch, Karl W. "The Commitment of National Legitimacy Symbols as a Verification Technique." *Journal of Arms Control* 1:4 (1963): 360–69.

1944   Helms, Richard. "Global Intelligence: The Democratic Society." *Vital Speeches* (May 15, 1971): 450–54.

1945   Hilsman, Roger. *Strategic Intelligence and National Decisions.* Glencoe, Ill.: Free Press, 1956.

1946   Howard, Michael. "Military Intelligence and Surprise Attack." *World Politics* 15 (July 1963): 701–11.

1947   Kalisch, Robert B. "Air Force Technical Intelligence." *Air University Review* 22 (July-Aug. 1971): 2–11.

1948   Lissitzyn, Oliver J. "Electronic Reconnaissance from the High Seas and International Law." *Naval War College Review* 22 (Feb. 1970): 26–34.

1949   Milly, George H. "A Proposed Approach to Arms Control: Unilateral, Extraterritorial Inspection." *Journal of Arms Control* 1:3 (1963): 219–23.

1950   Platt, Washington. *Strategic Intelligence Production.* New York: Praeger, 1957.

1951   Ransom, Harry H. *Central Intelligence and National Security.* Cambridge: Harvard Univ. Press, 1958.

1952   Vagts, Alfred. "Attachés and the Limitation of Armaments." *The Military Attaché.*

Princeton: Princeton Univ. Press, 1967, pp. 273–78.

1953 Wusserman, Benno. "The Failure of Intelligence Prediction." *Political Studies* 8 (June 1960): 156–69.

Records Evaluation

1954 Bornstein, Morris. "Inspection of Economic Records as an Arms Control Technique." *Journal of Conflict Resolution* 7:3 (1963): 404–12.

1955 Burkhead, Jesse. "The Control of Disarmament by Fiscal Inspection." In Seymour Melman, ed., *Inspection for Disarmament.* New York: Columbia Univ. Press, 1958, pp. 75–84.

1956 Johnsen, Katherine. "Better Soviet Budget Evaluation Sought." *Aviation Week & Space Technology* (Nov. 3, 1975): 21–22.

1957 Orear, Jay. "Non-Physical Inspection Techniques." *International Affairs* [Moscow] 7 (May 1961): 67–69.

1958 Polanyi, John C. "First Step—Sealed Records Caches?" *Disarmament and Arms Control* 1 (Summer 1963): 3–19.

1959 Singer, J. David. "Inspecting for Weapons Production: A Modest Computer Simulation." *Journal of Peace Research* 2:1 (1965): 18–38.

1960 ———. "Media Analysis in Inspection for Disarmament." *Journal of Arms Control* 1:3 (1963): 248–60.

International Supervision

1961 [Canada]. "The International Control of the Military Use of Atomic Energy." *External Affairs* [Ottawa] 7 (Mar. 1955): 83–94.

1962 Cavers, David F. "An Interim Plan for International Control of Atomic Energy." *Bulletin of the Atomic Scientists* 7 (Jan. 1951): 13–16.

1963 ———. "International Control of Armaments: Analysis and Proposition." *Annals of the Amer. Acad. of Pol. & Soc. Sci.* 296 (Nov. 1954): 117–30.

1964 Clark, Sen. Joseph S. "World Disarmament: An Enforceable World Law." *Vital Speeches* (Sept. 1, 1964): 688–92.

1965 Finkelstein, Lawrence S. "The United Nations and Organizations for the Control of Armaments." *International Organization* 16 (Winter 1962): 1–19.

1966 Fox, William T. R. "The International Control of Atomic Weapons." In Bernard Brodie, *The Absolute Weapon.* New York: Harcourt, Brace, 1946, pp. 169–203.

1967 Frase, Robert W. "International Control of Nuclear Weapons." *Annals of the Amer. Acad. of Pol. & Soc. Sci.* 290 (Nov. 1953): 16–26.

1968 Hydeman, Lee M., and William H. Berman. *International Control of Nuclear Maritime Activities.* Ann Arbor: Univ. of Michigan Law School, 1960.

1969 Ikle, Fred C., et al. *Alternative Approaches to the International Organization of Disarmament.* R–391–ARPA. Santa Monica, Ca.: Rand, 1962.

1970 Mohn, Paul. "Problems of Truce Supervision." *International Conciliation*, no. 478 (Feb. 1952): 1 ff.

1971 Myrdal, Alva. "The International Control of Disarmament." *Scientific American* 231 (Oct. 1974): 21–33.

1972 Nogee, Joseph L. "Soviet Policy Toward International Control of Atomic Energy." *American Political Science Review* 56 (Jan. 1962): 506–07.

1973 ———. *Soviet Policy Toward International Control of Atomic Energy.* Notre Dame: Univ. of Notre Dame Press, 1961.

1974 Oppenheimer, J. Robert. "International Control of Atomic Energy." *Foreign Affairs* 24 (Jan. 1948): 239–52.

1975 Palfrey, John G. "U.S. Approach to International Safeguards." *Nuclear Energy* (Apr. 1966): 107–11.

1976 [U.S.]. "International Control of Atomic Energy: Various Statements." *U.S. Department of State Bulletin* (Nov. 7, 1949): 686–90.

1977 U.S. Congress. Joint Committee on Atomic Energy. *The Hydrogen Bomb and International Control: Technical and Background Information.* Washington, D.C.: G.P.O., 1950.

1978   U.S. Library of Congress. Legislative Reference Service. *Should Weapons Systems Be Placed Under International Control?* Washington, D.C.: G.P.O., 1964. [Also appeared as Sen. Doc. 72, 88th Cong., 2d Sess., 1964.]

1979   Wainhouse, David W. *International Peace Observation.* London: Oxford Univ. Press, 1966.

INSPECTION & VERIFICATION

1980   Cory, Robert H., Jr. "International Inspection: From Proposals to Realization." *International Organization* 13 (Autumn 1959): 495–504.

1981   Latter, Richard. *Capabilities and Limitations of a Geneva Type Control System.* Santa Monica, Ca.: Rand, 1960.

1982   Linde, Hans A. "Organization of a 'Mixed' National and International Inspectorate." *Verification and Response in Disarmament Agreements.* Washington, D.C.: Institute for Defense Analyses, 1962, Annex II: 72–84. [Reprinted in Richard J. Barnet and Richard A. Falk, eds., *Security in Disarmament.* Princeton: Princeton Univ. Press, 1965, pp. 80–106.]

1983   Noel-Baker, Philip J. "International Inspection of Armed Forces." *British Speeches of the Day* 4 (Dec. 1946): 739–48.

1984   Schelling, Thomas C. "Arms Control: Proposal for a Special Surveillance Force." *World Politics* 12 (Oct. 1960): 1–18.

SAFEGUARDS FOR NUCLEAR MATERIALS

See also Chapter 12, Controlling Proliferation of Nuclear Weapons, Inspection & Supervision.

1985   Beaton, Leonard. "Safeguards on Plutonium." *Nature* [London] (Dec. 31, 1966): 1517–19.

1986   Bechhoefer, Bernhard G. "Plowshare Control." In Bennett Boskey and Mason Willrich, eds., *Nuclear Proliferation: Prospects for Control.* New York: Dunellen, 1970, pp. 103–15.

1987   Brady, David, and Phillip Althoff. "The Politics of Regulation: The Case of the Atomic

Energy Commission and the Nuclear Industry." *American Politics Quarterly* 1 (July 1973): 361–84.

1988   Fisher, Adrian S. "U.S. Urges Expanded Safeguards Over Peaceful Nuclear Activity." *U.S. Department of State Bulletin* (Aug. 22, 1966): 281–83.

1989   Gorove, Stephen. "Controls Over Atoms-For-Peace: Some Facts and Implications for Nuclear Disarmament." *Louisiana Law Review* 27 (Dec. 1966): 36–42.

1990   Hosmer, Craig. "Some Plain Talk on Safeguards." *Nuclear News* 13 (July 1970): 35–37.

1991   Imai, Ryukichi. *Nuclear Safeguards.* Adelphi Paper, no. 86. London: Institute for Strategic Studies, 1972.

1992   Kratzer, Myron B. "A New Era for International Safeguards." *Nuclear News* 14 (Feb. 1971): 40–43.

1993   McKnight, Allan D. *Atomic Safeguards: A Study in International Verification.* New York: U.N. Institute for Training and Research, 1971.

1994   ———. *Nuclear Non-Proliferation: IAEA and Euratom.* Occasional paper, no. 7. New York: Carnegie Endowment for International Peace, 1970.

1995   Miranda, Ugo. "Safeguard and Control Techniques for Nuclear Materials." *Euro-Spectra* 8 (Dec. 1969): 112–18.

1996   Morgan, Frank. "The International Control of Nuclear Materials." *Atom* 188 (June 1972): 105–08.

1997   Palfrey, John G. "Assurance of International Safeguards." In Bennett Boskey and Mason Willrich, eds., *Nuclear Proliferation.* New York: Dunellen, 1970, pp. 81–96.

1998   Pendley, Robert E. "International Safeguards on Nuclear Materials: A Study of Attitudes and Negotiations Concerning International Control over National Activities." Ph.D. diss., Northwestern Univ., 1968.

1999   Richardson, James L. "Controls Over Peaceful Nuclear Programs: A Review." *Journal of Conflict Resolution* 11:4 (1967): 497–503.

2000   Scoville, Herbert, Jr. "Technical Capabilities of Safeguards." In Bennett Boskey and

Mason Willrich, eds., *Nuclear Proliferation.* New York: Dunellen, 1970, pp. 53–60.

2001 SIPRI. *Safeguards Against Nuclear Proliferation.* New York: Humanities Press, 1975.

2002 Sisco, Joseph J. "United States Reviews Problems of Control of Peaceful Uses of Atomic Energy." *U.S. Department of State Bulletin* (Jan. 8, 1968): 63–65.

2003 Symington, Sen. Stuart. "The Nuclear Safeguards Delusion." *Congressional Record* 121 (July 15, 1975): S12610–13.

2004 Willrich, Mason. *Civil Nuclear Power and International Security.* New York: Praeger, 1972.

2005 ———. "International Control of Civil Nuclear Power." *Bulletin of the Atomic Scientists* 23 (Mar. 1967): 31–38.

2006 ———. "Safeguarding Atoms for Peace." *American Journal of International Law* 60 (Jan. 1966): 34–54.

2007 ———, ed. *International Safeguards and Nuclear Industry.* Baltimore: Johns Hopkins Press, 1973.

INTERNATIONAL ATOMIC ENERGY AGENCY
(IAEA)

For IAEA reports and studies, contact U.S. Atomic Energy Commission, Washington, D.C.

2008 Gmelin, W., et al. *A Technical Basis for International Safeguards.* IAEA A/CONF 49/ 773. Vienna, 1971.

2009 IAEA. *The Structure and Content of Agreements between the Agency and States Required in Connection with the Treaty on the Non-Proliferation of Nuclear Weapons.* IAEA INFCIRC/153. Vienna, 1971.

2010 U.S. Atomic Energy Commission. *Safeguards and Nuclear Materials Management: An Annotated Bibliography of Selected Literature.* No. 1141. Washington, D.C.: G.P.O., 1969.

2011 Abou-Ali, Sayed Anwar. "Système des Garanties de l'Agence Internationale de l'Energie Atomique." *Revue Egyptienne de Droit International* 26 (1970): 58–87.

2012 Australia. Department of External Affairs. "Australia and the IAEA." *Current Notes on International Affairs* 41 (Mar. 1970): 104–13.

2013 Bechhoefer, Bernhard. "Negotiating the Statute of the International Atomic Energy Agency." *International Organization* 13 (Spring 1959): 38–59.

2014 ———, and Eric Stein. "Atoms for Peace: The New International Atomic Energy Agency." *Michigan Law Review* 55 (Apr. 1957): 747–98.

2015 Cole, Sterling. "Needed: A Rebirth of the IAEA." *Nuclear News* 9 (Sept. 1966): 19–20.

2016 "Evolution of IAEA Safeguards." *International Atomic Energy Agency Bulletin* 7 (June 1965): 3–11.

2017 Gellert, Leslie. "The IAEA: Ten Years of Slow But Solid Progress." *Federation of American Scientists* (F.A.S.) *Newsletter* 20 (Mar. 1967): 5–6.

2018 Gorove, Stephen. "Maintaining Order Through On-Site Inspection: Focus on the IAEA." *Western Reserve Law Review* 18 (July 1967): 1525–47.

2019 Hall, John A. "The Safeguards Role of the International Atomic Energy Agency." *Disarmament* 7 (Sept. 1965): 11–16.

2020 [IAEA]. "International Atomic Energy Agency Report." *U.N. Monthly Chronicle* 5 (Dec. 1968): 41–43.

2021 Joshi, M. "Dead or Alive? International Atomic Energy Agency." *Bulletin of the Atomic Scientists* 17 (Mar. 1961): 95–98.

2022 McKnight, Allan D. *Atomic Safeguards: A Study in International Verification.* New York: U.N. Institute for Training and Research, 1971.

2023 ———. "IAEA Safeguards Inspection." *Neue Technik: New Techniques* 9 (Oct. 1967): 198–204.

2024 Quester, George H. "The Vienna Agency." *The Politics of Nuclear Proliferation.* Baltimore: Johns Hopkins Press, 1973, pp. 211–32.

2025 Ramming, Hans. "The International Atomic Energy Agency in Vienna." *Disarmament* 7 (Sept. 1965): 7–10.

2026 Scheinman, Lawrence. *Arms Control Special Studies Program*. Vol. 3: *The IAEA as a Political System: Implications for Arms Control*. ACDA Report WEC–126. Los Angeles: Univ. of California, Security Studies Project, 1968.

2027 ———. "Nuclear Safeguards, the Peaceful Atom, and the IAEA." *International Conciliation*, no. 572 (Mar. 1969): 1 ff.

2028 Seaborg, Glenn T. "General Conference of the International Atomic Energy Agency Holds 13th Session at Vienna." *U.S. Department of State Bulletin* (Oct. 20, 1969): 329–33.

2029 ———. "General Conference of the International Atomic Energy Agency Holds 14th Session at Vienna." *U.S. Department of State Bulletin* (Oct. 26, 1970): 485–91.

2030 ———. "The International Atom: A New Appraisal." *U.S. Department of State Bulletin* (Mar. 3, 1969): 173–84; (Mar. 10, 1969): 199–211.

2031 ———. "An International Challenge." *Bulletin of the Atomic Scientists* 26 (Nov. 1970): 5–7.

2032 ———. "The Promise of the International Atomic Energy Agency." *Science* (Oct. 13, 1967): 226–30.

2033 Stoessinger, John G. "Atoms for Peace: The International Atomic Energy Agency." In Arthur N. Holcombe, ed., *Organizing Peace in the Nuclear Age*. New York: New York Univ. Press, 1959, pp. 117–33.

2034 Szasz, Paul C. "International Atomic Energy Agency Safeguards." In Mason Willrich, ed., *International Safeguards and Nuclear Industry*. Baltimore: Johns Hopkins Press, 1973, pp. 73–141.

2035 U.S. Congress. Joint Committee on Atomic Energy. Hearings: *Agreement for Cooperation between the United States and the International Atomic Energy Agency*. 86th Cong., 1st Sess., 1959.

2036 ———. Hearings: *Participation Act of the International Atomic Energy Agency, S. 2341*. 85th Cong., 1st Sess., 1957.

2037 ———. Hearings: *Statute of the International Atomic Energy Agency*. 85th Cong., 1st Sess., May 10, 14, 15, 20, 1957.

2038 ———. Hearings: *U.S. Policy Toward the International Atomic Energy Agency*. 87th Cong., 2d Sess., Aug. 2, 1962.

2039 ———. Report: *Report of the Conferences on the Statute of the International Atomic Energy Agency by Congressional Advisors*. 85th Cong., 1st Sess., 1957.

2040 Whetten, Lawrence L. "The Relations of the International Atomic Energy Agency with Other International Organizations." Ph.D. diss., New York Univ., 1963.

EURATOM

2041 Ailleret, Col. Charles. "De l'Euratom au Programme Atomique National." *Revue de Défense Nationale* (Nov. 1956): 1319–27.

2042 Boulanger, W. "Das Verifikationsabkommen IAEA-Euratom." *Atomwirtschaft—Atomtechnik* 17 (Sept.–Oct. 1972): 510–11.

2043 "Euratom Guards Against Misuse of Nuclear Fuel: Community Controls are Automatic, Direct and Obligatory." *European Community* 93 (June 1966): 14–15.

2044 Gorove, Stephen. "Inspection and Control in Euratom." *Bulletin of the Atomic Scientists* 23 (Mar. 1967): 41–46.

2045 Helmont, Jacques Van. "Existing Arrangements for International Control of Warlike Material—2: Euratom." *Disarmament and Arms Control* 2 (Winter 1963–64): 43–56.

2046 Isayev, N. "Euratom: A Weapon of the Arms Race." *International Affairs* [Moscow] 9 (Jan. 1963): 86–90.

2047 Saeland, Einar. "Existing Arrangements for International Control of Warlike Material–4: The European Nuclear Energy Agency." *Disarmament and Arms Control* 2 (Summer 1964): 250–61.

2048 Scheinman, Lawrence. "Euratom and the IAEA." In Bennett Boskey and Mason Willrich, eds., *Nuclear Proliferation*. New York: Dunellen, 1970, pp. 63–79.

2049 Spaak, Fernand. "Euratom Safeguards." *Euratom Bulletin* 5 (Dec. 1966): 106–08.

2050 U.S. Congress. Joint Committee on Atomic Energy. Hearings: *Agreements for Cooperation with Euratom*. 85th Cong., 2d Sess., Jan. 21, 22, 1958.

2051 ———. Hearings: *Agreements for Cooperation with Euratom.* 86th Cong., 1st Sess., 1959.

2052 ———. Hearings: *Proposed Euratom Agreements* [with Associated Documents and Materials]. 2 pts. 85th Cong., 2d Sess., July 22–24, 29, 30, 1958.

2053 ———. Hearings: *To Provide for Cooperation with the European Atomic Energy Community.* 85th Cong., 1st Sess., 1957.

2054 ———. Report: *Proposed Euratom Agreement: Index to Hearings.* 85th Cong., 2d Sess., 1958.

Bilateral Controls

2055 Gorove, Stephen. "Controls Over Atoms-for-Peace Under Canadian Bilateral Agreements with Other Nations." *Denver Law Center Journal* 42 (Winter 1965): 41–49.

2056 Seaborg, Glenn T. "Existing Arrangements for International Control of Warlike Material—5: The United States Program of Bilateral Safeguards." *Disarmament and Arms Control* 2 (Autumn 1964): 422–32.

Compliance & Evasion

The historical section provides a few examples of the interwar concern with compliance and evasion; for additional references, see Part Two, *Accords, Proposals & Treaties.*

HISTORICAL ASSESSMENTS

2057 Burns, Richard Dean. "Inspection of the Mandates, 1919–1941." *Pacific Historical Review* 37 (Nov. 1968): 445–62.

2058 Carroll, Berenice A. "Germany Disarmed and Rearming, 1925–1935." *Journal of Peace Research* 3:2 (1966): 114–24.

2059 Einsten, Lewis. "Disarmament and Bootleg Armaments." *North American Review* 233 (Jan. 1932): 25 ff.

2060 Giddings, Ralph L., Jr. "Secret Weapons." *Military Review* 49 (Jan. 1969): 80–89.

2061 Gumbel, E. J. "Disarmament and Clandes-

tine Rearmament under the Weimar Republic." In Seymour Melman, ed., *Inspection for Disarmament.* New York: Columbia Univ. Press, 1958, pp. 203–19.

2062 Historical Evaluation and Research Organization (HERO). *Responses to Violations of Arms Control and Disarmament Agreements: Study "Riposte."* 3 vols. ACDA Report GC–177. Washington, D.C.: G.P.O., 1964.

2063 League of Nations. Conference for the Reduction and Limitation of Armaments [1932–1934]. Committee on Guarantees of Execution. *Documents, 1–4.* Geneva, 1934.

2064 Street, O. "Reduction of Armaments and International Guarantees." *Outlook* (Nov. 23, 1921): 465–67.

2065 U.S. Senate. Committee on the Judiciary. Staff Study: *Soviet Political Treaties and Violations.* Sen. Doc. 85. 84th Cong., 1st Sess., 1955.

2066 Wilds, Thomas. "How Japan Fortified the Mandated Islands." *U.S. Naval Institute Proceedings* 81 (Apr. 1955): 401–07.

CONTEMPORARY ISSUES

2067 Barnet, Richard J. "The Cuban Missile Crisis and Disarmament: Implications for Inspection and Enforcement." In Richard J. Barnet and Richard A. Falk, eds., *Security in Disarmament.* Princeton: Princeton Univ. Press, 1965, pp. 139–54.

2068 ———. "Violations of Disarmament Agreements." *Disarmament and Arms Control* 1 (Summer 1963): 33–48.

2069 Batten, James K. *Arms Control· and the Problem of Evasion.* Princeton: Princeton Univ., Center of International Studies, 1962.

2070 Chayes, Abram. "An Inquiry into the Workings of Arms Control Agreements." *Harvard Law Review* 85 (Mar. 1972): 905–69.

2071 "Disarmament: Enforcement of Disarmament: The Problem of the Response." [R. D. Fisher, comments; R. A. Falk, J. T. McNaughton, R. J. Barnet, discussion.] *American Society of International Law Proceedings* 56 (1962): 1–18.

2072 Fischer, Roger. "Responding to Disarmament Violations." *Bulletin of the Atomic Scientists* 18 (Sept. 1962): 22.

2073 Giddings, Ralph L., Jr. "Enforcement of Arms Control Agreements." *Military Review* 49 (Dec. 1969): 31–38.

2074 Goldblat, Jozef. *The Implementation of International Disarmament Agreements.* Stockholm: SIPRI, 1973.

2075 Greenberg, Daniel S. "Arms Control: U.S., British Conduct Big Troop Inspection Experiment." *Science* (Oct. 4, 1968): 106–07.

2076 Henkin, Louis. "Enforcement of Arms Control: Some Basic Considerations." *Journal of Arms Control* 1:3 (1963): 184–90.

2077 Ikle, Fred C. "After Detection—What?" *Foreign Affairs* 39 (Jan. 1961): 208–20.

2078 ———. "Deterring Violations of Arms Control Agreements." *Disarmament* 8 (Dec. 1965): 14–16.

2079 ———. *The Violation of Arms Control Agreements: Deterrence vs. Detection.* RM–1609–ARPA. Santa Monica, Ca.: Rand, Aug. 1960.

2080 Katz, Amrom H. *Hiders and Finders: An Approach to Inspection and Evasion Technology.* P–2432. Santa Monica, Ca.: Rand, Apr. 1961. [Reprinted in Ernest W. Lefever, ed., *Arms and Arms Control.* New York: Praeger, 1962, pp. 199–207.]

2081 Lyons, Gene M. "The Problem of Compliance Under Arms Control Agreements." *Journal of Conflict Resolution* 7:3 (1963): 351–58.

2082 Marshall, Charles Burton. "Hide and Seek: Some Dour Thoughts on Inspection." *New Republic* (Nov. 24, 1962): 14–17.

2083 ———. "A Primer on Inspection [excerpt]." *Verification and Response in Disarmament Agreements.* Washington, D.C.: Institute for Defense Analyses, 1962, Annex II: 97–102.

2084 Millis, Walter. "The Role of Police Forces in Response to Violations." In Richard J. Barnet and Richard A. Falk, eds., *Security in Disarmament.* Princeton: Princeton Univ. Press, 1965, pp. 286–319.

2085 Neild, Robert. "Cheating in a Disarmed World." *Disarmament and Arms Control* 1 (Autumn 1963): 133–43.

2086 O'Sullivan, Thomas C. "What if Nobody Cheats?" In James E. Dougherty and John F. Lehman, Jr., eds., *The Prospects for Arms Control.* New York: MacFadden-Bartell, 1965, pp. 197–204.

2087 Rivlin, Gershon. "Some Aspects of Clandestine Arms Production and Arms Smuggling." In Seymour Melman, ed., *Inspection for Disarmament.* New York: Columbia Univ. Press, 1958, pp. 191–202.

2088 "Should U.S. Risk Unenforced Disarmament?" [Yes, by August Hecksher; No, by Thomas K. Finletter.] *Foreign Policy Bulletin* (Aug. 15, 1955): 180–82.

2089 Sohn, Louis B. "Adjudication and Enforcement in Arms Control." In Donald G. Brennan, ed., *Arms Control, Disarmament, and National Security.* New York: Braziller, 1961, pp. 365–78.

2090 ———. "Enforcement of Disarmament Controls with Respect to States which Have Not Ratified A Disarmament or Arms Control Treaty." *Arms Control and Disarmament* 1 (1968): 99–107.

2091 ———. "A General Survey of Responses to Violations." *Journal of Arms Control* 1:2 (1963): 95–104.

2092 Szalita, Alberta B. "Some Comments on Psychological Aspects of Evasion and Disarmament." In Seymour Melman, ed., *Inspection for Disarmament.* New York: Columbia Univ. Press, 1958, pp. 251–60.

2093 Szarvas, Robert F. "No Place to Hide." *NATO's Fifteen Nations* 15 (Aug.–Sept. 1970): 76–80.

2094 Walsh, John B. "Technical Considerations Relating to the Covert Production and Employment of Electronic Missile Guidance Systems Under a Massive Disarmament Inspection." In Seymour Melman, ed., *Inspection for Disarmament.* New York: Columbia Univ. Press, 1958, pp. 120–29.

SURPRISE ATTACK

2095 Burns, Arthur Lee. "The International Consequences of Expecting Surprise." *World Politics* 10 (July 1958): 512–36.

2096 Kissinger, Henry A. "Arms Control, Inspection and Surprise Attack." *Foreign Affairs* 38 (July 1960): 557–75.

2097   Lall, Betty Goetz. "Diminishing the Danger of Surprise Attack in Europe." *Bulletin of the Atomic Scientists* 20 (Mar. 1964): 31–34.

2098   "Now, Instant Warning if U.S. is Attacked." *U.S. News & World Report* (Nov. 15, 1971): 108–09.

2099   Russett, Bruce M. "Cause, Surprise and No Escape." *Journal of Politics* 24 (Feb. 1962): 3–22.

2100   Schelling, Thomas C. *Surprise Attack and Disarmament.* P–1574. Santa Monica, Ca.: Rand, 1958. [Reprinted in *Bulletin of the Atomic Scientists* 15 (Dec. 1959): 413–18.]

2101   U.N. General Assembly. *Report of the Conference of Experts for the Study of Possible Measures Which Might be Helpful in Preventing Surprise Attack and for the Preparation of a Report Thereon to Governments.* U.N. Doc. A/4078–S/4145, Annexes 6, 7, 12. New York: Jan. 5, 1959.

CONTROLLING R&D

2102   Bowen, Russell J. "Soviet Research and Development: Some Implications for Arms Control Inspection." *Journal of Conflict Resolution* 7:3 (1963): 426–48.

2103   Hunter, Holland. "The Control of Unknown Arms." *Journal of Conflict Resolution* 7:3 (1963): 413–25.

2104   ———. *The Control of Unknown Arms.* Ann Arbor: Univ. of Michigan Press, 1963.

2105   Kolker, M., et al. *Unilateral Control of Military Technology.* Project Unicorn, BR–2248. Bedford, Mass.: Raytheon, 1963.

2106   Pitman, George R., Jr. *The Detection of R&D Activities Leading to New Military Capabilities.* El Segundo, Ca.: Aerospace Corp., 1964.

THEFT OF FISSIONABLE MATERIALS

2107   Abrahanson, Dean E. "Nuclear Theft and Nuclear Parks." *Environment* 16 (July–Aug. 1974): 5, 43.

2108   Adelson, Alan M. "Please Don't Steal the Atomic Bomb." *Esquire* (May 1969): 130–33, 144.

2109   Boyd, James H. "Can the Theft of Fissionable Materials and Their Use in Weapons be Prevented Under a Disarmament Program?" In Seymour Melman, ed., *Inspection for Disarmament.* New York: Columbia Univ. Press, 1958, pp. 109–19.

2110   Conrad, Thomas M. "Do-it-yourself A-bomb." *Commonweal* (July 25, 1969): 455–57.

2111   ———. "Radioactive Malevolence." *Bulletin of the Atomic Scientists* 30 (Feb. 1974): 16–20.

2112   Flood, Michael. "Nuclear Sabotage." *Bulletin of the Atomic Scientists* 32 (Oct. 1976): 29–38.

2113   Frank, Forrest R. "An International Convention Against Nuclear Theft." *Bulletin of the Atomic Scientists* 31 (Dec. 1975): 51.

2114   ———. "Nuclear Terrorism and the Escalation of International Conflict." *Naval War College Review* 28 (Fall 1976): 12–27.

2115   [Gillette, Robert]. "GAO Calls Security Lax at Nuclear Plants." *Science* (Dec. 6, 1974): 906–07.

2116   ———. "Nuclear Safeguards: Holes in the Fence." *Science* (Dec. 14, 1973): 1112–14.

2117   Ingram, Timothy H. "Nuclear Hijacking: Now Within the Grasp of Any Bright Lunatic." *Washington Monthly* 4 (Jan. 1973): 20–28.

2118   Krieger, David. "Terrorists and Nuclear Technology." *Bulletin of the Atomic Scientists* 31 (June 1975): 28–34.

2119   Larus, Joel. *Nuclear Weapons Safety and the Common Defense.* Columbus: Ohio State Univ. Press, 1967.

2120   Leachman, Robert A., and Phillip Althoff, eds. *Preventing Nuclear Theft: Guidelines for Industry and Government.* New York: Praeger, 1972.

2121   Ognibene, Peter J. "Homemade Nukes." *New Republic* (May 25, 1974): 10–11.

2122   Panati, Charles. "A Do-it-yourself A-Bomb." *Newsweek* (Mar. 10, 1975): 42 ff.

2123 Ribicoff, Sen. Abraham. "Nuclear Theft and Homemade Bombs." *Congressional Record* 120 (May 2, 1974): S6902.

2124 ———. "The Threat of Nuclear Theft and Sabotage." *Congressional Record* 120 (Apr. 30, 1974): S6621–30.

2125 Shapley, Deborah. "Plutonium Reactor Proliferation Threatens a Nuclear Black Market." *Science* (Apr. 9, 1971): 143–46.

2126 Willrich, Mason. "Terrorists Keep Out! The Problem of Safeguarding Nuclear Materials in a World of Malfunctioning People." *Bulletin of the Atomic Scientists* 31 (May 1975): 12–16.

2127 ———, and Theodore B. Taylor. *Nuclear Theft: Risks and Safeguards.* Cambridge, Mass.: Ballinger, 1974.

2128 Wohlstetter, Albert. "Terror on a Grand Scale." *Survival* 17 (May–June 1976): 98–104.

INTERNATIONAL POLICING

2129 Bechhoefer, Bernhard G. "United Nations Procedures in Case of Violations of Disarmament Agreements." *Journal of Arms Control* 1:3 (1963): 191–202.

2130 Fisher, Roger D. "International Police: A Sequential Approach to Effectiveness and Control." In Richard J. Barnet and Richard A. Falk, eds., *Security in Disarmament.* Princeton: Princeton Univ. Press, 1965, pp. 240–85.

2131 Grinyov, O. "Who Wants an International Police Force?" *International Affairs* [Moscow] 4 (Dec. 1958): 63–67.

2132 Kirk, Grayson. "Problems of International Policing." *Headline Series*, no. 64. New York: Foreign Policy Assoc., 1947.

2133 Marshall, Charles Burton. "Character and Mission of a United Nations Peace Force, Under Conditions of General and Complete Disarmament." *American Political Science Review* 59 (June 1965): 350–64.

2134 Morgenthau, Hans J. "The Impartiality of the International Police." In Richard J. Barnet and Richard A. Falk, eds., *Security in Disarmament.* Princeton: Princeton Univ. Press, 1965, pp. 320–40.

2135 Osgood, Robert E. *An International Military Force in a Disarming and Disarmed World.* Washington, D.C.: Institute for Defense Analyses, 1963.

2136 Purdom, Tom. "Reduction in Arms." *Fantasy and Science Fiction* (Aug. 1967): 4–27.

2137 Vladimirov, S. "Disarmament and the Plans for Establishing an International Police Force." *International Affairs* [Moscow] 6 (Apr. 1960): 44–49.

2138 Waskow, Arthur I., and Paul Kecskmeti. "Could Disarmament be Policed?" *Commentary* 36 (Nov. 1963): 394–98.

SELF-ENFORCING AGREEMENTS

2139 Fisher, Roger D. "Internal Enforcement of International Rules." In Seymour Melman, ed., *Disarmament: Its Politics and Economics.* Boston: American Academy of Arts & Sciences, 1962, pp. 99–120.

2140 Hammond, Paul Y. "Some Difficulties of Self-Enforcing Arms Agreements." *Journal of Conflict Resolution* 6:2 (1962): 103–15.

2141 Shestov, V. "The Main Disarmament Problem." *International Affairs* [Moscow] 16 (Oct. 1970): 35–38.

2142 Werkheiser, Don. "Disarmament Without Trust." *Journal of Human Relations* 19:2 (1971): 176–83.

SANCTIONS

2143 Blymyer, William H. "Peace Maintenance by Economic Isolation." *World Unity* 4 (Apr. 1929): 40–49.

2144 Bonn, M. J. "How Sanctions Failed." *Foreign Affairs* 15 (Jan. 1937): 350–61.

2145 Bornstein, Morris. "Economic Sanctions as Responses to Arms Control Violations." *Journal of Arms Control* 1:3 (1963): 203–18.

2146 ———. "Economic Sanctions and Rewards in Support of Arms Control Agreements." *American Economic Review* 58 (May 1968): 417–27.

2147 Brück, Otto. *Les Sanctions en Droit International Public.* Paris: Pedone, 1933.

2148 Clark, Evans, ed. *Boycotts and Peace: A Report by the Committee on Economic Sanctions.* New York: Harper, 1932.

2149 Crandall, Samuel B. *Treaties: Their Making and Enforcement.* Washington, D.C.: John Byrne, 1916.

2150 Doxey, Margaret P. *Economic Sanctions and International Enforcement.* New York: Oxford Univ. Press, 1971.

2151 Hadjuos, D. N. *Les Sanctions Internationales de la Société des Nations.* Paris: M. Giard, 1920.

2152 Martin, W. "Sanctions and Disarmament." *Annals of the Amer. Acad. of Pol. & Soc. Sci.* 126 (July 1926): 49–53.

2153 Miller, David Hunter. "Sanctions." *Annals of the Amer. Acad. of Pol. & Soc. Sci.* 126 (July 1926): 45–48.

2154 Mitrany, David. *The Problem of International Sanctions.* London: H. Milford, 1925.

2155 Nantet, Jacques. *Les Sanctions dans le Pacte de la S.D.N.* Paris: Editions Domat Montchrestien, 1936.

2156 Wild, Payson S., Jr. *Sanctions and Treaty Enforcement.* Cambridge: Harvard Univ. Press, 1934.

Six

Special Issues: Economic Consequences of Disarmament, Negotiations, Science & Technology, Bureaucratic Politics & the Military-Industrial Complex, & Legal & Psychological Dimensions

THESE "SPECIAL ISSUES" are ones that have affected arms control and disarmament (AC&D) policies and public attitudes toward these policies. In the early 1960s, it was charged by some critics that capitalist nations could not accept disarmament without seriously damaging their economy. Consequently other observers have argued that AC&D negotiations were not serious anyhow, that they were undertaken essentially for propaganda purposes or that they were pointless because "the Russians could not be trusted." Now in the 1970s, more attention is being focused on the "technological imperative" of weapons research and the role played by "bureaucratic politics" in their deployment. It is charged that unchecked weapons technology renders AC&D negotiations pointless because new, more deadly weapons are being drafted and deployed while diplomats are seeking control of the older obsolete weapons.

In the early 1960s the academic community became very much concerned with the "economic consequences" of possible AC&D treaties. Today there are relatively few people who sustain this interest—largely because few observers expect any substantial reductions in defense spending in the foreseeable future. Yet these early writings do identify and analyze most of the pertinent issues connected with the economic impact of AC&D. Both Emile Benoit and Kenneth E. Boulding have written extensively and perceptively about this matter; consequently, their co-edited *Disarmament and the Economy* (1963) provides an excellent introduction to issues.

While most of this bibliography deals with varied AC&D "negotiations," the items listed here seek to analyze the general negotiatory process which can be applied to AC&D issues. A perusal of the items indicates that a need exists for more recent research. Coral Bell's *Negotiation from Strength* (1963) is a sound introduction to this idea. The notion of "parity" in weapons is an old one in AC&D efforts; the index will suggest additional sources.

One of the gravest problems confronting current AC&D efforts is that its focus does not include weapons under development—that the development of weapons often seems to occur because of a "technological imperative," rather than because of need. Ralph Lapp's *Arms Be-*

yond Doubt: The Tyranny of Weapons Technology (1970) suggests the general nature of the dilemma, while G. T. Allison and F. A. Morris' "Armaments and Arms Control: Exploring the Determinants of Military Weapons" in *Daedalus* (1975) argues for a revision of AC&D priorities.

"Bureaucratic politics" is among the several analytical methods used to investigate the development of AC&D policies. Graham Allison's *Essence of Decision* (1971) provides an excellent introduction to this method. Closely related to defense spending decisions, and consequently AC&D policies, is the "military-industrial complex." Among the flood of books and essays are popular criticisms such as R. J. Barnet's *The Economy of Death* (1970), R. E. Lapp's *The Weapon Culture* (1969), and S. Lens' *The Military-Industrial Complex* (1970). A more sophisticated view may be found by comparing the above with C. Wright Mills' *The*

Power Elite (1956), Seymour Melman's *Pentagon Capitalism* (1970), and J. S. Baumgartner's *The Lonely Warriors: The Case for the Military-Industrial Complex* (1970). (A somewhat allied idea, the "merchants of death" thesis, is developed in Chapter 11, Controlling Arms Manufacture & Traffic, below.)

The legal and psychological dimensions of AC&D have been played down by most general accounts. International lawyers, however, have been concerned about the role of law in AC&D matters; thus given the scope of this bibliography, one should expect to find such references in several chapters. Consult the table of contents or index for a complete listing. G. Clark and L. B. Sohn have offered their views in *World Peace Through World Law* (1964). Sociologists, psychologists, and others have argued heatedly over whether human nature makes war inevitable, but they have raised more questions than they have answered.

Economic Consequences of Disarmament

BIBLIOGRAPHIES

2157 Meeker, Thomas A. *The Military-Industrial Complex: A Source Guide to the Issues of Defense Spending and Policy Control.* Los Angeles: California State Univ., Center for the Study of Armament & Disarmament, 1973.

2158 Roswell, Judith. *Arms Control, Disarmament, and Economic Planning: A List of Sources.* Los Angeles: California State Univ., Center for the Study of Armament & Disarmament, Aug. 1973.

2159 Saltman, Juliet. "Economic Consequences of Disarmament." *Peace Research Reviews* 4 (Apr. 1972): 1–88.

2160 U.S. Arms Control & Disarmament Agency. *Selected Bibliography on the Economic Aspects of Disarmament, 1961–August 1963.* Washington, D.C.: G.P.O., 1963.

2161 ———. Legislative Reference Service. *Economic Aspects of Disarmament: A Bibliography.* Washington, D.C.: G.P.O., 1963.

GENERAL ECONOMIC CONSEQUENCES

Historical to 1945

2162 Boulding, Kenneth E., and Alan Gleason. "War as an Investment: The Strange Case of Japan." *Papers of the Peace Research Society* (International) 3 (1964): 1–17.

2163 French, B. L. "Naval Reduction: What it Means in Money." *Current History* 31 (Jan. 1930): 711–17.

2164 Knight, John. "The Financial Consequences of Rearmament." *Labour Monthly* 19 (June–Oct. 1937): 353–358, 411–415, 491–496, 564–569, 634–638.

2165 Lewis, Willmott. "Our Financial and Economic Policies and Armament." *Annals of the Amer. Acad. of Pol. & Soc. Sci.* 144 (July 1929): 143–45.

2166 Stone, William T. "Economic Consequences of Rearmament." *Foreign Policy Reports* (Oct. 1, 1938): 158–72.

2167 "What Disarmament Means to Industry." *American Industry* (Nov. 1921): 7–21.

Contemporary, Since 1945

2168 Alexander, Archibald S. "Economic Aspects of Arms Control." *Temple Law Quarterly* 38 (Winter 1965): 152–58.

2169 ———. "The Problem and the Opportunity." *Bulletin of the Atomic Scientists* 20 (Apr. 1964): 8–10.

2170 Benoit, Emile. "Affording Disarmament: An Analysis, a Mode, Some Proposals." *Columbia University Forum* 5 (Winter 1962): 4–10.

2171 ———. "The Costs of Disarmament: A Weapons Freeze vs. Disarmament." *Current* 52 (Oct. 1964): 45–47.

2172 ———. "Economic Adjustments to Arms Control." *Journal of Arms Control* 1:2 (1963): 105–11.

2173 ———. "Economic Consequences of Disarmament." *Disarmament* 4 (Dec. 1964): 11–14.

2174 ———. "The Economics of Disarmament— Would Adjustment be Difficult?" *Challenge* 10 (June 1962): 91–113.

2175 ———, and Kenneth Boulding, eds. *Disarmament and the Economy.* New York: Harper & Row, 1963.

2176 Boulding, Kenneth E. "Economic Implications of Arms Control." In Donald G. Brennan, ed., *Arms Control, Disarmament, and National Security.* New York: Braziller, 1961, pp. 153–64.

2177 Callahan, Geraldine. "Economic Aspects of Disarmament." *Business Literature* 38 (Feb. 1966): 11–12.

2178 "Economic Hazards of Arms Reductions: What We Must Pay for a Normal Economy in a Stable World." *Nation* (Mar. 28, 1959): 265–78.

2179 *Economic and Social Consequences of Disarmament.* Vienna: International Institute for Peace, 1962.

2180 Economist Intelligence Unit, Ltd. *The Economic Effects of Disarmament.* Toronto: Univ. of Toronto Press, 1963.

2181 Feinstein, Otto. "Disarmament: Economic Effects." *Current History* 47 (Aug. 1964): 81–87.

2182 "The Financing of Disarmament." *Journal of Finance* 18 (May 1963): 113–60.

2183 Fishman, Leslie. "Economic Plan for Disarmament." *Bulletin of the Atomic Scientists* 18 (Mar. 1962): 37–38.

2184 Foster, William C. "The Economics of Arms Control and Disarmament." *U.S. Department of State Bulletin* (July 1, 1963): 7–11.

2185 "Fourteenth Pugwash Symposium: Economic and Social Aspects of Disarmament." *Pugwash Newsletter* 9 (July 1971): 6–15.

2186 Ganguli, B. N. "Economic Consequences of Disarmament [Part 1]." *India Quarterly* 8 (Oct.–Dec. 1962): 323–54.

2187 ———. "Economic Consequences of Disarmament [Part 2]." *India Quarterly* 9 (Jan.– Mar. 1963): 21–65.

2188 Harris, Seymour E. "The Economics of Disarmament." *Current History* 33 (Oct. 1957): 216–20.

2189 Hart, Albert G., et al. "Predicaments of Peace." *Harper's* 236 (June 1968): 86–88, 90–91.

2190 Hoeber, Francis P. "The Economic Impacts of Disarmament." *Orbis* 7 (Fall 1963): 631–47.

2191 Lall, Betty Goetz. "Arms Reduction Impact." *Bulletin of the Atomic Scientists* 22 (Sept. 1966): 41–44.

2192 Leontief, Wassily W. "Alternatives to Armament Expenditures." *Bulletin of the Atomic Scientists* 20 (June 1964): 19–21.

2193 ———, and Marvin Hoffenberg. "The Economic Effects of Disarmament." *Scientific American* 204 (Apr. 1961): 47–55.

2194 Levine, Robert A. "General Disarmament As a Policy Goal: Economic Aspects." In James E. Dougherty and John F. Lehman, Jr., eds., *The Prospects for Arms Control.* New York: MacFadden-Bartell, 1965, pp. 163–70.

2195 Melman, Seymour, ed. *Disarmament: Its Politics and Economics.* Boston: American Academy of Arts & Sciences, 1962.

2196 ———. "Economics of Armament and Disarmament." *New University Thought* 2 (Spring 1962): 79–92.

2197 Mills, Edwin S. "The Economic Effects of Arms Control." In Charles A. Barker, ed., *Problems of World Disarmament.* Boston: Houghton Mifflin, 1963, pp. 143–57.

2198 Morris, Jacob. "Disarmament and the Rate of Profit." *Science and Society* 26 (Summer 1962): 326–31.

2199 Nathan, Otto. "The Economics of Permanent Peace." *Bulletin of the Atomic Scientists* 19 (June 1963): 21–24.

2200 Patel, Surendra J. "Economic Consequences

of Disarmament." *Bulletin of the Atomic Scientists* 18 (Nov. 1962): 7–12.

2201 Perk, W. "If Disarmament Were to Come." *World Trade Union Movement* [London] 4 (Apr. 1960): 11–14.

2202 Piel, Gerard. "The Economics of Disarmament." *Bulletin of the Atomic Scientists* 16 (Apr. 1960): 117–122, 126.

2203 Rosen, Sumner N. "The New Orthodoxy on Disarmament Economics." *Correspondent* 33 (Winter 1965): 61–69.

2204 Royce, William S. "Economy of Disarmament." *Nation* (Sept. 8, 1962): 105–09.

2205 Schelling, Thomas C. "Experts Report on Economics of a Disarmed World." *U.N. Review* 9 (Apr. 1962): 22–24.

2206 U.N. Department of Economics and Social Affairs. *Economic and Social Consequences of Disarmament.* 2 vols. New York, 1962.

2207 U.S. Arms Control & Disarmament Agency. *Economic Impacts of Disarmament: Report to the U.S. Arms Control and Disarmament Agency.* ACDA Pub. 2. Washington, D.C.: G.P.O., Jan. 1962.

2208 ———. *Economic and Social Consequences of Disarmament: U.S. Reply to the Inquiry of the Secretary General of the United Nations.* Washington, D.C.: G.P.O., 1962. [Reprinted in *Documents on Disarmament, 1962.* Washington, D.C.: G.P.O., 1963, I: 217–75.]

2209 ———. *Economic and Social Consequences of Disarmament: U.S. Reply to the Inquiry of the Secretary General of the United Nations* [with revised statistical tables]. ACDA Pub. 21. Washington, D.C.: G.P.O., 1964.

2210 ———. *United States Report to Secretary General Thant on the Economic Consequences of Disarmament, March 26, 1968.* ACDA Pub. 52. Washington, D.C.: G.P.O., Sept. 1968. [Reprinted in *Documents on Disarmament, 1968.* Washington, D.C.: G.P.O., 1969, pp. 196–203.]

2211 Ward, Barbara. "Disarm Against a Sea of Troubles." *Development Forum* 1 (Feb. 1973): 1–5.

Soviet (Marxist) View

2212 Apremont, B. "Economie Sovietique et le Désarmement." *Politique Etrangère* [Paris] 24 (1959): 587–90.

2213 Glagolev, Igor S. *The Effects of Disarmament on the Economy.* Moscow: Science Publishing, 1964.

2214 Gromov, L. "Disarmament and Employment." *International Affairs* [Moscow] 7 (May 1961): 52–59.

2215 ———, and V. Strigachev. "Invalid Economic 'Arguments' About Disarmament." *International Affairs* [Moscow] 8 (Sept. 1962): 32–39.

2216 ———. "Some Economic Aspects of Disarmament." *International Affairs* [Moscow] 6 (Mar. 1960): 26–34.

2217 Ivanov, K., et al. "Economic Programme for Disarmament." *International Affairs* [Moscow] 8 (Dec. 1962): 8–16; 9 (Jan. 1963): 19–34.

2218 Kaigl, Vladimir. "Aspects Economiques du Désarmement." *Nouvelle Revue Internationale* [Paris] 3 (Nov. 1960): 16–30.

2219 ———. "The Economic Possibility of Disarmament." *World Marxist Review* 3 (Nov. 1960): 16–22.

2220 Lange, O. "Disarmament and the World Economy." *Polish Perspectives* [Warsaw] 3 (Oct. 1960): 3–9.

2221 Marzani, Carl, and Victor Perlo. *Dollars and Sense of Disarmament.* New York: Marzani & Munsell, 1960.

2222 Perlo, Victor. "Economic Consequences of Disarmament." *New World Review* 28 (June 1960): 29–34.

2223 Popovic, N. "Economic Aspects of the Problem of Disarmament." *Review of International Affairs* [Belgrade] (Dec. 1, 1957): 4–6.

2224 Rubinstein, Modest I. *If the Arms Race Were Stopped.* London: Soviet News, 1958.

2225 ———. "Economic Problems of Peaceful Coexistence." *Kommunist* 13 (Sept. 1959): 85–96.

2226 Urbar, Ludek. "Some Economic Aspects of Disarmament." *World Marxist Review* 6 (Aug. 1963): 23–29.

2227 Wieczinski, Joseph L. "Economic Consequences of Disarmament: The Soviet View." *Russian Review* 27 (July 1968): 275–85.

View from Other Countries

2228 Adams, E. G. *Economic Effects of Disarmament: The Example of Canada.* Vienna: International Institute for Peace, Apr. 1963.

2229 Bacskai, Tamas. *The Armament Race and the Developing Countries.* Vienna: International Institute for Peace, June 1967.

2230 Duisenberg, W. F. *The Economic Consequences of Disarmament in the Netherlands.* Assen, The Netherlands: Van Gorcum, 1965. [Also in *Journal of Peace Research* 2:2 (1965): 177–86.]

2231 Gromov, L. "Britain: The Economic Aspects of Disarmament." *International Affairs* [Moscow] 9 (June 1963): 52–58.

2232 Joenniemi, Pertti. "An Analysis of the Economic Consequences of Disarmament in Finland." *Papers of the Peace Research Society* (International) 13 (1970): 29–46.

2233 Mezerik, Avrahm G. *Disarmament: Impact on Underdeveloped Countries, Political, Social and Economic.* New York: International Review Service, 1961.

2234 Rosenbluth, Gideon. *The Canadian Economy and Disarmament.* Toronto: St. Martin's Press, 1967.

IMPACT OF DEFENSE SPENDING

Historical to 1945

2235 Beaver, Daniel R. "Newton D. Baker and the Genesis of the War Industries Board, 1917–1918." *Journal of American History* 52 (June 1965): 43–58.

2236 Crowell, Benedict, and Robert F. Wilson. *The Armies of Industry: Our Nation's Manufacture of Munitions for a World in Arms, 1917–1918.* 2 vols. New Haven: Yale Univ. Press, 1921.

2237 Crowell, J. Franklin. *Government War Contracts.* New York: Oxford Univ. Press, 1923.

2238 Cuff, Robert D. "A 'Dollar-a-Year Man' in Government: George N. Peek and the War Industries Board." *Business History Review* 41 (Winter 1967): 404–20.

2239 Himmelberg, Robert F. "The War Industries Board and the Antitrust Question in November 1918." *Journal of American History* 52 (June 1965): 59–74.

2240 Hudson, Manley O. "Private Enterprise and Public War." *New Republic* (Nov. 16, 1921): 26–30. [Supplement.]

2241 Jefferson, Charles E. "Military Preparedness as a Peril to Democracy." *Annals of the Amer. Acad. of Pol. & Soc. Sci.* 46 (1916): 228–36.

2242 U.S. Senate. Special Committee to Study Problems of American Small Business. Report: *Economic Concentration and World War II.* 79th Cong., 2d Sess., 1946.

Contemporary, Since 1945

2243 Adams, Benson D. "The Arms Race and Defense Spending." *Orbis* 14 (Winter 1971): 1037–43.

2244 Art, Robert J. *The TFX Decision.* Boston: Little, Brown, 1968.

2245 Augustine, Norman R. "Military R&D: There is a Return on the Investment." *Government Executive* 7 (Nov. 1975): 43.

2246 Benoit, Emile. "The Monetary and Real Costs of National Defense." *American Economic Review* 58 (May 1968): 398–416.

2247 ———, and H. Lubek. "World Defense Expenditures." *Journal of Peace Research* 3:2 (1966): 97–113.

2248 Boulding, Kenneth E. "Requirements for a Social Systems Analysis of the Dynamics of the World War Industry." *Papers of the Peace Research Society* (International) 9 (1968): 1–8.

2249 Buehler, Col. V. M. "Economic Impact of Defense Programs." *Statistical Reporter* 68 (July 1967): 68.

2250 Clayton, James L., comp. *The Economic Impact of the Cold War: Sources and Readings.* New York: Harcourt, Brace & World, 1970.

2251 Clifford, Clark M. "The Defense Establishment, Domestic Development." *Vital Speeches* (Nov. 1, 1968): 1.

2252 Cranston, Sen. Alan. "The Budget Process: Defense Expenditures." *Congressional Record* 121 (Oct. 29, 1975): S18890–93.

2253 Dempsey, Richard, and Douglas Schmude. "Occupational Impact of Defense Spending." *Monthly Labor Review* 94 (Dec. 1971): 12–15.

2254 *The Economics of Defense Spending: A Report.* Washington, D.C.: U.S. Chamber of Commerce, Committee on Economic Policy, 1965.

2255 Hitch, Charles J. "The Defense Sector: Its Impact on American Business." In Jacob K. Javits et al., *The Defense Sector and the American Economy.* New York: New York Univ. Press, 1968, pp. 27–34.

2256 ———, and Roland McKean. *The Economics of Defense in the Nuclear Age.* Cambridge: Harvard Univ. Press, 1960.

2257 Javits, Sen. Jacob K.; Charles J. Hitch; and Arthur F. Burns. *The Defense Sector and the American Economy.* New York: New York Univ. Press, 1968.

2258 Kane, Francis X. "Arms Control and Defense Spending." *Strategic Review* 1 (Spring 1973): 33–37.

2259 Kaufman, Richard F. "Pentagon Procurement: Billion-Dollar Grab-Bag." *Nation* (Mar. 17, 1969): 328–32.

2260 Korb, Lawrence J. "The Bicentennial Defense Budget: A Critical Appraisal." *Armed Forces and Society* 2 (Fall 1975): 128–39.

2261 McCarthy, Terence. "The Garrison Economy." *Columbia University Forum* 9 (Fall 1966): 27–32.

2262 Melman, Seymour. *Our Depleted Society.* New York: Holt, Rinehart & Winston, 1965.

2263 ———. *The Permanent War Economy: American Capitalism in Decline.* New York: Simon & Schuster, 1974.

2264 ———. "Ten Propositions on the War Economy." *American Economic Review* 62 [Pt. 2: *Papers and Proceedings*] (May 1972): 312–18.

2265 ———. "Too Much Defense Spending?" *Challenge* 11 (June 1963): 4–7.

2266 Miksche, Ferdinand O. "The Economics of Self-Destruction." *Atlas* 18 (Dec. 1969): 24–25.

2267 Russett, Bruce M. "The Revolt of the Masses: Public Opinion on Military Expenditures." *Peace, War, and Numbers.* Beverly Hills, Ca.: Sage, 1972.

2268 Segel, Frank W. "Capital Allocation Criteria for Defense Contractors." Ph.D. diss., George Washington Univ., 1972.

2269 Shepler, Cora E. "United States Defense Expenditures Abroad." *Survey of Current Business* 42 (Jan. 1962): 14–16.

2270 Stockfish, J. A., ed. *Planning and Forecasting in the Defense Industries.* Belmont, Ca.: Wadsworth, 1962.

2271 Tarshis, Lorie. "The Arithmetic of Defense Spending." *Nation* (Mar. 28, 1959): 267–71.

2272 Truppner, W. C. *Estimated Shipments, Value-Added and Employment on Defense Work in Selected Industries—1963.* Internal Note N–188. Arlington, Va.: Institute for Defense Analyses, 1964.

2273 U.S. Arms Control & Disarmament Agency. *Defense Dependency of the Metalworking Machinery and Equipment Industry and Disarmament Implications.* Resources Management Corporation, ACDA Report E–130. Washington, D.C.: G.P.O., 1969.

2274 ———. *The Economic Impact of Reductions in Defense Spending: Summary of Research Prepared for . . . [the ACDA].* Washington, D.C.: G.P.O., July 1, 1972.

2275 ———. *The Timing of the Impact of Government Expenditures.* Univ. of Pittsburgh, ACDA Report E–157. Washington, D.C.: G.P.O., 1970.

2276 U.S. Congress. Joint Economic Committee. *Background Material on Economic Aspects of Military Procurement and Supply.* Washington, D.C.: G.P.O., 1964.

2277 ———. Hearings: *Impact of Defense Procurement.* 86th Cong., 2d Sess., Jan. 28–30, 1960.

2278 ———. Hearings: *Progress Made By the Department of Defense in Reducing the Impact of Military Procurement on the Economy.* 87th Cong., 1st Sess., June 12, 1961.

2279 ———. Report: *The Military Budget and National Economic Priorities Report, Together With Supplementary Views.* 91st Cong., 1st Sess., 1969.

2280 ———. Report: *National Security and the American Economy in the 1960's.* Study Paper no. 18. 86th Cong., 2d Sess., 1960.

2281 Weidenbaum, Murray L. "Defense Expenditures and the Domestic Economy." In Edwin Mansfield, ed., *Defense, Science, and Public Policy*. New York: Norton, 1968.

2282 ——. *The Economics of Peacetime Defense*. New York: Praeger, 1974.

2283 ——. "The Impact of Military Procurement on American Industry." In J. A. Stockfish, ed., *Planning and Forecasting in the Defense Industries*. Belmont, Ca.: Wadsworth, 1962.

2284 Welsh, Edward C. "Arms Budgets and the Space Frontier." *Air Force and Space Digest* 47 (July 1964): 43–44.

2285 Wilson, E. Raymond. *The Economic and Political Impact of Military Spending on the U.S. Economy*. Washington, D.C.: Friends Committee on National Legislation, 1961.

Regional & State Impact

2286 Arrington, L. J. *The Defense Industry of Utah*. Logan: Utah State Univ., 1965.

2287 Bolton, Roger E. *Defense Purchases and Regional Growth*. Washington, D.C.: Brookings Institution, 1966.

2288 Bowen, Brent R. "Defense Spending in Alaska." *Alaskan Review of Business and Economic Conditions* 8 (July 1971): 1–16.

2289 Clayton, James L. "Defense Spending: Key to California's Growth." *Western Political Quarterly* 15 (June 1962): 280–93.

2290 Husing, John E. "The Relative Impact of Civilian vs. Military Defense Payrolls on a Small Region, 1964–1968." Ph.D. diss., Claremont Graduate School, 1971.

2291 *The Impact of Large Installations on Nearby Areas: Accelerated Growth*. Beverly Hills, Ca.: Sage, 1968.

2292 Isard, Walter, and James Ganschow. *Awards of Prime Military Contracts by County, State and Metropolitan Area of the United States, Fiscal Year 1960*. Philadelphia: Regional Science Research Institute, n.d.

2293 Karaska, Gerald J. "Interregional Flows of Defense-Space Awards." *Papers of the Peace Research Society* (International) 5 (1966): 45–62.

2294 Osterbend, Carter C. "Impact of Aerospace and Defense Programs on Florida's Economy." *Business and Economic Dimensions* 3 (Apr. 1967): 1–8.

2295 Steiner, George A. *National Defense and Southern California, 1961–1970*. Los Angeles: Southern California Associates, Committee for Economic Development, 1961.

2296 Tiebout, Charles M. "The Regional Impact of Defense Expeditures: Its Measurement and Problems of Adjustment." In Roger E. Bolton, ed., *Defense and Disarmament: The Economics of Transition*. Englewood Cliffs, N.J.: Prentice-Hall, 1966, pp. 125–39.

2297 U.S. Arms Control & Disarmament Agency. *The Regional and Industrial Distribution of Defense Subcontracting and Indirect Procurement*. Department of Labor, ACDA Report E/RA–69. Washington, D.C.: G.P.O., 1970.

2298 Weidenbaum, Murray L., and Ben Chiehliu. "Effect of Disarmament on Regional Income Distribution." *Journal of Peace Research* 3:1 (1966): 89–92.

2299 Wu Yuan-li, et al. *Fluctuations in Defense Spending and Their Economic Impact on Hawaii*. Hanna: Univ. of Hawaii, Economics Research Center, 1965.

U.S. War/Peace Economics

2300 Benoit, Emile. "Alternatives to Defense Production." In Amitai Etzioni and Martin Wenglinisky, eds., *War and Its Prevention*. New York: Harper & Row, 1970, pp. 99–126.

2301 Bolton, Roger E., ed. *Defense and Disarmament: The Economics of Transition*. Englewood Cliffs, N.J.: Prentice-Hall, 1966.

2302 Boulding, Kenneth E. *National Priorities: Military, Economic, and Social*. Washington, D.C.: Public Affairs Press, 1969.

2303 *The Economic Necessity of Disarmament*. Vienna: International Institute for Peace, 1966.

2304 Gilmore, John S., et al. *Defense Systems Resources in the Civil Sector*. ACDA Report E–103. Washington, D.C.: G.P.O., 1967.

2305 Grampp, William D. "Defense and Disarmament: Some Economic Surprises." *Michigan Business Review* 16 (Jan. 1964): 10–16.

2306 Nadler, Eugene. "Some Economic Disadvantages of the Arms Race." *Journal of Arms Control* 1:3 (1963): 597–602.

2307 Schelling, Thomas C. "Arms Control Will Not Cut Defense Costs: What Would Arms Control Mean for U.S. Economy, How Would it Affect the Federal Budget?" *Harvard Business Review* 39 (Mar.–Apr. 1961): 6–8.

Economic Impact of Disarmament

2308 Aptheker, Herbert, ed. *A Symposium: Disarmament and the American Economy: Studies in the Ideology, Politics and Economics of Disarmament in the U.S.A.* New York: New Century Publishers, 1960.

2309 Baran, Paul A. "The Choice Before Us. . . ." *Nation* (Mar. 28, 1959): 265–67.

2310 Benoit, Emile. "The Economic Impact of Disarmament in the United States." In Seymour Melman, ed., *Disarmament: Its Politics and Economics.* Boston: American Academy of Arts & Sciences, 1962, pp. 134–57.

2311 ———. "The Propensity to Reduce the National Debut Out of Defense Savings." *American Economic Review* 51 (May 1961): 455–59.

2312 ———. "Would Disarmament Mean a Depression?" *New York Times Magazine* (Apr. 28, 1963): 44–50.

2313 Chase, Stuart. "Peace, It's Terrible! Economic Consequences of Peace, It Could Be Wonderful!" *Progressive* 24 (Feb. 1960): 17–19.

2314 Colm, Gerhard. "Economic Implications of Disarmament." *Illinois Business Review* 14 (July 1967): 6–8.

2315 Davis, Richard M. "Issues in Arms Control and Employment." *Northwest Review* 5 (Summer 1962): 33–40.

2316 Fishman, Betty G., and Leslie Fishman. "Disarmament: How Will the Economy Respond?" *Quarterly Review of Economics and Business* 2 (Aug. 1962): 15–23.

2317 Grampp, William D. "False Fears of Disarmament." *Harvard Business Review* 42 (Jan.–Feb. 1964): 28–30.

2318 Knorr, Klaus E. "We Can Afford Disarmament—If We Make the Right Political Decisions." *Challenge* 8 (Jan. 1960): 62–65.

2319 Kokat, Robert G. "Some Implications of the Economic Impact of Disarmament on the Structure of American Industry." *Kyklos* 19:3 (1966): 481–502.

2320 Lall, Betty Goetz. "New Frontiers of Urban Excellence?" *Bulletin of the Atomic Scientists* 22 (Mar. 1966): 37–40.

2321 Lewis, David V. "Could Business Cope with Peace?" *Business Horizons* 6 (Spring 1963): 25–33.

2322 Lombardi, Ricardo. "Disarmament and the American Economy." *Review of International Affairs* [Belgrade] (Mar. 1, 1960): 10–12.

2323 Lumer, Hyman. "Disarmament and the American Economy." *Political Affairs* 39 (Jan. 1960): 22–34.

2324 Melman, Seymour. "Labor's Economic Stake in Disarmament." *I.U.D. Digest* [Industrial Union Department, AFL-CIO] 3 (Fall 1958): 27–32.

2325 ———. "Peace Without Depression." *Saturday Review* (Dec. 2, 1961): 19–22, 75.

2326 National Planning Assoc. *Can the American Economy Adjust to Arms Control?* Washington, D.C., 1960. [Summarized in *Looking Ahead* 8 (Mar. 1960): 5–7.]

2327 Newcomer, Mabel. "The Economics of Disarmament: Expansion in Civilian Markets at Home and Abroad." *Vital Speeches* (Feb. 1, 1957): 230–34.

2328 Piel, Gerard. "Can Our Economy Stand Disarmament?" *Atlantic Monthly* (Sept. 1962): 35–40.

2329 Pratt, J. A. "Economic Implications of Disarmament." *Pittsburgh Business Review* 8 (Sept. 1964): 1–3.

2330 "The Promises of Peace." *Business Week* (July 27, 1968): 56–58.

2331 Rosen, Sumner N. "Disarmament and the Economy." *War/Peace Report* 6 (Mar. 1966): 12–14.

2332 Seligman, Ben B. "Can the U.S. Convert to Peace?"·*Dissent* 7 (Winter 1960): 12–16.

2333 Sweezy, Paul M. "Power Blocks to a Peace Economy." *Nation* (Mar. 28, 1959): 275–78.

2334 "Swords to Plowshares: What $25 Billion Could Do For Mankind." *Newsweek* (Mar. 20, 1961): 42.

2335 [U.S.]. "Announcement by President Johnson: Formation of a Committee on the Economic Impact of Defense and Disarmament, December 21, 1963." *Documents on Disarmament, 1963.* Washington, D.C.: G.P.O., 1964, pp. 649–51.

2336 ———. *Report of the Committee on the Economic Impact of Defense and Disarmament.* [Submitted to Pres. Johnson, July 30, 1965]. Washington, D.C.: G.P.O., 1965.

2337 Weidenbaum, Murray L. "Economic Adjustments to Disarmament." *University of Washington Business Review* 22 (Feb. 1963): 3–11.

2338 ———. "The Economic Impact of an Arms Cut: Comment." *Review of Economics and Statistics* 49 (Nov. 1967): 612–13.

2339 ———. "Industrial Impact of Disarmament: An Exploratory Analysis." *American Journal of Economics and Sociology* 22 (Oct. 1963): 513–26.

2340 ———. "Reductions in Defense Spending: The Problem and the Government Response." *University of Washington Business Review* 24 (Apr.–June 1965): 5–12.

Reliance on Defense Spending

2341 Anderson, Richard M. "Anguish in the Defense Industry." *Harvard Business Review* 47 (Nov.–Dec. 1969): 162–164 ff.

2342 Benoit, Emile. "Will Defense Cuts Hurt Business." *Michigan Business Review* 8 (Mar. 1957): 1–6.

2343 Blacksby, F. T., and D. C. Paige. "Defense Expenditure—Burden or Stimulus?" *Survival* 2 (Nov.–Dec. 1960): 242–46.

2344 Bolton, Roger E. "Defense Spending: Burden or Prop?" *Defense and Disarmament.* Englewood Cliffs, N.J.: Prentice-Hall, 1966, pp. 1–33.

2345 Boulding, Kenneth E. "Can We Afford a War-less World?" *Saturday Review* (Oct. 6, 1962): 17–20.

2346 Harris, Seymour. "Can We Prosper Without Arms?" *New York Times Magazine* (Nov. 8, 1959): 20–24.

2347 Ikle, Doris M. *How Arms Controls Would Affect the National Security Budget.* P–2255. Santa Monica, Ca.: Rand, 1961. [Summarized in *Air Force* (Oct. 1961): 38–39.]

2348 Kast, Fremont, and Jim Rosenzweig. "Could We Afford Disarmament?" *Business and Society* (Autumn 1961): 16–24.

2349 Kaufman, Richard F. "MIRVing the Boondoggle: Contracts, Subsidy and Welfare in the Aerospace Industry." *American Economic Review* 62 [Pt. 2: *Papers and Proceedings*] (May 1972): 288–95.

2350 Klein, Lawrence R. "The Role of War in the Maintenance of American Economic Prosperity." *Proceedings of the American Philosophical Society* (Dec. 30, 1971): 507–11.

2351 Melman, Seymour. "Economic Alternatives to Arms Prosperity." *Annals of the Amer. Acad. of Pol. & Soc. Sci.* 351 (Jan. 1964): 10–16.

2352 ———. *The War Economy of the United States: Readings on Military Industry and Economy.* New York: St. Martin's Press, 1971.

2353 Reich, Michael. "Does the U.S. Economy Require Military Spending?" *American Economic Review* 62 [Pt. 2: *Papers and Proceedings*] (May 1972): 296–303.

2354 *Report From Iron Mountain on the Possibility and Desirability of Peace.* New York: Dial Press, 1967.

2355 Swomley, John M., Jr. "Why We Can't Afford to Disarm." *Fellowship* (July 1, 1962): 12–16, 29.

2356 Weidenbaum, Murray L. "Arms and the American Economy: A Domestic Convergence Hypothesis." *American Economic Review* 58 (May 1968): 428–37.

2357 "What will Take Up the Slack?" *Business Week* (July 18, 1964): 50–67.

Impact of Defense Realignment

2358 Dyckman, John W. "Some Regional Development Issues in Defense Program Shifts." *Papers of the Peace Research Society* (International) 2 (1965): 191–203.

2359 Isard, Walter, and Eugene Schooler. "An Economic Analysis of Local and Regional Impacts of Reduction of Military Expenditures." *Papers of the Peace Research Society* (International) 1 (1964): 15–44.

2360 Leontief, Wassily W., et al. "The Economic Impact—Industrial and Regional—Of an Arms Cut." *Review of Economics and Statistics* 47 (Aug. 1965): 217–41.

2361 "Military Cutbacks Will Send Tremors Through Industry." *Business Week* (Dec. 6, 1969): 91, 94, 96.

2362 Mosbeck, E. J. "Information on the Impact of Reductions in Defense Expenditures on the Economy." *Quarterly Review of Economics and Business* 5 (Fall 1965): 47–65.

2363 Murphy, Charles J. V. "The Defense Industry is Facing Trouble." *Fortune* 70 (Aug. 1964): 140–42 ff.

2364 Oberdorfer, Don. "Where the Cutback Cuts Deep." *Saturday Evening Post* (Sept. 12, 1964): 17–24.

2365 Udis, Bernard, ed. *The Economic Consequences of Reduced Military Spending.* Lexington, Mass.: D. C. Heath, 1973.

2366 U.S. Arms Control & Disarmament Agency. *Adjustments of the U.S. Economy to Reductions in Military Spending.* Report E–156. Boulder: Univ. of Colorado, Dec. 1970.

2367 ———. *Adjustments to Reduced National Defense Expenditures in New Mexico.* Report E–58. Kirschner Associates, July 1971.

2368 ———. *Ammunition Production for Vietnam: Impact on South-East Kansas.* Report E–142. Midwest Research Institute, Feb. 1970.

2369 ———. *Community Readjustment to Reduced Defense Spending: Case Studies of Potential Impact on Seattle-Tacoma, Baltimore, and New London-Groton-Norwich.* National Planning Assoc., ACDA Report E–57. Washington, D.C.: G.P.O., 1965.

2370 ———. *Survey of Economic Models for Analysis of Disarmament Impacts.* Report E–59. Ann Arbor: Univ. of Michigan, July 1965.

2371 U.S. Department of Defense. *The Challenge of Change.* Washington, D.C.: G.P.O., 1965.

2372 Weidenbaum, Murray L. "Adjusting to a Defense Cutback: Public Policy Toward Business." *Quarterly Review of Economics and Business* 4 (Spring 1964): 7–14.

2373 Witze, Claude. "Defense Cutback—What It Means to Industry." *Air Force and Space Digest* 53 (Jan. 1970): 45–49.

Base Closures

2374 Loveday, Douglas F. *The Role of U.S. Military Bases in the Philippine Economy.* Memo RM–5801–ISA. Santa Monica, Ca.: Rand, Apr. 1971.

2375 Lynch, John E. *Local Economic Development After Military Base Closures.* New York: Praeger, 1970.

2376 Terner, Ian D. *The Economic Impact of a Military Installation on the Surrounding Area: A Case Study of Fort Devens and Ayer, Massachusetts.* Boston: Federal Reserve Bank of Boston, 1965.

2377 U.S. Arms Control & Disarmament Agency. *Economic Impact of Military Base Closings.* 2 vols. Report E–90. Lawrence: Univ. Press of Kansas, Apr. 1970.

2378 U.S. President's Economic Adjustment Committee. *Economic Recovery: Community Response to Defense Decisions to Close Bases.* Washington, D.C.: Defense Office of Economic Adjustment, 1975.

Contract Cancellations

2379 Rainey, R. B., Jr., et al. *Seattle's Adaptation to Recession.* R–1353–NSF. Santa Monica, Ca.: Rand, Sept. 1973.

2380 Reid, R. J., and W. L. K. Schwarz. *Space and Defense Spending Cutback: The Economic Impact of Space and Defense Spending on the Minneapolis-St. Paul Metropolitan Area.* Minneapolis: North Star Research and Development Institute, 1970.

2381 U.S. Arms Control & Disarmament Agency. *A Case Study of the Effects of the Dyna-Soar Contract Cancellation upon Employees of the Boeing Company in Seattle, Washington.* Washington (State) Employment Security Department, ACDA Report E/RA–13. Washington, D.C.: G.P.O., 1965.

Unemployment Problems

2382 "Defense Cuts Bring a New Kind of Job Crisis." *U.S. News & World Report* (May 18, 1964): 80 ff.

2383 Fulton, Joseph F. "Employment Impact of Changing Defense Programs." *Monthly Labor Review* 87 (May 1964): 508–17.

2384 Oliver, Richard P. "The Employment Effect of Defense Expenditures." *Monthly Labor Review* 90 (Sept. 1967): 10–11.

2385 ———. "Employment Effects of Reduced Defense Spending." *Monthly Labor Review* 94 (Dec. 1971): 3–11.

2386 Oppenheimer, Martin. "Disarmament and Unemployment in the U.S." *Gandhi Marg* 43 (July 1963): 211–18.

2387 Riefler, Roger F., and Paul B. Downing. "Regional Effect of Defense Effort on Employment." *Monthly Labor Review* 91 (July 1968): 1–8.

2388 Treires, James J. "Arms and Employment: Kicking the Defense Habit." *Nation* (Feb. 23, 1970): 200–204.

2389 U.S. Arms Control & Disarmament Agency. *Characteristics of Potential Unemployment Problems in Vietnam Procurement Reductions.* Report E–168. Research Analysis Corp., June 1970.

2390 ———. *Pensions and Severance Pay for Displaced Defense Workers.* Report E–138. Urbana: Univ. of Illinois, Institute of Labor and Industrial Relations, July 1969.

2391 ———. *Post Layoff Experiences.* Vol. 1: *Republic Aviation Workers.* Vol. 2: *The Transferability of Defense Job Skills to Non-Defense Occupations.* Report E–69. State of New York, Department of Labor, Aug. 1966.

2392 ———. *Reemployment Experiences.* Report E–67. Martin Marietta, Dec. 1966.

2393 ———. *Reemployment Experiences of Defense Workers: A Statistical Analysis of the Boeing, Martin and Republic Lay-offs.* Univ. of Colorado, ACDA Report E–113. Washington, D.C.: G.P.O., 1968.

ECONOMIC CONVERSION

2394 "Aerospace: A New Life for a Billion-Dollar Industry?" *U.S. News & World Report* (May 24, 1965): 109–10.

2395 "As Plutonium Fades, AEC Calls Industry In." *Business Week* (Dec. 26, 1964): 58–64.

2396 Bernstein, Barton J. "The Debate on Industrial Conversion." *American Journal of Economics and Sociology* 26 (Apr. 1967): 159–72.

2397 Booth, Paul R. *Converting America: Economic Conversion and the War on Poverty.* Ann Arbor: Center for Research on Conflict Resolution, 1965.

2398 Carter, Luther J. "Swords into Ploughshares: Hanford Makes the Switch." *Science* (Mar. 6, 1970): 1357–58, 1360–61.

2399 Christodoulou, Aris P. *Conversion of Nuclear Facilities from Military to Civilian Uses: A Case Study in Hanford, Washington.* New York: Praeger, 1970.

2400 Cox, Donald W. *The Perils of Peace: Conversion to What?* Philadelphia: Chilton Books, 1965.

2401 "Defense Conversion." *New Englander* (Mar. 1965): 13–15, 32–35.

2402 "Defense and Disarmament." *American Economic Review* 53 (May 1953): 413–51.

2403 DuBoff, Richard B. "Converting Military Spending to Social Welfare: The Real Obstacles." *Quarterly Review of Economics and Business* 12 (Spring 1972): 7–22.

2404 Goldberger, A. A. "Conversion: The Magnitude of the Task." *Nation* (Mar. 28, 1959): 271–75.

2405 Isard, Walter, and S. Czmanski. "A Model for the Projection of Conversion Potentialities." *Papers of the Peace Research Society* (International) 5 (1966): 1–14.

2406 Lall, Betty Goetz. "Conversion of Defense Resources." *Bulletin of the Atomic Scientists* 22 (Jan. 1966): 46–48.

2407 Lockheed Aircraft Corp. "The Disarmament Outlook for a Large Defense Contractor." In Roger E. Bolton, ed., *Defense and Disarmament.* Englewood Cliffs, N.J.: Prentice-Hall, 1966, pp. 114–24.

2408 Mack-Forlist, Daniel M., and Arthur Newman. *The Conversion of Shipbuilding from Military to Civilian Markets.* New York: Praeger, 1970.

2409 Manning, Rip. "Focus on Grand Prairie." *Nation* (Mar. 28, 1959): 269.

2410 Marine, Gene. "Focus on Santa Monica." *Nation* (Mar. 28, 1959): 273.

2411 Melman, Seymour, ed. *The Defense Economy: Conversion of Industries and Occupations to Civilian Needs.* New York: Praeger, 1970.

2412 ———. *The Peace Race.* New York: Ballantine, 1961.

2413 Members of Congress for Peace Through Law. "Report on Economic Conversion: An Issue for the Seventies." *Congressional Record* 117 (Oct. 27, 1971): S16872–74.

2414 Mottur, Ellis R. *Conversion of Scientific and Technical Resources: Economic Challenge— Social Opportunity.* Monograph no. 8. Washington, D.C.: George Washington Univ., Program on Policy Studies in Science & Technology, Mar. 1971.

2415 Pick, Eric G. "Economic Aspects of Converting the Military Electronics Industry to Civilian Uses." Ph.D. diss., Columbia Univ., 1963.

2416 Raymond, Richard C. "Problems of Industrial Conversion." In Seymour Melman, ed., *Disarmament: Its Politics and Economics.* Boston: American Academy of Arts & Sciences, 1962, pp. 158–76.

2417 Schafers, Ted. "Focus on St. Louis." *Nation* (Mar. 28, 1959): 270.

2418 Ullmann, John E., ed. *Potential Civilian Markets for the Military-Electronics Industry: Strategies for Conversion.* New York: Praeger, 1970.

2419 U.S. Arms Control & Disarmament Agency. *Defense Systems Resources in the Civil Sector.* Report E–103. Denver: Denver Univ., Denver Research Institute, July 1967.

2420 ———. *Industrial Conversion Potential in the Shipbuilding Industry.* Report E–66. Midwest Research Institute, May 1966.

2421 "U.S. Arms Industry Could Shift to Peacetime Production." *War/Peace Report* 2 (Nov. 1962): 4–7.

2422 U.S. Senate. Committee on Labor and Public Welfare. Report: *Convertibility of Space and Defense Resources to Civilian Needs: A Search for New Employment Potentials.* 88th Cong., 2d Sess., 1964.

2423 Weidenbaum, Murray L. "Shifting from Defense to Non-Defense Spending." *Papers of the Peace Research Society* (International) 5 (1966): 15–43.

2424 ———. "The Transferability of Defense Industry Resources to Civilian Use." In Roger E. Bolton, ed., *Defense and Disarmament.* Englewood Cliffs, N.J.: Prentice-Hall, 1966, pp. 101–13.

Worker Skills

2425 Bluestone, Irving. "Problems of the Worker in Industrial Conversion." *Journal of Arms Control* 1:3 (1963): 589–96.

2426 Cambern, John R. "Skill Transfers: Can Defense Workers Adapt to Civilian Occupations." *Monthly Labor Review* 92 (June 1969): 21–25.

2427 U.S. Arms Control & Disarmament Agency. *The Potential Transfer of Industrial Skills from Defense to Non-Defense Industries.* 2 vols. Report E–102. State of California, Department of Labor, June 1968.

2428 ———. *The Transferability and Retraining of Defense Engineers.* Report E–110. Stanford, Ca.: Stanford Research Institute, Nov. 1967.

Diversification

2429 Barber, Arthur. "Some Thoughts on Diversification." *Signal* 19 (Apr. 1965): 26–29.

2430 Barlow, Derek. "A Million-Dollar Diversification Plan." *Electronics* (Apr. 5, 1965): 122–23.

2431 Barney, Walter. "Instruments Outlook: Growth and Diversification." *Electronics* (Aug. 8, 1966): 110–14.

2432 Beller, William S. "Firms Urged to Diversify While Defense Spending is High." *Missiles and Rockets* (May 9, 1966): 34, 36–37.

2433 Gilmore, John S., and Dean C. Coddington. "Diversification Guides for Defense Firms." *Harvard Business Review* 44 (May–June 1966): 144–55.

2434 Miller, Thomas G. *Strategies for Survival in the Aerospace Industry.* Cambridge, Mass.: Arthur D. Little, 1964.

2435   Ullmann, John E. "Alternatives to Arma-ments." *Saturday Review* (May 4, 1963): 13.

2436   U.S. Arms Control & Disarmament Agency. *Defense Industry Diversification: An Analysis with Twelve Case Studies.* Report E–68 by Denver Research Institute. Washington, D.C.: G.P.O., 1966.

2437   Walsh, John B. "Oak Ridge: Twenty Years After, Diversification is the Goal." *Science* (Nov. 12, 1965): 863–65.

Research & Development

2438   Berkowitz, Marvin. *The Conversion of Military-Oriented Research and Development to Civilian Uses.* New York: Praeger, 1970.

2439   Freeman, C. *Economic Effects of Disarma-ment: Research and Development.* Vienna: International Institute for Peace, Apr. 1963.

2440   Howell, R. P., et al. *The Economic Impact of Defense R&D Expenditures: In Terms of Value Added and Employment Generated, An Exploratory Study.* Stanford, Ca.: Stan-ford Research Institute, Feb. 1966.

2441   Nelson, Richard R. "Adjusting Research and Development." *Bulletin of the Atomic Scien-tists* 20 (Apr. 1964): 15–19.

2442   ———. "Impact of Arms Reduction on Re-search and Development." *American Economic Review* 53 (May 1963): 435–46.

2443   SIPRI. *Resources Devoted to Military Re-search and Development: An International Comparison.* New York: Humanities Press, 1972.

2444   Solo, Robert A. "Gearing Military R&D to Economic Growth." *Harvard Business Re-view* 40 (Nov.–Dec. 1962): 49–54.

2445   U.S. National Science Foundation. *National Patterns of R&D Resources, Funds and Manpower in the United States, 1953–1968.* Washington, D.C.: G.P.O., 1967.

2446   U.S. Senate. Committee on Labor and Public Welfare. Report: *The Impact of Federal Re-search and Development Policies upon Sci-entific and Technical Manpower.* 89th Cong., 2d Sess., 1966.

Negotiations: Process, Politics, & Propaganda

NEGOTIATORY PROCESS

See also, Chapter 3, General Surveys, United States.

2447   Bartos, Otomar J. "How Predictable are Negotiations?" *Journal of Conflict Resolu-tion* 11:4 (1967): 481–96.

2448   Bell, Coral. *Negotiation from Strength.* New York: Knopf, 1963.

2449   Benoit, Emile. "The Conditions of Disarma-ment." *Antioch Review* 15 (Fall 1955): 362–74.

2450   Bonham, G. Matthew. "Simulating Interna-tional Disarmament Negotiations." *Journal of Conflict Resolution* 15:3 (1971): 299–315.

2451   Bull, Hedley. "The Scope for Super-Power Agreement." *Arms Control and National Security.* New York: Hudson Institute, 1969.

2452   Cheney, John, et al. "The Effects of Com-municating Threats and Promises Upon the Bargaining Process." *Journal of Conflict Resolution* 16:2 (1972): 99–107.

2453   Craig, Gordon A. "Totalitarian Approaches to Diplomatic Negotiation." In A. O. Sarkissian, ed., *Studies in Diplomatic History and His-toriography in Honour of G. P. Gooch, C.H.* London: Longmans, 1961, pp. 107–25.

2454   Druckman, D. "Human Factors in Interna-tional Negotiations." *Sage Professional Pa-pers in International Studies* [No. 02–020] 2 (1973): 1–96.

2455   "Dynamics of the Bargaining Process in a Bureaucratic Age [Symposium Discussion]." In William R. Kintner and Robert L. Pfaltzgraff, Jr., eds., *SALT: Implications for Arms Control in the 1970's.* Pittsburgh: Pittsburgh Univ. Press, 1973, pp. 187–96.

2456   Fisher, Roger D. "Constructing Rules that Affect Governments." In Donald G. Brennan, ed., *Arms Control, Disarmament, and Na-tional Security.* New York: Braziller, 1961, pp. 56–67.

2457   Gabelic, Andro. "General, Not Bloc Approaches." *Review of International Affairs* [Belgrade] (July 5, 1971): 25–27.

2458 Hornstein, Harvey A., and David W. Johnson. "The Effects of Process Analysis and Ties to His Group Upon the Negotiator's Attitudes Toward the Outcomes of Negotiations." *Journal of Applied and Behavioral Science* 2 (Oct.–Dec. 1966): 449–63.

2459 Ignatieff, George. "Negotiating Arms Control." *International Journal* 30 (Winter 1975): 92–101.

2460 Ikle, Fred C. *How Nations Negotiate.* New York: Harper & Row, 1964.

2460a ———, and Nathan Leites. "Political Negotiation as a Process of Modifying Utilities." *Journal of Conflict Resolution* 6:1 (1962): 19–28.

2461 Jack, Homer A. "Disarmament as a Career." *War/Peace Report* 7 (Jan. 1967): 14–16.

2462 Jensen, Lloyd. "Approach-Avoidance Bargaining in the Test-Ban Negotiations." *International Studies Quarterly* 12 (June 1968): 152–60.

2463 Korhonen, Keijo T. "Disarmament Talks as an Instrument of International Politics." *Cooperation and Conflict* 5:3 (1970): 152–67.

2464 Martin, Anthony D. *Negotiation Strategies for Arms Control: Some Alternatives for the Next Decade and Beyond.* Santa Monica, Ca.: Southern California Arms Control & Foreign Policy Seminar, 1972.

2465 Niezing, Johan. "On the History of Disarmament Negotiations: Some Sociological Comments." *International Spectator* (July 8, 1969): 1237–50.

2466 Plischke, Elmer. "Summit Diplomacy: Its Uses and Limitations." *Virginia Quarterly Review* 48 (Summer 1972): 321–44.

2467 Sawyer, Jack, and Harold Guetzkow. "Bargaining and Negotiating in International Relations." In Herbert C. Kelman, ed., *International Behavior: A Social-Psychological Analysis.* New York: Holt, Rinehart & Winston, 1965.

2468 Schelling, Thomas C. "Reciprocal Measures for Arms Stabilization." In Donald G. Brennan, ed., *Arms Control, Disarmament, and National Security.* New York: Braziller, 1961, pp. 167–86.

2469 ———. "Signals and Feedback in the Arms Dialogue." *Bulletin of the Atomic Scientists* 21 (Jan. 1965): 5–10.

2470 ———. *The Strategy of Conflict.* Cambridge: Harvard Univ. Press, 1960.

2471 Singer, Eugene. "A Bargaining Model for Disarmament Negotiations." *Journal of Conflict Resolution* 7:2 (1963): 21–25.

2472 Stevens, Carl M. "On the Theory of Negotiation." *Quarterly Journal of Economics* 72 (1950): 77–97.

2473 Stone, Jeremy J. *Strategic Persuasion: Arms Limitations Through Dialogue.* New York: Columbia Univ. Press, 1967.

2474 Vayrynen, Raimo. "Prospects for Arms Limitation Talks: Negotiations, Asymmetries and Neutral Countries." *Coexistence* 9 (Mar. 1972): 1–15.

NEGOTIATORY POLITICS

For additional accounts, see Chapter 3, *General Surveys;* therein are extended sections on the United States and the Soviet Union. Also see Chapter 4 for League of Nations and United Nations accounts.

2475 Alexandrov, V. "Western Diplomacy Zigzags on Disarmament." *International Affairs* [Moscow] 6 (Aug. 1960): 56–60.

2476 Bechhoefer, Bernhard G. "Negotiating with the Soviet Union." In Donald G. Brennan, ed., *Arms Control, Disarmament, and National Security.* New York: Braziller, 1961, pp. 269–81.

2477 Bronfenbrenner, Urie. "The Mirror Image in Soviet-American Relations." *Journal of Social Issues* 17:3 (1961): 45–46.

2478 Bull, Hedley. "Disarmament and the International System." *Australian Journal of Politics and History* 5:2 (1959): 41–50.

2479 Burns, E. L. M. *A Seat at the Table.* Toronto: Clarke, Irwin, 1972.

2480 Campbell, John C. "Negotiations with the Soviets: Some Lessons of the War Period." *Foreign Affairs* 34 (Jan. 1956): 305–19.

2481 Cohen, Benjamin V. "Disarmament and Political Settlement." *New Leader* (July 1, 1957): 16–18.

2482   Cory, Robert H., Jr. "Images of United States Disarmament Policy in the International Disarmament Negotiating System." *Journal of Conflict Resolution* 7:3 (1963): 560–68.

2483   Craig, Gordon A. "Technique of Negotiation." In Ivo J. Lederer, ed., *Russian Foreign Policy: Essays in Historical Perspective.* New Haven: Yale Univ. Press, 1962.

2484   Dennett, Raymond, and Joseph E. Johnson, eds. *Negotiating With the Russians.* Boston: World Peace Foundation, 1951.

2485   Dunn, Frederick S. "Peace Strategies in an Unstable World." *Yale Review* 37 (Winter 1948): 226–40.

2486   Fedder, Edwin H. "Communication and American-Soviet Negotiating Behavior." *Background* 8 (Aug. 1964): 105–20.

2487   Garris, Jerome, and Laurie Wiseberg. *Security Studies Project.* Vol. 7: *Trends in International Polarity: Implications for Arms Control.* ACDA Report WEC-126. Los Angeles: Univ. of California, Arms Control Special Studies Program, 1968.

2488   Jensen, Lloyd. *The Postwar Disarmament Negotiations: A Study in American-Soviet Bargaining Behavior.* Ph.D. diss., Univ. of Michigan, 1963.

2489   ———. "Soviet-American Bargaining Behavior in the Postwar Disarmament Negotiations." *Journal of Conflict Resolution* 7:3 (1963): 522–41.

2490   Kertesz, Stephen D. "Reflections on Soviet and American Negotiating Behavior." *Review of Politics* 19 (Jan. 1957): 3–36.

2491   Kulski, Waldyslaw W. "Soviet Diplomatic Techniques." *Russian Review* 19 (July 1960): 217–26.

2492   Lall, Arthur S. *How Communist China Negotiates.* New York: Columbia Univ. Press, 1968.

2493   ———. "The Nonaligned in Disarmament Negotiations." *Bulletin of the Atomic Scientists* 20 (May 1964): 17–21.

2494   Leites, Nathan. *Styles in Negotiations: East and West on Arms Control, 1958–1961.* RM–2838 ARPA. Santa Monica, Ca.: Rand, Nov. 1961.

2495   Lvov, M. "Motion in a Circle." *International Affairs* [Moscow] 10 (Apr. 1964): 15–19.

2496   Mates, L. "The Big Powers and Disarmament." *Review of International Affairs* [Belgrade] (Feb. 16, 1960): 1–3.

2497   Pipes, Richard. *International Negotiation: Some Operational Principles of Soviet Foreign Policy.* Washington, D.C.: G.P.O., 1972. [Memorandum for Senate, Subcommittee on National Security and International Operations.]

2498   Price, Charles C. "A Look at Disarmament." *Bulletin of the Atomic Scientists* 14 (June 1958): 229–31.

2499   Rapacki, Adam. "Socialist Diplomacy of Peace in the World Arena." *World Marxist Review* 5 (June 1962): 12–18.

2500   Triska, Jan F., and David D. Finlay. "Soviet-American Relations: A Multiple-Symmetry Model." *Journal of Conflict Resolution* 9:2 (1965): 37–53.

2501   U.S. Senate. Committee on Government Operations. *The Soviet Approach to Negotiations: Selected Writings.* Washington, D.C.: G.P.O., 1969.

2502   Wedge, Bryant, and Cyril Muromcew. "Psychological Factors in Soviet Disarmament Negotiations." *Journal of Conflict Resolution* 9:2 (1965): 18–36.

2503   ———. *Soviet Negotiating Behavior at the Geneva Disarmament Conference.* Princeton: Institute for the Study of National Behavior, 1963.

2504   Young, Kenneth T. *Negotiations with the Chinese Communists: United States' Experience, 1953–1967.* New York: McGraw-Hill, 1968.

U.S. Suspicions of Soviet Union

2505   Baldwin, Hanson W. "Russia and Arms: A Dark Case History." *New York Times* (Feb. 14, 1960).

2506   Berkes, Ross N. "American Fears of the Soviet Union." *Current History* 42 (May 1962): 287–90, 301.

2507   "Do Talks With Russia Pay Off?" *U.S. News & World Report* (May 20, 1955): 35–37.

2508 Eastland, Sen. James O. "Will Russia Honor Any New Agreements?" *U.S. News & World Report* (Aug. 5, 1955): 88–90.

2509 Katz, Amrom H. "The Stumbling Block of Soviet Secrecy." *War/Peace Report* 2 (Oct. 1962): 10.

2510 Lowenthal, Richard. "Negotiate With Russia? What's the Use?" *New York Times Magazine* (Sept. 10, 1961): 21 ff.

2511 Neal, Fred Warner. *Disarmament and the Communist Threat.* Philadelphia: American Friends Service Committee, 1962.

2512 Steibel, Gerald L. *How Can We Negotiate With the Communists?* New York: National Strategy Information Center, 1972.

PROPAGANDA & NEGOTIATIONS

2513 Barghoorn, Frederick C. *Soviet Foreign Propaganda.* Princeton: Princeton Univ. Press, 1964, pp. 101–14.

2514 Haven, Andrew. "The Time Factor in Soviet Foreign Policy." *Problems of Communism* 5 (Jan.–Feb. 1956): 1–8.

2515 Kaplan, Morton A. "Psychological One-Upmanship." *New Leader* (Oct. 19, 1959): 10–12.

2516 Lawson, R. C. "UN: Disarmament and Propaganda." *Current History* 22 (Apr. 1952): 216–20.

2517 Luard, Evan. *Peace and Opinion.* London: Oxford Univ. Press, 1962.

2518 Nogee, Joseph L. "Propaganda and Negotiation: The Case of the Ten-Nation Disarmament Committee." *Journal of Conflict Resolution* 7:3 (1963): 510–21.

2519 Orwant, Jack E. "Effects of Derogatory Attacks in Soviet Arms Control Propaganda." *Journalism Quarterly* 49 (Spring 1972): 107–15.

2520 Rudzinski, Alexander W. "Soviet Peace Offensives." *International Conciliation,* no. 490 (Apr. 1953): 175–225.

2521 U.S. Senate. Committee on Foreign Relations. Hearings: *Psychological Aspects of International Relations.* 89th Cong., 2d Sess., 1966.

2522 ———. Committee on Judiciary. Staff Study: *Soviet Disarmament Propaganda and the Strange Case of Marshal Grechko.* 93d Cong., 2d Sess., 1974.

2523 Whitten, John B., and Arthur Larson. *Propaganda: Toward Disarmament in the War of Words.* Dobbs Ferry, N.Y.: Oceana, 1964.

Science, Technology & AC&D

2524 Agnew, Harold M. "Technological Innovation: A Necessary Deterrent of Provocation?" *Air Force & Space Digest* 50 (May 1967): 66–70.

2525 Brodie, Bernard. "Military Demonstration and Disclosure of New Weapons." *World Politics* 5 (Jan. 1953): 281–301.

2526 Bush, Vannevar. *Modern Arms and Free Men: A Discussion of the Role of Science in Preserving Democracy.* New York: Simon & Schuster, 1949.

2527 Calder, Nigel. *Technopolis: Social Control of the Uses of Science.* London: Panther, 1970.

2528 ———, ed. *Unless Peace Comes: A Scientific Forecast of New Weapons.* New York: Viking, 1968.

2529 Clemens, Walter C., Jr. "The Ecology of Weaponry." *Bulletin of the Atomic Scientists* 26 (Sept. 1970): 27–31.

2530 Deutsch, Karl W. "The Impact of Science and Technology on International Politics." *Daedalus* 88 (Fall 1959): 669–85.

2531 Ellul, Jacques. "The Technological Order." *Technology and Culture* 3 (Fall 1962): 394–99.

2532 Erickson, John, ed. *The Military-Technical Revolution.* New York: Praeger, 1966.

2533 Feld, Bernard T., et al., eds. *Impact of New Technologies on the Arms Race.* Cambridge: M.I.T. Press, 1971.

2534 Fuller, Gen. J. F. C. *Armament and History.* New York: Scribner's, 1945.

2535 ———. *The Conduct of War, 1789–1961.* New Brunswick: Rutgers Univ. Press, 1961.

2536 Green, Harold P. "The New Technological Era: A View from the Law." *Bulletin of the Atomic Scientists* 23 (Nov. 1967): 12–18.

2537   Hoffmann, Frederic de. "Pure Science in the Service of Wartime Technology." *Bulletin of the Atomic Scientists* 31 (Jan. 1975): 41 ff.

2538   Holley, I. B., Jr. *Ideas and Weapons.* New Haven: Yale Univ. Press, 1953.

2539   Kanter, Arnold, and Stuart J. Thorson. "The Weapons Procurement Process: Choosing Among Competing Theories." *Public Policy* 20 (Fall 1972): 479–524.

2540   Kintner, William R., and Harvey Sicherman. "Technology and International Politics: The Crisis of Wishing." *Orbis* 15 (Spring 1971): 13–27.

2541   Klare, Michael T. "Science for the Pentagon: The Secret Thinkers." *Nation* (Apr. 15, 1968): 503–04.

2542   Knorr, Klaus E., and Oskar Morgenstern. *Science and Defense: Some Critical Thoughts on Military Research and Development.* Princeton: Princeton Univ. Press, 1965.

2543   Lapp, Ralph E. *Arms Beyond Doubt: The Tyranny of Weapons Technology.* New York: Cowles, 1970.

2544   Larson, David L. *The Puritan Ethic in United States Foreign Policy.* New York: Van Nostrand, 1966, pp. 14–20.

2545   Liddell Hart, B. H. *The Evolution of Warfare.* London: Faber & Faber, 1946.

2546   Morse, John H. "New Weapons Technologies: Implications for NATO." *Orbis* 19 (Summer 1975): 497–513.

2547   Mumford, Lewis. *Values for Survival.* New York: Harcourt, Brace, 1946.

2548   O'Sullivan, Thomas C. "Weapons and Technology." *Current History* 47 (July 1964): 6–11, 50–51.

2549   Pokrovsky, Maj. Gen. G. I. *Science and Technology in Contemporary War.* Trans. by R. L. Garthoff. New York: Praeger, 1959.

2550   Possony, Stefan T., and J. E. Pournelle. *The Strategy of Technology: Winning the Decisive War.* New York: Dunellen, 1970.

2551   Scott, Richard. "Does Technology Determine Policy?" *Current* 109 (Aug. 1969): 45.

2552   Sherwin, C. W. "Securing Peace Through Military Technology." *Bulletin of the Atomic Scientists* 12 (May 1956): 159–64.

2553   Singer, Dorothea W. "On a 16th Century Cartoon Concerning the Devilish Weapon of Gunpowder: Some Medieval Reactions to Guns and Gunpowder." *Ambix* [The Journal of the Society for the Study of Alchemy & Early Chemistry] (1959): 25–33.

2554   Singer, J. David. "Weapons Technology and International Stability." *Centennial Review* 5 (Fall 1961): 415–35.

2555   Spencer, Daniel L. *Military Transfer of Technology.* Report prepared for APOSR. Washington, D.C.: Department of Air Force, Mar. 1967.

2556   "Technological Change and the Strategic Arms Race [symposium discussion]." In William R. Kintner and Robert L. Pfaltzgraff, Jr., eds., *SALT: Implications for Arms Control in the 1970's.* Pittsburgh: Pittsburgh Univ. Press, 1973, pp. 107–24.

2557   U.S. Arms Control & Disarmament Agency. *Worldwide Effects of Nuclear War . . . Some Perspectives.* Washington, D.C.: G.P.O., 1975.

2558   U.S. Senate. Committee on Foreign Relations. *Developments in Military Technology and Their Impact on United States Strategy and Foreign Policy.* Staff Study, no. 8. Washington, D.C.: G.P.O., 1959.

2559   Veale, Frederick J. P. *Advance to Barbarism: The Development of Total Warfare From Serajevo to Hiroshima.* New York: Devin-Adair, 1968.

2560   Wheeler, Hugh. "Effects of War on Industrial Growth." *Society* 12 (1975): 48–52.

2561   Wolper, Roy S. "Rhetoric of Gunpowder and the Idea of Progress." *Journal of the History of Ideas* 31 (Oct.–Dec. 1970): 589–98.

SCIENTISTS & MORAL RESPONSIBILITY

See also Chapter 10, Regulating & Outlawing of Weapons & War, Chemical-Biological Weapons, Responsibility of Scientists.

2562   Basov, Nikolai. "The Scientist's Social Responsibility." *New Times* [Moscow], no. 42 (Oct. 1976): 26–27.

2563   Boffery, Philip M. "Plutonium: Its Morality Questioned by National Council of Churches." *Science* (Apr. 23, 1976): 356–59.

2564 Burhop, E. H. S. "Scientists and Soldiers." *Bulletin of the Atomic Scientists* 30 (Nov. 1974): 4–8.

2565 ———. "The Social Responsibility of the Scientist." *Scientific World* 18 (Spring 1974): 20–23.

2566 Chapin, Seymour L. "A Case of Arms Control in the French Enlightenment." *Journal of the History of Ideas* 27 (Apr.–June 1966): 285–95.

2567 Cox, Donald W. *America's New Policy Makers: The Scientists' Rise to Power.* Philadelphia: Chilton, 1964.

2568 Dorfer, Ingemar. *Systems 37 Viggen: Arms, Technology and the Domestication of Glory.* Oslo: Universitetsforlaget, 1973.

2569 Dupre, J. S., and S. A. Lakoff. "Arms and the Scientist." *Science and the Nation: Policy and Politics.* Englewood Cliffs, N.J.: Prentice-Hall, 1962, pp. 81–103.

2570 Eide, Asbjorn. "Technical Warfare Against the Weak and the Conscience of the Scientist." *Bulletin of Peace Proposals* 3:4 (1972): 362–66.

2571 Fairbairns, Zoe. "War Research at British Universities." *New Scientist* (Aug. 8, 1974): 312–15.

2572 Feld, Bernard T. "Human Values and the Technology of Weapons." *Zygon* 8:1 (1973): 48–58.

2573 Gilpin, Robert. *American Scientists and Nuclear Weapons Policy.* Princeton: Princeton Univ. Press, 1962.

2574 Gleditsch, Nils P. "Six Arguments Against Research for the Military." *Bulletin of Peace Proposals* 6:2 (1975): 172–75.

2575 Lasswell, Harold D. "Must Science Serve Political Power?" *American Psychologist* 25 (Feb. 1970): 117–23.

2576 Lorenz, Konrad. "On Killing Members of One's Own Species." *Bulletin of the Atomic Scientists* 26 (Oct. 1970): 2–5.

2577 Messing, Aubrey R. "University Campus: Why Military-Sponsored Research?" *Military Review* 52 (Dec. 1972): 54–62.

2578 Montgomery, Viscount. "The Ethics of War." *A History of Warfare.* London: Collins, 1968.

2579 Nef, John U. *War and Human Progress.* New York: Norton, 1963.

2580 Nelkin, Dorothy. *The University and Military Research: Moral Politics at M.I.T.* Ithaca: Cornell Univ. Press, 1972.

2581 Nelson, Bryce. "Bulletin of the Atomic Scientists: Thirty Years of Clockwatching." *Science* (Dec. 12, 1975): 1070–73.

2582 ———. "M.I.T.'s March 4: Scientists Discuss Renouncing Military Research." *Science* (Mar. 1969): 1175–78.

2583 Nieburg, H. L. *In the Name of Science.* Chicago: Quadrangle, 1970.

2584 Phillips, Warren. "Military Support for Social Science Research: A Rejoinder." *Bulletin of Peace Proposals* 6:2 (1975): 176–79.

2585 Rabinowitch, Eugene. "Responsibilities of Scientists in the Atomic Age." *Bulletin of the Atomic Scientists* 15 (Jan. 1959): 2–7.

2586 Rapoport, Anatol. "Classified Military Research and the University." In F. N. Trager and P. S. Kronenberg, eds., *National Security and American Society: Theory, Process, and Policy.* Wichita: Univ. Press of Kansas, 1973.

2587 Reid, R. W. *Tongues of Conscience: War and the Scientist's Dilemma.* London: Constable, 1969.

2588 Rose, Steven, and H. Rose. "Knowledge and Power." *New Scientist* (Apr. 17, 1969): 108–09.

2589 Roubiczek, Paul. *Ethical Values in the Age of Science.* London: Cambridge Univ. Press, 1969.

2590 Smith, Alice Kimball. *A Peril and a Hope: The Scientists' Movement in America, 1945–1947.* Cambridge: M.I.T. Press, 1971.

2591 Strickland, Donald A. *Scientists in Politics: The Atomic Scientists Movement, 1945–1946.* Lafayette: Purdue Univ. Press, 1968.

2592 Thomas, Sen. Elbert D. "Atomic Bombs in International Society: Will It Brutalize the Men Who Wield It?" *American Journal of International Law* 39 (Oct. 1945): 736–43.

2593 ———. "Morals." *Air Affairs* 1 (Mar. 1947): 413–15.

2594   Weinberg, Alvin M. "The Many Dimensions of Scientific Responsibility." *Bulletin of the Atomic Scientists* 32 (Nov. 1976): 21–25.

2595   Wohlstetter, Albert. "Scientists, Seers and Strategy." *Foreign Affairs* 41 (Apr. 1963): 466–78.

2596   York, Herbert F. "The Debate Over the Hydrogen Bomb." *Scientific American* 233 (Oct. 1975): 106–13.

2597   Zuckerman, Sir Solly. *Scientist and War: The Impact of Science on Military and Civil Affairs.* New York: Harper & Row, 1967.

SCIENCE & AC&D

2598   Doty, Paul. "The Community of Science and the Search for Peace." *Science* (Sept. 10, 1971): 998–1002.

2599   Feld, Bernard T. "Scientists' Role in Arms Control." *Bulletin of the Atomic Scientists* 26 (Jan. 1970): 7–8, 47–48.

2600   Kuczynski, Jurgen. "International Scientific Co-operation and the Limitation of Armaments." *Scientific World* 12:4–5 (1968): 29–31.

2601   Noel-Baker, Philip J. "Science and Disarmament." *Impact of Science on Society* 15:4 (1965): 211–46.

2602   Piel, Gerard. "Science, Disarmament and Peace." *Bulletin of the Atomic Scientists* 14 (June 1958): 217–19.

2603   Schooler, Dean. "Scientists in an Extra-National Arena: Disarmament and Arms Control Policy." *Science, Scientists and Public Policy.* New York: Free Press, 1971, pp. 103–12.

2604   Wiesner, Jerome B. *Where Science and Politics Meet.* New York: McGraw-Hill, 1961.

TECHNOLOGY & AC&D

2605   Abt, Clark C. "Controlling Future Arms." *Disarmament and Arms Control* 3 (Spring 1965): 19–40.

2606   ———. "The Design of Weapons Systems for Arms Control." In James E. Dougherty and John F. Lehman, Jr., eds., *The Prospects for Arms Control.* New York: MacFadden-Bartell, 1965, pp. 222–41.

2607   Barber, Arthur. "Some Industrial Aspects of Arms Control." *Journal of Conflict Resolution* 7:3 (1963): 491–94.

2608   Biddle, W. F. *Weapons Technology and Arms Control.* New York: Praeger, 1972.

2609   Coffey, Joseph I., and Jerome Laulicht. *The Implications for Arms Control of Perceptions of Strategic Weapons Systems.* 6 vols. ACDA/E-163. Washington, D.C.: ACDA, Nov. 1971.

2610   Craven, John P. "The Design of Weapons Systems for an Arms Control Environment." *Journal of Arms Control* 1:1 (1963): 14–17.

2611   Dyson, Freeman J. "Arms Control and Technological Change." In Morton A. Kaplan, ed., *SALT: Problems and Prospects.* Morristown, N.J.: General Learning Press, 1973, pp. 201–19.

2612   Garwin, Richard. "Impact of New Technologies on U.S. Defense and Arms Control Policy." *Congressional Record* 122 (June 14, 1976): H5821–23.

2613   Gelber, Harry G. "Technical Innovation and Arms Control." *World Politics* 26 (July 1974): 509–41.

2614   May, Michael M. *Strategic Arms Technology and Doctrine Under Arms Limitation Agreements.* Research Memo no. 37. Princeton: Princeton Univ., Center of International Studies, Oct. 1972.

2615   O'Neal, Russell D. "Industry, Society, and Arms Control." *Journal of Conflict Resolution* 7:3 (1963): 464–68.

2616   Raser, John R. "Weapons Design and Arms Control: The Polaris Example." *Journal of Conflict Resolution* 9:4 (1965): 450–62.

2617   Rodberg, Leonard S. "Limiting Strategic Technology: The Need for National Self-Restraint." *Bulletin of the Atomic Scientists* 25 (Nov. 1969): 36–38.

2618   Rosebury, Theodor. "Technology and the Failure of Disarmament." *Minority of One* 10 (Mar. 1968): 23–27.

2619   U.S. Arms Control & Disarmament Agency. *Implications of Future Weapons Technology on Arms Control and Disarmament.* ACDA

Report ST–51. New York: Hudson Institute, 1965.

2620   Yanarella, Ernest J. "The 'Technological Imperative' and the Arms Race." *Peace and Change* 3 (Spring 1975): 3–16.

Applied Mathematics & AC&D

2621   Anscombe, F. J., et al. *Applications of Statistical Methodology to Arms Control and Disarmament*. Princeton, N.J.: Mathematica, Inc., 1963.

2622   MacQueen, James B. *Security Studies Project*. Vol. 8: *A Statistical Analysis of Some International Confrontations: Implications for Arms Control*. ACDA/WEC–12. Los Angeles: Univ. of California, Arms Control Special Studies Program, 1968.

2623   Saaty, Thomas L. *Mathematical Models of Arms Control and Disarmament: Application of Mathematical Structure in Politics*. New York: Wiley, 1968.

2624   ———. "A Model for the Control of Arms." *Operations Research* 12 (July–Aug. 1964): 586–609.

2625   Tashjean, John E. "Research on Arms Control: Both the USA and the USSR Are Too Technocratic to Know How to Subject Arms Problems to Policy Science and Political Wisdom." *American Behavioral Scientist* 6 (Jan. 1963): 15–17.

Bureaucratic Politics & the Military-Industrial Complex

AC&D & BUREAUCRATIC POLITICS

2626   Allison, Graham T. *Essence of Decision: Explaining the Cuban Missile Crisis*. Boston: Little, Brown, 1971.

2627   ———, and Frederic A. Morris. "Armaments and Arms Control: Exploring the Determinants of Military Weapons." *Daedalus* 104 (Summer 1975): 99–129.

2628   Armacost, Michael H. *The Politics of Weapon Innovation: The Thor-Jupiter Controversy*. New York: Columbia Univ. Press, 1969.

2629   "Arms Control and Disarmament at the White House." *Bulletin of the Atomic Scientists* 22 (Feb. 1966): 43–45; 22 (Mar. 1966): 33–37.

2630   Art, Robert J. "Bureaucratic Politics and American Foreign Policy: A Critique." *Policy Sciences* 4 (Dec. 1973): 467–90.

2631   ———. "Restructuring the Military-Industrial Complex: Arms Control in International Perspective." *Public Policy* 22 (Fall 1974): 423–59.

2632   Aspin, Rep. Les. "Parliamentary Control of Defense: The American Example." *Survival* 15 (July–Aug. 1973): 166–70.

2633   Bundy, McGeorge. "The Presidency and the Peace." *Foreign Affairs* 42 (Apr. 1964): 354–65.

2634   Campbell, John F. *The Foreign Affairs Fudge Factory*. New York: Basic Books, 1971.

2635   Chayes, Abram. "Bureaucracy: An Ally in Arms Control." *Survival* 14 (July–Aug. 1972): 183–87.

2636   Clark, Sen. Joseph S. "Congress and Disarmament." *Bulletin of the Atomic Scientists* 19 (Sept. 1963): 3–7.

2637   ———. "The Influence of Congress in the Formulation of Disarmament Policy." *Annals of the Amer. Acad. of Pol. & Soc. Sci.* 342 (July 1962): 147–53.

2638   Coffin, Tris. "Senate Probes United States Stand on Disarmament." *New Leader* (May 5, 1958): 3–5.

2639   Davis, Saville R. "Recent Policy Making in the United States Government." In Donald G. Brennan, ed., *Arms Control, Disarmament, and National Security*. New York: Braziller, 1961, pp. 379–90.

2640   D'Ombrain, Nicholas J. "Decision-Making: Science or Craft?" *Journal of the Royal United Services Institution* 116 (Sept. 1971): 56–58.

2641   Gelb, Leslie H., and Morton H. Halperin. "Diplomatic Notes: The Ten Commandments of the Foreign-Affairs Bureaucracy." *Harper's* 244 (June 1972): 28, 30–32, 36–37.

2642   Greenwood, Ted. *Making the MIRV: A Study of Defense Decision-Making*. Cambridge, Mass.: Ballinger, 1975.

2643 Gustavson, M. R. "Evolving Strategic Arms and the Technologist." *Science* (Dec. 5, 1975): 955–58.

2644 Halperin, Morton H. "Clever Briefers, Crazy Leaders and Myopic Analysts." *Washington Monthly* 6 (Sept. 1974): 42–49.

2645 ———. "The Decision to Deploy the ABM: Bureaucratic and Domestic Politics in the Johnson Administration." *World Politics* 25 (Oct. 1972): 62–95.

2646 ———. "Why Bureaucrats Play Games." *Foreign Policy*, no. 2 (Spring 1972): 70–90.

2647 ———, and Arnold Kanter. *Readings in American Foreign Policy: A Bureaucratic Perspective.* Boston: Little, Brown, 1973.

2648 ———, et al. *Bureaucratic Politics and Foreign Policy.* Washington, D.C.: Brookings Institution, 1974.

2649 Hamilton, Andrew. "Arms Talks: In-Group Debate on the Technical Issues." *Science* (Apr. 10, 1970): 234–36.

2650 Hammond, Paul Y. "Super Carriers and B–36 Bombers: Appropriations, Strategy and Politics." In Harold Stein, ed., *American Civil-Military Decisions.* Tuscaloosa: Univ. of Alabama Press, 1963, pp. 471–567.

2651 Herold, Robert C., and Shane E. Mahoney. "Military Hardware Procurement: Some Comparative Observations on Soviet and American Policy Processes." *Comparative Politics* 6 (July 1974): 571–99.

2652 Hilsman, Roger. *The Politics of Policy Making in Defense and Foreign Affairs.* New York: Harper & Row, 1971.

2653 Holloway, David. "Technology and Political Decision in Soviet Armaments Policy." *Journal of Peace Research* 11:4 (1974): 257–80.

2654 Kurth, James R. "Why We Buy the Weapons We Do." *Foreign Policy*, no. 11 (Summer 1973): 33–56.

2655 Lall, Betty Goetz. "Arms Control In Congress, 1966." *Bulletin of the Atomic Scientists* 22 (Dec. 1966): 35–37.

2656 ———. "Congress Considers Impact of Defense Reduction." *Bulletin of the Atomic Scientists* 20 (Feb. 1964): 31–32.

2657 Laurence, Edward J. "The Changing Role of Congress in Defense Policy-Making." *Journal of Conflict Resolution* 20:2 (1976): 213–53.

2658 Leacacos, John P. "Kissinger's Apparat." *Foreign Policy*, no. 1 (Winter 1971–72): 3–27.

2659 Lincoln, James B. "Weapons Systems Acquisition Process." *Military Review* 51 (Aug. 1971): 40–52.

2660 Lucas, William A., and Raymond H. Dawson. *The Organizational Politics of Defense.* Occasional paper, no. 2. Pittsburgh: Univ. of Pittsburgh, International Studies Assoc., 1974.

2661 Marshall, A. W. *Bureaucratic Behavior and the Strategic Arms Competition.* Santa Monica, Ca.: California Arms Control & Foreign Policy Seminar, 1971.

2662 Medalia, Jonathan E. "Congress and the Political Guidance of Weapons Procurement." *Naval War College Review* 27 (Fall 1975): 12–31.

2663 Rathjens, George W., et al. *Nuclear Arms Control Agreements: Process and Impact.* Washington, D.C.: Carnegie Endowment for International Peace, 1974.

2664 Robinson, Clarence A., Jr. "Civil Role in Weapon Efforts Scrutinized." *Aviation Week & Space Technology* (Nov. 17, 1975): 18–20.

2665 Rock, Vincent P. *The Statesman's Approach to Disarmament.* Washington, D.C.: Institute for Defense Analyses, 1963.

2666 Schilling, Warner R.; Paul Y. Hammond; and Glenn H. Snyder. *Strategy, Politics and Defense Budgets.* New York: Columbia Univ. Press, 1962.

2667 Spingarn, Jerome H. "The Humphrey Subcommittee: Was it Worthwhile?" *Bulletin of the Atomic Scientists* 13 (June 1957): 224–27.

2668 Steinbruner, John, and Barry Carter. "Organizational and Political Dimensions of the Strategic Posture: The Problems of Reform." *Daedalus* 104 (Summer 1975): 131–54.

2669 Tarr, David W. "Military Technology and the Policy Process." *Western Political Quarterly* 18 (Mar. 1965): 135–48.

2670 Wadsworth, James J., and Josephine W. Pomerance. "How the Pentagon Blocks Arms Pacts." *Current* 133 (Oct. 1971): 45–47.

2671 Yarmolinsky, Adam. "The President, Congress, and Arms Control." In S. G. Sarkesian, ed., *The Military-Industrial Complex.* Beverly Hills, Ca.: Sage, 1972.

2672 York, Herbert. *The Advisors: Oppenheimer, Teller and the Superbomb.* San Francisco: Freeman, 1976.

2673 ———. *Race to Oblivion: A Participant's View of the Arms Race.* New York: Simon & Schuster, 1970.

Military-Industrial Complex

2674 Armeson, Robert B. *Total War and Compulsory Labor: A Study of the Military-Industrial Complex in Germany during World War I.* The Hague: Nijhoff, 1964.

2675 Barnet, Richard J. *The Economy of Death.* New York: Atheneum, 1970.

2676 Baumgartner, John Stanley. *The Lonely Warriors: Case for the Military-Industrial Complex.* Los Angeles: Nash, 1970.

2677 Boulding, Kenneth E., ed. *Peace and the War Industry.* Chicago: Aldine-Atherton, 1970.

2678 Brailsford, Henry N. *The War of Steel and Gold: A Study of Armed Peace.* London: Bell, 1914.

2679 Carey, Omer L., ed. *The Military-Industrial Complex and the United States Foreign Policy.* Pullman: Washington State Univ. Press, 1969.

2680 Cockran, Bert. *The War System.* New York: Macmillan, 1965.

2681 Davis, Kenneth S., ed. *Arms, Industry and America.* New York: H. W. Wilson, 1971.

2682 Donovan, James A. *Militarism, U.S.A.* New York: Scribner's, 1970.

2683 Duscha, Julius. *Arms, Money and Politics.* New York: Ives Washburn, 1965.

2684 Hickman, Martin B., ed. *The Military and American Society.* Beverly Hills, Ca.: Glencoe, 1971.

2685 Jordan, David Starr. *War and Waste.* Garden City, N.Y.: Leipsic, 1918.

2686 Kaufman, Richard F. *The War Profiteers.* Indianapolis: Bobbs-Merrill, 1970.

2687 Klare, Michael T., comp. *The University-Military Complex. A Directory and Related Documents.* Berkeley, Ca.: North American Congress on Latin America, 1969.

2688 Lapp, Ralph E. *The Weapons Culture.* Baltimore: Penguin, 1969.

2689 Lasley, Jack. *The War System and You.* Chapel Hill: Univ. of North Carolina, Institute for International Studies, 1965.

2690 Lens, Sidney. *The Military-Industrial Complex.* Philadelphia: Pilgrim Press, 1970.

2691 Melman, Seymour. *Pentagon Capitalism.* New York: McGraw-Hill, 1970.

2692 ———. *The War Economy of the United States: Readings on Military, Industry and Economy.* New York: St. Martin's Press, 1971.

2693 Mills, C. Wright. *The Power Elite.* New York: Oxford Univ. Press, 1956.

2694 Perlo, Victor. *Militarism and Industry: Arms Profiteering in the Missile Age.* New York: International Publishers, 1963.

2695 Proxmire, Sen. William. *Report From Wasteland: America's Military-Industrial Complex.* New York: Praeger, 1970.

2696 Pursell, Carroll W., Jr., ed. *The Military-Industrial Complex.* New York: Harper & Row, 1972.

2697 Russett, Bruce M. *What Price Vigilance? The Burdens of National Defense.* New Haven: Yale Univ. Press, 1970.

2698 Sarkesian, Sam G., ed. *The Military-Industrial Complex.* Beverly Hills, Ca.: Sage, 1972.

2699 Stockfish, J. A. *Plowshares into Swords: Managing the American Defense Establishment.* New York: Mason & Lipscomb, 1973.

2700 Suall, Irwin. *The American Ultras: The Extreme Right and the Military-Industrial Complex.* New York: New American Library, 1962.

2701 Adams, Walter. "The Military-Industrial Complex and the New Industrial State." *American Economic Association, Papers & Proceedings* 58 (May 1968): 652–65.

2702 ———, and William J. Adams. "The Military-Industrial Complex: A Market Structure Analysis." *American Economic Review* 62 (May 1972): 279–87.

2703 Armstrong, Richard. "Military-Industrial Complex: Russian Style." *Fortune* (Aug. 1, 1969): 84–87 ff.

2704 Aspaturian, Vernon V. "The Soviet Military-Industrial Complex: Does It Exist?" *Journal of International Affairs* 26 (Spring 1972): 1–28.

2705 Biderman, Albert. "Retired Soldiers Within and Without the Military-Industrial Complex." In Sam G. Sarkesian, ed., *The Military-Industrial Complex* Beverly Hills, Ca.: Sage, 1972.

2706 Bix, Herbert P. "The Security Treaty System and the Japanese Military-Industrial Complex." *Bulletin of the Concerned Asian Scholars* 2 (Jan. 1970): 30–53.

2707 Boulding, Kenneth E. "The Role of the War Industry in International Conflict." *Journal of Social Issues* 23 (Jan. 1967): 47–61.

2708 Cobb, Stephen. "Defense Spending and Defense Voting in the House: An Empirical Study of an Aspect of the Military-Industrial Complex Thesis." *American Journal of Sociology* 82 (July 1976): 163–82.

2709 Cooling, B. Franklin, III. "The Formative Years of the Naval-Industrial Complex: Their Meaning for Studies of Institutions Today." *Naval War College Review* 27 (Mar.–Apr. 1975): 53–62.

2710 "Defense Department Lists Leading 100 Contractors for Fiscal 1975." *Aviation Week & Space Technology* (Feb. 2, 1976): 54–57.

2711 Eckhardt, William. "The Military-Industrial Personality." *Journal of Contemporary Revolutions* 3 (Fall 1971): 74–87.

2712 Gard, Robert G., Jr. "The Military and American Society." *Foreign Affairs* 49 (July 1971): 698–710.

2713 Gottlieb, Sanford. "A State Within a State: What is the Military-Industrial Complex?" *Dissent* 18 (Oct. 1971): 492–502.

2714 Hall, Martin. "A State Ruled By a Military-Industrial Complex." *International Affairs* [Moscow] 16 (June 1970): 80–83.

2715 Jahn, Egbert. "The Role of the Armaments Complex in Soviet Society (Is There a Soviet Military-Industrial Complex?)." *Journal of Peace Research* 12:3 (1975): 179–94.

2716 Koistinen, Paul A. C. "The Military-Industrial Complex in Historical Perspective: The Interwar Years." *Journal of American History* 56 (Mar. 1970): 819–39.

2717 ———. "The 'Military-Industrial Complex' in Historical Perspective: World War I." *Business History Review* 41 (Winter 1967): 378–403.

2718 Krell, Gert. "Military-Industrial Complex: Armaments Policy and the National Priorities Debate in the 92nd U.S. Senate 1971–72." *Instant Research on Peace and Violence* 5:1 (1975): 97–107.

2719 Krylov, Konstantin K. "Soviet Military-Economic Complex." *Military Affairs* 51 (Nov. 1972): 89–97.

2720 Larson, Arthur D. "The Military-Industrial Complex and Antimilitarism: The Role of Retired Officer Employment." *Air University Review* 23 (July–Aug. 1972): 26–33.

2721 Lee, William T. "The 'Politico-Military-Industrial Complex' of the U.S.S.R." *Journal of International Affairs* 26 (Spring 1972): 73–86.

2722 Lowry, Ritchie P. "To Arms: Changing Military Roles and the Military-Industrial Complex." *Social Problems* 18 (Summer 1970): 3–16.

2723 McGovern, Sen. George S. "And Now That the American Dream is Safely in the Hands of the Military-Industrial Establishment, We Wake to a New Decade." *Esquire* (Dec. 1969): 189 ff.

2724 Melman, Seymour. "The Pentagon Budget as War Policy: Or How to Cut War Expenditures to the Bone." *Dissent* 16 (June 1969): 477–83.

2725 Meyerson, Martin. "Price of Admission into the Defense Business." *Harvard Business Review* 45 (July–Aug. 1967): 111–23.

2726 Migolatyev, A. "The Military-Industrial Complex and the Arms Race." *International Affairs* [Moscow] 21 (Oct. 1975): 63–71.

2727 "The Military-Industrial Complex." *Newsweek* (June 9, 1969): 74–87.

2728 "Military-Industrial Complex: The Facts vs. the Fictions." *U.S. News & World Report* (Apr. 21, 1969): 60–63.

2729 "The Military-Industrial Complex: USSR/ USA." *Journal of International Affairs* 26 (Spring 1972): 1 ff.

2730 Ognibene, Peter J. "Defense Contractors' Devil Theory." *New Republic* (Jan. 27, 1973): 21–23.

2731 Perlo, Victor. "Arms Profiteering." *New Republic* (Feb. 7, 1970): 23–25.

2732 Pilisuk, Marc, and Thomas Hayden. "Is There a Military-Industrial Complex Which Prevents Peace?" *Journal of Social Issues* 21 (July 1965): 67–117.

2733 Powers, Lt. Col. Patrick W. "Butter for the Guns." *Military Review* 45 (Dec. 1965): 79–86.

2734 Proxmire, Sen. William. "Former Defense Brass Flock to Defense Industry." *Congressional Record* 122 (Jan. 28, 1976): S699–701.

2735 Raymond, Jack. "Growing Threat of a Military-Industrial Complex." *Harvard Business Review* 46 (May–June 1968): 53–64.

2736 Sherrill, Robert. "The War Machine." *Playboy* (May 1970): 134 ff.

2737 Slater, Jerome, and Terry Nardin. "The Military-Industrial Complex Muddle." *Yale Review* 65 (Autumn 1975): 1–23.

2738 Speilman, Karl F. "Defense Industrialists in the USSR." *Problems of Communism* 25 (Sept.–Oct. 1976): 52–69.

2739 Weidenbaum, Murray L. "The Defense-Space Complex: Impact on Whom?" *Challenge* 13 (Apr. 1965): 43–46.

2740 Wolf, Charles, Jr. *Military-Industrial Simplicities, Complexities and Realities.* P–4747. Santa Monica, Ca.: Rand, Dec. 1971.

Legal and Psychological Dimensions

LEGAL DIMENSIONS

See also Chapter 5, Special Issues: Inspection, Verification & Supervision, Legal Aspects; and Chapter 10, Outlawing & Regulating Weapons & War, International Law & Weapons; and CBW & International Law.

2741 Cavers, David F. "Legal Planning Against the Risk of Atomic War." *Columbia Law Review* 55 (Feb. 1955): 127–57.

2742 Clark, Grenville. *A Plan for Peace.* New York: Harpers, 1950.

2743 ———, and Lewis B. Sohn. *Peace Through Disarmament and Charter Revision.* Dublin, N.H.: Privately printed, 1956.

2744 ———. *World Peace Through World Law.* 2d ed. Rev. Cambridge: Harvard Univ. Press, 1964.

2745 Eide, Asbjorn. "International Law, Dominance, and the Use of Force." *Journal of Peace Research* 11:1 (1974): 1–20.

2746 Lusky, Louis. "Four Problems in Lawmaking for Peace [a Critique of Clark and Sohn]." *Political Science Quarterly* 80 (Sept. 1965): 341–56.

2747 Yuter, S. C. "The Role of World Law in Arms Control." *Bulletin of the Atomic Scientists* 25 (Oct. 1969): 23–25.

International Law & AC&D

2748 Bartos, Milan. "Legal Aspects of Disarmament." *Review of International Affairs* [Belgrade] (Jan. 16, 1960): 8–10.

2749 ———. "Problem of Disarmament and International Law." *Review of International Affairs* [Belgrade] (Apr. 16, 1956): 4–5.

2750 Bathhurst, M. E. "Legal Aspects of the International Control of Atomic Energy." *British Yearbook of International Law*, no. 24 (1947): 1–32.

2751 Bogdanov, Oleg V. "Disarmament in the Light of International Law." *Soviet Yearbook of International Law* (1958): 93–127.

2752 Clark, Grenville. "The Need for Total Disarmament Under Enforceable Law." *Current History* 47 (Aug. 1964): 93–96, 115.

2753 Clark, Sen. Joseph S. "Disarmament and World Law." *War/Peace Report* 5 (Oct. 1965): 9–10.

2754 ———. "World Disarmament: An Enforceable World Law." *Vital Speeches* (Sept. 1, 1964): 688–92.

2755 Cohen, Benjamin V. "Disarmament and International Law." *U.S. Department of State Bulletin* (May 26, 1952): 834–37.

2756 Esgain, Albert J. "The Legal Aspects of Arms Control and Disarmament Treaties." *Temple Law Quarterly* 38 (Winter 1965): 133–51.

2757 Falk, Richard A. "Respect for International Law and Confidence in Disarmament." In Richard J. Barnet and Richard A. Falk, eds., *Security in Disarmament*. Princeton: Princeton Univ. Press, 1965, pp. 204–25.

2758 Fisher, Adrian S. "Arms Control and Disarmament in International Law." *Virginia Law Review* 50 (Nov. 1964): 1200–19.

2759 Freeman, Harrop A., and Stanley Yarker. "Disarmament and Atomic Control: Legal and Non-Legal Problems." *Cornell Law Quarterly* 43 (Winter 1958): 132–35.

2760 Gaefrath, B. "Disarmament and International Law." *Scientific World* 16:1 (1972): 8–9.

2761 Gotlieb, Allen. *Disarmament and International Law: A Study of the Role of Law in the Disarmament Process*. Toronto: Canadian Institute of International Affairs, 1965.

2762 Kuznetsov, V. "Disarmament and International Law." *International Affairs* [Moscow] 19 (Mar. 1973): 107–09.

2763 Larson, Arthur. "Arms Control Through World Law." In Donald G. Brennan, ed., *Arms Control, Disarmament, and National Security*. New York: Braziller, 1961, pp. 423–38.

2764 Partan, Daniel G. *Individual Responsibility Under a Disarmament Agreement in American Law*. Durham, N.C.: Duke Rule of Law Research Center, 1965. [Reprinted in *Minnesota Law Review* 49 (Apr. 1965): 889–955.]

2765 Rhyne, Charles S. "Disarmament and Arms Control." *International Law: The Substance, Processes, Procedures and Institutions for World Peace with Justice*. Washington, D.C.: CLB Publishers, 1971, pp. 595–609.

2766 Stein, Eric. "Legal Restraints in Modern Arms Control Agreements." *American Journal of International Law* 66 (Apr. 1972): 255–89.

PSYCHOLOGICAL ASPECTS

2767 Alvik, Trond. "The Development of Views on Conflict, War and Peace among School Chil-

dren." *Journal of Peace Research* 5:2 (1968): 171–95.

2768 Cousins, Norman. "Security and the Individual." *International Affairs* [Moscow] 7 (Feb. 1961): 51–57.

2769 David, Robert N. "The International Influence Process: How Relevant is the Contribution of Psychologists?" *American Psychologist* 21:3 (Mar. 1966): 236–43.

2770 Deutsch, M. "Psychological Alternatives to War." *Journal of Social Issues* 18:2 (1962): 97–119.

2771 Eckhardt, William. "Psychology of War and Peace." *Journal of Human Relations* 16:2 (1968): 239–49.

2772 Farber, Irving J. "Psychological Aspects of Mass Disasters." *National Medical Association Journal* 59 (Sept. 1967): 340–45.

2773 Frank, Jerome D. "Psychological Aspects of the Nuclear Arms Race." *Bulletin of the Atomic Scientists* 32 (Apr. 1976): 22–24.

2774 ———. *Sanity and Survival: Psychiatric Aspects of War and Peace*. New York: Random House, 1967.

2775 Jeffries, Vincent. "Political Generations and the Acceptance or Rejection of Nuclear Warfare." *Journal of Social Issues* 30:3 (1974): 119–36.

2776 Meerloo, Joost A. M. *That Difficult Peace*. New York: Channel Press, 1961.

2777 Oldendorf, W. H. "On the Acceptability of a Device as a Weapon." *Bulletin of the Atomic Scientists* 18 (Jan. 1962): 35–37.

2778 Pear, T. H., ed. *Psychological Factors of Peace and War*. New York: Philosophical Library, 1950.

2779 Waelder, Robert. *Psychological Aspects of War and Peace*. Geneva: Geneva Research Centre, 1939. [Also listed as, *Geneva Special Studies* 10:2 (1939).]

2780 White, Ralph K. "Three Not-So-Obvious Contributions of Psychology to Peace." *Journal of Social Issues* 25:4 (1969): 23–39.

Aggression, Violence & War

2781 Angell, Robert S. "The Sociology of Human Conflict." In E. McNeil, ed., *The Nature of*

Human Conflict. Englewood Cliffs, N.J.: Prentice-Hall, 1965, pp. 91–115.

2782   Ardrey, Robert. *The Territorial Imperative: A Personal Inquiry into Animal Origins of Property and Nations.* New York: Atheneum, 1966.

2783   Bernard, Jessie, et al. *The Nature of Conflict.* Paris: UNESCO, 1957.

2784   Brinkman, August. "The Biological Background of War: Thoughts of a Biologist." *Army Quarterly* 102 (July 1972): 427–37.

2785   Cantril, Hadley, ed. *Tensions That Cause Wars.* Urbana: Univ. of Illinois Press, 1950.

2786   Carthy, J. D., and R. J. Ebling, eds. *The Natural History of Aggression.* New York: Academic Press, 1964.

2787   Clark, Robert A. "Psychiatrists and Psychoanalysts on War." *American Journal of Psycho-therapy* 19 (Oct. 1965): 540–58.

2788   Coblentz, S. A. *From Arrow to Atomic Bomb: The Psychological History of War.* New York: Beechhurst Press, 1953.

2789   Daniels, David N., et al., eds. *Violence and the Struggle for Existence.* Boston: Little, Brown, 1970.

2790   Dunn, Frederick S. *War and the Minds of Men.* New York: Harper, 1950.

2791   Durbin, E. F. M., and J. Browlby. *Personal Aggressiveness and War.* New York: Columbia Univ., 1939.

2792   Feshback, Seymour. "The Function of Aggression and the Regulation of Aggressive Drive." *Psychological Review* 71 (July 1964): 257–72.

2793   Frank, Jerome D. "Group Psychology and the Elimination of War." *Journal of Group Psychotherapy* 14:1 (1964): 41–48.

2794   Freud, Anna. "Comments on Aggression." *International Journal of Psychoanalysis* 53:2 (1972): 163–71.

2795   Fried, Morton, et al., eds. *War: The Anthropology of Armed Conflict and Aggression.* Garden City, N.Y.: Natural History Press, 1968.

2796   Gorer, Geoffrey. "Ardrey on Human Nature." *Encounter* 28 (June 1967): 66–71.

2797   ———. "Man Has No Killer Instinct." *New York Times Magazine* (Nov. 27, 1966): 47 ff.

2798   Heimann, Paul, and Arthur F. Valenstein. "The Psychoanalytical Concept of Aggression: An Integrated Summary." *International Journal of Psychoanalysis* 53:1 (1972): 31–35.

2799   Huxley, Julian. "Is War Instinctive—And Inevitable?" *New York Times Magazine* (Feb. 10, 1946): 59–60.

2800   Ilfeld, F. W., and R. J. Metzner. "Environment Theories of Violence." In David N. Daniels et al., eds., *Violence and the Struggle for Existence.* Boston: Little, Brown, 1970, pp. 79–96.

2801   Johnson, Roger N. *Aggression in Man and Animals.* Philadelphia: W. B. Saunders, 1972.

2802   Laussier, Andre. "Panel on 'Aggression.' " *International Journal of Psychoanalysis* 53:1 (1972): 13–19.

2803   Lehman, D. S. "A Critique of Konrad Lorenz's Theory of Instinctive Behavior." *Quarterly Review of Biology* 28 (Dec. 1953): 337–63.

2804   Lorenz, Konrad. *On Aggression.* New York: Bantam, 1967.

2805   Mead, Margaret. "The Psychology of Warless Man." In A. Larson, ed., *Warless World.* New York: McGraw-Hill, 1963, pp. 131–42.

2806   ———. "Warfare is Only an Invention: Not a Biological Necessity." *Asia* 40 (Aug. 1940): 402–05.

2807   Montagu, M. F. A., ed. *Man and Aggression.* New York: Oxford Univ. Press, 1968.

2808   Moskas, Charles C. "Civilized Warfare: Why Men Fight." In James P. Spardley and D. McCurdy, eds., *Conformity and Conflict.* Boston: Little, Brown, 1971.

2809   Nicolai, Georg Friedrich. *The Biology of War.* Trans. by C. A. Grande and J. Grande. New York: Century, 1918.

2810   Pearl, Raymond. "Some Biological Considerations About War." *American Journal of Sociology* 46 (Jan. 1941): 487–503.

2811   Usdin, Gene, ed. *Perspectives on Violence.* New York: Brunner, Mazel, 1971.

2812   Woods, Frederick A. "The Biology of War." *Forum* 74 (Oct. 1925): 533–42.

Psychology & AC&D

2813 Bass, Bernard M. "Socio-Psychological Implications of Disarmament." *Pittsburgh Business Review* 8 (Sept. 1964): 4–5.

2814 Frank, Jerome D. "Emotional and Motivational Aspects of the Disarmament Problem." *Journal of Social Issues* 17:3 (1961): 20–27.

2815 ———. "Psychological Aspects of the Disarmament Problem." In Charles A. Barker, ed., *Problems of World Disarmament*. Boston: Houghton Mifflin, 1963, pp. 82–97.

2816 McDougall, William. "Psychology, Disarmament and Peace." *North American Review* 219 (May 1924): 577–91.

2817 Niezing, Johan. *Sociology, War and Disarmament: Studies in Peace Research*. Rotterdam: Rotterdam Univ. Press, 1970.

2818 Pilisuk, Marc, and Anatol Rapoport. "Stepwise Disarmament and Sudden Destruction in a Two-Person Game: A Research Tool." *Journal of Conflict Resolution* 7:1 (1964): 36–49.

2819 Rosenbaum, Max, et al. "Psychotherapy and Nuclear Disarmament." *Journal of the Long Island Consultation Center* 5:1 (1967): 19–25.

2820 Seed, Philip. *The Psychological Problem of Disarmament*. London: Housmans, 1966.

2821 Singer, J. David. "Threat Perception and the Armament-Tension Dilemma." *Journal of Conflict Resolution* 2:2 (1958): 90–105. [Reprinted in John C. Garnett, ed., *Theories of Peace and Security*. New York: Macmillan, 1970, pp. 149–59.

2822 Suinn, Richard W. "The Disarmament Fantasy: Psychological Factors That May Produce Warfare." *Journal of Human Relations* 15:1 (1967): 36–42.

2823 Van Alta, Lester C. "Arms Control = Human Control." *American Psychologist* 18:1 (1963): 37–46.

Part Two

ACCORDS, PROPOSALS & TREATIES

Seven

Limitation of Weapons & Personnel

PROPOSALS AND AGREEMENTS aimed at "disarmament"—that is, the limitation and/or reduction of weapons and military personnel—usually are assumed to be modern ideas. While it is true that there has been a vastly increased effort in this direction since the First World War, this chapter suggests a historical continuity in this approach to arms control.

Sufficient agreements exist from earlier days to provide for certain historical comparisons. Those students of arms control interested in *imposed* disarmament may wish to compare the Treaty of Zama (201 B.C.), in which Rome imposed harsh limits on Carthage's military forces, and the Franco-Prussian Treaty (1808), in which Napoleon placed limits on the defeated Prussian army, with the dismantling of the military forces of the defeated nations after World Wars I and II. Other researchers concerned with naval limitation may wish to compare the Anglo-French Naval Pact (1787), although satisfactory information is as yet scarce on this accord, and the Argentine-Chile naval pact (1902) with those negotiations and agreements of the 1920s and 1930s.

The search for a peaceful world following the holocaust of World War I led to an intensive examination of the basic issues surrounding the limiting of armies and navies. These diplomatic endeavors took essentially two approaches. The first involved the major international institutions—the League of Nations and later the United Nations—and took a "global" view of the issues. Negotiations here were directed toward broad, multilateral agreements that would affect most of the nations of the world. (These efforts, though largely unsuccessful, did result in an extensive airing of most issues involved in general disarmament; sources on the League and U.N. process are listed in Chapter 4.)

The second approach was more restricted and less ambitious. It focused on the specific interests and priorities of a few nations, but resulted in somewhat greater successes. The most conspicuous example of this approach is the naval limitation treaties—the major accords signed at Washington (1922) and London (1930), and the bilateral pacts between Turkey and Greece (1930), Turkey and Russia (1931), and Great Britain and Germany (1935). (General studies evaluating the various effects of naval limitation during the interwar decades are listed in Chapter 3.)

After World War II there initially seemed to be considerable interest in disarmament. Consequently, there was public enthusiasm for disarming Germany, Japan and the other belligerent powers. The institutionalization of this effort is found in the Japanese Constitution (1946). Efforts to limit and control the newly discovered atomic bomb—the so-called Baruch Plan (1946)—found favor in official and public circles. In 1962, both the United States and the Soviet Union offered plans calling for "general and complete disarmament" (GCD), but these proposals were soon quietly dropped from active consideration.

The emphasis shifted, early in the 1960s from general disarmament schemes aimed at placing extensive limitations on military forces to bilateral or small group negotiations designed to limit specific weapons systems.

Agreements, Proposals & Treaties to 1914

Treaty of Zama (201 B.C.)

For text of treaty, see Guglielmo Ferrero and Corrado Barbagallo, *A Short History of Rome* (New York: Capricorn Books, 1964), p. 190; Livy, *The War With Hannibal*, Bk 30, Aubrey de Selincourt, trans. (Baltimore: Penguin Classics, 1965), pp. 65–66.

Documents

2824 Appian. *Appian's Roman History.* Vol. 1. Trans. by Horace White. New York: Macmillan, 1922, pp. 527–49. [Loeb edition.]

2825 Livy. *Summaries.* Vol. 14. Trans. by Alfred C. Schlesinger and Russell M. Geer. Cambridge: Harvard Univ. Press, 1959, pp. 25–31. [Loeb edition.]

2826 Polybius. *The Histories.* Vol. 6. Trans. by W. R. Paton. Cambridge: Harvard Univ. Press, 1954. [Loeb edition.]

2827 Strabo. *The Geography of Strabo.* Vol. 3. Ed. & trans. by Horace Leonard Jones. Cambridge: Harvard Univ. Press, 1959, pp. 185–87. [Loeb edition.]

General Accounts

2828 Armstrong, Donald. *The Reluctant Warriors.* New York: Crowell, 1966.

2829 Ferrero, Guglielmo, and Corrado Barbagallo. *A Short History of Rome.* New York: Capricorn Books, 1964, pp. 190–91, 230–35, 239–41.

2830 Mommsen, Theodor. *The History of Rome.* 3 vols. Glencoe, Ill.: Free Press, n.d. (1854); II: 359–68; III: 237–58.

2831 Scullard, Howard H. *A History of the Roman World.* New York: Barnes & Noble, 1961, pp. 301–04.

2832 Warmington, B. H. *Carthage.* Baltimore: Penguin Books, 1964, pp. 235, 244–55.

Anglo-French Naval Pact (1787)

For text of treaty, see Geo. Fred. de Martens, *Recueil de Traits*, 2d ed. (Göttingen: Dans La Librairie de Dieterich, 1818), IV: 279.

Documents

2833 Auckland, Lord William. *The Journal and Correspondence of William, Lord Auckland* [formerly William Eden]. London: Richard Bentley, Publisher in Ordinary to Her Majesty, 1861, I: 172–308, 519–533.

2834 Browning, Oscar, ed. *Despatches from Paris, 1784–1790: Selected and Edited from the Foreign Office Correspondence.* Camden Third Series, vol. 1 (1784–1787). London: Offices of the Society, 1909, pp. 249–63.

2835 *Parliamentary History of England: From the Earliest Period to the Year 1803.* London: T. C. Hansard, 1816, Vol. 26, cols. 1224–1305.

General Accounts

2836 Adams, Ephraim D. *The Influence of Grenville on Pitt's Foreign Policy, 1787–1798.* Washington, D.C.: Carnegie Endowment for International Peace, 1904, pp. 4–7.

2837 Ehrman, John. *The Younger Pitt.* New York: E. P. Dutton, 1969, pp. 528–38.

2838 Gifford, John. *A History of the Political Life of the Right Honourable William Pitt: Including Some Account of the Times in Which He Lived.* London: T. Cadell & W. Davies, Strand, 1809, I: 427–66.

2839 Rose, John Holland. *Life of William Pitt.* New York: Harcourt, Brace, 1924, pp. 368–82.

2840 Ward, A. W., and G. P. Gooch, eds. *The Cambridge History of British Foreign Policy, 1783–1919.* New York: Macmillan, 1922, I: 170–77.

FRANCO-PRUSSIAN TREATY (1808)

For text of treaty, see *Recueil des Traites de la France,* 24 vols. (Paris, 1864–1907), II: 272–73.

General Accounts

2841 Henderson, Ernest F. *A Short History of Germany.* 2 vols. New York: Macmillan, 1916, II: 235–322.

2842 Rosinski, Herbert. *The German Army.* New York: Praeger, 1966, pp. 52–53.

2843 Shanahan, William O. *Prussian Military Reforms, 1786–1813.* New York: Columbia Univ. Press, 1945, pp. 98–99, 109 ff.

2844 Showalter, Dennis E. "Manifestation of Reform: Rearmament of the Prussian Infantry, 1806–1813." *Journal of Modern History* 44 (Sept. 1972): 364–80.

2845 Simon, Walter M. *The Failure of the Prussian Reform Movement, 1807–1819.* Ithaca: Cornell Univ. Press, 1955, pp. 14, 18–19.

OTTOMAN'S LIMITATION OF EGYPTIAN ARMS (1841)

For text of this *Ferman,* and subsequent ones of 1866, 1873, and 1879, see Sir Thomas E. Holland, *European Concert in the Eastern Question* (Oxford: Clarendon Press, 1885), pp. 110–14, 114–16, 125–28; and J. C. Hurewitz, *Diplomacy in Near and Middle East,* 2 vols. (Princeton, N.J.: Van Nostrand, 1956), I: 121–23, 174–77.

General Accounts

2846 Anderson, M. S. *The Eastern Question, 1774–1923.* London: Macmillan, 1966.

2847 Charles-Roux, F. *Thiers et Mehemet-Ali: La Grande Crise Orientale et Européenne de 1840–1841.* Paris: PION, 1951.

2848 Cromer, Earl of. *Modern Egypt.* 2 vols. London: Macmillan, 1908.

2849 Dodwell, Henry Herbert. *The Founder of Modern Egypt: A Study of Muhammad' Ali.* Cambridge: Univ. Press, 1931.

2850 Hunter, W. P. *Expedition to Syria.* 2 vols. London: Henry Colburn, 1842, II: 186–287.

2851 Marlowe, John. *Anglo-Egyptian Relations, 1800–1853.* London: Cresset, 1954.

2852 Marriott, J. A. R. "Mehemet Ali of Egypt." *The Eastern Question.* Oxford: Clarendon Press, 1918, pp. 222–45.

2853 Sabry, M. *L'Empire Egyptien sous Mohamed-Ali et la Question d'Orient, 1811–1849.* Paris: P. Geuthner, 1930.

2854 Webster, Sir Charles K. *The Foreign Policy of Palmerston, 1830–1841.* 2 vols. New York: Humanities Press, 1969, II: 753–58.

ARGENTINA-CHILE NAVAL LIMITATION
CONVENTION (1902)

For text of convention, see Great Britain, Foreign
Office, *British and Foreign State Papers* (London:
Harrison, 1902–1903), XCV: 758–65; XCVI: 311–12.

Documents

2855   Argentine Republic. Ministerio de Relaciones
Exteriores y Culto. *Memoria de Relaciones
Exteriores y Culto Presentada al Honorable
Congreso Nacional Correspondiente al Ano
1903–1904.* Buenos Aires: Taller Tipografico
de la Penitenciaria Nacional, 1904.

2856   Chile. Ministerio de Relaciones Exteriores,
Culto, y Colonizacion. *Memoria de Re-
laciones Exteriores, Culto, y Colonizacion
Presentada al Congreso Nacional de 1902.*
Santiago: Imprenta Nacional, 1903.

2857   ————. *Memoria de Relaciones Exteriores,
Culto, y Colonizacion Presentada al Con-
greso Nacional de 1903.* Santiago: Imprenta
Nacional, 1904.

General Accounts

2858   Billard, Armand. *L'Arbitrage et la Limita-
tion des Armements, les Traites passes le 28
Mai, 1902 entre le Chile et la Republique
Argentine.* Paris, 1910.

2859   Burr, Robert N. "The Balance of Power in
Nineteenth-Century South America: An
Exploratory Essay." *Hispanic American
Historical Review* 25 (Feb. 1955): 37–60.

2860   ————. *By Reason or Force: Chile and the
Balancing of Power in South America,
1830–1905.* Berkeley: Univ. of California
Press, 1965, pp. 245–59.

2861   Gonzáles, Joaquín V. *Los Tratados de Paz de
1902 ante el Congreso. . . .* Buenos Aires:
Imprenta "Didot" de Féliz Lajouance y Cía,
1904.

2862   Huneeus y Gana, Jorge. *La Amistad
Chileno-Argentina: El Verdadero Origen de
los Pactos de Mayo.* Santiago: Imprenta
Litografía Encuadernación Barcelona, 1908.

2863   Tagle, Enrique. *Los Tratados de Paz entre
La República Argentina y Chile: la opinión
argentina.* Buenos Aires: Tipo-Lito Calileo,
1902.

2864   World Peace Foundation. "Chile and Argentina." *League of Nations Monthly Summary*
4 (Oct. 1921): 404–19.

Agreements, Proposals & Treaties, Interwar Years

For more general information about the issues of
arms control and disarmament during these two
decades, see Chapter 3, Historical Issues, Interwar
Years, and Chapter 4, League of Nations & United
Nations. The former contains, additionally, sections
on general assessments of naval limitation.

ARMISTICES (1918)

For texts, see Treaty of Versailles (1919), Documents.

General Accounts

2865   Maurice, Sir Frederick. *The Armistices of
1918.* London: Oxford Univ. Press, 1943.

2866   Nelson, K. L. "What Colonel House Overlooked in the Armistice." *Mid-America* 5:12
(1969): 75–91.

2867   Nudant, Charles. "Journal du President de la
Commission Interalliee de L'Armistice
1918–1919." *Revue de France* 4 (1925), pts
4–5.

2868   Rudin, Harry R. *Armistice, 1918.* New Haven: Yale Univ. Press, 1944.

2869   Shartle, Col. Samuel G. *Spa, Versailles,
Munich: An Account of the Armistice Commission.* Philadelphia: Dorrance, 1941.

2870   Weygand, Gen. Maxime. "Le Marechal Foch
et l'Armistice." *Revue des Deux Mondes*
(Nov. 1, 1938): 5–29.

TREATY OF VERSAILLES (1919)

For text of treaty, see Fred L. Israel, ed., *Major
Peace Treaties of Modern History, 1648–1967* (New
York: Chelsea House, 1967), II: 1363–83.

Documents

2871 Conference of Ambassadors. Paris. *Processed Minutes*. No. 1–327, January 26, 1920–January 12, 1931. 99 reels. Microfilm. Stanford, Ca.: Hoover Institution Microfilms.

2872 France. Ministere des Affaires Etrangeres. *Documents Diplomatiques: Documents Relatifs aux Negociations Concernant les Garanties de Securite Contre une Aggression de l'Allemagne, 10 Janvier 1919–7 Decembre 1923*. Paris: Imprimerie Nationale, 1924.

2873 Lapradelle, Albert G. de, ed. *La Paix de Versailles*. 12 vols. Paris: Les Editions Internationales, 1929–1939.

2874 League of Nations. Council. *Rules Adopted for the Exercise of the Right of Investigation Provided for by the Treaties of Versailles, Saint-Germain, Trianon and Neuilly.* 1926.IX.17. Geneva, 1926.

2875 Mantoux, Paul. *Les Deliberations du Conseil des Quatre*. 2 vols. Paris: Editions du Centre National de la Recherche Scientifique, 1955.

2876 Miller, David Hunter. *My Diary at the Conference of Paris*. 12 vols. New York: Appeal Printing, 1924. (Available in microfilm.)

2877 U.S. Department of State. *Foreign Relations of the United States: The Paris Peace Conference, 1919*. 13 vols. Washington, D.C.: G.P.O., 1942–1947.

2878 Woodward, E. L., and Rohan Butler, eds. *Documents on British Foreign Policy, 1919–1939*. First series, 8 vols. London: H.M.S.O., 1947–1958.

Paris Peace Conference

2879 Albrecht-Carrié, René. *Italy at the Paris Peace Conference*. New York: Columbia Univ. Press, 1938.

2880 D'Abernon, Viscount. *Versailles to Rapallo, 1920–1922*. New York: Doubleday, Doran, 1929.

2881 Daniels, Josephus. *The Wilson Era: Years of War and After, 1917–1923*. Chapel Hill: Univ. of North Carolina Press, 1946.

2882 Foch, Ferdinand. *The Memoirs of Marshal Foch*. Trans. by Col. T. B. Mott. New York: Doubleday, Doran, 1931.

2883 Glazebrook, G. P. de T. *Canada at the Paris Peace Conference*. New York: Oxford Univ. Press, 1942.

2884 Hankey, Lord. *The Supreme Control at the Paris Peace Conference, 1919*. London: Allen & Unwin, 1963.

2885 Lansing, Robert. *The Peace Negotiations: A Personal Narrative*. Boston: Houghton Mifflin, 1921.

2886 Lloyd George, David. *The Truth About the Peace Treaties*. 2 vols. London: Gollancz, 1938.

2887 Luckau, Alma. *The German Delegation at the Paris Peace Conference*. New York: Columbia Univ. Press, 1941.

2888 Marston, Frank S. *The Peace Conference of 1919: Organization and Procedure*. New York: Oxford Univ. Press, 1944.

2889 Nicholson, Harold. *Peacemaking 1919*. London: Constable, 1933.

2890 Noble, George B. *Policies and Opinions at Paris, 1919*. New York: Macmillan, 1935.

2891 Riddell, George A. *Lord Riddell's Intimate Diary of the Peace Conference and After, 1918–1923*. New York: Reynal & Hitchcock, 1934.

2892 Rothwell, V. H. *British War Aims and Peace Diplomacy, 1914–1918*. Oxford: Clarendon Press, 1971.

2893 Seymour, Charles, ed. *The Intimate Papers of Colonel House*. Vol. 4: *The Ending of the War*. Boston: Houghton Mifflin, 1928.

2894 ———. *Letters from the Paris Peace Conference*. New Haven: Yale Univ. Press, 1965.

2895 Tardieu, André. *The Truth About the Treaty*. Indianapolis: Bobbs-Merrill, 1921.

2896 Temperly, H. W. V., ed. *A History of the Peace Conference of Paris*. 6 vols. London: Oxford Univ. Press, 1924.

2897 Thompson, John M. *Russia, Bolshevism, and the Versailles Peace*. Princeton: Princeton Univ. Press, 1966.

2898 Tillman, Seth P. *Anglo-American Relations at the Paris Peace Conference of 1919*. Princeton: Princeton Univ. Press, 1961.

After Versailles Treaty

2899   Birdsall, Paul. *Versailles Twenty Years After*. New York: Reynal & Hitchcock, 1941.

2900   Jordan, W. M. *Great Britain, France and the German Problem: 1918–1939*. London: Oxford Univ. Press, 1943.

2901   Mowat, Charles L. *Britain Between the Wars, 1918–1940*. Chicago: Univ. of Chicago Press, 1955.

2902   Wolfers, Arnold. *Britain and France Between Two Wars: Conflicting Strategies of Peace Since Versailles*. New York: Harcourt, Brace, 1940.

German Disarmament

2903   Blucher, Princess Evelyn. "Disarmament of Germany: As Viewed by the Germans." *Nineteenth Century and After* 88 (Nov. 1920): 797–803.

2904   Boyle, Thomas E. "France, Great Britain and German Disarmament, 1919–1927." Ph.D. diss., State Univ. of New York, Stony Brook, 1972.

2905   Burns, Richard Dean, and Donald Urquidi. *Disarmament in Perspective*. 4 vols. Vol. 1: *Disarmament and the Peace Settlement*. Washington, D.C.: G.P.O., 1968.

2906   "Disarmament and the Peace Treaties: French and German Views." *Bulletin of International News* (Dec. 4, 1930): 1035–39.

2907   Genevey, Pierre. "Le Désarmement apres le Traité de Versailles." *Politique Etrangère* 32:1 (1967): 87–112.

2908   King, Jere C. *Foch vs. Clemenceau: France and German Disarmament, 1918–1919*. Cambridge: Harvard Univ. Press, 1960.

2909   Lowry, Francis B. "The Generals, the Armistice, and the Treaty of Versailles, 1919." Ph.D. diss., Duke Univ., 1963.

2910   Meinck, Gerhard. *Die Entwicklung der Militärischen Luftfahrt in Deutschland 1920–1933: Planung und Massnahmen sur Schaffung einer Flieger-truppe inder Riichswehr*. Stuttgart: Deutsches Verlags-Anstalt, 1962.

2911   Moll, Kenneth L. "Writing on Water with a Fork: 1919 Disarmament Efforts at Versailles." *Military Review* 44 (Aug. 1964): 29–37.

2912   Montgelas, M. "Germany's Burdens Under the Peace Settlements." *Current History* 27 (Feb. 1928): 660–68.

2913   Morgan, Gen. John H. *Assize of Arms: Being the Story of the Disarmament of Germany and Her Rearmament*. New York: Oxford Univ. Press, 1946.

2914   Oertzen, Friedrich Wilhelm von. *Das ist die Abrustung: Der Hohn der Abrustungsartikel von Versailles*. Oldenburg: G. Stalling, 1931.

2915   Reboul, Célestin A. *Non, l'Allemagne n'a pas Desarmé*. Paris: Lavauzelle, 1932.

2916   Schwendemann, Karl. *Versailles nach 15 Jahren: Der Stand der Revision des Versailler Diktate*. Berlin: Zentralverlag, 1935.

2917   Smith, Arthur L., Jr. "Le Désarmement de l'Allemagne en 1919: Les Vues du Général von Seeckt." *Revue Historique* 228 (Dec. 1962): 17–34.

Interallied Control Commission

2918   Apex. *The Uneasy Triangle: Four Years of the Occupation*. London: J. Murray, 1931.

2919   Bingham, Gen. Sir F. R. "Work with Allied Commission of Control in Germany, 1919–1924." *Journal of the Royal United Services Institution* 69 (Nov. 1924): 747–63.

2920   Carroll, Berenice A. "Germany Disarmed and Rearming, 1925–1935." *Journal of Peace Research* 3:2 (1966): 114–24.

2921   Cramon, August Frederick von. *Fort mit den Interalliierten Kontrollkommissionen*. Berlin: A. Scherl, 1922.

2922   Fox, John P. "Britain and the Inter-Allied Military Commission of Control, 1925–1926." *Journal of Contemporary History* 4 (Apr. 1969): 143–64.

2923   "German Criticism of Allied Methods." *Literary Digest* (Jan. 9, 1926): 16.

2924   "German Views of the End of Arms Control." *Literary Digest* (Mar. 5, 1927): 17.

2925   Guhr, Hans. *Sieben Jahre Interalliierte Militarkontrolle*. Breslau: W. G. Korn, 1927.

2926   League of Nations. "Disarmament: Application of Article 198 of the Treaty of Versailles." *Official Journal* 7 (Dec. 1926): 1629–43.

2927   ———. "[Dissolution of] Inter-allied Aeronautical Control in Germany." *Official Journal* 9 (May 1928): 608.

2928   ———. "Dissolution of the Inter-allied Military Commission of Control in Germany." *Official Journal* 8 (Sept. 1927): 1058.

2929   ———. "Dissolution of the Inter-allied Naval Commission of Control." *Official Journal* 6 (Mar. 1925): 304–05.

2930   ———. "Exercise of the Right of Investigation in the States Subjected to Investigation by the Treaties of Versailles, St. Germain, Trianon and Neuilly." *Official Journal* 5 (Oct. 1924): 1342–43, 1348–49, 1587–95; 6 (Feb. 1925): 133, 136–43, 147, 155; 6 (Apr. 1925): 489, 608–11; 6 (July 1925): 863–64; 7 (July 1926): 870; 8 (Feb. 1927): 162.

2931   Morgan, Gen. John H. "The Disarmament of Germany and After." *Quarterly Review* 242 (Oct. 1924): 415–57.

2932   Nollet, Gen. Charles. *Une Experience de Désarmement: Cinq Ans de Controle Militaire en Allemagne.* Paris: Gallimard, 1932.

2933   Roddie, Steward. *Peace Patrol.* New York: Putnam's, 1933.

2934   Roques, Paul. *Le Controle Militaire Interallie en Allemagne.* Paris: Bergen Levrault, 1927.

2935   Salewski, Michael. *Entwaffnung und Militarkontrolle in Deutschland, 1919–1927.* Munich: R. Oldenburg Verlag, 1966.

Russo-German Military Collaboration

2936   Carsten, Francis L. "The Reichswehr and the Red Army, 1920–1933." *Survey* 44–45 (Oct. 1962): 115–32.

2937   Dyck, Harvey L. *Weimar Germany and Soviet Russia, 1926–1933.* New York: Columbia Univ. Press, 1967.

2938   Freund, Gerald. *Unholy Alliance: Russian-German Relations from the Treaty of Brest-Litovsk to the Treaty of Berlin.* London: Chatto & Windus, 1957.

2939   Gatzke, Hans W. "Russo-German Military Collaboration during the Weimar Republic." *American Historical Review* 63 (Apr. 1958): 565–79.

2940   Hallgarten, George F. W. "General von Seeckt and Russia, 1920–1922." *Journal of Modern History* 21 (Mar. 1949): 28–34.

2941   Melville, Cecil F. *The Russian Face of Germany: An Account of the Secret Military Relations Between the German and Soviet-Russian Governments.* London: Wishart, 1932.

2942   Rosebaum, Kurt. *Community of Fate: German-Soviet Diplomatic Relations, 1922–1928.* Syracuse: Syracuse Univ. Press, 1965.

2943   Smith, Arthur L., Jr. "The German General Staff and Russia, 1919–1926." *Soviet Studies* 8 (Oct. 1956): 125–33.

2944   Spalki, Karl. "Begegnungen Zwischen Reichswehr und Roter Armee." *Aussenpolitik* 9 (July 1958): 506–13.

2945   Speidel, Helm. "Reichswehr und Rote Armee." *Vierteljahrshefte für Zeitgeschichte* 1 (1953): 9–45.

German Rearmament

2946   Banse, Ewald. *Germany Prepares for War.* New York, Harcourt, Brace, 1934.

2947   Bywater, Hector C. "The Rebirth of German Sea Power." *Nineteenth Century and After* 105 (Feb. 1929): 161–70.

2948   Carroll, Berenice A. *Design for Total War: Arms and Economics in the Third Reich.* The Hague: Mouton, 1968.

2949   Castellan, Georges. *Choix des Documents sur le Konzern Krupp et le Réarmement de l'Allemagne, 1918–1943.* Thesis. Paris: Faculté des Lettres, 1952.

2950   ———. *Le Rearmement Clandestin du Reich, 1930–1935: Vu par le 2e Bureau de L'Etat Major Francaise.* Paris: Plon, 1954.

2951   Gatzke, Hans W. *Stresemann and the Rearmament of Germany.* Baltimore: Johns Hopkins Press, 1954.

2952   "Germany and Rearmament." *Bulletin of International News* (Feb. 15, 1934): 499–509.

2953 "Germany's Secret Army Plans." *Living Age* (Dec. 3, 1931): 572–80.

2954 Graux, Lucien. *Histoire des Violations du Traité de Paix.* 4 vols. Paris: G. Crès, 1921–1927.

2955 "Great Britain and German Rearmament." *Bulletin of International News* (Mar. 1, 1934): 535–45; (Apr. 12, 1934): 631–41.

2956 Groener, Gen. Wilhelm. "German Military Power Since Versailles." *Foreign Affairs* 11 (Apr. 1933): 434–46.

2957 Gröner, Erich. *Die Schifte der Deutschen Kriegsmarine und Luftwaffe, 1939–1945.* Munich: J. F. Lehmanns, 1954.

2958 Gumbel, E. J. "Disarmament and Clandestine Rearmament Under the Weimar Republic." In Seymour Melman, ed., *Inspection for Disarmament.* New York: Columbia Univ. Press, 1958, pp. 203–19.

2959 Homze, Edward L. *Arming the Luftwaffe: The Reich Air Ministry and the German Aircraft Industry, 1919–1939.* Lincoln: Univ. of Nebraska Press, 1976.

2960 Hubatsch, Walther. *Der Admiralsstab und die Obersten Marinebehörden in Deutschland, 1848–1945.* Frankfurt: Bernard & Graefe, 1958.

2961 Klotz, Helmut. *Germany's Secret Armaments.* Trans. by H. J. Stenning. London: Jarrolds, 1934.

2962 Lore, Ludwig. "How Germany Arms." *Harper's* 168 (Apr. 1934): 505–17.

2963 Meinck, Gerhard. *Hitler und die Deutsche Aufrüstung.* Wiesbaden: Franz Steiner Verlag, 1959.

2964 Nelson, Walter H. *Germany Rearmed.* New York: Simon & Schuster, 1972.

2965 Overy, R. J. "Transportation and Rearmament in the Third Reich." *Historical Journal* 16 (June 1973): 389–409.

2966 Pilant, Paul. *L'Etat Actuel des Armements Allemands.* Paris: Querelle, 1932.

2967 Raeder, Adm. Erich. "Gegenwartsfragen der Reichsmarine." *Die Woche* [Berlin] (Oct. 29, 1932): 1326–32.

2968 Robertson, E. M. *Hitler's Pre-War Policy and Military Plans, 1933–1939.* New York: Citadel Press, 1963.

2969 Rosinski, Herbert. "Rebuilding the Reichswehr." *Atlantic Monthly* (Feb. 1944): 95–100.

2970 Schuddekopf, Otto E. *Das Heer und die Republik: Quellen zur Politik der Reichswehrführung 1918 bis 1933.* Hanover & Frankfurt: Norddeutsche Verlagsanstalt U. Goedel, 1955.

2971 Stolfi, Russel H. "Reality and Myth: French and German Preparations for War, 1933–1940." Ph.D. diss., Stanford Univ., 1966.

2972 Thomas, George R. *Geschichte der Deutschen Wehr-und-Rustungwirtschaft, 1918–1943/45.* Boppard: Boldt, 1966.

2973 Vogelsang, Thilo. "Neue Dokumente zur Geschichte der Reichswehr, 1930–1933." *Vierteljahrshefte für Zeitgeschichte* 2 (1954): 397–436.

2974 Volker, Karl-Heinz. "Die geheime Luftrüstung der Reichswehr und ihre Auswirkung auf den Flugzeugbestand der Luftwaffe bis zum Beginn des Zweiten Weltkrieges." *Wehrwissenschaftliche Rundschau* 12 (1962): 540–50.

2975 Woodman, Dorothy, ed. *Hitler Rearms: An Exposure of Germany's War Plans.* London: John Lane, 1934.

TREATY OF ST. GERMAIN-EN-LAYE (1919)

For text of treaty restricting military forces of Austria, see Lawrence Martin, *The Treaties of Peace, 1919–1923,* 3 vols. (New York: Carnegie Endowment for International Peace, 1924), I: 267–460.

Documents

2976 Temperly, H. W. V., ed. *A History of the Peace Conference of Paris.* 6 vols. London: Oxford Univ. Press, 1924, IV: 141–56, 389–411.

2977 U.S. Department of State. *Foreign Relations of the United States: The Paris Peace Conference, 1919.* 13 vols. Washington, D.C., 1942–1947, V: 888; VI: 258; VII: 875–87.

General Accounts

2978   Almond, Nina, and R. H. Lutz, eds. *The Treaty of St. Germain: A Documentary History of Its Territorial and Political Clauses.* Stanford: Stanford Univ. Press, 1935.

2979   Burns, Richard Dean, and Donald Urquidi. "Disarming the Vanquished: Austria, Hungary and Bulgaria." *Disarmament In Perspective, 1919–1939.* 4 vols. ACDA/RS-55. Washington, D.C.: G.P.O., 1968, I: 87–117.

2980   Dillon, E. J. *The Inside Story of the Peace Conference.* New York: Harpers, 1920, pp. 464–68.

2981   League of Nations. "Despatch of Arms to Austria." *Official Journal* 14 (Mar. 1933): 398–400.

2982   ———. "Execution of the Military, Naval, and Air Clauses in the Treaties of Peace: Article 159 of the Treaty of St. Germain. . . ." *Official Journal* 5 (July 1924): 920–22; 5 (Oct. 1924): 1298–99, 1315–17; 5 (Nov. 1924): 1658.

2983   ———. "Inter-Allied Military Control in Austria [terminated]." *Official Journal* 10 (Aug. 1929): 1276–77; 11 (May 1930): 384.

2984   ———. "The Position of the Council . . . in Regard to Article 159 of the Treaty of St. Germain. . . ." *Official Journal* 5 (July 1924): 1010–13.

2985   Marston, Frank S. *Peace Conference of 1919: Organization and Procedure.* London: Oxford Univ. Press, 1944, pp. 200–15.

Treaty of Neuilly (1919)

For text of treaty restricting military forces of Bulgaria, see Lawrence Martin, *The Treaties of Peace, 1919–1923,* 3 vols. (New York: Carnegie Endowment for International Peace, 1924), II: 653–788.

Documents

2986   Temperly, H. W. V., ed. *A History of the Peace Conference of Paris.* 6 vols. London: Oxford Univ. Press, 1924, IV: 166–70, 411–15.

2987   U.S. Department of State. *Foreign Relations of the United States: The Paris Peace Conference, 1919.* 13 vols. Washington, D.C.: G.P.O., 1942–1947, V: 627–38, 653–65, 877–88; VII: 736–37, 747–60; VIII: 634; IX: 523, 955–56, 961–64.

General Accounts

2988   Burns, Richard Dean, and Donald Urquidi. "Disarming the Vanquished: Austria, Hungary and Bulgaria." *Disarmament In Perspective, 1919–1939.* 4 vols. ACDA/RS-55. Washington, D.C.: G.P.O., 1968, I: 87–117.

2989   Drake, Edison J. "Bulgaria at the Paris Peace Conference: A Diplomatic History of the Treaty of Neuilly-Sur-Seine." Ph.D. diss., Georgetown Univ., 1967.

2990   Gewehr, Wesley M. *The Rise of Nationalism in the Balkans, 1800–1930.* New York: Holt, Rinehart & Winston, 1931, pp. 96–100.

2991   "Hungarian Law on War Materials: Import and Export Restrictions." *Board of Trade Journal and Commercial Gazette* (May 8, 1930): 629–37.

2992   League of Nations. "Application of Article 89 of the Treaty of Neuilly." *Official Journal* 9 (Mar. 1928): 298–309.

2993   ———. "Control of the Observance by Bulgaria of the Military and Air Clauses of the Treaty of Neuilly." *Official Journal* 4 (June 1923): 670–78.

2994   ———. "Execution by Bulgaria of the Military Clauses of the Treaty of Peace of Neuilly." *Official Journal* 6 (Mar. 1925): 304.

2995   ———. "Execution of the Military, Naval and Air Clauses in the Treaties of Peace: Article . . . 104 of the Treaty of Neuilly." *Official Journal* 5 (July 1924): 920–24; 5 (Oct. 1924): 1298–99, 1315–17; 5 (Nov. 1924): 1658.

2996   ———. "Inter-Allied Control in Bulgaria." *Official Journal* 9 (Mar. 1928): 324.

2997   ———. "The Position of the Council . . . in Regard to Article . . . 104 of the Treaty of Neuilly." *Official Journal* 5 (July 1924): 1010–13.

Treaty of Trianon (1920)

For text of treaty restricting military forces of Hungary, see Lawrence Martin, *The Treaties of*

Peace, 1919–1923, 3 vols. (New York: Carnegie Endowment for International Peace, 1924), I: 461–652.

Documents

2998 Temperly, H. W. V., ed. *A History of the Peace Conference of Paris*. 6 vols. London: Oxford Univ. Press, 1924, IV: 158–63, 415–27.

2999 U.S. Department of State. *Foreign Relations of the United States: The Paris Peace Conference, 1919*. 13 vols. Washington, D.C.: G.P.O., 1942–1947, V: 627–38, 653–65, 877–88; VII: 736–37, 747–60; VIII: 634; IX: 523, 955–56, 961–64.

General Accounts

3000 Apponyi, Albert, et al. *Justice for Hungary*. London: Longmans, Green, 1928.

3001 Bandholtz, Maj. Gen. Harry H. *An Undiplomatic Diary: By the American Member of the Inter-Allied Military Mission to Hungary, 1919–1920*. New York: Columbia Univ. Press, 1933.

3002 Burns, Richard Dean, and Donald Urquidi. "Disarming the Vanquished: Austria, Hungary and Bulgaria." *Disarmament In Perspective, 1919–1939*. 4 vols. Washington, D.C.: G.P.O., 1968, I: 87–117.

3003 Deak, Francis. *Hungary at the Paris Peace Conference*. New York: Columbia Univ. Press, 1942.

3004 Donald, Robert. *The Tragedy of Trianon*. London: T. Butterworth, 1928, pp. 288–90.

3005 Ignostus, Paul. *Hungary*. London: Praeger, 1972, pp. 154, 159–63, 265–66.

3006 League of Nations. "Application of Article 128 of the Treaty of Trianon." *Official Journal* 9 (Mar. 1928): 310–23.

3007 ———. "Dissolution of the Inter-Allied Military Commission of Control in Hungary." *Official Journal* 8 (Sept. 1927): 1058–59.

3008 ———. "Execution of the Military, Naval and Air Clauses in the Treaties of Peace: Article . . . 143 of the Treaty of Trianon. . . ." *Official Journal* 5 (July 1924): 920–22; 5 (Oct. 1924): 1298–99, 1315–17; 5 (Nov. 1924): 1658; 6 (Feb. 1925): 133.

3009 ———. "The Position of the Council . . . in Regard to Article . . . 143 of the Treaty of Trianon. . . ." *Official Journal* 5 (July 1924): 1010–13.

3010 ———. "Right of Investigation in Virtue of the Treaties of Peace." *Official Journal* 6 (Feb. 1925): 230–33.

3011 ———. Council. *Request of the Governments of Czechoslovakia, Roumania and the Kingdom of the Serbs, Croats and Slovenes for the Consideration by the Council of the Incident Which Occurred on January 1st, 1928, at the Szent-Gotthard Railway-Station on the Austro-Hungarian Frontier: Report to the Council by the Committee of Three*. C.199.1928.IX. Geneva, 1928.

Washington Naval Treaty (1922)

For text of treaty, see Charles I. Bevans, *Treaties and Other International Agreements of the United States of America* [multilateral] (Washington, D.C.: G.P.O., 1969), II: 351–71.

Documents

3012 Canada. Delegate to the Conference on the Limitation of Armament, Washington, D.C., 1921–1922. *Report of the Canadian Delegate including Treaties and Resolutions*. Sessional paper, no. 47. Ottawa: F. A. Acland, 1922.

3013 France, Ministère des Affaires Etrangères. *Conference de Washington, Juillet 1921–Fevrier 1922*. Paris: Imprimerie Nationale, 1923.

3014 Great Britain. Foreign Office. *Conference on Limitation of Armaments, Washington, 1921–1922* [treaties, resolutions, etc.]. Cmd. 1627. London: H.M.S.O., 1922.

3015 U.S. *Conference on the Limitation of Armaments, Washington, November 12, 1921–February 6, 1922*. Washington, D.C.: G.P.O., 1922.

3016 ———. Department of State. *Conference on the Limitation of Armament: Subcommittees*. Washington, D.C.: G.P.O., 1922.

3017 ———. *Report of the American Delegation of the Proceedings of the Conference on the Limitation of Armament*. Washington, D.C.: G.P.O., 1922.

3018 U.S. House. Committee on Foreign Affairs. Hearings: *Disarmament . . . on H.J. Res. 424, Authorizing and Empowering the President to Invite All Nations to Send Delegates to a Convention to Provide for Disarmament.* 66th Cong., 3d Sess., Jan. 14, 15, 1921.

3019 ————. Committee on Naval Affairs. Hearings: *Naval Policy of the United States: Including Discussions on Limitation of Armaments. . . .* 66th Cong., 3d Sess., 1921.

3020 U.S. Senate. Committee on Foreign Relations. *Conference on the Limitation of Armaments.* Sen. Doc. 126. 67th Cong., 2d Sess., 1922.

General Accounts

3021 Abbott, Alden H. "The League's Disarmament Activities and the Washington Conference." *Political Science Quarterly* 37 (Mar. 1922): 1–24.

3022 Abbott, Ernest H. "Stop-Now Policy." *Outlook* (Nov. 30, 1921): 508–11.

3023 Annunzio, Gabriele d'. *International Naval Disarmament Conferences at Washington and Genoa, November 1921–April 1922.* New York: Vanni, 1950.

3024 Buell, Raymond L. *The Washington Conference.* New York: D. Appleton, 1922.

3025 Bywater, Hector C. "The Limitation of Naval Armaments." *Atlantic Monthly* (Feb. 1922): 259–69.

3026 Dingman, Roger. *Power In the Pacific: The Origins of Naval Arms Limitation, 1914–1922.* Chicago: Univ. of Chicago Press, 1976.

3027 Gardiner, William H. "Naval View of the Conference." *Atlantic Monthly* (Apr. 1922): 521–30.

3028 Hinds, A. W. "Sea Power and Disarmament." *North American Review* 214 (Nov. 1921): 588–93.

3029 Hoag, Charles L. *Preface to Preparedness: The Washington Disarmament Conference and Public Opinion.* Washington, D.C.: American Council on Public Affairs, 1941.

3030 Klachko, Mary. "Anglo-American Naval Competition, 1918–1922." Ph.D. diss., Columbia Univ., 1962.

3031 Kolodkin, Milton A. "Russian Interests at the Washington Conference on the Limitation of Armaments, 1921–1922: With Special reference to United States' Policy." M.A. thesis, Columbia Univ., 1955.

3032 Lawton, L. "Evasions of Washington." *Fortnightly Review* 117 (Feb. 1922): 292–99.

3033 McCall, S. W. "The Washington Conference." *Atlantic Monthly* (Mar. 1922): 386–94.

3034 Obregon, A. "Washington Conference." *English Review* 34 (Jan. 1922): 73–76.

3035 Oulahan, R. V. "Personnel of the Arms Conference." *Current History* 15 (Nov. 1921): 185–93.

3036 Sales, Peter M. "American-Australian Relations and the Washington Disarmament Conference." *Australian Outlook* 27 (Dec. 1973): 329–38.

3037 Schornstheimer, G. "The Case Against the Naval Treaty." *Current History* 17 (June 1923): 401–06.

3038 Simonds, Frank H. "From Washington to Geneva." *Review of Reviews* 65 (Feb. 1922): 147–54.

3039 ————. "What was Gained at Washington." *Review of Reviews* 65 (Mar. 1922): 261–71.

3040 Sullivan, Mark. *The Great Adventure at Washington: The Story of the Conference.* New York: Doubleday, Page, 1922.

3041 Tarbell, Ida M. *Peacemakers, Blessed and Otherwise: Observations, Reflections and Irritations at an International Conference.* New York: Macmillan, 1922.

3042 Trask, David. *Anglo-American Naval Policies, 1917–1918.* Columbia: Univ. of Missouri Press, 1972.

3043 Vinson, John Chalmers. "The Problem of Australian Representation at the Washington Conference for the Limitation of Naval Armaments." *Australian Journal of Politics and History* 4:2 (1958): 155–64.

3044 Wells, Herbert G. *Washington and the Riddle of Peace.* New York: Macmillan, 1922.

3045 Wickersham, George W. "Has the Conference Succeeded?" *Forum* (Jan. 1922): 54–63.

3046 Wright, Quincy. "Washington Conference." *Minnesota Law Review* 6 (Mar. 1922): 279–99.

3047 Zeballos, Estanislao. "Conference on the Limitation of Armaments." *Inter-America* 5 (Apr. 1922): 210–13.

Anglo-Japanese Pact (1902)

3048 Boulger, D. C. "Anglo-Japanese Alliance." *Contemporary Review* 126 (Sept. 1920): 326–33.

3049 Brailsford, J. A. "Anglo-Japanese Alliance: An Australian View." *Nation* (Aug. 31, 1924): 234.

3050 Brobner, J. B. "Canada, the Anglo-Japanese Alliance and the Washington Conference." *Political Science Quarterly* 50 (Mar. 1935): 45–48.

3051 Chang, Chung-fu. *The Anglo-Japanese Alliance.* Baltimore: Johns Hopkins Press, 1931.

3052 Dolliver, J. P. "Significance of the Anglo-Japanese Alliance." *North American Review* 176 (May 1902): 594–605.

3053 Fry, Michael G. *Illusions of Security: North Atlantic Diplomacy, 1918–1922.* Toronto: Univ. of Toronto Press, 1972.

3054 ———. "The North Atlantic Triangle and the Abrogation of the Anglo-Japanese Alliance." *Journal of Modern History* 39 (Mar. 1967): 46–64.

3055 Galbraith, John S. "The Imperial Conference of 1921 and the Washington Conference." *Canadian Historical Review* 29 (June 1948): 143–52.

3056 Nish, Ian H. *Alliance in Decline: A Study in Anglo-Japanese Relations, 1908–1923.* London: Athlone Press (Univ. of London), 1972.

3057 ———. *The Anglo-Japanese Alliance: The Diplomacy of Two Island Empires, 1894–1907.* London: Athlone Press (Univ. of London), 1966.

3058 Okamoto, T. "American-Japanese Issues and the Anglo-Japanese Alliance." *Contemporary Review* 127 (Mar. 1921): 354–60.

3059 Peffer, N. "The Menace of the Anglo-Japanese Alliance." *Nation* (Nov. 9, 1921): 529–30.

3060 Rosen, F. "Vale the Anglo-Japanese Alliance." *Living Age* (Feb. 11, 1922): 325–27.

3061 Spinks, Charles N. "The Termination of the Anglo-Japanese Alliance." *Pacific Historical Review* 6 (Dec. 1937): 321–40.

3062 Stead, A. "Anglo-Japanese Agreement from Japanese Point of View." *Contemporary Review* 108 (Mar. 1902): 437–45.

3063 Tate, Merze, and Fidele Foy. "More Light on the Abrogation of the Anglo-Japanese Alliance." *Political Science Quarterly* 75 (Dec. 1959): 532–54.

3064 Vinson, John Chalmers. "The Imperial Conference of 1921 and the Anglo-Japanese Alliance." *Pacific Historical Review* 31 (Aug. 1962): 257–66.

Japanese Mandates

3065 Blakeslee, George H. "Mandates of the Pacific." *Foreign Affairs* 1 (Sept. 1922): 98–115.

3066 Burns, Richard Dean. "Inspection of the Mandates, 1919–1941." *Pacific Historical Review* 37 (Nov. 1968): 445–562.

3067 Gilchrist, Huntington. "The Japanese Islands: Annexation or Trusteeship?" *Foreign Affairs* 22 (July 1944): 635–42.

3068 Wilds, Thomas. "How Japan Fortified the Mandated Islands." *U.S. Naval Institute Proceedings* 81 (Apr. 1955): 401–07.

National Views—France

3069 Abbott, Ernest H. "France at the Conference." *Outlook* (Oct. 19, 1921): 248–49.

3070 Archimbaud, Léon. *La Conférence de Washington: 12 Novembre 1921–6 Fevrier 1922.* Paris: Payot, 1923.

3071 Ballou, Cmdr. Sidney. "French Point of View." *Outlook* (Jan. 25, 1922): 136–37.

3072 Cogniet, A. "Les Enseignements de la Guerre Navale et les Raisons Techniques de la Conference de Washington." *Mercure de France* (Oct. 15, 1923): 414–15.

3073 Degouy, J. B. "Après Washington et après Genes." *Revue des Deux Mondes* (June 1, 1922): 639–66.

3074   Huddleston, S. "France, Her Politicians, and the Washington Conference." *Atlantic Monthly* (Dec. 1921): 830–42.

3075   Hurd, Archibald S. "Is the Washington Naval Treaty Doomed?" *Fortnightly Review* (Jan. 1, 1923): 13–27.

3076   La Bruyère, René. "French Naval Ideas." *Atlantic Monthly* (June 1922): 826–33.

3077   ———. "La Marine francaise et le desarmement: avant la conference de Washington." *Revue des Deux Mondes* (Nov. 1, 1921): 118–32.

3078   ———. "Notre Détresse Navale." *Revue des Deux Mondes* (Aug. 15, 1921): 881–94.

3079   ———. "La Politique Navale de Washington." *Journal des Debats* (Apr. 7, 1922): 555–56.

3080   Lauzanne, S. "France, the Good Milch Cow." *Forum* (June 1922): 461–66.

3081   Le Chartier, G. "Choses Vues à Washington." *Revue des Deux Mondes* (Dec. 15, 1921): 913–30.

3082   Lippman, J. "Why France Cannot Disarm." *Current Opinion* (Mar. 1922): 317–20.

3083   Socas, Roberto E. "France, Naval Armament and Naval Disarmament, 1918–1922." Ph.D. diss., Columbia Univ., 1965.

3084   White, Donald G. "The French Navy and the Washington Conference." *Naval War College Review* 21 (Nov. 1969): 33–44.

National Views—Great Britain

3085   Abbott, Ernest H. "Britain at the Conference." *Outlook* (Nov. 2, 1921): 335–37.

3086   ———. "British 'Propaganda' and French 'Imperialism.'" *Outlook* (Jan. 11, 1922): 51–53.

3087   Birn, Donald S. "Britain and France at the Washington Conference, 1921–1922." Ph.D. diss., Columbia Univ., 1964.

3088   ———. "Open Diplomacy at the Washington Conference of 1921–1922: The British and French Experience." *Comparative Studies in Society and History* (July 1970): 297–319.

3089   Hurd, Archibald S. "Britain's Naval Policy." *Review of Reviews* 64 (Aug. 1921): 201–02.

3090   ———. "The British Fleet Dips its Ensign." *Fortnightly Review* 117 (Mar. 1922): 396–409.

3091   ———. "The Washington Conference and the Naval Issue." *Fortnightly Review* 116 (Nov. 1921): 717–26.

3092   ———. "The Washington Naval Standards: War Fleet of Four Million Tons." *Fortnightly Review* 117 (Jan. 1922): 106–21.

3093   Louis, William Roger. "The Washington Conference." *British Strategy in the Far East, 1919–1939.* Oxford: Clarendon Press, 1971, pp. 79–108.

3094   Scammell, J. M. "The New British Naval Base at Singapore." *Current History* 19 (Dec. 1923): 114–18.

3095   Wester-Wemyss, Lord. "And After Washington." *Nineteenth Century and After* 91 (Mar. 1922): 405–16.

National Views—Japan

3096   Abbott, Ernest H. "Japan at the Conference." *Outlook* (Oct. 12, 1921): 209–11.

3097   Asada, Sadao. "Japan's 'Special Interests' and the Washington Conference, 1921–1922." *American Historical Review* 67 (Oct. 1961): 62–70.

3098   Aston, G. "Japan and Singapore." *Nineteenth Century and After* 92 (Aug. 1923): 177–87.

3099   Bywater, Hector C. "Japan: A Sequel to the Washington Conference." *U.S. Naval Institute Proceedings* 49 (May 1923): 811–27.

3100   ———. "Naval Construction in Japan." *Scientific American* 126 (Jan. 1922): 25–26.

3101   Gardiner, William H. "Why Japan Would be Mistress of the Sea." *World's Work* (Dec. 1921): 212–17.

3102   Ichihashi, Yamato. *The Washington Conference and After: A Historical Survey.* Stanford: Stanford Univ. Press, 1928.

3103   Iyenaga, Toyokichi. "How Japan Views the Arms Conference." *Current History* 16 (Apr. 1922): 22–26.

3104   Kawakami, Kiyoshi K. *Japan's Pacific Policy: Especially in Relation to China, the Far East, and the Washington Conference.* New York: E. P. Dutton, 1922.

3105   Kinney, H. W. "Puzzled Japan." *Outlook* (Aug. 24, 1921): 641–42.

3106   Silver, Capt. Steven M., and Thomas H. Etzold. "Tactical Implications of the Washington Naval Conference." *U.S. Naval Institute Proceedings* 99 (Sept. 1973): 109–11.

National Views—United States

3107   American Federation of Labor. *Disarmament: The American Federation of Labor: Its Declarations and Actions in Support of Disarmament and International Peace. From the Official Records.* Washington, D.C., 1921.

3108   Braisted, William R. *The United States Navy in the Pacific, 1909–1922.* Austin: Univ. of Texas Press, 1971.

3109   Buckley, Thomas H. *The United States and the Washington Conference, 1921–1922.* Knoxville: Univ. of Tennessee Press, 1970.

3110   Buell, Raymond L., and Dudley W. Knox. "Did the U.S. Benefit by the Washington Conference? Pro and Con." *Congressional Digest* 4 (Jan. 1925): 133.

3111   Bullard, Arthur. *The ABC's of Disarmament and the Pacific Problems.* New York: Macmillan, 1921.

3112   Dingman, Roger. *Statesmen, Admirals and SALT: The United States and the Washington Conference, 1921–1922.* Santa Monica, Ca.: California Arms Control & Foreign Policy Seminar, Dec. 1972.

3113   Eberle, Adm. Edward W. "A Few Reflections on Our Navy and Some of Its Needs." *U.S. Naval Institute Proceedings* 50 (Sept. 1924): 1399–1407.

3114   Fiske, Adm. Bradley A. "Limitation of Armament, Uncensored Statement." *Harper's* 151 (July 1925): 129–30.

3115   ———. "Strongest Navy, Reply to Wester-Wemyss and Admiral Sims." *Current History* 16 (July 1922): 557–63.

3116   Gardiner, William H. "Some American Naval Views." *Fortnightly Review* (Mar. 1, 1923): 353–73.

3117   ———. "The Philippines and Sea Power." *North American Review* 216 (Aug. 1922): 165–73.

3118   Knapp, H. S. "The Limitation of Armament at the Conference of Washington." *U.S. Naval Institute Proceedings* 49 (May 1923): 768–76.

3119   Knox, Dudley W. *The Eclipse of American Sea Power.* New York: American Army and Navy Journal, 1922.

3120   Maddox, R. J. "Borah and the Battleships." *Idaho Yesterday* 9:2 (1965): 20–27.

3121   Overstreet, Capt. L. M. "Danger of Disarming America." *U.S. Naval Institute Proceedings* 50 (Sept. 1924): 1492–98.

3122   Pratt, Adm. William V. "Case for the Naval Treaty." *Current History* 18 (Apr. 1923): 1–5.

3123   ———. "Some Considerations Affecting Naval Policy." *U.S. Naval Institute Proceedings* 48 (Nov. 1922): 1845–62.

3124   Schornstheimer, G. "Our Navy Unready for War." *Current History* 17 (Jan. 1923): 624–31.

3125   Sims, Adm. William S. "Status of the United States Navy." *Current History* 16 (May 1922): 184–94.

3126   Sprout, Harold, and Margaret Sprout. *Toward a New Order of Sea Power: American Naval Policy and the World Scene, 1918–1922.* Princeton: Princeton Univ. Press, 1940.

3127   Stevens, William O. "Scrapping Mahan." *Yale Review* 12 (Apr. 1923): 528–42.

3128   Turnbull, A. D. "The United States a Second-Class Naval Power." *Current History* 19 (Mar. 1924): 969–83.

3129   Vinson, John Chalmers. *The Parchment Peace: The United States and the Washington Conference, 1921–1922.* Athens: Univ. of Georgia Press, 1955.

3130   Yardley, Herbert O. *The American Black Chamber* [Breaking the Japanese code during conference]. Indianapolis: Bobbs-Merrill, 1931.

GENOA CONFERENCE (1922)

Soviet delegate, M. Chicherin, opened conference (April 10) by calling for the "general iimitation of armaments" and the outlawing of gas and aerial warfare.

Documents

3131 Great Britain. Foreign Office. *Papers Relating to the International Economic Conference, Genoa, April–May, 1922.* Cmd. 1667. London: H.M.S.O., 1922.

3132 ———. *Resolutions Adopted by the Supreme Council at Cannes, January 22 as the Basis of the Genoa Conference.* Cmd. 1621. London: H.M.S.O., 1922.

3133 *International Economic Conference of Genoa. Provisional Verbatim Record. First Plenary Session.* Genoa, 1922.

3134 U.S.S.R. *Genoa Conference: Stenographic Account, Materials and Documents.* Moscow: Commissariat of Foreign Affairs, 1922.

General Accounts

3135 Fischer, Louis. "The Genoa Conference." *The Soviets in World Affairs.* 2 vols. 2d ed. Princeton: Princeton Univ. Press, 1951, I: 318–54.

3136 Mills, John Saxon. *The Genoa Conference.* New York: Dutton, 1922.

3137 Royal Institute of International Affairs. *Survey of International Affairs, 1920–1923.* London: Oxford Univ. Press, 1927, pp. 25–33.

MOSCOW DISARMAMENT CONFERENCE (1922)

Soviet government proposed military reductions and limitations to its neighbors; no agreement was reached.

Documents

3138 U.S.S.R. *Conference de Moscou pour la limitation des armaments.* Moscow: Commissariat du Peuple aux Affaires Etrangeres, 1923.

3139 ———. *Official Report of the Commissariat of Foreign Affairs for the Year, 1922.* Moscow: People's Commissar for Foreign Affairs, 1923.

General Accounts

3140 Clemens, Walter C., Jr. "Origins of the Soviet Campaign for Disarmament: The Soviet Position on Peace, Security and Revolution at the Genoa, Moscow and Lausanne Conferences, 1922–1923." Ph.D. diss., Columbia Univ., 1961.

3141 Fischer, Louis. "Disarmament and Bolshevism." *The Soviets in World Affairs.* 2 vols. 2d ed. Princeton: Princeton Univ. Press, 1951, I: 374–81.

3142 Strong, Anna L. "Disarmament Fails in Moscow." *Nation* (Feb. 7, 1923): 158–60.

3143 Toupine, A. "La Conference de Moscou sur le Désarmement." *L'Europe Nouvelle* (Dec. 30, 1922): 52.

CENTRAL AMERICAN ARMS LIMITATION TREATY (1923)

For text of treaty, see T. N. Dupuy and G. M. Hammerman, eds., "Convention on the Limitation of Armaments of Central American States, Washington, Feb. 7, 1923," *A Documentary History of Arms Control and Disarmament* (New York: Bowker, 1973), pp. 123–24.

Documents

3144 U.S. Department of State. *Conference on Central American Affairs, December 4, 1922 to February 7, 1923.* Washington, D.C.: G.P.O., 1923.

General Accounts

3145 "Central American Peace Treaties." *Current History* 17 (Mar. 1923): 1040.

3146 Scott, J. B. "The Central American Conference." *American Journal of International Law* 17 (Apr. 1923): 313–19.

SANTIAGO INTER-AMERICAN CONFERENCE (1923)

U.S. attempted to extend the "Washington naval limitation principles" to Latin American nations, with no success.

Documents

3147 U.S. Department of State. *Report of Delegates of United States to Fifth International Conference of American States Held at Santiago, Chile, March 25–May 3, 1923, with Appendices.* Washington, D.C.: G.P.O., 1924.

3148 *Verbatim Record of the Plenary Sessions of the Fifth International Conference of American States.* 2 vols. Santiago, 1923–1925.

General Accounts

3149 "Fifth Inter American Conference at Santiago." *Current History* 18 (May 1923): 185–88.

3150 "Fifth Pan American Conference at Santiago." *Bulletin of the Pan American Union* 57 (Aug. 1923): 109–78.

3151 Grieb, Kenneth J. "The United States and the Fifth Pan American Conference." *Inter-American Review of Bibliography* 20:2 (1970): 157–68.

3152 Livermore, Seward W. "Battleship Diplomacy in South America, 1905–1925." *Journal of Modern History* 16 (Mar. 1944): 31–48.

3153 Nieto, Don Rafael. "Why the Santiago Conference Failed." *Living Age* (Aug. 11, 1923): 247–50.

3154 "Uncle Sam Under Suspicion." *Living Age* (June 2, 1923): 495–96.

3155 "Was the Fifth Pan-American Conference a Failure?" *Pan-American Magazine* 283 (Oct. 1923): 164–68.

3156 "Washington's Disillusionment at Santiago." *Living Age* (Aug. 11, 1923): 250–53.

ROME NAVAL CONFERENCE (1924)

An attempt to extend the principles of the Washington naval treaty to nonsignatory nations.

Documents

(Documents may be found in League of Nations, *Official Journal* 5 (Apr. 1924): 697–714.)

3157 League of Nations. *Draft Convention for the Extension of the Washington Naval Treaty to the Nonsignatory Powers Members of the League of Nations.* Geneva, 1922.

3158 ———. *Extension to Non-signatory States of the Principles of the Treaty of Washington for the Limitation of Naval Armaments.* C.76. 1924. Geneva, 1924.

General Accounts

3159 Berens, E. A. "Statement to the Press [by Soviet delegate]." *Russian Review* (Apr. 15, 1924): 320–21.

3160 Bywater, Hector C. "A Sequel to the Washington Conference." *Atlantic Monthly* (Feb. 1923): 240–49.

3161 League of Nations. "Extension of the Principles of the Washington Naval Treaty to Non-Signatory Nations." *Official Journal* 4 (Nov. 1923): 1476–77.

3162 ———. "Limitation of Naval Armaments [Rome Conf.]." *Official Journal* 5 (July 1924): 998.

3163 ———. "Observations of the Governments on the Report on the Session of the Naval Sub-Commission of the Permanent Advisory Commission . . . . Held at Rome, Feb. 14–25, 1924." *Official Journal* 5 (Aug. 1924): 1040–47; 5 (Sept. 1924): 1177–79.

3164 Royal Institute of International Affairs. *Survey of International Affairs, 1924.* London: Oxford Univ. Press, 1928, pp. 77–80.

GENEVA NAVAL CONFERENCE (1927)

An unsuccessful conference called by President Calvin Coolidge to extend naval limitations begun at Washington in 1922.

Documents

3165 Coolidge, Pres. Calvin. "Message on Naval Armaments with Text of Memorandum." *Current History* 25 (Mar. 1927): 912–15.

3166 [Great Britain.] *Geneva Conference for the Limitation of Naval Armaments, June–August 1927: Speeches in Plenary Session by the Right Hon. W. C. Bridgeman, M.P., First Lord of the Admiralty.* Cmd. 2964. London: HMSO, 1927.

3167 U.S. Senate. Hearings: *Alleged Activities at the Geneva Conference . . . pursuant to S. Res. 114.* [Shearer episode.] 71st Cong., 1st Sess., 1928.

3168 ——. *Records of the Conference for the Limitation of Naval Armaments Held at Geneva, Switzerland from June 20 to August 4, 1927.* Sen. Doc. 55. 70th Cong., 1st Sess., 1928.

General Accounts

3169 Allen, Robert S. "Mr. Shearer Likes a Big Navy." *Nation* (Oct. 9, 1929): 378–79.

3170 Butler, Thomas S. "America Misled by Five Power Naval Treaty." *Current History* 26 (Apr. 1927): 86–92.

3171 ——. "Don't Give Up the Ships." *North American Review* 224 (June 1927): 214–22.

3172 ——. "Where the Arms Conference Failed: A World Portrait." *Literary Digest* 92 (Jan. 1927): 7.

3173 Custer, Ben Scott. *The Geneva Conference for the Limitation of Naval Armament, 1927.* Ph.D. diss., Georgetown Univ., 1948.

3174 "Disarmament and the Five Naval Powers." *Foreign Policy Association Information Service* (Mar. 20, 1927): 17–32.

3175 Dubay, Robert W. "The Geneva Naval Conference of 1927: A Study of Battleship Diplomacy." *Southern Quarterly* 8 (Jan. 1970): 177–200.

3176 Gatewood, R. D. "Sea Power and American Destiny." *U.S. Naval Institute Proceedings* 53 (Oct. 1927): 1076–80.

3177 Gerould, James T. "Disagreement at Conference on Naval Disarmament." *Current History* 26 (Aug. 1927): 792–97.

3178 ——. "Disarmament Negotiations." *Current History* 26 (May 1927): 267–69.

3179 ——. "Failure of Three Power Naval Conference." *Current History* 26 (Sept. 1927): 945–49.

3180 ——. "Naval Powers' Reception of the American Proposal." *Current History* 26 (Apr. 1927): 93–98.

3181 Hooker, Richard. "The Geneva Naval Conference." *Yale Review* 17 (Jan. 1928): 263–80.

3182 Howe, Walter B. "Why the United States asks Naval Equality." *U.S. Naval Institute Proceedings* 53 (Oct. 1927): 1056–58.

3183 "The International Naval Situation." *Foreign Policy Association Information Service* (Jan. 6, 1928): 310–31.

3184 Jones, Adm. Hilary P. "Reduction and Limitation of Armaments." *Annals of the Amer. Acad. of Pol. & Soc. Sci.* 138 (July 1928): 173–78.

3185 Jouvenel, Henry E. "France and Italy." *Foreign Affairs* 5 (July 1927): 538–52.

3186 Kawakami, Kiyoshi K. "The Hidden Conflict at the Three-Power Naval Conference." *Current History* 27 (Oct. 1927): 106–11.

3187 Noel-Baker, Philip J. *Disarmament and the Coolidge Conference.* London: Hogarth Press, 1927.

3188 Rodgers, Rear Adm. William L. "American Naval Policy and the Tri-Power Conference at Geneva, 1927." *U.S. Naval Institute Proceedings* 54 (July 1928): 572–78.

3189 Wheeler-Bennett, John W. "The Geneva Conference, 1927." *Disarmament and Security Since Locarno, 1925–1931.* London: Allen & Unwin, 1932, pp. 103–27.

ANGLO-FRENCH COMPROMISE (1928)

For text of compromise, see *Documents on British Foreign Policy, 1919–1939*, series IA (London: Oxford Univ. Press, 1973), V: 681, 775, 779–81.

Documents

3190 France. Ministère des Affaires Etrangères. *Limitation des Armements Navals. Trente-cinq Pieces Relatives aux Travaux Preparatoires du Désarmement et a la Limitation des Armements Navals. 21 Mars 1927–6 Octobre 1928.* Paris: Imprimerie des Journaux Officiels, 1928.

3191 Great Britain. Foreign and Commonwealth

Office. *Documents on British Foreign Policy, 1919–1939.* Series IA. London: Oxford Univ. Press, 1973, V: 602–928.

3192   ———. Foreign Office. *Papers Regarding the Limitation of Naval Armaments.* London: H.M.S.O., 1928.

General Accounts

3193   "The Anglo-French Accord." *Foreign Policy Association Information Service* (Nov. 23, 1928): 389–93.

3194   "The Anglo-French Project for Limitation of Armament: British White Paper, Address of Viscount Grey of Fallodon, Debate in the House of Lords." *International Conciliation,* no. 246 (Jan. 1929): 3–79.

3195   Carlton, David. "The Anglo-French Compromise on Arms Limitation, 1928." *Journal of British Studies* 8 (May 1969): 141–62.

3196   Gerould, James T. "America Rejects Franco-British Naval Accord: With Text of Note." *Current History* 29 (Nov. 1928): 306–10.

3197   ———. "Anglo-American Differences on Naval Disarmament." *Current History* 29 (Jan. 1929): 667–68.

3198   Glasgow, George. "The Anglo-French Gaffe." *Contemporary Review* 134 (Nov. 1928): 645–53.

3199   ———. "The Epitaph of a Compromise." *Contemporary Review* 134 (Dec. 1928): 777–89.

3200   Royal Institute of International Affairs. *Survey of International Affairs, 1928.* London: Oxford Univ. Press, 1929: 61–80.

3201   Wheeler-Bennett, John W. "Anglo-French Compromise." *Disarmament and Security Since Locarno, 1925–1931.* London: Allen & Unwin, 1932: pp. 127–42.

London Naval Conference (1930)

For text of treaty, see Charles I. Bevans, *Treaties and Other International Agreements of the United States of America, 1776–1949* [multilateral] *(Washington, D.C.: G.P.O., 1969), II: 1055–75.*

Documents

3202   Australia. Delegation to the Naval Conference. *Limitation of Naval Armament: Report of the Australian Delegate.* Canberra: H. J. Green, 1930.

3203   Great Britain. Foreign Office. *Documents of the London Naval Conference, 1930. . . .* London: H.M.S.O., 1930.

3204   U.S. Department of State. *London Naval Conference: Speeches and Press Statements by Members of the American Delegation, Jan. 20–Apr. 29, 1930.* Conf. Series no. 3. Washington, D.C.: G.P.O., 1930.

3205   ———. *Proceedings of the London Naval Conference of 1930 and Supplementary Documents.* Conf. Series no. 6. Washington, D.C.: G.P.O., 1930.

3206   U.S. Senate. Report: *Limitation and Reduction of Naval Armament.* Pts 1, 2. Sen. Doc. 1080. 71st Cong., 2d Sess., 1930.

3207   U.S. Senate. Committee on Foreign Relations. Hearings: *Treaty on the Limitation of Naval Armaments.* 71st Cong., 2d Sess., May 12–28, 1930.

3208   ———. Committee on Naval Affairs. Hearings: *London Naval Treaty of 1930.* 71st Cong., 2d Sess., May 14–29, 1930.

General Accounts

3209   Angell, Norman. "Naval Politics at London." *Nation* (Feb. 5, 1930): 146–47.

3210   ———. "The Ultimate Politics of the Conference." *Contemporary Review* 137 (Mar. 1930): 273–80.

3211   Arnold-Forster, D. "The Naval Conference." *Fortnightly Review* 132 (Mar. 1930): 289–309.

3212   ———. "The New Entente: Parity in Prospect." *Fortnightly Review* 134 (Nov. 1929): 629–35.

3213   Atkinson, James D. "The London Naval Conference of 1930." Ph.D. diss., Georgetown Univ., 1949.

3214   Barnes, H. E. "Disarmament: London Naval Conference Balked by Imperialist Designs." *Labor Age* (Mar. 1930): 14–17.

3215   Bellairs, Cmdr. Carlyon W. *The Naval Conference and After.* London: Faber & Faber, 1930.

3216   Brailsford, Henry N. "Battleship in the Conference." *New Republic* (Feb. 19, 1930): 16–18.

3217   Bywater, Hector C. "The London Naval Conference." *Nineteenth Century and After* 106 (Dec. 1929): 717–30.

3218   Dewar, Capt. Alfred C. "The London Naval Treaty." *Brassey's Naval and Shipping Annual* (1931): 69–84.

3219   Dewar, Adm. K. G. B. "The Naval Conference of 1930." *Nineteenth Century and After* 107 (Mar. 1930): 285–99.

3220   Dorling, Henry F. "The Naval Treaty and After." *Nineteenth Century and After* 109 (Apr. 1931): 414–28.

3221   Dow, H. E. "The United States and Sea Power." *U.S. Naval Institute Proceedings* 55 (Feb. 1929): 131–36.

3222   Drury-Lowe, S. R. "The Naval Conference and After." *Contemporary Review* 137 (May 1930): 545–54.

3223   ———. "Prospects of the Five Power Naval Conference." *Contemporary Review* 137 (Jan. 1930): 7–12.

3224   Dutt, R. Palme. "The Naval Conference and the Crisis of Capitalism." *Communist Review* 2 (Mar. 1930): 109–17; 9 (Aug. 1930): 735–43.

3225   Eggleston, F. W. "Disarmament and the Pacific." *Pacific Affairs* 3 (Dec. 1930): 1095–1108.

3226   French, Burton L. "Naval Reduction: What it Means in Money." *Current History* 31 (Jan. 1930): 711–17.

3227   Gatch, Lt. Cmdr. T. L. "The London Naval Conference." *U.S. Naval Institute Proceedings* 56 (Sept. 1930): 822–26.

3228   Gerould, James T. "Naval Disarmament Conference." *Current History* 32 (Mar. 1930): 1187–91.

3229   Glasgow, George. "The Five Power Conference." *Contemporary Review* 136 (Dec. 1929): 782–90.

3230   ———. "The Naval Conference." *Contemporary Review* 137 (Mar. 1930): 373–88.

3231   Harley, J. E. "The Main Issue in Disarmament." *Fortnightly Review* 133 (June 1930): 751–60.

3232   Houghton, Alanson B. "Causes of Anglo-American Differences, III: An American Plea for Understanding." *Current History* 32 (May 1930): 203–05.

3233   Howland, Charles P. "Navies and Peace: An American View." *Foreign Affairs* 8 (Oct. 1929): 30–40.

3234   ———. "Politics and Ships at London." *Yale Review* 19 (June 1930): 668–87.

3235   Hughes, Charles P. "The Modern Naval Cruiser and Its Varied Uses." *Congressional Digest* 8 (Jan. 1929): 4–5.

3236   "Limitations of Naval Armaments: With Pro and Con Discussion." *Congressional Digest* 8 (Oct. 1929): 225–51.

3237   MacKay, R. A. "Political Implications of the London Conference." *Queen's Quarterly* 37 (Summer 1930): 532–42.

3238   "Naval Pact as Viewed by the Nations." *Current History* 32 (June 1930): 441–62.

3239   Percival, Franklin G. "The Cruiser Problem." *U.S. Naval Institute Proceedings* 56 (May 1930): 387–99.

3240   Phayre, Ignatius. "The 'Big Navy' of the United States." *Quarterly Review* [London] 252 (Jan. 1929): 147–69.

3241   Read, Conyers. "More Light on the London Naval Treaty of 1930." *American Philosophical Society Proceedings* (Sept. 9, 1949): 290–308.

3242   ———. "Recent United States and British Government Publications on the London Naval Conference of 1930." *American Historical Review* 54 (1948–1949): 307–14.

3243   Shaw, Roger. "The London Naval Conference of 1930." Ph.D. diss., Fordham Univ., 1946.

3244   Sidebottom, Herbert. "The London Naval Treaty." *Nineteenth Century and After* 107 (June 1930): 754–62.

3245   Simonds, Frank H. "Britannia Shares the Waves." *Review of Reviews* 81 (June 1930): 52–55.

3246   ———. "What was Wrong at the London Conference?" *Review of Reviews* 81 (May 1930): 40–45.

3247 Stone, William T. "The London Naval Conference, Jan. 21–Apr. 22, 1930." *Foreign Policy Association Information Service* (May 28, 1930): 101–30.

3248 Taylor, E. A. "A Criticism of the Naval Conference." *English Review* 50 (June 1930): 681–88.

3249 ———. "The Naval Conference." *Empire Review* 51 (Mar. 1930): 176–82.

3250 Wainhouse, David W. "The Joker in the Naval Treaty." *Nation* (May 28, 1930): 634–36.

3251 Wallin, Homer N. "Permissible Building Programs Under the London Naval Treaty." *U.S. Naval Institute Proceedings* 56 (Dec. 1930): 1074–79.

3252 Wheeler-Bennett, John W. "The London Naval Conference, 1930." *Disarmament and Security Since Locarno, 1925–1931.* London: Allen & Unwin, 1932, pp. 195–215.

3253 Whitten, John B. "The London Naval Conference." *Current History* 32 (June 1930): 441–46.

3254 Wilbur, Curtis D. "Naval Developments Since 1921." *Congressional Digest* 8 (Jan. 1929): 1–3, 32.

3255 Williams, Benjamin H. *The London Naval Conference: Its Background and Results.* Pittsburgh: Univ. of Pittsburgh Press, 1930.

Anglo-American Differences (1929)

3256 Aldis, Graham. "Kellogg, Cruisers and Sanity." *Virginia Quarterly Review* 5 (Apr. 1929): 171–81.

3257 "Anglo-American Naval Competition." *Literary Digest* (Dec. 29, 1928): 13–14.

3258 "Anglo-American Naval Situation." *Editorial Research Reports* (Sept. 28, 1929): 751–67.

3259 Buell, Raymond L. "Anglo-American Naval Understanding." *Foreign Policy Association Information Service* 5 (Mar. 1929): 175–92.

3260 Buesst, Tristan. "Anglo-American Relations: An Australian View." *International Affairs* [London] 8 (Nov. 1929): 605–16.

3261 "Cruiser Victory that May Mean Disarmament: Issues Behind the Cruiser Controversy: Germany's Vest-Pocket Dreadnought." *Literary Digest* (Feb. 16, 1929): 5–8, 9–11, 13.

3262 Davis, John W. "Anglo-American Relations and Sea Power." *Foreign Affairs* 7 (Apr. 1929): 345–55.

3263 Dulles, Allen W. "The Threat of Anglo-American Naval Rivalry." *Foreign Affairs* 7 (Jan. 1929): 173–82.

3264 Dutt, R. Palme. "The Causes of Anglo-American Differences—Dangers of War." *Current History* 30 (May 1929): 189–99.

3265 Gerould, James T. "America and Britain Reach Preliminary Agreement on Naval Reduction." *Current History* 31 (Oct. 1929): 149–50.

3266 Glasgow, George. "Anglo-American Relations." *Contemporary Review* 136 (Aug. 1929): 242–47.

3267 Godfrey, James L. "Anglo-American Naval Conversations Preliminary to the London Naval Conference of 1930." *South Atlantic Quarterly* 49 (July 1950): 303–16.

3268 Kellogg, Paul U. "Pacts, Cruisers and—Then What?" *Survey* (Mar. 1, 1929): 732–34.

3269 Kenworthy, J. M. "The New Entente." *Fortnightly Review* 136 (Nov. 1929): 620–28.

3270 "Practical Steps Toward Armament Limitation—The Action of Great Britain and the United States in Curtailing Navies." *Commercial and Financial Chronicle* (July 27, 1929): 536–38, 562–63.

3271 Wilson, P. W. "Causes of Anglo-American Rivalry." *Current History* 30 (May 1929): 199–202.

Parity & Ratios

3272 Angell, Norman. "Parity or Reduction." *Nation* (Mar. 5, 1930): 266–68.

3273 Gardiner, William H. "Naval Fleet Ratios." *Review of Reviews* 69 (Mar. 1924): 305–08.

3274 Knox, Dudley W. "Naval Reduction and Parity." *Scientific American* 141 (Oct. 1929): 320–22.

3275 ———, and B. B. Wygant. "Five-Five-Three." *Outlook* (Dec. 13, 1922): 668–71.

3276 "Magic in the Hoover Naval Yardstick: European Reservations of our Naval Bomb-Shell." *Literary Digest* (May 11, 1929): 5–7, 17.

3277 "Naval Reduction and the Yardstick." *Economist* (July 27, 1929): 157–58.

3278 Noel-Baker, Philip J. "Problem of the Ratio." *Disarmament.* London: Hogarth Press, 1926, pp. 245–274.

3279 O'Connor, Raymond G. "The Yardstick and Naval Disarmament in the 1920's." *Mississippi Valley Historical Review* 45 (Dec. 1958): 441–62.

3280 Rodman, Hugh. "Emphasis on Parity in Navies Explained." *United States Daily* (Oct. 30, 1929): 2125.

3281 Simonds, Frank H. "Question of Naval Parity." *Review of Reviews* 80 (Aug. 1929): 60–62.

3282 ———. "What is Naval Parity?" *Review of Reviews* 78 (Nov. 1928): 502–04.

3283 Vickery, H. L. "Naval Yardstick." *Foreign Affairs* 8 (Oct. 1929): 142–44.

National Views—Great Britain

3284 Carlton, David. *MacDonald vs. Henderson: The Foreign Policy of the Second Labour Government.* London: Macmillan, 1970.

3285 Cobb, Cyril. "Navy and Disarmament." *Empire Review* 50 (Nov. 1929): 329–34.

3286 Dewar, Adm. K. G. B. "The End of the Naval Conference." *Nineteenth Century and After* 107 (May 1930): 606–09.

3287 Geraud, André. "British Policy as Seen by a Frenchman." *International Affairs* [London] 9 (Mar. 1930): 154–79.

3288 Graham, Gladys M. "The House of Lords Debates the London Naval Treaty." *Quarterly Journal of Speech* 16 (Nov. 1930): 414–20.

3289 Kerr, Philip. "Navies and Peace: A British View." *Foreign Affairs* 8 (Oct. 1929): 20–29.

3290 MacDonald, J. Ramsay. "The London Naval Conference, 1930." *International Affairs* [London] 9 (July 1930): 429–51.

3291 Richmond, Adm. Sir Herbert W. "Immediate Problems of Naval Reduction." *Foreign Affairs* 9 (Apr. 1931): 371–88.

3292 Steed, H. Wickham. "How the Results are Viewed in Each Nation, II: Great Britain." *Current History* 32 (June 1930): 449–51.

National Views—France, Italy, etc.

3293 Bouy, Raymond. *Le Désarmement Naval: La Conférence de Londres.* Paris: Press Universitaires, 1931.

3294 "Canada and the Problem of Naval Disarmament." *International Affairs* [London] 8 (Sept. 1929): 433–44.

3295 Cardona y Prieto, Pedro Maria. *La Conferencia y el Tratado Maritimo-Naval de Londres (1930) desde el Punto de Vista Español.* Madrid, 1931.

3296 Dell, Robert. "France Wins at London." *Nation* (May 7, 1930): 542–43.

3297 Docteur, J. "Results of the London Naval Conference, III: France." *Current History* 32 (June 1930): 451–53.

3298 Geraud, André [Pertinax]. "The London Naval Conference—A French View." *Foreign Affairs* 8 (July 1930): 519–32.

3299 Lyautey, Pierre. "After the London Conference: A French View." *Nineteenth Century and After* 108 (July 1930): 25–35.

3300 Mosca, Rudolfo. *Il Disarmo Navale e la Conferenza di Londra.* Pavia, 1931.

3301 Schanzer, Carlo. "Results of the London Naval Conference, IV: Italy." *Current History* 32 (June 1930): 454–57.

National Views—Japan

3302 "How Japan Wants Naval Reduction." *Literary Digest* (Nov. 2, 1929): 16–17.

3303 Kawakami, Kiyoshi K. "Japan and the Naval Pact." *Nation* (June 25, 1930): 727–29.

3304 ———. "The London Naval Conference as Viewed from Japan." *Nineteenth Century and After* 106 (Dec. 1929): 731–42.

3305 ———. "Results of the London Naval Conference, V: Japan." *Current History* 32 (Dec. 1930): 458–60.

3306 Mayer-Oakes, Thomas F. *Fragile Victory: Prince Saionji and the 1930 London Treaty*

Issue. From the Memoirs of Baron Harada Kumao. Detroit: Wayne State Univ. Press, 1968.

3307 ———. "Prince Saionji and the London Naval Conference of 1930." Ph.D. diss., Univ. of Chicago, 1955.

3308 Oliver, John Burrell. "Japan's Role in the Origins of the London Naval Treaty of 1930: A Study in Diplomatic History." Ph.D. diss., Duke Univ., 1954.

3309 Osumi, Mineo. "The London Conference and Japanese Psychology." *Japan Magazine* 20 (July 1930): 381–82.

3310 ———. "What Japan Thinks." *Congressional Digest* 8 (Jan. 1929): 6.

National Views—United States

3311 Hart, Albert B. "President Hoover's Challenge to Big Navy Propaganda." *Current History* 31 (Oct. 1929): 156–58.

3312 Hill, David Jayne. "How the Result is Viewed in Each Nation, I: The United States." *Current History* 32 (June 1930): 446–49.

3313 "Hoover Administration Appeals for Further Limitation of Naval Armaments." *Congressional Digest* 8 (Oct. 1929): 235–38.

3314 Kinkaid, Cmdr. T. C. "Present Problems of Naval Reduction." *U.S. Naval Institute Proceedings* 57 (July 1931): 949–54.

3315 Knox, Dudley W. "The London Treaty and American Naval Policy." *U.S. Naval Institute Proceedings* 57 (Aug. 1931): 1079–88.

3316 Lippmann, Walter. "The London Naval Conference—An American View." *Foreign Affairs* 8 (July 1930): 499–518.

3317 Lovette, Leland P. "Naval Policy at the Crossroads." *U.S. Naval Institute Proceedings* 56 (Apr. 1930): 269–80.

3318 O'Connor, Raymond G. *Perilous Equilibrium: The United States and the London Naval Conference of 1930.* Lawrence: Univ. Press of Kansas, 1962.

3319 Talbot, Melvin F. "Our Navy Under the London Treaty." *Atlantic Monthly* (Sept. 1930): 410–19.

3320 "The United States Senate and the London Naval Treaty." *Bulletin of International News* (July 31, 1930): 767–81.

3321 Wickersham, George W. "America's Naval Challenge." *Current History* 30 (Apr. 1929): 31–37.

3322 Wilson, John R. M. "Herbert Hoover and the Armed Forces: A Study of Presidential Attitudes and Policy." Ph.D. diss., Northwestern Univ., 1971.

Franco-Italian Negotiations, 1930–1931

3323 Engely, Giovanni. *The Politics of Naval Disarmament.* Trans. by H. V. Rhodes. London: Williams & Norgate, 1932.

3324 "Franco-Italian Naval Negotiations." *International News Bulletin* (Apr. 23, 1931): 1255–62.

3325 Great Britain. Foreign Office. *Memorandum on the Results of the Negotiations with France and Italy for the Reduction and Limitation of Naval Armaments, February-March 1931.* Cmd. 3812. London: H.M.S.O., 1931.

3326 Stone, William T. "The Franco-Italian Naval Dispute." *Foreign Policy Reports* (June 24, 1931): 78–85.

3327 Swing, Raymond Gram. "The Controversy Between France and Italy." *Congressional Digest* 8 (June–July 1930): 166, 192.

TURKO-GREEK NAVAL PROTOCOL (1930)

For text of protocol, see League of Nations, *Treaty Series* (London: Harrison, 1931–1932), vol. 125, p. 21.

3328 Burns, Richard Dean, and Seymour L. Chapin. "Near Eastern Naval Limitation Pacts, 1930–1931." *East European Quarterly* 3 (Mar. 1970): 72–87.

3329 Collins, J. Walter. "The Turco-Greek Rapprochement." *Contemporary Review* 139 (Feb. 1931): 203–08.

3330 "Greece and Turkey Friends." *Literary Digest* (July 19, 1930): 16.

3331   Miller, William. "The Greco-Turkish Friendship." *Contemporary Review* 140 (Dec. 1931): 718–26.

3332   Pallis, Alexander A. "The End of the Greco-Turkish Fund." *Contemporary Review* 138 (Oct. 1930): 615–20.

3333   Royal Institute of International Affairs. *Survey of International Affairs, 1930.* London: Oxford Univ. Press, 1931, pp. 158, 165–66.

TURKO-SOVIET NAVAL PROTOCOL (1931)

For text of protocol, see Leonard Shapiro, ed., *Soviet Treaty Series* (Washington, D.C.: Georgetown Univ. Press, 1955), II, doc. no. 347.

3334   Burns, Richard Dean, and Seymour L. Chapin. "Near Eastern Naval Limitation Pacts, 1930–1931." *East European Quarterly* 3 (Mar. 1970): 72–87.

3335   "A New Russo-Turkish Love Feast." *Literary Digest* (Apr. 25, 1931): 15.

3336   Wheeler-Bennett, John W. *Disarmament and Security Since Locarno, 1925–1931.* London: Allen & Unwin, 1932, pp. 231–33.

LEAGUE'S ONE-YEAR ARMAMENTS TRUCE (1931)

For text of League of Nations resolution, see John W. Wheeler-Bennett, ed., *Documents on International Affairs, 1931* (London: Humphrey Milford, 1932), pp. 40–41.

Documents

3337   League of Nations. *Armaments Truce.* C. 919.M.484.1931.IX (Conf. D. 35). Geneva, 1931. [Also in League of Nations. *Official Journal* 14 (Jan. 1933): 131–50.]

3338   ———. Assembly. Third Committee. *Armaments Truce: Information on the Position of Armaments in Various Countries.* Report of the Third Committee to the Assembly. A.93.1931.IX. Rapporteur, M. de Madariaga. Geneva, 1931.

3339   U.S. Department of State. *Foreign Relations of the United States, 1931.* Washington, D.C.: G.P.O., 1946, I: 440–50.

General Accounts

3340   League of Nations. "Armaments Truce [renewal]." *Official Journal* 14 (Jan. 1933): 120–28; 14 (Mar. 1933): 401.

3341   Myers, Denys P. *World Disarmament: Its Problems and Prospects.* Boston: World Peace Foundation, 1932, pp. 104–29.

3342   Navy League of the United States. *The League of Nations Proposal for a One-Year Naval Holiday and Senator Swanson's Five-Year Plan.* Washington, D.C., 1931.

3343   Royal Institute of International Affairs. *Survey of International Affairs, 1931.* London: Oxford Univ. Press, 1932, pp. 294–98.

ANGLO-GERMAN NAVAL AGREEMENT (1935)

For text of agreement, see Great Britain, Foreign Office, *British and Foreign State Papers* (London: Harrison, 1941–1948), vol. 139, pp. 182–85.

Documents

3344   U.S. Department of State. *Documents on German Foreign Policy, 1918–1945.* Washington, D.C.: G.P.O., 1957, Ser. C, Vols. III, IV.

General Accounts

3345   Bloch, Charles. "Great Britain, German Rearmament, and the Naval Agreement of 1935." In Hans W. Gatzke, ed., *European Diplomacy Between Two Wars, 1919–1939.* Chicago: Quadrangle, 1972, pp. 125–51. [Originally published as "La Grand-Bretagne Face au Rearmement Allemand et l'Accord Naval de 1935." *Revue D'Histoire de la Deuxieme Guerre Mondiale* 63 (Juillet 1966).]

3346   Burns, Richard Dean, and Donald Urquidi. "Anglo-German Naval Pact, 1935." *Disarmament In Perspective, 1919–1939.* 4 vols. Washington, D.C.: G.P.O., 1968, III: 185–213.

3347   Churchill, Winston. "The Anglo-German Naval Agreement." *While England Slept.* New York: Putnam's, 1938, pp. 217–20.

3348 Geraud, André [Pertinax]. "France and the Anglo-German Naval Treaty." *Foreign Affairs* 14 (Oct. 1935): 51–61.

3349 Papp, Nicholas G. "The Anglo-German Naval Agreement of 1935." Ph.D. diss., Univ. of Connecticut, 1969.

3350 Watt, Donald C. "The Anglo-German Naval Agreement of 1935: An Interim Judgment." *Journal of Modern History* 28 (June 1956): 155–75.

London Naval Treaty (1936)

For text of treaty, see Trevor N. Dupuy and Gay M. Hammerman, eds., *A Documentary History of Arms Control and Disarmament* (New York: Bowker, 1973), pp. 262–72.

Documents

3351 Great Britain. Foreign Office. *Documents of the London Naval Conference, 1935* [December 1935–March 1936]. London: H.M.S.O., 1936.

3352 U.S. Department of State. *The London Naval Conference 1935: Report of the Delegates of the United States of America, Text of the London Naval Treaty of 1936 and Other Documents.* Conf. Series no. 24. Washington, D.C.: G.P.O., 1936.

3353 U.S. Senate. Committee on Foreign Relations. Hearings: *Relative to a Treaty for the Limitation of Naval Armament and the Exchange of Information Concerning Naval Construction, Together with the Protocol.* 74th Cong., 2d Sess., May 14, 1936.

General Accounts

3354 Buell, Raymond L. "Rivalry in the Pacific." *Foreign Policy Bulletin* (Nov. 9, 1934): 1–2.

3355 Bywater, Hector C. "The Coming Struggle for Sea Power." *Current History* 41 (Oct. 1934): 9–16.

3356 "France Ratifies London Treaty." *U.S. Naval Institute Proceedings* 63 (Sept. 1937): 1347–48.

3357 "The Naval Conference." *Contemporary Review* 148 (Nov. 1935): 742–48.

3358 Nevins, Allan. "The London Naval Talks." *Current History* 41 (Dec. 1934): 327–29.

3359 Pelz, Stephen E. *Race to Pearl Harbor: The Failure of the Second London Naval Conference and the Onset of World War II.* Cambridge: Harvard Univ. Press, 1974.

3360 Popper, David H. "End of Naval Disarmament." *Foreign Policy Reports* (Oct. 23, 1935): 202–23.

3361 Wescott, Allan. "The Naval Situation." *U.S. Naval Institute Proceedings* 61 (Sept. 1935): 1311–12.

3362 Wolf, William T. "London Naval Disarmament Conference, 1935–1936." Ph.D. diss., Univ. of California, 1962.

National Views—Japan

3363 Buell, Raymond L. "Behind Japan's Demands." *New York Times*, Nov. 18, 1934.

3364 Kato, Adm. Kanji. "Fundamentals of Disarmament." *Contemporary Japan* 4 (Mar. 1936): 487–95.

3365 Nomura, Adm. Kichisaburo. "Japan's Demands for Naval Equality." *Foreign Affairs* 13 (Jan. 1935): 196–203.

3366 Roosevelt, Nicholas. "Japan's Challenge to American Policy." *Asia* 35 (Feb. 1935): 76–81.

3367 Swing, Raymond Gram. "On Being a Nuisance to Japan." *Nation* (Nov. 14, 1934): 558–59.

National Views—Great Britain

3368 Richmond, Adm. Sir Herbert W. "Naval Problems of 1935." *Foreign Affairs* 13 (Oct. 1934): 45–54.

3369 Thorne, Christopher. "The Shanghai Crisis of 1932: The Basis of British Policy." *American Historical Review* 75 (Oct. 1970): 1616–39.

3370 Thursfield, H. G. "The Naval Conference, 1935–1936." *Nineteenth Century and After* 119 (June 1936): 734–47.

National Views—United States

3371   Berg, Meredith W. "Admiral William H. Standley and the Second London Naval Treaty, 1934–1936." *Historian* 33 (Feb. 1971): 215–36.

3372   ———. "The United States and the Breakdown of Naval Limitation, 1934–1939." Ph.D. diss., Tulane Univ., 1966.

3373   Davis, Norman H. "London Naval Treaties." *Vital Speeches* (Apr. 20, 1936): 465–66.

3374   ———. "The New Naval Agreement." *Foreign Affairs* 14 (July 1936): 578–83.

3375   Holmes, Wilfred J. "The Foundation of Naval Policy." *U.S. Naval Institute Proceedings* 60 (Apr. 1934): 457–69.

3376   Pratt, Adm. William V. "The Setting for the 1935 Naval Conference." *Foreign Affairs* 12 (July 1934): 541–52.

3377   Standley, Adm. William H. "The Future of Arms Limitation." *U.S. Naval Institute Proceedings* 62 (July 1936): 1391–96.

3378   ———, and R. A. Collins. "Should the United States Navy Be Built up to Treaty Strength?" *Congressional Digest* 13 (Apr. 1934): 120–22.

3379   Stirling, Adm. Yates, Jr. "Naval Preparedness in the Pacific." *U.S. Naval Institute Proceedings* 60 (May 1934): 601–08.

BILATERAL TREATIES EXTENDING 1936
NAVAL PRINCIPLES (1937–1939)

Anglo-German Naval Pact (1937)

3380   Great Britain. Foreign Office. *Agreement between His Majesty's Government in the United Kingdom and the German Government Providing for the Limitation of Naval Armament and the Exchange of Information concerning Naval Construction, London, July 17, 1937.* Cmd. 5519, 5637. London: H.M.S.O., 1937.

3381   ———. *Protocol Modifying the Anglo-German Agreement of July 17, 1937 for Limitation of Naval Armament, London, June 30, 1938.* Cmd. 5738. London: H.M.S.O., 1938.

Anglo-Soviet Naval Pact (1937)

3382   Great Britain. Foreign Office. *Agreement between His Majesty's Government in the United Kingdom and the Government of the Union of Soviet Socialist Republics Providing for the Limitation of Naval Armament and the Exchange of Information concerning Naval Construction, London, July 17, 1937.* Cmd. 5518, 5679. London: H.M.S.O., 1937.

3383   ———. *Protocol Modifying the Anglo-Soviet Agreement of July 17, 1937 for the Limitation of Naval Armament, London, July 6, 1938.* Cmd. 5794, 6074. London: H.M.S.O., 1938.

Agreements, Treaties & Proposals, 1945–

POST-WORLD WAR II PEACE TREATIES

3384   Kalijarvi, Thorsten V., ed. "Peace Settlements of World War II." *Annals of the Amer. Acad. of Pol. & Soc. Sci.* 257 (May 1948): 1–202.

3385   ———. "Settlements of World Wars I and II Compared." *Annals of the Amer. Acad. of Pol. & Soc. Sci.* 257 (May 1948): 194–202.

3386   Leiss, Amelia C., ed. *European Peace Treaties After World War II: Negotiations and Texts of Treaties with Italy, Bulgaria, Hungary, Rumania, and Finland.* Boston: World Peace Foundation, 1954.

3387   Roucek, Joseph S. "The Bulgarian, Rumanian, and Hungarian Peace Treaties." *Annals of the Amer. Acad. of Pol. & Soc. Sci.* 257 (May 1948): 97–105.

3388   Wheeler-Bennett, John W., and Anthony Nicholls. "The Paris Conference and the Five Peace Treaties." *The Semblance of Peace: The Political Settlement After the Second World War.* London: Macmillan, 1972, pp. 419–64.

TREATY OF PEACE—ITALY (1947)

For text of treaty, see "Allied and Associated Powers and Italy: Treaty of Peace, Feb. 10, 1947,"

American Journal of International Law: Supplement 42 (Apr. 1948): 47–143.

3389   Albrecht-Carrie, René. "The Italian Treaty." *Annals of the Amer. Acad. of Pol. & Soc. Sci.* 257 (May 1948): 76–86.

3390   Great Britain. Foreign Office. *Protocol on the Establishment of a Four-Power Naval Commission, the Disposal of Excess Units of the Italian Fleet, and the Return by the Soviet Union of Warships on Loan, Paris, 10th February 1947.* Cmd. 7078. London: H.M.S.O., 1947.

3391   ———. *Protocol on the Establishment of a Four-Power Naval Commission. . . .* Cmd. 7353. London: H.M.S.O., 1948.

3392   Sottile, A. "Le Traité de Paix avec l'Italie: le Traité de Paix avec la Roumanie." *Revue de Droit International* [Geneva] 25 (Jan.–Mar. 1947): 18–30.

3393   U.S. Department of State. *Foreign Relations of the United States, 1946.* Washington, D.C.: G.P.O., 1970. III: 1 ff; IV: 1–62, 117–216, 889–917; V: 825–90.

Treaty of Peace—Bulgaria (1947)

For text of treaty, see "Allied and Associated Powers and Bulgaria: Treaty of Peace, Feb. 10, 1947," *American Journal of International Law: Supplement* 42 (July 1948): 203–23.

3394   U.S. Department of State. *Foreign Relations of the United States, 1946.* Washington, D.C., G.P.O., 1970. III: 1 ff.; IV: 95–101, 238–48, 478–525, 927–36.

3395   ———. *Foreign Relations of the United States, 1947.* Washington, D.C.: G.P.O., 1972. IV: 1–51.

3396   ———. *Foreign Relations of the United States, 1948.* Washington, D.C.: G.P.O., 1974. IV: 279–398.

Treaty of Peace—Finland (1947)

For text of treaty, see "Allied and Associated Powers and Finland: Treaty of Peace, Feb. 10, 1947," *American Journal of International Law: Supplement* 42 (July 1948): 203–23.

3397   U.S. Department of State. *Foreign Relations of the United States, 1946.* Washington, D.C.: G.P.O., 1970. III: 1 ff.; IV: 109–16, 282–98, 568–91, 949–56.

3398   Wuorinen, John H. "The Finnish Treaty." *Annals of the Amer. Acad. of Pol. & Soc. Sci.* 257 (May 1948): 87–96.

Treaty of Peace—Hungary (1947)

For text of treaty, see "Allied and Associated Powers and Hungary: Treaty of Peace, Feb. 10, 1947," *American Journal of International Law: Supplement* 42 (Oct. 1948): 225–51.

3399   U.S. Department of State. *Foreign Relations of the United States, 1946.* Washington, D.C.: G.P.O., 1970. III: 1 ff.: IV: 102–08, 249–81, 526–68, 937–48.

3400   ———. *Foreign Relations of the United States, 1947.* Washington, D.C.: G.P.O., 1972. IV: 1–51.

3401   ———. *Foreign Relations of the United States, 1948.* Washington, D.C.: G.P.O., 1974. IV: 279–398.

Treaty of Peace—Rumania (1947)

For text of treaty, see "Allied and Associated Powers and Roumania: Treaty of Peace, Feb. 10, 1947," *American Journal of International Law* 42 (Oct. 1948): 252–77.

3402   Ciurea, Emile C. *Le Traité de Paix avec la Roumanie du 10 Fevrier 1947.* Paris: Pedone, 1954.

3403   U.S. Department of State. *Foreign Relations of the United States, 1946.* Washington, D.C.: G.P.O., 1970. III: 1 ff.; IV; 63–94, 217–37, 430–77, 918–26.

3404   ———. *Foreign Relations of the United States, 1947.* Washington, D.C.: G.P.O., 1972. IV: 1–51.

3404a   ———. *Foreign Relations of the United States, 1948.* Washington, D.C.: G.P.O., 1974. IV: 279–398.

JAPANESE CONSTITUTION (1947)

For text of Article Nine of the Constitution of Japan, see Trevor N. Dupuy and Gay M. Hammerman, eds., *A Documentary History of Arms Control and Disarmament* (New York: Bowker, 1973), p. 313.

Documents

3405   Supreme Commander for Allied Powers. *Political Reorientation of Japan.* 2 vols. Washington, D.C.: G.P.O., 1949.

Constitutional Prohibition

3406   Blakeslee, George H. *The Far Eastern Commission: A Study of International Cooperation, 1945–1952.* Far Eastern Series no. 60. Washington, D.C.: G.P.O., 1953.

3407   Inomata, Kozo. "In Defense of the Constitution." *Contemporary Japan* 24:4/6 (1956): 200–215.

3408   McNelly, Theodore. "American Influence and Japan's No-War Constitution." *Political Science Quarterly* 67 (Dec. 1952): 589–98.

3409   ———. "The Japanese Constitution: Child of the Cold War." *Political Science Quarterly* 74 (June 1959): 176–93.

3410   ———. "The Renunciation of War in the Japanese Constitution." *Political Science Quarterly* 77 (Sept. 1962): 350–78.

3411   Miyasawa, Toshiyoshi. "The Constitution in Trouble." *Japan Quarterly* 6 (July–Sept. 1959): 291–96.

3412   Nakasone, Yasuhiro. "Reasons for Constitutional Revision." *Contemporary Japan* 24:7/8 (1956): 401–13.

3413   Nishijima, Yoshiji. "The Peace Constitution Controversy." *Japan Quarterly* 10 (Jan.–Mar. 1963): 18–27.

3414   Nixon, Vice Pres. Richard M. "To the Japanese People." *Contemporary Japan* 22:7/9 (1953): 363–78.

3415   Quigley, Harold S. "Japan's Constitutions: 1890 and 1947." *American Political Science Review* 41 (Oct. 1947): 865–74.

3416   ———. "Revising the Japanese Constitution." *Foreign Affairs* 39 (Oct. 1960): 11–26.

3417   Sato, Tatsuo. "The Origins and Development of Japanese Constitution." *Contemporary Japan* 24: 4/6 (1956): 175–87, 271–87.

3418   Sissions, D. C. S. "The Pacific Clause of the Japanese Constitution: Legal and Political Problems of Rearmament." *International Affairs* [London] 37 (Jan. 1961): 45–59.

3419   "Tug-of-War Over Article IX of the Constitution." *Japan Quarterly* 6 (Jan.–Mar. 1959): 140–45.

3420   Ward, Robert E. "The Commission and Prospects for Constitutional Change in Japan." *Journal of Asian Studies* 24 (May 1965): 401–29.

3421   ———. "Origins of the Japanese Constitution." *American Political Science Review* 50 (Dec. 1956): 980–1010.

3422   Williams, Justin. "Making the Japanese Constitution: A Further Look." *American Political Science Review* 59 (Sept. 1965): 665–79.

3423   Yokota, Kisaburo. "Renunciation of War in the New Japanese Constitution." *Japanese Annual of International Law* 4 (1960): 16–31.

Public Opinion

3424   Emmerson, John K., and Leonard Humphreys. *Will Japan Rearm? A Study in Attitudes.* Washington, D.C.: American Enterprise Institute for Public Policy Research, Dec. 1973. [Hoover Institution Press, 1975.]

3425   Kawai, Kazuo. "Japanese Views on National Security." *Pacific Affairs* 23 (Jan. 1950): 115–27.

3426   Lifton, Robert J. *History and Human Survival: Essays on the Young and Old, Survivors and the Dead, Peace and War, and on Contemporary Psychohistory.* New York: Random House, 1970.

3427   Mendel, Douglas, Jr. "A Nation Against Arms." *Far Eastern Economic Review* (Mar. 26, 1970): 35–36.

3428   ———. "Security Without Arms." *Far Eastern Economic Review* (Jan. 16, 1969): 102–03.

3429 Morris, Ivan I. "Significance of the Military in Postwar Japan." *Pacific Affairs* 3 (Mar. 1958): 3–21.

3430 Naoki, Kobayashi. "The Japanese People and the Peace Article." *Japan Quarterly* 13 (Oct.–Dec. 1966): 444–54.

3431 Seidensticker, Edward. "Japanese Views on Peace." *Far Eastern Survey* (June 13, 1951): 119–24.

3432 "SPJ's Policy on National Security." *Japan Socialist Review* (Nov. 15, 1969): 11–22.

3433 "We Condemn Arguments for 'Independent Defense.'" *Japan Socialist Review* (Dec. 1–15, 1969): 7–18.

Rearmament—Self-Defense Forces

3434 Auer, James E. "Japan's Maritime Self-Defense Force: An Appropriate Maritime Strategy." *Naval War College Review* 24 (Dec. 1971): 3–20.

3435 ———. *The Postwar Rearmament of Japanese Maritime Forces: 1945–1971.* New York: Praeger, 1973.

3436 Beecher, William. "Military Reawakening in Japan." *Army* 21 (Mar. 1971): 10–17.

3437 Billings, Gilbert M. "Japan's Air Self-Defense Force." *Air University Review* 16 (July–Aug. 1965): 60–71.

3438 Buck, James H. "The Japanese Self-Defense Forces." *Asian Survey* 7 (Sept. 1967): 597–613.

3439 Clark, Gregory. "At the Whim of the Shisei." *Far Eastern Economic Review* (July 23, 1970): 23–26.

3440 Connell, Lewis E. "Economic Imperatives Influencing Japan's Military Force Levels." *Naval War College Review* 24 (Nov. 1971): 49–54.

3441 Cordier, Sherwood S. "Japan: Present and Potential Military Power." *U.S. Naval Institute Proceedings* 93 (Nov. 1967): 68–78.

3442 Iwashima, Hisao. "Japan's Defense Policy." *Strategic Review* 3 (Spring 1975): 17–24.

3443 Jen, Ku-ping. "Japanese Militarism on the Road Back." *Peking Review* (Dec. 10, 1965): 5–8.

3444 Maki, John M. "Japan's Rearmament: Progress and Problems." *Western Political Quarterly* 7 (Dec. 1955): 545–68.

3445 Matsuura, Col. Noboru. "Japan's Defense Forces." *Military Review* 51 (Feb. 1971): 48–55.

3446 McBride, James H. *Japan's Self-Defense Forces: Background and Evolution.* Au-203–70–ASI. Maxwell Air Force Base, Ala.: U.S. Air Univ., 1971.

3447 Okumiya, Masatake. "Japan's Self-Defense Forces." *U.S. Naval Institute Proceedings* 91 (Dec. 1965): 26–35.

3448 Rhee, T. C. "Japan: 'Security' and 'Militarism.'" *World Today* 27 (Sept. 1971): 390–400.

3449 Seymour, Robert L. "Japan's Self-Defense: The Naganuma Case and Its Implications." *Pacific Affairs* 47 (Winter 1974–75): 421–37.

3450 Strope, W. E. "On Japanese Naval Rearmament." *U.S. Naval Institute Proceedings* 82 (June 1956): 575–84.

3451 Takizawa, Makoto. "Japanese Rearmament: A Dilemma in the Search for Peace and Security." Ph.D. diss., Florida State Univ., 1967.

3452 Uchida, Adm. Kazutomi. "The Rearmament of the Japanese Maritime Forces." *Naval War College Review* 26 (Nov.–Dec. 1973): 41–48.

3453 Weinstein, Martin E. "Japanese Air Self-Defense Force: Restrained, but Powerful." *Air Force and Space Digest* 50 (Dec. 1967): 56–60, 63.

3454 ———. *Japan's Postwar Defense Policy, 1947–1968.* Studies of the East Asian Institute. New York: Columbia Univ. Press, 1971.

3455 Yiu, Myung-kum. "The Prospects of Japanese Rearmament." *Current History* 60 (Apr. 1971): 231–36, 245.

GERMAN DISARMAMENT & REARMAMENT (1945–1954)

Directive for disarmament of Germany is contained in the "Protocol of the Proceedings of the Crimea [Yalta] Conference, Feb. 11, 1945," see Article 12 (a). See also, West German Renunciation of Nuclear & CB Weapons (1954) in Chapter 10.

Documents—Disarmament

3456 Germany (British Zone). *Progress of De-militarisation in the British Zone of Occupa-tion of Germany.* 2 pts. Berlin, 1946.

3457 Oppen, B. R., ed. *Documents on Germany Under Occupation, 1945–1954.* London: Ox-ford Univ. Press, 1955.

3458 U.S. Department of State. "Agreement Be-tween the Governments of the United States, France and the United Kingdom on Prohib-ited and Limited Industries in the Western Zones of Germany." *U.S. Department of State Bulletin* (Apr. 24, 1949): 526–31.

3459 ———. "Directive of the Organization of the Military Security Board for the Western Zones of Germany, Issued by the U.S., U.K., and France." *U.S. Department of State Bul-letin* (Feb. 13, 1949): 195–97. [Sec. 1, 2, & 3 detail responsibility to ensure disarmament.]

3460 ———. "Occupation Statute for the Western Zones of Germany." *U.S. Department of State Bulletin* (April 17, 1949): 499–501. [Sec. 2 (a) relates to disarmament.]

3461 ———. "Protocol of the Proceedings of the Crimea (Yalta) Conference, Feb. 11, 1945." *U.S. Department of State Press Release,* no. 239. Mar. 24, 1947. [Amends Art. 12 (a) relat-ing to disarmament of Germany.]

3462 U.S. Embassy. Great Britain. *Disarmament of the German Aircraft Industry.* London: Joint Report of Economic Objective Unit, Economic Warfare Division of American Em-bassy, and Research and Analysis Branch, Office of Strategic Services, 1944.

3463 U.S. Foreign Economic Administration. Enemy Branch. *A Program for German Economic and Industrial Disarmament.* Study submitted to the Subcommittee on War Mobilization, Committee on Military Af-fairs, U.S. Senate, Apr. 1946. 79th Cong., 2d Sess., 1946. Appendix, pp. 379–660.

3464 ———. *Study of the FEA Drafting Commit-tee on the Separation From Germany of the Ruhr-Rhineland Territory as a Disarma-ment Measure.* T.I.D. Project 22. Wash-ington, D.C.: G.P.O., 1945.

3465 U.S. Senate. Committee on Foreign Rela-tions. *Documents on Germany, 1944–1959.* 86th Cong., 1st Sess., 1959.

General Accounts

3466 Clay, Gen. Lucius. *Decision in Germany.* New York: Doubleday, 1950.

3467 Colby, Reginald E. *De Wonde wan Europa.* Amsterdam: Holdert, 1950.

3468 Davidson, Eugene. *The Death and Life of Germany: An Account of American Occupa-tion.* New York: Knopf, 1959.

3469 Gareau, Frederick H. "A Critical Examina-tion of United States Policy Toward German Industrial Disarmament." Ph.D. diss., American Univ., 1957.

3470 "German Disarmament and European Recon-struction." *Political Quarterly* 13 (Oct. 1942): 349–61.

3471 Gollancz, Victor. *In Darkest Germany.* Chicago: Regnery, 1947.

3472 Hansenack, Wilhelm. *Dismantling in the Ruhr Valley: Menace to European Recovery.* Cologne: Westdeutscher Verlag, 1949.

3473 Kirk, Grayson, ed. *Postwar German Disar-mament.* New York: Council on Foreign Re-lations, 1944.

3474 Mosely, Philip E. "Dismemberment of Ger-many: The Allied Negotiations from Yalta to Potsdam." *Foreign Affairs* 28 (Apr. 1950): 487–98.

3475 Moulton, Harold B., and Louis Marlio. *The Control of Germany and Japan.* Washington, D.C.: Brookings Institution, 1944.

3476 Pollack, James. "American Policy Towards Europe." *Foreign Policy Reports* (Nov. 1, 1967): 198–206.

3477 ———, and James H. Musir. *Germany Under Occupation.* Ann Arbor: Geo. Wahr, 1947.

3478 Royal Institute of International Affairs. *Sur-vey of International Affairs, 1939–1946.* London: Oxford Univ. Press, 1956, pp. 162–83, 253–65.

3479 Sielger, Heinrich von, ed. *Dokumentation zur Abrüstung und Sicherheit von 1943 bis 1959.* Bad Godesberg: "Archiv der Gegen-wart," 1960.

3480 Smith, Arthur L., Jr. "Churchill et l'Armée Allemande, 1945." *Revue d'Histoire de la*

Deuxième Guerre Mondiale 93 (Jan. 1974): 65–78.

3481   Strauss, Harold. "The Division and Dismemberment of Germany: From the Casablanca Conference to the Establishment of East Germany." Ph.D. diss., Univ. Geneva, 1952.

3482   U.S. Department of State. *Foreign Relations of the United States: Conferences at Cairo and Tehran, 1943.* Washington, D.C.: G.P.O., 1961.

3483   ———. *Conferences at Malta and Yalta, 1945.* Washington, D.C.: G.P.O., 1955.

3484   Villard, O. G. "Disarmament of Germany." *Rotarian* 66 (June 1945): 18–20.

3485   Warburg, James P. *Germany: Bridge or Battleground.* London: Heinemann, 1947.

3486   Wettig, Gerhard. *Entmilitarisierung und Wiederbewaffnung in Deutschland, 1943–1955.* Munich: R. Oldenburg, 1967.

3487   Willis, Frank R. *The French in Germany, 1945–1949.* Stanford: Stanford Univ. Press, 1962.

Morgenthau Plan

3488   Hull, Cordell. *Memoirs of Cordell Hull.* 2 vols. New York: Macmillan, 1948. II: 1602–22.

3489   Morgenthau, Henry, Jr. *Germany Is Our Problem.* New York: Harper, 1945.

3490   Stimson, Henry L., and McGeorge Bundy. *On Active Service in Peace and War.* New York: Harper, 1948, pp. 568–83.

3491   U.S. Department of State. *Foreign Relations of the United States: Quebec Conference.* Washington, D.C.: G.P.O., 1961.

Potsdam Conference

3492   Feis, Herbert. *Between War and Peace: The Potsdam Conference.* Princeton: Princeton Univ. Press, 1960, pp. 74–77, 235–58.

3493   Gareau, Frederick H. "A Critical Examination of United States Policy Towards German Industrial Disarmament." Ph.D. diss., American Univ., 1957, pp. 44–72.

3494   U.S. Department of State. *Foreign Relations of the United States: Conference of Berlin (Potsdam), 1945.* 2 vols. Washington, D.C.: G.P.O., 1960.

Rearmament—Documents

3495   "Agreement on Rearming Western Germany (Sept. 18, 1950), [and other pertinent documents]." *Current History* 20 (Feb. 1951): 106–10; 20 (Mar. 1951): 173–74.

3496   German Federal Republic. *The Security of the Federal Republic of Germany and the Development of the Federal Armed Forces.* Bonn: Federal Minister of Defense, 1974.

3497   *Soviet Efforts for Peace in Europe and Against German Rearmament: Documents.* London: Soviet News, 1955

3498   U.S. Department of State. "Note from the American Ambassador at Moscow to the Soviet Foreign Minister, on the Remilitarization of East Germany, May 23, 1950." *U.S. Department of State Bulletin* (June 5, 1950): 918–20.

Rearmament—General Accounts

3499   Arnot, R. P. "Re-militarizing West Germany and Japan." *Labour Monthly* 33 (Feb. 1951): 65–71.

3500   Baudissin, Wolf Graf von. "The New German Army." *Foreign Affairs* 34 (Oct. 1955): 1–13.

3501   Bussche, Axel. "German Rearmament: Hopes and Fears." *Foreign Affairs* 32 (Oct. 1953): 68–79.

3502   Clement, Alain. "Why are the West Germans Reluctant to Rearm?" *Reporter* [Gr. Br.] (Nov. 7, 1950): 32–34.

3503   Cornides, Wilhelm. *Die Weltmachte und Deutschland: Geschichte der jungsten Vergangenheit, 1945–1955.* Tübingen: Wunderlich Verlag, 1957.

3504   Craig, Gordon A. "Germany and NATO: The Rearmament Debate, 1950–1958." In Klaus Knorr, ed., *NATO and American Security.* Princeton: Princeton Univ. Press, 1959.

3505   Dallin, David J. "France and German Rearmament." *New Leader* (Oct. 15, 1951): 9–10.

3506 Deutsch, Karl W., and Lewis J. Edinger. *Germany Rejoins the Powers*. Stanford: Stanford Univ. Press, 1959.

3507 Edinger, Lewis J. *West German Armament*. Maxwell Air Force Base, Ala.: Air Univ. Press, 1955.

3508 "Four Views of German Rearmament." *Reporter* [Gr. Br.] (May 23, 1950): 9–20.

3509 Germany [Democratic Republic]. *West Germany Prepares War of Revenge: Facts on the Rebirth of German Militarism in the Bonn State*. Berlin, 1954(?).

3510 "Germany's New Army: No. 1 in Europe Again." *U.S. News & World Report* (Sept. 12, 1966): 69–70.

3511 Grosser, Alfred. *The Colossus Again: Western Germany From Defeat to Rearmament*. New York: Praeger, 1955.

3512 Hammond, Paul Y. "NSC-68: Prologue to Rearmament." In W. R. Schilling et al., eds., *Strategy, Politics, and Defense Budgets*. New York: Columbia Univ. Press, 1962.

3513 Kopp, Fritz. *Chronik de Wiederbewaffnung in Deutschland* [1945–1958]. Koln: Markus Verlag, 1958.

3514 Martin, Laurence W. "American Decision to Rearm Germany." In Harold Stein, ed., *American Civil-Military Decisions*. Birmingham: Univ. of Alabama Press, 1963.

3515 McGeehan, Robert J. *The German Rearmament Question: American Diplomacy and European Defense After World War II*. Urbana: Univ. of Illinois Press, 1971.

3516 Moch, Jules S. *Histoire du Rearmement Allemand depuis 1950*. Paris: Robert Laffont, 1965.

3517 Naves, Allen S. "German Rearmament and the European Balance." *Current History* 38 (Jan. 1960): 24–29.

3518 Neuberg, Howard G. "West Germany: Our Capable European Ally." *Military Review* 51 (Apr. 1971): 35–45.

3519 Onslow, C. G. D. "West German Rearmament." *World Politics* 3 (July 1951): 450–85.

3520 Pol, Heinz. "NATO joins the Wehrmacht." *Nation* (July 29, 1961): 44–48.

3521 Schubert, Klaus V. *Wiederbewaffnung und Westintegration*. Stuttgart: Deutsches Verlags-Anstalt, 1970.

3522 Schuman, Fredrick L. "The Soviet Union and German Rearmament." *Annals of the Amer. Acad. of Pol. & Soc. Sci.* 311 (July 1957): 57–83.

3523 Simpson, Benjamin M., III. "The Rearming of Germany, 1950–1954: A Linchpin in the Political Evolution of Europe." *Naval War College Review* 24 (May 1971): 76–90.

3524 Speier, Hans. "German Rearmament and the Old Military Elite." *World Politics* 6 (Jan. 1954): 147–68.

3525 Waldman, Eric. *The Goose Step is Verboten*. New York: Free Press, 1964.

3526 Zacharias, E. M., and Cecil Brown. "Should We Rearm Germany and Japan?" *Town Meeting* (Aug. 22, 1950): 1–16.

Baruch Plan (1946)

For text of draft, see "The Baruch Plan," *Documents on Disarmament, 1945–1959*, 2 vols. (Washington, D.C.: G.P.O., 1960), I: 7–16.

Documents

3527 Molotov, V. M. *Speeches at the General Assembly of the United Nations . . . New York, October-December, 1946*. Moscow: Foreign Languages Publishing House, 1948.

3528 U.S. Department of State. *International Control of Atomic Energy and the Prohibition of Atomic Weapons: Recommendations of the United Nations Atomic Energy Commission*. Dept. of State Pub. 3646. Washington, D.C.: G.P.O., Oct. 1949.

3529 ———. *A Report on the International Control of Atomic Energy: Prepared for the Secretary of State's Committee on Atomic Energy by a Board of Consultants*. [The Acheson-Lilienthal Report] Dept. of State Pub. 2498. Washington, D.C.: G.P.O., 1946. [Reprinted frequently.]

3530 U.S. Joint Committee on Atomic Energy. Hearings: *Development and Control of Atomic Energy* [on S. 1717]. 79th Cong., 2d Sess., 1946.

3531   ———. Hearings: *Investigating Problems Relating to the Development, Use, and Control of Atomic Energy* [on S. 179]. 5 pts. 80th Cong., 1st Sess., 1947.

For additional references, see Chapter 3, general accounts to 1975, Contemporary Issues, Since 1945; and Chapter 4, League of Nations & United Nations.

3532   Baruch, Bernard M. *Baruch: The Public Years.* New York: Holt, Rinehart & Winston, 1960.

3533   Bresler, Robert J. "American Policy Toward International Control of Atomic Energy, 1945–1946." Ph.D. diss., Princeton Univ., 1964.

3534   Gard, Robert G., Jr. "Arms Control Policy Formulation and Negotiation, 1945–1946." Ph.D. diss., Harvard Univ., 1961.

3535   Hewlett, Richard, and Oscar Anderson. *The New World, 1939–1946.* University Park: Pennsylvania State Univ. Press, 1962, pp. 531–619.

3536   Lieberman, Joseph I. *The Scorpion and the Tarantula: The Struggle to Control Atomic Weapons, 1945–1949.* Boston: Houghton Mifflin, 1970.

3537   Lilienthal, David E. *Journals of. . . .* Vol. 2: *The Atomic Energy Years, 1945–1950.* New York: Harper & Row, 1964.

3538   Newman, James R., and Byron S. Miller. *The Control of Atomic Energy.* New York: McGraw-Hill, 1948.

3539   Osborn, Frederick H. "Negotiating on Atomic Energy." In R. Dennett and J. E. Johnson, eds., *Negotiating With the Russians.* Boston: World Peace Foundation, 1951, pp. 209–36.

3540   Snyder, James R. "Sharing the Atom: An American Dilemma." Ph.D. diss., Univ. of Kentucky, 1962.

3541   U.S. House. Committee on Foreign Affairs. Staff Study: *The Failure of the Baruch Plan.* 92d Cong., 1st Sess., 1972.

3542   Woodward, E. L. *Some Political Consequences of the Atomic Bomb.* New York: Oxford Univ. Press, 1946.

3543   Acheson, Dean G., et al. "International Control of Atomic Energy." *U.S. Department of State Bulletin* (May 5, 1946): 774–77.

3544   ———. "Safeguarding Atomic Energy Against Misuse." *U.S. News* (May 3, 1946): 57–59.

3545   "Atom Control Program: Monopoly in an International Agency as Basis Proposed by U.S. Board for Discussion." *U.S. News & World Report* (Apr. 5, 1946): 67–72.

3546   Baruch, Bernard M. "The American Proposal for International Control." *Bulletin of the Atomic Scientists* 2 (July 1946): 3–5, 10.

3547   ———. "International Control of Atomic Energy." *Air Affairs* 3 (Spring 1950): 313–19.

3548   Clark, Sen. Joseph S. "The Disarmament Question." *Political Affairs* 26 (Feb. 1947): 122–31.

3549   Gromyko, Andrei. "A Defense of the Soviet Control Plan." *Bulletin of the Atomic Scientists* 4 (June 1948): 191–92.

3550   Harley, J. E. "Revival of Efforts for Reduction and Control of World Armaments." *World Affairs Interpreter* 18 (Apr. 1947): 70–82.

3551   Lilienthal, David E. "How Atomic Energy Can Be Controlled." *Bulletin of the Atomic Scientists* 2 (Oct. 1946).

3552   Molotov, V. M. "Inspection of World Arms: Russia Accepts Principle." *World Reports* (Dec. 10, 1946): 43–44.

3553   Osborn, Frederick H. "The Search for Atomic Control." *Atlantic Monthly* (Apr. 1948): 48–50.

3554   "Principles Governing General Regulation and Reduction of Armaments." *U.S. Department of State Bulletin* (Dec. 22, 1946): 1137–42.

3555   Shawcross, Hartley. "Inspection of World Arms: Britain Urges Abolition of Veto." *World Reports* (Dec. 10, 1946): 44–45.

3556   Turlington, Edgar W. "International Control of the Atomic Bomb." *American Journal of International Law* 40 (Jan. 1946): 165–67.

3557   Viner, Jacob. "The Implications of the Atomic Bomb for International Relations." *Proceedings of American Philosophical Society* (Jan. 29, 1946): 53–58.

KOREAN MILITARY ARMISTICE (1953)

For terms of the armistice, see U.S. Department of State, "Multilateral—Military Armistice in Korea, Panmunjom, July 27, 1953." *United States Treaties and Other International Agreements* 4:1 (1953): 234–354.

General Accounts

3558 Berger, Carl. *The Korean Knot: A Military-Political History.* Philadelphia, 1957.

3559 Clark, Gen. Mark W. *From the Danube to the Yalu.* New York: Harper, 1954.

3560 Fischer, Alfred Joachim. "L'armistice de Coree, Negociations Preliminaires et Suite." *Chronique de Politique Etrangère* [Brussels] 6 (Nov. 1953): 760–64; 7 (Jan. 1954): 18–80.

3561 George, Alexander L. "American Policymaking and the North Korean Aggression." *World Politics* 7 (1954–1955): 209–32.

3562 Gervals, André. "Les Armistices Palestiniens, Coreens et Indochinois et leurs Enseignements." *Annuaire Français de Droit International* [Paris] 2 (1956): 97–121.

3563 Goodrich, Leland M. *Korea: A Study of United States Policy in the United States.* New York: Council on Foreign Relations, 1956.

3564 Henderson, Gregory. *Korea: The Politics of the Vortex.* Cambridge: Harvard Univ. Press, 1968.

3565 Joy, Adm. Charles Turner. *How Communists Negotiate.* New York: Macmillan, 1955.

3566 Sawyer, Robert K. *Military Advisors in Korea: KMAG in Peace and War.* Washington, D.C.: G.P.O., 1962.

3567 Stone, I. F. *The Hidden History of the Korean War.* New York: Monthly Review Press, 1952.

3568 U.S. Department of State. *A Historical Summary of United States-Korean Relations.* Pub. 7446. Washington, D.C.: G.P.O., 1962.

3569 ———. *The Korean Problem at the Geneva Convention, April 26–June 15, 1954.* International Conf. Series II, Far Eastern no. 4. Washington, D.C.: G.P.O., 1954.

3570 ———. *The Record on Korean Unification.* Pub. 7084. Washington, D.C.: G.P.O., 1960.

3571 U.S. Senate. Committee on Foreign Relations. Report: *The U.S. and the Korean Problem: Documents, 1943–1953.* Sen. Doc. 74. 83d Cong., 1st Sess., 1953.

3572 Vatcher, William H. *Panmunjom: The Story of the Korean Military Armistice Negotiations.* New York: Praeger, 1958.

Neutral Nations Supervisory Commission

3573 Attia, Gamal El Din. *Les Forces Armées des Nations-Unies en Coree et au Moyen-Orient.* Geneva: Droz, 1963.

3574 Bindschedler, Robert D. "Les Commissions Neutres Instituees par l'Armistice de Coree." *Annuaire Suisse de Droit International* [Zurich] 10 (1953): 89–130.

3575 "Excerpts from May 4 Memorandum to Korean Military Armistice Commission." *U.S. Department of State Bulletin* (June 21, 1954): 944–47.

3576 Freymond, Jacques. "Supervising Agreements: The Korean Experience." *Foreign Affairs* 37 (Apr. 1959): 496–503.

3577 Kriebel, P. Wesley. "Korea: The Military Armistice Commission, 1965–1970." *Military Affairs* 36 (Mar. 1972): 96–99.

3578 "Reply to Sweden and Switzerland on Korean Supervisory Commission." *U.S. Department of State Bulletin* (Mar. 14, 1955): 429.

3579 "UN Command Cites Violations of Korean Armistice Agreement." *U.S. Department of State Bulletin* (Aug. 1, 1955): 191–96.

3580 "UN Command in Korea Announces Intention to Replace Old Weapons [Suspends 'arms control' terms]." *U.S. Department of State Bulletin* (July 8, 1957): 58–59.

3581 Wainhouse, David W. *International Peace Observation: A History and Forecast.* Baltimore: Johns Hopkins Press, 1966, pp. 342–57.

3582 "Withdrawal of NNSC Teams from South Korea." *U.S. Department of State Bulletin* (June 11, 1956): 967–70.

GENEVA ACCORDS ON INDOCHINA (1954 & 1973)

For text of accords, see Great Britain, *Papers and Accounts*, Misc. no. 20 (1954) Cmd. 9239. [Reprinted in Richard A. Falk, ed., *The Vietnam War and International Law*, 3 vols. (Princeton: Princeton Univ. Press, 1968) I: 543–73.]

Bibliography

3583 Leitenberg, Milton, and Richard Dean Burns, eds. *The Vietnam Conflict*. Santa Barbara, Ca.: ABC–Clio, 1973.

Documents

3584 Cameron, Allan W., comp. *Vietnam Crisis: A Documentary History, 1940–1956*. Ithaca: Cornell Univ. Press, 1971.

3585 Democratic Republic of Vietnam. *Documents Relatifs a l'Execution des Accords de Geneve concernant le Viet-Nam*. Hanoi: Ministry of Foreign Affairs, 1956.

3586 Great Britain. Foreign Office. *Documents Relating to British Involvement in the Indo-China Conflict, 1954–1965*. Cmd. 2834. London: H.M.S.O., 1965.

3587 *The Pentagon Papers: The Senator Gravel Edition*. 5 vols. Boston: Beacon, 1971–1972.

General Accounts

3588 Bator, Victor. *Vietnam, A Diplomatic Tragedy: Origins of U.S. Involvement*. London: Faber & Faber, 1965.

3589 Brandon, Henry H. *Anatomy of Error: The Inside Story of the Asian War on the Potomac, 1954–1969*. Boston: Gambit, 1969.

3590 Buttinger, Joseph. *Vietnam: A Dragon Embattled*. 2 vols. New York: Praeger, 1967.

3591 Fall, Bernard B. "The Cease-Fire in Indochina: An Appraisal." *Far Eastern Survey* 23 (Sept. 1954): 135–39; 23 (Oct. 1954): 152–55.

3592 ———. "That Geneva Agreement: How the French Got Out of Vietnam." *New York Times Magazine* (May 2, 1965): 28–29, 113–19.

3593 ———. *Viet-Nam Witness, 1953–1966*. New York: Praeger, 1966.

3594 Guillain, Robert. *La Fin des Illusions: Notes d'Indochine, Fevrier–Juillet 1954*. Paris: Centre d'Etude de Politique Etrangère, 1954.

3595 Gurtov, Melvin. *The First Vietnam Crisis, Chinese Strategy and United States Involvement, 1953–1954*. New York: Columbia Univ. Press, 1967.

3596 Hannon, John S., Jr. "A Political Settlement for Vietnam: The 1954 Geneva Conference and Its Current Implications." *Virginia Journal of International Law* 8 (Dec. 1967): 20–65.

3597 Lacouture, Jean, and Philippe Devillers. *End of a War: Indochina 1954*. New York: Praeger, 1969.

3598 Lancaster, Donald. *The Emancipation of French Indochina*. London: Oxford Univ. Press, 1961.

3599 Mecklin, John. *Mission in Torment: An Intimate Account of the U.S. Role in Vietnam*. Garden City, N.Y.: Doubleday, 1965.

3600 Randle, Robert F. *Geneva 1954: The Settlement of the Indochinese War*. Princeton: Princeton Univ. Press, 1969.

3601 Sar Desai, D. R. *Indian Foreign Policy in Cambodia, Laos, and Vietnam, 1947–1964*. Los Angeles: Univ. of California Press, 1968.

3602 Ton That Thien. "The Geneva Agreements and Peace Prospects in Vietnam." *India Quarterly* 12 (Oct.–Dec. 1956): 375–88.

International Control Commission— General

3603 Australia. Department of External Affairs. "Special Report of the International Control Commission in Viet Nam." *Current Notes on International Affairs* 33 (June 1962): 25–35.

3604 Blais, Edmond. "The International Commission for Supervision and Control in Indo-China." M.A. thesis, Georgetown Univ., 1959.

3605 Dai, Poeliu. "Canada's Role in the International Commission for Supervision and Control in Viet Nam." *Canadian Year Book of International Law* 4 (1966): 161–77.

3606   Democratic Republic of Vietnam. *La Politique d'Intervention et d'Agression des Etats-Unis au Sud.* Hanoi: Ministry of Foreign Affairs, 1962.

3607   Hannon, John S., Jr. "The International Control Commission Experience and the Role of an Improved International Supervisory Body in the Vietnam Settlement." *Virginia Journal of International Law* 9 (Dec. 1968): 20–65.

3608   Holmes, J. "Techniques of Peacekeeping in Asia." In A. Buchan, ed., *China and the Peace of Asia.* New York: Praeger, 1965: 231–49.

3609   Karpikhim, A. "The United States Takes Over in South Viet-Nam." *International Affairs* [Moscow] 2 (Apr. 1956): 83–91.

3610   ———. "The U.S.A. Sabotages the Geneva Agreements on Indochina." *International Affairs* [Moscow] 5 (1959): 57–62.

3611   Maneli, Mieczyslau. *War of the Vanquished: A Polish Diplomat in Vietnam.* New York: Harper & Row, 1971.

3612   Martin, Paul. *Canada and the Quest for Peace.* New York: Columbia Univ. Press, 1967, ch. 2.

3613   Murti, B. S. N. *Vietnam Divided: The Unfinished Struggle.* New York: Asia Publishing House, 1964.

3614   Naravane, A. S. "The International Commission for Vietnam." *Journal of the United Service Institution of India* 94 (Apr. 1964): 159–67.

3615   New Zealand. Department of External Affairs. "International Supervisory Commissions in Indo-China." *External Affairs Review* 8 (Oct. 1958): 1–6.

3616   Republic of Vietnam. *Violations of the Geneva Agreements by the Viet-Minh Communists.* Saigon, 1959.

3617   Thee, Marek. *Notes of a Witness: Laos and the Second Indochinese War.* New York: Vintage, 1973.

3618   U.S. Department of State. *Aggression from the North: The Record of North Vietnam's Campaign to Conquer South Vietnam.* Washington, D.C.: G.P.O., 1965.

3619   Wainhouse, David W. *International Peace Observation: A History and Forecast.* Baltimore: Johns Hopkins Press, 1966: 489–524.

International Control Commission— Reports

For a full listing of the I.C.C.'s *Official Reports*, relating to South Vietnam, Cambodia, and Laos, see Milton Leitenberg and Richard Dean Burns, eds., *The Vietnam Conflict* (Santa Barbara, Ca.: ABC–Clio, 1973), pp. 36–38.

1973 Vietnam Truce

For text, see "American-Vietnamese Agreement and Protocols, 27 January 1973," *Survival* 15 (Mar.–Apr. 1973): 81–97.

3620   Branfman, Fred. "Indochina—the Illusion of Withdrawal: Behind the Celebrations of Progress a Policy of Covert War." *Harper's* 243 (May 1973): 65–76.

3621   Cady, John F. *The History of Post-war Southeast Asia: Independence Problems.* Athens: Ohio Univ. Press, 1975.

3622   Culhane, Clair. "How Canada Torpedoed the Peace in Vietnam." *Canadian Dimension* 9 (July 1973): 6–7.

3623   Dobell, W. M. "A 'Sow's Ear' in Vietnam [Int'l Control Commission]." *International Journal* 29:3 (1974): 356–92.

3624   Goodman, Allen F. "South Vietnam: War Without End." *Asian Survey* 15 (Jan. 1975): 70–84.

3625   Porter, Gareth. *A Peace Denied: The United States, Vietnam and the Paris Agreement.* Bloomington: Indiana Univ. Press, 1975.

3626   Ravenal, Earl C. "Consequences of the End Game in Vietnam." *Foreign Affairs* 53 (July 1975): 651–67.

3627   Serong, F. P. "Vietnam's Menacing Cease-Fire." *Conflict Studies* 6 (Nov. 1974): 1–19.

3628   Terzani, Tiziano. *Giai Phong! The Fall and Liberation of Saigon.* New York: St. Martin's Press, 1976.

3629   Thies, W. J. "Searching For Peace: Vietnam and the Question of How Wars End." *Polity* 7 (Sept. 1975): 304–33.

3630 Thompson, Sir Robert. *Peace Is Not At Hand.* New York: McKay, 1974.

SOVIET DISARMAMENT PLAN (1955)

For text of plan, see "Soviet Proposal Introduced in the Disarmament Subcommittee: Reduction of Armaments, the Prohibition of Atomic Weapons, and the Elimination of the Threat of War, May 10, 1955," *Documents on Disarmament, 1945–1956* (Washington, D.C.: G.P.O., 1960), I: 456–567.

3631 Alexeyev, A. "The U.S.S.R. Disarmament Proposal: A Major Contribution to Peace." *International Affairs* [Moscow] 1 (July 1955): 14–23.

3632 Bogdanov, Oleg V. "International Disarmament Control." *New Times* [Moscow] (Jan. 23, 1955): 4–8.

3633 "Disarmament: Proposals and Negotiations," *World Today* 11 (Aug. 1955): 334–48.

3634 Finletter, Thomas K. "What kind of Disarmament?" *Vital Speeches* (Oct. 1, 1955): 1506–09.

3635 Frye, William R. "Disarmament, Diplomacy, and the Flames of Hell." *Reporter* (July 12, 1956): 10–14.

3636 ———. "The Disarmament Turning Point." *Bulletin of the Atomic Scientists* 12 (May 1956): 166–68.

3637 Fuller, Gen. J. F. C. "Soviet Disarmament Plan Called Dangerous Fraud." *U.S. News & World Report* (July 22, 1955): 88–90.

3638 Martin, Paul. "Recent Developments in Disarmament." *International Journal* 11 (Spring 1956): 79–84.

3639 "The New Soviet Disarmament Plan and the New Policy Shift it Represents." *New Republic* (May 23, 1955): 6–8.

3640 "U.S. Will Not Give Up Her Bombs." *New Republic* (Aug. 29, 1955): 3–4.

3641 Wadsworth, James J. "The U.S. Position on Disarmament." *U.S. Department of State Bulletin* (Oct. 3, 1955): 530–33.

3642 "What's all the Talk About Disarmament?" *U.S. News & World Report* 41 (Dec. 1956): 38–40.

U.S./U.S.S.R. PROPOSALS FOR GCD (1962)

For text of proposals on general and complete disarmament, see *Documents on Disarmament, 1962,* 2 vols. (Washington, D.C.: G.P.O., 1963) U.S.S.R. proposal, I: 103–26; U.S. proposal, I: 351–81. See also, Chapter 2, Survey of AC&D Issues.

3643 Bailey, Norman A. "Is Khrushchev's Disarmament Suggestion Merely a Bluff?" *Magazine of Wall Street* (Jan. 28, 1961): 499–501 ff.

3644 "Comparison of Disarmament Treaties: Summary Comparison of U.S. and USSR Treaties on General and Complete Disarmament, as Submitted . . . March and April 1962." *Bulletin of the Atomic Scientists* 18 (Sept. 1962): 8–9.

3645 "Controversy Over 'General and Complete Disarmament' and International Arms Control: Pro & Con." *Congressional Digest* 43 (Aug.–Sept. 1964): 193–224.

3646 DeWeerd, Harvey A. "Disarmament: Comparison of Soviet and Western Proposals." *Bulletin of the Atomic Scientists* 16 (Oct. 1960): 336–39.

3647 Falk, Richard A. "The Control of International Violence in a Disarming World." *Legal Order in a Violent World.* Princeton: Princeton Univ. Press, 1968: 441–531.

3648 Frye, William R. "K's Disarmament Plan: Pie-in-Sky?" *Foreign Policy Bulletin* (Oct. 15, 1959): 17.

3649 Hudson, Richard. "Should the United States Accept the Soviet Disarmament Plan." *War/Peace Report* 2 (May 1962): 3–5.

3650 Institute for Strategic Studies. *Disarmament and European Security: the Effects of Implementing the First Stage of the Soviet Draft Treaty and the United States Proposals on General and Complete Disarmament.* 2 vols. London: ISS, 1963.

3651 Kyle, Keith. "Disarmament: Is Khrushchev's Proposal 'Unthinkable'?" *New Republic* (Jan. 2, 1961): 11–15.

3652 Margolis, Howard. "Disarmament: America is Finding that Its Proposals Have Less Appeal Than Those of the Soviet Union." *Science* (Oct. 14, 1960): 1000–1001.

3653 McVitty, Marion H. *A Comparison and Evaluation of Current Disarmament Proposals as of March 1, 1964.* New York: World Law Fund, 1964.

3654 Orear, Jay. "Outline of Basic Provisions of a Treaty on General and Complete Disarmament in a Peaceful World, Submitted by the United States Delegation . . ., Geneva, April 18, 1962." *American Journal of International Law* 56 (July 1962): 899–949.

3655 Rusk, Dean. "U.S. Outlines Initial Proposals of Program for General and Complete Disarmament." *U.S. Department of State Bulletin* (Apr. 2, 1962): 531–36.

3656 [U.S.] "U.S. Pledges Full Support to Task of Achieving General and Complete Disarmament." *U.S. Department of State Bulletin* (Dec. 10, 1962): 890–96.

3657 U.S. Arms Control & Disarmament Agency. *Blueprint for the Peace Race: Outline of Basic Provisions of a Treaty on General and Complete Disarmament in a Peaceful World.* Washington, D.C.: G.P.O., 1962.

3658 ———. *Disarmament: The New U.S. Initiative.* ACDA Pub. 8. Washington, D.C.: G.P.O., 1962.

3659 ———. *Disarmament: Two Approaches—A Comparison of U.S. and U.S.S.R. Disarmament Proposals.* ACDA Pub. 1. Washington, D.C.: G.P.O., 1962.

3660 U.S. Department of State. *Freedom from War: The United States Program for General and Complete Disarmament in a Peaceful World.* Dept. of State Pub. 7277. Washington, D.C.: G.P.O., 1961.

3661 [U.S.S.R.] "Communication of the Soviet Government Regarding the Bilateral Soviet-American Negotiations on Disarmament Submitted to the 16th General Assembly." *International Affairs* [Moscow] 7 (Oct. 1961): 127–46.

3662 ———. *The Soviet Stand on Disarmament: A Collection of Nineteen Basic Soviet Documents on General and Complete Disarmament. . . .* New York: Crosscurrents Press, 1962.

3663 Wolfers, Arnold, et al. *The United States in a Disarmed World: A Study of the U.S. Outline for General and Complete Disarmament.* Baltimore: Johns Hopkins Press, 1966.

LIMITING PRODUCTION OF FISSIONABLE MATERIAL (1964)

For text of accord, see "Reducing Nuclear Materials Production," *Current History* 47 (July 1964): 47–48.

3664 Fisher, Adrian S. "U.S. Views on Nuclear Weapon Material Cutoff Agreement and Verification of Comprehensive Nuclear Test Ban." *U.S. Department of State Bulletin* (May 12, 1969): 409–13.

3665 Foster, William C. "U.S. Calls for Exploration of 'Freeze' Concept." *U.S. Department of State Bulletin* (Mar. 2, 1964): 350–52.

3666 ———. "U.S. Discusses Proposed Safeguards for Cutoff and Transfer of Fissionable Material and Nuclear Weapons Destruction." *U.S. Department of State Bulletin* (June 6, 1966): 901–06.

3667 ———. "U.S. Outlines Cutoff and Verification Provisions to Halt Production of Fissionable Materials for Nuclear Weapons Use." *U.S. Department of State Bulletin* (July 27, 1964): 123–27.

3668 "Khrushchev-Johnson Notes on the Use of Arms." *Current History* 46 (June 1964): 357–63.

3669 Lall, Betty Goetz. "Questions and Answers on the U.S. Production Freeze Proposal." *Bulletin of the Atomic Scientists* 20 (Dec. 1964): 30–34.

3670 Wainhouse, David W., et al. *Arms Control Agreements: Design for Verification and Organization.* Baltimore: Johns Hopkins Press, 1968, pp. 11–42.

U.N. PROPOSAL FOR WORLD DISARMAMENT CONFERENCE (1965–)

For text of resolution, see "General Assembly Resolution 2030 (xx): Question of Convening a World Disarmament Conference, November 29, 1965," A/RES/2030 (xx), Nov. 30, 1965, *Documents on Disarmament 1965* (Washington, D.C.: G.P.O., 1966), p. 585.

3671 Arkadev, Nikolai N. "In the Interest of General Security [G.C.D.]." *New Times* [Moscow] 38 (Sept. 1971): 4–5.

3672 ———. "Towards a World Disarmament Conference." *New Times* [Moscow] 31 (July 1972): 4–6.

3673 Babovic, Bogdan. "The World Disarmament Conference." *Review of International Affairs* [Belgrade] (July 5–20, 1965): 15–16.

3674 Demin, V. "Soviet Call for 5-Power Nuclear Talks: A Step Toward Nuclear Disarmament." *Current Digest of the Soviet Press* (Aug. 24, 1971): 5 ff.

3675 "Disarmament—Point At Issue." *Peking Review* (Nov. 17, 1972): 7–9.

3676 Foster, William C., and Arthur J. Goldberg. "U.S. Agrees to Discuss Holding of World Disarmament Conference." *U.S. Department of State Bulletin* (Dec. 27, 1965): 1029–34.

3677 "Government of the People's Republic of China Statement, July 30, 1971 [rejecting USSR's proposed 5 nation nuclear conference]." *Peking Review* (Aug. 13, 1971): 5.

3678 Gromyko, Andrei. "Soviet Union Calls for World Disarmament Conference: Letter to U.N. Secretary-General U Thant." *Soviet News* (Sept. 14, 1971): 1–2. [Annotated in *Bulletin of Peace Proposals* 4 (1971): 323.]

3679 Israelyan, Y. "New Soviet Initiative on Disarmament." *International Affairs* [Moscow] 20 (Nov. 1974): 19–25.

3680 Jack, Homer A. "Toward a World Disarmament Conference." *Review of International Affairs* (Feb. 20, 1966): 6–7.

3681 ———. "UNDC: For a World Disarmament Conference." *Bulletin of the Atomic Scientists* 21 (Sept. 1965): 39–40.

3682 ———. "A World Disarmament Conference." *Disarmament* 11 (Sept. 1966): 11–15.

3683 ———. "A World Disarmament Conference?" *Bulletin of the Atomic Scientists* 29 (Feb. 1973): 33–35.

3684 Phillips, Christopher H. "U.S. Gives Views on Question of World Disarmament Conference." *U.S. Department of State Bulletin* (Jan. 24, 1972): 109–12.

3685 Sims, Nicholas A. "UN Deadlocks and Delaying Tactics: The First Three Years of the Soviet Proposal for a World Disarmament Conference, 1971–1974." *Millenium* 4 (Autumn 1975): 113–31.

3686 Stoleshnikov, A. "Disarmament: The Possibilities of a World Forum." *International Affairs* [Moscow] 17 (Dec. 1971): 18–22.

3687 Vayrynen, Raimo. "Towards a World Disarmament Conference." *Instant Research on Peace and Violence* 6:1–2 (1976): 81–88.

MUTUAL BALANCED FORCE REDUCTION (1968–)

Initially proposed by NATO in 1968, negotiations for an MBFR continued through 1976 without agreement.

Documents

3688 U.S. Arms Control & Disarmament Agency. *Selected Background Documents Relating to Mutual and Balanced Force Reductions.* Washington, D.C.: G.P.O., 1973–. [Pt. 1, Disarmament Document Series, Reference no. 611, May 17, 1973; Pt. 2, no. 619, Nov. 1973; Pt. 3, no. 637, May 5, 1975.]

3689 U.S. House. Committee on Foreign Affairs. Hearings: *U.S. Forces In NATO.* 93d Cong., 1st Sess., 1973.

3690 U.S. Senate. Committee on Foreign Relations. Hearings: *U.S. Forces in Europe.* 93d Cong., 1st Sess., 1973.

General Accounts, 1968–1972

3691 Bellany, Ian. "Balancing Mutual Force Reductions." *Nature* [London] (Dec. 10, 1971): 361–62.

3692 Bertram, Christoph. *Mutual Force Reduction in Europe: The Political Aspects.* Adelphi Paper, no. 84. London: Institute for Strategic Studies, Jan. 1972.

3693 Brenner, Michael J. "Decouping, Disengagement and European Defense." *Bulletin of the Atomic Scientists* 28 (Feb. 1972): 38–42.

3694 Buntinx, Henry M. V. "Symmetrical Force Reduction vs. European Collective Security." *NATO's Fifteen Nations* 15 (Oct.–Nov. 1970): 29–33.

3695 Clemens, Walter C., Jr. "Mutual Balanced Force Reductions." *Military Review* 51 (Oct. 1971): 3–11.

3696 Cliffe, Trevor. *Military Technology and the European Balance*. Adelphi Paper, no. 89. London: Institute for Strategic Studies, 1972.

3697 Crezien, B. J. "Truppenverminderung und Osteuropa." *Wehrkunde* 21 (Sept. 1972): 441–46.

3698 Enthoven, Alain C. "Arms and Men: The Military Balance in Europe." *Interplay* 2 (Oct. 1969): 11–14.

3699 Goos, David. "Est-il Possible de Réduire les Forces Militaires des Deux Blocs?" *Revue Politique et Parlementaire* 74 (Jan. 1972): 39–42.

3700 Hill, Roger J. "MBFR Prelude: Explorations Before Negotiations." *NATO Review* 20 (July–Aug. 1972): 3–4.

3701 ———. "Mutual and Balanced Force Reductions: The State of a Key Alliance Policy." *NATO Review* 19 (Sept.–Oct. 1971): 17–20.

3702 Hunt, Kenneth. "The Problem of Mutual Balanced Force Reduction." *Canadian Defense Quarterly* 1:3 (1971–1972): 10–16.

3703 Hunter, Robert E. "Mutual and Balanced Force Reductions: The Next Step in Detente?" In Herbert Scoville et al., *The Arms Race: Steps Toward Restraint*. New York: Carnegie Endowment for International Peace, 1972, pp. 39–58. [*International Conciliation*, no. 587.]

3704 Kock, Maj. F. H. C. "Problems of Comparing Force Levels." *NATO Review* 19 (Mar.–Apr. 1971): 19–22.

3705 Kostko, Yu. "Mutual Force Reduction in Europe." *Survival* 14 (Sept.–Oct. 1972): 236–38.

3706 Lehmann, Hans. "Sicherheit—Sowjetisch." *Politische Studien* 23 (May–June 1972): 277–85.

3707 McKenney, Lt. Edward A., Jr. "Mutually Balanced Force Reduction: The Complex Problem." *Naval War College Review* 24 (June 1972): 29–41.

3708 Morris, C. E. "Problems of European Security." *Army Quarterly* 101 (July 1971): 396–401.

3709 Nerlich, Uwe. "Die Rolle beiderseitiger Truppenverminderung in der Europäischen Sicherheitspolitik." *Europa-Archiv* (Mar. 10, 1972): 161–68.

3710 "La Réduction Equilibrée des Forces et l'Aménagement de la Sécurité en Europe dans le Contexte Politique Actuel." *Politique Etrangère* 5 (1970): 499–516.

3711 Smart, Ian. *MBFR Assailed: A Critical View of the Proposed Negotiation on Mutual and Balanced Force Reductions in Europe*. Peace Studies Program Occasional Paper, no. 3. Ithaca: Cornell Univ., 1972.

3712 Stanley, Timothy W., and Darnell M. Whitt. "Mutual Force Reductions." *Detente Diplomacy: United States and European Security in the 1970's*. Cambridge, Mass.: Dunellen, 1970, pp. 53–67.

3713 Steinhopp, Gen. Johannes. "The Road to Detente." *Atlantic Community Quarterly* 10 (Winter 1972–73): 446–56.

3714 Wieck, Hans-George. "Perspektiven für MBFR in Europa." *Aussenpolitik* 22 (Nov. 1971): 641–45.

3715 ———. "Politische und Militärische Probleme Ausgewogener Truppenreduzierungen in Europa." *Europa-Archiv* (Nov. 25, 1970): 807–14.

General Accounts, 1973–1976

3716 Ball, Robert. "Rethinking the Defense of Europe." *Fortune* 87 (Feb. 1973): 60–65 ff.

3717 Borgart, Peter. "Increasingly Relevant to MBFR: The Air Attack Potential of the Warsaw Pact." *International Defense Review* 9 (Apr. 1976): 193–97.

3718 Canby, Steven. *The Alliance and Europe. Part 4: Military Doctrine and Technology*. Adelphi Papers, no. 109. London: Institute for Strategic Studies, 1975.

3719 Clark, Donald L. "What's An MBFR?" *Air University Review* 27 (July–Aug. 1976): 51–64.

3720 Coffey, Joseph I. "Arms Control and the Military Balance in Europe." *Orbis* 17 (Spring 1973): 132–54.

3721 ———. "Detente, Arms Control and European Security." *International Affairs* [London] 52 (Jan. 1976): 39–52.

3722 ———. *New Approaches to Arms Reductions in Europe*. Adelphi Papers, no. 105. London: Institute for Strategic Studies, 1974.

3723 Facer, Roger. *The Alliance and Europe.* Part 3: *Weapons Procurement in Europe— Capabilities and Choices.* Adelphi Papers, no. 108. London: Institute for Strategic Studies, 1975.

3724 Hamlett, Bruce D. "Mutual Balanced Force Reductions in Europe: An Alternative to Unilateral American Withdrawal." *Towson State Journal of International Affairs* 7 (Spring 1973): 109–20.

3725 Harned, Joseph W., et al. "Conference on Security and Cooperation in Europe and Negotiations on Mutual Balanced Force Reductions." *Atlantic Community Quarterly* 11 (Spring 1973): 7–54.

3726 Hill, Roger J. "MBFR." *International Journal* 29 (Spring 1974): 242–55.

3726a ———. "MBFR Progress: Commitment to Negotiations." *NATO Review* 21 (Sept.–Oct. 1973): 5.

3727 Holst, Johan J. "Mutual Force Reductions in Europe: Arms Control and the European Political Process." *Survival* 15 (Nov.–Dec. 1973): 283–88.

3728 Horhager, Axel. "The MBFR Talks: Problems and Prospects." *International Defense Review* 9 (Apr. 1976): 189–92.

3729 Hunt, Brig. Kenneth. *The Alliance and Europe.* Part 2: *Defense with Fewer Men.* Adelphi Papers, no. 98. London: Institute for Strategic Studies, Summer 1973.

3730 Jenner, Peter. "MBFR—Some of the Issues Involved." *NATO Review* 21 (Nov.–Dec. 1973): 8–10.

3731 Johnson, David. "Military Confrontation in Europe: Will the MBFR Talks Work?" *Defense Monitor* 5:10 (1975): 1–8.

3732 Khlestov, O. "Mutual Force Reductions in Europe." *Survival* 16 (Nov.–Dec. 1974): 293–98.

3733 Klaiber, Wolfgang, et al. *Era of Negotiations: European Security and Force Reductions.* Lexington, Mass.: D.C. Heath, 1973.

3734 Luns, Joseph M. A. H. "Prospects for the Alliance." *NATO Review* 22 (Feb.–Mar. 1974): 3–7.

3735 "Multilateral Exploratory Talks on MBFR in Vienna." *NATO Review* 21 (Jan.–Feb. 1973): 3–4.

3736 Newhouse, John. "Stuck Fast." *Foreign Affairs* 51 (Jan. 1973): 353–66.

3737 Ranger, Robin. "MBFR: Political or Technical Arms Control?" *World Today* 30 (Oct. 1974): 411–18.

3738 Rattinger, Hans. "Armaments, Detente, and Bureaucracy: The Case of the Arms Race in Europe." *Journal of Conflict Resolution* 19:4 (1975): 571–95.

3739 Rosenthal, Rep. Benjamin S. "America's Move." *Foreign Affairs* 51 (Jan. 1973): 380–91.

3740 Rostow, Eugene V. "Atlantic Relations: Perspectives towards the Future." *NATO Review* 21 (Mar.–Apr. 1973): 7–10.

3741 Ruehl, Lothar. "Beiderseitige Truppenverminderungen in Europa. Grundlagen, Moglichkeiten und Grenzen vom MBFR-Verhandlungen." *Europa-Archiv* (May 25, 1973): 325–40.

3742 ———. "The Negotiations on Force Reductions in Central Europe." *NATO Review* 24 (Oct. 1976): 18–25.

3743 ———. "Die Wiener Verhandlungen uber Truppenverminderungen in Ost und West." *Europa-Archiv* (Aug. 10, 1974): 507–18.

3744 Ruth, Friedrich. "Die Wiener Vorgespräche über Truppenverminderung: Verlauf und Ergebnis." *Europa-Archiv* (Sept. 25, 1973): 643–50.

3745 "SALT and MBFR: The Next Phase." *Survival* 17 (Jan.–Feb. 1975): 14–24.

3746 Senghaas, Dieter. "Arms Race by Arms Control." *Bulletin of Peace Proposals* 4:4 (1973): 359–79.

3747 SIPRI. *Force Reductions In Europe.* New York: Humanities Press, 1974.

3748 Van Delden, Rembert. "A Status Report on Mutual and Balanced Force Reductions." *NATO's Fifteen Nations* 21 (Aug.–Sept. 1976): 20–21.

3749 Willot, Albert. "Mutual and Balanced Force Reductions in Europe." *NATO Review* 21 (Jan.–Feb. 1973): 5–9.

3750 Wyle, Frederick S. "European Security: Beating the Numbers Game." *Foreign Policy* 10 (Spring 1973): 41–54.

3751   Yochelson, John. "MBFR: The Search for an American Approach." *Orbis* 18 (Spring 1973).

Soviet View

3752   Caldwell, Lawrence T. *Soviet Security Interests in Europe and MBFR.* Santa Monica, Ca.: California Seminar on Arms Control & Foreign Policy, 1976.

3753   Erickson, John. "MBFR: Force Levels and Security Requirements." *Strategic Review* 1 (Summer 1973): 28–43.

3754   Griswold, Lawrence. "Mutual Balanced Force Reductions Much Better for Russia?" *Sea Power* 16 (May 1973): 18–22.

3755   Gromyko, Andrei. "U.S. Heavyweight in the European Ring." *International Affairs* [Moscow] 17 (Feb. 1971): 16–23.

3756   Krementsov, M., and G. Starko. "Military Bases in Foreign Territories." *New Times* [Moscow] (May 21, 1955): 18–21.

3757   "The Soviet View of Mutual Balanced Force Reductions." *East-West Digest* 8 (July 1972): 497–500.

3758   Tomilin, Y. "The Problems of Armed Forces Reductions in Europe." *International Affairs* [Moscow] 19 (Mar. 1973): 37–42.

3759   "Trends in Warsaw Pact Military Developments." *NATO Review* 21 (July–Aug. 1973): 8–11.

3760   "Views on Arms Cutbacks in Central Europe." *Current Digest of the Soviet Press* (Nov. 1, 1972): 8–9.

3761   Wolfe, Thomas W. *Soviet Attitudes Toward MBFR and the USSR's Military Presence in Europe.* P-4819. Santa Monica, Ca.: Rand, Apr. 1972.

NATO & European Balance

3762   Booth, Kenneth. "Security Makes Strange Bedfellows: NATO's Problems from a Minimalist Perspective." *Royal United Services Institute for Defense Studies Journal* 120 (Dec. 1975): 3–14.

3763   Brosio, Manlio. "Will NATO Survive Detente?" *Atlantic Community Quarterly* 9 (Summer 1971): 143–55.

3764   Brown, Neville. "The Tactical Air Balance in Europe." *World Today* 28 (Sept. 1972): 385–92.

3765   Canby, Steven. "NATO Muscle: More Shadow than Substance." *Foreign Policy* 9 (Fall 1972): 38–49.

3766   Komer, R. W. "Treating NATO's Self-Inflicted Wound." *Foreign Policy*, no. 13 (Winter 1973–74): 34–48.

3767   Lawrence, Richard D., and Jeffrey Record. *U.S. Force Structure in NATO: An Alternative.* Washington, D.C.: Brookings Institution, 1974.

3768   Palmer, Joseph. "NATO Lives or Dies by the Sea." *NATO's Fifteen Nations* 19 (Oct.–Nov. 1974): 20–23.

3769   Pfaltzgraff, Robert L., Jr. "NATO and European Security: Prospects for the 1970's." *Orbis* 15 (Spring 1971): 154–77.

3770   Stambuk, George. "Foreign Policy and the Stationing of American Forces Abroad." *Journal of Politics* 25 (Aug. 1963): 472–88.

3771   U.S. Senate. Committee on Armed Services. Hearings: *European Defense Cooperation.* 94th Cong., 2d Sess., 1976.

3772   Yeremenko, A. "The Strategic and Political Value of Military Bases." *International Affairs* [Moscow] 6 (Nov. 1960): 57–61.

Mansfield Resolutions

3773   Center for Defense Information. "U.S. Forces for Europe: Need for Phased Reduction." *Defense Monitor* 2:5 (1973): 1–10.

3774   Clayton, B. A. "U.S. Force Reduction? The Implications for Europe." *Journal of the Royal United Services Institution* 117 (Sept. 1972): 55–61.

3775   Enthoven, Alain C. "U.S. Forces in Europe: How Many? Doing What?" *Foreign Affairs* 52 (Apr. 1975): 513–32.

3776   Fried, Edward R. "The Financial Cost of Alliance." In John Newhouse et al., *U.S. Troops in Europe: Issues, Costs, and Choices.* Washington, D.C.: Brookings Institution, 1971, pp. 102–44.

3777   Griffin, William E. "Why American Troops

Should Remain in Europe." *Reader's Digest* (May 1970): 121–25.

3778 Harrison, Stanley L. "Congress and President: NATO Troop Reduction Conflict." *Military Review* 51 (Sept. 1971): 13–24.

3779 Leonard, James F. "U.S. States Views on Conventional Arms Restraints." *U.S. Department of State Bulletin* (Sept. 20, 1971): 309–15.

3780 "Majority Would Reduce U.S. Troop Commitment to NATO." *Gallup Opinion Index*, Report no. 101 (Nov. 1973): 14–21.

3781 Mansfield, Sen. Mike J. "Reduction of U.S. Forces in Europe." *Congressional Record* 113 (Jan. 19, 1967): S997–1011.

3782 Newhouse, John. "U.S. Troops in Europe: Issues and Alternatives." *Atlantic Community Quarterly* 9:4 (1971): 460–75.

3783 ———, et al. *U.S. Troops in Europe: Issues, Costs and Choices.* Washington, D.C.: Brookings Institution, 1971.

3784 Radovanovic, Ljubomir. "New Developments in the Problem of Disarmament." *Review of International Affairs* [Belgrade] (June 5, 1971): 7–9.

3785 Resor, Stanley R. "United States Forces in Europe: Mutual Reduction." *Vital Speeches* (May 15, 1970): 456–59.

3786 Richardson, Elliot L., and Sen. Mike Mansfield. "American Forces in Europe: The Pros and Cons." *Atlantic Community Quarterly* 8 (Spring 1971): 5–13 ff.

3787 Watt, Donald C. "Balanced Force Reductions and the American Military Withdrawal From Germany." *United Service Institution Journal* 115 (June 1970): 42–44.

3788 Yochelson, John N. "The American Military Presence in Europe: Current Debate in the United States." *Orbis* 15 (Fall 1971): 784–807.

Tactical Nuclear Weapons In Europe

3789 Atkeson, Brig. Gen. Edward B. "Precision Guided Munitions: Implications for Detente." *Parameters* 5:2 (1976): 75–87.

3790 Bennett, W. S., et al. "A Credible Nuclear-Emphasis Defense for NATO." *Orbis* 17 (Summer 1973): 463–79.

3791 Brenner, Michael J. "Decoupling, Disengagement and European Defense." *Bulletin of the Atomic Scientists* 28 (Feb. 1972): 38–42.

3792 ———. "Tactical Nuclear Strategy and European Defense: A Critical Reappraisal." *International Affairs* [London] 51 (Jan. 1975): 25–43.

3793 Cohen, Samuel T. "Tactical Nuclear Weapons and U.S. Military Strategy." *Orbis* 15 (Spring 1971): 178–93.

3794 Davidson, Charles N. "Tactical Nuclear Defense: The West German View." *Parameters* 5:1 (1974): 47–57.

3795 Davis, Paul C. "A European Nuclear Force: Utility and Prospects." *Orbis* 17 (Spring 1973): 110–31.

3796 Dyer, Philip W. "Will Tactical Nuclear Weapons Ever Be Used?" *Political Science Quarterly* 88 (June 1973): 214–29.

3797 Ellis, Maj. Ronald I. "Beyond Deterrence: A Rational Approach to the Deployment of Tactical Nuclear Weapons in Europe." *Field Artillery* 64 (Nov.–Dec. 1974): 38–45.

3798 Gormley, Dennis M. "NATO's Tactical Nuclear Option: Past, Present, and Future." *Military Review* 53 (Sept. 1973): 3–18.

3799 Gray, Colin S. "Deterrence and Defence in Europe: Revising NATO's Theatre Nuclear Posture." *Strategic Review* 3 (Spring 1975): 58–69.

3800 ———. "Mini-nukes and Strategy." *International Journal* 29:2 (1974): 216–41.

3801 ———. "Theater Nuclear Weapons: Doctrines and Postures." *World Politics* 27 (Jan. 1976): 300–314.

3802 Heisenberg, Wolfgang. *The Alliance and Europe:* Part 1: *Crisis Stability in Europe and Theatre Nuclear Weapons.* Adelphi Papers, no. 96. London: International Institute for Strategic Studies, Summer 1973.

3803 Karber, Phillip A. "Nuclear Weapons and 'Flexible Response.'" *Orbis* 14 (Summer 1970): 284–97.

3804 Martin, Laurence. "Theatre Nuclear Weapons and Europe." *Survival* 16 (Nov.–Dec. 1974): 268–76.

3805   Miettinen, Jorma K. "Recent Developments in Tactical Nuclear Weapons and Their Bearing on Nuclear Non-Proliferation." *Instant Research on Peace and Violence* 3:4 (1975): 225–30.

3806   ———. "Time for Europeans to Debate the Presence of Tactical Nukes." *Bulletin of the Atomic Scientists* 32 (May 1976): 18–22.

3807   Nelson, Sen. Gaylord. "Report on Tactical Nuclear Weapons." *Congressional Record* 117 (July 20, 1971): S11625–628.

3808   Nerlich, Uwe. *The Alliance and Europe. Part 5: Nuclear Weapons and East-West Negotiations*. Adelphi Papers, no. 120. London: International Institute for Strategic Studies, 1976.

3809   Norman, Lloyd. "The Reluctant Dragon: NATO's Fears and Need For New Nuclear Weapons." *Army* 24:2 (1974): 16–21.

3810   Pincus, Walter. "Congress and Tactical Nukes." *New Republic* (Oct. 12, 1974): 19–20.

3811   ———. "Nukes Nobody Needs." *New Republic* (Apr. 20, 1974): 17.

3812   Polk, James H. "The Realities of Tactical Nuclear Warfare." *Orbis* 17 (Summer 1973): 439–47.

3813   Record, Jeffrey. *U.S. Nuclear Weapons in Europe: Issues and Alternatives*. Washington, D.C.: Brookings Institution, 1974.

3814   ———, and Richard D. Lawrence. *U.S. Force Posture in Europe: An Alternative*. Washington, D.C.: Brookings Institution, 1974.

3815   Santilli, Col. Joseph F., Jr. "NATO Strategy Updated: A First Use Policy." *Military Review* 54 (Mar. 1974): 3–20.

3816   Schmitz, Rep. John G. "NATO and the Neutron Bomb." *Congressional Record* 116 (Dec. 30, 1970): E10880–85.

3817   Schneider, Barry R. "30,000 U.S. Nuclear Weapons." *Defense Monitor* 4:2 (1975): 1–12.

3818   Stowe, Maj. Wain W. "Atomic Demolition Munitions." *National Defense* 59 (May–June 1975): 467–70.

3819   U.S. Congress. Joint Atomic Energy Subcommittee on Military Applications. Hearings: *Military Applications of Nuclear Technology*. 2 pts. 93d Cong., 1st Sess., 1973.

3820   U.S. Senate. Committee on Foreign Relations. Hearings: *Nuclear Weapons and Foreign Policy*. 93d Cong., 1st Sess., 1973.

3821   ———. Staff Report: *U.S. Security Issues in Europe: Burden Sharing and Offset, MBFR and Nuclear Weapons*. 93d Cong., 1st Sess., 1973.

3822   York, Herbert F. "The Nuclear 'Balance of Terror' in Europe." *Bulletin of the Atomic Scientists* 32 (May 1976): 16–17.

Eight

Limitation of Weapons (the SALT Era, 1969–1976)

THE STRATEGIC ARMS Limitation Talks (SALT) have marked the coming-of-age of the "arms controllers" (as contrasted with the "disarmers"). While previous efforts—such as the Baruch Plan (1946) and the proposals for general and complete disarmament (1962)—sought broad, multilateral reductions and control of nuclear forces, the SALT approach focused on the limitation of specific weapons systems through secret, bilateral negotiations between the United States and the Soviet Union. While this superpower diplomacy has resulted in the placing of some restrictions and limits on certain weapons, there is a mounting criticism of this selective approach. (The critiques are listed in Arms Control vs. Disarmament in Chapter 2.)

For those individuals who are relative newcomers to the SALT era, the first sections below will be helpful. The essays by Richard Dean Burns, "The SALT Talks in Historical Perspective," and Walter C. Clemens, Jr., "Nicholas II to SALT II," suggest certain historical comparisons. An excellent introduction to the initial phase of SALT is John Newhouse's book, *Cold Dawn: The Story of SALT*.

The SALT agreements were the result of extended, secret deliberation. Consequently, there was an outpouring of contemporary criticism, observations, and suggestions, most of which were written in ignorance of matters actually under discussion, and a large sample of these are listed in chronological order. The signing of the initial SALT accords, in 1972, brought to light the nature and direction of these negotiations; it also prompted criticism from all sides. In 1975, some of the SALT critics accused the Soviet Union of violating certain pledges.

SALT I succeeded in restricting more severely defensive missile systems (ABMs) than offensive missiles. That this was a controversial issue can be seen from the heated debate, prior to and after the signing of the treaty. Nevertheless, subsequent negotiations on the ABMs resulted in still further reductions (see the protocol signed in 1974).

When the superpower deliberations began anew after 1972, to draft a more definitive treaty limiting offensive nuclear weapons, public and academic argument continued. These arguments focused on SALT's underlying assumptions regarding the nature of strategic nuclear policy (deterrence), and whether or not SALT agreements were stimulating rather than reducing the nuclear arms race. The United States government insisted that weapons systems on the drawing board must continue to be developed and employed in order to provide "bargaining chips" which would bring the Soviet Union to terms. The Vladivostok Agreement (1974) became a particular source of irritation to those who looked to SALT to bring about reductions in offensive nuclear weapons. However, the deployment of cruise missiles may greatly alter the SALT effort.

Students of SALT who wish to pursue either argument will find listed below a sampling of essays dealing with the fundamental aspects and assumptions underlying various strategic concepts and the nature of arms races.

Historical Comparisons

3823 Bull, Hedley. *Strategic Arms Limitations: The Precedent of the Washington and London Naval Treaties*. Occasional paper. Chicago: Univ. of Chicago, Center for Policy Study, 1971.

3824 Burns, Richard Dean. "The SALT Talks in Historical Perspective." *Revue Militaire Générale* [Paris] 8 (Oct. 1970): 365–84.

3825 Clemens, Walter C., Jr. "Nicholas II to SALT II: Continuity and Change in East-West Diplomacy." *International Affairs* [London] 49 (July 1973): 385–401.

3826 Dingman, Roger. *Statesmen, Admirals and SALT: The United States and the Washington Conference, 1921–1922*. Santa Monica, Ca.: California Arms Control & Foreign Policy Seminar, 1972.

3827 Watt, Donald C. "Historical Light on SALT: Parallels with Inter-War Naval Arms Control." *Round Table* 245 (Jan. 1972): 29–35.

General Accounts

3828 Kaplan, Morton A., ed. *SALT: Problems and Prospects*. Morristown, N.J.: General Learning Press, 1973.

3829 Kintner, William R., and Robert L. Pfaltzgraff, Jr., eds. *SALT: Implications for Arms Control in the 1970's*. Pittsburgh: Univ. of Pittsburgh Press, 1973.

3830 Newhouse, John. *Cold Dawn: The Story of SALT*. New York: Holt, Rinehart & Winston, 1973.

3831 Pfaltzgraff, Robert L., Jr., ed. *Contrasting Approaches to Strategic Arms Control*. Lexington, Mass.: D. C. Heath, 1974.

3832 Willrich, Mason, and John B. Rhinelander, eds. *SALT: The Moscow Agreements and Beyond*. New York: Free Press, 1974.

3833 Wolfe, Thomas W. *The SALT Experience: Its Impact on U.S. and Soviet Strategic Policy and Decisionmaking*. R1686–PR. Santa Monica, Ca.: Rand, 1975.

3834 Beavers, Cmdr. Roy L., Jr. "SALT I." *U.S. Naval Institute Proceedings* 100 (May 1974): 204–219.

3835 Becker, Benjamin M. "The Myth of Arms Control and Disarmament." *Bulletin of the Atomic Scientists* 27 (Apr. 1971): 5–8 ff.

3836 Carter, Luther J. "Strategic Arms Limitation (I): The Decades of Frustration." *Science* (Jan. 31, 1975): 327–30.

3837 ———. "Strategic Arms Limitation (II): 'Leveling Up' to Symmetry." *Science* (Feb. 21, 1975): 627–32.

3838 Coffey, Joseph I. "The Limitation of Strategic Armaments." *Yearbook of World Affairs* 26 (1972): 128–51.

3839 Doty, Paul, et al. "The Race to Control Nuclear Arms." *Foreign Affairs* 55 (Oct. 1976): 119–32.

3840 Gellner, J. "Seeking Nuclear Arms Control: The Hard Lessons of SALT." *International Perspectives* [Canada] (Nov.–Dec. 1972): 43–47.

3841 Hayden, Eric W. "Soviet-American Arms Negotiations, 1960–1968: A Prelude to SALT." *Naval War College Review* 24 (Jan. 1972): 65–82.

3842 Hayes, Richard E. "The Inherent Inadequacy of SALT: The Inapplicability of a Bipolar Solution to a Multilateral Problem." *Western Political Quarterly* 24 (Dec. 1973): 631–48.

3843 Institute for Strategic Studies. *Soviet-American Relations and World Order: Arms Limitations and Policy.* Adelphi Paper, no. 65. London, Feb. 1970.

3844 Kahan, Jerome H. "Limited Agreements and Long-Term Stability: A Positive View Toward SALT." *Stanford Journal of International Studies* 7 (Spring 1972): 64–86.

3845 Lapp, Ralph E. "The Vicious Acronyms." *New Republic* (June 21, 1969): 15–19.

3846 Perle, Richard N. *Superpower Postures in SALT: The Language of Arms Control.* Occasional paper. Chicago: Univ. of Chicago, Center for Policy Study, 1971.

3847 Rathjens, George W., and G. B. Kistiakowsky. "The Limitation of Strategic Arms." *Scientific American* 222 (Jan. 1970): 19–29.

3848 Roberts, Chalmers M. "The ABCs of FBS and SALT and MBFR and CES." *Survival* 13 (Sept. 1971): 303–06.

3849 Slocombe, Walter B. "[Review of John Newhouse's *Cold Dawn: The Story of SALT.*]" *Yale Law Journal* 83 (Nov. 1973): 209–20.

3850 Van Cleave, William R. "The SALT Papers: A Torrent of Verbiage or a Spring of Capital Truths [Review of John Newhouse's *Cold Dawn: The Story of SALT*]." *Orbis* 17 (Winter 1974): 1396–1401.

SALT (I), 1969–1972

3851 Rogers, William P. "Secretary Rogers Discusses Forthcoming U.S.-U.S.S.R. Talks on Curbing Strategic Arms." *U.S. Department of State Bulletin* (Nov. 10, 1969): 389–94.

3852 ———. "U.S. and Soviet Union Conclude Preliminary Strategic Arms Limitation Talks." *U.S. Department of State Bulletin* (Jan. 12, 1970): 28–29.

3853 Smith, Gerard C. "United States and Soviet Union Begin Second Phase of Strategic Arms Limitation Talks." *U.S. Department of State Bulletin* (May 4, 1970): 572–73.

3854 ———. "United States and the Soviet Union Conclude Second Phase of Strategic Arms Limitation Talks." *U.S. Department of State Bulletin* (Aug. 31, 1970): 245–46.

3855 ———. "United States and Soviet Union Begin Third Phase of Strategic Arms Limitation Talks." *U.S. Department of State Bulletin* (Nov. 23, 1970): 651–52.

3856 ———. "U.S. and U.S.S.R. Conclude Third Phase of Strategic Arms Limitation Talks." *U.S. Department of State Bulletin* (Jan. 11, 1971): 55.

3857 ———. "U.S. and Soviet Union Begin Fifth Phase of SALT Talks." *U.S. Department of State Bulletin* (July 26, 1971): 98.

3858 ———. "U.S. and U.S.S.R. Conclude Fifth Phase of Strategic Arms Limitation Talks." *U.S. Department of State Bulletin* (Oct. 18, 1971): 403–04.

3859 ———. "U.S. and Soviet Union Begin Sixth Phase of SALT Talks." *U.S. Department of State Bulletin* (Dec. 6, 1971): 659–60.

3860 ———. "U.S. and U.S.S.R. Conclude Sixth Round of Strategic Arms Limitation Talks." *U.S. Department of State Bulletin* (Feb. 28, 1972): 278.

General—through 1969

3861 Bertram, Christoph. "Vor den Sowjetisch-Amerikanischen Rustungsgesprachen. Aussichten und Auswirkungen von 'SALT'." *Europa-Archiv* (Oct. 25, 1969): 717–26.

3862   Boyd, Andrew. "The SALT and the Earth." *Vista* 5 (July–Aug. 1969): 24–31.

3863   Brown, Harold. "Strategic Weapons: Security Through Limitations." *Foreign Affairs* 47 (Apr. 1969): 422–32.

3864   Bundy, McGeorge. "To Cap the Volcano." *Foreign Affairs* 48 (Oct. 1969): 1–20.

3865   "Courtship with Missiles." *Agenor* 14 (Dec. 1969): 48–53.

3866   Dougherty, James E. "A Nuclear Arms Agreement: What Shape Might It Take?" *War/Peace Report* 9 (Dec. 1969): 8–11, 16–18.

3867   Foster, William C. "Strategic Weapons: Prospects for Arms Control." *Foreign Affairs* 47 (Apr. 1969): 413–21.

3868   Fromm, Joseph. "Pitfalls for U.S. in Arms Talks." *U.S. News & World Report* (Nov. 10, 1969): 28–29.

3869   Getler, Michael. "Arms Control and the SS-9." *Space/Aeronautics* 52 (Nov. 1969): 38–47.

3870   Kabermann, Heinz. "Was ist von SALT zu Erwarten? Die Kosten der Friedlichen Koexistenz." *Politische Welte* 132 (Aug. 1969): 17–20.

3871   Lall, Betty Goetz. "Missile Control: Hope and Chimera?" *Dissent* 16 (May–June 1969): 225–30.

3872   "Looking for the Next Agreement." *Nature* [London] (Nov. 22, 1969): 737–38.

3873   Luchsinger, Fred. "Dialogue Between Giants." *Swiss Review of World Affairs* 19 (Dec. 1969): 2–3.

3874   Nielsen, Walter. "Was ist SALT—Strategisch und Politisch?" *Aussenpolitik* 20 (Sept. 1969): 537–46.

3875   Panofsky, Wolfgang K. H. "Strategic Arms Limitation." *Congressional Record* 115 (Nov. 18, 1969): S34537–540.

3876   "Real Issues in the U.S.-Russian Arms Talks." *U.S. News & World Report* (Dec. 1, 1969): 64–65.

3877   "U.S., Soviet Union to Hold Preliminary Discussions of 'Strategic Arms Limitation Talks.'" *Survey of China Mainland Press* (Nov. 13, 1969): 27–28.

3878   Vernant, Jacques. "Un Pas Vers le Désarmement?" *Revue de Defense Nationale* 24 (Aug.–Sept. 1968): 1308–12.

3879   Woollacott, Martin. "What Prospects for Arms Talks?" *Current* 109 (Aug. 1969): 43–45.

General—1970

3880   "Another Round of SALT." *Nature* [London] (Nov. 7, 1970): 489–90.

3881   Brown, Neville. "An Unstable Balance of Terror?" *World Today* 26 (Jan. 1970): 38–46.

3882   Bull, Hedley. "The Scope for Soviet-American Agreement." *Soviet-American Relations and World Order: Arms Limitations and Policy.* Adelphi Paper, no. 65. London: Institute for Strategic Studies, Feb. 1970.

3883   Bunn, George. "Missile Limitation: By Treaty or Otherwise?" *Columbia Law Review* 70 (Jan. 1970): 1–47.

3884   "Can the SALT Talks Succeed?" *Current* 119 (June 1970): 60–62.

3885   Cantrell, Burton N. "Misconceptions Concerning Nuclear Weapons." *Christian Century* (Oct. 14, 1970): 1219–20.

3886   Cook, Don. "Towards a New Congress of Vienna? Salt in Old Wounds." *Encounter* 35 (Sept. 1970): 53–60.

3887   DeVolpi, Alexander. "Expectations from SALT." *Bulletin of the Atomic Scientists* 26 (Apr. 1970): 6–8, 30–34.

3888   Geneste, Marc. "Les Conversations sur la Limitation des Armes Strategiques." *Revue Militaire Générale* [Paris] 6 (June 1970): 3–25.

3889   Gharekhann, C. R. "The Strategic Arms Limitation Talks." *India Quarterly* 26 (July–Sept. 1970): 239–48.

3890   ———. "Strategic Arms Limitation Talks—II." *India Quarterly* 26 (Oct.–Dec. 1970): 389 ff.

3891   Hamilton, Andrew. "Arms Talks: In-Group Debate on the Technical Issues." *Science* (Apr. 10, 1970): 234–36.

3892   ———. "Strategic Arms Talks: What is Negotiable?" *Science* (Mar. 27, 1970): 1707–08.

3893 Harrigan, Anthony. "The SALT Talks: Round Two." *National Review* (Apr. 7, 1970): 360.

3894 Hermges, David. "SALT: Eine Grosse Hoffnung." *Die Zukunft* 9/10 (May 1970): 11–12.

3895 Herzfeld, Charles M. "Innovation and Restraint." *Soviet-American Relations and World Order: Arms Limitations and Policy.* Adelphi Paper, no. 65. London: Institute for Strategic Studies, Feb. 1970.

3896 Hosmer, Rep. Craig. "The SALT Talks." *Congressional Record* 116 (May 18, 1970): H4478–79.

3897 Jonas, Anne M. "The SALT Negotiations: Keeping Hope in Line With Reality." *Air Force & Space Digest* 53 (Mar. 1970): 39–42.

3898 Lendvai, Paul. "Kleine Hoffnungen—Grosse Gefahren." *Die Zukunft* 9/10 (May 1970): 10–11.

3899 Lewis, Richard A. "SALT in Vienna: The Waltz of the Powers." *Bulletin of the Atomic Scientists* 26 (Sept. 1970): 19–21.

3900 Menos, Dennis. "Beyond SALT." *Military Review* 50 (June 1970): 91–97.

3901 "Mild Throw on Disarmament." *Nature* [London] (Jan. 17, 1970): 211–12.

3902 Nielsen, Walter. "SALT: Umkehr oder Kreuzweg?" *Aussenpolitik* 21 (Oct. 1970): 603–15.

3903 Pribicevic, Novak. "Second Round of Talks on Strategic Nuclear Arms." *Review of International Affairs* [Belgrade] (May 5, 1970): 10–11.

3904 "Prospects for SALT." *Nature* [London] (Mar. 28, 1970): 1178–79.

3905 "Pugwash Worth Its Weight in SALT." *Nature* [London] (Sept. 19, 1970): 1185–86.

3906 Raven, Wolfram von. "Das Gesprach der Giganten: Betrachtungen zu den SALT in Wien." *Revue Militaire Générale* [Paris] 8 (Oct. 1970): 395–414.

3907 Rougeron, Camille. "La Limitacion de los Armamentos Estrategicos." *Revista de Politica Internacional* 108 (Mar.–Apr. 1970): 15–34.

3908 Schneider, Mark B. "Red Missiles and SALT." *Ordnance* 55 (Nov.–Dec. 1970): 254–56.

3909 ———. "Two Views on Disarmament: Strategic Arms Limitation." *Military Review* 50 (Mar. 1970): 20–28.

3910 Schwarz, Urs. "Vor Neuen Verhandlungen uber Rustungsschrankungen." *Schweizer Monatshefte* 50 (Apr. 1970): 22–29.

3911 Scoville, Herbert, Jr. *Toward a Strategic Arms Limitation Agreement.* New York: Carnegie Endowment for International Peace, 1970.

3912 Smart, Ian. "The Strategic Arms Limitation Talks." *World Today* 26 (July 1970): 296–305.

3913 ———. "Worum Geht es bei SALT." *Merkur: Deutsche Zeitschrift für Europaisches Denken* 24 (Aug. 1970): 701–08.

3914 Stone, Jeremy J. "When and How to Use SALT." *Foreign Affairs* 48 (Feb. 1970): 262–73.

3915 Strauss, Lewis L. "Thoughts on Helsinki." *National Review* (Dec. 29, 1970): 1398.

3916 "Two Power Standard." *Round Table* 237 (Jan. 1970): 3–6.

3917 "What's at Stake as U.S. and Russia Meet on Arms." *U.S. News & World Report* (Apr. 20, 1970): 61–62.

General—1971

3918 Bebler, Ales. "SALT Talks and the Public." *Review of International Affairs* [Belgrade] (June 5, 1971): 6–7.

3919 Brunner, Dominique. "Sind die SALT zum Scheitern Verurteilt?" *Allgemeine Schweizerische Militarzeitschrift* 137 (Feb. 1971): 77–78, 81–84.

3920 Chalfont, Lord Arthur G. J. "SALT: Not Quite a Breakthrough." *New Statesman* (May 28, 1971): 729.

3921 Dzialas, Rudolf. "Aspekte des Strategischen Gleichgewichts." *Wehrkunde* 20 (Sept. 1971): 449–53.

3922 Fromm, Joseph. "Real Issue in Arms Talks." *U.S. News & World Report* (Mar. 22, 1971): 26.

3923 Gabelic, Andro. "Agreement on SALT Negotiations." *Review of International Affairs* [Belgrade] (June 5, 1971): 10–12.

3924 Kahan, Jerome H. "Strategies for SALT." *World Politics* 23 (Jan. 1971): 171–88.

3925 Perl, Martin L. "SALT and Its Illusions." *Bulletin of the Atomic Scientists* 27 (Dec. 1971): 7–12.

3926 [Pugwash Conference.] "SALT and International Security." *Bulletin of the Atomic Scientists* 27 (Dec. 1971): 17–19.

3927 Rathjens, George W. "A Breakthrough in Arms Control?" *Bulletin of the Atomic Scientists* 27 (June 1971): 4–5.

3928 Scoville, Herbert, Jr. "The Limitation of Offensive Weapons." *Scientific American* 224 (Jan. 1971): 15–25.

3929 Spinrad, Bernard I. "Implications of SALT." *Bulletin of the Atomic Scientists* 27 (Jan. 1971): 22–27.

3930 "Those Arms Talks." *Economist* (Dec. 4, 1971): 52–53.

3931 Vukadinovic, Radovan. "The Fourth Round of SALT Coming Up." *Review of International Affairs* [Belgrade] (Jan. 20, 1971): 21–23.

SALT I Pacts (1972)

For text, "Interim Agreement Between the United States of America and the Union of Soviet Socialist Republics on Certain Measures with Respect to the Limitation of Strategic Offensive Arms, Moscow, May 26, 1972," and "Protocol to the Interim Agreement . . ., Moscow, May 26, 1972," U.S. ACDA, *Arms Control and Disarmament Agreements* (Washington, D.C.: G.P.O., 1975), pp. 139–42; also in *International Legal Materials* 11 (July 1972): 791–96.

The above have been further defined by "SALT: Agreed Interpretations and Unilateral Statements, May 26, 1972," *Arms Control and Disarmament Agreements* (Washington, D.C.: G.P.O., 1975), pp. 143–49; "Agreement on the Establishment of a Standing Consultative Commission to Promote the Implementation of Certain Arms Control Agreements," *International Legal Materials* 12 (Jan. 1973): 46–61.

Documents

3932 U.S. House. Committee on Armed Services. Hearings: *Supplementary Hearings on De-*fense Procurement Authorization Relating to SALT Agreement. 92d Cong., 2d Sess., 1972.

3933 ———. Committee on Foreign Affairs. Hearings: *Agreement on Limitation of Strategic Offensive Weapons.* 92d Cong., 2d Sess., 1972.

3934 U.S. Senate. Committee on Foreign Relations. Hearings: *Strategic Arms Limitation Agreements.* 92d Cong., 2d Sess., June 19–29, July 20, 1972.

3935 ———. Report: *Agreement on Limitation of Strategic Offensive Weapons.* Rpt. no. 93–979. 92d Cong., 2d Sess., 1972.

Statements

3936 "Interim Agreement on Limitation of Strategic Offensive Weapons." *Congressional Record* 118 (Sept. 14, 1972): S14868–913.

3937 Mansfield, Sen. Mike J. "The Nixon-Brezhnev Treaty." *Congressional Record* 118 (June 19, 1972): S9596–608.

3938 "President Nixon and Dr. Kissinger Brief Members of Congress on Strategic Arms Limitation Agreements." *U.S. Department of State Bulletin* (July 10, 1972): 37–49.

3939 "President Signs Joint Resolution on Offensive Arms Agreement." *U.S. Department of State Bulletin* (Oct. 23, 1972): 466.

3940 "Secretary Rogers Urges Senate Support of the ABM Treaty and Interim Agreement on Strategic Offensive Arms." *U.S. Department of State Bulletin* (July 10, 1972): 50–55.

3941 "Strategic Arms Limitation Agreements Enter Into Force." *U.S. Department of State Bulletin* (Oct. 23, 1972): 467–69.

Jackson Amendment

3942 "Both Sides of Great Debate Over Nuclear Weapons." *U.S. News & World Report* (July 3, 1972): 58–63.

3943 Gottlieb, Sanford. "Scoop and Henry: The Arms Debate." *Dissent* 21 (Fall 1974): 473–76.

3944 "The Jackson Amendment." *New Republic* (Sept. 30, 1972): 11 ff.

3945 Jackson, Sen. Henry M. "SALT: An Analysis and a Proposal." *Air Force Magazine* 57

(Feb. 1974): 30–31. [Also in *Congressional Record* 119 (Dec. 4, 1973): S21757–759.]

3946 ———. "SALT: Some Basic Questions." *Sea Power* 15 (July–Aug. 1972): 18–19.

3947 Ognibene, Peter J. *Scoop: The Life and Politics of Henry M. Jackson.* New York: Stein & Day, 1975.

3948 Scoville, Herbert, Jr. "An 'Iffy' Arms Control Agreement." *New Republic* (Jan. 18, 1975): 19–21.

3949 Teller, Edward. "Should the Senate Ratify the SALT Accords?" *National Review* (July 7, 1972): 744–45, 758.

Assessments

3950 Acciaioli, Nicolo. "Gli Accordi SALT." *Rivista di Studi Politici Internazionali* 39 (Apr.–June 1972): 168–71.

3951 "After the Kremlin Ball." *Economist* (June 3, 1972): 13–14.

3952 Allen, Gary. "Our Security: The Department of Defense." *American Opinion* 15 (July–Aug. 1972): 1–5 ff.

3953 Baldwin, Hanson W. "Will SALT Succeed?" *Reader's Digest* (Nov. 1972): 100–04.

3954 Brennan, Donald G. *Arms Treaties With Moscow: Unequal Terms Unevenly Applied?* New York: National Strategy Information Center, 1975.

3955 ———. "When the SALT Hit the Fan." *National Review* (June 23, 1972): 685–92.

3956 Brosio, Manlio. "A European Leader Assesses the Threat from Russia Now." *U.S. News & World Report* (Aug. 28, 1972): 45–47.

3957 Center for Defense Information. "SALT and Afterward." *Defense Monitor* (June 30, 1972): 1–8.

3958 Coffin, Tristram. "More a Pause Than a Pact." *Nation* (June 12, 1972): 742–43.

3959 Feld, Bernard T. "The Trouble with SALT." *Saturday Review of Science* 55 (Nov. 1972): 54–57.

3960 Frank, Lewis A. "The SALT Swindle." *New Guard* 12 (Sept. 1972): 4–6.

3961 Galtung, Johan. "The SALT Armament Agreement." *Bulletin of Peace Proposals* 3:4 (1972): 291–93.

3962 Goldblat, Jozef. *Strategic Arms Limitation.* SIPRI Research Report 1:5. New York: Humanities Press, Sept. 1972.

3963 Gray, Colin S. "SALT I: How *Not* to Control Strategic Arms." *National Defense* 58 (Jan.–Feb. 1974): 321–25.

3964 Hall, Gus. "A Correct Policy at the Right Time." *World Marxist Review* [Canada] 16:9 (1973): 66–71.

3965 Heinl, Col. Robert D., Jr. "SALT Saves the Air Force." *Armed Forces Journal* 109 (Aug. 1972): 9 ff.

3966 Hoeber, Francis P. *SALT I: The Morning After.* P-4867. Santa Monica, Ca.: Rand, July 1972.

3967 Kintner, William R., and Robert L. Pfaltzgraff, Jr. "Assessing the Moscow SALT Agreements." *Orbis* 16 (Summer 1972): 341–60.

3968 ———. "The Strategic Arms Limitation Agreements of 1972: Implications for International Security." *SALT: Implications for Arms Control in the 1970's.* Pittsburgh: Pittsburgh Press, 1973, pp. 385–404.

3969 Klein, Herbert G. "The Meaning of the Nuclear Arms Limitation Agreements." *Association Management* 24 (July 1972): 63–64 ff.

3970 Kurzban, Ira. "Peace: Slogan or Plan? Nixon Ignores Arms Conversion." *Nation* (Sept. 25, 1972): 241–44.

3971 Loosbrock, John F. "The SALT Agreements." *Air Force Magazine* 55 (July 1972): 6.

3972 Metcalf, Arthur G. "SALT: An Egregious Folly?" *Washington Report* [American Security Council] (June 12, 1972): 1–4.

3973 Murphy, Charles J. V. "What We Gave Away in the Moscow Arms Agreements." *Fortune* 86 (Sept. 1972): 110–115 ff.

3974 Rathjens, George W. "The SALT Agreements: An Appraisal." *Bulletin of the Atomic Scientists* 28 (Nov. 1972): 8–11.

3975 Rhinelander, John B. "An Overview of SALT I." *American Journal of International Law* 67 (Nov. 1973): 29–34.

3976 ———. "The SALT I Agreements." In Mason Willrich and John B. Rhinelander, eds., *SALT: The Moscow Agreements and Be-*

yond. New York: Free Press, 1974, pp. 125–58.

3977 Scoville, Herbert, Jr. "Strategic Forum: The SALT Agreements." *Survival* 14 (Sept.–Oct. 1972): 210–19.

3978 "They're Equal Enough." *Economist* (June 3, 1972): 14–15.

3979 Van Cleave, William R. "Implications of Success or Failure of SALT." In William R. Kintner and Robert L. Pfaltzgraff, Jr., eds., *SALT: Implications for Arms Control in the 1970's.* Pittsburgh: Pittsburgh Univ. Press, 1973, pp. 313–36.

3980 Viktorov, V. "Agreements of Historic Importance." *International Affairs* [Moscow] 18 (Aug. 1972): 14–20.

3981 Wesson, Robert G. "The Soviet-American Arms Limitation Agreement." *Russian Review* 31 (Oct. 1972): 334–44.

3982 "What the Treaty With Russia Does to U.S. Defenses." *U.S. News & World Report* (Oct. 2, 1972): 32–33.

3983 Whiting, Allen S. "SALT on the Dragon's Tail." *New Republic* (Sept. 9, 1972): 11–13.

3984 Witze, Claude. "Look Before You Leap." *Air Force Magazine* 55 (Sept. 1972): 22–24.

3985 ———. "SALT: In a Wound, It Hurts." *Air Force Magazine* 55 (Oct. 1972): 13–14.

Verification

3986 Bates, Col. Asa, Jr. "The SALT Standing Consultative Commission: An American Analysis." *Millenium* 4 (Autumn 1975): 132–45.

3987 Beecher, William. "Spy Satellites Will Moniter [SALT] Pacts." *Sea Power* 15 (July–Aug. 1972): 20–24.

3988 Carter, Luther J. "Strategic Weapons: Verification Keeps Ahead of Arms Control." *Science* (Mar. 14, 1975): 936–39.

3989 Drew, H. A. W. "The Verification of Strategic Arms Agreements." *Hawk: Independent Journal of R.A.F.* 35 (Feb. 1974): 45–50.

3990 Lodal, Jan N. "Verifying SALT." *Foreign Policy*, no. 24 (Fall 1976): 40–64.

3991 Robinson, Clarence A., Jr. "SALT Proposals Facing Hurdles." *Aviation Week & Space Technology* (Dec. 9, 1974): 12–13.

3992 ———. "U.S. Weighs SALT Proposals [on verification]." *Aviation Week & Space Technology* (June 23, 1975): 12–14.

3993 Scoville, Herbert, Jr. "A Leap Forward in Verification." In Mason Willrich and John B. Rhinelander, eds., *SALT: The Moscow Agreements and Beyond.* New York: Free Press, 1974, pp. 160–82.

3994 Stubbs, Gilbert S. "On-Site Inspection: The Key Issue in SALT." *Washington Report* [American Security Council] (Apr. 28, 1972): 1–4.

3995 U.S. Arms Control & Disarmament Agency. *Development of Models for Analysis of the Influence of Mobile Nuclear Forces on Arms Control Agreements.* ACDA Rpt. WEC-172. 2 vols. Chicago: Museum of Science & Industry, 1970.

Violations

3996 Eaker, Lt. Gen. Ira C. "USSR Warned on SALT." *Air Force Times* (Jan. 2, 1974): 45–50.

3997 Gray, Colin S. "SALT I Aftermath: Have the Soviets Been Cheating?" *Air Force Magazine* 58 (Nov. 1975): 28–33.

3998 Gwertzman, Bernard. "Soviet Concedes Arms Violation." *New York Times*, May 25, 1976.

3999 Kissinger, Henry. "Secretary Kissinger's News Conference of December 9." *U.S. Department of State Bulletin* (Jan. 5, 1976): 1–12.

4000 Klass, Philip J. "Anti-Satellite Laser Use Suspected." *Aviation Week & Space Technology* (Dec. 8, 1975): 12–13.

4001 Laird, Melvin. "Is This Detente?" *Reader's Digest* (July 1975): 54–57.

4002 "Newest Delta Sub Pivotal in Latest SALT Violation." *Aviation Week & Space Technology* (May 24, 1976): 20–21.

4003 Robinson, Clarence A., Jr. "Another SALT Violation Spotted." *Aviation Week & Space Technology* (May 31, 1976): 12–14.

4004 ———. "Kissinger Deliberately Concealing SALT Violations, Zumwalt Claims." *Aviation Week & Space Technology* (Dec. 8, 1975): 13–16.

4005 ———. "SALT 'Hold' Said to Hit Cabinet." *Aviation Week & Space Technology* (Jan. 5, 1976): 12–14.

4006 ———. "Soviets Hiding Submarine Work." *Aviation Week & Space Technology* (Nov. 11, 1974): 14–16.

4007 ———. "Soviet Treaty Violations." *Aviation Week & Space Technology* (Oct. 21, 1974): 14–15. [Also see issues for Nov. 11, 25, 1974, and Feb. 3, 1975.]

4008 Szulc, Tad. "Have We Been Had? Secret Violations of the SALT Deal." *New Republic* (June 7, 1975): 11–15.

4009 U.S. House. Committee on Armed Services. Hearings: *Full House Consideration of Overall National Security Programs and Related Budget Requirements.* 94th Cong., 1st Sess., 1975, pp. 235–78.

4010 U.S. Senate. Committee on Armed Services. Hearings: *Soviet Compliance with Certain Provisions of the 1972 SALT I Agreements.* 94th Cong., 1st Sess., 1975.

4011 Zumwalt, Elmo R. "Zumwalt Disputes Policy on SALT." *Aviation Week & Space Technology* (Jan. 19, 1976): 46–50.

Salt (II), 1972–1976

4012 Aaron, David. "A New Concept." *Foreign Policy* 17 (Winter 1974–75): 157–65.

4013 Bailey, Sidney D. "Prospect for Arms Limitation." *Bulletin of Peace Proposals* 3:4 (1972): 356–61.

4014 Ball, Desmond. "The Pinch of SALT: Strategic Arms Limitation from Moscow to Vladivostok." *Australian Outlook* 29 (Aug. 1975): 231–42.

4015 Barcia, Emilio. "La 'Détente,' el SALT y el Futuro Equilibrio Atómico." *Revista de Politica Internacional* 143 (Jan.–Feb. 1976): 33–70.

4016 Baugh, William H. "Arms Reducing Possibilities for the SALT II Negotiations and Beyond: An Operations Analysis." *American Journal of Political Science* 20 (Feb. 1976): 67–95.

4017 Booth, Kenneth. "The Strategic Arms Limitation Talks: A Stock-taking." *World Survey* 73 (Jan. 1975): 1–17.

4018 Brindel, Col. Charles L. "The Implications of SALT Agreements in the 1970s." *Military Review* 55 (June 1975): 39–48.

4019 Buckley, Sen. James L. "On SALT II." *National Review* (Mar. 15, 1974): 312–17.

4020 ———. "The Score on SALT." *Aviation Week & Space Technology* (Sept. 8, 1975): 11.

4021 Burt, Richard. "SALT After Vladivostok." *World Today* 31 (Feb. 1975): 57–65.

4022 Calogero, Francesco. "A Scenario for Effective SALT Negotiations." *Bulletin of the Atomic Scientists* 29 (June 1973): 16–22.

4023 Clark, John J. "Salt and the Criteria of Arms Control." *Royal United Services Institute for Defense Studies Journal* 118 (Mar. 1973): 34–38.

4024 Coffey, Joseph I. "The Savor of SALT." *Bulletin of the Atomic Scientists* 29 (May 1973): 9–15.

4025 Crane, Rep. Philip. "The SALT Negotiations." *Congressional Record* 122 (Aug. 10, 1976): H8671–74.

4026 Doty, Paul. "Strategic Arms Limitation After SALT I." *Daedalus* 104 (Summer 1975): 63–74.

4027 Feld, Bernard T. "Looking to SALT-II." *Bulletin of the Atomic Scientists* 28 (June 1972): 2–3 ff.

4028 Firmage, Edwin B., and David J. Henry. "Vladivostok and Beyond: SALT I and the Prospects for SALT II." *Columbia Journal of Transnational Law* 14:2 (1975): 221–67.

4029 Gelber, Harry G. "Technische und Politische Ambivalenzen in den SALT-Abkommen." *Europa-Archiv* (Mar. 25, 1973): 187–200.

4030 Gray, Colin S. "Defense and Negotiation— The Strategic Arms Limitation Talks." *Air Force Magazine* 57 (Jan. 1974): 32–36.

4031 ———. "A Problem Guide to SALT II." *Survival* 17 (Sept.–Oct. 1975): 230–34.

4032 ———. "SALT and the American Mood." *Strategic Review* 3 (Summer 1975): 41–51.

4033 Hamlett, Bruce D. "SALT: The Illusion and the Reality." *Strategic Review* 3 (Summer 1975): 67–78.

4034 Harrington, Rep. Michael. "On Strategic Arms Accords: Predictable and Inconsequential." *Congressional Record* 120 (July 9, 1974): H6283–85.

4035 Holum, John. "The SALT Sell: Or, Who Will Bell the Pentagon?" *Nation* (Mar. 20, 1976): 326–30.

4036 Jackson, Sen. Henry M. "SALT II: Taking a More Sober Approach." *Army* 23:4 (1973): 5–6 ff.

4037 Kruzel, Joseph. "SALT II: The Search for a Follow-On Agreement." *Orbis* 17 (Summer 1973): 334–63.

4038 Metcalf, Arthur G. "SALT-II: Some Principles." *Strategic Review* 1 (Summer 1973): 6–16.

4039 ———. "SALT II and Offensive Force Levels." *Orbis* 18 (Summer 1974): 465–81.

4040 ———. "Soviet Sea-Based Forces and SALT." *Survival* 17 (Jan.–Feb. 1975): 9–13.

4041 Ognibene, Peter J. "Upsetting SALT II: Unruly Bombers, Unseen Missiles." *New Republic* (Jan. 24, 1976): 8–11.

4042 Panofsky, Wolfgang K. H. "From SALT I to SALT II." *Survey* 19 (Spring 1973): 160–87.

4043 Pfaltzgraff, Robert L., Jr. "The SALT II Issues." *Astronautics & Aeronautics* 12 (Feb. 1974): 18–24.

4044 ———, and Jacquelyn K. Davis. *SALT II: Promise or Precipice.* Miami: Univ. of Miami, Center for Advanced International Studies, 1976.

4045 "Politics, SALT and the Way Ahead." *Nature* [London] (Aug. 25, 1972): 423–24.

4046 "Prospects for Strategic Arms Limitation [SALT]." *Survival* 16 (Mar.–Apr. 1974): 54–74.

4047 Proxmire, Sen. William. "Proxmire SALT II Proposals." *Congressional Record* 120 (Feb. 5, 1974): S1195–97.

4048 Rathjens, George W. "The Prospects for SALT II." *SIPRI Yearbook of World Armament and Disarmament, 1973.* New York: Humanities Press, 1973, pp. 40–58.

4049 Roberts, Adam. "The Moscow Summit and Arms Control." *World Today* 30 (Aug. 1974): 315–18.

4050 Robinson, Clarence A., Jr. "Backfire Draws Focus in SALT." *Aviation Week & Space Technology* (Aug. 25, 1975): 14–15.

4051 ———. "Cabinet Shifts May Speed SALT." *Aviation Week & Space Technology* (Nov. 10, 1975): 12–14.

4052 ———. "SALT Extension Trades Pondered." *Aviation Week & Space Technology* (May 27, 1974): 14–15.

4053 ———. "Soviets Make New SALT Bid." *Aviation Week & Space Technology* (Feb. 2, 1976): 12–15.

4054 Rowen, Henry S. "Implications of SALT Agreement Detailed." *Aviation Week & Space Technology* (Sept. 15, 1975): 52–54.

4055 Scoville, Herbert, Jr. "Arms Control: What Are the Next Moves?" *International Conciliation*, no. 587 (Mar. 1972): 9–16.

4056 ———. "Beyond SALT I." *Foreign Affairs* 50 (Apr. 1972): 488–500.

4057 ———. "Next Steps in Limiting Strategic Arms." *Bulletin of the Atomic Scientists* 27 (Mar. 1972): 9–11.

4058 Shulman, Marshall D. "Comment [on SALT]." *Survey* 19 (Spring 1973): 175–82.

4059 Simmons, Henry T. "Problems and Prospects for a SALT II Arms Control Agreement." *Interavia* 30 (Aug. 1975): 854–58.

4060 Slocombe, Walter B. "Controlling Strategic Nuclear Weapons." *Foreign Policy Association* [Headline Series], no. 226 (June 1975): 1–63.

4061 Slominski, Col. Martin J. "SALT Facets." *Military Review* 54 (Jan. 1974): 82–88.

4062 Smith, Gerard C. "SALT After Vladivostok." *Journal of International Affairs* 29 (Spring 1975): 7–18.

4063 Starr, Richard F. "Comment [on SALT]." *Survey* 19 (Spring 1973): 183–87.

4064 Warnke, Paul C. "Possible Outcomes of SALT II." *American Journal of International Law* 67 (Nov. 1973): 41–48.

4065 Weiler, Lawrence D. "The Status of SALT: A Perspective." *Arms Control Today* 4 (Dec. 1974): 1–4.

4066   York, Herbert F. "Reducing the Overkill." *Survival* 16 (Mar.–Apr. 1974): 70–74.

Bargaining Chip Concept

4067   Gray, Colin S. "Of Bargaining Chips and Building Blocks: Arms Control and Defense Policy." *International Journal* 28 (Spring 1973): 266–96.

4068   Kane, Joseph, and Frank Merrick. "Arming to Disarm in the Age of Detente." *Time* (Feb. 11, 1974): 15–24.

4069   Larionov, V. "Bargain Chips? Equal Security and Washington's 'Policy of Strength' Relapses." *New Times* [Moscow] 37 (Sept. 1972): 28–29.

4070   Stone, I. F. "The Big Build-up Nixon is Putting Over on Us." *New York Review of Books*, July 20, 1972, p. 9.

4071   Woolsey, R. James. "Chipping Away at the Bargains." *Daedalus* 104 (Summer 1975): 175–86.

Parity vs. Superiority

For historical perspective, see Chapter 7, Limitation of Weapons & Personnel, London Naval Conference (1930), Parity & Ratios.

4072   Brennan, Donald G., et al. "The Great Nuclear Debate: Parity vs. Superiority." *War/Peace Report* 8 (Oct. 1968): 3–10.

4073   Brock, William E. "The Shifting Balance." *Ordnance* 56 (Mar.–Apr. 1972): 366–68.

4074   Goldhamer, Herbert. *The Soviet Union in a Period of Strategic Parity.* R-889-PR. Santa Monica, Ca.: Rand, Nov. 1971.

4075   Gray, Colin S. "Strategic 'Superiority' in Superpower Relations." *Military Review* 51 (Dec. 1971): 8–21.

4076   Holst, Johan J. "Parity, Superiority or Sufficiency? Some Remarks on the Nature and Future of the Soviet-American Strategic Relationship." *Soviet-American Relations and World Order: Arms Limitations and Policy.* Adelphi Paper, no. 65. London: Institute for Strategic Studies, Feb. 1970.

4077   Kolkowicz, Roman. "Strategic Parity and Beyond." *World Politics* 23 (Apr. 1971): 445–51.

4078   Lane, Gen. Thomas A. "Why Parity?" *Strategic Review* 1 (Summer 1973): 25–27.

4079   Larsen, Larry J. "The Delusion of Strategic Parity." *U.S. Naval Institute Proceedings* 91 (Oct. 1965): 46–53.

4080   Moulton, Harland B. *From Superiority to Parity: The United States and the Strategic Arms Race, 1961–1971.* Westport, Conn.: Greenwood, 1973.

4081   Pierre, Andrew J. "The Dynamics of Parity." *Air Force Magazine* 44 (Jan. 1971): 49–51.

4082   Scoville, Herbert, Jr. "Schlesinger's 'Sufficiency': A New Arms Race Ahead?" *New Republic* (Jan. 19, 1974): 19–21.

4083   Slocombe, Walter B. *The Political Implications of Strategic Parity.* Adelphi Paper, no. 77. London: Institute for Strategic Studies, 1971.

4084   Ulsamer, Edgar. "Soviet Objective: Technological Supremacy." *Air Force Magazine* 57 (June 1974): 22–27.

4085   Wolfers, Arnold. "Superiority in Nuclear Weapons: Advantages and Limitations." *Annals of the Amer. Acad. of Pol. & Soc. Sci.* 290 (Nov. 1953): 7–15.

WASHINGTON SUMMIT (1973)

4086   [Brezhnev-Nixon.] "Basic Principles of Negotiations on Further Limitation of Strategic Offensive Weapons." *Survival* 15 (Sept.–Oct. 1973): 244–48.

4087   "Joint Soviet-American Communique." *Soviet Military Review* 7 (July 1973): 51–55.

4088   Lodgaard, Sverre. "The Washington Summit and Disarmament." *Bulletin of Peace Proposals* 4:3 (1973): 195–97.

4089   Rubinstein, Alvin Z. "Soviet-American Relations in Transition." *Current History* 65 (Oct. 1973): 150–54, 180–81.

VLADIVOSTOK AGREEMENT (1974)

4090   Bar-Levav, Doron. "Vladivostok Arms Race." *Nation* (Apr. 12, 1975): 424–25.

4091   Barnaby, Frank. "The Ford-Brezhnev Agreement Assessed." *New Scientist* (Dec. 5, 1974): 734–36.

4092 Bingham, Rep. Jonathan B. "Resolution Re Vladivostok Agreement." *Congressional Record* 121 (Feb. 6, 1975): H687–88.

4093 Carter, Luther J. "Beyond Vladivostok: The Feasibility and the Policies of Arms Reductions." *Science* (Apr. 11, 1975): 130–33.

4094 Dornan, James E., Jr. "Maybe No Agreement Would be Better." *Armed Forces Journal International* 112 (Jan. 1975): 28–32.

4095 Jackson, Sen. Henry. "Vladivostok and Strategic Arms Reduction." *Congressional Record* 121 (Mar. 26, 1975): S5038–39.

4096 Johansen, Robert C. *The Vladivostok Accord: A Case Study of the Impact of U.S. Foreign Policy on the Prospects for World Order Reform.* Princeton: Princeton Univ., Center for International Studies, 1976.

4097 Kennedy, Sen. Edward M. "Senate Resolution 20: Submission of a Resolution Promoting Strategic Arms Control." *Congressional Record* 121 (Jan. 17, 1975): S462–64.

4098 Kissinger, Henry A. "The Vladivostok Accord: Background Briefing . . . , Dec. 3, 1974." *Survival* 17 (July–Aug. 1975): 191–98.

4099 "Kissinger Sums Up '74." *Newsweek* (Dec. 30, 1974): 29–32.

4100 Long, Franklin A. "Should We Buy the Vladivostok Agreement?" *Bulletin of the Atomic Scientists* 31 (Feb. 1975): 5–6.

4101 Nacht, Michael L. "The Vladivostok Accord and American Technological Options." *Survival* 17 (May–June 1975): 106–13.

4102 Nikolayev, N. "The Vladivostok Meeting: Important Progress." *International Affairs* [Moscow] 21 (Feb. 1975): 3–9.

4103 Nitze, Paul H. "Vladivostok and SALT II." *Review of Politics* 37 (Apr. 1975): 147–60.

4104 Schwartz, Charles. "Helping the Pentagon Aim Right." *Bulletin of the Atomic Scientists* 30 (Nov. 1974): 9–13.

4105 U.S. House. Committee on International Relations. Hearings: *The Vladivostok Accord: Implications to U.S. Security, Arms Control and World Peace.* 94th Cong., 1st Sess., June 24–25, July 8, 1975.

4106 Zablocki, Rep. Clement J. "Concurrent Resolution With Respect to Certain Arms Control and Disarmament Negotiations." *Congressional Record* 121 (July 30, 1975): H7929–30.

4107 ———. "Gerard Smith on Arms Control Implications of Vladivostok." *Congressional Record* 121 (Apr. 18, 1975): H1864–65.

SALT: Related Political Issues

NEGOTIATIONS

4108 Bowie, Robert R. "The Bargaining Aspects of Arms Control: The SALT Experience." In William R. Kintner and Robert L. Pfaltzgraff, Jr., eds., *SALT: Implications for Arms Control in the 1970's.* Pittsburgh: Pittsburgh Univ. Press, 1973, pp. 127–39.

4109 Brown, Neville. "The Adverse Partnership: The U.S. and Russia Learn to Talk." *New Middle East* 23 (Aug. 1970): 17–21.

4110 Dougherty, James E. "SALT and the Future of International Politics." In William R. Kintner and Robert L. Pfaltzgraff, Jr., eds., *SALT: Implications for Arms Control in the 1970's.* Pittsburgh: Pittsburgh Univ. Press, 1973, pp. 337–67.

4111 "Dynamics of the Bargaining Process in a Bureaucratic Age [Symposium and Discussion]." In William R. Kintner and Robert L. Pfaltzgraff, Jr., eds., *SALT: Implications for Arms Control in the 1970's.* Pittsburgh: Pittsburgh Univ. Press, 1973, pp. 187–96.

4112 Gelber, Harry G. "Nuclear Arms and the Pacific." *Australian Outlook* 25 (Dec. 1971): 295–308.

4113 ———. *Nuclear Weapons, the Pacific, and SALT.* Occasional paper. Chicago: Univ. of Chicago, Center for Policy Study, 1971.

4114 Israelyan, Y. "International Detente and Disarmament." *International Affairs* [Moscow] 20 (May 1974): 24–29.

4115 Joshua, Wynfred. "SALT and the Middle East." In William R. Kintner and Robert L. Pfaltzgraff, Jr., eds., *SALT: Implications for Arms Control in the 1970's.* Pittsburgh: Pittsburgh Univ. Press, 1973, pp. 237–54.

4116 Kaplan, Morton A. "SALT and the International System." *SALT: Problems and Prospects.* Morristown, N.J.: General Learning Press, 1973, pp. 1–25.

4117 Kincade, William H. "Thinking About Arms Control and Strategic Weapons." *World Affairs* 136 (Spring 1974): 364–76.

4118 Kintner, William R. "Arms Control for a Five-Power World." In William R. Kintner and Robert L. Pfaltzgraff, Jr., eds., *SALT: Implications for Arms Control in the 1970's.* Pittsburgh: Pittsburgh Univ. Press, 1973, pp. 167–86.

4119 Kolkowicz, Roman. "Strategic Elites and Politics of Superpowers." *Aussenpolitik* 23 (Apr. 1972): 210–29.

4120 Nitze, Paul H. "SALT: The Strategic Balance Between Hope and Skepticism." *Foreign Policy* 17 (Winter 1974–75): 136–56.

4121 ———. "Soviet's Negotiating Style Assayed." *Aviation Week & Space Technology* (Feb. 17, 1975): 40–43; (Feb. 24, 1975): 63–69; (May 12, 1975): 7.

4122 Prince, Howard T., II. "SALT, National Security and International Politics." *Journal of International & Comparative Studies* 4 (Winter 1971): 14–27.

4123 U.S. Arms Control & Disarmament Agency. *The Implications for Arms Control of Perceptions of Strategic Weapons.* ACDA Rpt. E–163. Pittsburgh: Univ. of Pittsburgh, 1971.

United States' View

4124 Allison, Graham T. "Cold Dawn and the Mind of Kissinger." *Washington Monthly* 6 (Mar. 1974): 38–49.

4125 Coffey, Joseph I. "American Interests in the Limitation of Strategic Arms." In William R. Kintner and Robert L. Pfaltzgraff, Jr., eds., *SALT: Implications for Arms Control in the 1970's.* Pittsburgh: Pittsburgh Univ. Press, 1973, pp. 55–94.

4126 Foster, William C. "New Hope for Disarmament." *Rotarian* 116 (May 1970): 26–30.

4127 Fromm, Joseph. "Kissinger-Schlesinger Feud: What It's All About." *U.S. News & World Report* (July 22, 1974): 22.

4128 Garwin, Richard L. *Superpower Postures in SALT: An American View.* Occasional paper. Chicago: Univ. of Chicago, Center for Policy Study, 1971.

4129 Hallett, Douglas. "Kissinger Dolosus: The Domestic Politics of SALT." *Yale Review* 64 (Dec. 1975): 161–74.

4130 Halperin, Morton H. "Prospects for SALT." *American Journal of International Law* 64 (Sept. 1970): 200–202.

4131 Humphrey, Hubert H. "An End to Nuclear Gamesmanship." *Bulletin of the Atomic Scientists* 28 (Mar. 1972): 12–15.

4132 Kraft, Joseph. "In Search of Kissinger." *Harper's* 242 (Jan. 1971): 54–61.

4133 Latting, James T. "The U.S. Approach to SALT." *Millenium* [London] 3 (Spring 1974): 76–82.

4134 Nixon, Pres. Richard M. "Strategic Arms Limitation Talks Open at Helsinki: Message. . . ." *U.S. Department of State Bulletin* (Dec. 15, 1969): 543–44.

4135 Orr, Samuel C. "Defense Report: National Security Council Network Gives White House Tight Rein over SALT Strategy." *National Journal* (Apr. 24, 1971): 877–86.

4136 ———. "Defense Report: Slow Pace of SALT Negotiations Prompts Proposals for Change in U.S. Position." *National Journal* (May 1, 1971): 947–59.

4137 Rogers, William P. "Strategic Arms Limitation Talks." *U.S. Department of State Bulletin* (Dec. 1, 1969): 465–68.

4138 Smith, Gerard C. "Can the Arms Talks Succeed?" *U.S. News & World Report* (Dec. 14, 1970): 62–63.

4139 ———, and Llewellyn Thompson. "Ambassador Smith Discusses Strategic Arms Limitation Talks." *U.S. Department of State Bulletin* (Jan. 26, 1970): 84–86.

4140 Stone, Jeremy J. "U.S. Military Policy: When and How to Use SALT." *Foreign Affairs* 48 (Jan. 1970): 262–73.

4141 U.S. Senate. Committee on Foreign Relations. Hearings: *ABM, MIRV, SALT, and the Nuclear Arms Race.* 91st Cong., 2d Sess., 1970.

4142 ———. Hearings: *The Limitation of Strategic Arms.* 2 pts. 91st Cong., 2d Sess., 1970.

4143 Weiler, Lawrence D. *The Arms Race, Secret Negotiations and the Congress.* Occasional paper 12. Muscatine, Ia.: Stanley Foundation, 1976.

U.S. VIEWS—FREEZE ON STRATEGIC VEHICLES

4144 Coffey, Joseph I. "An Over-All Freeze on Strategic Forces." *Disarmament* 11 (Sept. 1966): 5–7, 21.

4145 Doty, Paul. "A Freeze on Strategic Delivery Systems." *Bulletin of the Atomic Scientists* 21 (Feb. 1965): 2–6.

4146 "The Elimination of Rockets as Nuclear Delivery Vehicles." *Disarmament and Arms Control* 1 (Autumn 1963): 184–88.

4147 Lederberg, Joshua. "A Freeze on Missile Testing." *Bulletin of the Atomic Scientists* 27 (Mar. 1971): 4–6 ff.

4148 Wainhouse, David W., et al. *Arms Control Agreements: Design for Verification and Organization.* Baltimore: Johns Hopkins Press, 1968, pp. 62–78.

SOVIET VIEWS

4149 Arkadev, Nikolai N. "Big Contribution to Curbing the Arms Race." *New Times* [Moscow] 23 (June 1972): 4–5.

4150 Barsukov, I. U. "Strange Position." *Current Digest of the Soviet Press* (Mar. 9, 1971): 27.

4151 Brezhnev, Leonid. "Soviet Statement on Disarmament." *Current History* 61 (Oct. 1971): 240.

4152 Burhop, E. H. S. "The Soviet Peace Policy: For Detente and Disarmament." *New World Review* 40 (Fall 1972): 33–44.

4153 Caldwell, Lawrence T. *Soviet Attitudes to SALT.* Adelphi Paper, no. 75. London: Institute for Strategic Studies, 1971.

4154 Clemens, Walter C., Jr. "Sakharov: A Man for Our Times." *Bulletin of the Atomic Scientists* 27 (Dec. 1971): 4–6.

4155 Cottrell, Alvin J. "Soviet Views of U.S. Overseas Bases." *Military Review* 43 (Nov. 1963): 23–34.

4156 Gallagher, Matthew P. "The Uneasy Balance: Soviet Attitudes Toward the Missile Talks." *Interplay* 3 (Dec. 1969–Jan. 1970): 20–25.

4157 ———, and Karl F. Speilman. *The Public Understanding of SALT in the Soviet Union: A Study of Soviet Propaganda Policy and the Awareness Levels of Selected Population Groups.* Prepared for U.S. Information Agency, P-760. Arlington, Va.: Institute for Defense Analyses, Mar. 1971.

4158 ———. *Soviet Decision-Making for Defense.* New York: Praeger, 1972.

4159 Garthoff, Raymond L. "SALT and the Soviet Military." *Problems of Communism* 25 (Jan.–Feb. 1975): 21–37.

4160 Holloway, David. "Strategic Concepts and Soviet Policy." *Survival* 13 (Nov. 1971): 364–69.

4161 Karenin, A. "On the Limitation of Strategic Weapons." *International Affairs* [Moscow] 20 (Sept. 1974): 13–21.

4162 Kharich, V. "The Strategic Arms Race in the U.S.A.: Reliance on Nuclear Might." *Current Digest of the Soviet Press* (Aug. 10, 1971): 7 ff.

4163 ———. "The Strategic Arms Race in the U.S.S.R.: Shunning a Realistic Approach." *Current Digest of the Soviet Press* (Aug. 10, 1971): 6–7.

4164 Kolkowicz, Roman. "SALT and the Kremlin: The Policy of Hold-and-Explore." *Interplay* 3 (Nov. 1970): 33–36.

4165 Lambeth, Benjamin S. "Moscow and the Missile Race." *Current History* 61 (Oct. 1971): 215–21, 242.

4166 ———. "The Soviet Strategic Challenge Under SALT I." *Current History* 63 (Oct. 1972): 150–55.

4167 Leitenberg, Milton. "Soviet Secrecy and Negotiations on Strategic Weapons Arms Control and Disarmament." *Bulletin of Peace Proposals* 5:4 (1974): 377–80.

4168 ———. "The U.S.S.R. and the Outcome of SALT-II: Postscript." *Bulletin of Peace Proposals* 6:1 (1975): 94–96.

4169 Milshetyn, M. A., and L. S. Semeyko. "SALT-II—A Soviet View." *Survival* 14 (Mar.–Apr. 1974): 63–70.

4170 Payne, Samuel B., Jr. "The Soviet Debate on Strategic Arms Limitation, 1969–1972." *Soviet Studies* 27 (Jan. 1975): 27–45.

4171 Ra'anan, Uri. "Soviet Decision-Making and the Strategic Balance: Some Reflections." In Robert L. Pfaltzgraff, Jr., ed., *Contrasting*

Approaches to Strategic Arms Control. Lexington, Mass.: D. C. Heath, 1974: 113–22.

4172 Shestov, V. "What is Hidden Behind the Propaganda Screen?" *Current Digest of the Soviet Press* (Mar. 2, 1971): 6–8.

4173 Shulman, Marshall D. "SALT and the Soviet Union." In Mason Willrich and John B. Rhinelander, eds., *SALT: The Moscow Agreements and Beyond.* New York: Free Press, 1974, pp. 101–21.

4174 Stakh, G. "Basic Principles of Negotiations on the Limitation of Strategic Offensive Arms." *International Affairs* [Moscow] 19 (Nov. 1973): 10–15.

4175 Viktorov, V. "Some Results and Prospects—On the Strategic Arms Limitation Talks." *Current Digest of the Soviet Press* (Aug. 3, 1971): 1–3, 11.

4176 Wolfe, Thomas W. *Impact of Economic and Technological Issues on the Soviet Approach to SALT.* P–4368. Santa Monica, Ca.: Rand, June 1970.

4177 ———. "Soviet Approaches to SALT." *Problems of Communism* 19 (Sept.–Oct. 1970): 1–10.

4178 ———. *Soviet Interests in SALT: Political, Economic, Bureaucratic and Strategic Contributions and Impediments to Arms Control.* P–4701. Santa Monica, Ca.: Rand, 1971.

4179 ———. "The Soviet Union and SALT." *World Today* 27 (Apr. 1971): 162–73.

4180 ———. "Die Sowjetunion und SALT: Der Einfluss Wirtschaftlicher und Militarischer Erwagungen auf die Haltung in den Gesprachen uber eine Begrenzung der Strategischen Rustungen." *Europa-Archiv* (Jan. 10, 1971): 17–29.

China, SALT and Nuclear Strategy

4181 Barnett, A. Doak. "A Nuclear China and U.S. Arms Policy." *Foreign Affairs* 48 (Apr. 1970): 427–42.

4182 Ermath, Fritz. "Moscow and the Chinese Missile." *Military Review* 47 (Apr. 1967): 40–46.

4183 Gelber, Harry G. "China and SALT." *Survival* 12 (Apr. 1970): 122–26.

4184 ———. "The Impact of Chinese ICBM's on Strategic Deterrence." *Orbis* 13 (Summer 1969): 407–34.

4185 ———. "Strategic Arms Limitations and the Sino-Soviet Relationship." *Asian Survey* 10 (Apr. 1970): 265–89.

4186 Halperin, Morton. *Chinese Nuclear Strategy: The Early Detonation Period.* Adelphi Papers, no. 18. London: Institute for Strategic Studies, 1965.

4187 Hsieh, Alice Langley. *Communist China and Nuclear Force.* Santa Monica, Ca.: Rand, Aug. 1963.

4188 ———. "Communist China and Nuclear Warfare." *China Quarterly* 38 (Apr.–June 1960): 1–12.

4189 Leocha, Adolph. "The Limiting Effect of Technology on Chinese Military Strategy." Ph.D. diss. Georgetown Univ., 1970.

4190 Liu, Leo Y. "China's Attitude Towards Her Nuclear Weapons." *China Report* 7 (May–June 1971): 34–42.

4191 ———. "A Nuclear China and World Order." *Dalhousie Review* 51 (Summer 1971): 228–39.

4192 Murphy, Charles H. "Mainland China's Evolving Nuclear Deterrent." *Bulletin of the Atomic Scientists* 28 (Jan. 1972): 28–35.

4193 Platte, William A. "Peking, Moscow and the SALT Talks." *Naval War College Review* 22 (May 1970): 93–111.

4194 Pollack, Jonathan D. "Chinese Attitudes Toward Nuclear Weapons, 1964–69." *China Quarterly* 50 (Apr.–June 1972): 244–71.

4195 Richardson, Alfred K. "The Evolution of Chinese Nuclear Strategy." *Military Review* 53 (Jan. 1973): 13–32.

4196 ———. "Future Chinese Nuclear Strategy and Capabilities." *Military Review* 53 (Feb. 1973): 2–18.

4197 Scalapino, Robert A. "The American-Soviet-Chinese Triangle: Implications for Arms Control." In William R. Kintner and Robert L. Pfaltzgraff, Jr., eds., *SALT: Implications for Arms Control in the 1970's.* Pittsburgh: Pittsburgh Univ. Press, 1973, pp. 141–66.

4198 Swamy, Subramanian. "China's Strategic Nuclear Capability." *United Service Institu-*

tion of *India Journal* 100 (Oct.–Dec. 1970): 464–74.

U.S.-Europe Relations

4199 Barker, A. J. "NATO and SALT." *Army Quarterly and Defense Journal* 103 (Jan. 1973): 134–39.

4200 Bennett, W. S.; R. R. Sandoval; and R. G. Shreffler. "A Credible Nuclear-Emphasis Defense for NATO?" *Orbis* 17 (Summer 1973): 463–79.

4201 Coffey, Joseph I. "Strategic Arms Limitations and European Security." *International Affairs* [London] 47 (Oct. 1971): 692–707.

4202 Duchêne, François. "SALT, the Ostpolitik and the Post-Cold War Context." *World Today* 26 (Dec. 1970): 500–511.

4203 ———. "SALT, die Ostpolitik und die Liquidierung des Kalten Krieges." *Europa-Archiv* (Sept. 10, 1970): 639–53.

4204 Finan, James S. "Europe, the Super Powers, and SALT." *Queen's Quarterly* 78 (Autumn 1971): 456–61.

4205 Grewe, Wilhelm. "The Effect of Strategic Agreements on European-American Relations." *Soviet-American Relations and World Order: Arms Limitation and Policy.* Adelphi Paper, no. 65. London: Institute for Strategic Studies, Feb. 1970.

4206 Kemp, Geoffrey, and Ian Smart. "SALT and European Nuclear Forces." In William R. Kintner and Robert L. Pfaltzgraff, Jr., eds., *SALT: Implications for Arms Control in the 1970's.* Pittsburgh: Pittsburgh Univ. Press, 1973, pp. 199–235.

4207 Pierre, Andrew J. "Nuclear Diplomacy: Britain, France and America." *Foreign Affairs* 49 (Jan. 1971): 283–301.

4208 ———. "The SALT Agreement and Europe." *World Today* 28 (July 1972): 281–88.

4209 ———. "Das SALT-Abkommen und Seine Auswirkungen auf Europa." *Europa-Archiv* (July 10, 1972): 431–41.

4210 Ruehl, Lothar. "Abschreckung und Abrüstung: SALT und Europa." *Monat* 22 (July 1970): 19–26.

4211 "SALT Makes Important Progress—NATO Consultation Continues." *NATO Letter* 18 (Oct.–Nov. 1970): 19–20.

4212 "Strategic Arms Limitations: Do the Europeans Need SALT?" *Agenor* 12 (Oct. 1969): 42–43.

4213 Wyle, Frederick S. "U.S., Europe, SALT, and Strategy." In Morton A. Kaplan, ed., *SALT: Problems and Prospects.* Morristown, N.J.: General Learning Press, 1973, pp. 136–68.

SALT Economics

Also see, SALT and the Arms Race, below.

4214 Brooke, Sen. Edward W. "National Security: Dollars, Demands, and Dilemmas." *Vital Speeches* (Nov. 1, 1969): 44–47.

4215 Desai, Meghnad. [Review of: Members of Congress for Peace Through Law, Military Spending Committee, *The Economics of Defense: A Bipartisan Review of Military Spending.*] *Survival* 15 (May–June 1973): 146–47.

4216 Epstein, William. "The Inexorable Rise of Military Expenditures." *Bulletin of the Atomic Scientists* 30 (Jan. 1975): 17–19.

4217 General Research Corp. *The Economic Consequences of SALT I: A National Assessment.* ACDA Rpt. E–224. Washington, D.C.: G.P.O., Aug. 1973.

4218 ———. *The Economic Consequences of SALT I: An Update.* Washington, D.C.: G.P.O., 1974.

4219 Kaufman, Richard F. "Defense Spending: The Dead Weight of SALT." *Nation* (Aug. 21, 1972): 106–10.

4220 Ognibene, Peter J. " 'Hedges,' Arms Control?" *New Republic* (June 24, 1972): 11–12.

4221 Owen, Henry. "The Weapons Debate." *Atlantic Monthly* (June 1972): 6 ff.

4222 Proxmire, Sen. William. "SALT Treaty Should Be Opposed Unless It Reduces Military Spending." *Congressional Record* 118 (June 12, 1972): S9164–66.

4223 Quanbeck, Alton H., and Barry M. Blechman. *Strategic Forces: Issues for the Mid-*

Seventies. Washington, D.C.: Brookings Institution, 1973.

4224 U.S. House. Committee on Armed Services. Hearings: *Supplementary Hearings on Defense Procurement Authorization Relating to SALT Agreement*. 92d Cong., 1st Sess., June 6, 13, 1971.

4225 U.S. Senate. Committee on Foreign Relations. Hearings: *Arms Control Implications of Current Defense Budget*. 92d Cong., 1st Sess., 1971.

4226 "Will $91 Billions for New Weapons Systems be Wasted?" *Defense Monitor* (May 15, 1973): 1–8.

SALT & NONPROLIFERATION

4227 Barnaby, Frank. "Salting Down Non-Proliferation." *New Scientist* (Mar. 4, 1971): 476–77.

4228 Beaton, Leonard. *Secondary and 'Almost Nuclear' Powers: How Do They Affect Strategic Arms Limitations?* Occasional paper. Chicago: Univ. of Chicago, Center for Policy Study, 1971.

4229 Clemens, Walter C., Jr. "SALT, the NPT, and U.S.-Japanese Security Relations." *Asian Survey* 10 (Dec. 1970): 1037–45.

4230 Imai, Ryukichi. "Japan and the World of SALT." *Bulletin of the Atomic Scientists* 27 (Dec. 1971): 13–16.

4231 Keys, Donald F. "Last Chance for U.S.-Soviet Pact." *War/Peace Report* 11 (Oct. 1971): 14–16.

4232 Muramatsu, Takeshi. "Japan's Choice." In William R. Kintner and Robert L. Pfaltzgraff, Jr., eds., *SALT: Implications for Arms Control in the 1970's*. Pittsburgh: Pittsburgh Univ. Press, 1973, pp. 281–94.

4233 Parker, Jerry. "Reflections on SALT." *Peace and Change* 1 (Fall 1972): 67–75. [Reprinted as *Reflections on SALT: The Legacy of the 1968 Nonproliferation Treaty*. Center Occasional Paper 1. Los Angeles: Center for the Study of Armament & Disarmament, 1973.]

4234 Quester, George H. "Implications of SALT Outcome for Potential 'Nth' Powers: Israel, India, and Others." In William R. Kintner and Robert L. Pfaltzgraff, Jr., eds., *SALT:*

Implications for Arms Control in the 1970's. Pittsburgh: Pittsburgh Univ. Press, 1973, pp. 255–79.

4235 "SALT, Proliferation, and International Security [Symposium Discussion]." In William R. Kintner and Robert L. Pfaltzgraff, Jr., eds., *SALT: Implications for Arms Control in the 1970's*. Pittsburgh: Pittsburgh Univ. Press, 1973, pp. 295–310.

4236 Symington, Sen. Stuart. "Nuclear Proliferation and Counterforce." *Congressional Record* 121 (Oct. 22, 1975): S18464–466.

SALT & TEST BAN

4237 Cohen, Samuel T. *SALT and the Test Ban: Parallels and Prospects*. Santa Monica, Ca.: California Arms Control & Foreign Policy Seminar, May 1973.

4238 Kistiakowsky, G. B., and Herbert F. York. "Strategic Arms Race Slowdown Through Test Limitations." *Science* (Aug. 12, 1974): 403–06.

SALT: Arms Race or Military Balance

4239 Legault, Albert, and George R. Lindsey. *The Dynamics of the Nuclear Balance*. Ithaca: Cornell Univ. Press, 1976.

4240 Luttwak, Edward. *The Strategic Balance, 1972*. New York: Library Press, 1972.

4241 ———. *The U.S.-U.S.S.R. Nuclear Weapons Balance*. Beverly Hills, Ca.: Sage, 1974.

4242 Members of Congress for Peace Through Law (MCPL). "Defending America: An Alternative U.S. Foreign Policy and Defense Policy Posture Statement." *Congressional Record* 122 (May 19, 1976): S7507–33.

4243 Middleton, Drew. *Can America Win the Next War?* New York: Scribner's, 1975.

4244 Polmar, Norman. *Strategic Weapons: An Introduction*. New York: Crane, Russak, 1975.

4245 Tsipis, Kosta. *Offensive Missiles*. SIPRI Paper 5. Stockholm: SIPRI, Aug. 1974.

4246 U.S. Congressional Budget Office. *SALT and the U.S. Strategic Forces Budget*. Background paper, no. 8. Washington, D.C.: G.P.O., 1976.

SALT & Strategic Balance

4247 American Enterprise Institute. "Who's First in Defense: The US or the USSR?" *AEI Round Table* (June 3, 1976): 1–39.

4248 Aspin, Rep. Les. "How to Look at the Soviet-American Balance." *Foreign Policy* 22 (Spring 1976): 96–106.

4249 Bennett, Ralph K. "U.S.-Soviet Military Balance: Who's Ahead?" *Reader's Digest* (Sept. 1976): 79–83.

4250 Gray, Colin S. "Foreign Policy and the Strategic Balance." *Orbis* 18 (Fall 1974): 706–27.

4251 ———. "SALT and the Strategic Balance." *Air Force Magazine* 55 (Dec. 1972): 53–55.

4252 Kemp, Rep. Jack. "The Soviet Military Threat to Our National Security: The Real Facts and Figures." *Congressional Record* 122 (June 16, 1976): H6008–13.

4253 Leggett, Rep. Robert L. "Two Legs Do Not a Centipede Make." *Armed Forces Journal International* 112 (Feb. 1975): 30–32.

4254 Pierre, Andrew J. "America Down, Russia Up: The Changing Political Role of Military Power." *Foreign Policy*, no. 4 (Fall 1971): 163–87.

4255 Ravenal, Earl C. "After Schlesinger: Something Has to Give." *Foreign Policy* 22 (Spring 1976): 71–95.

4256 Schneider, Mark B. "SALT and the Strategic Balance, 1974." *Strategic Review* 2 (Fall 1974): 41–47.

4257 Sienkiewicz, Stan. "Gambling with the Strategic Balance." *Ripon Forum* 7 (June 1971): 17–19, 22.

4258 Stevenson, Sen. Adlai E., III. "Imbalance of Strategic Forces Between United States and Soviet Union." *Congressional Record* 122 (Mar. 11, 1976): S3298–309.

4259 "Strategic Arms: Worries and Cold Comfort." *Astronautics & Aeronautics* 14 (Apr. 1976): 6–11.

4260 Taylor, John W. R. "World Missiles, 1971." *Flight International* (Mar. 18, 1971): 374–93.

4261 U.S. Senate. Committee on Government Operations. Report: *The Changing American-Soviet Strategic Balance: Some Political Implications.* [By Uri Ra'anan]. 92d Cong., 2d Sess., 1972.

4262 "U.S.-Soviet Strategic Forces Detailed." *Aviation Week & Space Technology* (Dec. 9, 1974): 13.

SALT & THE ARMS RACE

Also see Economic Consequences of Disarmament, Impact of Defense Spending, Reliance on Defense Spending, in Chapter 6.

General Aspects

4263 Ball, Desmond V. "The Strategic Missile Programme of the Kennedy Administration, 1961–1963." Ph.D. diss., Australian National Univ., 1972.

4264 Bellany, Ian. "The Central Balance: Arms Race and Arms Control." In Carsten Holbraad, ed., *Super Powers and World Order.* Canberra: Australian National Univ. Press, 1971, pp. 41–63.

4265 "Big Shifts Ahead for U.S. Nuclear Arsenal." *U.S. News & World Report* (June 12, 1972): 22–24.

4266 Bottome, Edgar M. *The Balance of Terror: A Guide to the Arms Race.* Boston: Beacon, 1971.

4267 ———. *The Missile Gap: A Study of the Formulation of Military and Public Policy.* Cranbury, N.J.: Fairleigh Dickinson Univ. Press, 1970.

4268 Brunner, Dominique. "Die Nukleare Stabilitat und der Rustungswettlauf—ein Schicksalhaftes Problem." *Allgemeine Schweizerische Militarzeitschrift* 136 (Mar. 1970): 136 ff.

4269 Bundy, McGeorge. "How to Wind Down the Nuclear Arms Race." *New York Times Magazine* (Nov. 16, 1969): 46–47 ff.

4270 ———. "The Nuclear Arms Race." *Survival* 11 (Sept. 1969): 270–72, 278.

4271 Carlton, David, and Carlo Schaerf, eds. *The Dynamics of the Arms Race.* New York: Wiley, 1975.

4272 Chalfont, Lord Arthur G. J. "Slowing Down the Missile Race." *New Statesman* (Aug. 28, 1970): 230–32.

4273 "The Chances for an End to the Arms Race." *U.S. News & World Report* (Feb. 3, 1969): 32–33.

4274 Demin, V. "Who Needs Another Round of the Arms Race?" *International Affairs* [Moscow] 17 (June 1971): 105.

4275 Dougherty, James E. "Arms and the Western Conscience." *Air Force and Space Digest* 47 (July 1964): 36–40.

4276 Enthoven, Alain C., and K. Wayne Smith. *How Much is Enough?* New York: Harper & Row, 1971.

4277 "The Essence of Armed Futility." *Orbis* 18 (Fall 1974): 689–700.

4278 Fink, Daniel J. "How Much is Enough?" *Current* 106 (Apr. 1969): 14–17.

4279 Fisher, Robert S. *Service Rivalry and the Arms Race.* Santa Monica, Ca.: Southern California Arms Control & Foreign Policy Seminar, 1972.

4280 Fleming, D. F. "What Follows the Arms Race?" *Journal of Politics* 14 (May 1952): 203–23.

4281 Gabelic, Andro. "Arms Race Indicators." *Review of International Affairs* [Belgrade] (Jan. 20, 1971): 23–24.

4282 Gray, Colin S. " 'Gap' Prediction and America's Defense Arms Race Behavior in the Eisenhower Years." *Orbis* 16 (Spring 1972): 257–74.

4283 Ikle, Fred C. "The Nether World of Nuclear Megatonnage." *Bulletin of the Atomic Scientists* 30 (Jan. 1975): 20–25.

4284 Kasprzak, John F. "Hope in a New 'Terror Balance.' " *Far Eastern Economic Review* (Feb. 26, 1972): 18–19.

4285 Lapp, Ralph E. *Kill and Overkill.* New York: Basic Books, 1962.

4286 Leitenberg, Milton. "The Present State of the World's Arms Race." *Bulletin of the Atomic Scientists* 28 (Jan. 1972): 15–21.

4287 McGovern, Sen. George S. "The Politics of the Arms Buildup." *Current* 106 (Apr. 1969): 18–21.

4288 Pinckney, Thomas C. "Overkill and Underthought." *Air University Review* 15 (July–Aug. 1964): 37–48.

4289 Plate, Thomas G. *Understanding Doomsday: A Guide to the Arms Race for Hawks, Doves and People.* New York: Simon & Schuster, 1971.

4290 Rathjens, George W. *The Future of the Strategic Arms Race: Options for the 1970's.* New York: Carnegie Endowment for International Peace, 1969.

4291 Ruina, J. D. "The Nuclear Arms Race: Diagnosis and Treatment." *Bulletin of the Atomic Scientists* 24 (Aug. 1968): 19–22.

4292 Schelling, Thomas C. "The State of the Arms Race." In James E. Dougherty and John F. Lehman, Jr., eds., *The Prospects for Arms Control.* New York: MacFadden-Bartell, 1965, pp. 50–58.

4293 SIPRI. *Strategic Arms Limitation: The SALT Agreements and the Future of the Arms Race.* New York: Humanities Press, 1972.

4294 Sivard, Ruth L. "The Arms Race: What It Costs." *New Republic* (Jan. 4, 11, 1975): 9–11.

4295 Viktorov, V., and V. Diomin. "The Arms Race and Its Effects." *International Affairs* [Moscow] 18 (July 1972): 40–43.

4296 Wiesner, Jerome B. "The Cold War Is Dead: But the Arms Race Rumbles On." *Bulletin of the Atomic Scientists* 23 (June 1967): 17–25.

4297 York, Herbert F. "A Personal View of the Arms Race." *Bulletin of the Atomic Scientists* 26 (Mar. 1970): 27–30.

4298 ———. *Race to Oblivion: A Participant's View of the Arms Race.* New York: Simon & Schuster, 1970.

Theoretical Aspects

4299 Brito, D. L. "A Dynamic Model of an Armaments Race." *International Economic Review* 13 (June 1972): 359–75.

4300 Brubaker, Earl R. "Economic Models of Arms Races: Some Reformulations and Extensions." *Journal of Conflict Resolution* 17:2 (1973): 187–206.

4301 Chase, P. E. "Control Theory and the Nuclear Arms Race." *General Systems Yearbook* 14 (1969): 137–50.

4302 ———. "The Relevance of Arms Race Theory to Arms Control." *General Systems Yearbook* 13 (1968): 91–98.

4303 Chatterjee, Partha. "Balance of Power In Alliances and Arms Races." Ph.D. diss., Univ. of Rochester, 1972.

4304 ———. "The Equilibrium Theory of Arms Races: Some Extensions." *Journal of Peace Research* 11:3 (1974): 203–12.

4305 Gray, Colin S. "Action and Reaction in the Nuclear Arms Race." *Military Review* 51 (Aug. 1971): 16–26.

4306 ———. "The Arms Race is About Politics." *Foreign Policy* 9 (Winter 1973): 117–31.

4307 ———. "The Arms Race Phenomenon." *World Politics* 24 (Oct. 1971): 39–79.

4308 ———. "How Does the Nuclear Arms Race Work?" *Cooperation and Conflict* 9:4 (1974): 285–96.

4309 ——— "Social Science and the Arms Race." *Bulletin of the Atomic Scientists* 29 (June 1973): 23–26.

4310 ———. "Urge to Compete: Rationales for Arms Racing." *World Politics* 26 (Jan. 1974): 207–33.

4311 Huntington, Samuel P. "Arms Races: Prerequisites and Results." In C. J. Friedrich and S. E. Harris, *Public Policy, 1958*. Cambridge: Harvard Univ. Press, 1958, VIII: 41–86.

4312 Joenniemi, Pertti. "Aspects on the Measurement of Armament Levels." *Cooperation and Conflict* 5:3 (1970): 141–51.

4313 Joynt, C. B. "Arms Races and the Problem of Equilibrium." *Yearbook of World Affairs* (1964): 23–40.

4314 Kahn, Herman. "The Arms Race and Some of Its Hazards." In Donald G. Brennan, ed., *Arms Control, Disarmament, and National Security*. New York: Braziller, 1961, pp. 89–121.

4315 Lambelet, John C. "Do Arms Races Lead to War? Some Preliminary Thoughts." *Journal of Peace Research* 12:2 (1975): 123–28.

4316 Luterbacher, Urs. "Arms Race Models: Where Do We Stand?" *European Journal of Political Research* (June 1975): 2–17.

4317 McGuire, Martin C. *Secrecy and the Arms Race: A Theory of the Accumulation of Strategic Weapons and How Secrecy Affects It*. Cambridge: Harvard Univ. Press, 1965.

4318 Panofsky, Wolfgang K. H. "Roots of the Strategic Arms Race: Ambiguity and Ignorance." *Bulletin of the Atomic Scientists* 27 (June 1971): 15–20.

4319 Pitman, George R., Jr. *Arms Races and Stable Deterrence*. ACDA Security Studies, no. 18. Los Angeles: Univ. of California, 1969.

4320 Rathjens, George W. "Constraints on the Nuclear Arms Race." In Bennett Boskey and Mason Willrich, eds., *Nuclear Proliferation: Prospects for Control*. New York: Dunellen, 1970.

4321 ———. "The Dynamics of the Arms Race." *Scientific American* 220 (Apr. 1969): 15–25.

4322 Richardson, Lewis. *Arms and Insecurity*. Pittsburgh: Boxwood Press, 1960.

4323 Smoker, Paul. "Trade, Defense and the Richardson Theory of Arms Race." *Journal of Peace Research* 2:3 (1965): 161–76.

4324 Steiner, Barry H. "Arms Race Processes and Hazards." Ph.D. diss., Columbia Univ.

4325 "Technological Change and the Strategic Arms Race." In William R. Kintner and Robert L. Pfaltzgraff, Jr., eds., *SALT: Implications for Arms Control in the 1970's*. Pittsburgh: Pittsburgh Univ. Press, 1973, pp. 107–24.

4326 Thee, Marek. "The Nuclear Arms Race: Trends, Dynamics, Control." *Instant Research on Peace and Violence* 6:1–2 (1976): 18–28.

4327 Wohlstetter, Albert. "Legends of the Strategic-Arms Race." *Strategic Review* 2 (Fall 1974): 67–92.

4328 ———. "Rivals, But No 'Race'." *Foreign Policy* 16 (Fall 1974): 48–81. ["Comments," pp. 82–92.]

4329 York, Herbert F. "The Arms Race and the Fallacy of the Last Move." *Bulletin of the Atomic Scientists* 25 (June 1969): 27–28.

4330 ———. "Controlling the Qualitative Arms Race." *Bulletin of the Atomic Scientists* 29 (Mar. 1973): 4–8.

Arms Race: Accelerated After SALT I

4331 Jennings, Col. Richard M. "Running the Qualitative Race (and Not Losing)." *Military Review* 55 (Oct. 1975): 58–68.

4332 Knoll, Erwin. "More Weapons for the 'Generation of Peace.'" *Progressive* 36 (Aug. 1972): 14–16.

4333 Leitenberg, Milton. "Le Developpement des Arsenaux Strategiques depuis SALT I." *Politique Etrangère* 39:4/5 (1974): 427–40.

4334 Myrdal, Alva. "It's the Qualitative Arms Race that Frightens US Most." *War/Peace Report* 13 (June 1974): 3–7.

4335 Ognibene, Peter J. "Arms Jitters." *New Republic* (Feb. 23, 1974): 16–18.

4336 Scoville, Herbert, Jr. "After Overkill: Enough is Enough." *Ramparts* 14 (July 1975): 28–30 ff.

4337 ———. "More, More, More Weapons." *New Republic* (Mar. 4, 1972): 14–16.

4338 Stone, I. F. "McGovern vs. Nixon on Arms Race." *New York Review of Books* (July 20, 1972): 9–10.

4339 Warnke, Paul C. "Apes on a Treadmill." *Foreign Policy* 18 (Spring 1975): 12–29.

Arms Race: Specific Weapons Systems

4340 Cossaboom, Bruce. "Senate Proposes Freeze on ABM, MIRV." *Armed Forces Journal* (Apr. 18, 1970): 7–8.

4341 Holloway, Gen. Bruce K. "Survival as a Free Country Depends on Modern Weapons." *U.S. News & World Report* (Dec. 27, 1971): 52–55.

4342 Rogoff, Donald L. "The Triad: Or Sea Basing? A Diversified Deterrent is Best." *Ordnance* 57 (Jan.–Feb. 1973): 289–92.

4343 Shapley, Deborah. "The B-1 and the Cruise Missile: To Have and Have Not." *Science* (July 23, 1976): 303–05.

4344 "Soviets Demand B-1, Trident End." *Aviation Week & Space Technology* (Apr. 15, 1974): 14–15.

4345 Ulsamer, Edgar. "Adjusting Triad to Mounting Soviet Threats." *Air Force Magazine* 56 (Apr. 1974): 54–58.

4346 ———. "SALT II's Gray-Area Weapon Systems." *Air Force Magazine* 59 (July 1976): 80–85.

4347 U.S. Senate. Committee on Foreign Relations. Hearings: *ABM, MIRV, SALT, and the Nuclear Arms Race.* 91st Cong., 2d Sess., 1970.

4348 York, Herbert F. "ABM, MIRV, and the Arms Race." *Science* (July 17, 1970): 257–60.

4349 Zelnick, C. Robert. "Waiting for Disarmament: Weapons We Can Live With—And Without." *Washington Monthly* 5 (May 1973): 28–36.

Backfire Bomber

4350 "Backfire Boggles SALT II." *Astronautics & Aeronautics* 14 (July–Aug. 1976): 21–23.

4351 Burke, Gerard K. "Backfire: Strategic Implications." *Military Review* 56 (Sept. 1976): 85–90.

4352 Panyalev, Georg. "Backfire—Soviet Counter to the American B-1." *International Defense Review* 7 (Oct. 1975): 639–42.

Cruise Missiles & Orbital Bombs

4353 "About 'World's Most Accurate Missile.'" *U.S. News & World Report* (June 7, 1975): 53.

4354 Aldridge, Robert C. "Cruise Missiles: More Pentagon Mischief." *Nation* (June 14, 1975): 710–13.

4355 Barnaby, Frank. "Will the Cruise Missile Torpedo SALT?" *New Scientist* (Dec. 18, 1975): 679–81.

4356 Burt, Richard. "The Cruise Missile and Arms Control." *Survival* 19 (Jan.–Feb. 1976): 10–17.

4357 "The Cruise Missile: A Weapon in Search of a Mission." *Defense Monitor* 5 (Sept. 1976): 1–7.

4358 Currie, Malcolm R. "The Case for Cruise Missiles." *Aviation Week & Space Technology* (Apr. 21, 1975): 9.

4359 Geddes, J. Philip. "The Sea Launched Cruise Missile." *Interavia* 31 (Mar. 1976): 260–64.

4360 Hayward, John T. "Perspective: Tactical Missile at Sea." *Government Executive* (Nov. 1974): 19 ff.

4361 McGovern, Sen. George, and Rep. Jonathan Bingham. "Long-Range Cruise Missiles, Some Implications of their Development and Deployment." *Congressional Record* 122 (May 11, 1976): S6903–08.

4362 Miller, Judith. "Calling Off the Cruise." *Progressive* 40 (Jan. 1976): 7–8.

4363 Miller, Raphael. "The Harpoon Missile System." *International Defense Review* 8 (Feb. 1975): 61–66.

4364 "Missile Argument." *Aviation Week & Space Technology* (Mar. 24, 1975): 18.

4365 O'Connell, D. P. "The Legality of Naval Cruise Missiles." *American Journal of International Law* 66 (May 1972): 785–94.

4366 Robinson, Clarence A., Jr. "Navy Spurs Cruise Missile Pace." *Aviation Week & Space Technology* (Nov. 24, 1975): 12–15.

4367 ———. "Single Cruise Missile Set for Varied Use." *Aviation Week & Space Technology* (Feb. 24, 1975): 19–20.

4368 Shapley, Deborah. "Cruise Missiles: Air Force, Navy Weapon Poses New Arms Issue." *Science* (Feb. 7, 1975): 416–18.

4369 Tsipis, Kosta. "The Arms Control Effect of Cruise Missiles." *Congressional Record* 122 (Mar. 9, 1976): H1817–18.

4370 ———. "The Long-Range Cruise Missile." *Bulletin of the Atomic Scientists* 31 (Apr. 1975): 14–26.

4371 U.S. Senate. Armed Services Committee. Hearings: *Fiscal Year 1975 Authorization for Military Procurement.* 93d Cong., 2d Sess., 1974, pt. 7, pp. 3619–90.

4372 Vershbow, Alexander R. "The Cruise Missile: The End of Arms Control?" *Foreign Affairs* 55 (Oct. 1976): 133–46.

4373 Weiler, Lawrence D. "Strategic Cruise Missiles and the Future of SALT." *Arms Control Today* 5 (Oct. 1975): 1–4.

4374 Yaffee, Michael L. "Cruise Missile Engine Design Pushed." *Aviation Week & Space Technology* (July 7, 1975): 41–43.

Mobile ICBMs

4375 "The SALT Process and Its Use in Regulating Mobile ICBMs." *Yale Law Journal* 84 (Apr. 1975): 1078–1100.

4376 "U.S. to Press Development." *Aviation Week & Space Technology* (Dec. 9, 1974): 12.

4377 Willenson, Kim, and Lloyd H. Norman. "Missiles on the Move." *Newsweek* (Feb. 16, 1976): 42.

MIRVs

4378 Davis, Lynn E., and Warner R. Schilling. "All You Ever Wanted to Know About MIRV and ICBM Calculations But Were Not Cleared to Ask." *Journal of Conflict Resolution* 17:2 (1973): 207–42.

4379 DeVolpi, Alexander. "MIRV: Gorgon Medusa of the Nuclear Age." *Bulletin of the Atomic Scientists* 26 (Jan. 1970): 35–38, 46.

4380 Greenwood, Ted. *Making the MIRV: A Study of Defense Decision-Making.* Cambridge, Mass.: Ballinger, 1975.

4381 Karber, Phillip A. "MIRV: Anatomy of an Enigma." *Air Force Magazine* 54 (Feb. 1971): 83–87.

4382 Kaye, G. D., and George R. Lindsey. "MIRV's and the Strategic Balance." *Nature* [London] (Aug. 15, 1970): 696–97.

4383 Kyle, Keith. "Putting SALT on MIRV's." *Listener* (Dec. 11, 1969): 813–14.

4384 Lapp, Ralph E. "Can SALT Stop MIRV?" *New York Times Magazine* (Feb. 1, 1970): 14–15 ff.

4385 Marzari, Frank. "The Derangement of MIRV." *International Journal* 26 (Autumn 1971): 753–70.

4386 McGuire, Michael. "MIRV, SALT and Strategic Stability: A Dual Approach." *Congressional Record* 116 (July 29, 1970): S26385–388.

4387 "The 'MIRVing' of Minuteman: Doubled Power for U.S." *U.S. News & World Report* (June 2, 1975): 27–28.

4388 Sartori, Leo. "The Myth of MIRV." *Survival* 11 (Dec. 1969): 382–89.

4389 Scoville, Herbert, Jr. "MIRV Control Is Still Possible." *Survival* 16 (Mar.–Apr. 1974): 54–59.

4390 Tammen, Ronald L. *MIRV and the Arms Race: An Interpretation of Defense Strategy.* New York: Praeger, 1973.

4391 U.S. Arms Control & Disarmament Agency. *A Feasibility Study of MIRV Simulation Inspection by Gravity Gradiometry.* ACDA Rpt. ST–171. Los Angeles: Hughes Aircraft Co., 1970.

4392 U.S. House. Committee on Foreign Affairs. Hearings: *Diplomatic and Strategic Impact of Multiple Warhead Missiles.* 91st Cong., 1st Sess., 1969.

4393 Whetten, Lawrence L. "Soviet Interests and MIRV Control." *Survival* 16 (Mar.–Apr. 1974): 59–63.

4394 York, Herbert F. "Multiple-Warhead Missiles." *Scientific American* 229 (Nov. 1973): 18–27.

4395 ———. *The Origins of MIRV.* SIPRI Research Report no. 9. Stockholm: SIPRI, Aug. 1973.

B-1 Bomber

4396 "B-1 Bomber Need Defended, Critics Hit." *Aviation Week & Space Technology* (Aug. 11, 1975): 53–55.

4397 Berman, Bob. "The B-1 Bomber: Is it Worth $92 Billion?" *Defense Monitor* 4:4 (June 1975): 1–4.

4398 Center for Defense Information. "The B-1: Does the U.S. Need It?" *Defense Monitor* 2 (Jan. 22, 1973): 1–8.

4399 "Does U.S. Need the B-1 Bomber?" *U.S. News & World Report* (Apr. 26, 1976): 63–64.

4400 Dulberger, Leon H. "Advanced Strategic Bombers." *Space/Aeronautics* 45 (June 1966): 62–75.

4401 Frisbee, John L. "The B-1 Blue Chip in the Deterrent Stock." *Air Force & Space Digest* 53 (Apr. 1970): 45–48.

4402 Geddes, J. Philip. "The B-1 Bomber: A Costly Essential." *International Defense Review* 8 (Apr. 1975): 195–200.

4403 ———. "Rockwell International's B-1 Bomber at a Critical Point." *Interavia* (Feb. 1975): 132–38.

4404 Goldwater, Sen. Barry. "An Answer to a B-1 Critic." *Congressional Record* 122 (July 30, 1976): S12889–891.

4405 Gunston, Bill. *Bombers of the West.* New York: Scribner's, 1973.

4406 Hoeber, Francis P. "The B-1: A National Imperative." *Strategic Review* 4 (Summer 1976): 111–17.

4407 London, Michael P. "B-1: The Last Bomber?" *Space/Aeronautics* 53 (Apr. 1970): 26–33.

4408 Lowe, George E. "The Only Option?" *U.S. Naval Institute Proceedings* 97 (Apr. 1971): 18–26.

4409 Martin, Gen. Abner B. "The B-1: Strategic Deterrence Into the Twenty-First Century." *Air University Review* 27 (Mar.–Apr. 1976): 2–14.

4410 McGovern, Sen. George S. "The Joint Strategic Bomber Study: A Stacked Deck for the B-1." *Congressional Record* 121 (June 4, 1975): S9663–65.

4411 ———. "Members of Congress for Peace Through Law, Report on the B-1 Bomber Program." *Congressional Record* 120 (May 20, 1974): S8655–74.

4412 ———. "1976: The Year to Stop the B-1." *Congressional Record* 122 (Apr. 1, 1976): S4766–68.

4413 Miller, Barry. "B-1 Countermeasures Face Milestone." *Aviation Week & Space Technology* (Apr. 12, 1976): 47–51.

4414 "New Bomber Runs Into Old Flak." *Business Week* (May 3, 1969): 43–44.

4415 Ognibene, Peter J. "The B-1 Ballyhoo." *New Republic* (June 17, 1972): 17–20.

4416 ———. "Hidden Costs of the B-1: Bombing Empty Holes." *New Republic* (May 12, 1973): 18–21.

4417 Proxmire, Sen. William. "B-1 Bomber, Part 1: Costs Rise and Performance Slips." *Congressional Record* 122 (Apr. 26, 1976): S5831–40.

4418 Quanbeck, Alton, and Arch Wood. *Modernizing the Strategic Force: Why and How.* Washington, D.C.: Brookings Institution, 1976.

4419 Rice, Berkeley. "The B-1 Bomber: The Very Model of a Modern Major Misconception." *Saturday Review* (Dec. 11, 1971): 20–22 ff.

4420 Robinson, Clarence A., Jr. "U.S.A.F. Manned Bomber Need Challenged." *Aviation Week & Space Technology* (Mar. 24, 1975): 18–19.

4421 Schneider, Barry R. "Is the B-1 Still Flying or Was It Shot Down This Summer?" *Bulletin of the Atomic Scientists* 32 (Oct. 1976): 6–7.

4422 Stewart, Gen. James T. "Evolving Strategic Air Power and B-1." *Astronautics & Aeronautics* 10 (June 1972): 22–29.

4423 Towell, Pat. "Senate Approves Minuteman Missile, Delays Procurement of B-1 Bomber Until 1977." *Congressional Quarterly Weekly Report* (May 29, 1976): 1396–1401, 1408–09.

4424 Ulsamer, Edgar. "B-1: Good Bargain for Deterrence." *Air Force Magazine* 57 (Dec. 1974): 38–40.

SSBM, ULMS & Trident Submarine

4425 Brown, Neville. "Deterrence from the Sea." *New Scientist* (Apr. 16, 1970): 127–32.

4426 Craven, John P. "Ocean Technology and Submarine Warfare." *Implications of Military Technology Into the 1970's.* Adelphi Paper, no. 46. London: International Institute for Strategic Studies, Mar. 1968.

4427 Hersh, Seymour M. "20,000 Guns Under the Sea." *Ramparts* 8 (Sept. 1969): 41–44.

4428 Holme, Thomas T. "The Soviet Submarine Threat: Past, Present, and Future." *U.S. Naval Institute Proceedings* 97 (Aug. 1971): 60–62.

4429 Leary, Frank. "ULMS: Strategic Emphasis Shifts Seaward." *Space/Aeronautics* 53 (June 1970): 24–33.

4430 ———. "ULMS: Will All the Targets Go to Sea?" *Armed Forces Management* 16 (May 1970): 36–40.

4431 Libby, Adm. Ruthven E. "The Role of the Submarine in the Strategic Balance." *Strategic Review* 1 (Spring 1973): 29–32.

4432 "Military Spending Report [ULMS Most Cost-Effective]." *Congressional Record* 116 (July 31, 1970): S12559–566.

4433 Sapolsky, Harvey M. *The Polaris System Development: Bureaucratic and Programmatic Success in Government.* Cambridge: Harvard Univ. Press, 1972.

4434 Scoville, Herbert, Jr. "Missile Submarines and National Security." *Scientific American* 226 (June 1972): 15–27.

4435 Shapley, Deborah. "Trident in Trouble: New Missile May Resemble Poseidon, After All." *Science* (Jan. 9, 1976): 50–51.

4436 Tsipis, Kosta, et al., eds. *The Future of the Sea-Based Deterrent.* Cambridge: M.I.T. Press, 1973.

4437 Wells, Paul. "The Trident Submarine Is an Unneeded Behemoth." *Challenge* 16 (Sept.–Oct. 1974): 53–55.

Anti-Submarine Warfare (ASW)

4438 "Anti-Submarine Warfare: The Envious Siege of Wat'ry Neptune." *Defense & Foreign Affairs* (Aug.–Sept. 1976): 60–65.

4439 Booda, Larry L. "DOD Gives ASW Surveillance Systems High Priority." *Undersea Technology* 13 (Jan. 1972): 31–32.

4440 ———. "Industry's Stake in Undersea Warfare." *Undersea Technology* 9 (Nov. 1971): 20–23, 34.

4441 ———. "Navy Continues Priority on Ocean Surveillance Systems." *Undersea Technology* 14 (Jan. 1973): 27–29.

4442 Bussert, James C. "Soviet ASW." *U.S. Naval Institute Proceedings* 98 (Aug. 1972): 112–16.

4443 Feld, Bernard T. "ASW—The ABM of the 1970's?" *Stanford Journal of International Studies* 7 (Spring 1972): 87–95.

4444 ———, and George W. Rathjens. "Anti-Submarine Warfare and the Sea-Based Deterrent: Opportunities for Arms Control?" *Survival* 15 (Nov.–Dec. 1973): 268–74.

4445 Garwin, Richard L. "Antisubmarine Warfare and National Security." *Scientific American* 227 (July 1972): 14–25.

4446 La Violette, Paul E., et al. "New Satellites Offer Great Potential for Ocean Data Collection." *Undersea Technology* 13 (Nov. 1972): 23–31.

4447 Leary, Frank. "The Anti-Sub Submarine." *Space/Aeronautics* 46 (July 1966): 52–66.

4448 ———. "Search for Subs." *Space/Aeronautics* 44 (Sept. 1965): 58–68.

4449 Murphy, Frank B. "Ocean Surveillance: New Weapon of Naval Warfare." *U.S. Naval Institute Proceedings* 97 (Feb. 1971): 39–41.

4450 Polmar, Norman. *Atomic Submarines.* Princeton, N.J.: Van Nostrand, 1963.

4451 ———. "Thinking About Soviet ASW." *U.S. Naval Institute Proceedings* 102 (May 1976): 108–29.

4452 Rose, William M. "Submarine vs. Antisubmarine." *Bulletin of the Atomic Scientists* 31 (Apr. 1975): 27–30.

4453 Smith, Capt. Robert H. "ASW: The Crucial Naval Challenge." *U.S. Naval Institute Proceedings* 98 (May 1972): 126–41.

4454 Tsipis, Kosta. *Tactical and Strategic Antisubmarine Warfare.* Cambridge: M.I.T. Press, 1974.

4455 Ulsamer, Edgar. "Soviets Step Up Antisubmarine Warfare Capabilities." *Air Force Magazine* 55 (Dec. 1972): 28.

4456 Winnefeld, Capt. James A., and Carl H. Builder. "ASW: Now or Never." *U.S. Naval Institute Proceedings* 97 (Sept. 1971): 18–25.

Anti-Ballistic Missile Systems (ABM)

ABM LIMITATION TREATY (1972)

For text of treaty, see "Treaty Between the United States of America and the Union of Soviet Socialist Republics on the Limitation of Anti-Ballistic Missile Systems, Moscow, May 26, 1972," *U.S. Treaties and Other Agreements* (Washington, D.C.: G.P.O., 1972), no. 23, pt. 4, pp. 3435–62. Also see "Protocol to the Treaty Between the United States of America and the Union of Soviet Socialist Republics on the Limitation of Anti-Ballistic Missile Systems, Moscow, July 3, 1974," U.S. Arms Control and Disarmament Agency, *Arms Control and Disarmament Agreements*, 2d ed. (Washington, D.C.: G.P.O., 1975), pp. 150–52.

4457 Adams, Benson D. *Ballistic Missile Defense.* New York: American Elsevier Publishing, 1971.

4458 ———. "McNamara's ABM Policy, 1961–1967." *Orbis* 12 (Spring 1968): 200–225.

4459 Barnaby, Frank, and A. Boserup, eds. *Implications of Anti-Ballistic Missile Systems.* Pugwash Monograph II. London: Souvenir Press, 1969.

4460 Bethe, Hans A. "The ABM, China and the Arms Race." *Bulletin of the Atomic Scientists* 25 (May 1969): 41–44.

4461 Boehm, George A. "Countdown for Nike-X." *Fortune* 72 (May 1965): 133–37, 192–200.

4462 Brennan, Donald G. "Missile Defense and Arms Control." *Disarmament* 14 (June 1967): 1–4.

4463 ———. "New Thoughts on Missile Defense." *Bulletin of the Atomic Scientists* 23 (June 1967): 10–15.

4464 ———. *Post Deployment Policy Issues in Ballistic Missile Defense.* Adelphi Paper, no. 43. London: Institute for Strategic Studies, 1968.

4465 Burnell, Bates C. "Safeguard—1971." *Military Engineer* 63 (Nov.–Dec. 1971): 386–88.

4466 Chayes, Abram, and Jerome B. Wiesner. *ABM: An Evaluation of the Decision to Display an Anti-Ballistic Missile System.* New York: Harper & Row, 1969.

4467 Coffey, Joseph I. "BMD Options: A Critical Appraisal—Arms Control and Ballistic Missile Defense." In James E. Dougherty and John F. Lehman, Jr., eds., *Arms Control for the Late Sixties.* Princeton: Van Nostrand, 1967, pp. 69–79.

4468 ———. "Chinese and Ballistic Missile Defense." *Bulletin of the Atomic Scientists* 21 (Oct. 1965): 17–19.

4469 Davis, Paul C. "The Coming Chinese Communist Nuclear Threat and the U.S. Sea-Based ABM Options." *Orbis* 11 (Spring 1967): 45–66.

4470 Dyson, Freeman J. "Defense Against Ballistic Missiles." *Bulletin of the Atomic Scientists* 20 (June 1964): 12–18.

4471 Foster, Richard B. "The Impact of Ballistic Missile Defense on Arms Control Prospects." In James E. Dougherty and John F. Lehman, Jr., eds., *Arms Control for the Late Sixties.* Princeton: Van Nostrand, 1967, pp. 80–92.

4472 Garwin, Richard L., and Hans A. Bethe. "Anti-Ballistic Missile Systems." *Scientific American* 218 (Mar. 1968): 21–31.

4473 Greenwood, Ted. *The Utility of Safeguard for the Defense of Minuteman.* C/72–16. Cambridge: M.I.T., Center for International Studies, Aug. 1972.

4474 Halperin, Morton H. *The Decision to Deploy the ABM: Bureaucratic and Domestic Politics in the Johnson Administration.* Washington, D.C.: Brookings Institution, 1971. [Also see, *World Politics* 25 (Oct. 1972): 62–95.

4475 Herzfeld, Charles M. "Ballistic Missile Defense: This Time for Real." *Nature* (Sept. 28, 1968): 1315–17.

4476 ———. "BMD and National Security." *Survival* 8 (Mar. 1966): 70–76.

4477 Holahan, James. "Antimissile Defense Takes Shape." *Military Review* 43 (Aug. 1963): 60–65.

4478 Hunter, Robert E. "The ABM: President Nixon's Safeguard Programme." *World Today* 25 (May 1969): 194–203.

4479 Kennedy, T. E., and M. M. Dembo. "Model Test for Safeguard." *Military Engineer* 63 (Nov.–Dec. 1971): 389–91.

4480 Lapp, Ralph E. "From Nike to Safeguard: A Biography of the ABM." *New York Times Magazine* (May 4, 1969): 29 ff.

4481 Lowenhar, Herman. "ABM Radars: Myth vs. Reality." *Space/Aeronautics* 52 (Nov. 1969): 56–64.

4482 Mansfield, Sen. Michael. "Protocol to the Treaty with the Union of Soviet Socialist Republics on the Limitation of Antiballistic Missile Systems." *Congressional Record* 121 (Nov. 6, 1975): S19471–474.

4483 Martin, Laurence W. "Ballistic Missile Defense and Arms Control." *Arms Control and Disarmament* 1 (1968): 61–67.

4484 ———. "Into the ABM Age." *Interplay* 1 (May 1967): 14–16.

4485 ———. "Strategic Implications of BMD." *Survival* 9 (July 1967): 216–19.

4486 Moldauer, Peter. "The ABM Comes to Town." *Bulletin of the Atomic Scientists* 25 (Jan. 1969): 4–6, 20.

4487 Morton, Louis. "The Anti-Ballistic Missile: Some Political and Strategic Considerations." *Virginia Quarterly Review* 42:1 (1966): 28–42.

4488 Ognibene, Peter J. "The ABC's of ABM." *Commonweal* (Mar. 19, 1971): 31–34.

4489 Rathjens, George W. "Is Safeguard Worth the Risk?" *Bulletin of the Atomic Scientists* 27 (Mar. 1971): 14–16.

4490 ———. "Is Safeguard Worth the Risk?" *Bulletin of the Atomic Scientists* 25 (June 1969): 23–24.

4491 Robinson, Clarence A., Jr. "Army Spurs Missile Defense Technology." *Aviation Week & Space Technology* (Apr. 22, 1974): 12–15.

4492 ———. "U.S. Pushes Expanded ABM Data Base." *Aviation Week & Space Technology* (Apr. 21, 1975): 18–20.

4493 Rodberg, Leonard S. "ABM—Some Arms Control Issues." *Bulletin of the Atomic Scientists* 23 (June 1967): 16–20.

4494 Russett, Bruce M. "The Complexities of Ballistic Missile Defense." *Yale Review* 56 (Mar. 1967): 354–67.

4495 Slater, Jerome. "The Case for Reviving the ABM." *New Leader* (July 7, 1975): 9–11.

4496 Stone, Jeremy J. "Antiballistic Missiles and Arms Control." *Containing the Arms Race.* Cambridge: M.I.T. Press, 1966, pp. 21–74.

4497 U.S. Congress. Joint Committee on Atomic Energy. Hearings: *Scope, Magnitude, and Implications of the United States Antiballistic Missile Program.* 90th Cong., 1st Sess., Nov. 6, 7, 1967.

4498 U.S. House. Committee on Appropriations. Hearings: *Safeguard Antiballistic Missile System,* 91st Cong., 1st Sess., 1969.

4499 U.S. Senate. Committee on Armed Services. Hearings: *Military Implications of the Treaty on the Limitation of Anti-Ballistic Missile Systems and the Interim Agreement on Limitation of Strategic Offensive Arms.* 92d Cong., 2d Sess., 1972.

4500 ———. Committee on Foreign Relations. Hearings: *Strategic and Foreign Policy Implications of ABM Systems.* 91st Cong., 1st Sess., 1969.

4501 ———. Report: *Treaty on Limitation of Anti-Ballistic-Missile Systems.* Ex. Rpt. no

92–28 to Ex. L, 92–2. 92d Cong., 2d Sess., 1972.

4502 Willrich, Mason. "ABM and Arms Control." *International Affairs* [London] 44 (Apr. 1968): 228–39.

4503 Yanarella, Ernest J. "Pentagon Decision-Making and Bureaucratic Politics in the ABM Controversy, 1955–1957." Ph.D. diss., Univ. of North Carolina, 1971.

U.S.S.R.

4504 Coffey, Joseph I. "The Soviet ABM and Arms Control." *Bulletin of the Atomic Scientists* 26 (Jan. 1970): 39–43.

4505 ———. "Soviet ABM Policy: The Implications for the West." *International Affairs* [London] 45 (Apr. 1969): 205–22.

4506 Crane, Robert D. "Soviet Military Policy During the Era of Ballistic Missile Defense." In Denis Dirscherl, ed., *The New Russia.* Dayton: Pflaum Press, 1968, pp. 157–70.

4507 Erickson, John. "The Fly in Outer Space: The Soviet Union and the Anti-Ballistic Missile." *World Today* 23 (Mar. 1967): 106–14.

4508 ———. "Soviet BMD." *Survival* 9 (May 1967): 152–57.

4509 Hahn, Walter F., and Alvin J. Cottrell. "Ballistic Missile Defense and Soviet Strategy." *Orbis* 9 (Summer 1965): 316–37.

4510 Holst, Johan J. *Some Observations on the Soviet Views of ABM and SALT.* New York: Hudson Institute, Jan. 1970.

4511 ———. *The Russians and "Safeguard."* New York: Hudson Institute, Apr. 1969.

4512 Klass, Philip J. "Strengthened U.S. ICBM Forces to Off-Set Soviet Missile Defense." *Aviation Week & Space Technology* (Feb. 6, 1967): 27–28.

4513 Schneider, Mark B. "Russia and the ABM." *Ordnance* 56 (Mar.–Apr. 1972): 372–74.

4514 Scoville, Herbert, Jr. "Upgrading Soviet SAM." *New Republic* (Oct. 9, 1971): 19–20.

4515 Talensky, Gen. Nikolai A. "Anti-Missile Systems and Disarmament." *International Affairs* [Moscow] 10 (Oct. 1964): 15–19. [See also, *Bulletin of the Atomic Scientists* 21 (Feb. 1965): 26–29.]

4516 Thomas, John. "The Role of Missile Defense in Soviet Strategy." *Military Review* 44 (May 1964): 46–58.

Europe

4517 Holst, Johan J. "BMD and European Perspectives." In Donald G. Brennan, *Post Deployment Policy Issues in Ballistic Missile Defense.* Adelphi Paper, no. 43. London: Institute for Strategic Studies, 1968, pp. 24–36.

4518 Martin, Laurence W. "Ballistic Missile Defense and Europe." *Bulletin of the Atomic Scientists* 23 (May 1967): 42–46.

ABM DEBATE (U.S.)

4519 Cahn, Anne H. *Eggheads and Warheads: Scientists and the ABM.* C/71-7. Cambridge: M.I.T., Center for International Studies, 1971.

4520 Center for the Study of Democratic Institutions. *Anti-Ballistic Missile: Yes or No?* New York: Hill & Wang, 1969.

4521 Coffey, Joseph I. "The Anti-Ballistic Missile Debate." *Foreign Affairs* 45 (Apr. 1967): 403–13.

4522 "Fighting the Great ABM Battle Again." *Nature* (Oct. 15, 1971): 442–43.

4523 Fulbright, Sen. J. William. "Foreign Policy Implications of the ABM Debate." *Bulletin of the Atomic Scientists* 25 (June 1969): 20–33.

4524 Holst, Johan J., and William Schneider, Jr. *Why ABM? Policy Issues in the Missile Defense Controversy.* New York: Pergamon, 1969.

4525 Jayne, Edward R., II. "The ABM Debate: Strategic Defense and National Security." Ph.D. diss., M.I.T., 1969.

4526 Martin, Laurence W. "The Great Missile Defense Debate." *Interplay* 3:1 (1969): 39–41.

4527 McDonald, Donald. "The Background of the ABM Debate." *Current* 106 (Apr. 1969): 3–5.

4528 McNamara, Robert S. "U.S. Nuclear Strategy Missile Defense." *Vital Speeches* (Oct. 1, 1967): 738–43.

4529 Moss, Norman. "McNamara's ABM Policy: A Failure in Communications." *Reporter* (Feb. 23, 1967): 34–36.

4530 Mossman, J. "Secretary McNamara's Comments on Risks of Antiballistic Missile System." *U.S. Department of State Bulletin* (Mar. 20, 1967): 442–47.

4531 Rabinowitch, Eugene, and Ruth Adams, eds. *Debate: The Antiballistic Missile.* Chicago: Bulletin of the Atomic Scientists, 1967.

4532 Rothstein, Robert. "The ABM Debate Continues." *Current* 107 (May 1969): 18–23.

4533 Wildavsky, Aaron. "The Politics of ABM." *Commentary* 48 (Oct. 1969): 55–59.

4534 Witze, Claude. "The Fight Over the ABM: Debate or Witch-Hunt?" *Air Force & Space Digest* 52 (Apr. 1969): 34–38.

4535 Yates, Sidney R. "Showdown on the ABM." *Bulletin of the Atomic Scientists* 25 (Mar. 1969): 29–37.

4536 Young, Elizabeth. "ABM: No Alternative to Politics." *Bulletin of the Atomic Scientists* 23 (June 1967): 47–89.

4537 Yuter, S. C. "The ABM Controversy: Law Meets Science Again." *Lex et Scientia* 6 (Oct.–Dec. 1969): 131–35.

Debate—Pro

4538 Brennan, Donald G. "The Case for Missile Defense." *Foreign Affairs* 47 (Apr. 1969): 433–48.

4539 Burnham, James. "AMS Campaign." *National Review* (Mar. 7, 1967): 238.

4540 ———. "Why Not an Antimissile Missile?" *National Review* (June 14, 1966): 567.

4541 Dyson, Freeman J. "A Case for Missile Defense." *Bulletin of the Atomic Scientists* 25 (Apr. 1969): 31–34.

4542 Gilpatric, Roswell L. "Our Defense Needs: The Long View." *Foreign Affairs* 42 (Apr. 1964): 366–78.

4543 Kahn, Herman. "Why We Should Go Ahead with ABM." *Fortune* 79 (June 1969): 120–121 ff.

4544 Kintner, William R., ed. *Safeguard: Why the ABM Makes Sense.* New York: Hawthorne Books, 1969.

4545 Lodge, Henry Cabot, Jr. "A Citizen Looks at the ABM." *Reader's Digest* (June 1970): 57–64.

4546 London, Michael P. "Safeguard: Is There a Choice?" *Space/Aeronautics* 52 (Nov. 1969): 48–55.

4547 McMahan, Richard H. "Rationales for Ballistic Missile Defense Policy." *Bulletin of the Atomic Scientists* 21 (Mar. 1965): 37–40.

4548 Schneider, Mark B. "MIRV and ABM: Why Our Defenses Are Down." *National Review* (May 19, 1970): 512–13.

4549 Teller, Edward. "BMD in a Strategy for Peace." In James E. Dougherty and John F. Lehman, Jr., eds., *Arms Control for the Late Sixties.* Princeton: Van Nostrand, 1967, pp. 99–114.

4550 Trainor, James. "Study Aids Case for Nike-X." *Missiles and Rockets* (Jan. 4, 1965): 12.

Debate—Con

4551 Brandon, Henry H. "New Missile Race?" *Saturday Review* (Jan. 28, 1967): 14, 16, 77.

4552 Carter, Luther J. "Antimissile Defense: Should Nike-X Be Deployed?" *Science* (Dec. 24, 1965): 1696–99.

4553 ———. "Antimissile Missile: Next Entry in the Arms Race?" *Science* (Nov. 25, 1966): 985–87.

4554 ———. "Missile Defense: LBJ's Bid to Curb Arms Race Gains Support." *Science* (Mar. 31, 1967): 1651–54.

4555 Halsted, Thomas A. "Lobbying Against the ABM, 1967–1970." *Bulletin of the Atomic Scientists* 27 (Apr. 1971): 23–28.

4556 Hersh, Seymour M. "The Great ABM Pork Barrel." *War/Peace Report* 8 (Jan. 1968): 3–9, 19.

4557 Inglis, David R. "The Anti-Ballistic Missile: A Dangerous Folly." *Saturday Review* (Sept. 7, 1968): 26–27, 55–56.

4558 ———. "Antimissile Drag-Race." *Saturday Review* (Feb. 25, 1967): 36, 95.

4559 ———. "Conservative Judgment and Missile Madness." *Bulletin of the Atomic Scientists* 24 (May 1968): 6–11.

4560 ———. "Missile Defense, Nuclear Spread, and Vietnam." *Bulletin of the Atomic Scientists* 23 (May 1967): 49–52.

4561 Kalkstein, Marvin. "Anti-ABM." *Trans-Action* 6 (June 1969): 23–28.

4562 Lall, Betty Goetz. "ABM Decision: $40 Billion for Antimissile Establishmentarianism." *Commonweal* (Apr. 21, 1967): 144–47.

4563 Stone, Jeremy J. "ABM—The Next MLF?" *Bulletin of the Atomic Scientists* 22 (July 1966): 20–21.

4564 ———. "The Anti-Missile Folly." *New Leader* (Jan. 2, 1967): 13–15.

4565 ———. "Beginning of the Next Round?" *Bulletin of the Atomic Scientists* 23 (Oct. 1967): 20–25.

4566 ———. *The Case Against Missile Defense.* London: Institute for Strategic Studies, Apr. 1968.

4567 Wiesner, Jerome B. "The Argument Against ABM." *Current* 106 (Apr. 1969): 6–9.

4568 ———. The Case Against an Anti-Ballistic Missile System." *Look* (Nov. 28, 1967): 17–25.

ABM & SALT

4569 American Security Council. *U.S.S.R. vs. U.S.A.: The ABM and the Changed Strategic Military Balance.* Washington, D.C.: Acropolis Books, 1969.

4570 Lapp, Ralph E. "SALT Chips and Safeguard." *New Republic* (Aug. 15, 1970): 14–17.

4571 Long, Franklin A. "Strategic Balance and the ABM." *Bulletin of the Atomic Scientists* 24 (Oct. 1968): 2–5.

4572 Martin, Laurence W. "Ballistic Missile Defense and the Strategic Balance." *The Year Book of World Affairs, 1967.* New York: Praeger, 1967, pp. 37–54.

4573 Schneider, Mark B. "Safeguard, Sufficiency and SALT." *Military Review* 51 (May 1971): 24–33.

4574 Young, Elizabeth. "Prospects for SALT and the ABM Debate." *World Today* 25 (Aug. 1969): 323–28.

ABM & NPT

4575 Frank, Lewis A. "ABM and Non-Proliferation: Related Issues." *Orbis* 11 (Spring 1967): 67–79.

4576 Inglis, David R. "Nuclear Threats, ABM Systems, and Proliferation." *Bulletin of the Atomic Scientists* 24 (June 1968): 2–4.

4577 Pay, Rex. "ABM Would Imperil Test Ban Treaty." *Technology Week* (Mar. 20, 1967): 14–15.

4578 Rothstein, Robert L. "The ABM, Proliferation and International Stability." *Foreign Affairs* 46 (Apr. 1968): 487–502.

SALT: Nuclear Strategy

SALT & STRATEGY

4579 Alsop, Stewart. "Our New Strategy: The Alternatives to Total War." *Saturday Evening Post* (Dec. 1, 1962): 13–18.

4580 Aron, Raymond. *The Great Debate: Theories of Nuclear Strategy.* Garden City, N.Y.: Doubleday, 1965.

4581 Bothwell, Frank E. "Is the ICBM Obsolete?" *Bulletin of the Atomic Scientists* 25 (Oct. 1969): 21–22.

4582 Brennan, Donald G. "A Start on Strategic Stabilization." *Bulletin of the Atomic Scientists* 25 (Jan. 1969): 35.

4583 Brodie, Bernard. *Strategy in the Missile Age.* Princeton: Princeton Univ. Press, 1959.

4584 Brown, Neville. *Nuclear War: The Impending Strategic Deadlock.* New York: Praeger, 1964.

4585 Carpenter, William, et al. *U.S. Strategy in the Event of a Failure of Detente.* Stanford: Stanford Research Institute, May 1976.

4586 Carter, Barry. "Nuclear Strategy and Nuclear Weapons." *Scientific American* 230 (May 1974): 20–31.

4587 Coffey, Joseph I. *Strategic Power and National Security.* Pittsburgh: Univ. of Pittsburgh Press, 1971.

4588 Cohen, S. T. "U.S. Strategic Nuclear Policy: Do We Have One?—Should There Be One?"

Air University Review 26 (Jan.–Feb. 1975): 12–25.

4589 Feigl, Hubert. "Die Technischen Komponenten der Rustungsdynamik: Technologische Aspekte der Gespräche Über Beschränkungen der Strategischen Waffen." *Europa-Archiv* (Nov. 10, 1969): 757–68.

4590 Frank, Lewis A. "Soviet Power After SALT I: A Strategic-Coercive Capability?" *Strategic Review* 2 (Spring 1974): 54–60.

4591 Freistter, Franz. "Strategie und SALT." *Osterreichische Militarische Zeitschrift* 8 (Sept.–Oct. 1970): 363–69.

4592 Fryklund, Richard. *100 Million Lives: Maximum Survival in a Nuclear War.* New York: Macmillan, 1962.

4593 Halperin, Morton H. *Defense Strategies for the Seventies.* Boston: Little, Brown, 1971.

4594 Harkabi, Y. *Nuclear War and Nuclear Peace.* Jerusalem: Israel Program for Scientific Translations, 1966.

4595 Hoeber, Amoretta M. "Some Myths About the Strategic Balance." *Air University Review* 26 (July–Aug. 1975): 85–91.

4596 Holloway, Gen. Bruce K. "Reflections on Nuclear Strategy and the Nixon Doctrine." *Strategic Review* 1 (Spring 1973): 7–14.

4597 Holst, Johan J. *Comparative U.S. and Soviet Deployments, Doctrines, and Arms Limitation.* Occasional paper. Chicago: Univ. of Chicago, Center for Policy Study, 1971.

4598 Jacobs, Walter D. "Soviet Strategic Effectiveness." *Journal of International Affairs* 26:1 (1972): 60–72.

4599 Johnson, David, and Gene LaRocque. "The Mythology of National Defense." *Bulletin of the Atomic Scientists* 30 (Sept. 1974): 21–26.

4600 Kahan, Jerome H. *Security in the Nuclear Age: Developing U.S. Strategic Arms Policy.* Washington, D.C.: Brookings Institution, 1975.

4601 Kahn, Herman. *On Thermonuclear War.* New York: Free Press, 1960.

4601a ———. *Thinking About the Unthinkable.* New York: Avon, 1962.

4602 Kane, Francis X. "Criteria for Strategic Weapons." *Strategic Review* 2 (Spring 1974): 44–53.

4603 Kemp, Geoffrey. *Nuclear Forces for Medium Powers: Part 1: Targets and Weapon Systems.* Adelphi Paper, no. 106. London: International Institute for Strategic Studies, 1974.

4604 ———. *Nuclear Forces for Medium Powers.* Pts. 2, 3: *Strategic Requirements and Options.* Adelphi Paper, no. 107. London: International Institute for Strategic Studies, 1974.

4605 Kintner, William R., and Harriet F. Scott. *The Nuclear Revolution in Soviet Military Affairs.* Norman: Univ. of Oklahoma Press, 1968.

4606 Lambeth, Benjamin S. "The Evolving Soviet Strategic Threat." *Current History* 69 (Oct. 1975): 121–25 ff.

4607 Licklider, Roy E. *The Private Nuclear Strategists.* Columbus: Ohio State Univ. Press, 1971.

4608 Lodal, Jan N. "Assuring Strategic Stability: An Alternative View." *Foreign Affairs* 54 (Apr. 1976): 462–81.

4609 Nitze, Paul H. "Assuring Strategic Stability in an Era of Detente." *Foreign Affairs* 54 (Jan. 1976): 207–32.

4610 Ognibene, Peter J. "Nuclear Game Plan at the Pentagon." *Saturday Review* (Apr. 17, 1976): 14–20.

4611 Portisch, Hugo. *Friede durch Angst: Augenzeuge in den Arsenalen des Atomkrieges.* Wien: Verlag Fritz Molden, 1970.

4612 Rivkin, Steven R. *The Hobbled Weapon: A Second-Strike-Only Force.* Cambridge: M.I.T., Center for International Studies, Apr. 1961.

4613 Ruehl, Lothar. "Die Strategische Debatte in den Vereinigten Staaten: Zur Modifikation der Amerikanischen Nuklearstrategie und den Rustungspolitischen Forderungen fur SALT II." *Europa-Archiv* (Dec. 10, 1974): 787–98.

4614 Smith, Gerard C. "SALT and Strategies." *Congressional Record* (May 20, 1974): S8580–84.

4615 Stanley, Timothy W., and Darnell M. Whitt. "Tactical Nuclear Weapons and SALT." *Detente Diplomacy: United States and European Security in the 1970's.* Cambridge, Mass.: Dunellen, 1970, pp. 67–71.

4616   Stein, Arthur. *Strategic Doctrine for a Post-SALT World.* Occasional paper, no. 4. Ithaca: Cornell Univ., Peace Studies Program, 1973–74.

4617   Sullivan, Robert R. "ABM, MIRV, SALT and the Balance of Power." *Midwest Quarterly* 13 (Autumn 1971): 11–36.

4618   U.S. Senate. Committee on Armed Services. Hearings: *Status of U.S. Strategic Power.* 2 pts. 90th Cong., 2d Sess., 1968.

4619   ———. Committee on Foreign Relations. Hearings: *Nuclear Weapons and Foreign Policy.* 93d Cong., 2d Sess., 1974.

4620   ———. Hearings: *U.S.-U.S.S.R. Strategic Policies.* 93d Cong., 2d Sess., Mar. 4, 1974.

4621   Van Cleave, William R., and Roger W. Barnett. "Strategic Adaptability." *Orbis* 18 (Fall 1974): 655–76.

4622   Waskow, Arthur I., ed. *The Debate Over Thermonuclear Strategy.* Lexington, Mass.: D. C. Heath, 1965.

4623   ———. *The Limits of Defense.* Garden City, N.Y.: Doubleday, 1962.

4624   Widder, Robert L. "Launch on Warning: A Counter to the Arms Race." *Air University Review* 21 (Jan.–Feb. 1970): 95–100.

4625   Winne, Col. Clinton H., Jr. "SALT and the Blue-Water Strategy." *Air University Review* 25 (Sept.–Oct. 1974): 25–35.

SALT & DETERRENCE

4626   Alfheldt, Horst, and Philipp Sonntag. "Stability and Deterrence Through Strategic Nuclear Arms." *Journal of Peace Research* 10:3 (1973): 245–50.

4627   Barnaby, Frank. "Technology and the Myth of Deterrence." *New Scientist* (Sept. 24, 1970): 618–20.

4628   Benson, Charles. "Deterrence Through Defense." *National Review* (Mar. 9, 1971): 251–59.

4629   Bohn, Lewis C. "Questioning Our Nuclear Strategy: Reconsidering Nuclear Deterrence." *Current History* 64 (Feb. 1973): 42–56.

4630   Brodie, Bernard. "The Anatomy of Deterrence." *World Politics* 11 (Jan. 1959): 173–92.

4631   Brodie, Richard A. "Deterrence Strategies: An Annotated Bibliography." *Journal of Conflict Resolution* 4:4 (1960): 443–57.

4632   Burns, Arthur Lee. "From Balance to Deterrence: A Theoretical Analysis." *World Politics* 9 (July 1957): 494–529.

4633   Buzzard, Adm. Anthony W. "Massive Retaliation and Graduated Deterrence." *World Politics* 8 (Jan. 1956): 228–37.

4634   Coffey, Joseph I. *Deterrence in the 1970's.* Denver: Univ. of Denver, 1971.

4635   Eliot, George Fielding. "X Factors in Deterrence." *Military Review* 44 (Sept. 1964): 22–30.

4636   Elliot, James D. "Deterrence and the Art of War." *Military Review* 51 (Oct. 1971): 48–51.

4637   Fisher, Roger D. "Making Threats is Not Enough." In Frank N. Trager and P. S. Kronenberg, eds., *National Security and American Society.* Wichita: Univ. of Kansas Press, 1973.

4638   George, Alexander L., and Richard Smoke. *Deterrence in American Foreign Policy: Theory and Practice.* New York: Columbia Univ. Press, 1974.

4639   Gray, Colin S. "Unsafe at Any Speed: A Critique of 'Stable Deterrence' Doctrine." *Journal of the Royal United Services Institute for Defense Studies* 118 (June 1973): 23–27.

4640   Green, Philip. *Deadly Logic: The Theory of Nuclear Deterrence.* Columbus: Ohio State Univ. Press, 1966.

4641   Haas, Gerhard. "Kernwaffenstrategie und Ideologie." *Wehrkunde* 20 (Sept. 1971): 458–61.

4642   Ikle, Fred C. "Can Nuclear Deterrence Last Out the Century?" *Foreign Affairs* 51 (Jan. 1973): 267–85.

4643   Jackson, Sen. Henry M. "Credible Deterrence in a SALT II Environment." *Air Force Magazine* 56 (Jan. 1973): 44–46.

4644   Jones, Roy E. *Nuclear Deterrence.* London: Humanities Press, 1968.

4645   Junter, Douglas E. "Some Aspects of a Decision-Making Model in Nuclear Deterrence Theory." *Journal of Peace Research* 12:3 (1975): 209–22.

4646 Kahan, Jerome H. "Stable Deterrence: A Strategic Policy for the 1970's." *Orbis* 15 (Summer 1971): 528–43.

4647 Kang, Young Hoon. "The Relationship Between the Development of Strategic Nuclear Weapons Systems and Deterrence Doctrine in the Soviet Union and Communist China." Ph.D. diss., Univ. of Southern California, 1973.

4648 Kaplan, Morton A. "The Calculus of Nuclear Deterrence." *World Politics* 9 (Oct. 1958): 20–43.

4649 Knight, Jonathan. "Risks of War and Deterrence Logic." *Canadian Journal of Political Science* 6:1 (1973): 22–36.

4650 Kupperman, Robert A., et al. "The Deterrence Continuum." *Orbis* 18 (Fall 1974): 728–49.

4651 Lambeth, Benjamin S. "Deterrence in the MIRV Era." *World Politics* 24 (Jan. 1972): 234–42.

4652 Maccoby, Michael. "Social Psychology of Deterrence." *Bulletin of the Atomic Scientists* 17 (Sept. 1961): 278–81.

4653 Milburn, Thomas W. "What Constitutes Effective Deterrence?" *Journal of Conflict Resolution* 3:2 (1959): 138–45.

4654 Phipps, Thomas E. "The Case for Deterrence." *Current History* 42 (May 1962): 275–80.

4655 Reed, Col. Robert H. "On Deterrence: A Broadened Perspective." *Air University Review* 26 (May–June 1975): 2–17.

4656 Rosecrance, Richard N. *Strategic Deterrence Reconsidered.* Adelphi Paper, no. 116. London: International Institute for Strategic Studies, 1975.

4657 Schelling, Thomas C. *Arms and Influence.* New Haven: Yale Univ. Press, 1966.

4658 ———. "The Waning of Deterrence." *Perspectives in Defense Management* (Autumn 1973): 47–55.

4659 Singer, J. David. "From Deterrence to Disarmament." *International Journal* 16 (Autumn 1961): 307–26.

4660 ———. "Stable Deterrence and Its Limits." *Western Political Quarterly* 15 (Sept. 1962): 449–64.

4661 Slay, Alton D. "MX, A New Dimension in Strategic Deterrence." *Air Force Magazine* 59 (Sept. 1976): 44–49.

4662 Snyder, Glenn H. *Deterrence and Defense: Toward a Theory of National Security.* Princeton: Princeton Univ. Press, 1961.

4663 ———. *Deterrence By Denial and Punishment.* Princeton: Princeton Univ. Press, 1959.

4664 Steinbruner, John D. "Beyond Rational Deterrence: The Struggle for New Conceptions." *World Politics* 28 (Jan. 1976): 223–45.

4665 Thompson, Col. Roy L., and Ralph N. Hoffman, Jr. "The Triad and Beyond: The Future of Strategic Deterrence." *Air University Review* 25 (July–Aug. 1974): 9–16.

4666 U.S. Arms Control & Disarmament Agency. *Arms Control Implications of Uncertainties in Possible Nuclear Exchange.* ACDA Rpt. ST–166. Washington, D.C.: G.P.O., 1970.

4667 Waskow, Arthur I. *The Limits of Defense.* Garden City, N.Y.: Doubleday, 1962.

4668 Wohlstetter, Albert. "The Delicate Balance of Terror." *Foreign Affairs* 37 (Jan. 1958): 211–34.

Mutually Assured Destruction (MAD)

4669 Backus, Cmdr. Paul H. "The Vulnerable Homelands." *U.S. Naval Institute Proceedings* 96 (Dec. 1970): 18–22.

4670 Chester, Conrad V., and Eugene P. Wigner. "Population Vulnerability: The Neglected Issue in Arms Limitation and the Strategic Balance." *Orbis* 18 (Fall 1974): 763–69.

4671 LaRocque, Adm. Gene R. *Security Through Mutual Vulnerability.* Occasional paper 2. Muscatine, Ia.: Stanley Foundation, 1973.

4672 Lens, Sidney. "A Special Report: The Doomsday Strategy." *Progressive* (Feb. 1976): 12–35.

4673 Panofsky, Wolfgang K. H. "The Mutual Hostage Relationship Between America and Russia." *Foreign Affairs* 51 (Oct. 1973): 109–18.

4674 Perle, Richard N. "Mutually Assured Destruction as a Strategic Policy." *American Journal of International Law* 67 (Nov. 1973): 39–40.

4675   Rodbert, Leonard. "The Great American Doom Machine." *Ramparts* 12 (May 1974): 10–19.

4676   Ruina, Jack. "SALT in a MAD World." *New York Times Magazine* (June 30, 1974): 8, 42–51.

4677   Russett, Bruce M. "Assured Destruction of What? A Countercombatant Alternative to Nuclear Madness." *Public Policy* 22:2 (1974): 121–38.

4678   ———. "Short of Nuclear Madness." *Worldview* 15 (Apr. 1972): 31–37.

4679   Steinbruner, John D. "Strategic Vulnerability: The Balance Between Prudence and Paranoia." *International Security* 1 (Summer 1976): 138–81.

4680   York, Herbert F., et al. "A Center Symposium: Mutually Assured Destruction [MAD]: A Dialogue About Death." *Center Report* 6:4 (1973): 3–6.

Flexible Response

4681   Arbatov, G. A. "The American Strategic Debate: A Soviet View." *Survival* 16 (May-June 1974): 133–34.

4682   Baker, John C. "Flexibility: The Imminent Debate." *Arms Control Today* 4:1 (Jan. 1974): 1–2.

4683   Beavers, Cmdr. Roy L., Jr. "Counterforce or Countervalue." *U.S. Naval Institute Proceedings* 100 (Apr. 1974): 19–25.

4684   Bethe, Hans A. "Hard Point vs. City Defense." *Bulletin of the Atomic Scientists* 25 (June 1969): 25–26.

4685   Brooke, Sen. Edward W. "MIRV, SALT and Strategic Stability: A Dual Approach." *Congressional Record* 116 (July 29, 1970): S16385–388.

4686   ———. "President Nixon Makes Major Contribution to Strategic Restraint." *Congressional Record* 116 (Apr. 23, 1970): S12698–699.

4687   Carlin, Capt. Robert J. "A 400-Megaton Misunderstanding." *Military Review* (Nov. 1974): 3–12.

4688   Collins, John M. *Counterforce and Countervalue Options Compared: A Military Analysis Related to Deterrence.* Washington, D.C.: Library of Congress, Congressional Research Service, Dec. 7, 1972.

4689   Davis, Lynn E. *Limited Nuclear Options: Deterrence and the New American Doctrine.* Adelphi Paper, no. 121. London: International Institute for Strategic Studies, 1976.

4690   Drell, Sidney D., and Frank von Hippel. "Limited Nuclear War." *Scientific American* 235 (Nov. 1976): 27–37.

4691   Ellis, Gen. Richard H., and Col. Frank B. Horton III. "Flexibility—A State of Mind." *Strategic Review* 14 (Winter 1976): 26–36.

4692   Gray, Colin S. "Nuclear Strategy: The Debate Moves On." *Journal of the Royal United Services Institute for Defense Studies* 121 (Mar. 1976): 44–50.

4693   King, Peter. "The New American Nuclear Debate: Flexible Madness or Inflexible Sanity?" *Australian Outlook* 29 (Aug. 1975): 220–30.

4694   Korb, Lawrence J. "The Issues and Costs of the New United States Nuclear Policy." *Naval War College Review* 27 (Nov.–Dec. 1974): 28–41.

4695   Luttwak, Edward. "Nuclear Strategy: The New Debate." *Commentary* 57 (Apr. 1974): 53–59.

4696   Martin, Laurence. "Changes in American Strategic Doctrine—An Initial Interpretation." *Survival* 16 (July–Aug. 1974): 158–64.

4697   Mayer, Col. Laurel A., and Ronald J. Stupak. "The Evolution of Flexible Response in the Post-Vietnam Era: Adjustment or Transformation?" *Air University Review* 27 (Nov.–Dec. 1975): 11–21.

4698   McIntyre, Sen. Thomas J. "Nuclear Policy Debate." *Congressional Record* (Mar. 28, 1974): S4663–68.

4699   Rathjens, George W. "Flexible Response Options." *Orbis* 18 (Fall 1974): 677–88.

4700   Schneider, Mark B. "Nuclear Flexibility and Parity." *Air Force Magazine* 57 (Sept. 1974): 76–78.

4701   Scoville, Herbert, Jr. "Flexible Madness?" *Sane World* (May 1974): 48–52.

4702   Szilard, Leo. " 'Minimal Deterrent' vs. Saturation Parity." *Bulletin of the Atomic Scientists* 20 (Mar. 1964): 6–12.

4703 Tsipis, Kosta. "Physics and Calculus of Countercity and Counterforce Nuclear Attacks." *Science* (Feb. 7, 1975): 393–97.

4704 Warnke, Paul C. "Apes on a Treadmill." *Foreign Policy*, no. 18 (Spring 1975): 12–29.

Accuracy of Missiles

4705 Brown, Thomas A. "Missile Accuracy and Strategic Lethality." *Survival* 18 (Mar.–Apr. 1976): 52–59.

4706 Davis, Lynn E., and Warner R. Schilling. "All You Ever Wanted to Know About MIRV and ICBM Calculations but Were Not Cleared to Ask." *Journal of Conflict Resolution* 17 (June 1973): 207–42.

4707 Intriligator, Michael D. "The Debate over Missile Strategy: Targets and Rates of Fire." *Orbis* 11 (Winter 1968): 1138–59.

4708 McGlinchey, Col. Joseph J., and Jakob W. Seelig. "Why ICBMs Can Survive a Nuclear Attack." *Air Force Magazine* 57 (Sept. 1974): 82–85.

4709 Tsipis, Kosta. "The Accuracy of Strategic Missiles." *Scientific American* 233 (July 1975): 14–23.

Counterforce

4710 Albert, Bernard S. "Constructive Counterpower." *Orbis* 20 (Summer 1976): 343–66.

4711 Alberts, Capt. D. J. "Counterforce in an Era of Essential Equivalence." *Air University Review* 26 (Mar.–Apr. 1975): 27–37.

4712 Ball, Desmond. *Deja Vu: The Return to Counterforce in the Nixon Administration.* Santa Monica, Ca.: California Seminar on Arms Control & Foreign Policy, Dec. 1974.

4713 Brower, Michael. "Controlled Thermonuclear War." *New Republic* (July 30, 1962): 9–15.

4714 ———. "Nuclear Strategy of the Kennedy Administration." *Bulletin of the Atomic Scientists* 18 (Oct. 1962): 34–41.

4715 Collins, John M. "Maneuver Instead of Mass: The Key to Assured Stability." *Orbis* 18 (Fall 1974): 750–62.

4716 Foye, Raymond, and John B. Phelps. *Counter-Force Calculations: Attack and Retaliation with Mixed Weapons Systems.* Columbus, Ohio: Mershon National Security Program, Nov. 1959.

4717 Frisbee, John L. "Counterforce Revisited." *Air Force Magazine* 57 (Feb. 1974): 2.

4718 Gray, Colin S. "Rethinking Nuclear Strategy." *Orbis* 17 (Winter 1974): 1145–60.

4719 Greenwood, Ted, and Michael L. Nacht. "The New Nuclear Debate: Sense or Nonsense." *Foreign Affairs* 52 (July 1974).

4720 Halperin, Morton H. *Limited War in the Nuclear Age.* New York: Wiley, 1963.

4721 ———. "The 'No Cities' Doctrine." *New Republic* (Oct. 8, 1962): 155–70.

4722 Herrmann, Rene. "Schlesingers Konkretisierung der Strategie 'realistischer Abschreckung.'" *Europa-Archiv* (Apr. 10, 1974): 205–15.

4723 Hoeber, Amoretta M., and Francis P. Hoeber. "The Case Against the Case Against Counterforce." *Strategic Review* 3 (Fall 1975): 54–63.

4724 Johansen, Robert C. "Countercombatant Strategy: A New Balance of Terror?" *Worldview* 17 (July 1974): 47–53.

4725 Kaplan, Morton A. *The Strategy of Limited Retaliation.* Policy Memorandum no. 19. Princeton: Princeton Univ., Center of International Studies, Apr. 1959.

4726 Klare, Michael T. "Making Nuclear War 'Thinkable.'" *Nation* (Apr. 13, 1974): 461–66.

4727 Leghorn, Col. Richard S. "No Need to Bomb Cities to Win War." *U.S. News & World Report* (Jan. 28, 1955): 78–94.

4728 Lowe, George E. "Balanced Forces or Counterforces: Does It Make a Difference?" *U.S. Naval Institute Proceedings* 88 (Apr. 1962): 23–33.

4729 Maxfield, David M. "Limited Nuclear War: Sane or Suicidal?" *Congressional Quarterly Weekly Report* (Aug. 9, 1975): 1743–49.

4730 May, Michael M. "Some Advantages of a Counterforce Deterrence." *Orbis* 14 (Summer 1970): 271–83.

4731 Moore, Col. William C. "Counterforce: Facts and Fantasies." *Air Force Magazine* 57 (Apr. 1974): 49–52.

4732 Osgood, Robert E. "Kinds of Counterforce." *Survival* 5 (Jan.–Feb. 1963): 23–26.

4733 Schroeder, Rep. Pat. "Shooting at Empty Silos." *Washington Monthly* 6 (May 1974): 43–47.

4734 Sherman, Robert. "The Fallacies of Counterforce." *Strategic Review* 3 (Spring 1975): 48–57.

4735 Ulsamer, Edgar. "The Realities of Limited Strategic Options." *Air Force Magazine* 57 (July 1974): 79–84.

4736 ———. "Upgrading USAF's ICBM's for the Counterforce Role." *Air Force Magazine* 57 (Feb. 1974): 56–60.

4737 U.S. Senate. Committee on Foreign Relations. Hearings: *Briefing on Counterforce Attacks.* 93d Cong., 2d Sess., 1975.

4738 Wagstaff, Peter C. "An Analysis of Cities-Avoidance Theory." *Stanford Journal of International Studies* 7 (Spring 1972): 162–72.

4739 "Why the Big Shift in U.S. Missile Targets?" *U.S. News & World Report* (Jan. 1974): 30–31.

Consequences of Nuclear War

4740 Boffery, Philip M. "Nuclear War: Federation Disputes Academy on How Bad Effects Would Be." *Science* (Oct. 17, 1975): 248–50.

4741 Burns, E. L. M. "Thinking About the Unthinkable." *Bulletin of the Atomic Scientists* 32 (Jan. 1976): 42–43.

4742 Feld, Bernard T. "The Consequences of Nuclear War." *Bulletin of the Atomic Scientists* 32 (June 1976): 10–13.

4743 Medalia, Jonathan E. "The New Nuclear Strategy: Battle of the Dead?" *Defense Monitor* (July 1976): 1–8.

4744 U.S. Arms Control & Disarmament Agency. *World Wide Effects of Nuclear War . . . Some Perspectives.* Washington, D.C.: G.P.O., 1976.

4745 U.S. Senate. Committee on Foreign Relations. Report: *Analyses of Affects of Limited Nuclear Warfare.* 94th Cong., 1st Sess., 1975.

4746 Warshawsky, Capt. A. S. "Radiation Battlefield Casualties—Credible!" *Military Review* 56 (May 1976): 3–10.

Civil Defense

4747 Aspin, Rep. Les. "Soviet Civil Defense: Myth and Reality." *Arms Control Today* 6 (Sept. 1976): 1–2 ff.

4748 Broyles, Arthur A. "Civil Defense: The New Debate." *Survival* 18 (Sept.–Oct. 1976): 217–24.

4749 ———, et al. "Civil Defense in Limited War—A Debate." *Physics Today* 29 (Apr. 1976): 44–56.

4750 Goure, Leon. *War Survival in Soviet Strategy: USSR Civil Defense.* Washington, D.C.: Center for Advanced International Studies, Univ. of Miami, 1976.

4751 Scott, Harriet F. "Civil Defense in the U.S.S.R." *Air Force Magazine* 59 (Oct. 1975): 29–33.

4752 Smith, Brig. Gen. Lynn D. "Our Neglected Civil Defense." *Army* 26 (July 1976): 12–20.

4753 U.S. Congress. Joint Committee on Defense Production. Hearings: *Civil Defense and Limited Nuclear War.* 94th Cong., 2d Sess., 1976.

4754 U.S. House. Committee on Armed Services. Hearings & Report: *Civil Defense Review.* 94th Cong., 2d Sess., 1976.

First Strike

4755 Federation of American Scientists. "First Use Deserves More Than One Decision Maker." *F.A.S. Public Interest Report.* Washington, D.C., Sept. 1975.

4756 Huntington, Samuel P. "To Choose Peace or War: Is There a Place for Preventive War in American Policy?" *U.S. Naval Institute Proceedings* 83 (Apr. 1957): 359–69.

4757 Lapp, Ralph E. "Fear of a First-Strike." *New Republic* (June 28, 1969): 21–24.

4758 ———. "SALT, MIRV and First Strike." *Bulletin of the Atomic Scientists* 28 (Mar. 1972): 21–26.

4759 Leghorn, Col. Richard S. "Must the U.S. Take the First Blow?" *U.S. News & World Report* (Dec. 13, 1957): 54–59.

4760 Russett, Bruce M. "No First Use of Nuclear Weapons: To Stay the Fateful Lightning." *Worldview* 19 (Nov. 1976): 9–11.

4761 Scoville, Herbert, Jr. "A Soviet First Strike?" *New Republic* (Oct. 2, 1971): 17–19.

4762 Smith, Maj. Gen. Dale O. "Preventive War: An Essay." *Aerospace Historian* 13 (Spring 1966): 15–16.

4763 Talensky, Gen. Nikolai A. " 'Preventive War'—Nuclear Suicide." *International Affairs* [Moscow] 8 (Sept. 1962): 10–16.

Deterrence & History (Pre-SALT)

4764 Bullough, Vern, et al. *Military Deterrence in History.* New York: S.U.N.Y. Press, 1974.

4765 ———. "The Roman Empire vs. Persia, 363–502: A Study of Successful Deterrence." *Journal of Conflict Resolution* 7:1 (1963): 55–68.

4766 Lowe, George E. "Twentieth-Century Deterrents and Deterrence." *Virginia Quarterly Review* 46:1 (1970): 27–45.

4767 Moore, Col. William C. "History, Vietnam, and the Concept of Deterrence." *Air University Review* 20 (Sept.–Oct. 1969): 58–63.

4768 Naroll, Raoul. "Deterrence in History." In Dean G. Pruitt and Richard C. Snyder, eds., *Theory and Research on the Causes of War.* Englewood Cliffs, N.J.: Prentice-Hall, 1969, pp. 150–64.

4769 Quester, George H. *Deterrence Before Hiroshima.* New York: Wiley, 1966.

4770 ———. *Nuclear Diplomacy: The First Twenty-Five Years.* New York: Dunellen, 1970.

4771 Russett, Bruce M. "Pearl Harbor: Deterrence Theory and Decision Theory." *Journal of Peace Research* 4:2 (1967): 89–109.

4772 Wolk, Herman S. "Roots of Strategic Deterrence." *Aerospace Historian* 19 (Sept. 1972): 137–44.

Ethics & Deterrence

4773 Beaven, J. "Morality, Expedience and the Hydrogen Bomb." *Twentieth Century* 157 (Apr. 1955): 297–312.

4774 Bennett, John C., ed. *Nuclear Weapons and the Conflict of Conscience.* New York: Scribner's, 1962.

4775 Burns, Arthur Lee. *Ethics and Deterrence: A Nuclear Balance Without Hostage Cities?* Adelphi Paper, no. 69. London: International Institute for Strategic Studies, 1970.

4776 Douglass, James W. "The Morality of Thermo-Nuclear Deterrence." *Worldview* 7 (Oct. 1964): 4–8.

4777 Kaplan, Morton A., ed. *Strategic Thinking and Its Moral Implications.* Chicago: Univ. of Chicago Press, 1973.

4778 Miller, Raphael. "The Metaphysical World of Strategic Systems." *Bulletin of the Atomic Scientists* 24 (Oct. 1968): 18–22.

4779 O'Brien, William V. *Nuclear War, Deterrence and Morality.* Westminster: Newman, 1967.

4780 Stein, Walter, ed. *Nuclear Weapons and Christian Conscience.* London: Merlin, 1961.

4781 Weizsäcker, Carl F. "The Ethical Problem of Modern Strategy." *Problems of Modern Strategy.* New York: Praeger, 1970.

4782 Wertheimer, Alan. "Deterrence and Retribution." *Ethics* 86 (Apr. 1976): 181–99.

4783 Winters, Francis X. "Ethical Considerations and National Security Policy." *Parameters: Journal of the U.S. Army War College* 5:1 (1975): 17–25.

Nine

Demilitarization, Denuclearization & Neutralization

THESE THREE IDEAS—demilitarization, denuclearization, and neutralization—have certain similar characteristics. Essentially, they all are expressions of a *geographical* approach to arms control and disarmament; that is, the limitation of military forces is defined more in geographical than numerical terms. If demilitarization and denuclearization imply the possession of few, if any, military forces within a defined area, neutralization suggests a restriction on the aggressive or offensive potential of a nation. Thus, these ideas combine a geographical approach with a passive or defensive military posture.

Demilitarization, as J. H. Marshall-Cornwall points out in his excellent *Geographic Disarmament* (1935), is one of the oldest, and certainly most frequently employed, arms control techniques. Its purpose has been to remove military forces or fortification, which are potentially or actually destabilizing, from a specified geographical area. Some past and current examples of this technique include:

1. Demilitarization of seas and lakes—the Aegean Sea in the Peace of Callias (c. 448 B.C.), the Black Sea Convention, and the Great Lakes in the Rush-Bagot Agreement (1817).

2. Demilitarization of canals and straits—the Suez in the Convention of Constantinople (1881), the Strait of Magellan Treaty (1881), and the Turkish Straits in the Lausanne Convention (1923).

3. Demilitarization of islands—Aland Island Convention (1856, 1921), Spitsbergen (1920), non-fortification of the Pacific Islands (1922), and the Antarctic pact (1959).

4. Demilitarization of borders—Norway-Sweden in the Karlstad Convention (1905), Finland-Russia in the Treaty of Tartu-Dorpat (1920), and the Korean Demilitarized Zone (1953).

Denuclearization, or the creation of "nuclear-free zones," is a modern version of demilitarization. Its obvious objective is to keep nuclear weapons out of stipulated geographical regions. A fine recent survey of this method is William Epstein's essay, "Nuclear-free Zones," in *Scientific American* (Nov. 1975). This article—as well as Unto Vesa's "The Revival of Proposals for Nuclear-Free Zones," in *Instant Research on Peace and Violence* 5:1 (1975)—summarizes the U.N.'s special report (Aug. 28, 1975) on nuclear-free zones. While many proposals have been offered over the years, successful negotiations have been limited to the Denuclearization of Outer Space (1967) and the Latin America Denuclearization Treaty (1967).

Neutralization has been employed both as an arms control technique and a Cold War political maneuver. While both approaches are developed in C. E. Black, et al., *Neutralization and World Politics* (1968), the sources listed below focus on the use of this concept in the former sense, that is, the employment of neutralization as an announced policy which restricts a nation's military forces to self-defense. In some instances this policy consists of a unilateral declaration, in others it is recognized by a treaty. Finland and Sweden have sought to establish their neutralization by unilateral declaration, while Switzerland (1815), Belgium (1831), Austria (1955) and Laos (1962) have registered their neutrality by formal agreement.

DEMILITARIZATION

4784 Bentov, M. "Demilitarization and 'Secure Borders.' " *New Outlook* (May 1971): 9–12.

4785 Bing, Richard N. "The Role of the Developing Nations in the Formulation of International Controls for Unoccupied Regions: Outer Space, the Ocean Floor, and Antarctica." Ph.D. diss., Tufts Univ., 1972.

4786 Burton, John W. "Regional Disarmament: Southeast Asia." *Disarmament and Arms Control* 1 (Autumn 1963): 155–68.

4787 Dougherty, James E. "Zonal Arms Limitation in Europe." *Orbis* 7 (Fall 1963): 478–517.

4788 Grigoryev, T., and O. Efendiev. "The Gibraltar Conflict." [A demilitarization proposal]. *International Affairs* [Moscow] 15 (Oct. 1969): 86–89.

4789 Humphrey, Hubert H. "Regional Arms Control Agreements." *Journal of Conflict Resolution* 7:3 (1963): 265–71.

4790 Klimenko, Boris M. *Demilitarizatsiia i Neitralizatsiia v Mezhdunarodnom Prave.* Moscow: Izd-vo IMO, 1963.

4791 Kulebiakin, V. "The Moon and International Law." *International Affairs* [Moscow] 17 (Sept. 1971): 54–57.

4792 Marshall-Cornwall, Maj. Gen. James H. *Geographic Disarmament: A Study in Regional Demilitarization.* London: Humphrey Milford, 1935.

4793 Orear, Jay. "Safeguarded Zonal Disarmament." *Journal of Conflict Resolution* 7:3 (1963): 398–403. [Also in *International Affairs* (Moscow) 9 (Mar. 1963): 95–98.]

4794 Sohn, Louis B. "Disarmament and Arms Control by Territories." *Bulletin of the Atomic Scientists* 17 (Apr. 1961): 130–33.

4795 ———. "Disarmament and Arms Control by Territories." In E. W. Lefever, ed., *Arms and Arms Control.* New York: Praeger, 1962, pp. 209–18.

4796 ———. "Phasing of Arms Controls: The Territorial Method." In David H. Frisch, ed., *Arms Reduction: Program and Issues.* New York: Twentieth Century Fund, 1961, pp. 123–27.

4797 Stone, Betty. "Regional Disarmament." *Bulletin of the Atomic Scientists* 17 (Sept. 1961): 295.

4798 Talensky, Gen. Nikolai A. "Sincere?—Yes. Realistic?—No." [Zonal disarmament]. *International Affairs* [Moscow] 9 (Mar. 1963): 98–100.

4799 Yeremenko, A. "Modern Strategy and Border Conflicts." *International Affairs* [Moscow] 10 (Mar. 1964): 6–8.

DISENGAGEMENT

4800 Acheson, Dean G. "The Illusion of Disengagement." *Foreign Affairs* 36 (Apr. 1958): 371–82.

4801 Dwan, Col. John E., II. "The Anatomy of Disengagement." *Military Review* 42 (Feb. 1962): 2–15.

4802 Hinterhoff, Maj. Eugene. *Disengagement.* London: Stevens & Sons, 1959.

4803 Kennan, George F. "Disengagement and Disarmament." *Survival* 2 (Jan.–Feb. 1960): 20–24.

4804 ———. Disengagement Revisited." *Foreign Affairs* 37 (Jan. 1959): 187–210.

4805 ———. *Russia, the Atom and the West.* New York: Harper, 1957.

4806 Power, Paul F., ed. *Neutralism and Disengagement.* New York: Scribner's, 1964.

4807 Schmidt, Helmut. *Military Disengagement in Central Europe.* T–122. Santa Monica, Ca.: Rand, 1960.

DENUCLEARIZATION/NUCLEAR-FREE ZONES

4808 Bendix Corp. *An Examination of Nuclear-Free Zones with Emphasis on Africa and Scandinavia.* Ann Arbor, 1966.

4809 Druto, Jan. "Le Probleme de la Denuclearisation." *Revue Militaire Générale* 6 (Feb. 1968): 193–202.

4810 Epstein, William. "Nuclear-free Zones." *Scientific American* 233 (Nov. 1975): 25–35.

4811 Huerlin, Bertel. "Nuclear-Free Zones." *Cooperation and Conflict* 1 (1966): 11–30.

4812 Khamutov, N. "No Nuclear Weapons." *International Affairs* [Moscow] 9 (Aug. 1963): 112–13.

4813 Melnikov, D. "Denuclearized Zones." *New Times* [Moscow] (July 3, 1963): 13–15.

4814 Petrov, M. "Non-Nuclear Zones: A Pressing Demand." *International Affairs* [Moscow] 13 (June 1967): 12–16.

4815 Smartsey, A. "Nuclear-Free Zones are a Vital Necessity." *International Affairs* [Moscow] 10 (May 1964): 35–39.

4816 U.N. Conference of the Committee on Disarmament. *Special Report of the Conference . . . Transmitting a Comprehensive Study of the Question of Nuclear-Weapons-Free Zones in All of Its Aspects.* CCD/476. Geneva, Aug. 28, 1975.

4817 U.S. Arms Control & Disarmament Agency. *Operational System Guidelines to Verify a Nuclear Free Zone Agreement.* ACDA Rpt. WEC–101. 6 vols. Los Angeles: North American Aviation, 1967.

4818 Vesa, Unto. "The Revival of Proposals for Nuclear-Free Zones." *Instant Research on Peace and Violence* 5:1 (1975): 42–51.

Northern Europe & Arctic

4819 Apunen, Osmo. "A Nordic Nuclear-Free Zone: The Old Proposal or a New One?" *Yearbook of Finnish Foreign Policy, 1974.* Helsinki: Finnish Institute of International Affairs, 1974, pp. 42–49.

4820 Armstrong, Terence. "Arms Control in the Arctic." *Nature* [London] (May 29, 1965): 865–66.

4821 Brodin, Katarina. "Scandinavia and Nuclear-Free Zones." *Disarmament* 16 (Dec. 1967): 21–25.

4822 Holst, Johan J. "Arms Limiting and Force Adjusting Arrangements in the Northern Cap Area." *Cooperation and Conflict* 7:2 (1972): 113–20.

4823 ———. "Nordic Nuclear-Free Zone Today." *Bulletin of Peace Proposals* 6:2 (1975): 148–49.

4824 Joenniemi, Pertti. "Why a Nordic Nuclear-Free Zone?" *Bulletin of Peace Proposals* 6:2 (1975): 150–51.

4825 Korhonen, Keijo T. "Regional Arms Control in Europe: A Nordic Nuclear-Free Zone?" [Summarized in] *Bulletin of Peace Proposals* 6:1 (1975): 62.

4826 Mumford, Col. Jay C. "Problems of Nuclear Free Zones: The Nordic Example." *Military Review* 56 (Mar. 1976): 3–10.

4827 *A Nuclear-Free Zone and Nordic Security.* [Special issue of *Ulkopolitiikka* in English]. Helsinki: Finnish Institute of International Affairs, 1975.

4828 Rich, Alexander, and Aleksandr P. Vinogradov. "Arctic Disarmament." *Bulletin of the Atomic Scientists* 20 (Nov. 1964): 22–23.

4829 Teplinskii, B. "The Arctic, the Pentagon and NATO." *New Times* [Moscow] (Feb. 19, 1965): 6–9.

Far East

4830 Carthew, Alistair. "Pacific Nuclear-Free Zone: N.Z. Dream Slowly Fading." *Christian Science Monitor,* Jan. 9, 1976.

4831 Clunies-Ross, Anthony I., and Peter King. *Australia and Nuclear Weapons: The Case for a Non-Nuclear Region in South East Asia.* Sydney: Sydney Univ. Press, 1966.

4832 United Nations Draft Resolution. "A Nuclear-Free Zone in the South Pacific." *Survival* 18 (Jan.–Feb. 1976): 32–33.

4833 Vladimirov, K., and A. Yefremov. "Peace Zone in the Far East." *International Affairs* [Moscow] 5 (June 1959): 18–23.

Mediterranean

4834 Kafman, A. "The Mediterranean—Seat of Atomic Danger." *International Affairs* [Moscow] 9 (June 1963): 31–35.

4835 Lewis, Jesse W., Jr. *The Strategic Balance in the Mediterranean.* Washington, D.C.: American Enterprise Institute for Public Policy Research, 1976.

4836 Mijovie, Milorad. "Denuclearization of the Mediterranean Basin." *Review of International Affairs* [Belgrade] (Aug. 5, 1964): 7.

4837 Palmer, Michael, and David A. Thomas. "Arms Control and the Mediterranean." *World Today* 27 (Nov. 1971): 495–502.

4838 Vladimirov, A. "NATO Military Bases in the Mediterranean." *International Affairs* [Moscow] 9 (July 1963): 105–07.

4839 Zoppo, Ciro. *Naval Arms Control in the Mediterranean.* Santa Monica, Ca.: California Seminar on Arms Control & Foreign Policy, Aug. 1975.

Middle East

4840 Fontaine, Andre. "Why not Disarm the Middle East?" *Western World* (Oct. 1957): 17–19.

4841 Oren, Mordecai. "What Are the Reasons for an Atom-Free Middle East?" *Al Hamishmar* [Tel-Aviv] (July 15, 1966): 3. [JPRS 37, 197: Translations on the Near East, 19 (Israel), Aug. 24, 1966, pp. 22–29.]

4842 Oteifi, G. "The Demilitarization of Sinai." *Review of International Affairs* [Belgrade] 5 (May 1971): 10–12.

4843 Rubinstein, Amnon. "A Plan for the Sinai: Something Less than Peace in Return for Something Less than Total Withdrawal." *New York Times Magazine* (Jan. 17, 1971): 12–13, 32, 36–37, 39.

4844 Teltsch, Kathleen. "Iran Asks U.N. Action to Keep Region Free of Nuclear Arms." *New York Times,* July 13, 1974.

NEUTRALIZATION

4845 Bacot, Bernard. *Des Neutralités Durables: Origine, Domaine et Efficacité.* Paris: Recueil Sircy, 1946.

4846 Black, Cyril E., et al. *Neutralization and World Politics.* Princeton: Princeton Univ. Press, 1968.

4847 Fiedler, H. *Der Sowjetische Neutralitatsbegriff im Theorie und Praxis.* Verlag fur Politik im Wirtschaft, 1959.

4848 Ganiushkin, B. V. *Neitralitet i Reprisoedinenie.* Moscow: Mezhdunarodnye Otnosheniia, 1965.

4849 Graham, Malbone W., Jr. "Neutralization as a Movement in International Law." *American Journal of International Law* 21 (Jan. 1927): 79–94.

4850 Greene, Fred. "Neutralization and the Balance of Power." *American Political Science Review* 47 (Dec. 1953): 1041–57.

4851 Klenberg, Jan. *The Cap and the Straits: Problems of Nordic Security.* [Occasional Paper, no. 18.] Cambridge, Mass.: Center for International Affairs, 1968.

4852 Ogley, Roderick, comp. *The Theory and Practice of Neutrality in the Twentieth Century.* London: Routledge & K. Paul, 1970.

4853 Sherman, Gordon E. "The Permanent Neutrality Treaties." *Yale Law Journal* 24 (Jan. 1915): 217–41.

4854 Strupp, Karl. *Neutralisation, Befriedung, Entmilitarisierung.* Stuttgart: W. Kohlhammer, 1933.

4855 Wicker, Cyrus F. *Neutralization.* London: H. Frowde, 1911.

4856 Wildhaber, Luzius. "Die Mitgliedschaft Dauernd Neutraler Staaten im UNO-Sicherheitsrat." *Osterreichische Zeitschrift fur Aussenpolitik* 11:3 (1971): 131–45.

Finland & Sweden

4857 Bonsdorff, Goran von. "Finnlands Neutralitat zu Beginn der siebziger Jahre." *Osterreichische Zeitschrift fur Aussenpolitik* 11:2 (1971): 114–20.

4858 Brodin, Katarina, et al. "The Policy of Neutrality: Official Doctrines of Finland and Sweden." *Cooperation and Conflict* 1:1 (1968): 18–51.

4859 Erfurth, Sigfried. "Finnlands Politik der Neutralitat." *Wehrkunde* 17 (Sept. 1968): 457–59.

4860 Fannon, Peter M. "On Swedish Neutrality." *SAIS Review* 15:4 (1971): 11–14.

4861 Fried, Anne. "Finlandization Is Not a Curse Word." *Worldview* 16 (Jan. 1973): 17–21.

4862 Gaustad, Lt. Col. Peter J. "Swedish Neutrality: Its Impact on NATO." *Military Review* 54 (Apr. 1974): 46–53.

4863 Jakobson, Max. *Finnish Neutrality.* New York: Praeger, 1969.

4864 Jansson, Jan-Magnus. "La Neutralité de la Finlande: Ses Perspectives Européennes." *Politique Etrangère* 36:4 (1971): 361–72.

4865 Jonasson, Axel E. "The Crimean War, the Beginning of Strict Swedish Neutrality, and the Myth of Swedish Intervention in the Baltic." *Journal of Baltic Studies* 4:3 (1973): 244–53.

4866 Niu, Sien-chong. "Sweden and Switzerland: A Comparative Study." *NATO's Fifteen Nations* 11 (June–July 1966): 90–97.

4867 Orvik, Nils. *Sicherheit auf Finnisch: Finnland und die Sowjetunion.* Stuttgart: Seewald, 1972.

4868 Palme, Olof. "Sweden: Neutrality, Not Silence." *Vital Speeches* (July 15, 1970): 578–80.

4869 "What Finlandisation Means." *Economist* (Aug. 4, 1973): 15–16.

4870 Wuorinen, John H. *A History of Finland.* New York: Columbia Univ. Press, 1965, pp. 300–05, 472–78.

4871 ———. "Neutralism in Scandinavia." *Current History* 31 (Nov. 1956): 276–80.

4872 Zartman, I. William. "Neutralism and Neutrality in Scandinavia." *Western Political Quarterly* 5 (June 1954): 125–60.

Black Sea: Defortification & Demilitarization

Many of the accounts dealing with questions of the Turkish Straits allude to Black Sea demilitarization, including Ottoman and Russian defortification as far west as the Danubian basin.

4873 Anderson, M. S. *The Eastern Question, 1774–1923.* London: Macmillan, 1966.

4874 Baddeley, J. F. *The Russian Conquest of the Caucasus.* London: Longmans, Green, 1908.

4875 Chamberlain, Joseph P. *The Danube.* Washington, D.C., 1918.

4876 Marriott, J. A. R. *The Eastern Question: An Historical Study in European Diplomacy.* 4th ed. Oxford: Clarendon Press, 1947.

4877 Sumner, B. H. *Peter the Great and the Ottoman Empire.* Oxford: Blackwell, 1949.

TREATY OF THE PRUTH (1711)

For text of treaty, see J. C. Hurewitz, *Diplomacy in the Near and Middle East*, 2 vols. (Princeton: Van Nostrand, 1956), I: 39–40.

4878 Florinsky, Michael T., *Russia: A History and an Interpretation.* New York: Macmillan, 1953, pp. 335–45.

4879 Marriott, J. A. R. *The Eastern Question*, Oxford: Clarendon Press, 1918, pp. 129–37.

4880 Sumner, B. H. *Peter the Great and the Ottoman Empire*. Oxford: Blackwell, 1949, pp. 37–44.

4881 Ubersberger, Hans. *Russlands Orientpolitik in den letzten zwei Jahrhunderten*. Stuttgart: Deutsches Verlags-Anstalt, 1913, pp. 49–118.

TREATY OF ADRIANOPLE (1713)

For accounts of treaty, see Treaty of the Pruth, above.

TREATY OF BELGRADE (1739)

For text of treaty, see J. C. Hurewitz, *Diplomacy in the Near and Middle East*, 2 vols. (Princeton: Van Nostrand, 1956), I: 47–51.

Documents

4882 Laugier, Marc Antoine. *Histoire des Negociations pour la Paix Conclue a Belgrade le 18 Septembre 1739*. 2 vols. Paris: Chez La Veuve Duchesne, 1768.

General Accounts

4883 Fisher, Alan W. *The Russian Annexation of the Crimea, 1772–1783*. London: Cambridge Univ. Press, 1970, pp. 23–25.

4884 Marriott, J. A. R. *The Eastern Question*. Oxford: Clarendon Press, 1947, pp. 138–42.

4885 Roider, Karl A., Jr. *The Reluctant Ally: Austria's Policy in the Austro-Turkish War, 1737–1739*. Baton Rouge: Louisiana State Univ. Press, 1972.

4886 Vandal, Albert. *Une Ambassade Francaise en Orient sous Louis XV, la Mission du Marquis de Villeneuve, 1728–1741*. Paris: E. Plon, Mourrit et cie., 1887, ch. 7.

PEACE OF KUCHUK KAINARJI (1774)

For text of treaty, see J. C. Hurewitz, *Diplomacy in the Near and Middle East*, 2 vols. (Princeton: Van Nostrand, 1956), I: 54–61.

4887 Anderson, M. S. *The Eastern Question, 1774–1923*. London: Macmillan, 1966, pp. 1–27.

4888 ———. "Great Britain and the Russo-Turkish War of 1768–1774." *English Historical Review* 69 (Jan. 1954): 39–58.

4889 ———. "The Great Powers and the Russian Annexation of the Crimea, 1783–4." *Slavonic and East European Review* 37 (Dec. 1958): 17–41.

4890 Fisher, Alan W. "The Treaty of Kucuk Kaynarca, 1774." *The Russian Annexation of the Crimea, 1772–1783*. London: Cambridge Univ. Press, 1970, pp. 51–56, 105–11.

4891 Marriott, J. A. R. *The Eastern Question*. Oxford: Clarendon Press, 1947, pp. 142–54.

BLACK SEA CONVENTION (1856)

For text of convention, see J. C. Hurewitz, *Diplomacy in the Near and Middle East*, 2 vols. (Princeton: Van Nostrand, 1956), I: 153–56.

4892 Marriott, J. A. R. *The Eastern Question*. Oxford: Clarendon Press, 1947, pp. 275–80.

4893 Puryear, Vernon J. "The Straits and the Preliminaries of Peace." *England, Russia and the Straits Question, 1844–1856*. Berkeley: Univ. of California Press, 1931, pp. 340–433.

PONTUS TREATY (1871)

For text of treaty, see J. C. Hurewitz, *Diplomacy in the Near and Middle East*, 2 vols. (Princeton: Van Nostrand, 1956), I: 173–74; E. Hertslet, *Map of Europe by Treaty* (London: Harrison, 1875), II: 1892–97.

4894 Mosse, Werner E. "The End of the Crimea System: England, Russia and the Neutrality of the Black Sea, 1870–1871. *Historical Journal* 4:2 (1961): 164–90.

4895 Sumner, B. H. *Russia and the Balkans, 1870–1880*. Oxford: Clarendon Press, 1937.

Canals and Straits

4896 Baxter, Richard R. "Passage of Ships Through International Waterways in Time of

War." *British Year Book of International Law* 31 (1954): 192–202.

4897   Higgins, A. Pearce, and C. J. Colombos. "Straits and Artificial Canals." *International Law of the Sea.* 2d rev. London: Longmans, Green, 1951, pp. 130–47.

4898   Siegfried, Andre. *Suez and Panama.* London: Jonathan Cape, 1940.

4899   Woosey, Theodore S. "Suez and Panama: A Parallel." *American Historical Association, Annual Report* 1 (1902): 307–12.

STRAIT OF MAGELLAN TREATY (1881)

For text of treaty, see *American Journal of International Law: Supplement* 3 (1909): 121–22.

4900   Abribat, Jean Marie. *Le Detroit de Magellan: Au Point de Vue International.* Paris: A Chevalier-Maresco, 1902.

4901   Burr, Robert N. *By Reason or Force: Chile and the Balancing of Power in South America, 1830–1905.* Berkeley: Univ. of California Press, 1965, pp. 154–55.

4902   Encina, Francisco A. *Historia de Chile desde la Prehistoria Hasta 1891.* 20 vols. Santiago: Editorial Nascimento, 1949–1952, vol. 17, pp. 431–41.

4903   Guzman, Escudero. *La Situation Juridique Internationale des Eaux du Detroit de Magellan.* Santiago: Imprenta Nascimento, 1930.

PANAMA CANAL

A series of agreements between the U.S. and Great Britain, beginning with the Clayton-Bulwer Treaty, which demilitarized proposed canal sites, and concluding with the second Hay-Pauncefote Treaty and Hay-Bunau-Varilla Treaty, which omitted the nonfortification clause.

4904   Arias, Harmodio. *The Panama Canal: A Study in International Law and Diplomacy.* London: P. S. King & Son, 1911.

4905   Huberich, C. H. *The Trans-Isthmian Canal: A Study in American Diplomatic History.* Humanists Series, no. 1. Austin, Tex.: *Bulletin of the Univ. of Texas,* no. 26, 1904.

4906   Keasbey, Lindley M. "The National Canal Policy." *American Historical Association, Annual Report* 1 (1902): 275–88.

4907   Mack, Gerstle. *The Land Divided: A History of the Panama Canal and Other Isthmian Canal Projects.* New York: Octagon, 1944.

4908   Mathews, S. T. The Nicaragua Canal Controversy: The Struggle for an American-Constructed and Controlled Transitway." Ph.D. diss., Johns Hopkins Univ., 1949.

4909   Miner, Dwight Carroll. *The Fight for the Panama Route: The Story of the Spooner Act and the Hay-Herran Treaty.* New York: Columbia Univ. Press, 1940.

4910   Oppenheim, L. F. *The Panama Canal Conflict Between Great Britain and the United States of America: A Study.* Cambridge: Univ. Press, 1913.

4911   Whiteley, J. G. "The Diplomacy of the United States in Regard to Central American Canals." *North American Review* 165 (Sept. 1897): 364–78.

4912   Williams, Mary W. *Anglo-American Isthmian Diplomacy, 1815–1915.* Washington, D.C.: Carnegie Endowment for International Peace, 1916 [1965].

Clayton-Bulwer Treaty (1850)

For text of the agreement, see U.S. Department of State, *Papers Relating to the Foreign Relations of the United States, 1901* (Washington, D.C.: G.P.O., 1902), pp. 237–41.

4913   Bourne, K. "The Clayton-Bulwer Treaty and the Decline of British Opposition to the Territorial Expansion of the United States, 1857–1860." *Journal of Modern History* 33 (Sept. 1961): 287–91.

4914   Hayt, Edwin C. *National Policy and International Law: Case Studies from American Canal Policy.* Denver: Univ. of Denver, 1966, pp. 5–26.

4915   Travis, Ira D. *The History of the Clayton-Bulwer Treaty.* Ann Arbor: Michigan Political Science Assoc., Jan. 1900.

4916   Van Alstyne, Richard W. "British Diplomacy and the Clayton-Bulwer Treaty, 1850–1860." *Journal of Modern History* 11 (June 1939): 149–83.

4917 Williams, Mary W. *Anglo-American Isthmian Diplomacy, 1815–1915*. New York: Russell & Russell, 1965, pp. 67–109.

Hay-Pauncefote Treaty (1901)

For text of treaty, see U.S. Department of State, *Papers Relating to the Foreign Relations of the United States, 1901* (Washington, D.C.: G.P.O., 1902), pp. 243–46.

4918 Hains, Peter C. "Neutralization of the Panama Canal." *American Journal of International Law* 3 (Apr. 1909): 354–94.

4919 Kennedy, Crammond. "The Canal Fortification and the Treaty." *American Journal of International Law* 5 (July 1911): 620–38.

4920 Knapp, H. S. "The Real Status of the Panama Canal as Regards Neutralization." *American Journal of International Law* 4 (Apr. 1910): 314–58.

4921 Latane, John H. "Neutralization Features of the Hay-Pauncefote Treaty." *American Historical Association, Annual Report* 1 (1902): 289–303.

4922 Mahan, Adm. Alfred T. "Fortify the Panama Canal." *North American Review* 193 (Mar. 1911): 331–39.

4923 Mowat, Robert B. *The Life of Lord Pauncefote*. Glasgow: Univ. Press, 1920, pp. 276–91.

4924 Olney, Richard. "Fortification of the Canal." *American Journal of International Law* 5 (Apr. 1911): 298–301.

4925 Padelford, Norman J. "American Rights in the Panama Canal." *American Journal of International Law* 34 (July 1940): 416–42.

4926 Siegfried, Andre. "The Canal and Its Military Defense." *Suez and Panama*. London: Jonathan Cape, 1940, pp. 370–82.

4927 Wambaugh, Eugene. "The Right to Fortify the Panama Canal." *American Journal of International Law* 5 (July 1911): 615–19.

CONVENTION OF CONSTANTINOPLE (1881)

For text of convention, and other treaties affecting the neutralization of the Suez Canal, see Sir Thomas E. Holland, *European Concert in the Eastern Ques-* *tion* (Oxford: Clarendon Press, 1885), pp. 60–69; J. C. Hurewitz, *Diplomacy in the Near and Middle East*, 2 vols. (Princeton: Van Nostrand, 1956), I: 201–05.

4928 Buell, Raymond L. "The Suez Canal and League Sanctions." *Geneva Special Studies* 6:3 (1935): 1–18.

4929 Hallberg, Charles W. *The Suez Canal: Its History and Diplomatic Importance*. New York: Columbia Univ. Press, 1931 [1974], pp. 278–349.

4930 Hoskins, H. L. "The Suez Canal as an International Waterway." *American Journal of International Law* 37 (July 1943): 373–85.

4931 Obieta, Joseph A. *The International Status of the Suez Canal*. The Hague: Nijhoff, 1960.

4932 Schonfield, Hugh J. *The Suez Canal in Peace and War, 1869–1969*. Coral Gables, Fla.: Univ. of Miami Press, 1969, pp. 44–74.

4933 *The Suez Canal: A Selection of Documents . . . November 30, 1954–July 26, 1956*. London: Society of Comparative Legislation & International Law, 1956.

LAUSANNE CONVENTION (1923)

For this demilitarization of the straits, see Turkish Straits, Treaty of Lausanne (1923).

Individual Treaties

PEACE OF CALLIAS (c. 448 B.C.)

For text of agreement, see Wade-Gerry, Henry T. "The Peace of Kallias," or Eddy, Samuel K. "On the Peace of Callias," below.

4934 Burn, Andrew R. *Persia and the Greeks: The Defense of the West, c. 546–478 B.C.* New York: St. Martin's Press, 1962, p. 563.

4935 Bury, John B. *A History of Greece to the Death of Alexander the Great*. Revised by Russell Meiggs. 3d ed. London: Macmillan, 1956, pp. 572–73.

4936 ———, et al. *Cambridge Ancient History*. 12 vols. London: Cambridge Univ. Press, 1927, V: 86–87, 470.

4937   Eddy, Samuel K. "On the Peace of Callias." *Classical Philology* (Jan. 1971): 9–14.

4938   Hammond, N. G. L. *A History of Greece to 322 B.C.* Oxford: Clarendon Press, 1959, pp. 301–03.

4939   Murison, C. L. "The Peace of Callias: Its Historical Context." *Phoenix* 25:1 (1971): 12–31.

4940   Wade-Gerry, Henry T. "The Peace of Kallias." *Essays in Greek History.* Oxford: Blackwell, 1958, pp. 201–32.

DECLARATION OF SWISS NEUTRALITY (1815)

For text of treaty guaranteeing Swiss neutrality, see Edmond Hertslet, *Map of Europe by Treaty*, 2 vols. (London: Harrison, 1875), I: 370–71.

4941   Bonjour, Edgar. *Swiss Neutrality: Its History and Meaning.* London: Allen & Unwin, 1946.

4942   D'Arcis, Max. *The Diplomatic Position of Switzerland.* Geneva: Radar Editions, n.d.

4943   Gibson, Hugh. "Switzerland's Position in Europe." *Foreign Affairs* 4 (Oct. 1925): 72–84.

4944   Grieve, W. P. "The Present Position of 'Neutral' States." *Transactions of the Grotius Society* 33 (1947): 100–102, 115–18.

4945   Hofer, Walther. *Neutrality as the Principle of Swiss Foreign Policy.* Trans. by M. Hattinger. Zurich: Schweizer Spiegel Verlag, 1957.

4946   McCrackan, W. D. *The Rise of the Swiss Republic.* Boston: Arena Publishing, 1892, pp. 354–63.

4947   Pointet, Pierre J. *La Neutralité de la Swisse et la Liberté de la Presse.* Zurich: Editions Polygraphiques, 1945.

4948   Robert, Denise. *Etude sur la Neutralité Swisse.* Zurich: Editions Polygraphiques, 1950.

4949   Vergotti, Jacques M. *La Neutralité de la Swisse.* Lausanne: Imprimerie la Concorde, 1954.

ANGLO-FRENCH TREATY (1713)

For text of treaty, which orders defortification of Dunkirk, and which is part of the Peace of Utrecht, see Fred L. Israel, *Major Peace Treaties of Modern History, 1648–1967*, 4 vols. (New York: Chelsea House 1967), I: 207.

4950   Broderick, Thomas. *A Complete History of the Late War in the Netherlands Together with an Abstract of the Treaty of Utrecht.* London: Printed for William Pearson by Thomas Ward in the Inner-Temple Lane, 1713.

4951   *The Compleat History of the Treaty of Utrecht, As also that of Gertruydenberg Containing All the Acts, Memorials, Representations, Complaints, Demands, Letters, Speeches, Treaties, Negotiations there to which are added the Treaties of Radstat and Baden.* 2 vols. London: Printed for A. Roper & S. Butler, next Bernard's Inn in Helborn, 1715.

4952   Gerard, James W. *The Peace of Utrecht.* New York: Putnam's, 1885.

4953   Steele, Sir Richard. *The Importance of Dunkirk Considered in Defence of the Guardian of August the 7th in a Letter to the Bailiff of Stockbridge.* London: Printed for A. Baldwin in Warwick-Lane, 1713.

4954   Toland, John(?). *Dunkirk or Dover: Or the Queen's Honour, The Nation's Safety, the Liberties of Europe, and the Peace of the World, All at Stake till that Fort or Port be Totally Demolished by the French.* London: Printed for A. Baldwin, near the Oxford-Arms in Warwick-Lane, 1713.

4955   Ward, A. W., et al., eds. *The Cambridge Modern History.* Vol. 5: *The Age of Louis XIV.* New York: Macmillan, 1908, pp. 437–43.

RUSH-BAGOT AGREEMENT (1817)

For text of "exchange of notes" regarding demilitarization of the Great Lakes, see David Hunter Miller, ed., *Treaties and Other International Acts of the United States of America* (Washington, D.C.: G.P.O., 1931), II: 645–54.

Documents

4956 Lowie, Walter, and W. S. Franklin, comps. *American State Papers & Foreign Relations: Documents Legislative and Executive of the Congress of the United States.* Washington, D.C.: G.P.O., 1934, IV: 203–06.

4957 U.S. Department of State. "Construction of Naval Vessels on the Great Lakes." *Treaties and Other International Acts Series.* No. 1836. Washington, D.C.: G.P.O., 1949, pp. 1–17.

4958 ———. "Naval Vessels on the Great Lakes." *U.S. Department of State Bulletin* (Mar. 15, 1941): 366–72.

General Accounts

4959 Boutell, Henry S. "Is the Rush-Bagot Convention Immortal?" *North American Review* 173 (Sept. 1902): 331–48.

4960 Callahan, James M. "Agreement of 1817: Reduction of Naval Forces upon the American Lakes." *Annual Report of the American Historical Association for the Year 1895.* Washington, D.C., 1896, pp. 369–92.

4961 ———. *The Neutrality of the American Great Lakes and Anglo-American Relations.* Baltimore: Johns Hopkins Univ., Studies in Historical & Political Sciences, 1898.

4962 Crosby, Ernest. "A Precedent for Disarmament." *North American Review* (Oct. 19, 1906): 776–79.

4963 Eayrs, James. "Arms Control on the Great Lakes." *Disarmament and Arms Control* 2 (Autumn 1964): 373–404.

4964 Falk, Stanley L. "Disarmament on the Great Lakes: Myth or Reality?" *U.S. Naval Institute Proceedings* 87 (Dec. 1961): 69–73.

4965 Foster, John W. *Limitation of Armament on the Great Lakes.* Washington, D.C.: Carnegie Endowment for International Peace, 1914.

4966 Hitsman, J. M. *Safeguarding Canada, 1763–1871.* Toronto: Univ. of Toronto Press, 1968.

4967 Levermore, Charles H. *Disarmament on the Great Lakes.* Boston: World Peace Foundation, 1914.

4968 McInnis, Edgar W. *The Unguarded Frontier: A History of American-Canadian Relations.* New York: Doubleday, Doran, 1942.

4969 Stacy, C. P. "The Myth of the Unguarded Frontier, 1815–1871." *American Historical Review* 56 (Oct. 1950): 1–18.

NEUTRALIZATION OF BELGIUM (1831)

For texts of inter-related treaties (1831–1839), see Edmond Hertslet, *Map of Europe by Treaty*, 2 vols. (London: Harrison, 1875), II: 856–57, 881–84, 979–93.

General Accounts

4970 Berthrong, Merrill G. "Disarmament in European Diplomacy, 1816–1870." Ph.D. diss., Univ. of Pennsylvania, 1958, ch. 2.

4971 Cecil, Algernon. *British Foreign Secretaries, 1807–1916.* New York: Putnam's, 1927, pp. 139–47.

4972 Frank, R. *Die Belgische Neutralitat.* Tubingen: J. C. B. Mohr, 1915.

4973 Great Britain. Foreign Office. *Neutrality of Belgium.* (Handbook no. 20) London: H.M.S.O., 1920.

4974 Hyde, Charles C. "Belgium and Neutrality." *American Journal of International Law* 31 (Jan. 1937): 81–85.

4975 Lingelbach, William E. "Belgian Neutrality: Its Origins and Interpretation." *American Historical Review* 39 (Oct. 1933): 48–72.

4976 Waxweiller, Emile. *Belgium and the Great Powers: Her Neutrality Explained and Vindicated.* New York: Knickerbocker Press, 1916, pp. 118–54.

4977 Webster, Sir Charles K. *The Foreign Policy of Palmerston, 1830–1841: Britain, the Liberal Movement and the Eastern Question.* 2 vols. New York: Humanities Press, 1969, I; 89–176.

World War I & Termination

Neutrality of Belgium was abandoned by the Treaty of Versailles, see Articles 31–40.

4978   Fuehr, Karl A. *The Neutrality of Belgium: A Study of the Belgian Case and its Aspects in Political History and International Law.* New York: Funk & Wagnalls, 1915.

4979   Garner, James W. "The German Invasion of Belgium." *International Law in the World War.* 2 vols. New York: Longmans, Green, 1920, I: 186–231.

4980   LeRoy, Andre R. *L'Abrogation de la Neutralite de la Belgique, ses Causes et ses Effets.* Paris, 1923.

4981   Norden, F. *Neutral Belgium and Germany.* Brussels: Richard Press, 1915.

4982   Waxweiller, Emile. *Belgium: Neutral and Loyal.* New York: Knickerbocker Press, 1915.

KARLSTAD CONVENTION (1905)

For text of convention between Norway and Sweden which demilitarized their border, see *American Journal of International Law: Official Documents* 1 (1907): 171–73.

4983   Hellner, Johannes. "La Conference de Carlstad d'Aout-Septembre 1905." *Le Nord* 3 (1940): 30–51.

4984   "The Karlstad Convention." *Nation* (Oct. 12, 1905): 295–96.

4985   Larsen, Karen. *A History of Norway.* Princeton: Princeton Univ. Press, 1948, pp. 484–92.

4986   Lindgren, Raymond E. "The Karlstad Conference." *Norway-Sweden: Union, Disunion, and Scandinavian Integration.* Princeton: Princeton Univ. Press, 1959, pp. 172–94.

4987   Vogt, Benjamin. "Les Negociations de Carlstad, 1905." *Le Nord* 3 (1940): 52–63.

TREATY OF VERSAILLES (1919)

For text of treaty reference, see Treaty of Versailles in Chapter 7. That section also contains references to documents, general sources, etc.

General Accounts

4988   Burns, Richard Dean, and Donald Urquidi. "The Versailles Treaty and Territorial De-

militarization." *Disarmament In Perspective 1919–1939.* 4 vols. ACDA Rpt. RS–55. Washington, D.C.: G.P.O., 1968, I: 60–86.

4989   Seymour, Charles. "Geography, Justice and Politics at the Paris Conference of 1919." In Ivo J. Lederer, ed., *The Versailles Settlement.* Boston: Heath, 1960.

Rhineland

4990   Czernin, Ferdinand. *Versailles, 1919.* New York: Putnam's, 1964, pp. 228–66.

4991   Dawson, William H. *Germany Under the Treaty.* London: Allen & Unwin, 1933, pp. 17–21, 64–65.

4992   Haskins, Charles H., and Robert H. Lord. *Some Problems of the Peace Conference.* Cambridge: Harvard Univ. Press, 1920, pp. 105–14, 128–32.

4993   League of Nations. "[Council Resolution Condemning Germany's Violation of Rhineland.]" *Official Journal* 17 (Apr. 1936): 340.

4994   Loury, Francis B. "The Generals, the Armistice, and the Treaty of Versailles, 1919." Ph.D. diss., Duke Univ., 1963, pp. 355–411.

4995   Tardieu, André. *The Truth About the Treaty.* London: Hodder & Stoughton, 1921, pp. 145–202, 233–49.

Saar

4996   Dawson, William H. *Germany Under the Treaty.* London: Allen & Unwin, 1933, pp. 300–27.

4997   Haskins, Charles H., and Robert H. Lord. *Some Problems of the Peace Conference.* Cambridge: Harvard Univ. Press, 1920, pp. 142–50.

4998   Kahlman, Richard von. "The Future of the Saar." *Foreign Affairs* 12 (Apr. 1934): 426–35.

4999   League of Nations. "Demilitarization of the [Saar] Territory." *Official Journal* 16 (Apr. 1935): 527–29.

5000   Tardieu, André. *The Truth About the Treaty.* London: Hodder & Stoughton, 1921, pp. 250–79.

Baltic Channel

5001   Czernin, Ferdinand. *Versailles, 1919.* New York: Putnam's, 1964, pp. 201–27.

5002   Dawson, William H. *Germany Under the Treaty.* London: Allen & Unwin, 1933, pp. 93–174.

5003   Jordan, W. M. "Great Britain, France and the Eastern Frontiers of Germany." In Ivo J. Lederer, ed., *The Versailles Settlement.* Boston: Heath, 1960, pp. 73–77.

5004   Martel, Rene. *The Eastern Frontier of Germany.* London: Williams & Norgate, 1930.

Heligoland

5005   Haskins, Charles H., and Robert H. Lord. *Some Problems of the Peace Conference.* Cambridge: Harvard Univ. Press, 1920, pp. 46–47.

TREATY OF TARTU (DORPAT) (1920)

For text of treaty between Finland and Russia, which demilitarized several areas along their border, see Leonard Shapiro, ed., *Soviet Treaty Series,* 2 vols. (Washington, D.C.: Georgetown Univ. Press, 1950–1955), I: 69–75. Revised by the Convention of Helsingfors (June 1, 1922) or the Russo-Finnish Convention of 1922.

5006   Burns, Richard Dean, and Donald Urquidi. "The Russo-Finnish Treaty of October, 1920." *Disarmament in Perspective, 1919–1939.* 4 vols. Washington, D.C.: G.P.O., 1968, II: 1–26.

5007   Condon, Richard W. "The Moscow Parenthesis: A Study of Finnish-German Relations, 1940–1941." Ph.D. diss., Univ. of Minnesota, 1969.

5008   Holsti, Kalevi J. "The Origins of Finnish Foreign Policy, 1918–1922: Rudolf Holsti's Role in the Formulation of Policy." Ph.D. diss., Stanford Univ., 1961.

5009   Screen, J. E. D. *Mannerheim: The Years of Preparation.* London: C. Hurst, 1970.

5010   Smith, Clarence J. *Finland and the Russian Revolution, 1917–1922.* Athens: Univ. of Georgia Press, 1958.

5011   Wuorinen, John H. *A History of Finland.* New York: Columbia Univ. Press, 1965, pp. 224–26, 306–12, 344–50.

SPITSBERGEN CONVENTION (1920)

For text of convention, see League of Nations, *Treaty Series* (London: Harrison, 1921), III, no. 1, p. 8.

5012   Burns, Richard Dean, and Donald Urquidi. "Insular Arms Control: Spitsbergen and the Aland Islands." *Disarmament In Perspective, 1919–1939.* 4 vols. Washington, D.C.: G.P.O., 1968, II: 27–63.

5013   Gray, Louis H. *Spitsbergen and Bear Island.* Washington, D.C.: G.P.O., 1919.

5014   Great Britain. Foreign Office. [Historical Section Handbooks, no. 36.] *Spitsbergen.* London: H.M.S.O., 1919.

5015   Mathisen, Trygve. *Svalbard in the Changing Arctic.* Oslo: Gyldendal, 1954.

5016   ———. *Svalbard i Internasjonal Politiikk, 1871–1925.* Oslo: Aschahoug, 1951.

5017   ———. *Svalbard in International Politics: The Solution of a Unique International Problem.* Oslo: Kommisjon hos Broggers bokte Forlag, 1954.

5018   Rabot, Charles. *A Qui Doit Appartenir le Spitsberg?* Paris: Masson, 1919.

5019   Stael-Holstein, Baron Lage Fapian Wilhelm. *Norway in Arcticum: From Spitsbergen to Greenland?* Copenhagen: Levin & Munksgaard, 1932.

5020   Teal, John J., Jr. "Europe's Northernmost Frontier." *Foreign Affairs* 29 (Jan. 1951): 263–75.

ALAND ISLANDS CONVENTION (1921)

Nonfortification of the Aland Islands was considered in negotiations for Treaty of Fredrikshamm (1809) and were first accepted in the Aland Islands Convention to the Treaty of Paris (1856). This concept was restated in the Brest-Litovsk Treaty (1918), in the Aland Islands agreement (1918), and in the 1921 convention. For text of this convention, see *American Journal of International Law; Supplement* 17 (1923): 1–6.

Documents

5021 League of Nations. *The Aaland Islands Question: Report Submitted to the Council of the League of Nations by the Commission of Rapporteurs.* Document de Conseil B7.21/68/106, Genève, le 16 Avril 1921. Geneva: Imprimerie Kundig, 1921.

5022 ———. "Report of International Committee of Jurists." *Official Journal* [Special Supplement no. 3] (Oct. 1920).

General Accounts

5023 Anderson, Otto. *Les Origines de la Question d'Aland: l'Aland en 1917–18.* Helsingfors: Imprimerie du Gouvernement, 1920.

5024 Barros, James. *The Aland Island Question: Its Settlement by the League of Nations.* New Haven: Yale Univ. Press, 1968.

5025 Bellquist, Eric C. "Some Aspects of Recent Foreign Policy of Sweden." *University of California International Relations Publications* 1:3 (1929): 289–301.

5026 Brown, Philip M. "The Aaland Islands Question." *American Journal of International Law* 15 (Apr. 1921): 268–72.

5027 Condon, Richard W. "The Moscow Parenthesis: A Study of Finnish-German Relations, 1940–41." Ph.D. diss., Univ. of Minnesota, 1969.

5028 Cullberg, Albin. *La Politique du Roi Oscar I, Pendant la Guerre de Crimée.* 2 vols. Stockholm: Författarens, 1912–1926.

5029 Danielson-Kalmari, J. R. *La Question des Iles d'Aland de 1914 a 1920.* Helsinki: Imprimerie du Gouvernement, 1921.

5030 "The Fortification of the Aland Islands." *American Journal of International Law* 2 (Apr. 1908): 397–98.

5031 Great Britain. Foreign Office. [Historical Section Handbooks.] *The Aland Islands.* London: H.M.S.O., 1920.

5032 Gregory, Charles N. "The Neutralization of the Aaland Islands." *American Journal of International Law* 17 (Jan. 1923): 64–76.

5033 League of Nations. "Aaland Islands [nonfortification and neutralization]." *Official Journal* 2 (Feb. 1922): 124–25.

5034 ———. "The Aaland Islands Question." *Official Journal* 2 (Sept. 1921): 691–705.

5035 ———. "Convention of 1921 for the Nonfortification and Neutralization of the Aland Islands: Measures Proposed by the Finnish and Swedish Governments." *Official Journal* 20 (May–June 1939): 257–60, 279–82, 284–89; 20 (Nov.–Dec. 1939): 509–42.

NONFORTIFICATION OF PACIFIC ISLANDS (1922)

For information regarding nonfortification of the Mandated Pacific Islands at the Washington Conference, see Washington Naval Treaty (1922) in Chapter 7.

KOREAN DEMILITARIZED ZONE (1953)

For information regarding the demilitarized zone created by the Korean Armistice Commission, see Korean Military Armistice (1953), Chapter 7.

VIETNAM DEMILITARIZED ZONE (1954)

For information regarding the demilitarized zone created by the Geneva Accords, see Geneva Accords on Indochina (1954 & 1973), Chapter 7.

AUSTRIAN STATE TREATY (1955)

For text of treaty, see U.S. Department of State, *United States Treaties and Other International Agreements* (Washington, D.C., 1955), VI, pt. 2, pp. 2369–535.

5036 Allard, Sven. *Russia and the Austrian State Treaty: A Case Study of Soviet Policy in Europe.* University Park: Pennsylvania State Univ. Press, 1970.

5037 Bader, William B. *Austria Between East and West, 1945–1955.* Stanford: Stanford Univ. Press, 1966.

5038 Ducos-Adler, Robert. "The Treaty Re-Establishing an Independent and Democratic Austrian State Signed at Vienna on 15 May 1955." *Journal du Droit International* [Paris] 83 (Apr.–June 1956): 293–379.

5039 Ewing, Blair G. *Peace Through Negotiation: The Austrian Experience.* Washington, D.C.: Public Affairs Press, 1966.

5040 Ferring, Robert L. "The Austrian State Treaty of 1955 and the Cold War." *Western Political Quarterly* 21 (Dec. 1968): 651–67.

5041 Grayson, Cary T., Jr. *Austria's International Position, 1938–1953: Re-Establishment of an Independent Austria.* Geneva: Librairie E. Droz, 1953.

5042 Gruber, Karl. *Between Liberation and Liberty.* Trans. by Lionel Kochan. London: Andre Deutsch, 1955.

5043 Hartel, Gunther E. *Austria: History of Allied Occupation, 1945–1955.* New York: J. Obolensky, 1962.

5044 Huemer, Oskar. "Active Policy of Neutrality." *Review of International Affairs* (Nov. 20, 1966): 16–17.

5045 Kunz, Josef L. "Austria's Permanent Neutrality." *American Journal of International Law* 50 (Apr. 1956): 418–25.

5046 ———. "The State Treaty With Austria." *American Journal of International Law* 49 (Oct. 1955): 535–42.

5047 Mosely, Philip E. "The Treaty With Austria." *International Organization* 4 (May 1950): 219–35.

5048 Murillo Rubiera, Fernando. "El Tratado de Estado Austriaco." *Cuadernos de Politica Internacional* [Madrid] 22 (1955): 17–43.

5049 O'Hara, Michael N. "Negotiating with the Russians: The Case of the Austrian State Treaty." Ph.D. diss., Univ. of California, Los Angeles, 1971.

5050 Seidl-Hohenveldern, Ignaz. "Die Wiederherstellung der vollen Unabhangigkeit Osterreichs durch den Staatsvertrag vom 15. Mai 1955." *Europa-Archiv* (Apr. 20, 1956): 8741–72.

5051 Siegler, Heinrich von. *Austria: Problems and Achievements, 1945–1963.* Bonn: Siegler, 1965.

5052 Verdross, Albert. "Austria's Permanent Neutrality and the United Nations Organization." *American Journal of International Law* 50 (Jan. 1956): 61–68.

5053 Waldheim, Kurt. *Der osterreichische Weg Aus der Isolation Zur Neutralitat.* Wien: Molden, 1971.

RAPACKI PROPOSALS (1957, 1962)

This idea centers on proposals made by Polish Foreign Minister Adam Rapacki on two occasions—Oct. 2, 1957 and Mar. 28, 1962—and, hence, is known as the "Rapacki Plan." For text of proposal, see "Polish Memorandum Submitted to the Committee of the Whole of the Eighteen-Nation Disarmament Committee: Rapacki Plan for Denuclearized and Limited Armaments Zone in Europe, March 28, 1962," *Documents on Disarmament, 1962* (Washington, D.C.: G.P.O., 1963), I: 201–05.

5054 Amoja, F. d'. "Piano Rapaki E Rapporti Fra I due Blocci." *Comunita Internazionale* [Rome] 14 (Oct. 1959): 604–25.

5055 "Background to the Rapacki Plan: Proposals about the Demilitarized Zone. . . ." *Labour Monthly* 40 (Mar. 1958): 123–26.

5056 Bierzanek, Remigiusz. "The Rapacki Plan: An Attempt to Find Reasonable Solutions." *Bulletin of the World Council of Peace* [Vienna] (Jan. 15, 1960): 8–9.

5057 Callus, Edward. "The Possibility of a Neutralized Zone in Central Europe." *Studies for a New Central Europe* 2:1 (1967–1968): 9–14.

5058 Dzelepy, E. N. *Desatomiser L'Europe? La Verite sur le "Plan Rapacki."* Brussels: Les Editions Politiques, Les Cahiers Politiques, 1958.

5059 Erven, L. "The Rapacki Plan." *Review of International Affairs* [Belgrade] (Jan. 16, 1958): 7–8.

5060 Grandchamp, R. "Le Plan Rapacki et les Grandes Puissances." *Revue de Defense Nationale* [Paris] 14 (Apr. 1958): 585–94.

5061 Howard, Michael. "Limited Armament Zones in Europe." *Bulletin of the Atomic Scientists* 17 (Feb. 1962): 9–14.

5062 Kowalewski, Jerzy. "The Atom-Free Zone and its Opponents." *Polish Perspectives* (May 1958): 11–18.

5063 Lachs, Manfred. "Poland's Quest for European Security." *International Affairs* [London] 35 (July 1959): 305–09.

5064 Lall, Betty Goetz. "On Disarmament Issues: The Polish Plan." *Bulletin of the Atomic Scientists* 20 (June 1964): 41–43.

5065 Lapter, Karol D. "Nuclear Freeze in Central Europe." *Disarmament and Arms Control* 2 (Summer 1964): 299–309.

5066 Noirot, P. "Le Plan Rapacki dans le Dialogue Est-Ouest." *Democratie Nouvelle* [Paris] 12 (Mar. 1958): 135–36.

5067 Pogodin, A. "Make Northern Europe a Peace Zone." *International Affairs* [Moscow] 8 (July 1962): 27–31.

5068 Rapacki, Adam. "Disarmament—The Polish Point of View." *Foreign Affairs Reports* [India] (Feb. 1963): 8–15.

5069 ———. "The Polish Plan for a Nuclear-free Zone Today." *International Affairs* [London] 39 (Jan. 1963): 1–12.

5070 ———. "Le Sens du Plan Polonais." *Democratie Nouvelle* [Paris] 12 (Feb. 1958): 79–82.

5071 Revol, J. "Le Plan Rapacki." *Revue Militaire Suisse* [Lausanne] 103 (Mar. 1958): 105–09.

5072 Sahovie, M. "The Rapacki Plan and International Law." *Review of International Affairs* [Belgrade] 9 (Mar. 1958): 7–8.

5073 Skowronski, Andrzej. "Legal Problems Relating to Denuclearization in the Polish Plans for an Atom-Free Zone and for Freezing Nuclear Armaments in Central Europe." *Polish Yearbook of International Law* 1 (1966–67): 45–64.

5074 "United States Replies to Polish Note on Rapacki Plan." *U.S. Department of State Bulletin* (May 19, 1958): 821–22.

5075 Wainhouse, David W., et al. "Gomulka Proposals and Rapacki Plan." *Arms Control Agreements: Designs For Verification and Organization.* Baltimore: Johns Hopkins Press, 1968, pp. 43–61.

5076 Windsor, Philip. "Arms Control in Central Europe." *Disarmament* 3 (Sept. 1964): 9–11.

ANTARCTIC TREATY (1959)

For text of treaty, see United Nations, *Treaty Series* (New York, 1962), vol. 422, no. 5778, pp. 71–102.

Documents

5077 U.S. Department of State. *The Conference on Antarctica: Washington, D.C., October 15–December 1, 1959.* International Organizations and Conference Series, no. 13. Washington, D.C.: G.P.O., 1960.

5078 ———. *United States Policy and International Cooperation in Antarctica. Message from the President of the United States Transmitting Special Report on United States Policy and International Cooperation in Antarctica.* Washington, D.C.: G.P.O., 1964. [Also printed as House Doc. 358, 88th Cong., 2d Sess.]

5079 U.S. President. [D. D. Eisenhower.] "U.S. Circular Note Regarding Antarctica." *U.S. Department of State Bulletin* (June 2, 1958): 910–12.

5080 ———. [J. F. Kennedy.] "Antarctic Treaty Enters into Force." *U.S. Department of State Bulletin* (July 10, 1961): 91.

5081 ———. [L. B. Johnson.] "U.S. Policy and International Cooperation in Antarctica." *U.S. Department of State Bulletin* (Sept. 21, 1964): 402–07.

5082 ———. [L. B. Johnson.] "President Johnson meets with Antarctic Policy Group." *U.S. Department of State Bulletin* (June 12, 1965): 1013–15.

5083 ———. [R. M. Nixon.] "U.S. Marks 10th Anniversary of Antarctic Treaty." *U.S. Department of State Bulletin* (July 19, 1969): 82–83.

5084 U.S. Senate. Committee on Foreign Relations. Hearings: *The Antarctic Treaty.* 86th Cong., 2d Sess., June 14, 1960.

General Accounts

5085 Amaro, M. "Symbol of Good Will: The Antarctic Treaty." *Americas* 19 (Feb. 1967): 1–9.

5086 Barrett, Raymond J. "The Antarctic Treaty in Operation." *Military Review* 49 (Mar. 1969): 28–34.

5087 Daniels, Paul C. "The Antarctic Treaty." *Bulletin of the Atomic Scientists* 26 (Dec. 1970): 11–15.

5088 Goldblat, Jozef. "Troubles in the Antarctic?" *Bulletin of Peace Proposals* 4:3 (1973): 286–88.

5089 Gould, Laurence M. *Antarctic in World Affairs.* New York: Foreign Policy Assoc., 1958.

5090 Hanessian, John. "The Antarctic Treaty, 1959." *International and Comparative Law Quarterly* 9 (July 1960): 436–75.

5091 Hanevold, Truls. "The Antarctic Treaty Consultative Meeting: Form and Procedure." *Cooperation and Conflict* 6:3/4 (1971): 183–99.

5092 Hayton, Robert D. "American Antarctic." *American Journal of International Law* 50 (July 1956): 583–610.

5093 ———. "The Antarctic Settlement of 1959." *American Journal of International Law* 54 (Apr. 1960): 349–71.

5094 ———. "Polar Problems and International Law." *American Journal of International Law* 52 (Oct. 1958): 746–65.

5095 Jessup, Philip. "Sovereignty in Antarctica." *American Journal of International Law* 41 (Jan. 1947): 117–18.

5096 ———, and Howard J. Taubenfeld. *Controls for Outer Space and the Antarctic Analogy.* New York: Columbia Univ. Press, 1959.

5097 Plott, Barry M. "The Development of United States Antarctic Policy." Ph.D. diss., Tufts Univ., 1969.

5098 Roucek, Joseph S. "The Strategic Aspects of Antarctica." *Social Studies* 57 (Dec. 1966): 297–303.

5099 Sollie, Finn. "The Political Experiment in Antarctica." *Bulletin of the Atomic Scientists* 26 (Dec. 1970): 16–21.

5100 Taubenfeld, Howard J. "The Antarctic Treaty of 1959." *Disarmament and Arms Control* 2 (Spring 1964): 136–49.

5101 ———. "A Treaty for Antarctic." *International Conciliation*, no. 531 (Jan. 1961): 245–322.

5102 Toma, D. "Soviet Attitude Towards the Acquisition of Territorial Sovereignty in the Antarctica." *American Journal of International Law* 50 (July 1956): 611–26.

Inspection

5103 Hanevold, Truls. "Inspections in Antarctica." *Cooperation and Conflict* 6:6 (1971): 106–11.

5104 U.S. Department of State. *Report of United States Observers of Antarctic Stations.* Washington, D.C.: G.P.O., 1971.

5105 ———. *Report of United States Observers on Inspection of Antarctic Stations—1963–64 Austral Summer Season.* Washington, D.C.: G.P.O., 1964.

5106 ———. "Secretary Appoints Observers for Antarctic Inspection." *U.S. Department of State Bulletin* (Dec. 16, 1963): 932.

5107 ———. "U.S. Observers Inspect Antarctic Stations." *U.S. Department of State Bulletin* (Apr. 17, 1967): 633–34.

5108 ———. "U.S. to Conduct Inspection in Antarctica." *U.S. Department of State Bulletin* (Sept. 30, 1963): 513.

5109 Wainhouse, David. "Peace Observation and Fact-Finding and the Antarctic Treaty Analogy." *International Peace Observation: A History and Forecast.* Baltimore: Johns Hopkins Press, 1966, pp. 526–34.

U.N. RESOLUTION ON DENUCLEARIZATION OF AFRICA (1961)

For text of resolution, see *Documents on Disarmament, 1961* (Washington, D.C.: G.P.O., 1962), pp. 647–48. Also see "Declaration on the Denuclearization of Africa by the . . . [O.A.U.], July 21, 1964," *Documents on Disarmament, 1964* (Washington, D.C.: G.P.O., 1965), pp. 294–95.

5110 "Denuclearization of Africa." *U.N. Monthly Chronicle* 2 (Dec. 1965): 70–72.

5111 Foster, William C. "The Denuclearization of Africa." *U.S. Department of State Bulletin* (Jan. 17, 1966): 103–05.

5112 Frisch, David H. "A Proposal for an African and Near-Eastern Zone Free from Certain Weapons." *Disarmament and Arms Control* 1 (Summer 1963): 66–73.

5113 Katz, Amrom. *African Disarmament: A Proposal Seconded.* Santa Monica, Ca.: Rand, 1964.

5114 Kolo, Alhaji Sule. "Nuclear-Free Zone Demanded." *New Africa* 13:7/8 (1971): 7.

5115 Mensah, J. H. "Regional Disarmament: Africa." *Disarmament and Arms Control* 1 (Autumn 1963): 171–83.

GENEVA ACCORDS ON LAOS (1962)

For text of agreement, see U.S. Department of State, "Multilateral Neutrality of Laos, Geneva,

July 18, 1962," *U.S. Treaties and Other International Agreements* 14:1 (Washington, D.C.: G.P.O., 1963), pp. 1104–67.

Bibliography

5116 Leitenberg, Milton, and Richard Dean Burns, eds. *The Vietnam Conflict.* Santa Barbara, Ca.: ABC–Clio, 1973, pp. 19–27.

Documents

5117 Great Britain. Secretary of State for Foreign Affairs. *International Conference on the Settlement of the Laotian Question, Geneva, May 12, 1961–July 23, 1962.* London: H.M.S.O., 1962. Cmnd. 1828.

5118 Rusk, Dean. "United States Outlines Program to Insure Genuine Neutrality for Laos." *U.S. Department of State Bulletin* (June 5, 1961): 846.

5119 ———. "Why Laos Is Critically Important." *U.S. Department of State Bulletin* (July 6, 1964): 3–5.

5120 U.S. Department of State. *The Situation in Laos.* Washington, D.C.: G.P.O., 1959.

General Accounts

5121 Burnham, James. "Laos and Containment: With Editorial Comment." *National Review* (Apr. 8, 1961): 207–13.

5122 Cousins, Norman. "Report from Laos." *Saturday Review* (Feb. 18, 1961): 12–18.

5123 Czyzak, John J., and Carl F. Salans. "The International Conference on the Settlement of the Laotian Question and Geneva Agreements of 1962." *American Journal of International Law* 57 (Apr. 1963): 300–317.

5124 ———. "The International Conference on Laos and the Geneva Agreement of 1962." *Journal of Southeast Asian History* 7:2 (1966): 27–47.

5125 Dommen, Arthur J. *Conflict in Laos: The Politics of Neutralization.* New York: Praeger, 1964.

5126 Fall, Bernard B. *Anatomy of a Crisis: The Laotian Crisis of 1960–1961.* Garden City, N.Y.: Doubleday, 1969.

5127 Fuzesi, Stephen. *Negotiating a Neutralization Treaty: Laos a Contemporary Test Case.* Princeton: Princeton Univ., Center of International Studies, 1967.

5128 Henderson, William, and F. N. Trager. "Showdown at Geneva: Cease-Fire in Laos." *New Leader* (May 22, 1961): 9–11.

5129 Hill, Kenneth L. "Laos: The Vientiane Agreement." *Journal of Southeast Asian History* 8:2 (1967): 257–67.

5130 ———. "President Kennedy and the Neutralization of Laos." *Review of Politics* 31 (July 1969): 353–69.

5131 Langer, Paul F. "Laos: Preparing for a Settlement in Vietnam." *Asian Survey* 9 (Sept. 1969): 69–74.

5132 Lee, Chae-Jin. "Communist China and the Geneva Conference on Laos: A Reappraisal." *Asian Survey* 9 (July 1969): 522–39.

5133 Modelski, George. *International Conference on the Settlement of the Laotian Questions, 1961–1962.* Vancouver: Univ. of British Columbia Press, 1962.

5134 Morley, Lorna. "Menaced Laos." *Editorial Research Reports* (Sept. 23, 1959): 717–34.

5135 Ritvo, Herbert. "A Neutral Laos: The Dangers." *New Leader* (Apr. 10, 1961): 6.

5136 Stevenson, Charles A. *The End of Nowhere: American Policy Toward Laos Since 1954.* Boston: Beacon, 1972.

5137 Trager, F. N. "Dilemma in Laos." *America* 105:15 (1961): 506–11.

5138 Zasloff, Joseph J. "Laos 1972: The War, Politics and Peace Negotiations." *Asian Survey* 11 (Jan. 1973): 60–75.

Violations of Treaty

5139 Black, Col. Edwin F. "Laos: A Case Study of Communist Strategy." *Military Review* 44 (Dec. 1964): 49–59.

5140 Branfman, Fred. "Presidential War in Laos, 1964–1970." In Nina S. Adams and Alfred W. McCoy, eds., *Laos: War and Revolution.* New York: Harper & Row, 1970, pp. 213–80.

5141 Haney, Walt. "The Pentagon Papers and the United States Involvement in Laos." *The*

Pentagon Papers: The Senator Gravel Edition. 4 vols. Boston: Beacon, 1972, IV: 248–93.

5142 Laos. Ministry of Foreign Affairs. *North Vietnamese Interference in Laos.* Vientiane, 1965.

5143 ———. *White Book on Violations of the Geneva Accords of 1962.* Vientiane, 1966.

5144 ———. *White Book on Violations of the Geneva Accords of 1962.* Vientiane, 1968.

5145 ———. *White Book on Violations of the Geneva Accords of 1962.* Vientiane, 1970.

5146 Porter, D. Gareth. "After Geneva: Subverting Laotian Neutrality." In Nina S. Adams and Alfred W. McCoy, eds., *Laos: War and Revolution.* New York: Harper & Row, 1970, pp. 179–212.

5147 Roland, Paul. "Laos: Anatomy of American Involvement." *Foreign Affairs* 40 (Apr. 1971): 533–47.

5148 Thee, Marek. *Notes of a Witness: Laos and the Second Indochinese War.* New York: Vintage, 1973.

5149 U.S. Department of State. "U.S. Reviews North Vietnamese Violations of Agreement on Laos." *U.S. Department of State Bulletin* (June 22, 1968): 817–20.

5150 Wainhouse, David W. *International Peace Observation.* Baltimore: Johns Hopkins Press, 1966, pp. 501–12.

GOMULKA PROPOSAL (1964)

For text of proposal to freeze nuclear arms in Central Europe, see "The Gomulka Proposals: The Complete Text, Made on March 5, 1964," *Current History* 47 (Aug. 1964): 107–08.

5151 Auberti, Michel. "Disengagement et Securite Europeenne: Les Plans d'Origine Polonaise." *Revue de Defense Nationale* 21 (Oct. 1965): 1542–77.

5152 "Poland's Nuclear Freeze Plan." *New York Times*, Mar. 21, 1964. [Editorial.]

5153 Szymanski, Zygmunt. "The Gomulka Plan." *New Times* [Moscow] 13 (Apr. 1, 1964): 4–5.

5154 ———. "The Gomulka Plan and Its Critics." *New Times* [Moscow] 49 (Dec. 9, 1964): 7–8.

5155 Underwood, Paul. "Poland Details Proposal to Freeze Atomic Arms." *New York Times*, Mar. 6, 1964.

5156 ———. "Warsaw Presses Weapons Freeze." *New York Times*, Mar. 1, 1964.

DENUCLEARIZATION OF OUTER SPACE (1967)

For text of treaty, see U.S. Arms Control & Disarmament Agency, *Documents on Disarmament, 1967* (Washington, D.C.: G.P.O., 1968), pp. 38–42. This treaty formalizes the earlier U.N. General Assembly Res. 1884 (XVIII), which prohibited the stationing of weapons of mass destruction in Outer Space, Oct. 17, 1963 (adopted by acclamation).

Bibliography

5157 U.S. Air Force. *Space Law Bibliography.* A.F. Pam. no. 110–1–4. Washington, D.C.: G.P.O., 1961.

5158 White, Irvin L.; Clifton E. Wilson; and John A. Vosburgh. *Law and Politics in Outer Space: A Bibliography.* Tucson: Univ. of Arizona Press, 1972.

Documents

5159 United Nations. *Official Records of the Committee on the Peaceful Uses of Outer Space.* New York, 1962–1970.

5160 ———. *Official Records of the Legal Subcommittee of COPUS.* New York, 1962–1970.

5161 ———. *Official Records of the Scientific and Technical Subcommittee of COPUS.* New York, 1962–1970.

5162 ———. General Assembly. *Report of the Ad Hoc Committee on the Peaceful Uses of Outer Space.* A/4141. New York, July 14, 1959.

5163 ———. *Report of the Committee on the Peaceful Uses of Outer Space.* A/7285. New York, 1968; A/7621. New York, 1969; A/8021. New York, 1970.

5164 U.S. House. Committee on Foreign Affairs. Hearings: *Relative to The Establishment of Plans for the Peaceful Exploration of Outer Space.* Res. 326. 85th Cong., 2d Sess., 1958.

5165 ——. Committee on Science and Astronautics. Hearings: *Defense Space Interests*. 87th Cong., 1st Sess., 1961.

5166 ——. Report: *U.S. Policy on the Control and Use of Outer Space: Report of the Committee on Science and Astronautics*. House Rpt. no. 353. 86th Cong., 1st Sess., 1959.

5167 U.S. Senate. Committee on Aeronautical and Space Science. *Documents on International Aspects of the Exploration and Use of Outer Space, 1954–1962*. Sen. Doc. 18. 88th Cong., 1st Sess., 1963.

5168 ——. Report: *International Cooperation and Organization for Outer Space*. 89th Cong., 1st Sess., 1965.

5169 ——. Report: *International Cooperation in Outer Space: A Symposium*. Sen. Doc. 92–57. 92d Cong., 1st Sess., 1971.

5170 ——. Report: *Space Treaty Proposals by the United States and the Union of Soviet Socialist Republics*. 89th Cong., 2d Sess., 1966.

5171 ——. *Treaty on Principles Governing the Activities of States in the Exploration and Use of Outer Space, including the Moon and other Celestial Bodies: Analysis and Background Data*. 90th Cong., 1st Sess., 1967.

5172 U.S. Senate. Committee on Foreign Relations. Hearings: *The Treaty on Outer Space*. Exec. D. 90th Cong., 2d Sess., Apr. 12, 1967.

General Accounts

5173 Bloomfield, Lincoln P., ed. *Outer Space: Prospects for Man and Society*. Englewood Cliffs, N.J.: Prentice-Hall, 1962.

5174 Goldsen, Joseph M., ed. *Outer Space in World Politics*. New York: Praeger, 1963.

5175 Jessup, Philip C., and Howard J. Taubenfeld. *Controls for Outer Space and the Antarctic Analogy*. New York: Columbia Univ. Press, 1959.

5176 Loosbrock, John F., ed. *Space Weapons*. New York: Praeger, 1959.

5177 Odishaw, Hugh. *The Challenges of Space*. Chicago: Univ. of Chicago Press, 1962.

5178 Schlafly, Phyllis, and Chester Ward. *Strike From Space: How the Russians May Destroy Us*. New York: Devin-Adair, 1966.

5179 White, Irvin L. *Decision-Making for Space: Laws and Politics in Air, Sea and Outer Space*. Lafayette: Purdue Univ. Press, 1970.

Pre-Treaty Accounts

5180 Abt, Clark C. "The Problems and Possibilities of Space Arms Control." *Journal of Arms Control* 1:1 (1963): 18–43.

5181 ——. "Space Denial: Costs and Consequences." *Air Force and Space Digest* 46 (Mar. 1963): 45–52.

5182 Berkner, Lloyd V. "Earth Satellites and Foreign Policy." *Foreign Affairs* 36 (Jan. 1959): 221–31.

5183 Brennan, Donald G. "Arms and Arms Control in Outer Space." In Lincoln Bloomfield, ed., *Outer Space: Prospects for Man and Society*. Englewood Cliffs, N.J.: Prentice-Hall, 1962, pp. 145–77.

5184 ——. "Why Outer Space Control." *Bulletin of the Atomic Scientists* 15 (May 1959): 198–202.

5185 Brownlie, Ian. "The Maintenance of International Peace and Security in Outer Space." *British Yearbook of International Law* 60 (1964): 1–31.

5186 Clemens, Walter C., Jr. "Arms Control for Outer Space." *Disarmament* 12 (Dec. 1966): 5–11.

5187 "The Cosmos Must be a Peace Zone." *International Affairs* [Moscow] 9 (Dec. 1963): 41–43.

5188 Crane, Robert D. "Basic Principles in Soviet Space Law: Peaceful Coexistence, Peaceful Cooperation and Disarmament." *Law and Contemporary Problems* 29 (Autumn 1964): 943–55.

5189 Dembling, Paul G., and Daniel M. Arons. "The Evolution of the Outer Space Treaty." *Journal of Air Law and Commerce* 33 (Summer 1967): 419–57.

5190 Etzioni, Amitai. "The Cold War in Orbit." *The Moon-doggle: Domestic and Interna-*

tional Implications of the Space Race. Garden City, N.Y.: Doubleday, 1964, pp. 114–48.

5191   Frye, Alton. *Space Arms Control: Trends, Concepts, and Prospects.* P–2873. Santa Monica, Ca.: Rand, 1964.

5192   Kemp, John M. *Evolution Toward a Space Treaty: An Historical Analysis.* Washington, D.C.: National Aeronautics & Space Administration, 1966.

5193   Kilmarx, Robert A. "The Soviet Space Program." *Current History* 45 (Oct. 1963): 200–204.

5194   Knorr, Klaus E. "On the International Implications of Outer Space." *World Politics* 12 (July 1960): 564–84.

5195   Lachs, Manfred. "Law-Making for Outer Space and Its Peaceful Use." *Disarmament* 8 (Dec. 1965): 1–4.

5196   Lall, Betty Goetz. "Cooperation and Arms Control in Outer Space." *Bulletin of the Atomic Scientists* 22 (Nov. 1966): 34–37.

5197   Langer, Elinor. "Disarmament on the Moon: The Prospects Look Good." *Science* (July 8, 1966): 153–54.

5198   Leavitt, William. "Space Technology: Today's Tool for Controlled Peace." *Air Force and Space Digest* 46 (Apr. 1963): 106–13.

5199   Lissitzyn, Oliver J. "The American Position on Outer Space and Antarctica." *American Journal of International Law* 53 (Jan. 1959): 126–32.

5200   Nelson, Bryce. "The Space Treaty: A Step in Easing U.S.-Soviet Tensions." *Science* (Dec. 16, 1966): 1430–31.

5201   Rehm, Georg W. *Rüstungskontrolle im Weltraum.* Dokumentation der Deutschen Gesellschaft fur Auswartige Politik, Bd. 3. Bonn: Siegler, 1965.

5202   Roth, Joseph P. "Who Owns the Unknown?" *Military Review* 44 (Dec. 1964): 13–19.

5203   Schwartz, Leonard E. "Control of Outer Space." *Current History* 47 (July 1964): 39–46.

5204   Simsarian, James. "Hark the Herald Angels Sing." *Economist* (Dec. 17, 1966): 1226.

5205   "Space and the Cold War." *Air Force & Space Digest* 46 (Apr. 1963): 35–39.

Post-Treaty Accounts

5206   Aldoshin, V. "Outer Space Must Be a Peace Zone." *International Affairs* [Moscow] 14 (Dec. 1968): 38–41.

5207   Barrett, Raymond J. "Outer Space and Air Space—The Difficulties in Definitions." *Air University Review* 24 (May–June 1973): 34–39.

5208   Cheng, Bin. "The 1967 Space Treaty." *Journal du Droit International* [Clunet] 95 (1968): 532–644.

5209   Clemens, Walter C., Jr. "Outer Space: Strategy and Arms Control." *Bulletin of the Atomic Scientists* 23 (Nov. 1967): 24–28.

5210   Cooper, John C. "Some Crucial Questions About the Space Treaty." *Air Force and Space Digest* 50 (Mar. 1967): 104–11.

5211   Darwin, H. G. "The Outer Space Treaty." *British Yearbook of International Law* 52 (1967): 278–89.

5212   Fawcett, J. E. S. "The Politics of the Moon." *World Today* 25 (Aug. 1969): 357–62.

5213   Finch, Edward R. "Outer Space for 'Peaceful Purposes.'" *American Bar Association Journal* 54 (Apr. 1968): 365–67.

5214   Goedhuis, D. "An Evaluation of the Leading Principles of the Treaty on Outer Space of 27/1/67." *Netherlands International Law Review* 15 (Summer 1968): 17–40.

5215   Haran, M. Chandrasek. "The Space Treaty." *Indian Journal of International Law* 7 (Jan. 1967): 61–66.

5216   Johnson, Pres. Lyndon B. "President Johnson Hails U.N. Accord on Treaty Governing Exploration of Outer Space." *U.S. Department of State Bulletin* (Dec. 26, 1966): 952–55.

5217   Levine, Bruce. "Weapons Prohibition in Space vs. Disarmament." *Minority of One* 9 (May 1967): 10–11.

5218   Mostafa, Kairy H. Y., and Ishaq R. Goreish. "Disarmament in Outer Space and the Space

Treaty." *Revue Egyptienne de Droit International* 27 (1971): 59–78.

5219   Orr, John M. "The Treaty on Outer Space: An Evaluation of the Arms Control Provisions." *Columbia Journal of Transnational Law* 7 (Fall 1968): 259–78.

5220   Piradov, A. S., and V. Rybakov. "First Space Treaty." *International Affairs* [Moscow] 13 (Mar. 1967): 21–26.

5221   Poulantzas, Nicholas. "The Outer Space Treaty of January 27, 1967: A Decisive Step Towards Arms Control, Demilitarization of Outer Space and International Supervision." *Revue Hellenique de Droit* 20 (1967): 66–83.

5222   Reinstanz, Gerhard. "The Space Treaty." *German Foreign Policy* 6:2 (1967): 147–52.

5223   Rusk, Dean, and Arthur J. Goldberg. "Secretary Rusk and Ambassador Goldberg Urge Senate Approval of Outer Space Treaty." *U.S. Department of State Bulletin* (Apr. 10, 1967): 600–612.

5224   Schwartz, H. "Real Tragedy of Man's Infancy in Space." *Saturday Review* (Oct. 25, 1969): 33–36.

5225   Smart, Jacob E. "Strategic Implications of Space Activities." *Strategic Review* 2 (Fall 1974): 19–24.

5226   "The Treaty on Outer Space: An Evaluation of the Arms Control Provisions." *Columbia Journal of Transnational Law* 7 (Fall 1968): 259–78.

5227   Vlassic, Ivan A. "The Space Treaty: A Preliminary Evaluation." *California Law Review* 55 (May 1967): 507–19.

5228   Zhukov, G. "Moon for All States." *Space World* (July 1968): 44–45.

United Nations' Role

5229   Cheng, Bin. "United Nations Resolutions on Outer Space: 'Instant' International Customary Law." *Indian Journal of International Law* 5 (1965): 23–48.

5230   Cooper, John C. "Self-Defense in Outer Space . . . and the United Nations." *Air Force & Space Digest* 45 (Feb. 1962): 51–56.

5231   Goldberg, Arthur J. "U.N. General Assembly Endorses Outer Space Treaty." *U.S. Department of State Bulletin* (Jan. 9, 1967): 78–84.

5232   Langer, Elinor. "United Nations: Space Committee Makes Little Headway Developing International Law for Space." *Science* (May 10, 1963): 621.

5233   "Peaceful Uses of Outer Space: Assembly Adopts Three Resolutions." *U.N. Monthly Chronicle* 4 (Jan. 1967): 35–46.

5234   "Peaceful Uses of Outer Space: General Assembly Adopts Resolutions." *U.N. Monthly Chronicle* 4 (Dec. 1967): 55–57.

5235   Schwartz, Leonard E. *International Organizations and Space Cooperation.* Durham: Duke Univ., World Rule of Law Center, 1962.

5236   Shepherd, L. R. "Needed for the 1970's: International Space Control Agency." *Astronautics & Aeronautics* 4 (Nov. 1966): 56–59.

5237   Simsarian, James. "Outer Space Cooperation in the United Nations." *American Journal of International Law* 57 (Oct. 1963): 854–67.

5238   Stevenson, Adlai E. "United Nations Adopts Resolutions of Cooperation in Outer Space." *U.S. Department of State Bulletin* (Dec. 30, 1963): 1005–15.

5239   "Test of UN Resolution on International Cooperation in the Peaceful Uses of Outer Space." *Flight* (Jan. 4, 1962): 7–8.

5240   "U.N. Calls on States to Refrain From Orbiting Weapons." *U.S. Department of State Bulletin* (Nov. 11, 1963): 754.

5241   Waldheim, Kurt. "United Nations Conference on the Peaceful Uses of Outer Space." *U.N. Monthly Chronicle* 5 (Feb. 1968): 59–62.

Military Implications of Space

5242   Alsop, Stewart. "Outer Space: The Next Battlefield." *Saturday Evening Post* (July 28, 1962): 15–19.

5243   Bicknell, Robert. "Proposed: A Military Space Policy." *Armed Forces Management* 8 (Aug. 1962): 22–24.

5244   Conrad, Thomas M. "Damocles' New Sword: Bombs in Orbit." *Commonweal* (Dec. 8, 1967): 332–34.

5245 "Does Russia's Space Program Pose a Threat to Our National Security?" *Air Force and Space Digest* 46 (Nov. 1963): 59–77.

5246 Erickson, John. "John Erickson on the Military Use of Space by the Russians." *Listener* (Feb. 20, 1969): 230–32.

5247 Fink, Daniel J. "The Military Space Program." *Vital Speeches* (June 15, 1966): 518–21.

5248 Frye, Alton. "Our Gamble in Space: The Military Danger." *Atlantic Monthly* (Aug. 1963): 46–50.

5249 Funk, Ben I. "Military Space—A Mid-Sixties Look." *Sperryscope* 16:3 (1964): 4–7.

5250 Gallavardin, Jean. "La Bombe Orbitale." *Strategie* 8 (Apr.–June 1966): 62–82.

5251 Gandilhon, Jean. "Tendances et Realisations Militaires en Politique Spatiale." *Revue Militaire Générale* 10 (Dec. 1965): 567–86.

5252 Getler, Michael. "Military Space." *Missiles and Rockets* (May 30, 1966): 24–86.

5253 Gilpatric, Roswell L. "Nation's Official Position on Military in Space." *Army-Navy-Air Force Journal and Register* 100 (Sept. 1962): 14–15.

5254 Haggerty, James J. "Soviet Space Program is Military Oriented." *Journal of the Armed Forces* (Nov. 13, 1965): 8, 12.

5255 "If Space Becomes a Battlefield—Will the U.S. be Ready?" *U.S. News & World Report* (Sept. 3, 1962): 35–37.

5256 Kushnevick, John P. "The Military—the Moon—and the Future." *Aerospace Management* 5 (June 1962): 56–60.

5257 Leary, Frank. "Antisatellite Defense." *Space/Aeronautics* 51 (June 1969): 45–54.

5258 Leavitt, William. "Mixed Hopes for the Military Space Mission." *Air Force & Space Digest* 46 (Sept. 1963): 71–72.

5259 ———. "Why the 'Orbital Bomb'?" *Air Force & Space Digest* 48 (Dec. 1965): 62–63.

5260 LeMay, Gen. Curtis E. "Military Implications of Space." *Vital Speeches* (May 15, 1962): 452–55.

5261 Mayhall, Gene, and D. O. Appleton. "Military Applications of Space are Inevitable." *Data* 13 (June 1968): 16–19.

5262 McMillan, Brockway. "The Military Role in Space." In C. I. Cummins and H. R. Lawrence, eds., *Technology of Lunar Exploration*. New York: Academic Press, 1963, pp. 961–68.

5263 "Operational Satellite Killers Need Non-Nuclear Destruct Device." *Missiles and Rockets* (Sept. 28, 1964): 10–11.

5264 "Orbital Weapons." *Nature* [London] (Dec. 2, 1967): 848.

5265 Robinson, Davis R. "Self-Restrictions in the American Military Use of Space." *Orbis* 9 (Spring 1965): 116–39.

5266 Royal Air Force College of Air Warfare. "Military Applications of Space." *Royal Air Force Quarterly* 13 (Winter 1973): 273–96.

5267 Schofield, B. B. "The Significance of Space in Western Defence." *Army Quarterly* 85 (Jan. 1963): 219–26.

5268 Senter, Raymond D. "That Attack From Space." *New Republic* (May 4, 1963): 17–19.

5269 ———. "Nuclear Weapons in Orbit." *New Republic* (Nov. 27, 1965): 11–12.

5270 Sleeper, Col. Raymond S. "The Technological Conflict." *Air University Quarterly Review* 14 (Winter–Spring 1962–63): 6–18.

5271 "Space and National Security: A Symposium." *Air Force & Space Digest* 45 (Nov. 1962): 62–74.

5272 Sponsler, George G. "The Military Role in Space." *Bulletin of the Atomic Scientists* 20 (June 1964): 31–34.

5273 "Thinking Matures on Military's Space Role." *Aviation Week* (July 23, 1963): 209–11.

5274 Thomas, Paul G. "Space Traffic Surveillance." *Space/Aeronautics* 48 (Nov. 1967): 75–86.

5275 Ulsamer, Edgar. "The Question of Soviet Orbital Bombs." *Air Force Magazine* 55 (Apr. 1972): 74–75.

5276 Welsh, Edward C. "Defense in Space." *Ordnance* 47 (May–June 1963): 656–58.

5277 Witze, Claude. "Let's Get Operational in Space." *Air Force & Space Digest* 48 (Oct. 1965): 80–84, 87–88.

5278 Zuckert, Eugene M. "Impact on Military Strategy." *General Electric Forum* 5 (July 1962): 14–17.

5279 Zygielbaum, Joseph L. "The Soviet Program for Military Applications in Space." *Journal of Astronautical Sciences* 13 (Jan.–Feb. 1966): 37–41.

Military Implications of Space—MOL

5280 Butz, J. S. "MOL: The Technical Promise and Prospects." *Air Force & Space Digest* 48 (Oct. 1965): 42–46.

5281 Cooper, John C. "The Manned Orbiting Laboratory: A Major Legal and Political Decision." *American Bar Association Journal* 51 (Dec. 1965): 1137–40.

5282 "Douglas Gets a Jump With MOL." *Business Week* (Dec. 25, 1965): 50–52.

5283 Getler, Michael. "McNamara Outlines MOL Schedule." *Missiles and Rockets* (Feb. 28, 1966): 14–16.

5284 Leavitt, William. "MOL: Evolution of a Decision." *Air Force & Space Digest* 48 (Oct. 1965): 35–41.

5285 Power, Gen. Thomas S. "Military Aspects of Manned Spaceflight." *Air Force & Space Digest* 46 (June 1963): 51–54.

Legal Issues

5286 Adams, Thomas R. "The Outer Space Treaty: An Interpretation in Light of the Non-Sovereignty Provision." *Harvard International Law Journal* 9 (Winter 1968): 140–57.

5287 Bhatt, S. "Legal Controls of the Exploration and Use of the Moon and Celestial Bodies." *Indian Journal of International Law* 8 (Jan. 1968): 33–48.

5288 Chiu, Hungdah. "Communist China and Law of Outer Space." *International and Comparative Law Quarterly* 16 (Oct. 1967): 1135–39.

5289 Christol, Carl Q. *The International Law of Outer Space.* International Law Studies. Vol. 55. Washington, D.C.: G.P.O., 1962.

5290 Crane, Robert D. "Law and Strategy in Space." *Orbis* 6 (Summer 1962): 281–300.

5291 ———. "Soviet Attitude Toward International Space Law." *American Journal of International Law* 56 (July 1962): 685–723.

5292 Fawcett, J. E. S. *International Law and the Uses of Outer Space.* Dobbs Ferry, N.Y.: Oceana, 1968.

5293 Gal, Gyula. *Space Law.* Dobbs Ferry, N.Y.: Oceana, 1969.

5294 Gardner, Richard N. "International Space Law and Free World Security." *Air Force & Space Digest* 47 (July 1964): 58–63.

5295 Gorove, Stephen. "Interpreting Article II of the Outer Space Treaty." In M. Schwarz, ed., *Proceedings of the 11th Colloquium on the Law of Outer Space.* Davis: Univ. of California Press, 1969, pp. 41–51.

5296 Kopal, Valdmir. "Treaty on Principles Governing the Activities of States in the Exploration and Use of Outer Space, including the Moon and other Celestial Bodies." *Yearbook of Air and Space Law* (1966): 463–84.

5297 Lay, S. Houston. "Observations on the Law of Activities in Space." *Utah Law Review* 9 (Summer 1965): 518–42.

5298 ———, and Howard J. Taubenfeld. *The Law Relating to Activities of Man in Space.* Chicago: Univ. of Chicago Press, 1970.

5299 McMahon, J. F. "Legal Aspects of Outer Space." *World Today* 18 (Aug. 1962): 328–34.

5300 Zhukov, G. "Practical Problems of Space Law." *International Affairs* [Moscow] 9 (May 1963): 27–30.

LATIN AMERICAN DENUCLEARIZATION TREATY (1967)

For text of treaty, see U.S. Arms Control & Disarmament Agency, *Documents on Disarmament, 1967* (Washington, D.C.: G.P.O., 1968), pp. 69–83.

Documents

5301 Garcia Robles, Alfonso. *The Denuclearization of Latin America.* New York: Carnegie Endowment for International Peace, 1967.

General Accounts

5302 Barnes, Peter. "Latin America: The First Nuclear Free Zone?" *Bulletin of the Atomic Scientists* 22 (Dec. 1966): 37–40.

5303 Bowser, Hallowell. "Denuclearization in Latin America." *Saturday Review* (May 20, 1967): 32.

5304 Eder, Linda. "Latin America Bans the Bomb." *Nation* (Mar. 20, 1967): 371–72.

5305 Eklund, Sigvard. "Treaty of Tlatelolco." *International Atomic Energy Bulletin* 11:5 (1969): 32–36.

5306 Espiell, Hector Gros. *En Torno al Tratado de Tlatelolco y la Proscripcion de las Armas Nucleares en la America Latina.* Mexico City: Publicaciones del Opanal, 1973.

5307 Garcia Robles, Alfonso. "The Denuclearization of Latin America." *Disarmament* 8 (Dec. 1965): 17–20.

5308 ———. "The Denuclearization of Latin America." *Review of International Affairs* (Nov. 5, 1966): 8–10.

5309 ———. "Mesures de Désarmement dans les Zones Particulières: le Traité Visant l'Interdiction des Armes Nucléaires en Amérique Latine." *Recueil des Cours* [The Hague] 133:2 (1971): 43–134.

5310 Glick, Edward B. "The Feasibility of Arms Control and Disarmament in Latin America." *Orbis* 9 (Fall 1965): 743–59.

5311 Gomez, Juan. "Make Latin America a Zone of Peace!" *World Marxist Review* 1 (Nov. 1958): 70–71.

5312 Gude, Edward W. *Political Implications of the Proposed Nuclear Free Zone in Latin America.* Bedford, Mass.: Raytheon, 1963.

5313 Hudson, Richard. "Latin American Advance toward a Nuclear-Free Zone." *War/Peace Report* 5 (Aug. 1965): 15.

5314 ———. "Latin Americans Sign Treaty to Prohibit Nuclear Weapons." *War/Peace Report* 7 (Apr. 1967): 15–16.

5315 ———. "Latin Americans Take Next Step Toward a Nuclear-Free Zone." *War/Peace Report* 5 (Oct. 1965): 15.

5316 ———. "Latin America Without Nuclear Weapons: The First Treaty on Denuclearized Zones." *Disarmament* 13 (Mar. 1967): 1–4.

5317 ———. "Latin Progress on a Nuclear Free Zone." *War/Peace Report* 6 (June–July 1966): 21.

5318 Jha, P. K. "Treaty for the Prohibition of Nuclear Weapons in Latin America, 1967: A Critical Appraisal." *Indian Journal of International Law* 8 (Jan. 1968): 63–73.

5319 Maratov, M. "Nuclear-Free Zone for Latin America." *International Affairs* [Moscow] 14 (July 1968): 34–39.

5320 Marini, Ruy M., and Olga Pellicer de Brody. "Militarismo y Desnuclearizacion en America Latina: El Caso de Brazil." *Foro Internacional* 8 (July–Sept. 1967): 1–24.

5321 Miller, Lynn H. *Security Studies Project.* Vol. 4: *The Denuclearization of Latin America.* ACDA Rpt. WEC–126. Los Angeles: Univ. of California, 1968.

5322 [People's Republic of China]. "China Respects and Supports Proposition for Latin American Nuclear-Weapons-Free Zone." *Peking Review* (Nov. 24, 1972): 7–8.

5323 ———. "Soviet Union Refuses to Commit Itself to Latin American Nuclear-Free Zone." *Peking Review* (Nov. 24, 1972): 9–10.

5324 Redick, John R. "Military Potential of Latin American Nuclear Energy Programs." *Sage Professional Papers in International Studies* 1:02–012 (1972).

5325 ———. "The Politics of Denuclearization: A Study of the Treaty for the Prohibition of Nuclear Weapons in Latin America." Ph.D. diss., Univ. of Virginia, 1970.

5326 Robinson, Davis R. "The Treaty of Tlatelolco and the United States: A Latin American Nuclear Free Zone." *American Journal of International Law* 64 (Apr. 1970): 282–309.

5327 SIPRI. "The Treaty for the Prohibition of Nuclear Weapons in Latin America." *SIPRI Yearbook of World Armament and Disarmament, 1969–1970.* New York: Humanities Press, 1970, pp. 218–56.

5328 Stimson, Hugh B., and James D. Cochrane. "The Movement for Regional Arms Control in Latin America." *Journal of Inter-American Studies and World Affairs* 13 (Jan. 1971): 1–17.

5329   [U.N.]. "Denuclearization of Latin America." *U.N. Monthly Chronicle* 5 (Jan. 1968): 25–26.

5330   ———. "Denuclearization of Latin America: Consideration in First Committee." *U.N. Monthly Chronicle* 4 (Nov. 1967): 18–22.

Protocol I to Treaty

5331   "Additional Protocol I to the Treaty for the Prohibition of Nuclear Weapons in Latin America, February 14, 1967." *International Legal Materials* 6 (May–June 1967): 533.

Protocol II to Treaty

5332   U.S. Department of State. "Multilateral: Additional Protocol II to the Treaty for the Prohibition of Nuclear Weapons in Latin America, Mexico, Feb. 14, 1967." *U.S. Treaties and Other International Agreements* 22:1 (Washington, D.C.: G.P.O., 1971): 754–86.

5333   U.S. Senate. Committee on Foreign Relations. Hearings: *Additional Protocol II to the Latin American Nuclear Free Zone Treaty.* 91st Cong., 1st Sess., Sept. 22, 1970, Feb. 3, 1971.

INDIAN OCEAN: A "ZONE OF PEACE" (1971)

For text of U.N. resolution, see "Resolution Declaring the Indian Ocean a Zone of Peace," 26th General Assembly, Res. 2892, Dec. 16, 1971, *Bulletin of Peace Proposals* 1 (1972): 18.

Zone of Peace Idea

5334   Barnds, William J. "Arms Race or Arms Control in the Indian Ocean?" *America* (Oct. 14, 1972): 280–82.

5335   "Chen Chu Expounds China's Principled Stand in Support 'Declaration of Indian Ocean as Peace Zone.'" *Survey of China Mainland Press* (Dec. 22, 1971): 116–18.

5336   Kaushik, Devendra. *The Indian Ocean: Towards a Peace Zone.* Delhi: Vikas Publications, 1972.

5337   Millar, Thomas B. "Review of Devandra Kaushik, *The Indian Ocean: Towards a Peace Zone.*" *Survival* 15 (May–June 1973): 150.

5338   Robbs, Peter. "Africa and the Indian Ocean." *Africa Report* 21 (Mar.–Apr. 1976): 41–45.

5339   Subrahmanyam, K., and J. P. Anand. "Indian Ocean as an Area of Peace." *India Quarterly* 27 (Oct.–Dec. 1971): 289–315.

5340   Wriggins, Howard. "Heading Off a New Arms Race: Let's Try to Neutralize the Indian Ocean." *War/Peace Report* 11 (Aug.–Sept. 1971): 7–11.

India's Interests

5341   Anand, Mulk R. "Will the Indian Ocean Develop Into 'The Power Vacuum' or Area of Peace?" *Indian & Foreign Review* (May 15, 1971): 9–10.

5342   Bindra, Capt. A. P. S. "The Indian Ocean as Seen by an Indian." *U.S. Naval Institute Proceedings* 96 (May 1970): 178–203.

5343   Chopra, Wg. Cmdr. Mahraj K. "Indian Ocean Strategy." *Military Review* 45 (May 1965): 85–95.

5344   Harrigan, Anthony. "India's Maritime Posture." *Military Review* 49 (Apr. 1969): 24–30.

5345   Hyder, K. "Strategic Balance in South and Southeast Asia." *Pakistan Horizon* 24:4 (1971): 11–29.

5346   Indian Council on World Affairs. *Defense and Security in the Indian Ocean Area.* Bombay: Asia Publishing House, 1957.

5347   Kahn, Rashid A. "Strategy in the Indian Ocean." *Pakistan Horizon* 18:3 (1965): 247–51.

5348   Kaul, Lt. Cmdr. Ravi. "The Indo-Pakistani War and the Changing Balance of Power in the Indian Ocean." *U.S. Naval Institute Proceedings* 99 (May 1973): 172–95.

5349   Misra, K. P. "International Politics and Security of the Indian Ocean Area." *International*

Studies [New Delhi] 12 (Jan.–Mar. 1973): 141–60.

5350   Poonawala, Rashida. "The Afro-Asian Ocean." *Pakistan Horizon* 24:4 (1971): 30–43.

5351   Subrahmanyam, K. "The Problem of India's Security in the Seventies." *United Asia* 22 (Sept.–Oct. 1970): 246–56.

5352   Vivekananda, B. "Naval Power in the Indian Ocean: A Problem in Indo-British Relations." *Round Table* 65 (Jan. 1975): 59–72.

Superpower Competition

5353   Adie, W. A. C. *Oil, Politics and Seapower: The Indian Ocean Vortex.* New York: Crane, Russak, 1975.

5354   Atkinson, James D. "Who Will Dominate the Strategic Indian Ocean Area in the 1970s?" *Navy* 11 (Sept. 1968): 22–26.

5355   Bindra, Capt. A. P. S. "Indian Ocean Vacuum: Fact or Fiction?" *NATO's Fifteen Nations* 16 (Feb.–Mar. 1971): 42–46.

5356   Boxhall, P. G. "The Strategic Use of Islands in a Troubled Ocean." *Royal United Services Institution Journal* 111 (Nov. 1966): 336–41.

5357   Braun, Dieter. "Der Indische Ozean in der Sicherheitspolitischen Diskussion." *Europa-Archiv* (Sept. 25, 1971): 645–58.

5358   Burt, Richard. "Strategic Politics and the Indian Ocean: A Review Article." *Pacific Affairs* 47 (Winter 1974–75): 509–14.

5359   Cottrell, Alvin J., and R. M. Burrell, eds. *The Indian Ocean: Its Political, Economic, and Military Importance.* New York: Praeger, 1972.

5360   ———, and R. M. Burrell. "Soviet-U.S. Naval Competition in the Indian Ocean." *Orbis* 18 (Winter 1975): 1109–28.

5361   Furlong, R. D. M. "Strategic Power in the Indian Ocean." *International Defense Review* 5 (Apr. 1972): 133–40.

5362   Ghebhardt, Alexander O. "Soviet and U.S. Interests in the Indian Ocean." *Asian Survey* 13 (Aug. 1975): 672–83.

5363   Gretten, Adm. Peter. "Sea Power in the Indian Ocean and Southern Atlantic." *NATO's Fifteen Nations* 14 (June–July 1969): 10–13.

5364   Griswold, Lawrence. "A Sea of Troubles." *Seapower* 17 (Dec. 1974): 14–19.

5365   Hutchinson, Alan. "Exotic Packaging." *Africa Report* 20 (Jan.–Feb. 1975): 53 ff.

5366   ———. "The Island Viewpoint." *Africa Report* 20 (Jan.–Feb. 1975): 50–52.

5367   Johnson, David. "The Indian Ocean: A New Naval Arms Race?" *Defense Monitor* (Apr. 1974): 1–12.

5368   Martin, Laurence W. "The New Power Gap in the Indian Ocean." *Interplay* 2 (Jan. 1969): 37–40.

5369   Millar, Thomas B. *The Indian and Pacific Oceans: Some Strategic Considerations.* Adelphi Paper, no. 57. London: Institute of Strategic Studies, 1969.

5370   Misra, K. P. "International Politics in the Indian Ocean." *Orbis* 18 (Winter 1975): 1088–108.

5371   Ratsimbazafy, Aristide. "The Indian Ocean: New Strategic Role." *Review Of International Affairs* [Belgrade] (Oct. 20, 1967): 18–19.

5372   Reau, Guy. "Les Grandes Puissances et L'Ocean Indien." *Revue de Défense Nationale* 27:10 (1971): 1464–79.

5373   Roschmann, Hans. "Lageentwicklung um den Indischen Ozean." *Wehrkunde* 18 (Sept. 1969): 446–52.

5374   "Russia-U.S. Showdown Coming? Behind the Big-Power Moves in Indian Ocean." *U.S. News & World Report* (Jan. 24, 1972): 32–34.

5375   Schofield, B. B. "The Strategic Importance of the Southern Oceans." *Revue Militaire Générale* [Paris] 9 (July 1971): 186–95.

5376   Simons, Sheldon W. "A Systems Approach to Security in the Indian Ocean Arc." *Orbis* 14 (Summer 1970): 401–42.

5377   U.S. House. Committee on Foreign Affairs. Report: *Means of Measuring Naval Power with Special Reference to U.S. and Soviet Activities in the Indian Ocean.* Washington, D.C.: G.P.O., May 12, 1974.

5378   Van der Kroef, Justus M. "Der Indische Ozean: Ein Neuer Schauplatz des Kalten Kriegs." *Schweizer Monatshefte* 49 (Nov. 1969): 737–41.

Soviet Union's Interests

5379 Becker, Abraham S. *Oil and the Persian Gulf in Soviet Policy in the 1970's.* P–4743–1. Santa Monica, Ca.: Rand, May 1972.

5380 Chalfont, Lord Arthur G. J. "Russia and the Indian Ocean: New Attitudes to Sea Power." *New Middle East* 44 (May 1972): 4–6.

5381 Chaplin, Dennis. "Somalia and the Development of Soviet Activity in the Indian Ocean." *Military Review* 55 (July 1975): 3–9.

5382 Cottrell, Alvin J., and R. M. Burrell. "The Soviet Navy and the Indian Ocean." *Strategic Review* 2 (Fall 1974): 25–35.

5383 Harrigan, Anthony. "Red Star Over the Indian Ocean." *National Review* (Apr. 20, 1971): 421–23.

5384 ———. "Soviets May 'Own' Indian Ocean if U.S. Doesn't Make Counter Move." *Navy* 12 (Dec. 1969): 14–18.

5385 Hopker, Wolfgang. "Der Indische Ozean im Visier des Kremls." *Aussenpolitik* 23 (June 1972): 355–64.

5386 Jukes, Geoffrey. *The Indian Ocean in Soviet Naval Policy.* Adelphi Paper, no. 87. London: International Institute of Strategic Studies, May 1972.

5387 ———. "The Soviet Union and the Indian Ocean." *Survival* 13 (1971): 370–75.

5388 Lavrentyev, Alexander. "The Soviet Perspective." *Africa Report* 20 (Jan.–Feb. 1975): 46–49.

5389 Linde, Gerd. *Die Sowjetunion im Indischen Ozean.* Koln: Bundesinstitut fur Ostwissenschaftliche und Internationale Studien, 1971.

5390 Millar, Thomas B. "Soviet Policies South and East of Suez." *Foreign Affairs* 49 (Oct. 1970): 70–80.

5391 O'Connor, Raymond G., and Vladimir P. Prokofieff. "Soviet Navy in the Mediterranean and Indian Ocean." *Virginia Quarterly Review* 49 (Autumn 1973): 481–93.

5392 Paone, Rocco M. "The Soviet Threat in the Indian Ocean." *Military Review* 50 (Dec. 1970): 48–55.

5393 Schratz, Paul R. "Red Star Over the Southern Sea [Indian Ocean]." *U.S. Naval Institute Proceedings* 96 (June 1970): 22–31.

5394 Symington, Sen. Stuart. "CIA Testimony on Soviet Presence in the Indian Ocean." *Congressional Record* 120 (Aug. 1, 1974): S14092–095.

5395 U.S. Senate. Armed Services Committee. Report: *Soviet Military Capability in Berbera, Somalia.* Washington, D.C.: G.P.O., 1975.

5396 Wheeler, Geoffrey, "The Indian Ocean Area: Soviet Aims and Interests." *Asian Affairs* 59:3 (1972): 270–74.

5397 Zumwalt, Adm. Elmo R. "Where Russian Threat Keeps Growing." *U.S. News & World Report* (Sept. 13, 1971): 72–77.

United States' Interests

5398 Badgley, John. "An American Policy to Accommodate Asian Interests in the Indian Ocean." *SAIS Review* 15:3 (1971): 2–10.

5399 Belashchenko, Capt. T. "U.S. Big Stick Over the Indian Ocean." *Soviet Military Review* 12 (Dec. 1969): 50–52.

5400 Butler, Olva B., et al. "A Committee Report of the Strategic Planning Study on U.S. Alternatives for an Indian Ocean Policy." *Naval War College Review* 21 (June 1969): 160–74.

5401 Cagle, Cmdr. Malcolm W. "The Neglected Ocean." *U.S. Naval Institute Proceedings* 84 (Nov. 1958): 54–61.

5402 "A Committee Report on the Strategic Planning Study of U.S. Alternatives For an Indian Ocean Area Policy." *Naval War College Review* 21 (June 1969): 160–74.

5403 Coye, Beth F., et al. "An Evaluation of U.S. Naval Presence in the Indian Ocean." *Naval War College Review* 23 (Oct. 1970): 34–52.

5404 Gannon, Edmond J. "Military Considerations in the Indian Ocean." *Current History* 63 (Nov. 1972): 218–21 ff.

5405 Griswold, Lawrence. "From Simonstown to Singapore." *U.S. Naval Institute Proceedings* 97 (Nov. 1971): 52–57.

5406 Heinl, Col. Robert D., Jr. "U.S. Flag Over Diego Garcia: Challenging the Soviet Fleet." *Armed Forces Journal* (Feb. 1, 1971): 13.

5407 Johnson, David. "Troubled Waters for the U.S. Navy." *Africa Report* 20 (Jan.–Feb. 1975): 8–10.

5408   Mansfield, Sen. Mike J. "Senate Resolution 1160—Resolution Disapproving Construction Projects on the Island of Diego Garcia." *Congressional Record* 121 (May 19, 1975): S8651–54.

5409   Maxfield, David M. "Senate Rejects Ban on Diego Garcia Project." *Congressional Quarterly Weekly Report* (Aug. 2, 1975): 1718–19.

5410   Mazing, V., and G. Sviator. "The U.S. Naval Buildup." *New Times* [Moscow] 5 (Feb. 1972): 8–9.

5411   Pell, Sen. Claiborne. "Diego Garcia." *Congressional Record* 120 (Feb. 7, 1974): S1452–53.

5412   Prina, L. Edgar. "At Last, A Base in the Indian Ocean." *Navy* 14 (Jan. 1971): 26–27.

5413   Rockcastle, Capt. Charles H. *The Indian Ocean: Involvement or Surrender?* Res. Rpt. 3865. Maxwell A.F.B., Ala.: Air War College, 1969.

5414   Schroeder, Richard C. "Indian Ocean Policy." *Congressional Quarterly* (Mar. 10, 1971): 189–206.

5415   Spiers, R. I. "U.S. National Security Policy and the Indian Ocean Area: Statement, July 28, 1971." *U.S. Department of State Bulletin* (Aug. 23, 1971): 199–203.

5416   Sullivan, Cmdr. Don M. *On The Need For an Indian Ocean Fleet.* Res. Rpt. 3691. Maxwell A.F.B., Ala.: Air War College, 1968.

5417   Tanham, G. K. "United States View." *International Affairs* [Moscow] 12 (Apr. 1966): 194–206.

5418   Unna, Warren. "Whom Do You Trust?: Justifying Diego Garcia." *New Republic* (Aug. 31, 1974): 10–11.

5419   U.S. House. Committee on International Relations. Hearings: *Diego Garcia, 1975: The Debate Over the Base and the Island's Former Inhabitants.* 94th Cong., 1st Sess., 1975.

5420   ———. Hearings: *The Indian Ocean: Political and Strategic Future.* 92d Cong., 1st Sess., 1971.

5421   ———. Hearings: *Proposed Expansion of U.S. Military Facilities in the Indian Ocean.* 93d Cong., 2d Sess., 1974.

5422   Withrow, Lt. Cmdr. John E., Jr. "Needed: A Credible Presence." *U.S. Naval Institute Proceedings* 92 (Mar. 1966): 52–61.

SEABED TREATY (1971)

For text of treaty, see "Treaty Banning Emplacement of Nuclear Weapons on the Seabed: Signed by 62 Nations at Washington," *U.S. Department of State Bulletin* (Mar. 8, 1971): 288–90.

Bibliography

5423   *Ocean Affairs Bibliography 1971: A Selected List Emphasizing International Law, Politics and Economics of Ocean Uses.* Ocean Series, no. 302. Washington, D.C.: Woodrow Wilson International Center for Scholars, 1971.

Documents

5424   Borgese, Elisabeth M., ed. *Pacem in Maribus.* Malta Conference Papers. New York: Dodd, Mead, 1972.

5425   U.N. *Legal Aspects of the Question of Reservation Exclusively for Peaceful Purposes of the Seabed and Ocean Floor and the Subsoil Thereof, Underlying the High Seas Beyond the Limits of National Jurisdiction and the Uses of their Resources in the Interest of Mankind.* A/AC 135/19, Add. 2. New York, 1968.

5426   ———. *Official Records of the Ad Hoc Committee on Peaceful Uses of the Seabed and Ocean Floor Beyond the Limits of National Jurisdiction.* A/7477, A/CI. New York, 1969.

5427   ———. *Official Records of the Committee on the Peaceful Uses of the Seabed and Ocean Floor Beyond the Limits of National Jurisdiction.* New York, 1969–1970.

5428   ———. *Official Records of the Legal Subcommittee of the Ad Hoc and Full Seabed Committees.* A/AC. 138/18–Add. 1. New York, 1968–1970.

5429   ———. *Official Records of the Scientific and Technical Subcommittee of the Ad Hoc and*

Full Seabed Committees. A/AC. 138/17/ SC2/6. New York, 1968–70.

5430 ———. *Report of the Ad Hoc Committee to Study Peaceful Uses of the Seabed and Ocean Floor Beyond Limits of National Jurisdiction.* A/7230, A/7622, A/8021. New York, 1968, 1969, 1970.

5431 ———. *Survey of National Legislation Concerning the Seabed and Ocean Floor and the Subsoil Thereof, Underlying the High Seas Beyond the Limits of National Jurisdiction.* A/AC 135/11; A/AC 138/9. New York, 1968, 1969.

5432 ———. "United Nations: General Assembly Resolutions Concerning the Seabed and Ocean Floor." *International Legal Materials* 10 (Jan. 1971): 220–30.

5433 "United States-Union of Soviet Socialist Republics: Draft Treaty on the Prohibition of the Emplacement of Nuclear Weapons and Other Weapons of Mass Destruction on the Seabed and Ocean Floor." *International Legal Materials* 9 (Mar. 1970): 392–95.

5434 U.S. Senate. Committee on Foreign Relations. Hearings: *Governing the Use of Ocean Space.* 90th Cong., 1st Sess., 1967.

5435 ———. Hearings: *Seabed Arms Control Treaty.* 92d Cong., 2d Sess., Jan. 27, 1972.

General Accounts

5436 Ahluwalia, S. S. "Peaceful Uses of the Sea-Bed." *India Quarterly* 27 (Apr.–June 1971): 149–52.

5437 Alexander, Robert J. "Oceanography and Future Naval Warfare." *U.S. Naval Institute Proceedings* 88:1 (June 1963): 66–73.

5438 Alvarez, Jose A. "Strategic Implications of Continental Shelves." *Naval War College Review* 21 (Nov. 1969): 48–68.

5439 Baker, Sam, and Kerry Gruson. "The Coming Arms Race Under the Sea." In Leonard S. Rodberg and Derek Shearer, eds., *The Pentagon Watchers: Students Report on the National Security State.* Garden City, N.Y.: Doubleday, 1970, pp. 335–70.

5440 Barry, James A., Jr. "Seabed Arms Control Issue, 1967–1971: A Superpower Symbiosis?" *Naval War College Review* 24 (Nov.–Dec. 1972): 87–101.

5441 Craven, John P. "Sea Power and the Sea Bed." *U.S. Naval Institute Proceedings* 92 (Apr. 1966): 36–52.

5442 Gorove, Stephen. "Toward Denuclearization of the Ocean Floor." *San Diego Law Review* 7 (July 1970): 504–19.

5443 Hanks, Robert J. "The Paper Torpedo." *U.S. Naval Institute Proceedings* 95 (May 1969): 27–34.

5444 Henkin, Louis. "The Sea-Bed Arms Treaty: One Small Step More." *Columbia Journal of Transnational Law* 10 (Spring 1971): 61–65.

5445 Hirdman, Sven. *Prospects for Arms Control in the Ocean.* SIPRI Research Report, no. 7. Stockholm: SIPRI, Oct. 1972.

5446 Hopmann, P. Terrence. "Bargaining in Arms Control Negotiations: The Seabed Denuclearization Treaty." *International Organization* 28 (Summer 1974): 313–43.

5447 Krieger, David. "Disarmament and Arms Control in Ocean Space." *Peace Research Reviews* 5 (May 1974): 48–52.

5448 Krieger, Walter W., Jr. "The United Nations Treaty Banning Nuclear Weapons and Other Weapons of Mass Destruction on the Ocean Floor." *Journal of Maritime Law & Commerce* 3 (Oct. 1971): 107–28.

5449 Kruger-Sprengel, Friedhelm. *The Role of NATO in the Use of the Sea and the Seabed.* Ocean Series, no. 304. Washington, D.C.: Woodrow Wilson International Center for Scholars, 1972.

5450 Lambert, Robert W., and John W. Syphax. *International Negotiations on the Seabed Arms Control Treaty.* ACDA Pub. 68. Washington, D.C.: G.P.O., May 1973.

5451 Loftas, Tony. "Decade for Ocean Escalation." *New Scientist* (July 2, 1970): 31–33.

5452 Maechling, Charles. "The Politics of the Ocean." *Virginia Quarterly Review* 47 (Autumn 1971): 505–17.

5453 Marx, Wesley. "The Deep-Sea Bed." *Atlantic Monthly* (Apr. 1969): 24, 26, 28, 30, 32, 37–38.

5454 "Military Use of the Ocean Space & the Continental Shelf." *Columbia Journal of Transnational Law* 7 (Fall 1968): 279–301.

5455 Myrdal, Alva. "Preserving the Oceans for Peaceful Purposes." *Recueil des Cours* [The Hague] 133:2 (1971): 1–14.

5456 Pavic, Radovan. "The Process of Demilitarization and the World Sea." *Review of International Affairs* [Belgrade] (Dec. 20, 1971): 23–25.

5457 Pfeiffer, Gerhard. "Zur Frage eines Internationalen Abkommens uber die Begrenzung der Meeresbodenrustung?" *Europa-Archiv* (Aug. 25, 1969): 581 ff.

5458 Purver, Ron. "Canada and the Control of Arms on the Seabed." *Canadian Yearbook of International Law* 13 (1975): 195–230.

5459 Schacky, Erwin Freiherr von, and Hans L. Waiblinger. "Der Meeresbodenvertrag vom 11. Februar 1971." *Europa-Archiv* (Sept. 25, 1971): 659–64.

5460 Selzer, Steven M. "The Seabed Arms Limitation Treaty: A Significant Development in Arms Control and Disarmament." *Journal of International Law & Economics* 6 (June 1971): 157–74.

5461 [U.N.]. "Ad Hoc Committee on Peaceful Uses of Seabed: Begins Second Session." *U.N. Monthly Chronicle* 5 (July 1968): 46–49.

5462 ———. "Reservation of Sea-Bed and Ocean Floor for Peaceful Purposes." *U.N. Monthly Chronicle* 5 (Jan. 1968): 28–34; 5 (Dec. 1968): 53–61.

5463 ———. *Sea-Bed: A Frontier of Disarmament.* Doc. no. E72.I.10. New York, 1972.

5464 "US, Soviet Union Cook-Up New Fraud of So-Called Prohibition of Emplacement of Nuclear Weapons on Sea-Bed and Ocean Floor." *Survey of China Mainland Press* (Oct. 29, 1969): 31.

5465 Young, Elizabeth. "To Guard the Sea." *Foreign Affairs* 50 (Oct. 1971): 136–47.

5466 ———. "Ocean Policy and Arms Control." *World Today* 26 (Sept. 1970): 401–07.

Soviet Union's Position

5467 Alekseev, A. "Prohibiting Military Use of the Sea-Bed." *International Affairs* [Moscow] 17 (1971): 60–62.

5468 Kalinkin, G. F. "Military Use of the Sea-Bed Should be Banned." *International Affairs* [Moscow] 15 (1969): 45–48.

5469 Orr, Samuel C. "Soviet Latin Opposition Blocks Agreement on Seabed Treaty." *National Journal* 2 (Sept. 1970): 1974–77.

5470 Tomilin, Iu. "Keeping the Sea-Bed Out of the Arms Race." *International Affairs* [Moscow] 16 (Jan. 1970): 41–45.

United States' Position

5471 Fisher, Adrian S. "U.S. Submits Draft Treaty Banning Emplacement of Nuclear Weapons on the Seabed." *U.S. Department of State Bulletin* (June 16, 1969): 520–24.

5472 Irwin, John N. "Department Urges Senate Approval of Seabed Arms Control Treaty." *U.S. Department of State Bulletin* (Mar. 6, 1972): 309–10.

5473 Leonard, James F. "United States Comments on Revisions in Draft Treaty Banning Emplacement of Nuclear Weapons on the Seabed." *U.S. Department of State Bulletin* (Dec. 1, 1969): 480–84.

5474 ———. "United States and U.S.S.R. Table Revised Draft Treaty Banning Emplacement of Nuclear Weapons on the Seabed." *U.S. Department of State Bulletin* (May 25, 1970): 663–67.

5475 ———. U.S. Discusses Verification Procedures Under the Draft Treaty Banning Emplacement of Nuclear Weapons on the Seabed." *U.S. Department of State Bulletin* (Nov. 17, 1969): 425–29.

5476 ———. "U.S. and U.S.S.R. Agree on Draft Treaty Banning Emplacement of Nuclear Weapons on the Seabed." *U.S. Department of State Bulletin* (Nov. 3, 1969): 365–68.

5477 Nixon, Pres. Richard M. "United States Policy for the Seabed." *U.S. Department of State Bulletin* (June 15, 1970): 737–41.

5478 Popper, David H. "The Deep Ocean Environment: U.S. and International Policy." *U.S. Department of State Bulletin* (Aug. 12, 1968): 171–77.

5479 ———. "U.N. Seabed Committee Concludes Spring Session." *U.S. Department of State Bulletin* (Apr. 21, 1969): 342–45.

5480   Rogers, William P. "Seabed Arms Control Treaty Transmitted to the Senate: Secretary Rogers' Report." *U.S. Department of State Bulletin* (Aug. 16, 1971): 185–87.

5481   Smith, Gerard C. "Ambassador Smith Presents U.S. Views on Seabed Proposal at Eighteen-Nation Disarmament Conference." *U.S. Department of State Bulletin* (Apr. 21, 1969): 333–37.

5482   Wiggins, James R. "U.S. Suggests Possible Steps by U.N. to Promote Peaceful Uses of the Deep Ocean Floor." *U.S. Department of State Bulletin* (Nov. 15, 1968): 554–58.

Legal Issues

5483   Alexander, Lewis M., ed. *The Law of the Sea: A New Geneva Conference. Proceedings of the Sixth Annual Conference . . . at the University of Rhode Island.* Kingston: Univ. of Rhode Island, 1972.

5484   ———. *The Law of the Sea: The United Nations and Ocean Management. Proceedings of the Fifth Annual Conference . . . at the University of Rhode Island.* Kingston: Univ. of Rhode Island, 1971.

5485   Andrassy, Jura, ed. *International Law and the Resources of the Sea.* New York: Columbia Univ. Press, 1970.

5486   Brown, Edward D. *Arms Control in Hydrospace: Legal Aspects.* Oceans Series, no. 301. Washington, D.C.: Woodrow Wilson International Center for Scholars, 1971.

5487   Burke, William T. "Comments on Current International Issues Relating to the Law of the Sea." *Natural Resources Lawyer* 4 (July 1971): 660–66.

5488   Gehring, Robert W. "Legal Rules Affecting Military Uses of the Seabed." *U.S. Military Law Review* 54 (Fall 1971): 168–224.

5489   Goralczyk, Wojciech. "The Legal Foundations of the Peaceful Uses of the Sea-Bed and the Ocean Floor." *Studies on International Relations* [Warsaw] 2 (1973): 75–114.

5490   Johnson, D. H. M. "Who Owns the Sea-Bed?" *New Scientist* (Feb. 20, 1969): 394–95.

5491   Loftas, Tony. "Ocean Law in Deep Water." *New Scientist* (Mar. 12, 1970): 519.

5492   Nanda, Veda P. "Some Legal Questions on the Peaceful Uses of Ocean Space." *Virginia Journal of International Law* 9 (May 1969): 343–408.

5493   Wilkes, Daniel. "The Use of World Resources Without Conflict: Myths About the Territorial Sea." *Wayne State Law Review* 14 (Spring 1968): 441–70.

SINAI PACT (1975)

For text of pact, see "Egypt-Israel: Agreement on the Sinai and Suez Canal," *International Legal Materials* 14 (Nov. 1975): 1450–69.

5494   Evron, Yair. *The Demilitarization of Sinai.* Jerusalem Papers on Peace Problems, no. 11. Jerusalem: Hebrew Univ., Leonard Davis Institute for International Relations, 1975.

5495   Goldsworthy, Peter J. "Neutralization of an Arab Palestine: The Key to a Settlement in the Middle East." *Australian Outlook* 29 (Apr. 1975): 97–108.

5496   U.S. House. Committee on International Relations. Hearings: *Middle East Agreements and the Early-Warning System in Sinai.* 94th Cong., 1st Sess., Sept. 8–25, 1975.

5497   U.S. Senate. Committee on Foreign Relations. Hearings: *Early Warning System in Sinai.* 94th Cong., 1st Sess., Oct. 6–7, 1975.

5498   Younger, Sam. "The Sinai Pact." *World Today* 31 (Oct. 1975): 391–94.

Ten

Regulating & Outlawing Weapons & War

AS THE WEAPONS of war have evolved from the crossbow to the H-bomb, various attempts have been made to restrict or outlaw their use. The Church's alleged outlawing of the Crossbow (1139) is the classic example of this arms control and disarmament technique. In subsequent centuries, particularly the 18th and 19th, the "rules of war" were frequently expanded to regulate and restrict the use of weapons against civilian populations. Weapons technology in the 20th century, however, eroded away these earlier barriers and reintroduced indiscriminate targeting. Thus, some critics of this modern trend have argued for outlawing or controlling specific weapons.

The basic arguments underlying these attitudes may be put simply. Those who urge control or abolition of weapons capable of vast, indiscriminate destruction argue with Polybius that "to destroy that for which war is undertaken, seems an act of madness, and madness of a very violent sort." On the other side are those who insist that there is an unwritten rule that governs the use of weapons: their employment is dictated almost exclusively by

their effectiveness. To assist in developing the debate over weapons, the sections below dealing with chemical-biological (C/B) warfare, submarines and aerial bombardment have been enlarged to include examples of their use.

The initial sections of this chapter feature lists of books and essays that reflect the development of international law regarding weapons. J. W. Garner's *International Law and the World War* (1920) examines alleged World War I violations, while several other essays survey the contemporary issues. (See Chapter 13 for additional references to the "rules of war"). G. Schwarzenberger's *The Legality of Nuclear Weapons* (1958) and N. Singh's *Nuclear Weapons and International Law* (1959) focus on the legality of weapons of mass destruction. The Soviet Union's proposal to outlaw nuclear weapons (1967) is employed here as a focal point for related issues.

Efforts to outlaw chemical and biological warfare began at the Hague Conferences (1899, 1907) but were stimulated again after each world war. Although the literature on this topic is voluminous, the most complete survey of these AC&D attempts and the issues involved is SIPRI's *The Problem of Chemical and Biological Warfare*, 6 vols. (1971–1974). These volumes are updated in the *SIPRI Yearbook of World Armament and Disarmament* (1968/69–). F. J. Brown's *Chemical Warfare: A Study in Restraints* (1968) and the Thomases' *Legal Limits on the Use of Chemical and Biological Weapons: International Law, 1899–1970* (1970) are excellent single-volume introductions.

The sinking of merchant ships without warning by submarines during World War I prompted a postwar movement to sharply restrict submarine activities. There are a number of fine accounts of these efforts, the most extensive of which is W. T. Mallison's *Studies in the Law of Naval Warfare: Submarines in General and Limited Wars* (1968). If a short survey is sufficient, then see the essays by R. D. Burns, "Regulating Submarine Warfare, 1921–41" in *Military Affairs* (1971) or W. H. Barnes, "Submarine Warfare and International Law" in *World Polity* (1960); disagreement with these rules is registered by A. M. Low in *The Submarine at War* (1942).

Aerial bombardment has been unchecked except for minimal efforts to apply the "rules of war." The total collapse of restraints can be traced during World War II from Britain's early use of "area bombing" to the U.S.'s dropping of A-bombs on Japan. H. DeSaussure's essay, "The Laws of Air Warfare: Are There Any?" *Naval War College Review* (1971), poses the essential question; Col. J. D. Terry's response in "The Evolving Law of Aerial Warfare" in *Air University Review* (1975) is an inadequate answer.

The "outlawing of war" was one of the more noble, if illusionary, undertakings of the interwar years. And yet, if mankind is ever to achieve peace, it will have to find a way to eliminate war. Walter Millis' *The Abolition of War* (1963) is a brilliant study of the problems that lie in a world beyond war. The impractical Kellogg-Briand Pact (1928) has been subjected to considerable historical criticism; R. H. Ferrell's *Peace in their Time* (1952) and J. C. Vinson's *William E. Borah and the Outlawry of War* (1957) expose the issues and politics connected with this venture.

Crossbows & Nuclear Weapons

INTERNATIONAL LAW & WEAPONS

5499 Bailey, Sidney D. *Prohibitions and Restraints in War*. New York: Oxford Univ. Press, 1972.

5500 Butz, J. S. "You Can't Ban Technology." *Air Force and Space Digest* 46:6 (June 1963): 34–37.

5501 Eide, Asbjorn. "Outlawing the Use of Some Conventional Weapons: Another Approach to Disarmament?" *Instant Research on Peace and Violence* 6:1–2 (1976): 39–51.

5502 Gardiner, Robert W. *The Cool Arm of Destruction: Modern Weapons and Moral Insensitivity*. Philadelphia: Westminister Press, 1974.

5503 Garner, James W. "Forbidden Weapons and Instrumentalities." *International Law and the World War*. 2 vols. London: Longmans, Green, 1920, I: 262–97.

5504 Halle, Louis. "Is War Obsolete? The Inhibiting Effect of Absolute Weapons." *New Republic* (Apr. 2, 1962): 13–17.

5505 Heydte, Baron F. A. von der. "Le Probleme que pose l'Existence des Armes de Destruction Massive et la Distinction entre les Objectifs Militaires et non Militaires en General."

Annuaire de l'Institut de Droit International [Session de Nice] 52, Bk II (1969).

5506 Joenniemi, Pertti. "Conventional Weapons: A Revived Issue [Prohibitions]." *Instant Research on Peace and Violence* 6:1–2 (1976): 29–38.

5507 Krepon, Michael. "Weapons Potentially Inhumane: The Case of Cluster Bombs." *Foreign Affairs* 52 (Apr. 1974): 595–611.

5508 Lumsden, Malvern. "Inhumane Weapons and Inhuman Warfare." *World Armament and Disarmament, SIPRI Yearbook 1973*. New York: Humanities Press, 1973, pp. 132–51.

5509 Mallison, William T., Jr. "The Laws of War and the Juridical Control of Weapons of Mass Destruction in General and Limited Wars." *George Washington Law Review* 36 (Dec. 1967): 308–46.

5510 Rhyne, Charles S. "Law for Weapons." *Tennessee Law Review* 26:1 (1958): 401–09.

5511 Sack, A. N. "ABC—Atomic, Biological, Chemical Warfare in International Law." *Lawyers Guild Review* 10 (Winter 1950): 161–80.

5512 ———. "Atomic Weapons and Non-Directed Missiles." *Revue Internationale de la*

Croix-Rouge, English Supplement [Geneva] 3 (Apr. 1950): 70–73.

5513   Schwarzenberger, George. "Self-Defense under the Charter of the United Nations and the Use of Prohibited Weapons." *International Law Association Report of the 50th Conference* (1962): 192–237.

5514   Singh, Nagendra. "The Laws of Land Warfare and Prohibited Weapons and Practices." *Indian Yearbook of International Affairs* 7 (1958): 3–52.

5515   SIPRI. *The Law of War and Dubious Weapons.* Stockholm: Almqvist & Wiksell, 1976.

5516   Smith, H. A. "Modern Weapons and Modern War." *Yearbook of World Affairs* 9 (1955): 222–47.

5517   Szilard, Leo. "My Trial as a War Criminal." *University of Chicago Law Review* 17 (Autumn 1949): 79–86.

5518   Vukas, Budislav. "Weapons of Mass Destruction and International Law." *Medunarodni Problemi* 23:1 (1971): 39–54.

INTERNATIONAL LAW & NUCLEAR WEAPONS

5519   Borchard, Edwin M. "The Atomic Bomb." *American Journal of International Law* 40 (Jan. 1946): 161–65.

5520   Brownlie, Ian. "Some Legal Aspects of the Use of Nuclear Weapons." *International And Comparative Law Quarterly* [London] 14 (Apr. 1965): 437–51.

5521   Cassagne-Serres, Blanca A. *Las Armas Atomicas y Bomba de Hidrogeno Frente al Derecho Internacional.* Buenos Aires: Perrot, 1954.

5522   Falk, Richard A. "Shimoda Case: A Legal Appraisal of the Atomic Attacks on Hiroshima and Nagasaki." *American Journal of International Law* 59 (Oct. 1965): 759–93.

5523   Furet, M. F. *Experimentation des Armes Nucléaires et Droit International Public.* Paris: A. Pedone, 1966.

5524   Galeski, B. "Arme Atomique et Droit International." *Polish Perspectives* [Warsaw] 4 (Aug.–Sept. 1961): 12–35.

5525   Hartley, Livingston. "False Parallel: Basic Difference Between Gas and Atomic Warfare." *Bulletin of the Atomic Scientists* 6 (June 1950): 172–73, 192.

5526   Korovin, Eugene A. "The A-Weapons vs. International Law." *International Affairs* [Moscow] 1 (May 1955): 45–55.

5527   Kunz, Josef L. "Atombombe und Volkerrecht." *Osterreichische Zeitschrift fur Offentliches Recht* [Vienna] 2 (Jan. 1950): 414–36.

5528   Lewy, Guenter. "Superior Orders, Nuclear Warfare and the Dictates of Conscience." In Richard A. Wasserstrom, ed., *War and Morality.* Belmont, Ca.: Wadsworth, 1970, pp. 115–34.

5529   Maggs, P. B. "Soviet Viewpoint on Nuclear Weapons in International Law." *Law and Contemporary Problems* 29 (Autumn 1964): 956–70.

5530   Meyrowitz, Henri. "Les Juristes devant l'Arme Nucléaire." *Revue Generale de Droit International Publiĉ* 67 (Oct.–Dec. 1963): 820–73.

5531   O'Brien, William V. "Legitimate Military Necessity in Nuclear War." *World Polity* 2 (1960): 35–120.

5532   ———. "Nuclear Warfare and the Law of Nations." In William J. Nagle, ed., *Morality and Modern Warfare.* Baltimore: Helicon Press, 1960, pp. 126–50.

5533   Radojkovic, M. "Les Armes Nucleaires et le Droit International." *Yearbook of World Affairs* 16 (1962): 197–215.

5534   Richstein, A. R. "Legal Rules in Nuclear Weapons Employments." *Military Review* 41 (July 1961): 91–98.

5535   Schwarzenberger, George. *The Legality of Nuclear Weapons.* London: Stevens, 1958.

5536   Singh, Nagendra. *Nuclear Weapons and International Law.* London: Stevens, 1959.

5537   ———. "The Right of Self-Defense in Relation to the Use of Nuclear Weapons." *Indian Yearbook of International Affairs* [Madras] 5 (1956): 3–37.

5538   Stowell, Ellery C. "The Laws of War and the Atomic Bomb." *American Journal of International Law* 39 (Oct. 1945): 784–88.

5539   Taylor, Telford. "Le Droit Penal International et la Guerre Atomique." *Revue de Droit International* [Sottile-Geneva] 29 (Jan.–Mar. 1951): 1–15.

5540   Thomas, Sen. Elbert D. "Atomic Bombs in International Society." *American Journal of International Law* 39 (Oct. 1945): 736–44.

5541   ———. "Atomic Warfare and International Law." *American Society of International Law: Proceedings* (1946): 84–89.

5542   Tyrrell, F. G. "Is the Use of the Atomic Bomb Justified?" *Vital Speeches* (Oct. 1, 1945): 767–68.

ECOCIDE

5543   Falk, Richard A. "Environmental Warfare and Ecocide." *Bulletin of Peace Proposals* 4:1 (1973): 80–96.

5544   Lewallen, J. *Ecology of Devastation: Indochina.* Baltimore: Penguin, 1971.

5545   Orians, G. H., and E. W. Pfeiffer. "Ecological Effects of War in Vietnam." *Science* (May 1, 1970): 544–54.

5546   Schell, O., Jr. "Silent Vietnam: How We Invented Ecocide and Killed a Country." *Look* (July 1971): 55, 57–58.

5547   SIPRI. *Ecological Consequences of the Second Indochina War.* Cambridge: M.I.T. Press, 1976.

5548   U.S. Joint Committee on Atomic Energy. Hearings: *Biological and Environmental Effects of Nuclear War.* 86th Cong., 1st Sess., 1959.

5549   Weisberg, B., ed. *Ecocide in Indochina: The Ecology of War.* San Francisco: Canfield Press, 1970.

5550   Westing, Arthur H. "Ecocide in Indochina." *Natural History* 80:3 (1971): 56–61, 88.

5551   ———. "Proscription of Ecocide: Arms Control and the Environment." *Bulletin of the Atomic Scientists* 30 (Jan. 1974): 24–27.

OUTLAWING THE CROSSBOW (1139)

For text of decision of the Second Lateran Council Decree, Canon 29, see Trevor N. Dupuy and Gay M. Hammerman, eds., *A Documentary History of Arms Control and Disarmament* (New York: Bowker, 1973), pp. 10–11.

5552   Hills, Lawrence D. "Unilateral Disarmament: 1139 A.D." *Nation* (Oct. 7, 1961): 220.

5553   Royse, M. W. *Aerial Bombardment and the International Regulation of Warfare.* New York: Harold Vinal, 1928, p. 166.

5554   Schroeder, H. J., ed. *Disciplinary Decrees of the General Councils.* St. Louis: Herder, 1937, p. 213.

SOVIET PROPOSAL OUTLAWING NUCLEAR WEAPONS (1967)

For text of Soviet draft convention, see "Soviet Draft Convention on the Prohibition of the Use of Nuclear Weapons, Sept. 22, 1967," *Documents on Disarmament, 1967* (Washington, D.C.: G.P.O., 1968), pp. 420–21. [See also U.N. General Assembly Resolution 1653 (XVI): *Declaration on the Prohibition of the Use of Nuclear and Thermonuclear Weapons, Nov. 24, 1961.*]

5555   Beaumont, Roger A. "Prospects for Nuclear Nullification." *Military Review* 49 (Oct. 1969): 29–35.

5556   "Convention on Prohibition of Nuclear Weapons: Consideration by First Committee." *U.N. Monthly Chronicle* 4 (Dec. 1967): 69–72.

5557   Daiches, David. "Renouncing Nuclear Weapons." In Quincy Wright et al., eds., *Preventing World War III.* New York: Simon & Schuster, 1962, pp. 83–86.

5558   Falk, Richard A. "Renunciation of Nuclear Weapons Use." In Bennett Boskey and Mason Willrich, eds., *Nuclear Proliferation: Prospects For Control.* New York: Dunellen, 1970, pp. 133–45.

5559   Fisher, Adrian S. "U.S. Gives Views on Soviet Proposal for Convention on 'Nonuse' of Nuclear Weapons." *U.S. Department of State Bulletin* (Jan. 1, 1968): 26–30.

5560   Frye, William R. "The Disarmament Turning Point." *Bulletin of the Atomic Scientists* 12 (May 1956): 166–68.

5561   Halperin, Morton H. *A Proposal for a Ban on the Use of Nuclear Weapons.* Special Studies Group, SM-4. Washington, D.C.: Institute for Defense Analyses, 1961.

5562　Heisenberg, Wolfgang. "Zum Verbot des Ersteinsatzes von Kernwaffen: Fesseling oder Entfesselung des Modernen Krieges?" *Europa-Archiv* (Nov. 10, 1974): 729–37.

5563　Kecskmeti, Paul. "Nuclear Abolitionism." *Commentary* 36 (July 1963): 43–48.

5564　Lvov, M. "Ban Nuclear Weapons." *International Affairs* [Moscow] 11 (Jan. 1965): 9–14.

5565　"New Worry for World: If Nuclear Weapons are Banned, Something Worse in Their Place?" *U.S. News & World Report* (May 30, 1958): 39–44.

5566　"Outlaw Atomic Weapons." *International Affairs* [Moscow] 3 (May 1957): 5–10.

5567　"Prohibition of Use of Nuclear Weapons." *U.N. Monthly Chronicle* 5 (Jan. 1968): 23–25.

5568　Read, Thornton. *A Proposal to Neutralize Nuclear Weapons*. Policy Memo, no. 22. Princeton: Princeton Univ., 1960.

5569　"UN World Poll: Should Absolute Weapons be Outlawed?" *U.N. World* 2 (Mar. 1948): 6.

5570　Wendt, Lt. Col. William R. "Outlaw the Atomic Bomb." *U.S. Naval Institute Proceedings* 75 (Mar. 1949): 334–35.

"No First Use" of Nuclear Weapons

5571　Aspin, Rep. Les. "Nonproliferation Treaty [non-use against non-nuclear states]." *Congressional Record* 121 (Nov. 4, 1975): H10623.

5572　"Exposing New U.S. Fraud Over Nuclear Weapons." *Peking Review* (June 24, 1966): 27–28.

5573　Falk, Richard A. "Thoughts in Support of a No-First-Use Proposal." *Legal Order in a Violent World*. Princeton: Princeton Univ. Press, 1968, pp. 425–35.

5574　Feld, Bernard T. "A Pledge: No First Use." *Bulletin of the Atomic Scientists* 23 (May 1967): 46–48.

5575　"First Use Deserves More Than One Decision-Maker." *F.A.S. Public Interest Report*. Washington, D.C.: Federation of American Scientists, Sept. 1975.

5576　Halperin, Morton H. "A Proposal for a Ban on the First Use of Nuclear Weapons." *Journal of Arms Control* 1:2 (1963): 112–23.

5577　Lenefsky, David. "No First Use of Nuclear Weapons—A Pledge." *Bulletin of the Atomic Scientists* 29 (Mar. 1973): 9

5578　Schandler, Herbert Y. *U.S. Policy on the Use of Nuclear Weapons, 1945–1975*. Congressional Research Service Pub. no. 75-175 F. Washington, D.C.: Library of Congress, Aug. 14, 1975.

5579　Schroeder, Rep. Pat. "When Should the United States Use Nuclear Weapons?" *Congressional Record* 121 (Oct. 3, 1975): H17514–515.

5580　Scoville, Herbert, Jr. " 'First Use' of Nuclear Weapons." *Arms Control Today* 5 (July–Aug. 1975): 1–3.

5581　Tucker, Robert W., et al. *Proposal for No First Use of Nuclear Weapons: Pros and Cons*. Princeton: Princeton Univ., Center of International Studies, 1963.

5582　Udall, Rep. Morris K. "Report to Members of Congress for Peace Through Law Denounces Nuclear Weapons First Use Strategy." *Congressional Record* 121 (July 31, 1975): H8023–25.

5583　Ullman, Richard H. "No First Use of Nuclear Weapons." *Foreign Affairs* 50 (July 1972): 669–83.

5584　U.S. House. Committee on International Relations. Hearings: *First Use of Nuclear Weapons: Preserving Responsible Control*. 94th Cong., 2d Sess., 1976.

5585　———. Report: *Authority to Order the Use of Nuclear Weapons (United States, United Kingdom, France, Soviet Union, People's Republic of China)*. 94th Cong., 1st Sess., 1975.

5586　Willrich, Mason. "No First Use of Nuclear Weapons: An Assessment." *Orbis* 9 (Summer 1965): 299–315.

Chemical-Biological Weapons

Bibliographies

5587　Robinson, Julian Perry, ed. *CBW: An Introduction and Bibliography*. Los Angeles:

California State Univ., Center for the Study of Armament & Disarmament, 1974.

5588 U.S. Library of Congress. *Chemical and Biological Warfare: U.S.S.R., A Bibliography.* Washington, D.C.: G.P.O., 1963.

5589 Wasan, R. P. "Chemical and Biological Warfare: A Selected Bibliography." *Institute for Defence Studies and Analyses Journal* [New Delhi] 2 (Jan. 1970): 365–78.

5590 Westing, Arthur H., ed. *Herbicides as Weapons: A Bibliography.* Los Angeles: California State Univ., Center for the Study of Armament & Disarmament, 1974.

Documents

5591 [League of Nations]. *Treatment of the Question of Chemical/Biological Warfare in the League of Nations: Review by the United Nations Secretariat* [Aug. 3, 1951]. Doc. no. A/AC.50/3. New York: United Nations, 1951.

5592 U.N. General Assembly. *Chemical and Bacteriological (Biological) Weapons and the Effects of their Possible Use.* Report of the Secretary-General. Doc. A/7575/Rev.1; S/9292/Rev.1. New York, 1969.

General Accounts

5593 American Academy of Arts & Sciences. *Proceedings of the Conference on Chemical and Biological Warfare, July 25, 1969.* Boston: House of the Academy, 1969.

5594 American Chemical Society. *Nonmilitary Defense: Chemical and Biological Defenses in Perspective.* Advances in Chemistry Series, no. 26. Washington, D.C.: American Chemical Society, 1960.

5595 Ch'en P'ei-Fu and Wang Chao-Ku. *Military Information Handbook: Introduction to Atomic, Chemical and Bacteriological Weapons.* [Translation of portions of Fan Jua-Hsueh Ping, Peking, 1957.] Washington, D.C.: U.S. Department of Army, 1959. [Available from National Technical Information Service as OTS 59 11275.]

5596 Clarke, Robin H. *The Silent Weapons: The Realities of Chemical and Biological Warfare.* New York: David McKay, 1968.

5597 Cookson, John, and Judith Nottingham, eds. *A Survey of Chemical and Biological Warfare.* London: Sheed & Ward, 1969.

5598 Cornish, M. D., and R. Murray, eds. *The Supreme Folly: Chemical and Biological Weapons.* London: NCLC Publishing Society, 1970.

5599 Hersh, Seymour M. *Chemical and Biological Warfare: America's Hidden Arsenal.* New York: Bobbs-Merrill, 1968.

5600 Lefebure, Maj. Victor. *The Riddle of the Rhine: Chemical Strategy in Peace and War.* New York: Dutton, 1923.

5601 ———. *Scientific Disarmament: A Treatment Based on the Facts of Armament.* London: Gollancz, 1931.

5602 Liepmann, Heinz. *Death From the Skies: A Study of Gas and Microbial Warfare.* London: Secker & Warburg, 1937.

5603 McCarthy, Richard D. *The Ultimate Folly: War by Pestilence, Asphyxiation and Defoliation.* New York: Random House, 1969.

5604 McCullough, James M. *Chemical and Biological Warfare: Issues and Developments During 1971.* Library of Congress, Congressional Research Service Report SP 71–261. Washington, D.C.: G.P.O., 1971.

5605 Prentiss, Augustin M. *Chemicals in War: A Treatise on Chemical Warfare.* New York: McGraw-Hill, 1937.

5606 Quimby, F. H., and M. E. Carlin. *Chemical and Biological Warfare: Some Questions and Answers.* Library of Congress, Legislative Reference Service Report SP 164. Washington, D.C.: G.P.O., 1969.

5607 Rose, Steven, ed. *CBW: Chemical and Biological Warfare.* Boston: Beacon, 1969.

5608 Rothschild, J. H. *Tomorrow's Weapons: Chemical and Biological.* New York: McGraw-Hill, 1964.

5609 SIPRI. *The Problem of Chemical and Biological Warfare.* 6 vols. New York: Humanities Press, 1971–1975. [Vol. 1: *The Rise of CB Weapons* (1971); Vol. 2: *CB Weapons Today* (1973); Vol. 3: *CBW and the Law of War* (1974); Vol. 4: *CB Disarmament Negotiations, 1920–1970* (1971); Vol. 5: *The Prevention of CBW* (1971); Vol. 6: *Technical*

Aspects of Early Warning and Verification (1975).]

5610   Templeton, James L., Jr. *A Credible Chemical Defense: Fact or Fantasy.* NTIS no. AD–A024976/3GA. Springfield, Va.: National Technical Information Service, 1975.

5611   Weizacker, Ernst-Ulrich von, ed. *BC-Waffen und Friedenspolitik.* Stuttgart, Klett, 1970.

Pre-1945 Essays

5612   Fradkin, Elvira K. "Chemical Warfare: Its Possibilities and Probabilities." *International Conciliation,* no. 248 (Mar. 1929): 109–92.

5613   ———. "Future of Poison Gas." *Current History* 15 (Dec. 1921): 419–22.

5614   Fries, Gen. Amos A. "Some Naval Aspects of Chemical Warfare." *U.S. Naval Institute Proceedings* 54 (Aug. 1928): 635–43.

5615   Lapoule, Albert. "Chemical Preparations for War." *Living Age* 335 (Dec. 1928): 254–56.

5616   Lefebure, Maj. Victor. "Chemical Warfare." *Journal of Royal United Services Institution* 73 (Aug. 1928): 492–505.

5617   McDowell, Edward C., Jr. "Poison Gas: Myth or Menace." *Current History* 44 (July 1936): 59–64.

5618   McLaughlin, E. F. "Poison Gas and the Civilian Front: Reply with Rejoinder." *New Republic* (Sept. 9, 1936): 131.

5619   Mills, J. E. "Chemical Warfare." *Military Engineering* 14 (July–Aug. 1922): 247–49.

5620   Worker, Gertrude. "Chemical and Bacteriological Warfare." *What Would Be the Character of a New War? Enquiry Organized by the Inter-Parliamentary Union.* London: Gollancz, 1933, pp. 354–91.

Post-1945 Essays

5621   "Biological and Chemical Warfare: An International Symposium." *Bulletin of the Atomic Scientists* 16 (June 1960): 226–56.

5622   Boffery, Philip M. "Nerve Gas: Dugway Accident Linked to Utah Sheep Kill." *Science* (Dec. 27, 1968): 1460–64.

5623   Briggs, Michael. "Chemical and Biological Warfare." *Humanist* 84 (July 1969): 201–06.

5624   Brodine, Virginia, et al. "The Wind From Dugway." *Environment* 2:1 (1969): 2–9.

5625   Carlat, Louis E. "Germs and Gases: Question Marks of Modern War." *Nuclear Information* 5 (Feb. 1963): 1, 7–11.

5626   "Chemical and Biological Warfare: A Special Issue." *Scientist & Citizen* 9 (Aug.–Sept. 1967). [Entire issue.]

5627   Creasy, Gen. William M. "Attack by Invisible Invader." *Army Information Digest* (Feb. 1958): 46–53.

5628   ———. "CBR: Invisible Attack." *NATO Civil Defense Bulletin* 5 (June 1959): 24–26.

5629   Edsall, John T., and Matthew S. Meselson. "CB Warfare: The Terrors of the New Weaponry." *Harvard Alumni Bulletin* (Mar. 11, 1967): 16–19, 30.

5630   Fair, Lt. Col. Stanley D. "Gas and a Just War." *Ordnance* 51 (Nov.–Dec. 1966): 272–76.

5631   Farer, Tom J. "Chemical and Biological Agents and Nuclear Weapons." *International Conciliation,* no. 582 (Mar. 1971): 18–24.

5632   Guest, Alex. "Chemical and Biological Warfare." *Marxist Quarterly* 17 (Spring 1966): 80–89.

5633   Haddow, Alexander. "On Bacteriological and Chemical Warfare." *New Scientist* (Feb. 12, 1959): 329–31.

5634   Hersh, Seymour M. "Chemical and Biological Weapons—The Secret Arsenal." *New York Times Magazine* (Aug. 25, 1968): 26–27, 82, 84–87, 90, 92.

5635   ———. "Germs and Gas as Weapons." *New Republic* (June 7, 1969): 13–16.

5636   ———. "On Uncovering the Great Nerve Gas Coverup." *Ramparts* 8 (June 1969): 12–18.

5637   Kennedy, William V. "CBR War—The X Factor." *Ordnance* 48 (1963): 50–52.

5638   McCarthy, Richard D. "Poison for Peace." *Commonweal* (June 6, 1969): 335–37.

5639   McIntyre, William R. "Chemical-Biological Warfare." *Editorial Research Reports* (Oct. 12, 1959): 757–73.

5640   Meselson, Matthew S., et al. "Symposium on Chemical and Biological Warfare." *Proceedings of the National Academy of Sciences* 65:1 (1970): 250–79.

5641 Miettinen, Jorma K. "The Chemical Arsenal." *Bulletin of the Atomic Scientists* 30 (Sept. 1974): 37–43.

5642 Mirimanoff, Jean. "The Red Cross and Biological and Chemical Warfare." *International Review of the Red Cross* 111 (June 1970): 301–15.

5643 Pfaltzgraff, Robert L., Jr. "Biological and Chemical Weapons." *Current History* 47 (July 1964): 18–24, 51–52.

5644 Robinson, Julian Perry. "The Special Case of Chemical and Biological Weapons." *Bulletin of the Atomic Scientists* 31 (May 1975): 17–23.

5645 Rose, Steven. "The Real Significance of CBW." *Journal of Instant Research on Peace and Violence* 2:1 (1972): 9–16.

5646 Rothschild, J. H. "Germs and Gas: The Weapons Nobody Dares Talk About." *Harper's* 218 (June 1959): 29–34.

5647 Saunders, David M. "The Biological/Chemical Warfare Challenge." *U.S. Naval Institute Proceedings* 91 (Sept. 1965): 46–51.

5648 Sibley, C. Bruce. "A CB Primer: Looking at the Chemical and Biological Warfare Scenarios." *Defense & Foreign Affairs*, no. 10 (1976): 6–12.

5649 Sidel, Victor W., and Robert M. Goldwyn. "Chemical and Biologic Weapons—A Primer." *New England Journal of Medicine* (Jan. 6, 1966): 21–27, 50–51.

5650 Stokes, J. D. "Chemical, Bacteriological and Radiological Warfare." *Journal of the Kentucky State Medical Association* 62 (1964): 24–30.

5651 Windom, Maj. Jackson. "Survival: Chemical Warfare." *Infantry* 60 (Jan.–Feb. 1970): 38–40.

5652 Windsor, Philip. "Gas: an ISS [Institute for Strategic Studies] View." *Survival* 7 (May–June 1965): 145–46.

NATIONAL POLICIES—UNITED STATES

5653 Beller, William S. "Forthright CBR Policy Urged." *Missiles and Rockets* (Apr. 19, 1965): 27–31.

5654 Bills, Maj. Ray W. "What Should be the United States' Position on Chemical Warfare Disarmament?" *Military Review* 55 (May 1975): 12–23.

5655 Boffery, Philip M. "CBW: Pressure for Control Builds in Congress, International Groups." *Science* (June 20, 1969): 1376–78.

5656 "Chemical-Biological Treaty Stalled in White House." *Congressional Quarterly Weekly Report* (July 24, 1970): 1917–19.

5657 Conway, Paul G. "An Analysis of Decision Making on United States Chemical and Biological Warfare Policies in 1969." Ph.D. diss., Purdue Univ., 1972.

5658 Fair, Lt. Col. Stanley D. "The Chemical Corps: Alive, Well and Visible." *Army* 22:4 (1972): 29–32.

5659 Gellner, Charles R. *International Prohibition of the Use of Chemical and Biological Weapons: A Survey of United States Policy.* Library of Congress, Legislative Reference Service Report F–374. Washington, D.C.: G.P.O., 1969.

5660 Goldhaber, Samuel Z. "CBW: Interagency Conflicts Stall Administration Action." *Science* (July 31, 1970): 454–56.

5661 Hamilton, Andrew. "CBW: Nixon Initiative on Treaty Anticipates Congressional Critics." *Science* (Dec. 5, 1969): 1250.

5662 Hart, Sen. Gary. "Senate Bill 1288 [prohibit development & production of chemical weapons]." *Congressional Record* 121 (Mar. 22, 1975): S4876–77.

5663 Hicks, Rep. Floyd. "Chemical Warfare and Biological Defense Programs." *Congressional Record* 121 (May 8, 1975): H3854–55.

5664 Kanegis, Arthur, "U.S. CBW Policy." *Liberation* 15 (Nov. 1970): 11–19.

5665 ———, and Lindsay Richards. "The Budget Gives the Game Away." *Nation* (Oct. 11, 1971): 337–40.

5666 Kastenmeier, Rep. Robert W. "Chemical Warfare: Pentagon Booby-trap." *Progressive* 23 (Dec. 1959): 19–21.

5667 Langer, Elinor. "Chemical and Biological Warfare: The Research Program." *Science* (Jan. 13, 1967): 174–77.

5668 ———. "Chemical and Biological Warfare: The Weapons and Policies." *Science* (Jan. 20, 1967): 299–303.

5669 Leonard, James F. "Control of Chemical and Biological Weapons." *U.S. Department of State Bulletin* (Sept. 21, 1970): 330–31.

5670 ———. "United States Explains Position on Chemical and Biological Warfare." *U.S. Department of State Bulletin* (Apr. 27, 1970): 552–57.

5671 Martin, Joseph, Jr. "United States Discusses Chemical Weapons and Other Arms Control Issues." *U.S. Department of State Bulletin* (June 5, 1972): 792–801.

5672 McCullough, James M. *Chemical and Biological Warfare: Issues and Developments During 1974.* Cong. Research Service Pub. 75–13 SP. Washington, D.C.: Library of Congress, Jan. 2, 1975.

5673 ———, and Blanchard Randall IV. *Chemical and Biological Warfare: Issues and Development During 1975.* Cong. Research Service Pub. UG 447, 76–30 SP. Washington, D.C.: Congressional Library, Jan. 5, 1976.

5674 McIntyre, Sen. Thomas. "Semiannual Report by the Department of Defense on Chemical and Biological Warfare Activities." *Congressional Record* 121 (Mar. 17, 1975): S3999–4008.

5675 ———. "Semiannual Report by the Department of Defense on Chemical and Biological Warfare Activities." *Congressional Record* 121 (Sept. 19, 1975): S16348–357.

5676 ———. "Senate Concurrent Resolution 68 —Submission of a Concurrent Resolution Relating to an International Treaty Banning Lethal Chemical Weapons." *Congressional Record* 121 (Oct. 2, 1975): S17348.

5677 Miller, O. N., et al. "Report of the Ad Hoc Advisory Committee on Chemical Corps Mission and Structure, August 6, 1955." *Armed Forces Chemical Journal* 10:6 (1959): 18–19, 28.

5678 Nixon, Pres. Richard M. "Chemical and Biological Defense Policies and Programs." *U.S. Department of State Bulletin* (Dec. 15, 1969): 541–43.

5679 Norman, Colin. "U.S. at Chemical War Crossroads." *Nature* (May 24, 1974): 301–02.

5680 Ottinger, Rep. Richard L. "Chemical Warfare—Brown Response." *Congressional Record* 121 (May 20, 1975): H4479.

5681 U.S. Department of Army. *Employment of Chemical and Biological Agents.* Army Field Manual FM 3–10. Washington, D.C.: G.P.O., 1966.

5682 ———. *Military Biology and Biological Warfare Agents.* Army Technical Manual TM 3–216. Washington, D.C.: G.P.O., 1956.

5683 ———. *Potential Biological Anti-Personnel Agents.* Army Training Manual EA 108.1. Washington, D.C.: G.P.O., 1970.

5684 U.S. House. Committee on Foreign Affairs. Hearings: *Chemical-Biological Warfare: U.S. Policies and International Effects.* 91st Cong., 1st Sess., Nov.–Dec. 1969.

5685 ———. Hearings: *International Implications of Dumping Poisonous Gas and Waste Into Oceans.* 91st Cong., 1st Sess., 1969.

5686 ———. Hearings: *U.S. Chemical Warfare Policy.* 93d Cong., 2d Sess., 1974.

5687 ———. Report: *Chemical-Biological Warfare: U.S. Policies and International Effects* [with appended study, *The Use of Tear Gas in War: A Survey of International Negotiations and U.S. Policy and Practice*]. 91st Cong., 2d Sess., 1970.

5688 U.S. House. Committee on Government Operations. Report: *Environmental Dangers of Open Air Testing of Lethal Chemicals.* 91st Cong., 1st Sess., 1969.

5689 ———. Committee on Merchant Marine and Fisheries. Hearings: *Ocean Disposal of Unserviceable Chemical Munitions.* 91st Cong., 2nd Sess., 1970.

5690 ———. Committee on Science and Astronautics. Hearings: *Chemical, Biological and Radiological Warfare Agents.* 86th Cong., 1st Sess., (1959), June 16, 22, 1960.

5691 ———. Report: *Research in CBR (Chemical, Biological and Radiological Warfare).* No. 815. 86th Cong., 1st Sess., 1959.

5692 U.S. Senate. Committee on Commerce. Hearings: *Dumping of Nerve Gas Rockets in the Ocean.* 91st Cong., 2nd Sess., 1970.

5693 ———. Committee on Foreign Relations. Hearings: *Chemical and Biological Warfare.* 91st Cong., 1st Sess., Apr. 30, 1969.

5694 ———. Committee on Labor and Public Welfare. Report: *Chemical and Biological*

Weapons: Some Possible Approaches for Lessening the Threat and Danger. Prepared by Library of Congress, Legislative Reference Service. 91st Cong., 1st Sess., 1969.

5695 Zablocki, Rep. Clement J. "Introduction of a Resolution Concerning an International Treaty on Chemical Warfare." *Congressional Record* 121 (Oct. 2, 1975): H9531.

NATIONAL POLICIES—SOVIET UNION

5696 Arkhangel'skiy, A. M., et al. *Bacteriological Weapons and How to Defend Against Them.* [Trans. of *Bakteriologicheskoye oruzhiye i zachchita ot nego.* Moscow: Military Pub. House, 1967.] Washington, D.C.: Joint Publications Research Service, 1967. [Available from NTIS as JPRS 42361.]

5697 Bogdanov, Oleg V. "For an Effective Ban on Chemical and Bacteriological Weapons." *Reprints from the Soviet Press* (Sept. 1970): 41–54.

5698 Bulat, R., et al. *Atomic, Biological, Chemical Warfare and Defense.* [Translation of *Atomska Bioloshka Hemiska Orushja i zashita.* Zagreb, 1960.] Washington, D.C.: Joint Publications Research Service, 1962. [Available from NTIS as JPRS 14282.]

5699 Malooley, Lt. Col. Rudolph S. "Gas is Not a Dirty Word in Soviet Army." *Army* 24:8 (1974): 21–23.

5700 Petrov, M. "An Important Aspect of Disarmament [Banning Chemical and Biological Weapons]." *International Affairs* [Moscow] 16 (Mar. 1970): 53–56.

5701 ———. "The Urgent Need to Prohibit Chemical and Biological Warfare." *International Affairs* [Moscow] 15 (Aug. 1969): 40–43.

5702 Pozdnyakov, V. "The Chemical Arm." In Basil H. Liddell Hart, ed., *The Soviet Army.* London: Weidenfeld & Nicolson, 1956, pp. 384–94.

5703 Rozhynastovskiy, T., and Z. Shultovsky. *Biological Warfare: The Threat and the Reality.* [Trans. from Russian.] Washington, D.C.: Joint Publications Research Service, 1960. [Available from U.S. Dept. of Commerce, Cat. no. 60–41. 126.]

5704 "Soviet Civil Defense Against CBR Attack." *Armed Forces Chemical Journal* 13:3 (May–June 1959): 16–19, 24.

5705 Tomilin, Y. "Chemical Weapons Must Be Outlawed." *International Affairs* [Moscow] 18 (June 1972): 8–12.

5706 Viney, D. E. "Research Policy: The Soviet Union." In Steven Rose, ed., *CBW: Chemical and Biological Warfare.* Boston: Beacon, 1969, pp. 130–37.

5707 Wade, Nicholas. "Biological Warfare: Suspicions of Soviet Activity." *Science* (Apr. 2, 1976): 38, 40.

BIOLOGICAL WARFARE

5708 Baldwin, Hanson W. *The Price of Power.* New York: Harpers, 1948, pp. 71–75, 340–45.

5709 Baroyan, O. V. "Bacterial Weapons: A Threat to Mankind." *Peace and the Sciences* 1 (July 1970): 31–41.

5710 "Biological Warfare Potentialities." *Armed Forces Chemical Journal* 3:4 (1949): 32, 39.

5711 Boffery, Philip M. "Detrick Birthday: Dispute Flares Over Biological Warfare Center." *Science* (Apr. 19, 1968): 285–88.

5712 Chisholm, B. "Biological Warfare: Demand for Answers." In M. Grodzius and E. Rabinowitch, eds., *The Atomic Age.* New York: Basic Books, 1963, pp. 178–82.

5713 Clews, John C. *The Communists' New Weapon—Germ Warfare.* London: Praeger, 1953.

5714 Engel, Leonard. "The Scope of Biological Warfare." *Nation* (July 26, 1947): 93–95.

5715 Fotherfill, Leroy D. "Biological Warfare and Its Defense." *Armed Forces Chemical Journal* 12:5 (1958): 4–6, 26, 28.

5716 Fox, L.A. "Bacterial Warfare." *Scientific Monthly* 55 (July 1942): 5–18.

5717 ———. "Bacterial Warfare: The Use of Biologic Agents in Warfare." *Military Surgeon* 72 (Mar. 1933): 189–207.

5718 "Germs Anyone?" *Commonweal* (Aug. 8, 1968): 475–76.

5719 "The Germs of Porton Down." *Economist* (July 14, 1962): 127–28.

5720 Gorer, P. A. "Bacterial Warfare." In D. Hall et al., *The Frustration of Science*. London: Norton, 1935.

5721 Heden, Carl-Goran. "Microbiological Weapons: The Infectious Dust Cloud." In Nigel Calder, ed., *Unless Peace Comes: A Scientific Forecast of New Weapons*. New York: Viking, 1968, pp. 147–65.

5722 Herriot, Roger M. "Biological Warfare." In Charles A. Barker, ed. *Problems of World Disarmament*. Boston: Houghton Mifflin, 1963, pp. 69–81.

5723 Hersh, Seymour M. "Dare We Develop Biological Weapons?" *New York Times Magazine* (Sept. 28, 1969): 28–29.

5724 ———. "Germ Warfare: For Alma Mater, God and Country." *Ramparts* 7 (Dec. 1969): 21–28.

5725 Lederberg, Joshua. "Biological Warfare: A Global Threat." *American Scientist* 59 (Mar.–Apr. 1971): 195–97.

5726 Malek, Ivan. "Biological Weapons." In Steven Rose, ed., *CBW: Chemical and Biological Warfare*. Boston: Beacon, 1969, pp. 48–59.

5727 ———. "Biological Weapons: Current Problems." *Scientific World* 11:6 (1967): 20–22.

5728 Mayer, R. L. "Epidemics and Bacteriological Warfare." *Scientific Monthly* 67 (Nov. 1948): 331–37.

5729 Merck, George W. "Official Report on Biological Warfare." *Bulletin of the Atomic Scientists* (Oct. 1, 1946): 16–18.

5730 ———. "Peacetime Implications of Biological Warfare." *Chemical and Engineering News* (May 25, 1946): 1346–49.

5731 Neinast, W. H. "United States Use of Biological Warfare." *Military Law Review* 24 (Apr. 1964): 1–45.

5732 Nopar, Robert E. "Plagues on Our Children: The Threat of Biological Warfare." *Clinical Pediatrics* 6 (Feb. 1967): 67–73.

5733 "The Pentagon Prepares for Germ Warfare." *Fellowship* (Jan. 1, 1960): 5–16.

5734 Piel, Gerard. "Biological Warfare: BW Uses Scourges of Disease and Famine as Weapons." *Life* (Nov. 18, 1946): 118–20.

5735 Pincher, C. "Biological Warfare." *Discovery* 11 (1950): 382–84.

5736 Rassweiler, Clifford F. "What's So Terrible About Germ Warfare?" *Saturday Evening Post* (Jan. 30, 1965): 12–14.

5737 Rosebury, Theodor. *Peace or Pestilence: Biological Warfare and How To Avoid It*. New York: Whittlesy House, 1949.

5738 Smith, Peter J. "Germ Warfare: The Plagues of Fort Detrick." *Spectator* (June 28, 1968): 886–87.

5739 Wedum, Arnold G. "Defensive Aspects of Biological Warfare." *Journal of the American Medical Association* (Nov. 27–30, 1956): 34–37.

INCENDIARY WARFARE

5740 Dreyfus, J. C. "Napalm and Its Effects on Human Beings." In K. Coates et al., eds., *Prevent the Crime of Silence*. London: Penguin, 1971, pp. 191–98.

5741 Fisher, George J. B. *Incendiary Warfare*. New York: McGraw-Hill, 1946.

5742 Greene, L. W. "Prewar Incendiary Bomb Development." *Chemical Corps Journal* I (Oct. 1947): 25–30.

5743 Hollingsworth, E. W. "The Use of Thickened Gasoline in Warfare." *Armed Forces Chemical Journal* 4:3 (1951): 26–32.

5744 Miller, W. L. "The Uses of Flame in Korea." *Combat Forces Journal* (Mar. 1954): 37–39.

5745 SIPRI. *Incendiary Weapons*. Cambridge: M.I.T. Press, 1975.

5746 U.N. Secretary-General. Report: *Napalm and Other Incendiary Weapons and All Aspects of Their Possible Use*. A/9027. New York, 1973.

5747 U.S. Department of Army. *Ground Flame Warfare*. FM 20-33. Washington, D.C.: G.P.O., 1970.

5748 Wilson, Andrew. *Flame Thrower*. London: Kimber, 1956.

CBW & ARMS CONTROL

5749 "Appoints Expert Group on Questions of Chemical & Bacteriological Weapons." *U.N. Monthly Chronicle* 6 (Feb. 1969): 7.

5750 Bull, Hedley. "Chemical and Biological Weapons: The Prospects for Arms Control." *Australian Outlook* 24 (Aug. 1970): 152–63.

5751 ———. "Disarmament and Chemical, Biological and Radiological Warfare." *The Control of the Arms Race*. London: Weidenfeld & Nicolson, 1961, pp. 123–44.

5752 Bunn, George. "Banning Poison Gas and Germ Warfare: Should the United States Agree?" *Wisconsin Law Review* 59:2 (1969): 375–420.

5753 ———. "The Banning of Poison Gas and Germ Warfare: The U.N. Role." *American Journal of International Law* 64 (Sept. 1970): 194–99.

5754 *The Control of Chemical and Biological Weapons*. New York: Carnegie Endowment for International Peace, 1971.

5755 Goodell, Charles E. *Targets for Further Disarmament: CBW*. Policy Paper Series, no. 2, CIS no. 4. New York: New York Univ., Center for International Studies, 1969.

5756 Gozze-gucetic, Vuko. "Chemical and Biological Weapons in the Disarmament Negotiations." *Medunarodni Problemi* 22:2 (1970): 77–94.

5757 Lederberg, Joshua. "The Control of Chemical and Biological Weapons." *Stanford Journal of International Studies* 7 (Spring 1972): 22–44.

5758 Lefebure, Maj. Victor. "Chemical Warfare: The Possibility of its Control." *Transactions of the Grotius Society* 7 (1921): 153–66.

5759 Margolis, Howard. "From Washington: Notes on Gas and Disarmament." *Bulletin of the Atomic Scientists* 21 (Nov. 1965): 30–32.

5760 Nelson, Bryce. "Arms Control: Demand for Decisions . . . and CBW." *Science* (Dec. 6, 1968): 1102, 1106–08.

5761 Noel-Baker, Philip J. *The Arms Race: A Programme for World Disarmament*. London: Stevens, 1958, pp. 320–59.

5762 Polanyi, John C. "CBW—What Hope For Restraint?" *International Journal* 25 (Autumn 1970): 766–78.

5763 [Pugwash Workshop]. "The Second Pugwash Chemical Warfare Workshop: Stockholm, Sweden." *Pugwash Newsletter* 12 (Aug. 1975): 170–77.

5764 ———. "The Third Pugwash Chemical Warfare Workshop, London." *Pugwash Newsletter* 13 (Apr. 1976): 188–202.

5765 Rosenhead, Jonathan. "CBW and Disarmament." *Labour Monthly* 52 (Jan. 1970): 15–18.

5766 Scammell, J. M. "Outlawry of Poison Gases in Warfare." *Current History* 30 (June 1929): 396–403.

5767 SIPRI. *Chemical Disarmament: New Weapons for Old*. New York: Humanities Press, 1975.

5768 U.S. Senate. Committee on Foreign Relations. Report: *Chemical-Biological-Radiological (CBR) Warfare and Its Disarmament Aspects*. 86th Cong., 2d Sess., 1960.

5769 Viney, D. E. "Constraining Chemical-Biological Warfare." *Disarmament* 15 (Sept. 1967): 1–4, 20–21.

Verification & Control

5770 [Germany, Federal Republic of. Foreign Ministry]. "Controlling Ban on Manufacture of Biological and Chemical Weapons." *NATO Letter* 18:7–8 (1970): 17–19.

5771 ———. "Surveillance of a Prohibition of Biological and Chemical Weapons." *Wehrkunde* 3 (1970): 152–54.

5772 Lundin, Johan. "Considerations on a Chemical Arms Control Treaty and the Concept of Amplified Verification." *FOA Reports* 7:1 (1973): 1–5.

5773 Midwest Research Institute. *Economic Monitoring of Arms Control Agreements: Chemical Warfare Agents*. ACDA Rpt. E-183. Kansas City, 1971.

5774 ———. *The Role of Phosphorus Control in Verification of a Ban on Nerve Agent Production: An Economic and Technical Analysis*. ACDA Rpt. E–204, ST–215. Kansas City, 1973.

5775 ———. *Verification Aspects of a Chemical and Biological Weapons Arms Control Agreement*. ACDA Rpt. AT–150. Kansas City, 1969.

5776 Pugwash Workshop. "Chemical Warfare [verification]." *Pugwash Newsletter* 13 (Apr. 1976): 189–95.

5777   SIPRI. *Chemical Disarmament: Some Problems of Verification.* New York: Humanities Press, 1973.

5778   ———. *Technical Aspects of Early Warning and Verification.* New York: Humanities Press, 1975.

CBW & INTERNATIONAL LAW

5779   Bernstein, Cyrus. "The Law of Chemical Warfare." *George Washington Law Review* 10 (June 1942): 889–915.

5780   Brownlie, Ian. "Legal Aspects of CBW." In Steven Rose, ed., *CBW: Chemical and Biological Warfare.* Boston: Beacon, 1969, pp. 141–54.

5781   Brungs, Bernard J. "The Status of Biological Warfare in International Law." *Military Law Review* 24 (Apr. 1964): 47–95.

5782   Ewing, R. H. "The Legality of Chemical Warfare." *American Law Review* 61 (Jan.–Feb. 1927): 58–76.

5783   Fuller, Jon W. "The Application of International Law to Chemical and Biological Warfare." *Orbis* 10 (Spring 1966): 247–73.

5784   Ipsen, Knut. "Chemical and Biological Weapons in International Law." In Ernst-Ulrich von Weizacker, ed., *BC-Waffen und Friedenspolitik.* Stuttgardt, Klett, 1970.

5785   Kelly, Maj. Joseph B. "Gas Warfare in International Law." *Military Law Review* (July 1960): 1–67. [Also issued as DA Pam 27–100–9, July 1960.]

5786   Khan, R. "Chemical and Bacteriological Weapons and International Law." *Indian Journal of International Law* 9 (Oct. 1969): 497–511.

5787   Meyrowitz, Henri. *Les Armes Biologiques et le Droit International.* Paris: Editions A. Pedone, 1968.

5788   ———. "Les Armes Psycho-chimiques et le Droit International." *Annuaire Français de Droit International* 10 (1964): 81–126.

5789   O'Brien, William V. "Biological/Chemical Warfare and the International Law of War." *Georgetown Law Journal* 51 (Fall 1962): 1–63.

5790   Thomas, Ann Van Wynen, and Aaron J. Thomas, Jr. *Development of International Legal Limitations on the Use of Chemical and Biological Weapons.* 2 vols. ACDA Rpt GC–128. Washington, D.C.: ACDA, Nov. 1968.

5791   ———. *Legal Limits on the Use of Chemical and Biological Weapons: International Law, 1899–1970.* Dallas: Southern Methodist Univ. Press, 1970.

5792   U.S. Department of State. *International Agreements to Outlaw Chemical and Bacteriological Weapons and the Record of the Use of Poison Gas.* Research Project 449. Washington, D.C.: Department of State, Historical Office, Nov. 1960.

RESPONSIBILITY OF SCIENTISTS

5793   American Assoc. of Scientific Workers. "Memorandum to the U.N.—On Bacterial Warfare." *Bulletin of the Atomic Scientists* 3 (Dec., 1947): 363–64.

5794   Brown, Martin, ed. *The Social Responsibility of the Scientist.* New York: Free Press, 1971.

5795   Burhop, E. H. S. "ABC Weapons: Disarmament and the Responsibility of the Scientist." *Scientific World* 16:1 (1972): 5–7.

5796   Chain, E. "Social Responsibility and the Scientist." *New Scientist* (Oct. 22, 1970): 166–70.

5797   Cousins, Norman. "CBR Versus Man." *Saturday Review* (July 23, 1960): 9, 12, 38, 39.

5798   "FAS Asks Clarification of U.S. Policies on Germ Warfare." *Bulletin of the Atomic Scientists* 8 (June 1952): 130.

5799   "FAS Statement on Biological and Chemical Warfare." *Bulletin of the Atomic Scientists* 20 (Oct. 1964): 46–47.

5800   Galston, A. W. "Science and Social Responsibility: A Case Study." *Annals of the New York Academy of Science* 196 (1972): 223–35.

5801   Graven, Jean. "Les Limites du Role et de la Responsabilité du Medecin dans la Guerre Biologique et Bacteriologique." *Revue Internationale de Droit Penal* [Paris] 23 (1952): 19–56.

5802 Heden, Carl-Goran. "A Professional Verdict Over BW." *New Scientist* (Sept. 10, 1970): 518–20.

5803 Humphrey, J. H. "Initiative Against Chemical and Biological Warfare." *New Scientist* (Sept. 29, 1966): 715–16.

5804 ———, and M. Meselson. " 'Ethical Problems' Preventing CBW." In Steven Rose, ed. *CBW: Chemical and Biological Warfare.* Boston: Beacon, 1969, pp. 99–102.

5805 Krickus, R. J. "On the Morality of Chemical/Biological War." *Journal of Conflict Resolution* 9:2 (1965): 200–210.

5806 Lappe, Marc. "Biological Warfare." In Martin Brown, ed., *The Social Responsibility of the Scientist.* New York: Free Press, 1971, pp. 96–118.

5807 Mayer, C. F. "The Hippocratic Oath, the Pledge of Geneva, and ABC Warfare." *Military Surgeon* 111 (Nov. 1952): 369. [Editorial.]

5808 Neilands, J. B. "Chemical Warfare." In Martin Brown, ed., *The Social Responsibility of the Scientist.* New York: Free Press, 1971, pp. 82–94.

5809 Powell, C. F. "Scientific Responsibility." In Steven Rose, ed., *CBW: Chemical and Biological Warfare.* Boston: Beacon, 1969, pp. 181–88.

5810 "[Pugwash Conference] On Biological and Chemical Warfare." *Bulletin of the Atomic Scientists* 15 (Oct. 1959): 337–39.

5811 "Pugwash International Conference of Scientists: Statement on Biological and Chemical Warfare." *Nature* (Oct. 3, 1959): 1018–19.

5812 Ramsey, Paul. *War and the Christian Conscience.* Durham: Duke Univ. Press, 1961, pp. 224–31, 320–24.

5813 Rose, Steven. "The Real Significance of CBW." *New Perspectives* 1 (Dec. 1971): 53–57.

5814 Rosebury, Theodor. "Medical Ethics and Biological Warfare." *Perspectives in Biology and Medicine* 6 (Summer 1963): 512–23.

5815 Rubbo, Sydney D. "The Lethal Knife— Chemical and Biological Warfare." *Australian Quarterly* 40 (Dec. 1968): 21–28.

5816 Ruttenberg, Charles L. "Political Behavior of American Scientists: The Movement Against Chemical and Biological Warfare." Ph.D. diss., New York Univ., 1972.

5817 Sidel, Victor W. "Medical Ethics." In Steven Rose, ed., *CBW: Chemical and Biological Warfare.* Boston: Beacon, 1969, pp. 44–47.

5818 Unwin, A. W. "Chemical and Biological Warfare." *Humanist* 82 (Aug. 1967): 230–33.

Protests Against CB Research

5819 Hersh, Seymour M. "Gas and Germ Warfare: The Controversy Over Campus Research Contracts." *New Republic* (July 1, 1967): 12–14.

5820 Marquand, Carl B., and William J. Sparks. "CBN War-Fare Research . . . and Human Welfare." *Ordnance* 50 (Jan.–Feb. 1966): 402–06.

5821 "Microbiologists Condemn Military Research in Biology." *Scientific World* 15:2 (1971): 21–23.

5822 Soddy, F. "Chemical Warfare, the Universities, and Scientific Workers." *Nature* 106 (Nov. 1920): 310.

5823 "Spice Rack and Summit: A Season's Discontent Over Classified Research." *Pennsylvania Gazette* 7 (1967): 14 ff.

5824 Synge, Ann. "Chemical and Biological Warfare." *New Blackfriars* 50 (Feb. 1969): 256–63.

5825 Walsh, John B. "Senate Imposes CBW Limitations, Cuts Defense Research." *Science* (Aug. 22, 1969): 778.

5826 Wingell, Bill. "Protests Mount on University of Pennsylvania's Warfare Research." *National Guardian* (Nov. 12, 1966): 3.

CHEMICAL-BIOLOGICAL ISSUES

Case for CB Weapons

5827 Anderson, Skinner E. "CS and Its Use." *Military Review* 51 (Jan. 1971): 64–68.

5828 "Benefits of CBR Research." *Illustrated Army Digest* 24 (Aug. 1969): 6–13.

5829 Dodson, C. A. "The Case for CBR." *Army* 12:1 (1961): 41–46.

5830 Fair, Lt. Col. Stanley D. "The Ghost of Ypres." *Army* 17:2 (1967): 51–55.

5831 Fries, Gen. Amos A. "The Future of Poison Gas." *Current History* 15 (Dec. 1921): 419–22.

5832 Gilchrist, Col. Harry L. "The Humanity of Chemical Warfare." *Military Surgeon* 57:5 (Nov. 1925): 529–38.

5833 Gundel, H. "The Case for CB Weapons." *Ordnance* 47 (Jan.–Feb. 1963): 435–37.

5834 Haldane, John B. S. *Callinicus: A Defence of Chemical Warfare.* London: Kegan Paul, Trench, Trubner, 1925.

5835 Harrigan, Anthony. "The Case for Gas Warfare." *National Review* (Apr. 9, 1963): 283–84.

5836 ———. "The Case for Gas Warfare." *Armed Forces Chemical Journal* 17:2 (1963): 12–13.

5837 "Humane Chemical Warfare." *Literary Digest* (Sept. 19, 1931): 28.

5838 "Humanity of Poison Gas." *Scientific American* (Mar. 29, 1919): 310.

5839 Kendall, James. *Breathe Freely: The Truth About Poison Gas.* New York: Appleton-Century, 1938.

5840 Kernan, Maj. W. F. "Poison Gas Myth." *American Mercury* 40 (Apr. 1937), pp. 410–15.

5841 ———. "In Praise of Poison." *Harper's Magazine* 175 (Aug. 1937): 329–32.

5842 Marriott, John. "Chemical and Biological Warfare." *International Defense Review* 2 (Apr. 1969): 170–74.

5843 Marsden, J. N. "Moral Aspects of CBR Warfare." *Armed Forces Chemical Journal* 17:2 (1963): 5–6, 8, 10–11.

5844 Rothschild, J. H. "Propaganda and Toxic War." *Ordnance* 50 (May–June 1966): 617–19.

5845 Schneir, W. "The Campaign to Make Chemical Warfare Respectable." *Reporter* (Oct. 1, 1959): 24–28.

5846 Stubbs, Marshal. "CBR—A Power for Peace." *Armed Forces Chemical Journal* 13:3 (1959): 8–10.

"Non-lethal" Psychochemical Agents

5847 Candlin, A. H. *Psycho-Chemical Warfare: The Chinese Communist Drug Offensive Against the West.* New Rochelle: Arlington House, 1973.

5848 Gershater, E. M. "Psychochemicals: A Weapon that Incapacitates but Doesn't Kill or Destroy." *Army* 12:1 (1961): 47–49.

5849 Goldman, Ralph M. "Psychochemical Weapons and Disarmament." *NATO's Fifteen Nations* 7:4 (1962): 98–101.

5850 Haas, A. D. "Is Agent BZ the Army's Secret Weapon for Bending the Minds of the Enemy?" *Science and Mechanics* (Oct. 1968): 43, 81–84.

5851 Hamm, Capt. Anthony B. "CS [tear gas] Can Save Lives." *Infantry* 59 (Nov.–Dec. 1969): 30–31.

5852 Hollyhock, W. M. "Weapons Against the Mind." *New Scientist* (Apr. 22, 1965): 224–26.

5853 Joyce, C. R. B. "Psychedelics." In Steven Rose, ed., *CBW: Chemical and Biological Warfare.* Boston: Beacon, 1969, pp. 35–44.

5854 Lieberman, E. James. "Psychochemicals as Weapons." *Bulletin of the Atomic Scientists* 18 (Jan. 1962): 11–14.

5855 Lindsey, Douglas, et al. " 'Off the Rocker' and 'on the floor' Nonlethal Chemical Agents." *Armed Forces Chemical Journal* 14:3 (1960): 8–9.

5856 MacArthur, J. C. " 'Psycho-chemical Warfare' and the Case of the Discombobulated Cat." *Armed Forces Chemical Journal* 13:1 (1959): 4–7.

5857 Meyrowitz, Henri. "Les Armes Psychochimiques et le Droit International." *Annuaire Français de Droit International* 10 (1964): 81–126.

5858 Nunn, A. C. "The Arming of an International Police Force." *Journal of Peace Research* 2:3 (1965): 187–91.

5859 Trainor, James. "DOD Weighs New War Concept." *Missiles and Rockets* (Oct. 5, 1964): 14.

5860 Yanka, D. E. "Mickey Finn on the Battlefield." *Army* 10:9 (1960): 28–29.

Herbicides

5861 "AAAS Board of Directors: A Statement on the Use of Herbicides in Vietnam." *Science* (July 19, 1968): 253–56.

5862 Boffery, Philip M. "Herbicides in Vietnam: AAAS Study Runs into a Military Roadblock." *Science* (Oct. 2, 1970): 42–45.

5863 ———. "Herbicides in Vietnam: AAAS Study Finds Widespread Devastation." *Science* (Jan. 8, 1971): 43–47.

5864 Constable, J., and Matthew S. Meselson. "Ecological Impact of Large Scale Defoliation in Vietnam." *Sierra Club Bulletin* 56:4 (1971): 4–9.

5865 "Defoliants, Deformities: What Risk?" *Medical World News* 11:9 (1970): 15–17.

5866 Fair, Lt. Col. Stanley D. "No Place to Hide: How Defoliants Expose the Viet Cong." *Army* 14:2 (1963–1964): 54–55.

5867 Galston, A. W. "Herbicides in Vietnam." *New Republic* (Nov. 25, 1967): 19–21.

5868 ———. "Military Uses of Herbicides in Vietnam." *New Scientist* (June 13, 1968): 583–84.

5869 Mayer, Jean E., and Victor W. Sidel. "Crop Destruction in South Vietnam." *Christian Century* (June 29, 1966): 829–32.

5870 McElheny, Victor. "Herbicides in Vietnam: Juggernaut Out of Control." *Technology Review* 73 (Mar. 1971): 12–13.

5871 Nelson, Bryce. "Herbicides in Vietnam: AAAS Board Seeks Field Study." *Science* (Jan. 3, 1969): 59–60.

5872 Shapley, Deborah. "Herbicides: AAAS Study Finds Dioxin in Vietnamese Fish." *Science* (Apr. 20, 1973): 285–86.

5873 Tschirley, Fred W. "Defoliation in Vietnam." *Science* (Feb. 21, 1969): 779–86.

5874 U.S. House. Committee on Science & Astronautics. Report: *A Technology Assessment of the Vietnam Defoliant Matter: A Case History.* Prepared by Library of Congress, Legislative Reference Service. 91st Cong., 1st Sess., 1969.

5875 "Viet Deformities: Will We Ever Know?" *Medical World News* 12:4 (1971): 4–5.

5876 Westing, Arthur H. "Ecological Effects of Military Defoliation on the Forests of South Vietnam." *BioScience* (Sept. 1, 1971): 893–98.

5877 Whiteside, Thomas. *The Withering Rain: America's Herbicidal Folly.* New York: Dutton, 1971.

Binary Chemical Weapons

5878 Henahan, John F. "The Nerve-Gas Controversy." *Atlantic Monthly* (Sept. 1974): 52–56.

5879 Hicks, Rep. Floyd. "Recent Legislative History of Binary Chemical Munitions." *Congressional Record* 121 (Sept. 22, 1975): H8959.

5880 Kanegis, Arthur. "The Hidden Arsenal: You Can't Keep a Deadly Weapon Down." *Washington Monthly* 2 (Dec. 1970): 24–26.

5881 Lundin, Johan. "The Scope and Control of Chemical Disarmament Treaties Particularly with Regard to Binary Chemical Weapons." *Cooperation and Conflict* 11:3–4 (1973): 145–53.

5882 "Nerve Gas—The Army's Latest Weapon." *Nature* (Oct. 5, 1973): 231–32.

5883 Ottinger, Rep. Richard L. "Binary Chemical Weapons: A Hazardous and Wasteful Expense." *Congressional Record* 121 (Mar. 14, 1975): H1170–1780.

5884 Robinson, Julian Perry. "Binary Weapons—A Mixed Problem." *New Scientist* (Apr. 5, 1973): 34–35.

5885 Shapley, Deborah. "Binary Program Wins a Narrow Escape." *Science* (Aug. 8, 1975): 440–41.

Past Uses of CBW

5886 Batten, James K. "Chemical Warfare in History." *Armed Forces Chemical Journal* 14:2 (1960): 16–17, 32.

5887 Miles, Wyndham D. "The Idea of Chemical Warfare in Modern Times." *Journal of the History of Ideas* 31 (Apr.–June 1970): 297–304.

5888 West, C. J. "The History of Poison Gases." *Science* 49 (Apr. 1915): 412–17.

Early Instances

5889   "Chemical Warfare Tried in Calais in Year 1410." *Science News Letter* (June 8, 1940): 361.

5890   Cheronis, N. D. "Chemical Warfare in the Middle Ages." *Journal of Chemical Education* 14 (Aug. 1937): 360–65.

5891   de Bellegarde, M. "Gas Warfare in Antiquity." *Living Age* 357 (Jan. 1940): 436–37.

5892   Derbes, V. J. "De Mussis and the Great Plague of 1348: A Forgotten Episode of Bacteriological Warfare." *Journal of the American Medical Association* (Apr. 4, 1966): 59–62.

5893   Dundonald, Earl of. *My Army Life.* London: Arnold, 1926, pp. 329–38.

5894   Knollenberg, Bernhard. "General Amherst and Germ Warfare." *Mississippi Valley Historical Review* 41 (Dec. 1954): 489–94.

5895   Kokatnor, V. R. "Chemical Warfare in Ancient India." *Journal of Chemical Education* 25 (May 1948): 268–74.

5896   Miles, Wyndham D. "I: Admiral Cochrane's Plans for Chemical Warfare." *Armed Forces Chemical Journal* 11:6 (1957): 22–23, 40.

5897   ———. "III: Chemical Warfare in the Civil War." *Armed Forces Chemical Journal* 12:2 (1958): 26–27, 33.

5898   ———. "IV: Stink Balls, Fire Rain, and Smoke Pots—Chemical Weapons in 1825." *Armed Forces Chemical Journal* 12:5 (1958): 34–36.

5899   ———. "IV [sic]: The Velvet-Lined Gas Mask of John Stenhouse." *Armed Forces Chemical Journal* 12:3 (1958): 24–25.

5900   ———. "VII: Suffocating Smoke at Petersburg." *Armed Forces Chemical Journal* 13:4 (1959): 34–35.

5901   Partington, J. R. *A History of Greek Fire and Gunpowder.* Cambridge: Heffer, 1960.

World War I

5902   Anderson, A. "Some Recollections of Porton in World War I." *Journal of the Royal Army Medical Corps* 118:3 (1972): 173–77.

5903   Auld, S. J. M. *Gas and Flame in Modern Warfare.* New York: Doran, 1918.

5904   Baldwin, Hanson W. "After Fifty Years the Cry of Ypres Still Echoes—'Gas!'" *New York Times Magazine* (Apr. 18, 1965): 29 ff.

5905   Clark, D. K. *Effectiveness of Chemical Weapons in WWI.* Bethesda, Md.: Johns Hopkins Univ. Operations Research Office, 1959. [Available from NTIS as AD 233081.]

5906   Cornubert, R. "La Guerre des Gaz: Generalites: l'oeuvre Francaise." *Revue Generale des Sciences* 31 (1920): 45–46.

5907   Florentin, D. "La Guerre des Gaz: l'Allemagne et la Guerre des Gaz." *Revue Generale des Sciences* 31 (1920): 237–50.

5908   Foulkes, C. H. *"Gas" The Story of the Special Brigade.* Edinburgh: Blackwood, 1936.

5909   ———. "Then and Now, I: Chemical Warfare in 1915." *Armed Forces Chemical Journal* 15:6 (1961): 4, 15–16.

5910   Fuller, Gen. J. F. C. *The Conduct of War, 1789–1961.* London: Eyre & Spottiswoode, 1961, pp. 172–77.

5911   ———. *The Reformation of War.* 2d ed. London: Hutchinson, 1923, pp. 108–11, 120–35, 143–45.

5912   Gilchrist, Col. Harry L. *A Comparative Study of World War Casualties from Gas and Other Weapons.* Washington, D.C.: G.P.O., 1928.

5913   Hanslian, R. *Der Chemische Krieg.* Berlin: Mittler, 1937.

5914   Miles, Wyndham D. "Fritz Haber, Father of Chemical Warfare." *Armed Forces Chemical Journal* 14:1 (1960): 28–29.

5915   SIPRI. *The Problem of Chemical and Biological Warfare.* 6 vols. New York: Humanities Press, 1971, I: 25–58, 125–40.

5916   Trumpener, Ulrich. "The Road to Ypres: The Beginnings of Gas Warfare in World War I." *Journal of Modern History* 47 (Sept. 1975): 460–80.

5917   Vedder, Edward B. *The Medical Aspects of Chemical Warfare.* Baltimore: Williams & Wilkins, 1925.

Italo-Ethiopian War, 1935–1936

5918   Barker, A. J. *The Civilizing Mission: The Italo-Ethiopian War, 1935–36.* London: Cassell, 1968, pp. 221–23.

5919   League of Nations. "Allegations Against Italy [use of gas]." *Official Journal* 17 (Apr. 1936): 370–71; 17 (July 1936): 778.

5920   Martelli, G. *Italy Against the World.* London: Chatto & Windus, 1937, pp. 232–35, 254–59.

5921   SIPRI. *The Problem of Chemical and Biological Warfare.* 6 vols. New York: Humanities Press, 1971, I: 142–46; IV: 175–89.

Sino-Japanese War, 1937–1945

5922   "Bacterial Warfare." *Chinese Medical Journal* 61 (July–Sept. 1943): 259–63.

5923   "Germ Warfare: Reports that the Japanese have Experimented in China." *New Republic* (Mar. 9, 1942): 315–16.

5924   "Invisible Weapon: Plague from Planes over the Chinese City of Changteh." *Time* (Mar. 9, 1942): 22–23.

5925   League of Nations. "Communications Received Concerning the Use of Poison Gas." *Official Journal* 19 (Aug.–Sept. 1938): 665–68; 19 (Nov. 1938): 863–65, 878–81.

5926   SIPRI. *The Problem of Chemical and Biological Warfare.* 6 vols. New York: Humanities Press, 1971, I: 147–52, 342–47; IV: 189–91.

World War II

5927   Alexandrov, G. "Lessons of the Past Are Not to be Forgotten." *International Affairs* [Moscow] 15 (1969): 76–78.

5928   Baxter, J. P. "Why Not Gas?" *Scientists Against Time.* Boston: Little, Brown, 1946, pp. 266–81.

5929   Brophy, Leo P., and George J. B. Fisher. *The Chemical Warfare Service: Organizing for War.* [In series] *United States Army in World War II: The Technical Services.* Washington, D.C.: G.P.O., 1959.

5930   ———; et al. *The Chemical Warfare Service: From Laboratory to Field.* [In series] *United States Army in World War II: The Technical Services.* Washington, D.C.: G.P.O., 1959.

5931   Brown, Frederic J. "Confirmation of Restraints, 1939–1942." *Chemical Warfare: A Study in Restraints.* Princeton: Princeton Univ. Press, 1968, pp. 191–262.

5932   Bush, Vannevar. *Modern Arms and Free Men: A Discussion of the Role of Science in Preserving Democracy.* New York: Simon & Schuster, 1949, pp. 140–46.

5933   Infield, G. B. *Disaster at Bari.* New York: Macmillan, 1971.

5934   Kleber, Brooks E., and Dale Birdsell, *The Chemical Warfare Service: Chemicals in Combat.* [In series] *United States Army in World War II: The Technical Services.* Washington, D.C.: G.P.O., 1966.

5935   Lindley, E. K. "Thoughts on the Use of Gas in Warfare." *Newsweek* (Dec. 20, 1943): 24.

5936   Ochsner, H. *History of German Chemical Warfare in World War II.* Part 1: *The Military Aspect.* Chemical Corps Historical Studies, no. 2 (P–004). Washington, D.C.: Historical Office, Chief of the Chemical Corps, 1949.

5937   Saunders, David M. "The Bari Incident." *U.S. Naval Institute Proceedings* 93 (Sept. 1967): 35–39.

5938   Schuyler, J. "Poison Gas: Terror Over Europe." *Current History* 51 (June 1940): 23–24, 62, 64.

5939   "Should the U.S. Use Gas?" *Time* (Jan. 3, 1944): 15.

5940   SIPRI. *The Problem of Chemical and Biological Warfare.* 6 vols. New York: Humanities Press, 1971, I: 153–57, 217–23, 294–335.

5941   Waitt, Capt. Alden H. "Why Germany Didn't Try Gas." *Saturday Evening Post* (Mar. 9, 1946): 17.

Korean War, 1950–1953

5942   Baker, E. R., et al. "Gas Warfare: Chemical Warfare in Korea." *Armed Forces Chemical Journal* 4:4 (1951): 3, 54–56.

5943   Bechhoefer, Bernhard G. *Postwar Negotiations for Arms Control.* Washington, D.C.: Brookings Institution, 1961, pp. 194–201.

5944   Clews, John C. *Communist Propaganda Techniques.* New York: Praeger, 1964.

5945   ———. *The Communists' New Weapon— Germ Warfare.* London: Praeger, 1953.

5946   Friedman, Bernard. "Germ Warfare: Is U.S. Using It in Korean War?" *New World Review* 20 (June 1952): 17–27.

5947   "Germ Warfare in Korea" [Reply by the Deputy United States Representative to the United Nations to Repeated Soviet Charges]. *Current History* 23 (Summer 1952): 172–78.

5948   *International Scientific Committee for the Investigation of the Facts Concerning Bacteriological Warfare in Korea and China, Report.* Peking, 1952.

5949   Mayo, C. W. "Germ Warfare Confessions." *U.S. Department of State Bulletin* (Nov. 9, 1953): 641–47.

5950   ———. "Investigation of Charges of Use of Bacteriological Warfare by UN Forces." *Quartermaster Review* 33 (Jan.–Feb. 1954): 8–9; 33 (Apr. 1954): 18–19, 131.

5951   SIPRI. *The Problem of Chemical and Biological Warfare.* 6 vols. New York: Humanities Press, 1971, IV: 196–221; V: 238–58.

Yemen Civil War, 1963–1967

5952   "How Nasser Used Poison Gas." *U.S. News & World Report* (July 3, 1967): 60.

5953   Meselson, Matthew S., and D. E. Viney. "CBW in Use: The Yemen." In Steven Rose, ed., *CBW: Chemical and Biological Warfare.* Boston: Beacon, 1969, pp. 99–102.

5954   Salvia, J. "Gas in Yemen." *Scientist and Citizen* 9 (Aug.–Sept. 1967): 149–52.

5955   Schmidt, D. A. *Yemen: The Unknown War.* London: The Bodley Head, 1968, pp. 257–73.

5956   SIPRI. *The Problem of Chemical and Biological Warfare.* 6 vols. New York: Humanities Press, 1971, I: 159–61, 336–41; IV: 243–47; V: 225–38.

5957   U.N. "Exchange of Communications with the Deputy Permanent Representative of Saudi Arabia to the United Nations." Security Council Document S/7842. New York, Apr. 6, 1967.

Indo-China War, 1961–1972

For an additional bibliographical survey, see Milton Leitenberg and Richard Dean Burns, eds., *The Vietnam Conflict* (Santa Barbara, Ca.: ABC–Clio, 1973), pp. 121–23. Also see Herbicides under Chemical-Biological Issues, above.

5958   Bach, Pham Van. "Law and the Use of Chemical Warfare in Vietnam." *Scientific World* 15:6 (1971): 12–14.

5959   Beecher, William. "Chemicals vs. the Viet Cong—(Right) or (Wrong)?" *National Guardsman* 20 (Feb. 1966): 3–6.

5960   Briantais, J. M. *Massacres: la Guerre Chimique en Asie de Sud-est.* Paris: François Maspero, 1970.

5961   Brindley, T. "A Legacy of Poison." *Far Eastern Economic Review* 79:9 (1973): 22–24.

5962   Do Xuan Sang. "U.S. Crimes of Chemical Warfare in South Vietnam." *U.S. War Crimes in Viet Nam.* Hanoi: Juridical Sciences Institute, State Commission of Social Sciences, 1968.

5963   Draw, J. "Lethal-gas Attack by Viet-Cong." *Daily Telegraph,* Apr. 7, 1970.

5964   Etzioni, Amitai. "More 'Humane' Warfare in Vietnam." *War/Peace Report* 6 (May 1966): 5–6.

5965   Guignard, J. P., et al. *Vietnam: Documents on Chemical and Bacteriological Warfare.* London: Dr. Philip Harvey, 1967.

5966   "How the State Department Tried to Explain Away the Use of 'Non-lethal' Gases." *I. F. Stone's Weekly* (Mar. 29, 1965): 2–3.

5967   Khan, M. F. "CBW in Use: Vietnam." In Steven Rose, ed., *CBW: Chemical and Biological Warfare.* Boston: Beacon, 1969, pp. 87–98.

5968   Lederer, E. "Report on Chemical Warfare in Vietnam." In K. Coates et al., eds., *Prevent the Crime of Silence.* London: Penguin, 1971.

5969   Meselson, Matthew S. "Tear Gas in Vietnam and the Return of Poison Gas." *Bulletin of the Atomic Scientists* 27 (Mar. 1971): 17–19.

5970   Neilands, J. B. "Chemical Warfare in Vietnam." *Peace and the Sciences* (July–Sept. 1969): 24–35.

5971   ———, et al. *Harvest of Death: Chemical Warfare in Vietnam and Cambodia.* New York: Free Press, 1972.

5972   ———. "Vietnam: Progress of Chemical War." *Asian Survey* 10 (Mar. 1970): 209–29.

5973 Nguyen Khac Vien, ed. "Chemical Warfare." *Vietnamese Studies* [Hanoi] 29 (1971).

5974 Rothschild, J. G. "Chemical and Biological Warfare in Vietnam." *Science* 167 (Apr. 1967): 167–68.

5975 Russell, Lord Bertrand."Chemical Warfare in Vietnam." *New Republic* (July 6, 1963): 30.

5976 Savitz, David. "Gas and Guerrillas—A Word of Caution." *New Republic* (Mar. 19, 1966): 13–14.

5977 "Silent Weapons: Role of Chemicals in Lower Case Warfare." *Army Digest* 23:11 (1968): 6–11.

5978 SIPRI. *The Problem of Chemical and Biological Warfare.* 6 vols. New York: Humanities Press, 1971, I: 162–210.

5979 Verwey, W. D. "Chemical Warfare in Vietnam: Legal or Illegal?" *Netherlands International Law Review* 18:2 (1971): 217–44.

Prohibitions on the Use of Poison

There have been several societies which evolved prohibitions against the use of poison in warfare.

5980 Bordwell, P. *The Law of War Between Belligerents.* Chicago: Callaghan, 1908, p. 12. [The Saracens.]

5981 Bühler, G., trans. *The Laws of Manu.* Oxford: Clarendon Press, 1886, p. 230. [Code of Manu.]

5982 Davie, Maurice R. *The Evolution of War: A Study of Its Role in Early Societies.* Port Washington, N.Y.: Kennikat Press, 1968, p. 182. [Primitive tribes.]

5983 Scott, J. B. *The Hague Conventions and Declarations of 1899 and 1907,* 3d ed. New York: Oxford Univ. Press, 1918, pp. 116–18. [Hague Conventions 1899 & 1907.]

General Accounts

5984 Fenwick, Charles G. *International Law.* New York: Appleton-Century, 1924, pp. 471–72.

5985 Garner, James W. *International Law and the World War.* 2 vols. London: Longmans, Green, 1920, I: 288–92.

5986 Grotius, Hugo. *The Law of War and Peace.* London: Peace Look Co., 1939, Bk. III, Ch. 4, Sec. 14–16.

5987 SIPRI. "Prohibition of Poison and Poisoned Weapons." *The Problem of Chemical and Biological Warfare.* 6 vols. New York: Humanities Press, 1973, III: 93–96.

5988 Thomas, Ann Van Wynen, and Aaron J. Thomas, Jr. "Poison and Poisoned Weapons." *Development of International Legal Limitations on the Use of Chemical and Biological Weapons.* 2 vols. ACDA Rpt. GC–128. Washington, D.C.: G.P.O., Nov. 1968, II: 57–67.

Hague Declarations Prohibiting Use of Gas (1899, 1907)

For text of these declarations, see Leon Friedman, *The Law of War,* 2 vols. (New York: Random House, 1972), I: 249–50.

5989 Greenspan, Morris. *The Modern Law of Land Warfare.* Berkeley: Univ. of California Press, 1959, pp. 315, 354–55.

5990 Stone, Julius. *Legal Controls of International Conflict.* New York: Rinehart, 1954, pp. 552–53, 609.

5991 Thomas, Ann Van Wynen, and Aaron J. Thomas, Jr. *Development of International Legal Limitations on the Use of Chemical and Biological Weapons.* 2 vols. ACDA Rpt. GC–128. Washington, D.C.: G.P.O., Nov. 1968, II: 53–67.

Washington Treaty on Noxious Gases (1922)

For text of this treaty, which also dealt with rules for submarine warfare, see U.S. Department of State, *Papers Relating to the Foreign Relations of the United States, 1922* (Washington, D.C.: G.P.O., 1938), I: 267–70.

Documents

5992 *Conference on the Limitation of Armaments, Washington, D.C., November 12, 1921– February 6, 1922.* Washington, D.C.: G.P.O., 1922, pp. 728–49.

5993 U.S. Senate. "Treaty on Submarines and Noxious Gases." *Congressional Record* 62 (Mar. 29, 1922): 4723–30.

General Accounts

5994 Brown, Frederic J. "The Washington Arms Conference." *Chemical Warfare: A Study in Restraints*. Princeton: Princeton Univ. Press, 1968, pp. 61–71.

5995 Kappen, T. M. "Chemical Warfare and Disarmament." *Independent* (Oct. 22, 1921): 73–74.

5996 Knapp, H. S. "Treaty No. 2 of the Washington Conference." *Political Science Quarterly* 39 (June 1922): 201–17.

5997 Lewis, W. L. "Is Prohibition of Gas Warfare Feasible?" *Atlantic Monthly* (June 1922): 834–40.

5998 McBride, R. S. "Chemical Warfare and the Arms Treaty." *Chemical Metallurgical Engineering* (Feb. 22, 1922): 351–53.

5999 Thorpe, Sir Edmund. "Chemical Warfare and the Washington Conference." *Journal of the Society of Chemical Industry* (Feb. 15, 1922): 43–44.

6000 "Will the Ban on Poison Gas End It?" *Literary Digest* (Jan. 21, 1922): 12.

GENEVA PROTOCOL ON CBW (1925)

For text of protocol, see League of Nations, "Prohibition of the Use in War of Asphyxiating, Poisonous or other Gases and of Bacteriological Methods of Warfare," *Treaty Series*, 205 vols. (London: Harrison, 1920–1946), vol. 94, p. 65.

Documents

6001 League of Nations. *Report of the Committee Appointed to Consider the Question of Chemical and Bacteriological Warfare.* In *Report of the Temporary Mixed Commission for the Reduction of Armaments.* Doc. A.16.1924. IX. Geneva, 1924.

6002 U.S. Senate. [Debate on Protocol.] *Congressional Record*, 69th Cong., 1st Sess., Dec. 9, 10, 13, 1926, pp. 141–54, 226–29, 363–68.

6003 ———. Committee on Foreign Relations. Hearings: *The Geneva Protocol of 1925.* 91st Cong., 2d Sess. (1972), Mar. 5–21, 1971.

6004 ———. Report: *Protocol for the Prohibition of the Use in War of Asphyxiating, Poisonous, or Other Gases, and of Bacteriological Methods of Warfare: Message from the President of the U.S., Transmitting the Protocol signed at Geneva, June 17, 1925.* Exec. J. 91st Cong., 2d Sess., 1971.

General Accounts

6005 Babinski, Witold, and Wladyslaw Jajko, eds. "General Kazimierz, the United States and the Ban on Bacteriological Weapons." *Polish Review* 15:2 (1970): 105–13.

6006 Bailey, Sidney D. [Geneva Protocol—1925.] *Prohibitions and Restraints in War.* New York: Oxford Univ. Press, 1972, pp. 126–30.

6007 Baxter, Richard R., and Thomas Buergenthal. "Legal Aspects of the Geneva Protocol of 1925." *American Journal of International Law* 64 (Oct. 1970): 853–79.

6008 Carlton, David, and N. Sims. "The CS Gas Controversy: Great Britain and the Geneva Protocol of 1925." *Survival* 13 (Oct. 1971): 333–40.

6009 "Fight Over Poison Gas." *Literary Digest* (Dec. 25, 1926): 8.

6010 Fujita, Hisakazu. "Ratification, par le Japon, du Protocole de Geneve de 1925." *Japanese Annual of International Law* 15 (1971): 81–96.

6011 Fulbright, Sen. J. William. "The Geneva Protocol of 1925." *Congressional Record* 117 (June 8, 1971): S18694–695.

6012 Johnston, L. Craig. "Ecocide and the Geneva Protocol." *Foreign Affairs* 49 (July 1971): 711–20.

6013 Lewis, W. L. "Poison Gas and Pacifists." *Independent* (Sept. 12, 1925): 289–91, 308.

6014 Madariaga, Salvador de. *Disarmament.* London: Oxford Univ. Press, 1929, pp. 158–64.

6015 Meselson, Matthew S. "Gas Warfare and the Geneva Protocol of 1925." *Bulletin of the Atomic Scientists* 28 (Feb. 1972): 33–37.

6016   Moore, John N. "Ratification of the Geneva Protocol on Gas and Bacteriological Warfare: A Legal and Political Analysis." *Virginia Law Review* 58 (Mar. 1972): 419–509.

6017   "Poison Gas and the Rules of War." *World's Work* 49 (Mar. 1925): 465–66.

6018   Rogers, William P. "The Department Urges Senate Approval of Geneva Protocol on Poisonous Gases and Biological Warfare." *U.S. Department of State Bulletin* (Mar. 29, 1971): 455–59.

6019   Shapley, Deborah. "Impact of Protocol Passage Diluted by Senate Compromise." *Science* (Jan. 17, 1975): 149.

6020   SIPRI. *The Problem of Chemical and Biological Warfare*. 6 vols. New York: Humanities Press, 1971, IV: 58–71.

6021   Westing, Arthur H. "Herbicides as Agents of Chemical Warfare: Their Impact in Relation to the Geneva Protocol of 1925." *Environmental Affairs* 1 (Nov. 1971): 578–86.

Geneva Disarmament Conference (1932)

These discussions did not lead to any new formal treaty arrangement; see League of Nations, above, for more on conference.

Documents

6022   League of Nations. Conference for the Reduction and Limitation of Armaments, Geneva 1932–1934. Special Committee on Chemical and Bacteriological Weapons. *Documents 1–38*. Geneva, 1932.

6023   ———. *Provisional Minutes*. 2d Sess., Geneva, Nov. 22–Dec. 13, 1932.

6024   ———. *Reply to the Questionnaire Submitted by the Bureau to the Special Committee*. Geneva, 1932.

6025   ———. *Report to the General Commission*. Geneva, 1932.

6026   ———. *Report Submitted to the Bureau on the Prohibition of Chemical Warfare and Violations of the Prohibition to Use Chemical, Bacteriological and Incendiary Weapons, in Execution of the Decision of Sept. 22, 1932*. Geneva, 1932.

General Accounts

6027   Brown, Frederic J. "World Disarmament Conference." *Chemical Warfare: A Study in Restraints*. Princeton: Princeton Univ. Press, 1968, pp. 110–20.

6028   Fradkin, Elvira K. *Poison Gas or Peace*. Washington, D.C.: National Council for Prevention of War, 1932.

6029   Mills, J. E. "Chemical Warfare." *Foreign Affairs* 10 (Apr. 1932): 444–52.

6030   Noel-Baker, Philip J. "Chemical Warfare." *Disarmament*. London: Hogarth, 1926 [1972], pp. 275–89.

6031   [Simon Resolution.] In John W. Wheeler-Bennett, ed., *Documents on International Affairs, 1932*. London: Oxford Univ. Press, 1933, pp. 178–80.

6032   SIPRI. *The Problem of Chemical and Biological Warfare*. 6 vols. New York: Humanities Press, 1971–1975, IV: 172–174.

6033   U.N. Secretariat. *Treatment of the Question of Chemical/Biological Warfare in the League of Nations: Review by the United Nations Secretariat*. Doc. A/AC.50/3. New York, Aug. 3, 1951. [Reprinted in U.S. Senate. Committee on Foreign Relations. *Disarmament and Security: A Collection of Documents, 1919–1955*. 84th Cong., 2d Sess., 1956, pp. 169–89.]

6034   "War Gas Not So Bad." *Literary Digest* (July 23, 1932): 25.

F. D. R.'s "No-First-Use" Declaration (1942)

For text of declaration, see "Use of Poison Gas," *U.S. Department of State Bulletin* (June 12, 1943): 507; and U.S. Naval War College, "Use of Poison Gas," *International Law Documents, 1942* (Washington, D.C.: G.P.O., 1943), pp. 85–86.

6035   Brophy, Leo P., and George J. B. Fisher. *The Chemical Warfare Service: Organizing for War*. Washington, D.C.: G.P.O., 1959, pp. 63–64.

6036   Brown, Frederic J. "Confirmation of Restraints, 1939–1942." *Chemical Warfare: A Study in Restraints*. Princeton: Princeton Univ. Press, 1968, pp. 196–207, 262–65.

6037 "Look Out for Gas: Roosevelt's Warning to Japan." *Time* (June 15, 1942): 23.

6038 Marshall, Jim. "We are Ready with Gas." *Collier's* (Aug. 7, 1943): 21, 59.

6039 "Plague on the Enemy?" *Newsweek* (Mar. 16, 1942): 75–76.

West German Renunciation of Nuclear & CB Weapons (1954)

For text of declarations, see *Documents on American Foreign Relations, 1954* (New York: Harpers, 1955), pp. 107–24, 145–65.

6040 Beaton, Leonard, and John Maddox. "Die Bundesrepublik und die Frage der Atomrustung." *Europa-Archiv* 21 (1962): 732 ff.

6041 "Bonn's Atomic Rearmament." *Economist* (Apr. 12, 1958): 95–97.

6042 "Bonn Seeking Additional Nuclear Weapons." *Aviation Week* (Oct. 18, 1965): 23–24.

6043 Brandt, Willy. "The Nuclear Age." *Vital Speeches* (Oct. 1, 1968): 750–52.

6044 Kelleher, Catherine M. "German Nuclear Dilemmas, 1956–1966." Ph.D. diss., M.I.T., 1967.

6045 ———. "The Issue of German Nuclear Armament." *Acad. of Pol. Sci. Proceedings* 29:2 (1968): 95–107.

6046 Legault, Albert. "Atomic Weapons for Germany?" *International Journal* 21 (Autumn 1966): 447–69.

6047 Mahncke, Dieter M. "Nuclear Participation: The Federal Republic of Germany and Nuclear Weapons, 1954–1966." Ph.D. diss., Johns Hopkins Univ., 1968.

6048 Menzel, Eberhard. *Legalitat oder Illegalitat der Anwendung von Atomwaffen.* Tubingen: Mohr, 1960.

6049 Osgood, Robert E. *NATO: The Entangling Alliance.* Chicago: Univ. of Chicago Press, 1962, pp. 96–98, 217–30.

6050 Speier, Hans. *German Rearmament and Atomic War.* Evanston, Ill.: Row, Peterson, 1957.

6051 Taler, Conrad. "Deutsche Industrie im Rustungschaft: Produktion Konventioneller Waffen . . . Vorspiel fur atome Rustung?" *Blatter fur Deutsche und Internationale Politik* 14 (Nov. 1969): 1169–80.

6052 Weizsäcker, Carl F. "Should Germany Have Atomic Arms?" *Bulletin of the Atomic Scientists* 13 (Oct. 1957): 283–86.

Multilateral Force (MLF)

6053 Bader, William B. "Nuclear Weapons Sharing and the 'German Problem.' " *Foreign Affairs* 44 (July 1966): 693–700.

6054 Brzezinski, Zbigniew. "Moscow and the M.L.F.: Hostility and Ambivalence." *Foreign Affairs* 43 (Oct. 1964): 126–34.

6055 Etzioni, Amitai. "The Multinational Force: Germany's Finger on the Atom?" *Nation* (Oct. 12, 1964): 208–11.

6056 Fontaine, Andre. "The ABC of MLF." *Reporter* (Dec. 31, 1964): 10–14.

6057 Hoag, Malcolm W. "Nuclear Strategic Options and European Force Participation." In R. N. Rosecrance, ed., *The Dispersion of Nuclear Weapons.* New York: Columbia Univ. Press, 1964, pp. 222–58.

6058 Hudson, Richard. "The Biddle and the M.L.F." *War/Peace Report* 4 (Aug. 1964): 7–8.

6059 Johnson, Maj. Gen. Max. "The Story of 'MLF': What it is and What's at Stake." *U.S. News & World Report* (Dec. 14, 1964): 44–45.

6060 Kenny, Capt. Edward T. "MLF: The New NATO Sword?" *U.S. Naval Institute Proceedings* 90 (Feb. 1964): 25–35.

6061 Kohl, Wilfrid L. "Nuclear Sharing in NATO and the Multilateral Force." *Political Science Quarterly* 80 (Mar. 1965): 88–109.

6062 Mulley, Frederick W. "NATO's Nuclear Problems: Control or Consultation?" *Orbis* 8 (Spring 1964): 21–35.

6063 Newhouse, John. "The Multilateral Force: An Appraisal." *Bulletin of the Atomic Scientists* 20 (Sept. 1964): 13–18.

6064 Osgood, Robert E. *The Case for the MLF: A Critical Evaluation.* Washington, D.C.: Washington Center for Foreign Policy Research, 1964.

6065 Slessor, Sir John. "Multilateral or Multinational: An Alternative to MLF." *Atlantic*

Community Quarterly 2 (Summer 1964): 285–91.

6066   Smith, Gerard C. "The Nuclear Defense of NATO." *U.S. Department of State Bulletin* (May 18, 1964): 783–90.

6067   Strauss, Franz-Josef. "Armement Atomique et Bundeswehr." *Revue Militaire Générale* 1 (May 1962): 556–57.

6068   Taylor, Edmond. "Behind De Gaulle's Veiled Threats." *Reporter* (Nov. 19, 1964): 30 ff.

6069   ———. "What Price MLF?" *Reporter* (Dec. 3, 1964): 12 ff.

6070   Werth, Alexander, "NATO Today: The Great Poker Game." *Nation* (Nov. 30, 1964): 399–401.

6071   Wiegele, Thomas C. "The Multi-Lateral Nuclear Force: A Study in the Politics of the Control of Nuclear Weapons." Ph.D. diss., Univ. of Pennsylvania, 1967.

6072   Williams, Alan L. "Is a European Nuclear Force Desirable?" *Atlantic Community Quarterly* 10 (Summer 1972): 185–87.

6073   Young, Wayland. "MLF—A West European View." *Bulletin of the Atomic Scientists* 20 (Nov. 1964): 19–21.

Third Protocol to Brussels Treaty (1954)

For text, see "Protocol III on the Control of Armaments, with Annexes, Paris, Oct. 23, 1954," *American Journal of International Law: Supplement* 49 (July 1955): 134–40.

6074   Coignard, Marcel. "Armament Control Carried Out by the Agency for Control of Armaments of the Western European Union." *Disarmament* 6 (June 1965): 5–8.

6075   Fletcher, Raymond. "Existing Arrangements for International Control of Warlike Material—Western European Union." *Disarmament and Arms Control* 1 (Autumn 1963): 144–54.

6076   ———. "Western European Union." In Wayland Young, ed. *Existing Mechanisms of Arms Control*. Oxford: Pergamon, 1966, pp. 1–12.

6077   Menzel, Eberhard. "Die Rüstungskontrolle der Westeuropäischen Union und das NATO System." *Europa-Archiv* 8 (1957): 9767–75.

6078   SIPRI. "The Terms Imposed on Germany [re: CB]." *The Problem of Chemical and Biological Warfare*. 6 vols. New York: Humanities Press, 1971–1975, VI: 215–19.

6079   Vreeden, D. C. "The Armaments Control Agency of the Western European Union." *NATO's Fifteen Nations* 15 (1960): 62–65.

U.N. Resolution on Tear Gas & Herbicides (1969)

For text of resolution, see "General Assembly Resolution, 2603 (XXIV): Question of Chemical and Bacteriological (Biological) Weapons, December 16, 1969," *Documents on Disarmament, 1969* (Washington, D.C.: G.P.O., 1970), pp. 716–19.

Documents

6080   U.N. General Assembly. *U.N. Resolution 2603A (Dec. 16, 1969)*. Doc. A/PV.1836. New York, 1969.

6081   U.S. Senate. ["The Debate, with Insertions for the Record, which preceded the Vote against Placing Restrictions on the Military Use of Herbicides in Vietnam."] *Congressional Record* 116 (Aug. 26, 27, 1970): S14240–258, S14419–424.

General Accounts

6082   Bazell, Robert J. "CBW Ban: Nixon Would Exclude Tear Gas and Herbicides." *Science* (Apr. 16, 1971): 246–48.

6083   Gellner, Charles R., and Leneice N. Wu. "The Use of Tear Gas in War: A Survey of International Negotiations and of U.S. Policy and Practice." In U.S. House. Subcommittee on National Security Policy and Scientific Development. Report: *Chemical-Biological Warfare: U.S. Policies and International Effects*. 91st Cong., 2d Sess., 1970, pp. 11–41.

6084   Goldblat, Jozef. "Are Tear Gas and Herbicides Permitted Weapons?" *Bulletin of the Atomic Scientists* 26 (Apr. 1970): 13–16.

6085   Jack, Homer A. "The United Nations and Chemical Warfare." *Christian Century* (Jan. 11, 1967): 60–62.

6086   "The Silent Arsenal: A United Nations Report on the Production, Use, and Effects of

Chemical and Bacteriological Weapons." *Saturday Review* (Sept. 27, 1969): 14–17, 43.

6087   Westing, Arthur H. "Herbicides in War: Current Status and Future Doubt." *Biological Conservation* 4 (Oct. 1972): 322–27.

NIXON'S UNILATERAL BAN ON BIOLOGICAL WEAPONS (1970)

For text of statement, see "White House Statement on the President's Decision to Renounce Toxins as a Method of War, February 14, 1970," *Documents on Disarmament, 1970* (Washington, D.C.: G.P.O., 1971), pp. 5–6.

6088   Beaton, Leonard. "A Ban on Germs." *Survival* 12 (Jan. 1970): 17–18.

6089   Boffery, Philip M. "Fort Detrick: A Top Laboratory is Threatened with Extinction." *Science* (Jan. 22, 1971): 262–64.

6090   ———. "Pine Bluff Saved, Detrick Critical." *Science* (Feb. 5, 1971): 462.

6091   "Detrick's Germs Gone, NCI's Viruses Due." *Medical World News* (July 23, 1971): 25.

6092   Glines, C. V. "Nixon's CBW Policy: Unilateral Disarmament?" *Armed Forces Management* 16 (Jan. 1970): 42–43, 45.

6093   Karber, Phillip A. "The Nixon Policy on CBW." *Bulletin of the Atomic Scientists* 28 (Jan. 1972): 22–27.

6094   Meselson, Matthew S. "Behind the Nixon Policy for Chemical and Biological Warfare." *Bulletin of the Atomic Scientists* 26 (Jan. 1970): 23–24, 26–34.

6095   "Nixon Converts Detrick to Cancer Research." *Army Research and Development News Magazine* 12:5 (1971): 1, 6–7.

6096   Rosebury, Theodor. "President Nixon's Statement on CBW." *Scientific World* 14:3 (1970): 9–10.

6097   Wade, Nicholas. "Russians Reserve Doubts: Is Fort Detrick Really de-Tricked?" *Science* (Aug. 11, 1972): 500.

6098   Yarmolinsky, Adam. *The Military Establishment: Its Impact on American Society.* New York: Harper & Row, 1971, pp. 103–104.

BIOLOGICAL WEAPONS CONVENTION (1972)

For text of convention, see U.S. Arms Control & Disarmament Agency, "Convention on the Prohibition of the Development, Production and Stockpiling of Bacteriological (Biological) and Toxin Weapons and on Their Destruction," *Arms Control and Disarmament Agreements: Texts and History of Negotiations* (Washington, D.C.: G.P.O., Feb. 1975), pp. 118–24.

Documents

6099   "Convention on Biological and Toxin Weapons Transmitted to the Senate." *U.S. Department of State Bulletin* (Sept. 4, 1972): 253–57.

6100   "UN: Draft Convention on the Prohibition of Bacteriological Weapons." *International Legal Materials* 10 (Nov. 1971): 1177–81.

6101   "UN: Draft Convention on the Prohibition of the Development, Production and Stockpiling of Bacteriological (Biological) and Toxin Weapons and on Their Destruction, Sept. 28, 1971." *American Journal of International Law* 66 (Apr. 1972): 451–54.

6102   "United Nations Proposals Concerning Chemical and Bacteriological Weapons: Question of Chemical and Bacteriological (biological) Weapons, Dec. 16, 1969." *International Legal Materials* 9 (Mar. 1970): 377–81.

6103   "United Nations: Questions of Chemical and Bacteriological Weapons." *International Legal Materials* 10 (May 1971): 630–47.

General Accounts

6104   Ailleret, Col. Charles. "Arme Biologique et Desarmement." *Revue de Defense Nationale* 11 (Aug.–Sept. 1955): 144–55.

6105   Aleksandrov, L., and V. Shestov. "Important Initiative of Socialist Countries [on Biological Weapons Ban]." *International Affairs* [Moscow] 17 (July 1971): 88–91.

6106   Fineberg, Richard A. "No More Chemical/Biological War?" *New Republic* (Dec. 2, 1972): 17–19.

6107   Goldblat, Jozef. "Biological Disarmament." *Bulletin of the Atomic Scientists* 28 (Apr. 1972): 6–10.

6108   Greenberg, Daniel S. "Test-Tube Warfare: The Fake Renunciation." *World Magazine* (Aug. 15, 1972): 26–28.

6109   Jack, Homer A. "Another First in Disarmament." *America* (Apr. 29, 1972): 460–61.

6110   Malek, Ivan, and Darel Raske. "Problems of Biological Disarmament." *Disarmament and Arms Control* 2 (Spring 1964): 150–56.

6111   McCarthy, Richard D. "Biological Warfare as National Policy: An Offensive Capability." *Vital Speeches* (Sept. 1, 1969): 681–83.

6112   Shestov, V. "Real Advance Towards Disarmament." *International Affairs* [Moscow] 18 (Mar. 1972): 9–14.

Negotiations

6113   "Geneva Disarmament Conference Agrees on Draft Text of Bacterial Weapons Convention." *U.S. Department of State Bulletin* (Nov. 1, 1971): 504–12.

6114   Lambert, Robert W., and Jean E. Mayer. *International Negotiations on the Biological-Weapons and Toxin Convention.* ACDA Pub. 78. Washington, D.C.: G.P.O., 1975.

6115   Lederberg, Joshua. "A Biological Weapons Race: International Cooperation." *Vital Speeches* (Oct. 1, 1970): 740–43.

6116   Leonard, James F. "U.S. Supports Inclusion of Toxins in Biological Warfare Convention." *U.S. Department of State Bulletin* (June 8, 1970): 731–32.

6117   ———. "U.S. and U.S.S.R. Table Draft Biological Weapons Convention at Geneva Disarmament Conference." *U.S. Department of State Bulletin* (Aug. 30, 1971): 221–26.

6118   Stulz, P.; H. Helbing; and S. Forster. "Resume of the Discussion at the Conference on ABC Weapons." *Scientific World* 16:3 (1972): 11–15.

6119   "U.N. Commends Biological Weapons Convention and Requests Continued Negotiations on Prohibition of Chemical Weapons." *U.S. Department of State Bulletin* (Jan. 24, 1972): 102–09.

6120   "United States Welcomes Soviet Move Toward Biological Weapons Ban." *U.S. Department of State Bulletin* (Apr. 26, 1971): 549.

Control & Verification

6121   Groupe, Vincent. "On the Feasibility of Control of Biological Weapons." In Seymour Melman, ed., *Inspection for Disarmament.* New York: Columbia Univ. Press, 1958, pp. 185–90.

6122   Hjertonsoon, Karin. "A Study on the Prospects of Compliance with the Convention on Biological Weapons." *Journal of Instant Research on Peace and Violence* 3:4 (1973): 211–24.

Restricting Submarine Warfare

Bibliographies

6123   Anderson, Frank J. *Submarines, Submariners, Submarining: A Checklist.* . . . Hamden, Conn.: Shoe String Press, 1963.

6124   National Research Council. Committee on Undersea Warfare. *An Annotated Bibliography of Submarine Technical Literature, 1557–1953.* Pub. 307. Washington, D.C.: G.P.O., 1954.

6125   Paine, Thomas O. *Submarining: Three Thousand Books and Articles.* Santa Barbara, Ca.: ABC–Clio for General Electric-TEMPO, Center for Advanced Studies, 1971.

Submarine Warfare

6126   Abbot, Henry L. *The Beginning of Modern Submarine Warfare Under Captain Lieutenant David Bushnell.* Hamden, Conn.: Archon Books, 1966.

6127   Andrade, Ernest, Jr. "Submarine Policy in United States Navy, 1914–1971." *Military Affairs* 35 (Apr. 1971): 50–56.

6128   Barnes, Robert H. *United States Submarines.* New Haven, Conn.: H. F. Morse Assoc., 1944.

6129   Bauer, Hermann. *The Submarine, Its Importance as Part of a Fleet, Its Position in International Law, Its Employment in War, Its Future.* Trans. by Hyman G. Rickover. Newport, R.I.: U.S. Naval War College, 1936.

6130   Casing, James. *Submarines.* London: Macmillan, 1951.

6131   Fyfe, Herbert C. *Submarine Warfare: Past and Present.* 2d ed. London: Richards, 1907.

6132   Jane, Frederick T. *The Torpedo in Peace and War.* London: Thackery, 1898.

6133   Kuenne, Robert. *The Attack Submarine: A Study of Strategy.* New Haven: Yale Univ. Press, 1955.

6134   Lake, Simon. *The Submarine in War and Peace.* London: Lippincott, 1918.

6135   Lewis, Cmdr. David D. *The Fight for the Sea: The Past, Present, and Future of Submarine Warfare in the Atlantic.* Cleveland: World, 1961.

6136   Parsons, William B. *Robert Fulton and the Submarine.* New York: Columbia Univ. Press, 1922.

6137   Polmar, Norman. *Atomic Submarines.* Princeton: Van Nostrand, 1963.

6138   Sapolsky, Harvey M. *The Polaris System Development: Bureaucratic and Programmatic Success in Government.* Cambridge: Harvard Univ. Press, 1972.

6139   Saville, Allison W. "The Development of the German U-Boat Arm, 1919–1935." Ph.D. diss., Univ. of Washington, 1963.

6140   Sleeman, Charles W. *Torpedoes and Torpedo Warfare.* Portsmouth: Griffin, 1880.

6141   Spindler, Arno. "The Value of the Submarine in Warfare." *U.S. Naval Institute Proceedings* 52 (May 1926): 835–54.

6142   Stambler, Irwin. *The Battle for Inner Space: Undersea Warfare and Weapons.* New York: St. Martin's Press, 1962.

6143   Sueter, Murray F. *The Evolution of the Submarine Boat, Mine and Torpedo: From the Sixteenth Century to the Present Time.* Portsmouth: Griffin, 1907.

6144   Woodbury, David O. *What the Citizen Should Know about Submarine Warfare.* New York: Norton, 1942.

6145   Zim, Herbert S. *Submarines.* New York: Harcourt, Brace, 1942.

American Civil War

6146   Barnes, John S. *Submarine Warfare, Offensive and Defensive, including a Discussion of the Offensive Torpedo System, Its Effects Upon Iron-Clad Ship Systems, and Influence Upon Future Naval Wars.* New York: Van Nostrand, 1869.

6147   Bolander, Louis M. "The 'Alligator' the First Federal Submarine of the Civil War." *U.S. Naval Institute Proceedings* 64 (June 1938): 845–54.

6148   Klonitz, Lt. Harry von. "The Confederate Submarine." *U.S. Naval Institute Proceedings* 63 (Oct. 1937): 1453–57.

6149   Merrill, James M. *The Rebel Shore: Story of Union Seapower in the Civil War.* Boston: Little, Brown, 1957.

6150   Robinson, William M., Jr. *The Confederate Privateers.* New Haven: Yale Univ. Press, 1928.

World War I

6151   Ajax [pseud.]. *The German Pirate: His Methods and Record.* London: Pearson, 1918.

6152   Bateman, Charles T. *U-Boat Devilry: Illustrating the Heroism and Endurance of Merchant Seamen.* London: Hodder & Stoughton, 1918.

6153   Carr, William J. C. *Good Hunting: Being Volume Three of "By Guess and By God."* London: Hutchinson, 1940.

6154   ———. *By Guess and By God. The Story of the British Submarines in the War.* New York: Doubleday, 1930.

6154a ———. *Hell's Angels of the Deep.* London: Hutchinson, 1932.

6155   Clark, William B. *When the U-Boats Came to America.* Boston: Little, Brown, 1929.

6156   Francois, J. P. A. *Duik boot en Volkenrecht.* Leiden: Nijhoff, 1919.

6157   Garner, James W. "Submarine Warfare." *International Law in the World War.* 2 vols. New York: Longmans, Green, 1920, I: 355–416.

6158   Gayer, Capt. A. "Summary of German Submarine Operations in the Various Theatres of War." *U.S. Naval Institute Proceedings* 52 (Apr. 1926): 621–59.

6159   Gibson, Richard H., and Maurice Prendergast. *The German Submarine War, 1914–1918.* New York: Smith, 1931.

6160 Higgins, A. Pearce. "Submarine Warfare." *British Yearbook of International Law* 1 (1920–1921): 149–65.

6161 Laurens, Adophe. *Histoire de la Guerre Sous-marine Allemande.* Paris: Societe d'Editions Geographiques, Maritimes, et Coloniales, 1930.

6162 Masters, David. *The Submarine War.* New York: Putnam's, 1935.

6163 Sims, Adm. William S. "The Truth about the German Submarine Atrocities." *Current History* 18 (June 1923): 355–63.

6164 Thomson, G. P. "The German Official Account of the Submarine War on Commerce." *Royal United Services Institution Journal* 77 (Aug. 1932): 504–08.

World War II

6165 Blair, Clay, Jr. *Silent Victory: The U.S. Submarine War Against Japan.* Philadelphia: Lippincott, 1975.

6166 Brou, Willy C. *Combat Beneath the Sea.* Trans. by Edward Fitzgerald. New York: Crowell, 1957.

6167 Busch, Harold. *U-Boats at War: German Submarines in Action, 1939–1945.* Trans. by L. P. R. Wilson. New York: Ballantine, 1955.

6168 Cocchia, Aldo. *The Hunters and the Huntea. Adventures of Italian Naval Forces.* Trans. by M. Gwyer. Annapolis: U.S. Naval Institute, 1958.

6169 Colby, Carroll B. *Submarine: Men and Ships of the U.S. Submarine Fleet.* New York: Coward-McCann, 1953.

6170 Cope, Harley F., and Walter Karig. *Battle Submerged: Submarine Fighters of World War Two.* New York: Norton, 1951.

6171 Cresswell, John. *Sea Warfare, 1939–1945: A Short History.* London: Longmans, 1950.

6172 Frank, Wolfgang. *The Sea Wolves: The Story of German U-Boats at War.* Trans. by R. O. B. Long. New York: Rinehart, 1955.

6173 Gilbert, Nigel J. "British Submarine Operations in World War II." *U.S. Naval Institute Proceedings* 89 (Mar. 1963): 73–81.

6174 Hart, Sydney. *Discharged Dead: A True Story of Britain's Submarines at War.* London: Oldham's, 1956.

6175 Hashimoto, Mochitsura. *Sunk: The Story of the Japanese Fleet, 1941–1945.* Trans. by E. H. M. Colegrave. New York: Holt, 1954.

6176 Isakov, Ivan S. *The Red Fleet in the Second World War.* Trans. by Jack Hural. London: Hutchinson, 1947.

6177 Lockwood, Charles A. *Sink 'Em All: Submarine Warfare in the Pacific.* New York: Dutton, 1951.

6178 Peillard, Léonce. *The Laconia Affair.* Trans. by Oliver Coburn. New York, Putnam's, 1963.

6179 Roscoe, Theodore. *United States Submarine Operations in World War Two.* Annapolis: U.S. Naval Institute, 1949.

6180 Thomas, David A. *Submarine Victory: The Story of British Submarines in World War Two.* London: Kimber, 1961.

Regulating Submarine Warfare

6181 Anderson, Capt. Walter S. "Submarines and Disarmament Conferences." *U.S. Naval Institute Proceedings* 53 (Jan. 1927): 50–69.

6182 Barnes, William H., III. "Submarine Warfare and International Law." *World Polity* 2 (1960): 121–202.

6183 Burns, Richard Dean. "Regulating Submarine Warfare, 1921–41: A Case Study in Arms Control and Limited War." *Military Affairs* 35 (Apr. 1971): 56–63.

6184 "Discussion of the Abolition of Submarines." *Transactions of the Grotius Society* 11 (1925): 65–78.

6185 Douglas, Lawrence H. "Submarine Disarmament, 1919–1936." Ph.D. diss., Syracuse Univ., 1970.

6186 Fawkes, G. B. H. "The Submarine and International Law." *Royal United Services Institution Journal* 77 (Nov. 1932): 744–47.

6187 Groeling, Dorothy T. "Submarines, Disarmament and Modern Warfare." Ph.D. diss., Columbia Univ., 1935.

6188 Hyde, C. C. "The Part of International Law in Further Limitation of Naval Armaments." *American Journal of International Law* 20 (Apr. 1926): 237–56.

6189   Kerr, Alex A. "International Law and the Future of Submarine Warfare." *U.S. Naval Institute Proceedings* 81 (Oct. 1955): 1105–10.

6190   Louvard, Jacques. *La Guerre Sous-Marine au Commerce.* Paris: Sirey, 1934.

6191   Low, Archibald M. "[a critique of submarine rules]." *The Submarine at War.* New York: Sheridan House, 1942, pp. 275–88.

6192   Mallison, William T., Jr. *Studies in the Law of Naval Warfare: Submarines in General and Limited Wars.* [U.S. Naval War College. *International Law Studies*, vol. 58.] Washington, D.C.: G.P.O., 1968.

6193   Miller, Capt. William O. "A New International Law for the Submarine?" *U.S. Naval Institute Proceedings* 92 (Oct. 1966): 96–103.

6194   Mori, K. *The Submarine in War: A Study of Relevant Rules and Problems.* New York: Stechert, 1931.

6195   Pollen, Sir A. J. H. "The Submarine." *Foreign Affairs* 5 (July 1927): 553–66.

6196   "Problems of Submarine Warfare Under International Law." *New York University Intramural Law* 22 (Jan. 1967): 136–51.

6197   "Report of the Committee on the Legal Status of Submarines." *Transactions of the Grotius Society* 14 (1928): 155–74.

6198   Robertson, Lt. H. B., Jr. "Submarine Warfare." *Judge-Advocate General Journal* (Nov. 1956): 3–9.

WASHINGTON TREATY ON SUBMARINES & NOXIOUS GASES (1922)

For text of treaty, see Trevor N. Dupuy and Gay M. Hammerman, eds., *A Documentary History of Arms Control and Disarmament* (New York: Bowker, 1973), pp. 120–21. Treaty was not ratified.

Documents

6199   *Conference on the Limitation of Armaments, Washington, November 12, 1921–February 6, 1922.* Washington, D.C.: G.P.O., 1922, pp. 596–618.

6200   *Conference on the Limitation of Armaments: Subcommittees.* Washington, D.C.: G.P.O., 1922.

6201   U.S. Senate. Committee on Foreign Relations. *Conference on the Limitation of Armaments.* Sen. Doc. 126. 67th Cong., 2d Sess., 1922, pp. 68, 264–65, 278–94, 311–12, 348–51, 413–14, 427–32.

General Accounts

See Chapter 7, Limitation of Weapons & Personnel, Washington Naval Treaty (1922), for general accounts which relate to the submarine issue at that conference.

6202   Anderson, Chandler P. "As If for an Act of Piracy." *American Journal of International Law* 16 (Apr. 1922): 260–61.

6203   Castex, Capt. Raoul. "Synthese de la Guerre Sous-Marine." *Revue Maritime* [New series] 1 (Jan., Feb., Mar., 1920): 1 ff., 161 ff., 305 ff.

6204   "The Civilizing of Warfare." *New Republic* 29 (Jan. 1922): 197–98.

6205   Cooper, Morris J. "The Future of the Submarine in International Law." *U.S. Naval Institute Proceedings* 48 (Mar. 1922): 337–46.

6206   Douglas, Lawrence H. "Submarines and the Washington Conference of 1921." *Naval War College Review* 26 (Mar.–Apr. 1974): 86–100.

6207   "France's Demand for Submarines." *Literary Digest* (Jan. 7, 1922): 7–9.

6208   La Bruyère, René. "La Question des Sous-Marins." *L'Europe Nouvelle* (Jan. 14, 1922): 43 ff.

6209   Roxburgh, R. F. "Submarines at the Washington Conference." *British Yearbook of International Law* 3 (1922–1923): 150–58.

6210   Sims, Adm. William S. "Changing Methods of Submarine Warfare." *Current History* 18 (Sept. 1923): 911–18.

6211   U.S. Senate. "Treaty on Submarines and Noxious Gases [ratification]." *Congressional Record* 67 (Mar. 29, 1922): 4723–30.

LONDON SUBMARINE RESTRICTIONS (1930)

Text of the 1930 agreement regulating submarine warfare is in the London Naval Treaty (1930), pt. 4, art. 22, cited in Chapter 7. Also see Chapter 7, Limitation of Weapons & Personnel, London Naval

Conference (1930), for general accounts which relate to the submarine issue.

6212 Castex, Capt. Raoul. "The Weapon of the Weak—A French View." *Royal United Services Institution Journal* 77 (Nov. 1932): 733–43.

6213 Richmond, Adm. Sir Herbert W. "The Weapon of the Weak—A British View." *Royal United Services Institution Journal* 77 (Aug. 1932): 497–503.

6214 "Submarine Code." *Outlook and Independent* (Apr. 23, 1930): 652.

6215 Wilson, G. G. "Armed Merchant Vessels and Submarines." *American Journal of International Law* 24 (Oct. 1930): 694–702.

SUBMARINE PROTOCOL (1936)

For text of the *Proces-Verbal* or Protocol of 1936, see "Proces-Verbal Relating to the Rules of Submarine Warfare as Set Forth in Part IV of the London Naval Treaty of 1930," *American Journal of International Law: Supplemental Official Documents* 31 (1937): 137–39.

6216 Hazlett, E. E. "Submarines and the London Treaty." *U.S. Naval Institute Proceedings* 62 (Dec. 1936): 1690–1702.

6217 Rickover, Adm. Hyman. "International Law and the Submarine." *U.S. Naval Institute Proceedings* 61 (Sept. 1935): 1213–27.

6218 Wilson, G. G. "The Submarine and Place of Safety." *American Journal of International Law* 35 (July 1941): 496–97.

NYON AGREEMENT (1937)

For text of accord, see "International Agreement for Collective Measures Against Piratical Attack in the Mediterranean by Submarines, Nyon, Sept. 14, 1937," *American Journal of International Law: Supplement* 31 (1937): 179, 182.

6219 Cortada, James W. "Ship Diplomacy and the Spanish Civil War: Nyon Conference, September 1937." *Il Politico* 4 (1972): 673–89.

6220 Genet, Raoul. "The Charge of Piracy in the Spanish Civil War." *American Journal of International Law* 32 (Apr. 1938): 253–63.

6221 League of Nations. "Appeal by the Spanish Government [re: Nyon Agreement]." *Official Journal* 18 (Dec. 1937): 914–19, 1161–66.

6222 "The Nyon Arrangements: Piracy by Treaty?" *British Yearbook of International Law* 19 (1938): 198–209.

6223 Padelford, Norman J. "Foreign Shipping During the Spanish Civil War." *American Journal of International Law* 32 (Apr. 1938): 264–79.

6224 Royal Institute of International Affairs. *Survey of International Affairs, 1937*. London: Oxford Univ. Press, 1938, II: 347–62.

Aerial Bombardment

For additional references, see Chapter 13, Rules of War & Stabilizing the International Environment.

BOMBING & INTERNATIONAL LAW

6225 Barclay, T. "Aircraft Bombs and International Law." *Nineteenth Century* 76 (Nov. 1914): 1032–38.

6226 DeSaussure, Hamilton. "Laws of Air Warfare: Are There Any?" *Air Force JAG Law Review* 12 (Fall 1970): 242–51.

6227 ———. "The Laws of Air Warfare: Are There Any?" *Naval War College Review* 23 (Feb. 1971): 35–47.

6228 Hazeltine, Harold D. *The Law of the Air.* London: Univ. of London Press, 1911.

6229 International Committee of the Red Cross. *Commission of Experts for the Legal Protection of Civilian Populations and Victims of War from the Dangers of Aerial Warfare and Blind Weapons.* Geneva, 1954.

6230 Peng, Ming-Nin. "Les Bombardements Aériens et la Population Civile depuis la Seconde Guerre Mondiale." *Revue Generale de l'Air* [Paris] 15 (1952): 302–11.

6231 ———. "La Definition de l'Aeronef Militaire." *Revue Française de Droit Aerien* [Paris] 10 (Apr.–June 1956): 121–68.

6232 ———. *Le Statut Juridique de l'Aeronef Militaire.* The Hague: Nijhoff, 1957.

6233 Phillips, C. P. "Air Warfare and Law: An Analysis of Legal Doctrines, Practices and

Policies." *George Washington Law Review* 21 (1953–1954): 311–35, 395–422.

6234   Royse, M. W. *Aerial Bombardment and the International Regulation of Warfare*. New York: Harold Vinal, 1928.

6235   Saunby, Air Marshal Sir Robert. "The Ethics of Bombing." *Air Force & Space Digest* 5 (June 1967): 49–53.

6236   Sibert, Marcel. "Remarques et Suggestions sur la Protection des Populations Civiles contre les Bombardements Aeriens." *Revue Generale de Droit International Public* [Paris] 59 (Apr.–June 1955): 177–92.

6237   Sloutzki, Nokhim M. "Le Bombardement Aerien des Objectifs Militaires." *Revue Generale de Droit International Public* [Paris] 61 (July–Sept. 1957): 353–81.

6238   Smith, E. C. "Legal Aspects of Surface and Aerial Warfare." *JAG Journal* (Sept., Oct. 1956): 9–10, 10–15.

6239   Spaight, James M. "Air Bombardment." *British Yearbook of International Law* 4 (1923–1924): 21–33.

6240   ———. *Air Power and the Cities*. New York: Longmans, Green, 1930.

6241   ———. *Air Power and War Rights*. 3d ed. London: Longmans, Green [1924], 1947.

6242   ———. *Air Power Can Disarm: A Sequel to Air Power and the Cities, 1930*. London: Pitman, 1948.

6243   Spetzler, E. *Luftkrieg und Menschlichkeit: Die Volkerrechtliche Stellung der Zivilpersonen im Luftkrieg*. Gottingen: Musterschmidt, 1956.

6244   Swint, William A. "The German Air-Attack on Rotterdam (14 May 1940), Revisited." *Aerospace Historian* 21 (Mar. 1974): 14–22.

6245   Terry, Col. Jay D. "The Evolving Law of Aerial Warfare." *Air University Review* 26 (Nov.–Dec. 1975): 22–37.

6246   Williams, P. W. "Legitimate Targets in Aerial Bombardment." *American Journal of International Law* 22 (July 1929): 570–81.

Open Cities

6247   Fisher, E. F. "Rome: An Open City." *Military Review* 45 (Aug. 1965): 71–77.

6248   Garner, James W. "Aerial Bombardment of Undefended Towns." *American Journal of International Law* 9 (Jan. 1915): 93–101.

6249   Jennings, R. Y. "Open Towns." *British Yearbook of International Law* 22 (1945): 258–64.

6250   Read, J. J., and Paul Salstrom. "The Free Cities Plan." *Humanist* 28 (Jan.–Feb. 1968): 12–15.

6251   Watson, Thomas J. "World Conference for Action on the Bombardment of Open Towns." *International Conciliation*, no. 343 (Oct. 1938): 337–96.

AERIAL BOMBING—HISTORICAL

6252   Bishop, William A. *Winged Warfare*. Garden City, N.Y.: Doubleday, 1967.

6253   Dillon, Richard T. "Some Sources for Faulkner's Version of the First Air War." *American Literature* 44:4 (1973): 629–37.

6254   Goyal, S. N. *Air Power in Modern Warfare*. Bombay: Thackery, 1952.

6255   Grey, Charles G. *Bombers*. London: Faber & Faber, 1942.

6256   Harr, K. G., Jr. "The Arsenals of Peace." *Air Force & Space Digest* 53 (Sept. 1970): 84–91.

6257   Macmillan, Norman. *Tales of Two Air Wars*. London: Bell, 1963.

6258   Pierce, Wasson O'Dell. *Air War: Its Psychological, Technical and Social Implications*. New York: Modern Age, 1939.

6259   Ross, Albert H. *War on Great Cities*. London: Faber & Faber, 1937.

6260   Saundby, Air Marshal Sir Robert. *Air Bombardment: The Story of Its Development*. New York: Harpers, 1961.

6261   Spaight, James M. *Air Power In the Next War*. London: Bles, 1938.

6262   Vander Els, Theodore. "The Irresistible Weapon." *Military Review* 51 (Aug. 1971): 80–90.

World War I

6263   "Aerial Warfare and International Law." *Review of Reviews* 51 (Jan. 1915): 97–98.

6264   Armani, Armando. *Ex Alto ad Signum: Aneddoti ed Episodi di Bombardamenti*

Aeri [1915–1918]. Roma: Tipografia del Senato, 1925.

6265 Barclay, T. "Law and the Bombardment of London." *English Review* 20 (May 1915): 225–30.

6266 ———. "Ruthless Warfare and Forbidden Methods." *Nineteenth Century* 76 (Dec. 1914): 1186–92.

6267 Fredette, Raymond H. *The First Battle For Britain, 1917–1918, and the Birth of the Royal Air Force.* London: Cassell, 1966.

6268 Garner, James W. "Aerial Warfare." *International Law and the World War.* 2 vols. London: Longmans, Green, 1920, I: 458–96.

6269 Jones, H. A. *The War in the Air.* 5 vols. Oxford: Clarendon Press, 1922–1937.

6270 Jourdain, M. "Air Raid Reprisals and Starvation by Blockade." *International Journal of Ethics* 28 (July 1918): 542–53.

6271 Lefranc, Jean Ablel. "Les Forces Aériennes Allemandes de Bombardement." *Revue Scientifique* 56 (1918): 99–104.

6272 Lehmann, Ernst A. *The Zeppelins: The Development of the Warship, with the Story of the Zeppelin Air Raids in the World War.* New York: J. H. Sears, 1927.

6273 Morris, Joseph. *The German Air Raids on Great Britain, 1914–1918.* London: Low & Marston, 1925.

6274 Norman, Aaron. *The Great Air War.* New York: Macmillan, 1968.

6275 Spaight, James M. *The Beginnings of Organized Air Power: A Historical Study.* London: Longmans, Green, 1927.

6276 Stiénon, C. "Les Raids des Zeppelins et l'Opinion Publique en Angleterre." *Revue Politique et Litteraire* (Feb. 10, 1917): 108–12.

6277 Sykes, Sir F. H. *Aviation in Peace and War.* London: E. Arnold, 1922.

6278 Thiéry, Maurice. *Paris Bombarde par Zeppelins, Gothas et Berthas.* Paris: E. de Boccard, 1921.

Interwar Years

6279 "Guernica as Art History." *Art News* 66 (Dec. 1967): 32–35.

6280 League of Nations. "Allegations Against Italy [bombing of hospitals and open cities in Ethiopia]." *Official Journal* 17 (Apr. 1936): 368–70, 372; 17 (July 1936): 778.

6281 ———. "Appeal by the Chinese Government." *Official Journal* 18 (Aug.–Sept. 1937): 655–57; 19 (Nov. 1938): 864, 879, 881–82; 20 (Mar.–Apr. 1939): 207–14; 20 (May–June 1939): 277; 20 (July–Aug. 1939): 346–55.

6282 ———. "Bombardment of the Civilian Populations [Chaco War]." *Official Journal* 15 (July 1934): 803–06.

6283 ———. "Reports of the Commission for the Investigation of Air Bombardment in Spain." *Official Journal* 20 (Jan. 1939): 28–34; 20 (Feb. 1939): 86–90, 96–99.

6284 ———. "[Resolution condemning bombing of open cities in Spain.]" *Official Journal* 18 (May–June 1937): 334. [Doc. C.269(1).1937. VII.]

6285 LeGoff, M. "Les Bombardements Aériens dans la Guerre Civile Espagnole." *Revue Générale de Droit International Public* 45 (Sept.–Oct. 1938): 581–606.

6286 Scovill, Elmer B. "The Royal Air Force, the Middle East, and Disarmament, 1919–1934." Ph.D. diss., Michigan State Univ., 1973.

6287 U.S. Department of State. *Papers Relating to the Foreign Relations of the United States: Japan, 1931–1941.* 2 vols. Washington, D.C.: G.P.O., 1943, I: 20–21; II: 491–99. [Protests Japanese bombing of Chinchow, etc.]

World War II

6288 Alexander, Richard G. "Experiment in Total War." *U.S. Naval Institute Proceedings* 82 (Aug. 1956): 837–47.

6289 Allen, Hubert R. *The Legacy of Lord Trenchard.* London: Cassell, 1972.

6290 Arnold, Gen. H. H. *Global Mission.* New York: Harpers, 1949.

6291 ———. *The War Reports.* Philadelphia: Lippincott, 1947.

6292 Caidin, Martin. *The Night Hamburg Died.* New York: Ballantine, 1960.

6293 ———. *A Torch to the Enemy: The Fire Raid on Tokyo.* New York: Ballantine, 1960.

6294 Craven, Wesley, and James Cate, eds. *The Army Air Forces in World War II.* 7 vols. Chicago: Univ. of Chicago Press, 1948–1958.

6295 Divine, D. *The Broken Wing: A Study in the British Exercise of Air Power.* London: Hutchinson, 1966.

6296 Emory, Sir Basil. *Mission Completed.* London: Methuen, 1957.

6297 Franklin, Noble. *The Bombing Offensive Against Germany: Outline and Perspective.* London: Faber, 1965.

6298 Harris, Arthur T. *Bomber Offensive.* London: Collins, 1947.

6299 Ikle, Fred C. *The Social Impact of Bomb Destruction.* Norman: Univ. of Oklahoma Press, 1958.

6300 Irving, David. [John Cawdell.] *The Destruction of Dresden.* New York: Ballantine, 1964.

6301 Krauskopf, Robert W. "The Army and the Strategic Bomber, 1930–1939 [B-17]." *Military Affairs* 22 (Feb. 1958): 208–15.

6302 MacIaac, David, ed. *The United States Strategic Bombing Survey.* 11 vols. New York: Garland, 1975.

6303 Middlebrook, M. *The Nuremberg Raid.* London: Allen Lane, 1973.

6304 Quester, George H. "Bargaining and Bombing during World War II in Europe." *World Politics* 15 (Apr. 1963): 417–37.

6305 Richards, D., and H. S. G. Saunders. *Royal Air Force, 1939–1945.* 3 vols. London: H.M.S.O., 1953–1954.

6306 Rumpf, Hans. *The Bombing of Germany.* New York: Holt, Rinehart & Winston, 1963.

6307 Sallager, F. M. *The Road to Total War: Escalation in World War II.* NR R–465–PR. Santa Monica, Ca.: Rand, Apr. 1969.

6308 Shandroff, Gary J. "The Evolution of Area Bombing in American Doctrine and Practice." Ph.D. diss., New York Univ., 1972.

6309 Smith, Maj. Gen. Dale O., and Stephen E. Ambrose. "Was the Bombing of Germany Worth the Cost? Yes . . . No." *American History Illustrated* (Apr. 1970): 4–9, 49–52.

6310 Snow, C. P. *Science and Government.* Cambridge: Harvard Univ. Press, 1961. [British decision on area bombing.]

6311 Spaight, James M. *Bombing Vindicated.* London: Bles, 1944.

6312 U.S. Strategic Bombing Survey. *Index to the Records of the United States Strategic Bombing Survey.* Washington, D.C.: G.P.O., 1947.

6313 Verrier, Anthony. *The Bomber Offensive.* New York: Macmillan, 1968.

6314 Webster, Sir Charles K., and Noble Franklin. *The Strategic Air Offensive Against Germany.* 4 vols. London: H.M.S.O., 1961.

WW II—Protests of Bombing

6315 Bellah, James W. "Bombing Cities Won't Win the War." *Harper's* 179 (Nov. 1939): 658–63.

6316 Ford, John C. "The Morality of Obliteration Bombing." *Theological Studies* 5 (Sept. 1944): 261–309. [Reprinted in R. A. Wasserstrom, ed., *War and Morality.* Belmont, Ca.: Wadsworth, 1970.]

6317 Gertsch, W. Darrell. "The Strategic Air Offensive and the Mutation of American Values, 1937–1945." *Rocky Mountain Social Science Journal* 11:3 (1975): 37–50.

6318 Gillis, James M. "Editorial Comment: Massacre by Bombing." *Catholic World* 159 (May 1944): 97–104.

6319 Hassler, R. Alfred. "Slaughter of the Innocent." *Fellowship* 10 (Feb. 1944): 19–21.

6320 Hopkins, George E. "Bombing and the American Conscience During World War II." *Historian* 28 (May 1966): 451–73.

WW II—Atomic Bomb

6321 Amrine, Michael. *The Great Decision: The Secret History of the Atomic Bomb.* New York: Putnam's, 1959.

6322 Baker, Paul. *The Atomic Bomb: The Great Decision.* New York: Holt, Rinehart & Winston, 1968.

6323 Bernstein, Barton. "Shatterer of Worlds: Hiroshima and Nagasaki." *Bulletin of the Atomic Scientists* 31 (Dec. 1975): 12–22.

6324 Blow, Michael. *The History of the Atomic Bomb.* New York: American Heritage Press, 1968.

6325 Clark, Ronald W. *The Birth of the Bomb.* London: Phoenix House, 1961.

6326 Compton, Arthur. *Atomic Quest: A Personal Narrative*. New York: Oxford Univ. Press, 1956.

6327 Goudsmit, Samuel A. *Also: The Story of a Mission*. New York: Schuman, 1947.

6328 Gowing, Margaret. *Britain and Atomic Energy, 1939–1945*. New York: St. Martin's Press, 1964.

6329 Groves, Gen. Leslie. *Now It Can Be Told: The Story of the Manhattan Project*. New York: Harper, 1962.

6330 Jungk, Robert. *Brighter Than a Thousand Suns: A Personal History of the Atomic Scientists*. New York: Harcourt, Brace, 1958.

6331 Lamont, Lansing. *Day of Trinity*. New York: Signet, 1967.

6332 Lifton, Robert J. "On Death and Death Symbolism: The Hiroshima Disaster." *Psychiatry* 27 (Aug. 1964): 191–210.

6333 Oughterson, A. W., and S. Warren. *Medical Effects of the Atomic Bomb in Japan*. New York: McGraw-Hill, 1956.

6334 Spaight, James M. *The Atomic Problem*. London: Barron, 1948.

6335 Teller, Edward. *The Legacy of Hiroshima*. Garden City, N.Y.: Doubleday, 1962.

6336 U.S. Strategic Bombing Survey. *Effects of Atomic Bombs on Hiroshima and Nagasaki*. Washington, D.C.: G.P.O., 1946.

WW II—Decision to Drop A-Bomb

6337 Alperovitz, Gar. *Atomic Diplomacy: Hiroshima and Potsdam*. New York: Simon & Schuster, 1965.

6338 Batchelder, Robert. *The Irreversible Decision, 1939–1950*. Boston: Houghton Mifflin, 1961.

6339 Feis, Herbert. *Japan Subdued: The Atomic Bomb and the End of the War In the Pacific*. Princeton: Princeton Univ. Press, 1961. [Rev. as *The Atomic Bomb and the End of World War II*. Princeton: Princeton Univ. Press, 1966.]

6340 Finney, Nat S. "How FDR Planned to Use the A-Bomb." *Look* (Mar. 14, 1950): 23–27.

6341 Giovannitti, Len, and Fred Freed. *The Decision to Drop the Bomb*. New York: Coward-McCann, 1965.

6342 Glazier, Kenneth M., Jr. "The Decision to Use Atomic Weapons Against Hiroshima and Nagasaki." *Public Policy* 18 (Summer 1970): 463–516.

6343 Hewlett, Richard. "The Debate About Hiroshima." *Military Affairs* 27 (Spring 1947): 25–30.

6344 ———, and Oscar Anderson. *The New World, 1939–1946*. University Park: Pennsylvania State Univ. Press, 1962.

6345 Horowitz, David J. "Hiroshima and the Cold War." *Liberation* 10 (Sept. 1965): 26–27.

6346 Morton, Louis. "The Decision to Use the Bomb." *Foreign Affairs* 35 (Jan. 1957): 334–53.

6347 Sherwin, Martin J. "The Atomic Bomb and the Origins of the Cold War: U.S. Atomic Energy Policy and Diplomacy, 1941–1945." *American Historical Review* 78 (Oct. 1973): 945–68.

6348 ———. *A World Destroyed: The Atomic Bomb and the Grand Alliance*. New York: Knopf, 1975.

6349 Smith, Alice Kimball. "Behind the Decision to Use the Atomic Bomb." *Bulletin of the Atomic Scientists* 14 (Oct. 1958): 288–312.

6350 Snowman, David. "President Truman's Decision to Drop the First Atomic Bomb." *Political Studies* [Gr. Br.] 14:3 (1966): 365–73.

6351 Stimson, Henry L. "The Decision to Use the Atomic Bomb." *Harper's* 194 (Feb. 1947): 97–107.

6352 "Was A-Bomb on Japan a Mistake?" *U.S. News & World Report* (Aug. 15, 1960): 62–76.

WW II—A-Bomb & Popular Opinion

6353 "America's Atomic Atrocity." *Christian Century* (Aug. 29, 1945): 974–76.

6354 Argus, Major. "Why the Japs Gave Up." *Infantry Journal* 57 (Nov. 1945): 8–13.

6355 Arnold, Gen. H. H. "Our Power to Destroy War." *Air Force* 28 (Oct. 1945): 9–10.

6356   Aron, Raymond. "Can War in the Atomic Age Be Limited?" *Confluence* 5 (July 1956): 99–114.

6357   "The Atomic Bomb." *Commonweal* (Aug. 31, 1945): 468–69.

6358   "Atomic Bomb: Asset or Threat?" *U.S. News* (Oct. 26, 1945): 93–98.

6359   Besse, Janet, and Harold D. Lasswell. "Our Columnists on the A-Bomb." *World Politics* 3 (Oct. 1950): 72–87.

6360   Compton, Karl. "If the Atomic Bomb Had Not Been Used." *Atlantic Monthly* (Dec. 1946): 54–56.

6361   "Fortune Survey: Use of Atomic Bomb." *Fortune* 32 (Dec. 1945): 305.

6362   [Gallup Poll on Use of Atomic Bomb]. *Public Opinion Quarterly* 9 (Fall 1945): 385.

6363   Gillis, James M. "The Atomic Bomb." *Catholic World* 161 (Sept. 1945): 449–52.

6364   Hersey, John R. *Hiroshima*. New York: Knopf, 1946.

6365   "Horror and Shame." *Commonweal* (Aug. 24, 1945): 443–44.

6366   Luft, John, and W. M. Wheeler. "Reaction to John Hersey's 'Hiroshima.'" *Journal of Social Psychology* 28 (Aug. 1948): 135–40.

6367   MacDonald, Dwight. "The Bomb." *Politics* 3 (Sept. 1945): 257–58.

6368   Mahoney, E. J. "Ethical Aspect of the Atomic Bomb." *Clergy Review* [London] 25 (Oct. 1945): 475–76.

6369   McReavy, Lawrence L. "An Anglican Verdict on the Atomic Bomb." *Clergy Review* [London] 30 (July 1948): 1–10.

6370   Merton, Thomas. *Original Child Bomb: Points for Meditation to be Scratched on the Walls of a Cave*. New York: New Directions, 1962.

6371   Montagu, M. F. A. "Racism, the Bomb, and World's People." *Asia and the Americas* 46 (Dec. 1946): 533–35.

6372   Morison, Samuel Eliot. "Why Japan Surrendered." *Atlantic* (Oct. 1960): 41–47.

6373   Mumford, Lewis. "Gentlemen: You are Mad." *Saturday Review of Literature* (Mar. 2, 1946): 5, 6.

6374   Ridenour, Louis. "What is the Crime of War?" *Saturday Review of Literature* (Nov. 2, 1946): 16.

6375   Sembower, John F. "Democracy and Science Fused by the Atomic Bomb." *Antioch Review* 5 (Winter 1945–46): 493–500.

6376   Smothers, Edgar R. "An Opinion on Hiroshima." *America* (July 5, 1947): 379.

6377   Winnacker, Rudolph A. "The Debate About Hiroshima." *Military Affairs* 11 (Spring 1947): 25–30.

6378   Yavenditti, Michael John. "The American People and the Use of Atomic Bombs on Japan, the 1940s." *Historian* 36 (Feb. 1974): 224–47.

6379   ———. "American Reaction to the Use of Atomic Bombs on Japan, 1945–1947." Ph.D. diss., Univ. of California, Berkeley, 1970.

6380   ———. "John Hersey and the American Conscience: The Reception of 'Hiroshima.'" *Pacific Historical Review* 43 (Feb. 1974): 24–49.

Korean War

6381   "Chinese Communists Protest: Charging American Planes Bombed Manchurian Cities." *Current History* 19 (Oct. 1950): 235.

6382   Collins, J. Lawton. *War in Peacetime: The History and Lessons of Korea*. Boston: Houghton Mifflin, 1969, pp. 200–204, 290–91.

6383   Futrell, Robert F. "Strategic Bombing Campaign." *The United States Air Force in Korea, 1950–1953*. New York: Duell, Sloan & Pearce, 1961, pp. 174–86.

6384   "Industry Bombing of Industries in North Korea." *Air University Quarterly Review* 5 (Winter 1951–52): 38–41.

6385   Jackson, R. *Air War Over Korea*. London: Allen, 1973.

6386   "Precision Bombing." *Air University Quarterly Review* 4 (Summer 1951): 58–65.

6387   Sleeper, Col. Raymond S. "Korean Targets for Medium Bombardment." *Air University Quarterly Review* 4 (Spring 1951): 18–31.

6388 Stewart, Gen. James T., ed. *Airpower: The Decisive Force in Korea.* Princeton: Van Nostrand, 1957.

6389 Weyland, Gen. Otto P. "The Air Campaign in Korea." *Air University Quarterly Review* 6 (Fall 1953): 3–28.

Vietnam War

For additional references, see M. Leitenberg and Richard Dean Burns, *The Vietnam Conflict: A Bibliography* (Santa Barbara, Ca.: ABC–Clio, 1973).

6390 Chaliand, Gerard. "Bombing of Dai Lai." *Liberation* 12 (Sept. 1967): 67–69.

6391 Flood, Charles B. *The War of the Innocents.* New York: McGraw-Hill, 1970.

6392 Greene, Jerry. "U.S. Airpower in Vietnam: Scalpel Rather than Broadsword." *Air Force and Space Digest* 48 (May 1965): 33–36.

6393 Harvey, F. *Air War: Vietnam.* New York: Bantam Books, 1967.

6394 Lacoste, Yves. "Bombing the Dikes." *Nation* (Oct. 9, 1972): 298–301.

6395 Littauer, Raphael, and Norman Uphoff, eds. *The Air War in Indochina.* 2d ed. Boston: Beacon, 1972.

6396 *The Pentagon Papers: Senator Gravel Edition.* 4 vols. Boston: Beacon, 1972, III: 269–388; IV: 1–276.

6397 Russett, Bruce M. "Vietnam and Restraints on Aerial Warfare." *Ventures* 9:1 (1969): 55–61. [Also in *Bulletin of the Atomic Scientists* 26 (Jan. 1970): 9–12.]

6398 Sights, Col. A. P., Jr. "Graduated Pressure in Theory and Practice." *U.S. Naval Institute Proceedings* 96 (July 1970): 40–45.

6399 Verrier, Anthony. "Strategic Bombing: The Lessons of World War II and the American Experience in Vietnam." *Royal United Services Institution Journal* 112 (May 1967): 157–61.

6400 Wald, George. "Our Bombs Fall on People." *Washington Monthly* 4 (May 1972): 8–10.

6401 Wharton, John F. "En Route to a Massacre?" *Saturday Review* (Nov. 4, 1967): 19–21.

DECLARATION PROHIBITING AERIAL BOMBARDMENT (1899, 1907)

For text of declaration, see William M. Malloy, comp., "Declaration Prohibiting the Discharge of Projectiles and Explosives from Balloons, Oct. 18, 1907," *Treaties, Conventions, International Acts, Protocols, and Agreements Between the United States of America and Other Powers, 1776–1909,* 2 vols. (Washington, D.C.: G.P.O., 1910), II: 2366–67. For documents and negotiations of the Hague conferences, see Rules of War, Hague Treaties (1899, 1907), in Chapter 13.

6402 Davis, George B. "Launching of Projectiles from Balloons." *American Journal of International Law* 2 (July 1908): 528–29.

6403 Ellis, Wilmot E. "Aerial-Land and Aerial-Maritime Warfare." *American Journal of International Law* 8 (Apr. 1914): 256–73.

6404 Garner, James W. *International Law and the World War.* London: Longmans, Green, 1920, pp. 419–20, 465–67.

6405 Hawthorne, H. L. "Balloons and Dirigibles in War." *Scientific American: Supplement* (Nov. 20, 1909): 330–31.

6406 Hildebrandt, A. "Dropping Projectiles from Balloons." *Scientific American: Supplement* (Mar. 6, 1909): 147.

6407 Kuhn, Arthur K. "Beginnings of an Aerial Law." *American Journal of International Law* 4 (Jan. 1910): 109–32.

6408 Royse, M. W. *Aerial Bombardment and the International Regulation of Warfare.* New York: Harold Vinal, 1928, pp. 22–122.

6409 Squier, G. O. "Present Status of Military Aeronautics." *Smithsonian Report* (1908): 117–33.

6410 Stone, Julius. *Legal Controls of International Conflict.* New York: Rinehart, 1954, pp. 615–23.

HAGUE DRAFT CONVENTION (1923)

For text of the draft convention, see "Hague Draft Rules for the Regulation of the Use of Aircraft and of Radio in Time of War," *American Journal of International Law: Supplement* 17 (1923): 242–50.

Documents

6411 Great Britain. *Draft Rules on Aerial Warfare.* Cmnd. 2201. London: H.M.S.O., 1924.

6412 ———. Foreign Office. *Documents on British Foreign Policy, 1919–1939.* 1st series. London: H.M.S.O., 1974, vol. 19, pp. 1039–1138.

6413 [The Hague. Commission of Jurists]. "Official Documents." *American Journal of International Law* 17 (Oct. 1923): 242–60.

6414 U.S. Department of State. *Foreign Relations of the United States, 1923.* Washington, D.C.: G.P.O., 1938, I: 69–87.

6415 ———. *Foreign Relations of the United States, 1925.* Washington, D.C.: G.P.O., 1940, I: 93–106.

General Accounts

6416 Colby, E. "Aerial Laws and War Targets." *American Journal of International Law* 19 (Oct. 1925): 702–15.

6417 Garner, James W. "Proposed Rules for the Regulation of Aerial Warfare." *American Journal of International Law* 18 (Jan. 1924): 56–81.

6418 Moore, John Bassett. "Rules of Warfare: Aircraft and Radio." *International Law and Some Current Illusions and Other Essays.* New York: Macmillan, 1924, pp. 182–288.

6419 Renaudel, Pierre. "Disarmament in the Air." *Labour Magazine* (Aug. 31, 1931): 154–57.

6420 Rodgers, Rear Adm. William L. "The Laws of War Concerning Aviation and Radio." *American Journal of International Law* 17 (Oct. 1923): 629–40.

6421 Royse, M. W. *Aerial Bombardment and the International Regulation of Warfare.* New York: Harold Vinal, 1928, pp. 213–14, 221–37.

LEAGUE OF NATIONS RESOLUTION OPPOSING BOMBING (1938)

For text of resolution, see League of Nations, *Official Journal, Special Supplement No. 183* (Records of the Nineteenth Ordinary Session of the Assembly Plenary Meetings, Text of the Debates), Geneva, Nov. 30, 1938, pp. 135–36.

Document

6422 League of Nations. Assembly. Third Committee. *Reduction and Limitation of Armament and Protection of Civilian Populations Against Bombing from the Air in Case of War.* Doc. A.69.1938.IX. Geneva, 1938.

General Accounts

6423 Keating, Fr. Joseph. "The Ethics of Bombing." *Catholic Mind* (July 22, 1938): 277–81.

6424 Maritain, Jacques. "War and the Bombardment of Cities." *Commonweal* (Sept. 2, 1938): 460–61.

6425 Mitchell, Jonathan. "Death Rides the Wind." *New Republic* (May 16, 1937): 63–64.

6426 Oxley, A. E. "Death From the Sky? Inaccuracy of Airplane Bombing Makes Possible Regrettable Violations of Rules of Warfare." *American Science* 159 (Oct. 1938): 173–75.

6427 Spaight, James M. "Non-Combatants and Air Attacks." *Air Law Review* 9 (1938): 372–76.

6428 Williams, F. S. "Modern War and the Civilian. What can International Law do About Bombing?" *Living Age* 353 (Dec. 1937): 295–98.

GENEVA DISARMAMENT CONFERENCE (1932)

These discussions did not lead to any new arms control arrangements regarding aerial bombardment; see League of Nations, above, for more on conference.

Documents

6429 League of Nations. Air Commission. Conference for the Reduction and Limitation of Armaments, Geneva, 1932–34. *Documents, 1–71.* Geneva, 1932–1935.

6430 ———. *Records of the Conference.* Series D, vol. 3: *Minutes of the Air Commission,* Geneva, 1932.

6431 ———. *Report to the General Commission, Called for by that Commission's Resolution dated April 22, 1932.* Geneva, 1932.

6432 ———. *Report Submitted to the Bureau on the Question of Air Forces, in Compliance with the Decision Taken on Sept. 26, 1932.* Geneva, 1932.

General Accounts

6433 Carlton, David. "The Problems of Civil Aviation in British Air Disarmament Policy, 1919–1934." *Royal United Services Institution Journal* 44 (Nov. 1966): 307–16.

6434 Colegrove, Kenneth W. *International Control of Aviation.* Boston: World Peace Foundation, 1930.

6435 Fradkin, Elvira K. *The Air Menace and the Answer.* New York: Macmillan, 1934.

6436 Garner, James W. "International Regulation of Air Warfare." *Air Law* 3:2 (1932): 103–26; 3:3 (1932): 309–23.

6437 Quindry, Frank E. "Aerial Bombardment of Civilians and Military Objectives." *Air Law* 2:4 (1931): 474–509.

6438 "Strafing New York from the Clouds." *Literary Digest* (June 8, 1929): 60–66.

Outlawing War

Documents

6439 U.S. Senate. Committee on the Judiciary. Hearings: *Constitutional Amendment Making War Legally Impossible.* S.J. Res. 100, Jan. 22, 1927. 69th Cong., 2d Sess., 1927.

6440 ———. Hearings: *Constitutional Amendment Making War Legally Impossible.* S.J. Res. 45, Apr. 12, 1930. 71st Cong., 2d Sess., 1930.

6441 ———. Hearings: *Constitutional Amendment Making War Legally Impossible.* S.J. Res. 24, Apr. 14, 1934. 73d Cong., 2d Sess., 1934.

General Accounts

6442 Bainton, Roland H. "From Outlawry of War to A-Bomb." *Christian Century* (Sept. 28, 1960): 1112–15.

6443 Brierly, J. L. "The Prohibition of War by International Law." *Agenda* 2 (Nov. 1943): 289–301.

6444 Feinberg, N. *The Legality of a "State of War" After the Cessation of the Hostilities Under the Charter of the United Nations and the Covenant of the League of Nations.* Jerusalem: Hebrew Univ., 1961.

6445 Gottlieb, Gidon. "The New International Law: Toward the Legitimation of War." *Ethics* 78 (Jan. 1968): 144–47.

6446 MacArthur, Douglas. "The Abolition of War." *Vital Speeches* 21 (June 1955): 1040–143.

6447 Millis, Walter. *The Abolition of War.* New York: Macmillan, 1963.

6448 Nikol'skii, Nikolai M. *Osnovnoi Vopros sovremennosti: Problema unichtozheniia voin.* Moscow: Izd-vo "Mezhdunarodnye Otnosheniia," 1964.

6449 Wright, Quincy. "The Outlawry of War and the Law of War." *American Journal of International Law* 47 (July 1953): 365–76.

6450 ———. *The Role of International Law in the Elimination of War.* Manchester: Univ. of Manchester Press, 1962.

KELLOGG-BRIAND TREATY (1928)

For text of treaty, see U.S. Department of State, *The General Pact for the Renunciation of War, Text of the Pact as Signed, Notes and Other Papers* (Washington, D.C.: G.P.O., 1928).

Documents

6451 Great Britain. Foreign Office. *Correspondence with the United States Ambassador Respecting the United States Proposal for the Renunciation of War.* Cmd. 3109. London: H.M.S.O., 1928.

6452 ———. *Further Correspondence with the Government of the United States Proposal for the Renunciation of War.* Cmd. 3153, continuation of Cmd. 3109. London: H.M.S.O., 1928.

6453 League of Nations. *Amendment of the Covenant of the League of Nations in Order to Bring it into Harmony with the*

Pact of Paris: Observations Submitted by Governments. A.11.1931.V.; A.11(a).1931.V. Geneva, 1931.

6454 ———. Assembly. First Committee. *Amendment of the Covenant of the League of Nations with a View to Bringing it into Harmony with the Pact of Paris: Report of the First Committee.* A.85.1930.V. Geneva, 1930.

6455 ———. *Amendment of the Covenant of the League of Nations with the Pact of Paris: Report of the First Committee to the Assembly.* A.86. 1931.VI. Geneva, 1931.

6456 ———. 10th Assembly, 1929. *Amendment of the Covenant of the League of Nations as a Result of the General Adhesion of the Members of the League to the Pact of Paris for the Renunciation of War: Extracts from the Records of the Tenth Ordinary Session of the Assembly.* C.499.M.163. 1929.V. Geneva, 1929.

6457 U.S. Department of State. *Notes Exchanged between France and the United States on the Subject of a Multilateral Treaty for the Renunciation of War, together with the Text of M. Briand's Original Proposal for a Pact of Perpetual Friendship.* Washington, D.C.: G.P.O., 1928.

6458 ———. *Notes Exchanged between the United States and Other Powers on the Subject of a Multilateral Treaty for the Renunciation of War.* June 20, 1927–July 20, 1928. Washington, D.C.: G.P.O., 1928.

General Accounts

6459 Butler, Nicholas Murray. *The Path to Peace: Essays and Addresses on Peace and Its Making.* New York: Scribner's, 1930.

6460 Gerould, James T., comp. *Selected Articles on the Pact of Paris: Officially the General Pact for the Renunciation of War.* New York: Wilson, 1929.

6461 Haase, Joachim. *Wandlung des Neutralitatsbegriffs.* Leipzig: R. Noake, 1932.

6462 Lysen, Arnoldus, ed. *Le Pacte Kellogg: Documents Concernant le Traité Multilateral Contre la Guerre, Signe a Paris le 27 aout 1928, Recueillis avec une Preface, un Tableau.* Leiden: A. W. Sijthoff, 1928.

6463 Miller, David Hunter. *The Peace Pact of Paris: A Study of the Briand-Kellogg Treaty.* New York: Putnam's, 1928.

6464 Moon, Parker T., ed. *The Preservation of Peace.* Proceedings of the Academy of Political Science, vol. 12, no. 2. New York: Columbia Univ. Press, 1929.

6465 Myers, Denys P. *Origin and Conclusion of the Paris Pact: The Renunciation of War as an Instrument of National Policy.* New York: Garland, 1929 [1972].

6466 Page, Kirby. *Renunciation of War.* New York: Doubleday, Doran, 1928.

6467 Shotwell, James T. *War as an Instrument of National Policy and Its Renunciation in the Pact of Paris.* New York: Harcourt, Brace, 1928.

6468 Wehberg, Hans. *The Outlawry of War: A Series of Lectures.* Trans. by E. H. Zeydel. Washington, D.C.: Carnegie Endowment for International Peace, 1931.

6469 Wheeler-Bennett, John W. *Information on the Renunciation of War, 1927–1928.* London: Allen & Unwin, 1928.

6470 Borchard, Edwin M. "The Multilateral Treaty for the Renunciation of War." *American Journal of International Law* 23 (Jan. 1929): 116–20.

6471 Brown, Philip M. "The Interpretation of the General Pact." *American Journal of International Law* 23 (Apr. 1929): 374–79.

6472 ———. "Japanese Interpretation of the Kellogg Pact." *American Journal of International Law* 27 (Jan. 1933): 100–102.

6473 Catt, Carrie Chapman. "The Outlawry of War." *Annals of the Amer. Acad. of Pol. & Soc. Sci.* 138 (July 1928): 157–63.

6474 Fish, Hamilton, Jr. "The Renunciation of War." *Annals of the Amer. Acad. of Pol. & Soc. Sci.* 138 (July 1928): 164–65.

6475 Howland, Charles P. "John Dewey and the Crusade to Outlaw War." *World Affairs* 138 (Spring 1976): 336 ff.

6476 Hyde, Charles C. "Secretary Hull on the Kellogg-Briand Pact." *American Journal of International Law* 35 (Jan. 1941): 117–18.

6477 Jessup, Philip C. "United States and Treaties for the Avoidance of War." *International Conciliation*, no. 239 (Apr. 1928): 179–245.

6478 Keen, F. N. "The Preamble of the Pact of Paris." *Transactions of the Grotius Society* 26 (1940): 165–82.

6479 Kellogg, Frank B. "Renunciation of War." *Review of Reviews* 78 (Dec. 1928): 595–601.

6480 ———. "The War Prevention Policy of the United States." *American Journal of International Law* 22 (Mar. 1928): 253–61.

6481 "Kellogg-Briand Pact: Intimative Kiss." *Congressional Record* 74 (Jan. 13, 1929): 1063–66, 1186–89.

6482 Kerr, Philip. "Pact or War—No Other Alternative." *Christian Century* (Jan. 3, 1929): 9–10.

6483 Lodge, Henry Cabot, Sr. "Meaning of the Kellogg Treaty." *Harper's* 158 (Dec. 1928): 32–41.

6484 Rooks, A. H. "On the Prevention of War." *U.S. Naval Institute Proceedings* 54 (Apr. 1928): 268–72.

6485 "Wars Are Over." *Independent* (May 26, 1928): 490–91.

6486 Wickersham, George W. "Making Real the Pact of Paris." *Century* 118 (May 1929): 141–47.

6487 ———. "Pact of Paris: A Gesture or a Pledge?" *Foreign Affairs* 7 (Apr. 1929): 356–71.

6488 Wright, Quincy. "Meaning of the Pact of Paris." *American Journal of International Law* 27 (Jan. 1933): 39–61.

Origins of the Pact

6489 Bingham, Sen. Hiram. "Is it Wise to Make War Illegal and Unconstitutional?" *Annals of the Amer. Acad. of Pol. & Soc. Sci.* 120 (July 1925): 142–46.

6490 Eddy, George S., and Kirby Page. *The Abolition of War: The Case Against War and Questions and Answers Concerning War.* New York: Doran, 1924.

6491 Fish, Hamilton, Jr. "Our Duty to Outlaw War." *Annals of the Amer. Acad. of Pol. & Soc. Sci.* 120 (July 1925): 152.

6492 Hapgood, Norman. "Psychology of Education in Outlawing War." *Annals of the Amer. Acad. of Pol. & Soc. Sci.* 120 (July 1925): 157–58.

6493 Hurd, William. "The Outlawing of War." *Annals of the Amer. Acad. of Pol. & Soc. Sci.* 120 (July 1925): 136–41.

6494 Levinson, Salmon O. *Outlawry of War: A Plan to Outlaw War.* 67th Cong., 2d Sess., Sen. Doc. 115. Washington, D.C.: G.P.O., 1922.

6495 McDonald, James G. "Steps Towards the Outlawry of War." *Annals of the Amer. Acad. of Pol. & Soc. Sci.* 120 (July 1925): 147–51.

6496 Morrison, Charles C. *The Outlawry of War: A Constructive Policy for World Peace.* Chicago: Willett, Clark & Colby, 1927.

6497 "Movement to Outlaw War: With Pro and Con Discussion." *Congressional Digest* 7 (Mar. 1928): 75–94.

6498 Robins, Raymond. "The Outlawry of War: The Next Step in Civilization." *Annals of the Amer. Acad. of Pol. & Soc. Sci.* 120 (July 1925): 153–56.

6499 Shotwell, James T. "Plans and Protocols to End War." *International Conciliation*, no. 208 (Mar. 1925): 5–35.

Historical Assessment

6500 Chamberlain, Waldo. "Origins of the Kellogg-Briand Pact." *Historian* 15 (Autumn 1952): 77–82.

6501 Ferrell, Robert H. *Peace in Their Time: The Origins of the Kellogg-Briand Pact.* New Haven: Yale Univ. Press, 1952.

6502 Hefley, J. Theodore. "War Outlawed: *The Christian Century* and the Kellogg Peace Pact." *Journalism Quarterly* 48 (Spring 1971): 26–32.

6503 Kneeshaw, Stephen J. "The Kellogg-Briand Pact: The American Reaction." Ph.D. diss., Univ. of Colorado, 1971.

6504 Stoner, John E. *S. O. Levinson and the Pact of Paris: A Study in the Techniques of Influence.* Chicago: Univ. of Chicago Press, 1943.

6505   Vinson, John Chalmers. *William E. Borah and the Outlawry of War.* Athens: Univ. of Georgia Press, 1957.

Disarmament & the Pact

6506   Drexel, Constance. *Disarmament, Security and Control: Draft of Convention for Disarmament, Security, and Control Based on the Kellogg Pact.* 74th Cong., 1st Sess., Sen. Doc. 33. Washington, D.C.: G.P.O., 1935.

6507   Gerould, James T. "Problems of Security, Disarmament and Renunciation of War." *Current History* 28 (Apr. 1928): 110–14.

6508   Harrison, Pat. *Cruiser Construction and the Kellogg Peace Pact.* Washington, D.C.: G.P.O., 1928.

6509   "Our Navy Not Affected by the Anti-War Pacts." *Literary Digest* (Aug. 25, 1928): 8–9.

6510   Pavichich, A. T. "Limitation of Armaments and the Outlawry of War." *Advocate of Peace* 89 (Feb. 1927): 93–99.

6511   "Peace Pact and Disarmament." *Nation* (Aug. 7, 1929): 132.

Special Issues

6512   Boye, Thorvald. "Shall a State Which Goes to War in Violation of the Kellogg-Briand Pact have a Belligerent's Rights in Respect of Neutrals?" *American Journal of International Law* 24 (Oct. 1930): 766–70.

6513   Buell, Raymond L. "Sea Law Under the Kellogg Pact." *New Republic* (May 15, 1929): 349–51.

6514   Capper, Sen. Arthur. "Making the Peace Pact Effective." *Annals of the Amer. Acad. of Pol. & Soc. Sci.* 144 (July 1929): 40–50.

6515   Chamberlain, Joseph P. "Equality of Belligerents and the Embargo Resolutions." *Annals of the Amer. Acad. of Pol. & Soc. Sci.* 144 (July 1929): 55–58.

6516   Fenwick, Charles G. "The Implications of Consultations in the Pact of Paris." *American Journal of International Law* 26 (Oct. 1932): 787–89.

6517   Geneva Research Center. "The Covenant and the Pact." *Geneva Special Studies* 1:9 (1930): 1–23.

6518   Kuhn, Arthur K. "The Economic Sanction of the Kellogg Pact." *American Journal of International Law* 24 (Jan. 1930): 83–88.

6519   Lauterpacht, Sir Hersh. "The Pact of Paris and the Budapest Articles of Interpretation." *Transactions of the Grotius Society* 20 (1934): 178–204.

6520   Myers, William S. "The Kellogg Pact: The Question of Sanctions." *Annals of the Amer. Acad. of Pol. & Soc. Sci.* 144 (July 1929): 59–62.

6521   Rodgers, Edith N. "How the Kellogg Peace Pact Can Be Made Effective." *Annals of the Amer. Acad. of Pol. & Soc. Sci.* 144 (July 1929): 51–54.

6522   Scelle, Georges. "Pacte Kellogg et Protocole Litvinov." *Le Monde Slave* 2:4 (1929): 1–32.

6523   Whitten, John B. "What Follows the Pact of Paris?" *International Conciliation*, no. 276 (Jan. 1932): 5–48.

6524   Wood, Bryce. "The Application of the Kellogg Pact [to the Leticia Dispute]." *The United States and Latin American Wars, 1933–1942.* New York: Columbia Univ. Press, 1966, pp. 197–205.

ARGENTINE ANTI-WAR TREATY (1933)

For text of treaty, see Charles I. Bevans, *Treaties and Other International Agreements of the United States of America, 1776–1949: Multilateral* (Washington, D.C.: G.P.O., 1969), III: 135–40.

6525   Borchard, Edwin M. "War, Neutrality, and Non-Belligerency." *American Journal of International Law* 35 (Oct. 1941): 618–25.

6526   Jessup, Philip C. "The Argentine Anti-War Pact." *American Journal of International Law* 28 (July 1934): 538–41.

6527   ———. "The Saavedra Lamas Anti-War Draft Treaty." *American Journal of International Law* 27 (Jan. 1933): 109–14.

6528   League of Nations. "Treaty of Non-Aggression and Conciliation Signed at Rio de Janeiro on October 10th, 1933." *Official Journal* 15 (Feb. 1934): 133–36.

6529   U.S. Department of State. *Foreign Relations of the United States, 1933.* Washington, D.C.: G.P.O., 1950, IV: 228–40.

Eleven

Controlling Arms Manufacture & Traffic

IN THE 1970s, many Americans, among them many arms controllers and members of Congress, have become increasingly concerned about the age-old problem of international "arms transfers"—modern arms control experts prefer this term to such old-fashioned ones as "arms traffic" or "arms trade." To many experts, legislators, and concerned citizens these arms tranfers contribute significantly to international instability and are, consequently, disruptive of world peace.

In the 1920s and 1930s, the targets of opponents of the arms trade were shadowy individuals or particular firms—the Sir Basil Zaharoffs and the Vickers or Du Pont companies. Their solution was to place the production of all war materials under government supervision, and this was virtually accomplished by the end of World War II. But the results were not what the reformers had hoped for, because now governments sponsored the arms traffic, the Pentagon becoming the world's largest arms merchant, while the Kremlin is a close second.

P. J. Noel-Baker's *The Private Manufacture of Armaments* (1936) or the extremely popular H. C. Englebrecht and F. C. Hanighen's *Merchants of Death* (1934) reflects the popular version of arms trade problems as seen in the interwar years. J. E. Wiltz's *In Search of Peace: The Senate Munitions Inquiry, 1934–1936* (1963) details the efforts of the Nye Committee to ferret out arms traders. The arms transfer issue of the 1970's is more complex; this may be seen in L. A. Frank's *The Arms Trade in International Relations* (1969), R. E. Harkavy's *The Arms Trade and International Systems* (1975) or J. Stanley and M. Pearton's *The International Trade in Arms* (1972). SIPRI's *The Arms Trade with the Third World* (1971), which is updated in its annual *SIPRI Yearbook of World Armament and Disarmament* (1968/69–), is an excellent source of data.

Attempts to control or prohibit the manufacture and/or transfer of weapons are many. The Old Testament reports an early, though ultimately unsuccessful, effort by the Philistines to prevent the Israelites from attaining iron weapons (1100 B.C.). Much in the same manner, the nuclear club has sought to use the Nonproliferation Treaty (1968) to limit the spread of nuclear weapons.

In the years between, several multilateral attempts have been made to halt or restrict the arms traffic. These efforts have been via treaties and embargoes; some of these episodes are included below. Often overlooked in the discussions to regulate or ban arms traffic are the views of arms recipients. Geoffrey Kemp's essays remedy this deficiency, particularly his "Arms Traffic and Third World Conflicts," *International Conciliation* (1970).

Bibliographies

6530 Johnsen, Julia E., comp. *The Government Control of Arms and Munitions.* New York: H. W. Wilson, 1934.

6531 League of Nations. "Supervision of the Trade and Private Manufacture of Arms and Munitions and Implements of War." *Annotated Bibliography on Disarmament and Military Questions.* Geneva, 1935, pp. 53–57.

6532 Matthews, Mary A., comp. *Traffic in Arms, Munitions, and Implements of War and Control of their Manufacture.* Washington, D.C.: Carnegie Endowment for International Peace, 1933.

6533 Meeker, Thomas A. *The Military-Industrial Complex: A Source Guide to the Issues of Defense Spending and Policy Control.* Los Angeles: California State Univ., Center for the Study of Armament & Disarmament, 1973.

6534 U.S. Library of Congress. Legislative Reference Service. *Limitation of International Traffic in Arms and Ammunition: Excerpts from Selected References Chronologically Arranged.* Washington, D.C.: G.P.O., 1946.

Arms Trade Issues to 1945

6535 League of Nations. *Armaments Year Book.* 15 vols. Geneva, 1924–1939/1940.

6536 ———. *Statistical Information on the Trade in Arms, Ammunition and Implements of War.* 15 vols. Geneva, 1924–1939/1940.

6537 Baccus, John H., ed. *Arms and Munitions.* New York: Noble, 1935.

6538 Cook, Blanche, et al., eds. *The International Trade in Armaments Prior to World War II.* New York: Garland, 1971.

6539 Gregory, Charles N. *Neutrality and Arms Shipments.* London: Darling, 1915.

6540 Hudson, Manley O. *Munitions Industry: International Regulation of the Trade in and Manufacture of Arms and Ammunition.* Washington, D.C.: G.P.O., 1935.

6541 Launay, Louis, and Jean Sennac. *Les Relations Internationales des Industries de Guerre.* Paris: Editions Republicaines, 1932.

6542 Laursen, Svend. *Rustningsindustrien: Staternes Kontrol med Vaabenhandel og Vaabenproducktion.* Copenhagen: Gyldendal, 1938.

6543 Molinari, D. L. *El Control Internacional del Trafico de Armas.* Buenos Aires: Imprenta Mercatali, 1924.

6544 Noel-Baker, Philip J. *The Private Manufacture of Armaments.* 2 vols. London: Gollancz, 1936.

6545 Perris, George H. *The War Traders.* London: National Peace Council, 1914.

6546   White, Freda. *Traffic In Arms*. 3d ed. London: League of Nations Union, 1932.

6547   "Arming the World?" *Nation* (Jan. 16, 1924): 51–52.

6548   Carnegie, David. "The Traffic In Arms." *Goodwill* [London] (Oct. 15, 1927): 136–40.

6549   ———, and George A. Drew. "Manufacture of Arms and Its Control." *Interdependence* 10 (July 1933): 77–94.

6550   "The Christian Conscience Confronts the Traffic In Arms." *Federal Council Bulletin* 16 (Feb. 1933): 2 ff.

6551   Dennis, William C. "The Right of Citizens of Neutral Countries to Sell and Export Arms and Munitions of War to Belligerents." *Annals of the Amer. Acad. of Pol. & Soc. Sci.* 60 (July 1915): 168–82.

6552   Drexel, Constance. "Armament Manufacture and Trade." *International Conciliation*, no. 295 (Dec. 1933): 1–27.

6553   Garner, James W. "The Sale and Exportation of Arms and Munitions of War to Belligerents." *American Journal of International Law* 10 (Oct. 1916): 749–97.

6554   Gregory, Charles N. "Neutrality and the Sale of Arms." *American Journal of International Law* 10 (July 1916): 543–55.

6555   Harley, J. E. "Moral Disarmament and the Traffic In Arms." *Institute of World Affairs Proceedings, 1934* (1935): 194–201.

6556   "How the Arms Traffic Is Stimulated by the Far Eastern Crisis." *China Weekly Review* (Jan. 7, 1933): 258.

6557   Hyde, Charles C. "The Arms Traffic from the Standpoint of International Law." *Acad. of Pol. Sci. Proceedings* 16 (Jan. 1935): 127 ff.

6558   "International Traffic in Arms and Ammunition." *Foreign Policy Association Information Service* (Aug. 12, 1933): 130–40.

6559   Lange, C. L. "Control of the Traffic In and the Manufacture of Arms and War Munition." *Inter-Parliamentary Bulletin* 6 (Nov. 1926): 148–55; 7 (Jan. 1927): 6–13.

6560   Lehmann-Russbu't, Otto. "The Arms Traffic: A Study in Confusing Statistics." *Disarmament* [Geneva] (March 6, 1933): 1 ff.

6561   Meister, Jurg. "Rustung und Kriegfuhrung im Burenkrieg 1898 bis 1902." *Allgemeine Schweizerische Militarzeitschrift* 138 (Sept. 1972): 478 ff.

6562   Moch, Edmund von. "An Argument Against the Exportation of Arms." *Annals of the Amer. Acad. of Pol. & Soc. Sci.* 60 (July 1915): 192–94.

6563   Morgan, Gen. John H. "Traffic in Arms." *New Statesman and Nation* (Nov. 26, 1932): 653 ff.

6564   Morgan, Laura P. "A Possible Technique of Disarmament Control." *Geneva Special Studies* 11:7 (1940): 1–96.

6565   "The Problem of Arms Traffic." *World Affairs* 97 (Dec. 1934): 206–09.

6566   Stimson, Ralph H. "The Private Manufacture of Arms." *Acad. of Pol. Sci. Proceedings* 16 (Jan. 1935): 127 ff.

6567   Stone, William T. "International Traffic in Arms and Ammunition." *Foreign Policy Reports* (Aug. 16, 1933): 130–40.

"MERCHANTS OF DEATH" THESIS

6568   Batty, Peter. *The House of Krupp*. New York: Stein & Day, 1966.

6569   Brockway, A. Fenner. *The Bloody Traffic*. London: Gollancz, 1933.

6570   ———. *Death Pays A Dividend*. London: Gollancz, 1944.

6571   Davenport, Guiles. *Zaharoff: High Priest of War*. New York: Lothrop, 1934.

6572   Dewar, George. *The Great Munitions Feat, 1914–1918*. London: Constable, 1921.

6573   Drew, George A. *Salesmen of Death*. 3d ed. Toronto: Women's League of Nations Assoc., 1933.

6574   Du Pont de Nemours & Company. *A History of the Du Pont Company's Relations with the United States Government, 1802–1927*. Wilmington: Du Pont, 1928.

6575   Engelbrecht, Helmuth C., and Frank C. Hanighen. *Merchants of Death*. New York: Dodd, 1934.

6576   Judd, C. D. *Traffic in Armaments*. Dallas: Southern Methodist Univ. Press, 1934.

6577 League of Nations Union. *The Manufacture of Arms*. Pamphlet no. 347. London, July 1933.

6578 Lehmann-Russbult, Otto. *War for Profits*. Trans. by P. Loving. New York: A. H. King, 1930.

6579 Lewinsohn, Richard. *The Profits of War through the Ages*. Trans. by G. Sainsbury. New York: Dutton, 1937.

6580 Mahlen, Narbert. *The Incredible Krupps*. New York: Holt, 1959.

6581 McCullagh, Francis. *Syndicates For War*. Boston: World Peace Foundation, 1911.

6582 Murray, H. Robertson. *Krupp's and the International Armaments Ring: The Scandal of Modern Civilisation*. London: Holden & Hardingham, 1915.

6583 Neumann, Robert. *Zaharoff: The Armaments King*. London: Allen & Unwin, 1935.

6584 Noel-Baker, Philip J. *Hawkers of Death: The Private Manufacture and Trade in Arms*. London: Labour Party, 1934.

6585 Rule, Victor A. *Chain the War-God!* Elkhart, Ind.: James A. Bell, 1935.

6586 Scott, J. D. *Vickers: A History*. London: Weidenfeld & Nicolson, 1962.

6587 Seldes, George. *Iron, Blood and Profits*. New York: Harper, 1934.

6588 Stevens, William S. *The Powder Trust, 1872–1912*. Philadelphia: Univ. of Pennsylvania, 1912.

6589 Trotter, Agnes A. "The Development of 'Merchants of Death' Theory of American Intervention in the First World War, 1914–1937." Ph.D. diss., Duke Univ., 1966.

6590 Union of Democratic Control. *The International Industry of War*. London, 1915.

6591 ———. *The Secret International: Armaments Firms at Work*. London, 1933.

6592 Waldman, Seymour. *Death and Profits*. New York: Harcourt, 1932.

6593 Widdrington, Percy E. T. *The Armaments Racket, Ecrasez l'Infame: An Appeal to the Christian Conscience*. Milwaukee: Morehouse, 1933.

6594 Abad, C. H. "Munitions Industries in World Affairs." *Scribner's Magazine* 94 (Sept. 1933): 176 ff.

6595 "Arms Manufacturers and the Public." *Foreign Affairs* 12 (July 1934): 639–53.

6596 "Arms and the Men." *Fortune* 9 (Mar. 1934): 53–57 ff.

6597 Black, F. R. "Profits of War." *Nation* (Aug. 1, 1932): 222 ff.

6598 Brockway, A. Fenner. "Armament Makers Conspiracy." *Christian Century* (Nov. 20, 1933): 1499–1501.

6599 Engelbrecht, Helmuth C. "The Bloody International." *World Tomorrow* 14 (Oct. 1931): 317–20.

6600 ———. "The International Armament Industry." *Annals of the Amer. Acad. of Pol. & Soc. Sci.* 175 (Sept. 1934): 73–81.

6601 ———. "The Traffic in Death." *World Tomorrow* (Oct. 5, 1932): 330–31.

6602 "Facts about Munitions Makers." *Army Ordnance* 14 (May–June 1932): 361–64.

6603 Friend, Vita, and Joseph Friend. "How the Arms Makers Work." *Forum* 90 (Nov. 1933): 278–84.

6604 Gunther, John. "Slaughter for Sale." *Harper's* 167 (May 1934): 649–59.

6605 Harris, Paul. "Give us Profits From Bigger and Better Wars: Says Public Enemy Number One." *News Bulletin* 12 (Jan. 1933): 1 ff.

6606 "International Ramifications of the Armaments Industry." *Labour Magazine* 11 (July–Aug. 1932): 99–104 ff.

6607 "Die Internationale Rustungsindustrie." *Betriebswart* (Apr. 30, 1932): 81–84.

6608 "J." "Arms Manufacturers and the Public." *Foreign Affairs* 12 (July 1934): 639–53.

6609 "Nationalize the Arms Industry!" *Nation* (Dec. 19, 1934): 726.

6610 Nickerson, Hoffman. "Munitions Makers and Common Sense." *Army Ordnance* 15 (Sept.–Oct. 1934): 71–74.

6611 "Promoting War for Profit." *Christian Century* (Feb. 28, 1934): 275–76.

6612   Russell, Charles E. "For Patriotism and Profits." *Pearson's Magazine* 30 (1913): 545–56.

6613   "Secret International Armaments Racket." *Living Age* 343 (Oct. 1932): 109–20.

6614   "Sino-Japanese War Profitable for Munitions Makers." *China Weekly Review* (Jan. 6, 1934): 250.

6615   Steel, Johannes. "World's Greatest Racket." *Nation* (June 6, 1934): 646–48.

6616   Stokes, R. R. "Accountants and Armaments Profits." *Accountant* (Sept. 10, 1938): 365–68.

6617   Strabolgi, Lord. "Europe's Boom in Armaments." *Current History* 45 (Feb. 1937): 54–57.

6618   "Taking the Profits Out of War." *Christian Century* (May 1, 1935): 566–68.

6619   Trebicock, Clive. "Legends of the British Armament Industry, 1890–1914." *Journal of Contemporary History* 5 (1970): 3–19.

6620   "War Profits Doomed." *Business Week* (Apr. 13, 1935): 9–10.

UNITED STATES & CONTROLS

6621   Atwater, Elton. *American Regulation of Arms Exports*. Washington, D.C.: Carnegie Endowment for International Peace, 1941. [Johnson Reprint Corp., 1971.]

6622   Graber, Elizabeth M. *The Control of Sales of Arms, Ammunition and Implements of War*. Sen. Doc. 19, 77th Cong., 1st Sess. Washington, D.C.: G.P.O., 1941.

6623   Green, Joseph C. "Supervising the American Traffic in Arms." *Foreign Affairs* 15 (July 1937): 729–44.

6624   Griffin, Alva L. "The Problem of the Control of Munitions Traffic: Efforts at Control in the U.S." M.A. thesis, Univ. of California, Los Angeles, 1935.

6625   Hudson, Manley O. "The Treaty-Making Power of the United States in Connection with the Manufacture of Arms and Ammunition." *American Journal of International Law* 28 (Oct. 1934): 736–39.

6626   Ludlow, James M. "Control of the International Traffic in Arms." *U.S. Department of State Bulletin* (June 24, 1944): 576–83.

6627   ———. "The National Munitions Control Board." M.A. thesis, Columbia Univ., 1940.

6628   Moore, John Bassett. "Restriction of Traffic in Firearms and Liquor." *Digest of International Law*. Washington, D.C.: G.P.O., 1906, II: 468–74.

6629   Stedman, Murray S. *Exporting of Arms: The Federal Arms Export Administration, 1935–1945*. New York: King's Crown Press, 1947.

6630   Stimson, Ralph H. *The Control of the Manufacture of Armaments*. Urbana: Univ. of Illinois Press, 1915.

6631   "Traffic in Arms, Ammunition and Implements of War." *U.S. Department of State Press Releases* (Sept. 17, 1938): 191–96.

6632   U.S. Department of State. *International Traffic in Arms: Laws and Regulations Administered by the Secretary of State Governing the International Traffic in Arms, Ammunition, and Implements of War, and Other Munitions of War*. Washington, D.C.: G.P.O., Oct. 10, 1935. [Frequently revised.]

6633   ———. *Memoranda for the Members of the American Delegation to the Conference on Limitation of Armament: Limitation of Armaments (Including the Private Manufacture of Arms)*. . . . Washington, D.C.: G.P.O., 1921.

6634   U.S. Senate. *Shipment of Arms to Mexico: Letter from the Secretary of War, Submitted in Response to Senate Resolution 193, Dated March 20, 1924*. . . . Sen. Doc. 104. 68th Cong., 1st Sess., 1924.

U.S. Inquiries

6635   Borah, Sen. William E. *Munition Manufacturers Should be Curbed*. Washington, D.C.: G.P.O., Mar. 5, 1934.

6636   Brown, Francis E. "The Crusading Mr. Nye." *Current History* 41 (Feb. 1935): 521–27.

6637   Chatfield, Charles. "Disarmament and the Devil Theories." *For Peace and Justice: Pacifism in America, 1914–1941*. Knoxville: Univ. of Tennessee Press, 1971, pp. 143–67.

6638   Engelbrecht, Helmuth C. *One Hell of a Business*. New York: McBride, 1934.

6639 Liveright, R. "Investigating Armaments." *Nation* (Apr. 4, 1934): 388.

6640 Scroggs, W. O. "The American and British Investigations." *Foreign Affairs* 15 (Jan. 1937): 320–29.

6641 "Senate Munitions Investigations." *Commercial and Financial Chronicle* (Sept. 15, 1934): 1636–38.

6642 Stone, William T. "The Munitions Industry: An Analysis of the United States Senate Investigations, Sept. 4–21, 1934." *Geneva Special Studies* 5:9 (1934): 1–20. [See also, *Foreign Policy Reports* (Jan. 21, 1935): 250–68.]

6643 U.S. Senate. Special Committee Investigating the Munitions Industry [Nye Committee]. Report: Munitions Industry: International Regulation of the Trade In and Manufacture of Arms and Ammunition. . . . 73d Cong., 2d Sess., 1935.

6644 ———. Report: *Munitions Industry: Report on Government Manufacture of Government Munitions.* . . . Sen. Rpt. no. 944, pt. 7. 74th Cong., 2d Sess., 1936.

6645 Wiltz, John E. *In Search of Peace: The Senate Munitions Inquiry, 1934–1936.* Baton Rouge: Louisiana State Univ. Press, 1963.

U.S. Neutrality Acts

6646 "The Arms Embargo Resolution and American Neutrality." *Yale Law Journal* 42 (May 1933): 1109–21.

6647 Borchard, Edwin M. "The Arms Embargo and Neutrality." *American Journal of International Law* 27 (Apr. 1933): 293–98.

6648 "Embargo Proposed on Arms Shipments to Nations Violating Peace Compact [Porter and Capper Resolutions]." *Advocate of Peace* 91 (Mar. 1929): 187–89.

6649 Jessup, Philip C. "The New Neutrality Legislation." *American Journal of International Law* 29 (Oct. 1935): 665–70.

6650 Langer, William L., and Evrett Gleason. *The Challenge to Isolation, 1937–1940: The World Crisis and American Foreign Policy.* New York: Harper, 1952, pp. 218–35.

6651 "The Porter and Capper Resolutions Against Traffic in Arms." *American Journal of International Law* 23 (Apr. 1929): 379–83.

6652 Reynolds, W. L. "Arms Embargo Road to War." *National Republic* 21 (June 1933): 3–4 ff.

6653 Schuman, Fredrick L. "The Arms Embargo and the Capper-Porter Resolution." *Foreign Notes* 4 (Mar. 1929): 22.

6654 U.S. House. Committee on Foreign Affairs. Hearings: *Exportation of Arms, Munitions, or Implements of War to Belligerent Nations.* 70th Cong., 1st Sess. (1929), Mar. 15–22, 1928.

6655 ———. Hearings: *Exportation of Arms or Munitions of War.* 73d Cong., 1st Sess., 1933.

6656 Woolsey, Lester H. "The Burton Resolution on Trade in Munitions of War." *American Journal of International Law* 22 (July 1928): 610–14.

6657 ———. "The Porter and Capper Resolutions Against Traffic in Arms." *American Journal of International Law* 23 (Apr. 1929): 379–83.

6658 Wright, Quincy. "The Future of Neutrality." *International Conciliation*, no. 242 (Sept. 1928): 28–31.

GREAT BRITAIN & CONTROLS

6659 Atwater, Elton. "British Control Over the Export of War Materials." *American Journal of International Law* 33 (Apr. 1939): 292–317.

6660 "Private Arms Trade." *Economist* (Nov. 7, 1936): 250–51.

6661 "Private Trade in Arms." *Economist* (Feb. 15, 1936): 346–47.

British Inquiries

6662 Great Britain. Home Office. Report: *Royal Commission on the Private Manufacture of and Trading in Arms* (1935–1936). Cmd. 5292. London: H.M.S.O., 1936.

6663 ———. Prime Minister. *Statement Relating to Report of the Royal Commission on the Private Manufacture of and Trading in Arms, 1935–1936.* Cmd. 5292 (1936). London: H.M.S.O., 1937.

6664 Laski, Harold. "The British Arms Inquiry." *Nation* (Mar. 4, 1936): 272–73.

6665 "The Private Manufacture of Arms." *Arbitrator* (Dec. 1932): 55.

6666 Vallance, Aylmer. "Arms and the Slump." *New Fabian Research Bureau Quarterly* (Summer 1937): 4–6.

LEAGUE & CONTROLS

6667 League of Nations. "Control of the Traffic in Arms and Ammunition." *Official Journal* 5 (Apr. 1924): 596; 5 (Oct. 1924): 1361–64; 6 (Feb. 1925): 132.

6668 ———. *Reduction of Armaments: Supervision of the Private Manufacture of Arms and Ammunition and Implements of War.* Geneva, 1928.

6669 ———. *Report of the Temporary Mixed Commission on Armaments.* A. 81. Geneva, 1921.

6670 ———. "Resolutions of the [5th to 10th] Assembly on Supervision of Manufacture of Arms and Ammunition." *Official Journal: Special Supplement*, nos. 21, 32, 43, 53, 63, 74 (Sept. 1924–Sept. 1929.)

6671 ———. Secretariat. *Ten Years of World Cooperation.* Geneva, 1930, pp. 114–20.

6672 ———. "Traffic in Arms and Ammunition: Request by the Persian Government." *Official Journal* 4 (Nov. 1923): 1502–03.

6673 Sloutzki, Nokhim M. *La Societe des Nations et le Controle du Commerce International, des Armes de Guerre* (1919–1938). Geneva: Dotation Carnegie pour la Paix Internationale, 1969.

League Inquiries

6674 Henderson, Arthur, et al. "The Private Manufacture of Armaments." *Disarmament* [Geneva] (July 1, 1932): 1 ff.

6675 League of Nations. *National Supervision of the Manufacture of and Trade in Arms: Action Taken on the Resolution Adopted by the Assembly of the League of Nations, Sept. 30, 1937.* 1938. IX.2. Geneva, 1938.

6676 ———. ". . . Private Manufacture of Arms and Ammunition and of Implements of War." *Official Journal* 7 (Feb. 1926): 219–27.

6677 ———. "Private Manufacture of Arms and Ammunition and of Implements of War." *Official Journal* 7 (Aug. 1926): 1042–68.

6678 ———. "Private Manufacture of Arms and Ammunition and of Implements of War: Circular Letter. . . . *Official Journal* 7 (Aug. 1926): 1042–68; 7 (Sept. 1926): 1146–50; 8 (May 1927): 626.

6679 ———. "Report of the Special Committee Appointed to Prepare Draft Convention on the Private Manufacture of Arms. . . ." *Official Journal* 8 (July 1927): 766–67, 846–59.

6680 ———. "Supervision of the Private Manufacture of Arms . . . : Resolution Adopted by Assembly." *Official Journal* 8 (Feb. 1927): 147–50.

6681 ———. "Supervision of the Private Manufacture of Arms and Ammunition and of Implements of War." *Official Journal* 8 (Oct. 1926): 1347–55.

6682 ———. *Supervision of the Private Manufacture and Publicity of the Manufacture of Arms and Ammunition and of Implements of War.* Geneva, 1929.

6683 ———. "Traffic in Arms and Control of the Private Manufacture of Arms and Munitions [Report]." *Official Journal* 5 (July 1924): 913–14.

6684 ———. "Work of the Special Commission for the Preparation of a Draft Convention on the Private Manufacture of Arms and Ammunition and of Implements of War. . . ." *Official Journal* 9 (Oct. 1928): 1584–88.

Arms Trade Issues Since 1945

6685 Benoit, Emile. *Defense and Economic Growth in Developing Countries.* Lexington, Mass.: Lexington Books, 1973.

6686 Blumenfeld, York. "International Arms Sales." *Editorial Research Reports* (Sept. 2, 1970): 649–66.

6687 Browne & Shaw Research Corp. *The Diffusion of Combat Aircraft, Missiles, and their Supporting Technologies.* Waltham, Mass., 1966.

6688 Hamer, John. "World Arms Sales." *Editorial Research Reports* (May 7, 1976): 325–41.

6689 Hoagland, John H. *World Combat Aircraft Inventories and Production, 1970–1975: Implications for Arms Transfer Policies.* Cambridge: M.I.T., Center for International Studies, 1970.

6690 Miller, Lynn H. *Security Studies Project.* Vol. 5: *The Reporting of International Arms Transfers.* ACDA Rpt. WEC–126. Los Angeles: Univ. of California, Arms Control Special Studies Program, 1968.

6691 SIPRI. *Arms Trade Registers: The Arms Trade With the Third World.* Cambridge: M.I.T. Press, 1975.

6692 ——. *SIPRI Yearbook of World Armament and Disarmament, 1968/1969–.* New York: Humanities Press, 1969–. [Annual.]

6693 U.S. Arms Control & Disarmament Agency. *World Military Expenditures and Arms Trade, 1963–1974.* ACDA Pub. 74. Washington, D.C.: G.P.O., 1975.

6694 U.S. Department of Defense. *Military Assistance and Foreign Military Sales Facts (1950–1970).* Washington, D.C.: G.P.O., 1970.

6695 Albrecht, Ulrich. *Der Handel mit Waffen.* Munich: Carl Hanser Verlag, 1971.

6696 ——. *Politik und Waffengeschafte: Rüstungsexporte in der BRD.* Munchen: C. Hanser, 1972.

6697 ——; D. Ernst; P. Lock; and H. Wulf. "Militarization, Arms Transfer and Arms Production in Peripheral Countries." *Journal of Peace Research* 12:3 (1975): 195–212.

6698 Beaton, Leonard, et al. *Arms Trade and International Politics.* Occasional paper, no. 13. Ottawa: Carleton Univ., School of International Affairs, Aug. 1971.

6699 Frank, Lewis A. *The Arms Trade in International Relations.* New York: Praeger, 1969.

6700 Harkavy, Robert E. *The Arms Trade and International Systems.* Cambridge, Mass.: Ballinger, 1975.

6701 Hoagland, John H., and P. A. Clapp. *Notes on Small Arms Traffic.* Cambridge: M.I.T., Center for International Studies, 1970.

6702 Johnson, George E. *International Armament.* 2 vols. Cologne: International Small Arms Publishing, 1965.

6703 Leiss, Amelia C. *Changing Patterns of Arms Transfers: Implications for Arms Transfer Policies.* Cambridge: M.I.T., Center for International Studies, 1970.

6704 Stanley, John, and Maurice Pearton. *The International Trade in Arms.* London: Chatto & Windus, 1972.

6705 Vayrynen, Raimo. *Arms Trade, Military Aid and Arms Production.* Basel: Herder Verlag, 1973.

6706 Albrecht, Ulrich. "On the Internationalization of the Arms Business." *Instant Research on Peace and Violence* 4:4 (Dec. 1973): 205–07.

6707 ——. "The Study of International Trade in Arms and Peace Research." *Journal of Peace Research* 9:2 (1972): 165–78.

6708 "The Arms Dealers: Guns for All." *Time* (Mar. 3, 1975): 34–44.

6709 "Arms Pushers of the World." *Atlas* 18 (Dec. 1969): 22–24.

6710 Bader, William B. "The Proliferation of Conventional Weapons." In Cyril E. Black and Richard A. Falk, comps., *The Future of the International Legal Order.* Vol. 3: *Conflict Management.* Princeton: Princeton Univ. Press, 1971, pp. 210–23.

6711 "The Booming World Trade in Arms." *Business Week* (May 23, 1970): 114–16 ff.

6712 Gray, Colin S. "The Arms Phenomenon: Definitions and Functions." *World Politics* 24 (Oct. 1971): 39–79.

6713 Haftendorn, Helga. "Der Internationale Waffentransfer und die Bemühungen um seine Einschränkung." *Europa-Archiv* (Jan. 25, 1971): 25–74.

6714 Harkavy, Robert E. "Comparison of the International Arms Trade in the Interwar and Postwar Periods." *Michigan Academician* 4:4 (1972): 445–60.

6715 James, Victor. "The Profits of Death." *Word* 1 (Winter 1965–66): 12–14 ff.

6716 Kemp, Geoffrey. "The Arms Dilemma." *International Conciliation*, no. 577 (Mar. 1970): 5–10.

6717 ——. "Dilemmas of the Arms Traffic." *Foreign Affairs* 48 (Jan. 1970): 274–84.

6718   ———. "The International Arms Trade: Supplier, Recipient and Arms Control Perspectives." *Political Quarterly* 42 (Oct.–Dec. 1971): 379–89.

6719   Klare, Michael T. "The Political Economy of Arms Sales." *Society* 11 (Sept.–Oct. 1974): 41–49.

6720   Kuebler, Jeanne. "Traffic in Arms." *Editorial Research Reports* (Apr. 28, 1965): 303–19.

6721   Leiss, Amelia C. "Comments on 'The Study of International Trade in Arms and Peace Research' by Ulrich Albrecht." *Journal of Peace Research* 9:2 (1972): 179–82.

6722   Martin, Laurence W. "The Arms Trade." *Listener* (Aug. 27, 1970): 274–75.

6723   Miksche, Ferdinand O. "Auswirkungen des Waffenhandels auf die Weltpolitik." *Wehr und Wirtschaft* (Oct. 20, 1968): 494–95.

6724   Rothschild, Emma. "The Boom in the Death Business." *New York Review of Books* (Oct. 2, 1975): 7–12.

6725   "Rustung: Da tummelt sich die Elite." *Spiegel* (July 3, 1972): 30 ff.

6726   Sivard, Ruth L. "Let Them Eat Bullets." *Bulletin of the Atomic Scientists* 31 (Mar. 1975): 6–10.

6727   Stone, William T. "International Arms Deals." *Editorial Research Reports* (Nov. 16, 1955): 791–808.

6728   "Weapons for All Nations." *Reader's Digest* (June 1975): 94–98.

"Merchants of Death" Thesis (Since 1945)

6729   Berkley, George E. "The Myth of War Profiteering." *New Republic* (Dec. 20, 1969): 15–18.

6730   Englemann, Bernt. *The Weapons Merchants.* Trans. by E. Detto. New York: Crown, 1968.

6731   "Eximbank Arms Sales." *Congressional Quarterly Weekly Report* (July 28, 1967): 1303–04.

6732   Ferrell, Robert H. "The Merchants of Death: Then and Now." *Journal of International Affairs* 26 (Spring 1972): 29–39.

6733   Fletcher, Raymond. "Where are the Merchants of Death?" *Twentieth Century* 171 (Spring 1963): 89–96.

6734   Gray, Colin S. "What is Good for General Motors. . . ." *Royal United Services Institution Journal* 117 (June 1972): 36–43.

6735   Hutton, J. Bernard. *The Traitor Trade.* New York: Obounsky, 1963.

6736   Itskov, Igor M. *Kontrakundisty vo vrakakh.* Moscow: Znanie, 1964.

6737   Manchester, William. *The Arms of Krupp, 1587–1968.* Boston: Little, Brown, 1969.

6738   "Now a Worldwide Boom in Sales of Arms." *U.S. News & World Report* (Jan. 22, 1973): 50–53.

6739   Perlo, Victor. *Militarism and Industry: Arms Profiteering in the Missile Age.* New York: International Publishers, 1963.

6740   Sherman, George. "The Pentagon's Merchants of Death." *Progressive* 31 (Nov. 1967): 30–33.

6741   Thayer, George. *The War Business: The International Trade in Armaments.* New York: Simon & Schuster, 1969.

6742   "Uneasy World Feeds Arms Trade: Commercial Arms Traffic Is Lively, Despite a Current Price Slump." *Business Week* (Sept. 19, 1959): 94.

Control of Arms Trade

6743   Bailey, Sidney D. "Can the Booming Arms Trade Be Halted?" *Christian Century* (Feb. 23, 1972): 220–22.

6744   Bloomfield, Lincoln P., and Amelia C. Leiss. "Arms Transfer and Arms Control." *Acad. of Pol. Sci. Proceedings* 29 (Mar. 1969): 37–54.

6745   ———. *Controlling Small Wars: A Strategy for the 1970's.* New York: Knopf, 1969.

6746   "Chucking Guns Around." *Economist* (July 8, 1967): 93–94.

6747   Culver, Sen. John C. "Need for an International Conference on Arms Sales." *Congressional Record* 121 (Sept. 23, 1975): S16510.

6748   Dobbs, Theodore B. "Munitions Control: U.S. Foreign Policy Into Action." *Newsletter* 75 (July 1967): 10–11.

6749   Gray, Colin S. "Traffic Control for the Arms Trade?" *Foreign Policy* 6 (Spring 1972): 153–69.

6750 Hansen, Erland B., and Jorgen W. Ulrich. "A Weapons Transfer System for Inter-Nation Conflict Regulation: A Proposal." In Bengt Hoglund and J. W. Ulrich, eds., *Conflict Control and Conflict Resolution.* Copenhagen: Munksgaard, 1972, pp. 156–73.

6751 Johnson, William A. *U.S. Military Aid Programs and Conventional Arms Control.* Santa Monica, Ca.: California Arms Control & Foreign Policy Seminar, Jan. 1973.

6752 Kemp, Geoffrey. "Regulating the Arms Trade." *Disarmament* 16 (Dec. 1967): 11–15.

6753 Klein, Jean. "Les Aspects Actuels de la Reglementation du Commerce des Armes." *Politique Etrangère* 34:2 (1969): 161–89.

6754 Leonard, James F. "U.S. States View on Conventional Arms Restraints." *U.S. Department of State Bulletin* (Sept. 20, 1971): 309–15.

6755 McArdle, Catherine. *The Role of Military Assistance in the Problem of Arms Control: The Middle East, Latin America and Africa.* Cambridge: Massachusetts Inst. Technol. Center for International Studies, 1964.

6756 Pomeroy, L. H. "The International Trade and Traffic in Arms: Its Supervision and Control." *U.S. Department of State Bulletin* (Feb. 6, 1950): 187–94; (Mar. 6, 1950): 357–64, 881; (Apr. 3, 1950): 507–15, 520.

6757 "Sondernummer Wehrbereitschaft, Rustungsproduktion und Waffenausfuhr." *Allgemeine Schweizerische Militarzeitschrift* 138 (June 1972): 297–352.

6758 Stanley, John. "The International Arms Trade: Controlled or Uncontrolled?" *Political Quarterly* 43:2 (1972): 155–68.

6759 Stubbs, Cmdr. G. D. "The International Arms Trade and Its Control." *Army Quarterly & Defense Journal* 103 (Jan. 1973): 200–210.

6760 Taylor, Trevor. "The Control of the Arms Trade." *International Relations* (May 1971): 903–12.

THE SUPPLIERS

6761 "The Arms Pushers: Booming World Arms Trade." *SANE World* 13 (Aug.–Sept. 1974): 1–48.

6762 Blechman, Barry M. "Handicapping the Arms Race." *New Republic* (Jan. 3, 10, 1976): 19–21.

6763 Cahn, Anne H. "Have Arms, Will Sell." *Bulletin of the Atomic Scientists* 31 (Apr. 1975): 10–12.

6764 Cobban, William. "Dealing Out Death Discreetly: The Traffic in Canadian Arms." *Saturday Night* 86 (Nov. 1971): 23–26.

6765 Daniels, Jeff. "Swedish Strike Power from SAAB." *Flight International* (Mar. 9, 1972): 360–62.

6766 "Germans Consider Non-NATO Weapons Sales." *Aviation Week & Space Technology* (Sept. 22, 1975): 16.

6767 Haftendorn, Helga. *Militärhilfe und Rüstungsexporte der BRD.* Düsseldorf: Bertleman Universitatsverlag, 1971.

6768 "Die Illegale Waffenausfuhr aus der Schweiz." *Flugwehr und Technik: Arme et Technique de l'Air* 31 (Jan.–Feb. 1969): 15–18.

6769 Klare, Michael T. "Political Economy of Arms Sales." *Bulletin of the Atomic Scientists* 32 (Nov. 1976): 11–13.

6770 Kurz, H. R. "Die Durch- und Ausfuhr von Kriegsmaterial aus der Schweiz." *Osterreichische Militarische Zeitschrift* 2 (Mar.–Apr. 1966): 109–16.

6771 Latour, Charles. "Armament Sales." *NATO's Fifteen Nations* 18 (Apr.–May 1973): 74–76 ff.

6772 Port, A. Tyler. "Co-operation on Arms Production: The Task Ahead." *NATO Review* 21 (May–June 1973): 13–17.

6773 "Schweiz: Rustungsproduktion und Waffenausfuhr." *Wehrkunde* 19 (Feb. 1970): 104–05.

6774 Stahle, Peter. "Im Dschungel des Waffenhandels: Bonner Geschafte mit Kriegsmaterial." *Zeit* (Sept. 5, 1967): 6.

6775 "Sweden's Arms Export Policy: Tight But Easing." *Armed Forces Journal* 110 (Feb. 1973): 56–57 ff.

6776 "Who Has Been Arming the Middle East?" *Business Week* (July 18, 1970): 72–73.

6777   Yefimov, S. "The Struggle of Monopolies on European Arms Market." *International Affairs* [Moscow] 7 (July 1961): 37–43.

Great Britain

See Treaties, Embargoes & Conventional Weapons, U.N. Embargo of Arms to South Africa (1963), below.

6778   Great Britain. Parliament. *Export of Surplus War Material.* Cmnd. 9676. London: H.M.S.O., 1956.

6779   Hickmott, J. R. "We Must Have Conventional British Weapons." *Contemporary Review* 210 (Apr. 1967): 171–72.

6780   "If We Don't Sell Those Arms." *Economist* (Nov. 21, 1970): 13–14.

6781   McDougall, D. "Wilson Government and the British Defense Commitment in Malaya-Singapore." *Journal of South Eastern Asian Studies* 4 (Sept. 1973): 229–40.

6782   Ramsden, J. M. "EEC and British Aerospace." *Flight International* (Jan. 20, 1972): 89–92.

6783   Watt, Donald C. "Britain Stirs It Up." *Spectator* (Sept. 16, 1966): 339–40.

France

6784   Alia, Josette. "Les Marchands de Mort." *Nouvel Observateur* (Nov. 19, 1970): 24–25.

6785   "Belgium Buy Spurs Mirage Sales." *Aviation Week & Space Technology* (Feb. 26, 1968): 16–17.

6786   Crocker, C. A. "France's Changing Military Interests." *Africa Review* 13 (June 1968): 16–24.

6787   "Die Franzosische Heereswaffenschau 1971: In Satory standen Panzerfahrzeuge und Raketenwerfer im Vordergrund." *Soldat und Technik* 14 (Sept. 1971): 498–505.

6788   Erven, L. "France in the Mediterranean." *Review of International Affairs* (Mar. 5, 1970): 10–13.

6789   "France Woos Libyans With Aid." *Africa Report* 15 (June 1970): 20–21.

6790   Kowitt, Sylvia. "The Politics of a Tacit Alliance: France-Israel Relations, 1956–1967." Ph.D. diss., Columbia Univ., 1970.

6791   Lamarche, Rene. "Death at Any Price—France: The Hard Sell." *Agenor* (Oct. 1974): 22–25.

6792   Leroy, Daniel. "La France Exportatrice des Missiles." *Science et Vie* 120 (Nov. 1971): 112–19.

6793   Manor, Yohanan. "Does France Have an Arms Export Policy?" *Res Publica* 16:5 (1974): 645–62.

6794   Ramsden, J. M. "France's Aircraft Industry." *Flight International* (Oct. 28, 1971): 685–700.

6795   "Record French Arms Exports in 1970." *International Defense Review* 4 (Apr. 1971): 113–14.

6796   "Will French Arms Boom Backfire?" *Business Week* (Feb. 1, 1969): 22.

United States

6797   Bryan, B. O. "Today's Pattern for Munitions Control." *U.S. Department of State Bulletin* (May 30, 1955): 884–89.

6798   Hout, Marvin J. "Munitions Export Control Policies and Procedures." *Defense Management Journal* 8 (July 1972): 49–52.

6799   Truman, Pres. Harry S. "Control of Exportation and Importation of Arms, Ammunition and Implements of War." *U.S. Department of State Bulletin* (Apr. 27, 1947): 750–57 ff.

6800   U.S. Arms Control & Disarmament Agency. *Compendium of U.S. Laws on Controlling Arms Exports.* Res. Rpt. 66–2. Washington, D.C.: G.P.O., May 1966.

6801   U.S. Department of State. *International Traffic in Arms: Laws and Regulations Administered by the Secretary of State Governing the International Traffic in Arms, Ammunition, and Implements of War.* Pub. 6587. 11th ed. Washington, D.C.: G.P.O., March 1958. [Frequently revised.]

U.S.—General Arms Sales

6802   "Aiming at the Arms Market Overseas: Technology and Lucrative Licensing Abroad

Put U.S. Ahead in Weapon Sales." *Business Week* (Dec. 3, 1966): 66–67 ff.

6803 "American Weapons Abroad: Sales Instead of Giveaways. . . ." *U.S. News & World Report* (July 27, 1970): 52–53.

6804 Anderson, Sally. "U.S. Military Assistance and Sales (U.S. Is Number One!)." *Defense Monitor* 3 (May 1974): 1–12.

6805 "Arms Sales: Nixon Doctrine May Boost U.S. Arms Sales Abroad." *Congressional Quarterly Weekly Report* (Mar. 6, 1970): 698–701.

6806 "Arms Sales and Foreign Policy." *Bulletin of the Atomic Scientists* 23 (Sept. 1967): 44–48.

6807 "Arms Sales and U.S. Foreign Policy." *Current* 86 (Aug. 1967): 33–41.

6808 Blake, Gen. Donald F. "A Realistic Look at USAF Military Assistance and Foreign Military Sales." *Air University Review* 22 (Nov.–Dec. 1970): 35–44.

6809 Catledge, Capt. Morris B., and Capt. Larrie F. Knudsen. "Foreign Military Sales: United States Involvement in Coproduction and Trends toward Codevelopment." M.A. theses, Air Institute of Technology, Air Univ., 1969.

6810 Eaker, Lt. Gen. Ira C. "Arms Sale Policies Hurt U.S. Interests." *Air Force Times* (Feb. 10, 1971): 13.

6811 Ellsworth, Robert. "Justifying Foreign Military Sales." *Aviation Week & Space Technology* (Apr. 19, 1976): 11.

6812 "Export Policies Relaxed on Technology [electronic warfare equipment]." *Aviation Week & Space Technology* (Jan. 27, 1975): 78–87.

6813 "Growing Export Markets: Weapons." *Forbes* (Feb. 1, 1966): 15–16.

6814 Habib, Philip C. "Department Testifies on Proposed Military Sales to Foreign Governments." *U.S. Department of State Bulletin* (Oct. 11, 1976): 447–51.

6815 Humphrey, Sen. Hubert H. "The Arms Transfer Problem." *Congressional Record* 122 (Feb. 17, 1976): S1685–86.

6816 Kaplan, Fred. "Still the Merchants of Death: Arms Sales and Foreign Policy." *Progressive* 40 (Mar. 1976): 22–25.

6817 Katzenbach, Nicholas de B. "U.S. Arms for the Developing World: Dilemmas of Foreign Policy." *U.S. Department of State Bulletin* 57 (Dec. 1967): 794–98.

6818 Kraar, Louis. "Grumman Still Flies for Navy, but it is Selling the World." *Fortune* 91 (Feb. 1976): 78–83, 142–46.

6819 Ligon, Walter B. "Foreign Military Sales." *National Defense* 60 (July–Aug. 1975): 30–32.

6820 Louscher, David J. "Foreign Military Sales: An Analysis of a Foreign Affairs Undertaking." Ph.D. diss., Univ. of Wisconsin, 1972.

6821 McCarthy, Sen. Eugene J. "Arms and the Man Who Sells Them." *Atlantic* (Oct. 1967): 82–86.

6822 ———. "The U.S. Supplier of Weapons to the World." *Saturday Review* (July 9, 1966): 13–15.

6823 "Military Sales Bolster Free World Defenses." *Armed Forces Management* 15 (Jan. 1969): 55–57.

6824 Miller, Judith. "Alarm Over Arms Sales." *Progressive* 39 (Dec. 1975): 6–7.

6825 Moran, Theodore. "A Primer on U.S. Arms Sales Around the World." *Ripon Forum* 5 (July 1969): 15–18.

6826 Morse, Col. David L. "Foreign Arms Sales: 2 Sides to the Coin." *Army* 26:1 (Jan. 1976): 14–21.

6827 Nilhart, Brooke. "Increased Foreign Military Sales Inescapable under Nixon Doctrine." *Armed Forces Journal* (Nov. 2, 1970): 22–25 ff.

6828 "Now: A World Wide Boom in Sales of Arms." *U.S. News & World Report* (Jan. 22, 1973): 50–53.

6829 Perlo, Victor. "Alliance of Militarists and Arms Manufacturers." *International Affairs* [Moscow] 15 (Sept. 1969): 19–25.

6830 Phalon, Philip A. "Military Sales Abroad." *National Defense* 61 (Sept.–Oct. 1976): 129–30.

6831 Powell, Craig. "Arms Sales Is More Than Just a Military Question." *Armed Forces Management* 14 (Jan. 1968): 72 ff.

6832   Szulc, Tad. "Kickback: Corruption in U.S. Arms Sales." *New Republic* (Apr. 17, 1976): 8–11.

6833   Taylor, Trevor. "President Nixon's Arms Supply Policies." *Yearbook of World Affairs* 26 (1972): 65–80.

6834   U.S. Congressional Budget Office. *Budgetary Cost Savings to the Department of Defense Resulting From Foreign Military Sales.* Washington, D.C., May 24, 1976.

6835   ———. *The Effect of Foreign Military Sales on the U.S. Economy.* Washington, D.C.: G.P.O., 1976.

6836   "Where Arms Ban Backfired on U.S." *U.S. News & World Report* (Jan. 22, 1973): 53–54.

6837   "Why Didn't We?" *Armed Forces Journal* (Apr. 25, 1970): 16–17.

6838   "Why the U.S. Is Pushing the Sale of Weapons." *U.S. News & World Report* (Oct. 11, 1965): 122.

U.S.—Military Assistance

6839   Barber, W. F., and C. N. Ronning. *International Security and Military Power.* Columbus: Ohio State Univ. Press, 1966.

6840   Brown, William A., Jr., and Redvers Opie. *American Foreign Assistance.* Washington, D.C.: Brookings Institution, 1953.

6841   Cleveland, Harlan, et al. *The Overseas Americans.* New York: McGraw-Hill, 1960.

6842   Draper Committee. *Report of the President's Committee to Study the Military Assistance Program.* Washington, D.C.: G.P.O., 1959.

6843   Furniss, Edgar C. *Some Perspectives on American Military Assistance.* Princeton: Princeton Univ. Press, 1957.

6844   Holcombe, John L., and Alan Berg. *MAP for Security.* Columbia: Univ. of South Carolina Press, 1957.

6845   Hovey, Harold A. *United States Military Assistance: A Study of Policies and Practices.* New York: Praeger, 1965.

6846   Lefever, Ernest W. *U.S. Military Training Programs for Developing Countries.* Washington, D.C.: Brookings Institution, 1966.

6847   Pranger, Robert J., and Dale R. Tahtinen. *Toward a Realistic Military Assistance Program.* Foreign Affairs Studies, no. 15. Washington, D.C.: American Enterprise Institute for Public Policy Research, Dec. 1974.

6848   Refson, J. S. *U.S. Military Training and Advice: Implications for Arms Transfer Policies.* Cambridge: M.I.T., 1970.

6849   Stamey, Roderick A., Jr. "The Origin of the U.S. Military Assistance Program." Ph.D. diss., Univ. of North Carolina-Chapel Hill, 1972.

6850   U.S. Arms Control & Disarmament Agency. *The Control of Local Conflict.* Cambridge: M.I.T., Center for International Studies, 1967.

6851   ———. Department of State. *The Military Assistance Program.* Pub. 3563. Washington, D.C.: G.P.O., 1949.

6852   Wolf, Charles, Jr. *Economic Impacts of Military Assistance.* P–4578. Santa Monica, Ca.: Rand, Feb. 1971.

6853   ———. *Military Assistance Programs.* P–3240. Santa Monica, Ca.: Rand, 1965.

6854   Baker, Marshall E. "The Case for Military Assistance." *Armed Forces Management* 5 (June 1959): 13–15.

6855   Connery, R. H., and Paul T. David. "The Mutual Defense Assistance Program." *American Political Science Review* 45 (June 1951): 321–47.

6856   Heymont, Irving. "U.S. Military Assistance Programs." *Military Review* 48 (Jan. 1968): 89–95.

6857   Hughes, Col. David R. "The Myth of Military Coups and Military Assistance." *Military Review* 47 (Dec. 1967): 3–10.

6858   Irwin, John N. "New Approaches in International Security Assistance." *U.S. Department of State Bulletin* (Feb. 22, 1971): 221–27.

6859   Jordan, Amos A., Jr. "Military Assistance and National Policy." *Orbis* 2 (Summer 1958): 236–51.

6860   Kintner, William R. "The Role of Military Assistance." *U.S. Naval Institute Proceedings* 87 (Mar. 1961): 76–84.

6861 Lefever, Ernest W. "The Military Assistance Training Program." *Annals of the Amer. Acad. of Pol. & Soc. Sci.* 424 (Mar. 1976): 85–95.

6862 Lemnitzer, Gen. Lyman L. "The Foreign Military Aid Program." *Acad. of Pol. Sci. Proceedings* 23 (1948–1950): 436–42.

6863 Lincoln, George A. "Forces Determining Arms Aid." *Acad. of Pol. Sci. Proceedings* 25 (May 1953): 263–72.

6864 Maxfield, David M. "Big Increase Authorized in Military Aid." *Congressional Quarterly Weekly Report* (Mar. 6, 1976): 540–42.

6865 Meyer, Charles A. "U.S. Military Activities in Latin America." *Inter-American Economic Affairs* 23 (Autumn 1969): 89–94.

6866 Netherland, Robert. "A Challenge in Teaching the Foreign Military Student." *U.S. Naval Institute Proceedings* (Mar. 1960): 78–85.

6867 Raymond, Daniel A. "Reflections on Mutual Defense Assistance Program." *Military Review* 35 (Aug. 1955): 31–44.

6868 Victor, A. H. "Military Aid and Comfort to Dictatorships." *U.S. Naval Institute Proceedings* 95 (Mar. 1969): 42–47.

6869 Warren, Robert H. "Military Assistance Program: Foreign Military Sales." *Vital Speeches* (July 15, 1969): 601–03.

6870 Windle, C., and T. Vallance. "Optimizing Military Assistance Training." *World Politics* 15 (Oct. 1962): 91–107.

6871 Winston, Donald C. "DOD Plan Would Separate Civil, Military Aid Request." *Aviation Week & Space Technology* (Dec. 25, 1967): 17–18.

6872 Wood, Gen. R. J. "Military Assistance and the Nixon Doctrine." *Orbis* 15 (Spring 1971): 247–74.

6873 ———. "Military Assistance Program." *Armed Forces Management* 11 (Nov. 1964): 105–06.

U.S.—Congress & Arms Transfers

6874 Aspin, Rep. Les. "To Establish An Annual Foreign Military Arms Sales Budget." *Congressional Record* 121 (June 12, 1975): E3116–17.

6875 Culver, Sen. John C. "Secretary Kissinger Responds on Arms Sales." *Congressional Record* 121 (Dec. 3, 1975): S20962–963.

6876 DuPont, Rep. Pierre. "US Arms Sales Policy: It's Time to Develop One." *Congressional Record* 121 (June 12, 1975): H5409–11.

6877 Gardner, Judy. "Congress Weighs New Controls on Arms Sales." *Congressional Quarterly Weekly Report* (Dec. 20, 1975): 2817–19.

6878 Harrison, Stanley L. "Congress and Foreign Military Sales." *Military Review* 51 (Oct. 1971): 79–87.

6879 Humphrey, Sen. Hubert H. "International Security Assistance and Arms Export Control Act of 1975." *Congressional Record* 121 (Nov. 13, 1975): S19880–890.

6880 ———. "S. 2662, The International Security Assistance and Arms Export Control Act of 1975." *Congressional Record* 121 (Dec. 9, 1975): S21430–435.

6881 "International Security Assistance and Arms Export Control Act of 1975." *Congressional Record* 122 (Feb. 4, 1976): S1255–87. [Also see, (Feb. 17, 1976): S1737–60 and (Feb. 18, 1976): S1868–1916.]

6882 Johnsen, Katherine. "Foreign Arms Sales Spur Congressional Surveillance." *Aviation Week & Space Technology* (June 23, 1975): 14–15.

6883 Kennedy, Sen. Edward. "Foreign Assistance Act of 1975: Amendment No. 1233–1236." *Congressional Record* 121 (Dec. 10, 1975): S21601–602.

6884 "Massive Congressional Review Could Cause Arms Export Cuts." *Aviation Week & Space Technology* 87 (July 31, 1967): 22.

6885 Maxfield, David M. "Vinnell Contract Triggers Arms Sales Debate." *Congressional Quarterly Weekly Report* (Mar. 29, 1975): 656–59.

6886 Mondale, Sen. Walter. "Senate Resolution 296—Submission of a Resolution Relating to Arms Sales." *Congressional Record* 121 (Nov. 6, 1975): S19396–399.

6887 Morgan, Rep. Thomas E. "Conference Report on H.R. 13680." *Congressional Record* 122 (June 16, 1976): H6034–35. [Text of International Security Assistance and Arms Export Control Act of 1976.]

6888 Nelson, Sen. Gaylord. "Foreign Assistance Act of 1975: Amendment No. 1228." *Congressional Record* 121 (Dec. 9, 1975): S21422–428.

6889 ———. "S.854 [Amendment for Foreign Military Arms Sales Act]." *Congressional Record* (Feb. 26, 1975): S2653–59.

6890 ———. "U.S. Arms Sales and the National Interest." *Congressional Record* (Sept. 23, 1975): S16507–510.

6891 "New Arms Sale Battle Looms in Congress: Congress Restricts Arms Sales to Developing Nations." *Congressional Quarterly Weekly Report* (Mar. 22, 1968): 596–600.

6892 Shuman, William. "Tighter Foreign Sales Controls Studied." *Aviation Week & Space Technology* (June 16, 1975): 20–21.

6893 Simmons, Henry T. "U.S. Arms Sales: Congress Steps on the Brake." *Interavia*, no. 10 (1976): 987–88.

6894 U.S. Arms Control & Disarmament Agency. *The International Transfer of Conventional Arms*. Rpt. to Congress. Washington, D.C.: G.P.O., Apr. 12, 1974.

6895 U.S. Department of Defense. *Foreign Military Sales and Military Assistance Facts*. Washington, D.C.: G.P.O., 1966–. [Annual report.]

6896 U.S. House. *Foreign Aid, Message from the President of the United States Transmitting Proposals to Redirect Our Efforts in Foreign Aid*. 91st Cong., 1st Sess., May 28, 1968.

6897 Committee on Banking and Currency. Hearings: *Export-Import Bank and Credit Sales of Defense Articles*. 90th Cong., 1st Sess., July 17, 1967.

6898 U.S. House. Committee on Foreign Affairs. Hearings: *To Amend the Foreign Military Sales Act*. 91st Cong., 2d Sess., Feb. 5, 17, 1970.

6899 ———. Hearings: *The Foreign Military Sales Act*. 90th Cong., 2d Sess., June 26, 27, 1968.

6900 ———. Hearings: *Foreign Assistance Act of 1969*. 91st Cong., 1st Sess., 1969.

6901 ———. Hearings: *Foreign Assistance Act of 1971*. 92d Cong., 1st Sess., 1971.

6902 ———. Hearings: *International Security Assistance Act of 1976*. 94th Cong., 2d Sess., 1976.

6903 ———. Hearings: *International Transfer of Conventional Arms: Report to Congress from U.S. Arms Control & Disarmament Agency Pursuant to Sec. 302 of Foreign Relations Authorization Act of 1972*. 93d Cong., 2d Sess., Apr. 12, 1974.

6904 ———. Hearings: *Military Assistance Training*. 91st Cong., 2d Sess., 1970.

6905 ———. Report: *Amending the Foreign Military Sales Act*. 91st Cong., 2d Sess., 1970.

6906 ———. Report: *Background Material: Foreign Assistance Act: Fiscal Year 1970*. 91st Cong., 1st Sess., 1969.

6907 ———. Report: *Conference Report on Foreign Assistance Act of 1968*. 90th Cong., 2d Sess., 1968.

6908 ———. Report: *Conference Report on Foreign Assistance Act of 1969*. 91st Cong., 1st Sess., 1969.

6909 ———. Report: *Military Assistance Training*. 92d Cong., 1st Sess., 1971.

6910 ———. Report: *Staff Memorandum on the Foreign Assistance Program Authorizations and Appropriations for Fiscal Year 1969*. 90th Cong., 2d Sess., 1968.

6911 U.S. Joint Economic Committee. Hearings: *Economic Issues in Military Assistance*. 92d Cong., 1st Sess., 1971.

6912 U.S. President. *U.S. Foreign Assistance in the 1970's: A New Approach*. Rpt. from Task Force on International Development. Washington, D.C.: G.P.O., 1970.

6913 U.S. Senate. Committee on Appropriations. Report: *United States Military Operations and Mutual Security Programs Overseas*. Rpt. of Sen. Dennis Chaves. 86th Cong., 2d Sess., 1960.

6914 ———. Committee on Banking and Currency. Hearings: *Export-Import Bank Participation and Financing in Credit Sales of Defense Articles*. 90th Cong., 1st Sess., July 25, 1967.

6915 ———. Report: *Export-Import Act Amendments of 1967*. 90th Cong., 1st Sess., 1967.

6916 ———. Committee on Foreign Relations. Hearings: *Foreign Assistance Act of 1968.* 90th Cong., 2d Sess., Mar. 13, 14, 1968.

6917 ———. Hearings: *Foreign Assistance Act, 1969.* 91st Cong., 1st Sess., July 14–18, Aug. 6, 1969.

6918 ———. Hearings: *Foreign Assistance Authorization: Arms Sales Issues.* 94th Cong., 1st Sess., 1976.

6919 ———. Hearings: *Foreign Military Sales.* 90th Cong., 2d Sess., June 20, 1968.

6920 ———. Hearings: *Foreign Military Sales Act Amendment, 1970, 1971.* 91st Cong., 2d Sess., Mar. 24, May 11, 1970.

6921 ———. Hearings: *Foreign Military Sales and Assistance Act, 1973.* 93d Cong., 1st Sess., May 2–8, 1973.

6922 ———. Report: *Amending the Foreign Military Sales Act.* 91st Cong., 2d Sess., 1970.

6923 ———. Report: *Foreign Assistance Act of 1968.* 90th Cong., 1st Sess., 1968.

6924 ———. Report: *Foreign Assistance Act of 1969.* 91st Cong., 1st Sess., 1969.

6925 ———. Staff Study: *Arms Sales and Foreign Policy.* 90th Cong., 1st Sess., Jan. 25, 1967.

6926 U.S. Senate. Special Committee to Study the Foreign Aid Program. Report: *Compilation of Studies and Surveys.* 85th Cong., 1st Sess., 1957.

6927 Winston, Donald C. "White House Battles to Block Export Ban." *Aviation Week & Space Technology* (Aug. 21, 1967): 21.

U.S.S.R.—Military Aid

6928 Alexandros, L. "Sowjetische Raketenschiffe im Mittelmeerraum." *Wehr und Wirtschaft* (Apr. 15, 1966): 257–59.

6929 Baker, Ross K. "Soviet Military Assistance to Tropical Africa." *Military Review* 48 (July 1968): 76–81.

6930 Einbeck, Eberhardt. "Moskaus Militarhilte an die Dritte Welt." *Aussenpolitik* 22 (May 1971): 300–313.

6931 Gasteyger, Curt. "Moscow and the Mediterranean." *Foreign Affairs* 46 (July 1968): 476–87.

6932 Gilbert, Stephan P. "Soviet-American Military Aid Competition in the Third World." *Orbis* 13 (Winter 1970): 1117–37.

6933 ———. "Wars of Liberation and Soviet Military Aid Policy." *Orbis* 10 (Fall 1966): 839–58.

6934 ———, and Wynfred Joshua. *Arms for the Third World: Soviet Military Aid Diplomacy.* Baltimore: Johns Hopkins Press, 1969.

6935 Pye, Lucien. "Soviet and American Styles in Foreign Aid." *Orbis* 9 (Summer 1960): 159–73.

6936 Ra'anan, Uri. *The USSR Arms the Third World: Case Studies in Soviet Foreign Policy.* Cambridge: M.I.T. Press, 1969.

6937 Ramazani, R. K. "Soviet Military Assistance to the Uncommitted Countries." *Midwest Journal of Political Science* (Nov. 1959): 356–73.

Europe

6938 Ashcroft, G. *Military Logistic Systems in NATO: The Goal of Integration.* Adelphi Papers, no. 62, 68. London: Institute for Strategic Studies, 1969, 1970.

6939 Beer, F. A. *Integration and Disintegration in NATO.* Columbus: Ohio State Univ. Press, 1969.

6940 Dubrovin, V. "Atlantic Fights on Arms Market." *International Affairs* [Moscow] 11 (Sept. 1965): 78–83.

6941 Edmonds, Martin. "International Collaboration in Weapons Procurement: The Implications of the Anglo-French Case." *International Affairs* [London] 43 (Apr. 1967): 252–64.

6942 Hovey, Harold A. *United States Military Assistance: A Study of Politics and Practices.* New York: Praeger, 1965, pp. 75–90.

6943 Schutze, W. *European Defense Cooperation and NATO.* Paris: Atlantic Institute, 1969.

6944 Simpson, John, and Frank Gregory. "West European Collaboration in Weapons Procurement." *Orbis* 16 (Summer 1972): 435–61.

6945 Stifani, Giuseppe. "Wo Bleibt die Abstimmung?" *Wehr und Wirtschaft* (Apr. 15, 1966): 191–92.

6946   Vandevanter, Gen. E., Jr. *Coordinated Weapons Production in NATO: A Study of Alliance Processes.* RN–5282–PR. Santa Monica, Ca.: Rand, 1967.

6947   Zwissler, Tilbert. "Probleme der Wehrwirtschaft und Rüstung." *Wehrkunde* 20 (May 1971): 231–36.

THIRD WORLD RECIPIENTS

6948   Albrecht, Ulrich. "Arms Trade With the Third World and Domestic Arms Production." *Instant Research on Peace and Violence* 6:1–2 (1976): 52–61.

6949   ———, and Birgit A. Sommer. "Deutsche Waffen fur die Dritte Welt." In *Militarhilfe und Entwicklungspolitik.* Hamburg: Rowohlt Verlag, 1972.

6950   ———; et al. "Armaments and Underdevelopment." *Bulletin of Peace Proposals* 3:2 (1972): 173–85.

6951   Barrett, Raymond J. "Arms Dilemma for the Developing World." *Military Review* 50 (Apr. 1970): 28–35.

6952   Bova, Sergio. "Il Commercio Della Armi E I Paesi del Terzo Mondo." *Quaderni di Sociologia* [Italy] 21:2 (1972): 217–26.

6953   Chaudhuri, Gen. J. N. "International Arms Trade: The Recipient's Problem." *Political Quarterly* 43 (July–Sept. 1972): 261–69.

6954   Cook, Fred J. "Deadly Contagion: Arms Sales to the Third World." *Nation* (Jan. 24, 1972): 106–09.

6955   Davinic, Prvoslav. "Basic Characteristics of Arms Trade with Developing Countries." *Medunarodni Problemi* 23:3 (1971): 55–92.

6956   Hanning, Hugh. "Lessons from the Arms Race." *Africa Report* 13 (Feb. 1968): 42–47.

6957   Hoagland, John H. "Arms in the Developing World." *Orbis* 12 (Spring 1968): 167–84.

6958   ———. "Arms in the Third World [a review]." *Orbis* 14 (Summer 1970): 500–504.

6959   "Increasing Weaponry Sales Struggle Seen." *Aviation Week & Space Technology* (Oct. 24, 1966): 386–95.

6960   Kemp, Geoffrey. "Arms Sales and Arms Control in the Developing Countries." *World Today* 22 (Sept. 1966): 386–95.

6961   ———. "Arms Traffic and Third World Conflicts." *International Conciliation*, no. 577 (Mar. 1970): 1–80.

6962   ———. *Classification of Weapons Systems and Force Designs in Less Developed Country Environments: Implications for Arms Transfer Policies.* Cambridge: M.I.T., Center for International Studies, 1970.

6963   ———. "Strategy, Arms and the Third World." *Orbis* 16 (Fall 1972): 809–15.

6964   Kennedy, Gavin. *The Military in the Third World.* New York: Scribner's, 1974.

6965   Leiss, Amelia C.; Geoffrey Kemp; et al. *Arms Transfers to Less Developed Countries.* Report C/70–1. Cambridge: M.I.T., Center for International Studies, Feb. 1970.

6966   Martin, Laurence W. "The Arms Trade with the Third World." *Arms and Strategy.* New York: David McKay, 1973, pp. 253–67.

6967   Massachusetts Institute of Technology. *Regional Arms Control Arrangements for Developing Nations: Arms and Arms Control in Latin America, the Middle East and Africa.* Cambridge: M.I.T., Center for International Studies, Sept. 1964.

6968   Menges, Constantine C. *Military Aspects of International Relations in Developing Areas.* P–3480. Santa Monica, Ca.: Rand, 1966.

6969   Miksche, Ferdinand O. "The Arms Race in the Third World." *Orbis* 13 (Spring 1968): 161–66.

6970   ———. "Rustungsgeschaft des Ostblocks mit der Dritten Welt." *Wehr und Wirtschaft* 15 (Sept. 1971): 438–39.

6971   Oberg, Jan. "Arms Trade with the Third World as an Aspect of Imperialism." *Journal of Peace Research* 12:3 (1975): 213–34.

6972   ———. "Third World Armament: Domestic Arms Production in Israel, South Africa, Brazil, Argentina, and India, 1950–75." *Instant Research on Peace and Violence* 5:4 (1975): 222–39.

6973   SIPRI. *The Arms Trade with the Third World.* New York: Humanities Press, 1971.

6974   Sutton, John L., and Geoffrey Kemp. *Arms to Developing Countries, 1945–1965.* Adelphi Paper, no. 28. London: Institute for Strategic Studies, Oct. 1966.

Africa

6975 Akehurst, Frederick S., ed. *Arms and African Development*. New York: Praeger, 1972.

6976 Bell, M. J. V. *Military Assistance to Independent African States*. Adelphi Paper, no. 15. London: Institute of Strategic Studies, 1964.

6977 "Can the Epidemic of Coups be Stopped?" *Toward Freedom* 15 (Mar. 1966): 3–4.

6978 Cervenka, Zdenek. "The Arms Trade in Africa." *Africa* 7 (Mar. 1972): 14–17.

6979 Cooley, John K. "From Mau Mau to Missiles." *African Forum* 2 (Summer 1966): 42–56.

6980 Edmonds, Martin. "Civil War and Arms Sales: The Nigeria-Biafran War and Other Cases." In Robin Higham, ed., *Civil Wars in the Twentieth Century*. Lexington: Univ. of Kentucky Press, 1972.

6981 Gutteridge, William F. "The Political Role of African Armed Forces: The Impact of Foreign Military Assistance." *African Affairs* 66 (Apr. 1967): 93–101.

6982 Jacob, A. "Israel's Military Aid to Africa, 1960–1966." *Journal of Modern African Studies* 9 (Aug. 1971): 165–87.

6983 Mazrui, Ali A. "African Radicalism and Arms Policy." *African Scholar* 1:4 (1970): 3–4.

6984 Minty, Abdul S. *South Africa's Defense Strategy*. London: Anti-Apartheid Movement, 1969.

6985 Shaw, Lt. Bryant P. "Military Assistance to Black Africa: Blessing or Curse?" *Air University Review* 23 (May–June 1972): 72–78.

6986 Shestakov, S. "Arms Build-up in South Africa and Rhodesia." *International Affairs* [Moscow] 22 (Sept. 1976): 142–43.

6987 Short, Philip. "Army Still Takes Biggest Slice of Uganda's Budget." *African Development* (Sept. 1972): 15–16.

6988 Whitaker, Paul M. "Arms and the Nationalists: Who Helps?" *Africa Report* 15 (May 1970): 12–14.

Asia

6989 Hovey, Harold A. *United States Military Assistance*. New York: Praeger, 1965, pp. 17–43.

6990 Jordan, Amos A., Jr. *Foreign Aid and the Defense of Southeast Asia*. New York: Praeger, 1962.

6991 Marsot, Alain G. "China's Aid to Cambodia." *Pacific Affairs* 43 (Summer 1969): 189–98.

6992 Nagashima, Shusuke. "Japan's Defense Rests on U.S. Technology." *Technology Week* (Dec. 6, 1966): 32–33.

6993 Polsky, Anthony. "Asia's Little Israel [Singapore]." *Far Eastern Review* (Sept. 11, 1969): 655–57.

6994 Smith, Alphonso. "Military Assistance in the Far East." *U.S. Naval Institute Proceedings* 86 (Dec. 1960): 40–48.

6995 Wurfel, David. "Foreign Aid and Social Reform in Political Development: A Philippine Case Study." *American Political Science Review* 53 (June 1959): 456–82.

Asia—India/Pakistan

6996 "Friends Have Their Uses." *Economist* (Aug. 5, 1967): 487–88.

6997 Guha, S. B. "Pakistan's Air Power." *Institute for Defense Studies and Analysis* [New Delhi] 2 (Oct. 1969): 124–49.

6998 Hasan, K. Sarwar. "The Background of American Aid to Pakistan." *Pakistan Horizon* 20:2 (1967): 120–26.

6999 ———. "United States Arms Policy in South Asia, 1965–1967." *Pakistan Horizon* 20:2 (1967): 127–36.

7000 Nilhart, Brooke. "Who Armed Pakistan?" *Armed Forces Journal* 109 (Nov. 1971): 50–52.

7001 Qureshi, Khalida. "Arms Aid to India and Pakistan." *Pakistan Horizon* 20:2 (1967): 137–50.

7002 Rajasekhariah, A. M., and V. T. Patil. "Soviet Arms Supply to Pakistan: Motives and Implications." *Modern Review* 123 (Oct. 1968): 706–10.

7003 Sharma, B. L. "Soviet Arms for Pakistan." *United Service Institution of India Journal* 98 (July–Sept. 1968): 223–38.

7004 Spain, James W. "Military Assistance for Pakistan." *American Political Science Review* 48 (Sept. 1954): 738–51.

7005   U.S. Senate. Committee on Foreign Relations. Hearings: *Arms Sales to Near East and South Asian Countries.* 90th Cong., 1st Sess., 1967.

Latin America

7006   Baines, John M. "U.S. Military Assistance to Latin America: An Assessment." *Journal of Inter-American Studies and World Affairs* 14 (Nov. 1972): 469–87.

7007   Brownlow, Cecil. "Brazil Looks Again to U.S. for Weapons." *Aviation Week & Space Technology* (Dec. 9, 1974): 21–22.

7008   ———. "Peru Military Build-up Worries Neighbors." *Aviation Week & Space Technology* (Dec. 2, 1974): 21–22.

7009   ———. "U.S., Europe Vie for Latin Fighter Order." *Aviation Week & Space Technology* (May 30, 1966): 26–27.

7010   Dame, H. *United States Military Assistance and Latin American Relations.* Washington, D.C.: American Univ., Center for Research in Social Systems, 1962.

7011   Einaudi, Luigi R., et al. *Arms Transfers to Latin America: Toward a Policy of Mutual Respect.* R–1173–Dos. Santa Monica, Ca.: Rand, June 1973.

7012   Estep, Raymond. *United States Military Aid to Latin America.* Maxwell A.F.B., Ala.: Air Univ., Documentary Research Division, 1966.

7013   Gailer, Col. Frank, Jr. "Air Force Missions in Latin America." *Air University Quarterly Review* 13 (Fall 1961): 45–58.

7014   Gebhardt, Herman P. "Komplexe Rustungsprobleme in Latinamerika." *Aussenpolitik* 19 (Apr. 1968): 220–29.

7015   Grant, Zalin B. "Alliance Against Revolution: Training, Equipping the Latin American Military." *New Republic* (Dec. 16, 1967): 13–14.

7016   Gruening, Sen. Ernest. "Export Trouble." *Nation* (Oct. 6, 1962): 194–96.

7017   Haahr, John C. "Military Assistance to Latin America." *Military Review* 49 (May 1966): 12–21.

7018   "Is There Really an Arms Race in Latin America?" *U.S. News & World Report* (Mar. 4, 1968): 52.

7019   Kaplan, Stephen S. "U.S. Arms Transfers to Latin America, 1945–1974: Rational Strategy, Bureaucratic Politics and Executive Parameters." *International Studies Quarterly* 19 (Dec. 1975): 339–431.

7020   Kemp, Geoffrey. "Rearmament in Latin America." *World Today* 23 (Sept. 1967): 375–84.

7021   ———. *Some Relationships Between U.S. Military Training in Latin America and Weapons Acquisitions Patterns: 1959–1969.* Cambridge: M.I.T., Center for International Studies, 1970.

7022   Klare, Michael T. "How to Trigger an Arms Race." *Nation* (Aug. 30, 1975): 137–42.

7023   ———. "The Politics of U.S. Arms Sales to Latin America." *Latin American Report* [NACLA] 9 (Mar. 1975): 12–17.

7024   Lieuwen, Edwin. *Arms and Politics in Latin America.* New York: Praeger, 1961.

7025   Loftus, Joseph E. *Latin American Defense Expenditures, 1938–1965.* R.M.–5310–IR–15A. Santa Monica, Ca.: Rand, Jan. 1968.

7026   Meyer, Charles A. "U.S. Military Assistance Policy toward Latin America." *U.S. Department of State Bulletin* (Aug. 4, 1969): 100–102.

7027   Ronfeldt, David F., and Luigi R. Einaudi. *Internal Security and Military Assistance to Latin America in the 1970's: A First Statement.* R–924–ISA. Santa Monica, Ca.: Rand, Dec. 1971.

7028   Rosenbaum, H. Jon. *Arms and Security in Latin America: Recent Developments.* Washington, D.C.: Woodrow Wilson International Center for Scholars, 1971.

7029   Sereseres, Caesar D. "Military Development and the United States Military Assistance Program for Latin America: The Case of Guatemala, 1960–1969." Ph.D. diss., Univ. of California, Riverside, 1972.

7030   Simcox, David E. "United States Military Assistance and Latin American Military Elites." M.A. thesis, American Univ., School of International Service, 1970.

7031   U.S. Department of State. *Arms Sales in Latin America.* Res. Study, RAAS–14. Washington, D.C.: Bureau of Intelligence & Research, June 1973.

7032 ———. "Inter-American Military Cooperation." *U.S. Department of State Bulletin* (Apr. 9, 1951): 574.

7033 ———. *Military Assistance to Latin America: Background.* Washington, D.C.: G.P.O., 1953.

7034 U.S. House. Committee on Foreign Affairs. Hearings: *Aircraft Sales in Latin America.* 91st Cong., 2d Sess., Apr. 29–30, 1970.

7035 U.S. Senate. Committee on Appropriations. Report: *United States Activities in Mexico, Panama, Peru, Chile, Argentina, Brazil, and Venezuela.* 87th Cong., 2d Sess., 1962.

7036 ———. Committee on Foreign Relations. Hearings: *United States Military Policies and Programs in Latin America.* 91st Cong., 1st Sess., June 24, July 8, 1969.

7037 ———. Report: *Survey of the Alliance for Progress, the Latin American Military.* 90th Cong., 1st Sess., 1967.

7038 Weaver, Jerry L. "Arms Transfers to Latin America: A Note on the Contagion Effect." *Journal of Peace Research* 11:3 (1974): 213–20.

7039 "Why U.S. Military Assistance Is Given to Argentina: Dictatorship of the U.S. Department of Defense." *Inter-American Economic Affairs* 21 (Autumn 1967): 81–89.

7040 Wolf, Charles, Jr. *The Political Effects of Military Programs: Some Indications from Latin America.* Santa Monica, Ca.: Rand, 1963.

7041 Wychoff, Theodore. "The Role of the Military in Latin American Military Politics." *Western Political Quarterly* 13 (Sept. 1960): 745–63.

7042 Zook, Capt. David H., Jr. "United States Military Assistance to Latin America." *Air University Review* 14 (Sept.–Oct. 1963): 82–85.

Middle East

7043 Alexandros, L. "Streifzug durch den nahen osten." *Wehr und Wirtschaft* (May 10, 1966): 293–95.

7044 "Arms and Alms." *Progressive* 40 (Oct. 1976): 9–10.

7045 "Arms Peddling." *New Republic* (Oct. 2, 1976): 7–8 ff.

7046 Brown, Neville. "Revolutionary Libya's Arms Potential . . . Who Will Benefit?" *New Middle East* 13 (Oct. 1969): 11–13.

7047 "Controlling the Middle East Arms Race." *Disarmament* 10 (June 1966): 1–6.

7048 Copley, Gregory. "Iran: The Psychopolitics of Arms: The Politics of Neighborliness." *Defense and Foreign Affairs* (Aug.–Sept. 1976): 6–17, 31.

7049 DeVore, Ronald M. "The Arab-Israeli Arms Race and the Super-powers." *Middle East* 66 (Feb. 1974): 70–73.

7050 ———. "The Arab-Israeli Military Balance." *Military Review* (Nov. 1973): 65–71.

7051 Duchêne, François. "The Arms Trade in the Middle East." *Political Quarterly* 44 (Oct.–Dec. 1973): 453–65.

7052 Evron, Yair. "French Arms Policy in the Middle East." *World Today* 26 (Feb. 1970): 82–90.

7053 Gharleb, Edmund. "U.S. Arms Supply to Israel during the War." *Journal of Palestine Studies* (Winter 1974): 114–21.

7054 Glassman, Jon D. *Arms for the Arabs: The Soviet Union and War in the Middle East.* Baltimore: Johns Hopkins Press, 1976.

7055 Hoagland, John H., and John B. Teeple. "Regional Stability and Weapons Transfer: The Middle Eastern Case." *Orbis* 9 (Fall 1965): 714–28.

7056 Hurewitz, J. C. *Middle East Politics: The Military Dimension.* New York: Praeger, 1969.

7057 Jabber, Fuad. "Not by War Alone: Curbing the Arab-Israeli Arms Race." *Middle East Journal* 28 (Summer 1974): 233–47.

7058 ———. "Petrodollars, Arms Trade, and the Pattern of Major Conflicts." In J. C. Hurewitz, ed., *Oil, the Arab-Israeli Dispute, and the Industrial World.* Boulder, Colo.: Westview Press, 1976, pp. 149–64.

7059 Kemp, Geoffrey. "The Military Build-up: Arms Control or Arms Trade?" *The Middle East and the International System.* Pt. 1:

The Impact of the 1973 War. Adelphi Paper, no. 114. London: International Institute for Strategic Studies, 1975, pp. 31–37.

7060   Klare, Michael T. "The Political Economy of Arms Sales." *Society* 11 (Sept.–Oct. 1974): 41–49.

7061   Lambelet, John C. "A Dynamic Model of the Arms Race in the Middle East, 1953–1965." *General Systems Yearbook* 16 (1971): 145–70.

7062   Meltzer, Ronald M. "The Middle East Arms Race: Suppliers and Recipients." M.A. thesis, San Diego State Univ., 1970.

7063   "Mid East: New Clashes, New Arms Shipments." *U.S. News & World Report* (Feb. 26, 1968): 58–59.

7064   Milstein, Jeffrey S. *Soviet and American Influences on the Arab-Israeli Arms Race: A Quantitative Analysis.* New Haven: Yale Univ. Press, 1970.

7065   Mistrorigo, Luigi. "In Margine Alla Guerra Arabo-Israeliani: Il Commercio della Armi." *Civitas* 24:11–12 (1973): 110–13.

7066   Morris, Joe A. "Pandora's Ammunition Box." *Nation* (Aug. 8, 1966): 109–12.

7067   Newcombe, Hanna. "The Case for an Arms Embargo." *War/Peace Report* 11 (Mar. 1971): 17–19.

7068   "Nixon Treads Cautiously in Middle East Arms Race." *Congressional Quarterly Weekly Report* (Mar. 27, 1970): 880–84.

7069   O'Ballance, Edgar. "Middle East Arms Race." *Army Quarterly* 88 (July 1964): 210–14.

7070   Pajak, Roger F. "Soviet Aid to Iraq and Syria." *Strategic Review* 4 (Winter 1976): 51–59.

7071   ———. "Soviet Arms and Egypt." *Survival* 17 (July–Aug. 1975): 165–73.

7072   ———. *Soviet Arms Aid in the Middle East.* Washington, D.C.: Georgetown Univ., Center for Strategic & International Studies, Jan. 1976.

7073   Peres, Shimon. *David's Sling.* New York: Random House, 1970.

7074   Shapiro, Walter. "Arming the Shah: Alms for the Rich." *Washington Monthly* 6 (Feb. 1976): 28–32.

7075   Smolansky, Oles M. "Moscow and the Arab-Israeli Sector." *Current History* 71 (Oct. 1976): 105–08 ff.

7076   ———. "The Soviet Setback in the Middle East." *Current History* 64 (Jan. 1973): 17–20.

7077   "Stocking the Arsenals of the Middle East." *Atlas* 17 (Jan. 1969): 42–43.

7078   "Tipping the Balance: Arms Balance in Middle East in Arabs' Favor." *Newsweek* (Apr. 29, 1968): 40.

7079   Wagner, Charles. *The Impact of Soviet Arms Introduction into the Middle East: A Missed Opportunity.* Santa Monica: California Arms Control & Foreign Policy Seminar, Mar. 1972. [Reprinted in Willard Beling, ed., *The Middle East: Quest for an American Policy.* New York: State Univ. of New York Press, 1973.]

7080   Weller, Jac. "Israeli Arms Productions." *Ordnance* 55 (May–June 1971): 540–44.

7081   Yodfat, A. Y. "Arms and Influence in Egypt: The Record of Soviet Military Assistance Since June 1967." *New Middle East* 10 (July 1969): 27–32.

Persian Gulf

7082   Berman, Bob, and Stefan H. Leader. "U.S. Arms to the Persian Gulf: $10 Billion Since 1973." *Defense Monitor* 4 (May 1975): 1–8.

7083   Kennedy, Sen. Edward M. "The Persian Gulf: Arms Race or Arms Control?" *Foreign Affairs* 54 (Oct. 1975): 14–35.

7084   Pearton, Maurice. "The Persian Gulf Has a Deadly Little Arms Race." *New York Times,* Dec. 15, 1974.

7085   Tahtinen, Dale R. *Arms in the Persian Gulf.* Washington, D.C.: American Enterprise Institute for Public Policy Research, Mar.–Apr., 1974.

7086   U.S. House. Committee on Foreign Affairs. Hearings: *The Persian Gulf, 1974: Money, Politics, Arms and Power.* 94th Cong., 1st Sess., 1975.

7087   ———. Hearings: *The Persian Gulf, 1975: The Continuing Debate on Arms Sales.* 94th Cong., 1st Sess., 1976.

Treaties, Embargoes & Conventional Weapons

7088 Atwater, Elton. "Administration of Export and Import Embargoes, 1935–1936." *Geneva Studies* 9:12 (1938): 1–64.

7089 Chamberlain, Joseph P. "The Embargo Resolutions and Neutrality: Text of the Resolutions, the Treaty of St. Germain and the Trade in Arms Convention." *International Conciliation*, no. 251 (June 1929): 259–342.

7090 ———. "Equality of Belligerents and the Embargo Resolutions." *Annals of the Amer. Acad. of Pol. & Soc. Sci.* 144 (July 1929): 55–58.

7091 Clark, Evans, ed. *Boycotts and Peace: A Report by the Committee on Economic Sanctions.* New York: Harper, 1932.

7092 Feidornowicz, de Georges. "Historical Survey of the Applications of Sanctions." *Transactions of the Grotius Society* 22 (1936): 117–31.

7093 Losman, Donald L. "International Boycotts: An Appraisal." *Politico* 37:4 (1972): 648–72.

7094 Patch, Buell W. "Boycotts and Embargoes." *Editorial Research Reports* (Mar. 17, 1932): 193–209.

7095 Siedman, J. I. "Munitions Manufacture and Arms Embargoes." *Editorial Research Reports* (June 1, 1934): 367–80.

7096 Weaver, Charles R. "Arms Embargoes and the Traffic in Munitions." *Editorial Research Reports* (May 11, 1933): 339–54.

ISRAEL DISARMED (1100 B.C.)

For text of account which suggests Israelites were disarmed, see Holy Bible (King James Version), I Samuel 13:19, 20.

7097 Burn, Andrew R. *Minoans, Philistines and Greeks, B.C. 1400–900.* New York: Knopf, 1930, pp. 160, 163–64.

7098 Hindson, Edmond E. *The Philistines and the Old Testament.* Grand Rapids: Baker Book House, 1971, pp. 109–10, 124, 150.

7099 Macalister, R. A. S. *History of the Philistine Nation.* London: British Academy, 1914, pp. 65, 96.

7100 ———. *The Philistines: Their History and Civilization.* The Schweich Lectures—1911. Chicago: Argonaut, 1965, pp. 125–26.

RESTRAINT OF ARMS TRADE TO CHINA (1919)

For text of this eight-power agreement to restrain sale of arms and munitions to Chinese factions, see W. Mallory, *Treaties, Conventions, International Acts, Protocols, and Agreements between the United States of America and Other Powers, 1910–1923* (Washington, D.C.: G.P.O., 1910–1938), III: 3821.

7101 Atwater, Elton. "China: The Arms Embargo Agreement of 1919." *American Regulation of Arms Exports.* Washington, D.C.: Carnegie Endowment for International Peace, 1941 [1971], pp. 122–43.

7102 Fox, Charles J. *The Arms Embargo Against China.* Tientsin: The North China Star, 1925.

7103 Reinsch, Paul S. *An American Diplomat in China.* New York: Doubleday, Page, 1922, pp. 341–42, 344–45.

7104 U.S. Department of State. *Papers Relating to the Foreign Relations of the United States, 1919.* Washington, D.C.: G.P.O., 1934, I: 290–92, 667–73; *1920*, I: 576–80, 741–42; *1922*, I: 725–45; *1923*, I: 606–16; *1924*, I: 530–43.

TREATY OF ST. GERMAIN (1919)

For text of treaty, see League of Nations, *Treaty Series* (London: Harrison, 1922), pp. 333–59.

Documents

7105 U.S. Department of State. *Foreign Relations of the United States, 1920.* Washington, D.C.: G.P.O., 1935, pp. 196–207; *1922*, I: 543–56; *1923*, I: 37–47; *1924*, I: 17–19 ff.

General Accounts

7106 Atwater, Elton. *American Regulation of Arms Exports.* Washington, D.C.: Carnegie Endowment for International Peace, 1941, pp. 172–75.

7107   "Convention for the Control of the Trade in Arms and Ammunition and Protocol, Signed at Saint-Germain-en-Laye, Sept. 10, 1919." *International Conciliation*, no. 164 (July 1921): 235–58.

7108   SIPRI. *The Arms Trade with the Third World.* New York: Humanities Press, 1971, pp. 91–93.

7109   "The United States and the St. Germain Treaties." *Foreign Policy Association Information Service* 4 (Jan. 1929): 425–36.

CONVENTION FOR SUPERVISION OF ARMS TRADE (1925)

For text of convention, see "Convention for the Supervision of Trade in Arms and War Munitions," *American Journal of International Law* 20 (Jan. 1926): 151–54. [Not ratified.]

Documents

7110   League of Nations. Secretariat. *Conference for the Supervision of the International Trade in Arms and Ammunition and in Implements of War—Preparatory Documents.* Doc. C.758.M.258.1924.IX. Geneva, 1924.

7111   ———. *Conference for the Supervision of the International Trade in Arms and Ammunition and in Implements of War—Proceedings.* Doc. A.13.1925.IX. Geneva, May 4–June 17, 1925.

7112   ———. *Supervision of the Private Manufacture of Arms and Ammunition and Implements of War—Report of the Third Committee.* Geneva, 1926.

7113   U.S. Senate. Committee on Foreign Relations. Hearings: *Supervision of International Trade in Arms, Convention for Supervision of International Trade in Arms and Ammunition and in Implements of War, Signed Geneva, Switzerland, June 17, 1925.* 69th Cong., 1st Sess., 1926.

7114   ———. Report: *Convention for Supervision of International Trade in Arms and Ammunition and Implements of War, Signed Geneva, Switzerland, June 17, 1925.* 73d Cong., 2d Sess., 1934.

7115   ———. "Debate and Ratification of the 1925 Arms Traffic Convention, with Reserva-

tions." 74th Cong., 1st Sess. *Congressional Record* 79 (June 6, 1935), pt. 8, pp. 8783–96.

General Accounts

7116   "Arms, Gas and Germs at Geneva." *Literary Digest* (July 4, 1925): 12.

7117   Baldwin, E. F. "Arms and the Man." *Outlook* 40 (Aug. 1925): 486–87.

7118   "Conference for Control of the International Traffic in Arms." *Editorial Research Reports* (Apr. 27, 1925): 225–35.

7119   "Conference for the Supervision of the International Trade in Arms and Ammunition and in Implements of War." *Advocate of Peace* 87 (Sept. 1925): 546–57.

7120   Lange, C. L. "Control of the Traffic in and the Manufacture of Arms and War Munitions." *Inter-Parliamentary Bulletin* 6 (Nov. 1926): 148–55.

7121   ———. "Control of the Traffic in and the Manufacture of Arms and War Munitions." *Inter-Parliamentary Bulletin* 7 (Jan. 1927): 6–13.

7122   League of Nations. "Conference for the International Control of the Trade in Arms." *League of Nations Monthly Summary* (June 15, 1925): 125–26.

7123   ———. "Conference for the Supervision of the International Trade in Arms and Ammunition and in Implements of War." *Official Journal* 6 (Aug. 1925): 1117–86.

7124   ———. "Letter from the Persian Government to the Secretary-General of the League [resents 1925 Convention]." *Official Journal* 12 (Aug. 1931): 1583–85.

7125   Miles, M. "International Traffic in Arms." *English Review* 32 (Jan. 1926): 37–47.

7126   Royal Institute of International Affairs. *Survey of International Affairs, 1925.* London: Oxford Univ. Press, 1926, pp. 69–71.

7127   "Supervision of the Private Manufacture of Arms and Ammunition and of Implements of War: Report of the [League's] Third Committee." *World Peace Foundation* (Sept. 17, 1926).

7128   "Traffic in Arms Conference." *World Tomorrow* (July 1925): 216.

7129 Wigmore, J. H. "Legislative Summary of the Sixth Assembly (1925) of the League of Nations." *Illinois Law Review* 20 (Jan. 1926): 475–83.

TREATY OF PARIS (1930)

For text of this agreement regulating the trade in arms and ammunition to Ethiopia, see League of Nations, *Official Journal* 12 (Mar. 1931): 547–57.

Documents

7130 League of Nations. "Dispute between Ethiopia and Italy: Coordination of Measures under Article 16 of the Covenant." *Official Journal: Special Supplement*, no. 145. Geneva, 1935.

7131 ———. "Dispute between Ethiopia and Italy: Coordination of Measures under Article 16 of the Covenant." *Official Journal: Special Supplement*, no. 150. Geneva, 1936.

7132 ———. "Note from Ministers of France, United Kingdom, and Italy to the Ethiopian Government, 1934." *Official Journal* 16 (Nov. 1935): 1479–80.

7133 ———. "Regulation of the Importation of Arms and Ammunition and of Implements of War into Abyssinia." C.713.1930.IX. *Official Journal* 12 (Mar. 1931): 547–57.

7134 ———. "Traffic in Arms and Ammunition [to Ethiopia]." *Official Journal* 16 (Nov. 1935): 1410–12.

7135 [Roosevelt, Pres. Franklin D.]. "Embargo by United States on Exports of Arms to Italy and Ethiopia: Proclamation. . . ." *Commercial and Financial Chronicle* (Oct. 12, 1935): 2366–67.

General Accounts

7136 Atwater, Elton. "Administration of Export and Import Embargoes, 1935–1936." *Geneva Studies* 9:6 (1938): 1–64.

7137 Braddick, H. B. "A New Look at American Policy during the Italo-Ethiopian Crisis, 1935–1936." *Journal of Modern History* 34 (Mar. 1962): 64–73.

7138 Costi, Robert L. "To Stop a War: Efforts by the League of Nations and the U.S. to Place Economic Restrictions on Italy during the Italo-Ethiopian War." Ph.D. diss., Univ. of Idaho, 1973.

7139 Harris, Brice, Jr. *The United States and the Italo-Ethiopian Crisis.* Stanford: Stanford Univ. Press, 1964, pp. 53–96.

7140 Highley, Albert E. *The Actions of the States Members of the League of Nations in Application of Sanctions Against Italy, 1935–1936.* Geneva: Geneva Research Centre, 1938.

7141 ———. "The First Sanctions Experiment: A Study of the League's Procedures." *Geneva Studies* 9:4 (July 1938): 7–63.

7142 Walters, Francis. *A History of the League of Nations.* 2 vols. London: Oxford Univ. Press, 1952, II: 623–91.

SINO-JAPANESE ARMS EMBARGO (1933)

A British effort to organize an embargo of arms to Far Eastern combatants—it failed.

7143 "Arms Embargo in the Far East." *Christian Century* (Mar. 15, 1933): 349–50.

7144 "British Arms Embargo." *Current History* 38 (Apr. 1933): 125–27.

7145 "Great Britain's Embargo on Arms to Japan and China." *Nation* (Mar. 8, 1933): 245 ff.

7146 Medlicott, W. N., et al. *Documents on British Foreign Policy, 1919–1939.* 2d series. London: H.M.S.O., XI: 379 ff.

7147 Rasmussen, O. D. "Arms Embargo and Armament Industry: What Pacifists Overlook." *China Critic* [Shanghai] (Jan. 19, 1933): 63–64.

7148 Thorne, Christopher. "The Quest for Arms Embargoes: Failure in 1933." *Journal of Contemporary History* 5:4 (1970): 129–49.

LEAGUE-SANCTIONED EMBARGO OF CHACO WAR (1934)

For text of League Resolution and responses by Nations, see League of Nations, "Dispute between Bolivia and Paraguay [May 19, 1934]," *Official Journal* 15 (July 1934): 765–66, 828–40; 15 (Nov. 1934): 1594–611.

Documents

7149 Argentina. Ministerio de Relaciones Exteriores y Culto. *La Conferencia de Paz del Chaco, 1935–1936.* Buenos Aires, 1939.

7150 League of Nations. "Dispute between Bolivia and Paraguay. . . ." *Official Journal: Special Supplement,* no. 124. Extracts from Records of the Fifteenth Ordinary Session of the Assembly. Geneva, 1934, pp. 28–46, 48–51, 167–68.

7151 ———. "Supply of Arms and War Material to Bolivia and Paraguay: Question of the Withdrawal of the Prohibition of that Supply." *Official Journal* 16 (July 1935): 905–08; 16 (Sept. 1935): 985–88; 16 (Dec. 1935): 1654–55.

7152 [Roosevelt, Pres. Franklin D.]. "Proclamation Prohibiting the Sale of Arms and Munitions of War to Bolivia and Paraguay, 1934." *American Journal of International Law* 28 (July 1934): 134–35.

7153 U.S. Department of State. *Chaco Peace Conference: Report of Delegation of United States to Peace Conference Held at Buenos Aires, July 1, 1935–January 23, 1939.* Washington, D.C.: G.P.O., 1940.

General Accounts

7154 "Arms and the Chaco." *Economist* (May 26, 1934): 1129–30.

7155 "Arms Traffic and the Chaco War." *Commercial and Financial Chronicle* (May 26, 1934): 3491–92.

7156 "Chaco Arms Embargo Still Unenforced." *Christian Century* 51 (June 1934): 819–20.

7157 Cooper, Russell, and Mary A. Mattison. "The Chaco Dispute." *Geneva Special Studies* 5:2 (1934): 1–25.

7158 Fenwick, Charles G. "The Arms Embargo Against Bolivia and Paraguay." *American Journal of International Law* 28 (July 1934): 534–38.

7159 Garner, William P. *The Chaco Dispute: A Study of Prestige Diplomacy.* Washington, D.C.: Public Affairs Press, 1966.

7160 Gillette, Michael L. "Huey Long and the Chaco War." *Louisiana History* 11 (Fall 1970): 293–311.

7161 Hudson, Manley O. "The Chaco Arms Embargo." *International Conciliation,* no. 320 (May 1936): 217–46.

7162 Kain, Ronald S. "Behind the Chaco War." *Current History* 42:5 (Aug. 1935): 468–74.

7163 ———. "The Chaco Dispute and the Peace System." *Political Science Quarterly* 50 (Sept. 1935): 321–42.

7164 Kirkpatrick, Helen P. "The League of Nations and Chaco Dispute." *Foreign Policy Reports* 12 (July 1934): 110–20.

7165 La Foy, M. "The Chaco Dispute and the League of Nations." Ph.D. diss., Bryn Mawr, 1941 [1946].

7166 Meister Jurg. "Der Krieg zwischen Bolivien und Paraguay, 1932–1935." *Schweizer Soldat* 47 (June 1972): 4–5.

7167 Rout, Leslie B. *Politics of the Chaco Peace Conference, 1935–1939.* Austin: Univ. of Texas Press, 1970.

7168 "The Traffic in Arms: The Chaco Report and Its Effects." *Manchester Guardian Weekly* (May 25, 1934): 405 ff.

7169 Walters, Francis. *A History of the League of Nations.* 2 vols. London: Oxford Univ. Press, 1952, II: 524–40.

7170 Wood, Bryce. *The United States and Latin American Wars, 1932–1942.* New York: Columbia Univ. Press, 1966, pp. 62–65 ff.

7171 Zook, Capt. David H., Jr. *The Conduct of the Chaco War.* New Haven: Yale Univ. Press, 1961.

Non-Intervention Committee (1937)

For text of "rules governing committee," see William E. Waters, *International Committee for the Application Regarding Non-Intervention in Spain* (New York: Exposition, 1971).

Documents

7172 League of Nations. "Appeal by the Spanish Government [for enforcement of non-intervention policy]." *Official Journal* 18 (Jan. 1937): 8–21, 35; 18 (Mar.–Apr. 1937): 262–64; 18 (May–June 1937): 317–26, 333–34; 18 (July 1937): 602–03.

7173 U.S. Department of State. *Documents on German Foreign Policy, 1918–1945.* Series D (1937–1945). Washington, D.C.: G.P.O., 1950, III: 423–95.

7174 ———. *Foreign Relations of the United States, 1936.* Washington, D.C.: G.P.O., 1954, II: 447–626; *1937*, I: 464–605; *1938*, I: 345–64.

General Accounts

7175 Allen, David E., Jr. "The Soviet Union and the Spanish Civil War, 1936–1939." Ph.D. diss., Stanford Univ., 1952.

7176 Beloff, Max. *The Foreign Policy of Soviet Russia, 1929–1941.* 2 vols. Norwich, Eng.: Page, 1949, II: 28–38.

7177 Belumelburg, Werner. *Kampf um Spanien: Die Geschichte der Legion Condor.* Berlin: Stalling, 1939.

7178 Busch, Fritz Otto. *Kampf vor Spaniens Kusten.* Leipzig: Schneider, 1939.

7179 Carlton, David. "Eden, Blum, and the Origins of Non-Intervention." *Journal of Contemporary History* 6:3 (1971): 40–55.

7180 Cattell, David C. *Soviet Diplomacy and the Spanish Civil War.* Berkeley: Univ. of California Press, 1957, pp. 14–70, 97–122.

7181 Cot, Pierre. *Triumph of Treason.* New York: Ziff-Doris, 1944, pp. 336–56.

7182 "Embargo on Arms to Spain: Letters to the *New York Times* by H. L. Stimson and C. C. Burlingham." *International Conciliation*, no. 348 (Mar. 1939): 117–38.

7183 Finch, G. A. "The United States and the Spanish Civil War." *American Journal of International Law* 31 (Jan. 1937): 74–80.

7184 Garner, James W. "Question of International Law in the Spanish Civil War." *American Journal of International Law* 31 (Jan. 1937): 66–73.

7185 "Lift the Embargo." *Nation* (Jan. 21, 1939): 77–78.

7186 Lore, Ludwig. "Has Britain Betrayed Spain?" *New Republic* (Mar. 3, 1937): 99–100.

7187 ———. "Intervention in Spain: How the Rebellion Started and What Kept It Going." *Current History* 45 (Nov. 1936): 40–45.

7188 Maisky, Ivan. *Spanish Notebooks.* Trans. by Ruth Kirsch. London: Hutchinson, 1966, pp. 27–37, 123–73, 184–203.

7189 Mowat, Robert B. *The Fight for Peace.* Bristol, Eng.: Arrowsmith, 1937.

7190 "Now It Can be Told." *Nation* (June 17, 1939): 688–89.

7191 Padelford, Norman J. *International Law and Diplomacy in the Spanish Civil Strife.* New York: Macmillan, 1939.

7192 "Pro-Fascist Neutrality." *Nation* (Jan. 9, 1937): 33–34.

7193 "Shipping Arms to Spain." *New Republic* (Jan. 13, 1937): 315–16.

7194 "Spanish Helpers: Extent of German, Italian and Red Intervention Revealed." *Newsweek* (June 12, 1939): 20–21.

7195 Thomas, Hugh. *The Spanish Civil War.* New York: Harper & Row, 1961, pp. 257–64, 394–98.

7196 Vedovato, Giuseppe. *Il Non Intervento in Spagna.* 3 vols. Florence: Studio Fiorentino di Politica Estera, 1940.

7197 Walters, Francis. *A History of the League of Nations.* 2 vols. London: Oxford Univ. Press, 1952, II: 721–30.

TRIPARTITE ARMS DECLARATION (1950)

For text of declaration, see "Tripartite Declaration Regarding Security in the Near East," *U.S. Department of State Bulletin* (June 5, 1950): 886.

Documents

7198 Hurewitz, J. C. "Statement by Prime Minister of 'abd-al-Nasir's Government [on Egypt-Czech Arms Purchase Agreement]." *Diplomacy in the Near and Middle East: A Documentary Record.* 2 vols. Princeton: Van Nostrand, 1956, II: 401–05.

7199 ———. "Tripartite [Britain, France and United States] Declaration on Security in the Arab-Israel Zone." *Diplomacy in the Near and Middle East.* 2 vols. Princeton: Van Nostrand, 1956, II: 308–11.

7200 Magnus, Ralph H., ed. "Peace and Stability in the Middle East: Tripartite Declaration of the United States, the United Kingdom and France [May 25, 1950]." *Documents on the Middle East.* Washington, D.C.: American Enterprise Institute for Public Policy Research, 1969, pp. 163–64.

7201   ———. "Reaffirmation of the Tripartite Declaration by the United States: Statement by the President [Nov. 9, 1955]." *Documents on the Middle East.* Washington, D.C.: American Enterprise Institute for Public Policy Research, 1969, pp. 166–67.

General Accounts

7202   Campbell, John C. *Defense of the Middle East: Problems of American Policy.* Rev. ed. New York: Harper & Row, 1960.

7203   "Common Front on the Middle East." *Time* (June 5, 1950): 24.

7204   Fitzsimons, Matthew A. *Empire by Treaty: Britain in the Middle East in the Twentieth Century.* Notre Dame: Univ. of Notre Dame Press, 1964.

7205   "Foreign Ministers Conference: Arms for the Middle East." *Current History* 19 (July 1950): 43–44.

7206   Gottheil, Fred M. "An Economic Assessment of the Military Burden of the Middle East: 1960–1970." *Journal of Conflict Resolution* 43:3 (1974): 502–13.

7207   Horelick, Arnold L. "Soviet Policy in the Middle East: Policy from 1955 to 1969." In P. Hammond and S. Alexander, eds., *Political Dynamics in the Middle East.* New York: American Elsevier, 1972, pp. 553–604.

7208   Hurewitz, J. C. *Middle East Politics: The Military Dimension.* New York: Praeger, 1969.

7209   Jabber, Fuad. "The Politics of Arms Transfer and Control: The Case of the Middle East." Ph.D. diss., Univ. of California, Los Angeles, 1974.

7210   Lehrman, Hal. "Arms for Arabs—And What for Israel? Dilemmas in the Search for a Middle East Balance of Power." *Commentary* 18 (Nov. 1954): 423–33.

7211   "Near East Solution?" *Nation* (June 3, 1950): 541–42.

7212   Quandt, William B. "United States Policy in the Middle East: Constraints and Choices." In P. Hammond and S. Alexander, eds., *Political Dynamics in the Near East.* New York: American Elsevier, 1972, pp. 489–551.

7213   Shrvadran, Benjamin. "Arms for the Middle East." *Middle Eastern Affairs* 1 (June–July 1950): 167–79.

U.N. Embargo of Arms to South Africa (1963)

For text of United Nations resolution, see United Nations, Security Council, *Official Records 18th Year, Supplement for July, August, and September 1963*, Doc. S/5386 (New York, 1964), pp. 73–74.

Documents

7214   U.N. General Assembly. *Report of the Special Committee on the Policies of Apartheid of the Government of South Africa, 18th Session.* A/5453, A/5497, A/6284, A/6864. New York, 1963.

7215   ———. *Special Committee on the Policies of Apartheid of the Government of the Republic of South Africa.* A/AC 115/SR. 345, 363, 365, 367, 371. New York, 1964.

7216   ———. Security Council. *Report of the Special Committee on the Policies of Apartheid of the Government of the Republic of South Africa.* S/8196/Add.1, S/6257, S/8843. New York, 1967.

7217   ———. *Security Council, 18th Year, Supplement for October, November, and December, 1963.* Doc. S/5438 & Add. 1–6. New York, 1964, pp. 7–40.

7218   U.S. House. Committee on Foreign Affairs. Hearings: *United States-South Africa Relations.* 4 pts. 89th Cong., 2d Sess., 1966.

General Accounts

7219   Abrous, A. "OAU and Arms Sales to South Africa." *Africa Quarterly* 11 (Apr.–June 1971): 2–10.

7220   "Apartheid and Atlantic Defense System." *Africa Today* 17 (Sept.–Oct. 1970): 40–42.

7221 "Arms Embargo Against South Africa and U.N. Security Council." *Indian and Foreign Review* (Aug. 1, 1970): 6–7.

7222 Bacskai, Tamas. "Apartheid . . . A Look Behind the Facade in South Africa." *Active Co-Existence* 13 (July–Sept. 1967): 1–13.

7223 Bunting, Brian. *The Rise of the South African Reich.* Baltimore: Penguin, 1969.

7224 "Foreign Investment in South Africa." *U.N. Monthly Chronicle* (June 1967): 50–51.

7225 Hollingsworth, J. Rogers. "Arms and Apartheid: The U.S. Should Cut Loose." *Nation* (Mar. 29, 1971): 390–94.

7226 Horwitz, Ralph. "South Africa: The Background to Sanctions." *Political Quarterly* 42 (June 1971): 163–76.

7227 Leiss, Amelia C., ed. *Apartheid and United Nations Collective Measures.* New York: Carnegie Endowment for International Peace, 1965.

7228 U.N. Security Council. "Resolution on Arms Embargo Against South Africa." *International Legal Materials* 9 (Sept. 1970): 1091–92.

7229 Venter, Al J. "South Africa's Military/Industrial Complex." *International Defense Review* 4 (Dec. 1971): 547–48.

7230 Walters, Ronald W. "The Formulation of the United States Foreign Policy towards Africa." Ph.D. diss., American Univ., 1971.

South Africa's Arms Trade

7231 "Arms for South Africa." *Intelligence Digest* 350 (Jan. 1968): 10–11.

7232 "Arms for South Africa." *Labour Research* 59 (Dec. 1970): 193–95.

7233 Christie, Michael J. *The Simonstown Agreements: Britain's Defense and the Sale of Arms to South Africa.* London: Africa Bureau, Sept. 1970.

7234 Coleman, Herbert J. "U.K. Rejects South Africa Defense Order." *Aviation Week & Space Technology* (Dec. 25, 1967): 20.

7235 Gruhn, Isebill W. *British Arms Sales to South Africa: The Limits of African Diplo-* *macy.* 3:3. Denver: Center on International Race Relations, Univ. of Denver, 1971–1972.

7236 Hinterhoff, Maj. Eugene. "Arms for South Africa." *NATO's Fifteen Nations* 16 (Feb.–Mar. 1971): 26–33.

7237 Hughes, Anthony. "Arms and South Africa." In Colin Legum, ed., *Africa Contemporary Record: Annual Survey and Documents, 1970–1971.* London: Rex Collings, 1971, pp. A3–A10, C16–C34.

7238 International Defense and Aid Fund. *South Africa: Arms and Apartheid.* London: Christian Action Publications, 1970.

7239 Kum Buo, Sammy. "Fortress South Africa." *Africa Report* 20 (Jan.–Feb. 1975): 11–16.

7240 Lipton, Merle. "British Arms for South Africa." *World Today* 26 (Oct. 1970): 427–34.

7241 Miers, Sue. "Notes on the Arms Trade and Government Policy in Southern Africa." *Journal of African History* 12:4 (1971): 571–77.

7242 "South Africa's Access to Armaments." *Strategic Survey, 1972.* London: International Institute for Strategic Studies, 1972.

Arguments Supporting Arms Trade with South Africa

7243 Rippon, Geoffrey. "South Africa and Naval Strategy: The Importance of South Africa." *Round Table* 239 (July 1970): 303–09.

7244 Spence, J. E. "South Africa and the Defense of the West." *Round Table* 241 (Jan. 1971): 15–23.

U.N. EMBARGO OF ARMS TO PORTUGAL (1963)

For text of United Nations resolution banning arms shipments to Portuguese colonies, see United Nations, Security Council, *Official Records, Supplement for July, Aug., Sept., 1963*, S/5448 (New York, 1964), pp. 55–56.

Documents

7245 U.N. Security Council. *Official Records, Supplement for Oct., Nov., Dec., 1963.* S/5448. New York, 1964, pp. 55–56.

General Accounts

7246   Davidson, Basil. "Arms and the Portuguese: NATO's Role." *Africa Report* 15 (May 1970): 10–11.

7247   Minter, William. "Allies in Empire: Part II—U.S. Military Involvement." *Africa Today* 17 (July–Aug. 1970): 28–32.

7248   Stanley, John, and Maurice Pearton. *The International Trade in Arms*. New York: Praeger, 1972, pp. 1965–72.

7249   U.S. House. Committee on Foreign Affairs. Hearings: *Implementation of the U.S. Arms Embargo* [Against Portugal and South Africa . . .]. 93d Cong., 1st Sess., 1973.

Twelve

Controlling Proliferation of Nuclear Weapons

NUCLEAR PROLIFERATION, A columnist recently noted, "is a subject that totally bores most people. But the fact remains that it could affect, quite decisively, whether by 1990 or so there will be any world left in which to be bored." These observations were prompted by SIPRI's projection that by 1980 nuclear power reactors at work in nations that do not now have nuclear weapons would be capable of producing enough plutonium each week to make 10 Nagasaki-type A-bombs.

Since 1960 there have been many similar warnings describing the perils of nuclear proliferation. William Epstein's *The Last Chance: Nuclear Proliferation and Arms Control* (1976) is the most recent of a number of excellent books which survey the dangers a lack of controls promises, and which illuminate the problems which must be overcome if controls are to become effective. The volumes by W. B. Bader, G. H. Quester, and M. Willrich, listed early in this chapter, elaborate the political and economic dilemmas that nations must deal with in order to achieve any substantive control over the nuclear spread.

A few writers have argued either that the problem of controlling proliferation is impossible—so one should learn to live in a world of nuclear-armed states—or that proliferation could, contrary to the popular view, enhance world peace by reestablishing the global balance-of-power—this time based on nuclear weapons. These criticisms of regulating proliferation can be found in F. O. Miksche, "The Case for Nuclear Sharing," *Orbis* (1961) and D. A. Robison, "Learning to Live with Nuclear Spread," *Air Force & Space Digest* (1966).

The problem of adequate verification and control systems ("safeguards") has ranked high among the many issues associated with regulating nuclear development in accordance with treaty restrictions. A. D. McKnight's many writings on this subject, such as *Nuclear Non-Proliferation: IAEA and Euratom* (1970), and G. H. Quester's "The Nuclear Nonproliferation Treaty and the International Atomic Energy Agency," *International Organization* (1969), illustrate the questions raised by the search for technical and political safeguards.

In 1975 a review conference was held by the nations signatory to the Nonproliferation Treaty of 1968, for the purpose of reexamining the premise of the treaty and for evaluating its functioning. Most analysts were pessimistic on the eve of the conference, and the essays reviewing the results of these discussions confirmed this initial view. W. Epstein's essays, as well as those of T. A. Halsted, convey that much shoring-up of the basic treaty must be done, and quickly, or efforts to control the proliferation of nuclear weapons will come to naught.

7250 Arms Control Assoc. *NPT: Paradoxes and Problems*. Washington, D.C.: Carnegie Endowment for International Peace, 1975.

7251 Bader, William B. *The United States and the Spread of Nuclear Weapons*. New York: Pegasus, 1968.

7252 Barnaby, Frank, ed. *Preventing the Spread of Nuclear Weapons*. Pugwash Monograph, no. 1. New York: Humanities Press, 1969.

7253 Beaton, Leonard. *Must the Bomb Spread?* London: Penguin, 1966.

7254 ———, and John Maddox. *The Spread of Nuclear Weapons*. New York: Praeger, 1962.

7255 Bendix Corp. *Problems of U.S. Defense Policy in a World of Nuclear Proliferation*. 2 vols. Ann Arbor, 1966.

7256 Boskey, Bennett, and Mason Willrich, eds. *Nuclear Proliferation: Prospects for Control*. New York: Dunellen, 1970.

7257 Buchan, Alastair, ed. *A World of Nuclear Powers*. Englewood Cliffs, N.J.: Prentice-Hall, 1966.

7258 Burns, Arthur Lee. *Power Politics and the Growing Nuclear Club*. Policy Memo, no. 20. Princeton: Princeton Univ., Center of International Studies, June 1959.

7259 Epstein, William. *The Last Chance: Nuclear Proliferation and Arms Control*. New York: Free Press, 1976.

7260 Fischer, George. *The Non-Proliferation of Nuclear Weapons*. Trans. by David Wiley. New York: St. Martin's Press, 1971.

7261 Jensen, Lloyd. *Return from the Nuclear Brink: National Interest and the Nuclear Non-Proliferation Treaty*. Lexington, Mass.: D. C. Heath, 1973.

7262 Kertesz, Stephen D., ed. *Nuclear Non-Proliferation in a World of Nuclear Powers*. Notre Dame: Univ. of Notre Dame Press, 1967.

7263 Lall, Betty Goetz. *Nuclear Weapons: Can Their Spread Be Halted?* New York: Council on Religion & International Affairs, 1965.

7264 Quester, George H. *The Politics of Nuclear Proliferation*. Baltimore: Johns Hopkins Press, 1973.

7265 Rakove, Milton L., ed. *Arms and Foreign Policy in the Nuclear Age*. New York: Oxford Univ. Press, 1972.

7266   Rosecrance, Richard N., ed. *The Dispersion of Nuclear Weapons: Strategy and Politics.* New York: Columbia Univ. Press, 1964.

7267   ———. *Problems of Nuclear Proliferation.* Los Angeles: Univ. of California Press, 1966.

7268   SIPRI. *Nuclear Proliferation Problems.* Cambridge: M.I.T. Press, 1974.

7269   U.S. Department of State. *Problems of Nuclear Proliferation: Technology and Politics.* [By R. N. Rosecrance.] Washington, D.C.: G.P.O., 1966.

7270   Van Cleave, William R. "Nuclear Proliferation: The Interaction of Politics and Technology." Ph.D. diss., Claremont Graduate School, 1967.

7271   Wentz, Walter B. *Nuclear Proliferation.* Washington, D.C.: Public Affairs Press, 1968.

7272   Willrich, Mason. *Non-Proliferation Treaty: Framework for Nuclear Arms Control.* Charlottesville, Va.: Michie, 1969.

7273   Zuckerman, Sir Solly; Alva Myrdal; and Lester B. Pearson. *The Control of Proliferation: Three Views.* Adelphi Paper, no. 29. London: Institute for Strategic Studies, 1966.

These essays are pre-treaty comments, suggestions, and evaluations of the problems; for later essays, see subsequent headings below.

7274   Aiken, Frank. "Can We Limit the Nuclear Club?" *Bulletin of the Atomic Scientists* 17 (Sept. 1961): 263–66.

7275   Aron, Raymond. "The Spread of Nuclear Weapons." *Atlantic Monthly* (Jan. 1965): 44–50.

7276   Beaton, Leonard. "Nuclear Proliferation." *Science Journal* 3 (Dec. 1967): 35–40.

7277   Bobrow, Davis B. "Realism about Nuclear Spread." *Bulletin of the Atomic Scientists* 21 (Dec. 1965): 20–22.

7278   Brennan, Donald G. "The Risks of Spreading Weapons: A Historical Case." *Arms Control and Disarmament* 1 (1968): 56–60.

7279   Brodie, Richard A. "Some Systematic Effects of the Spread of Nuclear Weapons Technology: A Study through Simulation of a Multi-Nuclear Future." *Journal of Conflict Resolution* 7:4 (1963): 663–753.

7280   Buchan, Alastair. "The Politics of Nonproliferation." *Listener* (May 11, 1967): 607–09.

7281   Bull, Hedley. "The Role of the Nuclear Powers in the Management of Nuclear Proliferation." In James E. Dougherty and John F. Lehman, Jr., eds., *Arms Control for the Late Sixties.* Princeton: Van Nostrand, 1967, pp. 143–50.

7282   Burns, E. L. M. "Can the Spread of Nuclear Weapons Be Stopped?" *International Organization* 19 (Autumn 1965): 851–69.

7283   Chalfont, Lord Arthur G. J. "Alternatives to Proliferation: Inhibition by Agreement." In Alastair Buchan, ed., *A World of Nuclear Powers.* Englewood Cliffs, N.J.: Prentice-Hall, 1966, pp. 123–42.

7284   ———. "Arms Control or Nuclear Anarchy?" *Review of International Affairs* (May 5, 1967): 3–6.

7285   ———. "Can We Make the World Drop the Bomb?" *Realities* [London] 190 (Sept. 1966): 34–37.

7286   ———. "On Non-Proliferation: Thinking Ahead with . . . Lord Chalfont." *International Science and Technology* 61 (Jan. 1967): 82–90.

7287   Cockcroft, Sir John D. "The Perils of Nuclear Proliferation." In Nigel Calder, ed., *Unless Peace Comes: A Scientific Forecast of New Weapons.* New York: Viking, 1968, pp. 30–42.

7288   "Coming: Nuclear Bombs for All Nations." *U.S. News & World Report* (Aug. 10, 1964): 48–51.

7289   Cook, Don. "Die Kunst der Non-Proliferation." *Der Monat* (July 1966): 5–12.

7290   Donnelly, Harold C. "How a Nuclear Nonproliferation Treaty Could Work." *Air Force and Space Digest* 50 (Feb. 1967): 52–54.

7291   ———. "Nuclear Proliferation: A Military Point of View." *Vital Speeches* (Jan. 1, 1967): 166–69.

7292   Feld, Bernard T. "The Nonproliferation of Nuclear Weapons." *Bulletin of the Atomic Scientists* 20 (Dec. 1964): 2–6.

7293 Foster, William C.; John A. Hall; and Ralph L. Powell. "Risks of Nuclear Proliferation." *Foreign Affairs* 43 (July 1965): 587–625.

7294 Goldstein, Walter. "Keeping the Genie in the Bottle: The Feasibility of a Nuclear Non-Proliferation Agreement." *Background* 9 (Aug. 1965): 137–46.

7295 ———. "Preventing the Spread of Nuclear Weapons." *War/Peace Report* 3 (Mar. 1965): 14–15.

7296 Griffiths, Franklyn. "Preventing the Spread of Nuclear Weapons." *International Journal* 20 (Autumn 1965): 524–29.

7297 Halperin, Morton H. "A Way to Stop the Spread of Nuclear Weapons." *War/Peace Report* 4 (Aug. 1964): 10–11.

7298 Harrison, Stanley L. "Aspects of Nuclear Diffusion." *Military Review* 42 (Sept. 1962): 92–99.

7299 Hoffman, Stanley. "Nuclear Proliferation and World Politics." In Alastair Buchan, ed., *A World of Nuclear Powers*. Englewood Cliffs, N.J.: Prentice-Hall, 1966, pp. 89–122.

7300 Kahn, Herman. "Nuclear Proliferation and Rules of Retaliation." *Yale Law Journal* 76 (Nov. 1966): 77–91.

7301 ———. "Suggestions for Long-Term Anti-Nuclear Policies." In James E. Dougherty and John F. Lehman, Jr., eds., *Arms Control for the Late Sixties*. Princeton: Van Nostrand, 1967, pp. 162–73.

7302 Kalkstein, Marvin. "Preventing the Spread of Nuclear Weapons." *Bulletin of the Atomic Scientists* 20 (Dec. 1964): 18–19.

7303 Kaysen, Carl, and Jeremy J. Stone. "Keeping the Lid on Nuclear Weapons." *New Republic* (Jan. 15, 1966): 13–14.

7304 Lall, Betty Goetz. "Next: A Proliferation Ban." *Bulletin of the Atomic Scientists* 22 (Jan. 1966): 42–45.

7305 Lvov, M. "A Time of Choice." *Current Digest of the Soviet Press* (Nov. 10, 1965): 21–22.

7306 Martin, Andrew, and Wayland Young. "Proliferation." *Disarmament and Arms Control* 3 (Autumn 1965): 107–34.

7307 Martin, Laurence W. "Non-Proliferation: Who'll Kill Cock Robin?" *Spectator* (Aug. 18, 1967): 183–84.

7308 Miksche, Ferdinand O. "The Case for Nuclear Sharing." *Orbis* 3 (Fall 1961): 292–305.

7309 Niu, Sien-chong. "The Nightmare of Nuclear Proliferation." *Atlantic Community Quarterly* 5 (Summer 1967): 223–33.

7310 "Non-Proliferation of Nuclear Weapons." *U.N. Monthly Chronicle* 2 (Nov. 1965): 18–23.

7311 Norstad, Gen. Lauris. "Who Should Control Nuclear Weapons." *U.S. News & World Report* (Oct. 5, 1964): 47–48.

7312 Robison, David A. "Learning to Live with Nuclear Spread." *Air Force and Space Digest* 49 (Aug. 1966): 56–57 ff.

7313 ———. "Softening the Impact of Nuclear Spread." *Air Force and Space Digest* 49 (Oct. 1966): 82–84 ff.

7314 Schulz, Joachim. "Non-Proliferation of Nuclear Weapons and International Law." *German Foreign Policy* 5:3 (1966): 187–97.

7315 Shestov, V. "No More Nuclear Powers: Concerning the Non-Proliferation of Nuclear Weapons." *International Affairs* [Moscow] 10 (Nov. 1964): 29–34.

7316 Shub, Anatole. "Non-Proliferation for Non-Scientists." *Encounter* 28 (May 1967): 85–90.

7317 Smyth, Henry D. "Nuclear Power and Proliferation." *U.S. Department of State Bulletin* (Jan. 3, 1966): 28–63.

7318 Spinelli, Altiero. "Notes on Non-Proliferation." *Atlantic Community Quarterly* 5 (Summer 1967): 223–33.

7319 Stewart, Charles T., Jr. "Dissemination of Nuclear Weapons." *Military Review* 44 (Oct. 1964): 3–8.

7320 Stone, Jeremy J. "On Proliferation: Where's the Danger?" *Bulletin of the Atomic Scientists* 21 (Nov. 1965): 18–21.

7321 Washburn, A. Michael. "Nuclear Proliferation in a Revolutionary International System." *Public International Affairs* 5 (Spring 1967): 111–33.

7322 "Why the Bombs Haven't Proliferated." *Economist* (Dec. 10, 1966): 1112–13.

7323 Willrich, Mason. "The Future of Nuclear Weapons Containment." *Virginia Quarterly* 42 (Autumn 1966): 497–511.

7324   Zoppo, Ciro E. "Nuclear Technology, Multipolarity and International Stability." *World Politics* 18 (July 1966): 579–606.

NTH COUNTRY DEBATE

7325   Baldwin, Hanson W. "If Sixteen Countries Had the Bomb." *New York Times Magazine* (Feb. 12, 1961): 7, 68–71.

7326   Burns, Arthur Lee. *The Rationale of Catalytic War.* Research Monograph, no. 3. Princeton: Princeton Univ., Center of International Studies, 1959.

7327   Davidson, William C., et al. *The Nth Country Problem and Arms Control: A Statement by the NPA Special Projects Committee on Security through Arms Control and a Technical Report.* Pamphlet no. 108. Washington, D.C.: National Planning Assoc., Jan. 1960.

7328   Davis, W. "Atomic Bomb Countries." *Science News Letter* (June 8, 1963): 359.

7329   Harrison, Stanley L. "Nth Nation Challenges: The Present Perspective." *Orbis* 7 (Spring 1965): 155–70.

7330   ———. *A Review of the Nth Nation Issue.* Res. Paper, P–80. Washington, D.C.: Institute for Defense Analyses, 1963.

7331   Hohenemser, Christoph. "The Nth Country Problem Today." In Seymour Melman, ed., *Disarmament: Its Politics and Economics.* Boston: American Academy of Arts & Sciences, 1962, pp. 238–76.

7332   Ikle, Fred C. *"Nth Countries" and Disarmament.* Rpt. P–1956. Santa Monica, Ca.: Rand, 1960. [Summarized in the *Bulletin of the Atomic Scientists* 16 (Dec. 1960): 391–94.]

7333   Inglis, David R. "The Fourth-Country Problem: Let's Stop at Three." *Bulletin of the Atomic Scientists* 15 (Jan. 1959): 22–26.

7334   "More Countries that Can Make Nuclear Bombs." *U.S. News & World Report* (Dec. 6, 1965): 50–51.

7335   Morgenstern, Oskar. "The Nth Country Problem." *Fortune* 63 (Mar. 1961): 136–37, 205–08.

7336   Schlesinger, James R. "Nuclear Spread." *Yale Review* 57 (Autumn 1967): 66–84.

7337   Tucker, Robert C. *Stability and the Nth Country Problem.* Study Memo, no. 5. Washington, D.C.: Institute for Defense Analyses, 1961.

From 2 to 5—Great Britain, France & China

7338   Augenstein, B. W. "The Chinese and French Programs for Development of National Nuclear Forces." *Orbis* 4 (Fall 1967): 846–63.

7339   Brown, Neville. "Anglo-French Nuclear Collaboration?" *World Today* 25 (Aug. 1969): 351–56.

7340   Joshua, Wynfred, and Walter F. Hahn. *Nuclear Policies: America, France and Britain.* The Washington Papers: Sage Policy Papers Series, vol. 1, no. 480009. Beverly Hills, Ca.: Sage, 1972–1973.

7341   Pierre, Andrew J. "Nuclear Diplomacy: Britain, France, and America." *Foreign Affairs* (Jan. 1971): 283–301.

NATO, MLF & Nonproliferation

7342   Boulton, J. W. "NATO and the MLF." *Journal of Contemporary History* 7:3 (1972): 275–94.

7343   Joiner, Harry M. "NATO and MLF." Ph.D. diss., Univ. of Kentucky, 1971.

7344   Magstadt, Thomas M. "NATO Nuclear Sharing and Non-Proliferation in Soviet Foreign Policy, 1960–1967." Ph.D. diss., Johns Hopkins Univ., 1972.

7345   Maratov, M. "Non-Proliferation and NATO Nuclear Plans." *International Affairs* [Moscow] 12 (Jan. 1966): 18–23.

7346   "Reflections on the Quarter: Nonproliferation and the Future of NATO." *Orbis* 9 (Fall 1965): 539–42.

7347   U.S. Department of Army. *Nuclear Weapons and the Atlantic Alliance: A Bibliographical Survey.* DA Pam 20–66. Washington, D.C.: G.P.O., 1965.

7348   ———. *Nuclear Weapons and NATO: Analytical Survey of Literature.* DA Pam 50–1. Washington, D.C.: G.P.O., 1970.

7349 Wohlstetter, Albert. "Nuclear Sharing: NATO and the Nth-Country." *Foreign Affairs* 39 (Apr. 1961): 361–71.

Great Britain

7350 DeWeerd, Harvey A. "The British Effort to Secure an Independent Deterrent." In Richard N. Rosecrance, ed., *The Dispersion of Nuclear Weapons.* New York: Columbia Univ. Press, 1964, pp. 87–100.

7351 Duncan, Francis. "Atomic Energy and Anglo-American Relations, 1946–1954." *Orbis* 12 (Winter 1969): 1188–1203.

7352 Goldberg, Alfred. "The Atomic Origins of the British Nuclear Deterrent." *International Affairs* [London] 40 (July 1964): 409–29.

7353 Rosecrance, Richard N. "British Incentives to Become a Nuclear Power." *The Dispersion of Nuclear Weapons.* New York: Columbia Univ. Press, 1964, pp. 48–65.

France

7354 Brown, Neville, "DeGaulle's Nuclear Dream." *New Scientist* (July 18, 1968): 139.

7355 ———. "Nuclear Matchmaking Across the Channel." *New Scientist* (June 19, 1969): 635–36.

7356 Fontaine, Andre. "What is French Policy?" *Foreign Affairs* 46 (Oct. 1966): 58–76.

7357 Griswold, Lawrence. "France: The Third Force?" *Sea Power* 16 (Aug. 1973): 137–39.

7358 Kohl, Wilfrid L. *French Nuclear Diplomacy.* Princeton: Princeton Univ. Press, 1971.

7359 Kolodziej, Edward A. "French Strategy Emergent." *World Politics* 19 (Apr. 1967): 417–42.

7360 McKnight, Allan D. "A French Love Affair with Atoms." *Australian Quarterly* 44 (Sept. 1972): 10–15.

7361 Mendl, Wolf. "The Debate over Defense Policy in France: With Special Reference to Nuclear Armament, 1945–1960." Ph.D. diss., Univ. of London, 1967.

7362 ———. *Deterrence and Persuasion: French Nuclear Armaments in the Context of National Policy, 1945–1969.* New York: Praeger, 1970.

7363 "The Political Background of the French A-Bomb." *Orbis* 4 (Fall 1960): 284–306.

7364 Sattler, Donald C. "Nuclear Proliferation: The French Case." *Naval War College Review* 18 (June 1966): 15–55.

7365 Scheinman, Lawrence. *Atomic Energy Policy in France under the Fourth Republic.* Princeton: Princeton Univ. Press, 1965.

7366 Zoppo, Ciro E. "France as a Nuclear Power." In Richard N. Rosecrance, ed., *The Dispersion of Nuclear Weapons.* New York: Columbia Univ. Press, 1964, pp. 113–56.

China

7367 Barcata, Louis. "China's Bomb Shakes India." *Atlas* 9 (Mar. 1965): 162–64.

7368 Barnett, A. Doak. "A Nuclear China." *Survival* 12 (July 1970): 216–26.

7369 ———. "A Nuclear China and U.S. Arms Policy." *Foreign Affairs* 48 (Apr. 1970): 427–42.

7370 Barnett, Col. James W., Jr. "What Price China's Bomb?" *Military Review* 47 (Aug. 1967): 16–23.

7371 "A Bombshell in China: The Dilemma of Indian Defenses." *Round Table* 218 (Mar. 1965): 114–17.

7372 Candlin, A. H. "The Chinese Nuclear Threat." *Army Quarterly and Defense Journal* 92 (Apr. 1966): 50–60.

7373 Cheng, Ch'ien. "A Dragon with Nuclear Teeth." *Military Review* 46 (Oct. 1966): 78–84.

7374 "China and the Bomb." *China Quarterly* 21 (Jan.–Mar. 1965): 74–107.

7375 "China Successfully Conducts Guided Missile-Nuclear Weapon Test." *Peking Review* (Oct. 28, 1966): 2–3.

7376 "China Successfully Conducts New Hydrogen Bomb Test." *Peking Review* (Jan. 3, 1969): 5–6.

7377 "China Successfully Explodes Its First Atom Bomb." *Peking Review* (Oct. 16, 1964): 2–4.

7378 "The Chinese A-Bomb." *Science* (Oct. 30, 1964): 601.

7379 "A Chinese Statement on Nuclear Proliferation." *Bulletin of the Atomic Scientists* 23 (May 1967): 53–54.

7380 Clemens, Walter C., Jr. "China's Nuclear Tests: Trends and Portents." *China Quarterly* 32 (Oct.–Dec. 1967): 111–31.

7381 Evans, Gordon H. "China and the Atom Bomb, I & II." *Royal United Services Institution Journal* 107 (Feb. 1962): 30–35; 107 (May 1962): 130–34.

7382 Feigl, Hubert. "China als Kernwaffenmacht: Pekings Entwicklungsstrategie für nukleare Waffen." *Europa-Archiv* (May 25, 1973): 341–52.

7383 Fix, Col. Joseph E., III. "China—The Nuclear Threat." *Air University Review* 17 (Mar.–Apr. 1966): 28–39.

7384 Frank, Lewis A. "Nuclear Weapons Development in China." *Bulletin of the Atomic Scientists* 22 (Jan. 1966): 12–15.

7385 Gelber, Harry G. *Nuclear Weapons and Chinese Policy.* Adelphi Paper, no. 99. London: International Institute for Strategic Studies, 1973.

7386 Halperin, Morton H. *China and the Bomb*, New York: Praeger, 1965.

7387 ———. *China and Nuclear Proliferation.* Chicago: Univ. of Chicago, Center for Policy Study, 1966.

7388 ———. "China and Nuclear Proliferation." *Bulletin of the Atomic Scientists* 22 (Nov. 1966): 4–10; 22 (Dec. 1966): 18–24.

7389 Hsieh, Alice Langley. "The Test at Lop Nor: Implications for Red China's Strategy." *Military Review* 46 (Mar. 1966): 86–94.

7390 James, Francis. "Mao's Wild, Wild West: China's Nuclear Zone—First on the Inside." *Atlas* 18 (Aug. 1969): 19–23.

7391 Johnson, Chalmers. "China's Manhattan Project." *New York Times Magazine* (Oct. 25, 1964): 23, 117–19.

7392 Kishida, Junnosuke. "Chinese Nuclear Development." *Survival* 9 (Sept. 1967): 298–304.

7393 Kramish, Arnold. "The Great Chinese Bomb Puzzle—And a Solution." *Fortune* 73 (June 1966): 157–58 ff.

7394 Minor, Michael S. "China's Nuclear Development Program." *Asian Survey* 16 (June 1976): 571–79.

7395 "Moscow's New Treachery Denounced by Jenmin Jih-Pao." *Survey of China Mainland Press* (Sept. 12, 1967): 34–35.

7396 "Nuclear Hoax Cannot Save U.S. Imperialists, Soviet Revisionists." *Survey of China Mainland Press* (Sept. 7, 1967): 25–27.

7397 Powell, Ralph L. "China's Bomb: Exploitation and Reactions." *Foreign Affairs* 43 (July 1965): 616–25.

7398 "Red China's Bomb: How It Alters Things in the World." *U.S. News & World Report* (Oct. 26, 1964): 48–50.

7399 Ryan, William, and Sam Summerlin. *The China Cloud.* Boston: Little, Brown, 1968.

7400 Wang, Chi. "Nuclear Research in Mainland China." *Nuclear News* 10 (May 1967): 16–20.

7401 "World of Atoms: Is Red China's H-Bomb A Product of the West?" *Atlas* 16 (Dec. 1968): 22–24.

7402 Yahuda, Michael B. "China's Nuclear Option." *Bulletin of the Atomic Scientists* 25 (Feb. 1969): 72–77.

7403 Young, Oran R. "Chinese Views on the Spread of Nuclear Weapons." *China Quarterly* 26 (Apr.–June 1966): 136–70.

7404 Yuter, S. C. "Preventing Nuclear Proliferation through the Legal Control of China's Bomb." *Orbis* 12 (Winter 1969): 1018–41.

NPT & Review Conference

NONPROLIFERATION TREATY (1968)

For text of treaty, see "Multilateral Treaty on the Non-Proliferation of Nuclear Weapons, July 1, 1968," *U.S. Treaties and Other International Agreements* 21:1 (1970), pp. 483–566. See also, United Nations, "General Assembly Resolution 1665 (XVI)

Prevention of the Wider Dissemination of Nuclear Weapons, Dec. 5, 1961," *Documents on Disarmament, 1961* (Washington, D.C.: G.P.O., 1962), p. 694.

Documents

Also see, U.N. Eighteen-Nation Disarmament Conference, *Records* from 1964 to present; cited under United Nations, above.

7405   Hartung, Arnold, ed. *Zum Atomsperrvertrag: Reden und Erklärungen sowie Dokumente zur Genfer Konferenz, zum NV-Vertrag und zum Europäischen Sicherungssystem.* Berlin: Berlin Verlag, 1969.

7406   U.S. Arms Control & Disarmament Agency. *International Negotiations on the Treaty on the Nonproliferation of Nuclear Weapons.* Pub. 48. Washington, D.C.: G.P.O., 1969.

7407   ———. *To Prevent the Spread of Nuclear Weapons: The United States Draft Treaty to Prevent the Spread of Nuclear Weapons.* Pub. 26. Washington, D.C.: G.P.O., Sept. 1965.

7408   U.S. Joint Committee on Atomic Energy. Hearings: *Nonproliferation of Nuclear Weapons.* Sen. Res. 179. 89th Cong., 2d Sess., Feb. 23, Mar. 1, 7, 1966.

7409   ———. Report: *Nonproliferation of Nuclear Weapons, April 28, 1966.* Sen. Rpt. no. 1141. 89th Cong., 2d Sess., 1966.

Negotiations

7410   Albonetti, Achille, "The NPT Draft under Scrutiny." *Survival* 9 (July 1967): 223–26.

7411   Brezaric, M. "The UN and Non-Proliferation of Nuclear Weapons." *Review of International Affairs* [Belgrade] (May 20, 1968): 12 ff.

7412   Bunn, George. "U.S. Non-Proliferation Policy." In James E. Dougherty and John F. Lehman, Jr., eds., *Arms Control for the Late Sixties.* Princeton: Van Nostrand, 1967, pp. 151–56.

7413   Burns, E. L. M. "The Nonproliferation Treaty: Its Negotiation and Prospects." *International Organization* 23 (Autumn 1969): 788–807.

7414   Cavalletti, Francesco. "An Italian Proposal of Nuclear Moratorium." In James E. Dougherty and John E. Lehman, Jr., eds. *Arms Control for the Late Sixties.* Princeton: Van Nostrand, 1967, pp. 157–61.

7415   *Disarmament: Negotiations and Treaties, 1946–1971.* Keesing's Research Report, no. 7. New York: Scribner's, 1972, pp. 243–62.

7416   Dougherty, James E. "The Non-Proliferation Treaty." *Russian Review* 25 (Jan. 1966): 10–23.

7417   Douglas, R. N. "United States Anti-Proliferation Policies in the 1960's." *Australian Outlook* 21 (Aug. 1967): 179–97.

7418   Feld, Bernard T. "The Nonproliferation Treaty: In the Cards for 1968?" *Bulletin of the Atomic Scientists* 24 (Mar. 1968): 34–35.

7419   Foster, William C. "Arms Control: A Non-Proliferation Treaty." *Vital Speeches* (Jan. 15, 1966): 199–202.

7420   Goldberg, Arthur J. "United States Discusses Security Assurances and Draft Nonproliferation Treaty." *U.S. Department of State Bulletin* (June 10, 1968): 755–61.

7421   ———. "U.S. Calls for Prompt Endorsement by the U.N. General Assembly of the Draft Treaty on the Nonproliferation of Nuclear Weapons." *U.S. Department of State Bulletin* (May 20, 1968): 635–45.

7422   ———, and William C. Foster. "United States Reviews Position on Nonproliferation of Nuclear Weapons." *U.S. Department of State Bulletin* (Dec. 12, 1966): 896–902.

7423   [Johnson, Pres. Lyndon B.]. "Eighteen-Nation Disarmament Committee Considers U.S. Draft Treaty to Prevent Spread of Nuclear Weapons." *U.S. Department of State Bulletin* (Sept. 20, 1965): 466–75.

7424   ———. "President Johnson Renews Call for Nonproliferation Treaty." *U.S. Department of State Bulletin* (Mar. 20, 1967): 447–48.

7425   ———, and William C. Foster. "Draft Treaty on Nonproliferation of Nuclear Weapons Submitted to Geneva Disarmament Conference." *U.S. Department of State Bulletin* (Sept. 11, 1967): 315–20.

7426   Keens-Soper, Maurice. "Negotiating Non-Proliferation." *World Today* 24 (May 1968): 189–96.

7427   Kintner, William R. "A Reappraisal of the Proposed Nonproliferation Treaty." *Orbis* 10 (Spring 1966): 138–51.

7428   Lambeth, Benjamin S. "Nuclear Proliferation and Soviet Arms Control." *Orbis* 14 (Summer 1970): 298–325.

7429   Larson, Arthur. "Last Chance on Nuclear Non-Proliferation?" *Saturday Review* (Oct. 7, 1967): 21–24.

7430   Moss, Norman. "Building a Shrine for Disarmament." *Reporter* (Oct. 7, 1965): 33–35.

7431   Nikolayev, N., and V. Shestov. "Decisive Round at Geneva." *International Affairs* [Moscow] 14 (Mar. 1968): 3–7.

7432   "Non-Proliferation Treaty: Committee Begins Debate." *U.N. Monthly Chronicle* 5 (May 1968): 36–42.

7433   Rothstein, Robert L. "Nuclear Proliferation and American Policy." *Political Science Quarterly* 82 (Mar. 1967): 14–34.

7434   Silard, John. "The Coming International Nuclear Security Treaty." In James E. Dougherty and John F. Lehman, Jr., eds., *Arms Control for the Late Sixties.* Princeton: Van Nostrand, 1967, pp. 185–94.

7435   Tucker, Robert C. "Proliferation and Soviet-American Relations." *Bulletin of the Atomic Scientists* 22 (Oct. 1966): 14–18.

7436   "U.S. Presents Amendments to Draft Treaty on Nonproliferation of Nuclear Weapons in 18-Nation Disarmament Committee." *U.S. Department of State Bulletin* (Apr. 25, 1966): 675–80.

7437   "U.S. and U.S.S.R. Submit Complete Draft Treaty on Nonproliferation of Nuclear Weapons to the Geneva Disarmament Conference." *U.S. Department of State Bulletin* (Feb. 5, 1968): 164–67.

7438   Vital, David. "Double-Talk or Double-Think? A Comment on the Draft Non-Proliferation Treaty." *International Affairs* [London] 44 (July 1968): 419–33.

7439   Walsh, John B. "Nuclear Spread: Quest for a Treaty Is Receiving New Attention." *Science* (July 21, 1967): 288–90.

7440   Wettig, Gerhard. "Funktionen eines Sperrvertrages in der Sowjetischen Politik." *Aussenpolitik* 19 (Jan. 1968): 9–23.

7441   ———. "Soviet Policy on the Nonproliferation of Nuclear Weapons, 1966–1968." *Orbis* 12 (Winter 1969): 1058–84.

Ratification

7442   Goldwater, Sen. Barry M. "Nuclear Weapons: Treaty on Non-proliferation." *Vital Speeches* (Feb. 15, 1969): 262–63.

7443   Hosmer, Rep. Craig. "The Nonproliferation Treaty: An Exercise in Futility." *Washington Report* [American Security Council] (Sept. 9, 1968): 1–4.

7444   [Johnson, Pres. Lyndon B.] "President Urges Senate Action on Nonproliferation Treaty." *U.S. Department of State Bulletin* (Nov. 4, 1968): 469–70.

7445   [Nixon, Pres. Richard M.]. "President Nixon Ratifies Nuclear Nonproliferation Treaty." *U.S. Department of State Bulletin* (Mar. 2, 1970): 228–29.

7446   ———. "Treaty on the Non-Proliferation of Nuclear Weapons: The President's Remarks, March 5, 1970." *Presidential Documents* (Mar. 9, 1970): 318–20.

7447   "Nonproliferation Treaty Signed by 56 Nations at White House Ceremony." *U.S. Department of State Bulletin* (July 22, 1968): 85–88.

7448   "On Nuclear Nonproliferation Treaty: Minor Senate Opposition Seen for Nuclear Treaty." *Congressional Quarterly Weekly Report* (Feb. 21, 1969): 286–90.

7449   "Pro and Con Discussion: Should the U.S. Senate Consent Now to Ratification of the Nuclear Nonproliferation Treaty?" *Congressional Digest* 48 (Jan. 1969): 1–9 ff.

7450   "Treaty on the Nonproliferation of Nuclear Weapons Enters into Force." *U.S. Department of State Bulletin* (Mar. 30, 1970): 410–14.

7451   U.S. Senate. Committee on Armed Services. Hearings: *Military Implications of the Treaty on the Non-Proliferation of Nuclear Weapons.* 91st Cong., 1st Sess., Feb. 27, 28, 1969.

7452 ———. Committee on Foreign Relations. Hearings: *Nonproliferation Treaty.* July 10–17—on Ex. H. 90th Cong., 2d Sess., 1968.

7453 ———. Hearings: *Treaty on Nonproliferation of Nuclear Weapons.* Feb. 18, 20—On Ex. H. 91st Cong., 2d Sess., 1969.

7454 ———. Report: *Treaty on the Nonproliferation of Nuclear Weapons.* Ex. Rpt., no. 91–1. 91st Cong., 1st Sess., 1969.

Analysis of Treaty

7455 Ahmed, Samir. "The Non-Proliferation Treaty: Pros and Cons." *Disarmament* 14 (June 1967): 18–20.

7456 Alekseev, A. "Non-Proliferation Treaty and Security." *International Affairs* [Moscow] 15 (Jan. 1969): 10–14.

7457 Ansberry, William F. "Non-Proliferation: A Second Example of the Partial Approach to Arms Control." *Arms Control and Disarmament: Success or Failure?* Berkeley, Ca.: McCutchan, 1969, pp. 73–102.

7458 Australia. Department of External Affairs. "Treaty on the Non-Proliferation of Nuclear Weapons." *Current Notes on International Affairs* 39 (June 1968): 234–40.

7459 Bunn, George. "The Nuclear Nonproliferation Treaty." *Wisconsin Law Review* 68:3 (1968): 766–85.

7460 Canada. Department of External Affairs. "Disarmament: Non-Proliferation Treaty." *External Affairs* 20 (Apr. 1968): 170–81.

7461 Chekhonin, B. "Who Profits from Obstruction of the Nuclear Nonproliferation Treaty?" *Reprints from the Soviet Press* (May 16, 1969): 47–50.

7462 Feld, Bernard T. "After the Nonproliferation Treaty—What Next?" *Bulletin of the Atomic Scientists* 24 (Sept. 1968): 2–3.

7463 Firmage, Edwin B. "Treaty on the Non-Proliferation of Nuclear Weapons." *American Journal of International Law* 63 (Oct. 1969): 711–46.

7464 Foster, William C. "The Nuclear Nonproliferation Treaty: A Preventive and a Positive Measure." *U.S. Department of State Bulletin* (June 24, 1968): 836–38.

7465 ———. "Obligations of the Parties to the Treaty on the Nonproliferation of Nuclear Weapons." *U.S. Department of State Bulletin* (Dec. 16, 1968): 637–43.

7466 Harrison, Stanley L. "The Elusive Goal of Nonproliferation." *U.S. Naval Institute Proceedings* 95 (Apr. 1969): 26–37.

7467 Hudson, Richard. "The N.P.T.: Nuclear Watershed." *Atlantic Community Quarterly* 6:3 (1968): 425–32.

7468 Kaplan, Morton A. "The Nuclear Non-Proliferation Treaty: Its Rationale, Prospects and Possible Impact on International Law." *Journal of Public Law* 18:1 (1969): 1–20.

7469 ———. "Weaknesses of the Nonproliferation Treaty." *Orbis* 12 (Winter 1969): 1042–57.

7470 Katzenbach, Nicholas de B. "The Nuclear Nonproliferation Treaty—A Vital Step in Bringing the Atom under Control." *U.S. Department of State Bulletin* (May 20, 1968): 646–50.

7471 "The New Kellogg." *Spectator* (Feb. 24, 1967): 211–12.

7472 Nikolaev, N. "Non-Proliferation and Peace." *New Times* [Moscow] 8 (Aug. 1968): 19–20.

7473 Northedge, F. S., and Vinod Kumar. "The Nuclear Non-Proliferation Treaty." *Political Scientist* 5 (July 1968): 1–13.

7474 [People's Republic of China]. "Another Deal Between the Two Nuclear Overlords, the U.S. and the Soviet Union." *Peking Review* (Nov. 18, 1966): 34–35.

7475 ———. "A Nuclear Fraud Jointly Hatched by the United States and the Soviet Union." *Peking Review* (June 21, 1968): 17–18.

7476 Pilai, Narayana. "Nuclear Moralities." *Far Eastern Economic Review* (June 20, 1968): 606–08.

7477 Pilkington, Betty. "Non-Proliferation: Two Views. Disarming, but not Disarming." *Commonweal* (Mar. 14, 1969): 721–22.

7478 Rao, R. Jaganmohana. "The Treaty on Non-Proliferation of Nuclear Weapons: A Critical Appraisal." *Eastern Journal of International Law* 2 (Oct. 1970): 188–97.

7479 Rogers, William P. "Department Emphasizes the Importance of the Nuclear Nonproliferation Treaty." *U.S. Department of State Bulletin* (Mar. 10, 1969): 189–90.

7480   Sherman, Michael E. *Nuclear Proliferation: The Treaty and After.* Toronto: Canadian Institute of International Affairs, 1968.

7481   Smith, Bruce L. R. "The Non-Proliferation Treaty and East-West Detente." *Journal of International Affairs* 22:1 (1968): 89–106.

7482   Subbarao, M. V. "A Course Towards Disarmament: Non-Proliferation Treaty." *United Asia* 20 (Mar.–Apr. 1968): 96–104.

7483   "United Nations General Assembly Commends Treaty on the Non-Proliferation of Nuclear Weapons." *U.S. Department of State Bulletin* (July 1, 1968): 3–11.

7484   U.N. *Treaty on the Non-Proliferation of Nuclear Weapons.* Doc. no. OPI/372. New York: Office of Public Information, 1969.

7485   U.S. Arms Control & Disarmament Agency. *Explanatory Remarks about the Draft Non-Proliferation Treaty.* Washington, D.C.: G.P.O., 1968.

7486   Willrich, Mason. "Treaty on Non-Proliferation of Nuclear Weapons: Nuclear Technology Confronts World Politics." *Yale Law Journal* 77 (July 1968): 1447–1519.

7487   Winsor, Curtin, Jr. "The Non-Proliferation Treaty: A Step toward Peace." *Orbis* 12 (Winter 1969): 1004–17.

7488   Young, Elizabeth. *The Control of Proliferation: The 1968 Treaty in Hindsight and Forecast,* Adelphi Paper, no. 56. London: Institute for Strategic Studies, 1969.

7489   Zavialov, L. "A Treaty Meeting the Interests of Peace." *International Affairs* [Moscow] 16 (June 1970): 70–71.

Strategic Implications

7490   Beaton, Leonard. "Implications of the Non-Proliferation Treaty on Deterrence and the Prospects for Disarmament." *Royal United Services Institution Journal* 114 (June 1969): 34–40.

7491   Coffey, Joseph I. "Strategy, Alliance Policy and Nuclear Proliferation." *Orbis* 11 (Winter 1968): 975–95.

7492   Kelleher, Catherine M. "The Non-Proliferation Treaty and European Security." *Studies for a New Central Europe* 2:4 (1968–1969): 298–301.

7493   Scheinman, Lawrence. "Security and a Transnational System: The Case of Nuclear Energy." *International Organization* 25 (Summer 1971): 626–54.

7494   Schlesinger, James R. "The Strategic Consequences of Nuclear Proliferation." *Reporter* (Oct. 20, 1966): 36–38.

7495   Van Cleave, William R. "The Nonproliferation Treaty and Fission-Free Explosion Research." *Orbis* 11 (Winter 1968): 1055–66.

7496   ———, and S. T. Cohen. "Nuclear Aspects of Future U.S. Security Policy in Asia." *Orbis* 19 (Fall 1975): 1152–80.

Inspection & Supervision

See also Chapter 5, Special Issues: Inspection, Verification & Supervision.

7497   Abu Bakr, Abdel. "IAEA Technical Co-Operation Activities: Africa." *International Atomic Energy Agency Bulletin* 18 (Feb. 1976): 33–39.

7498   Botzian, Rudolf. "Die Internationale Atomenergie-Organisation und der Kernwaffen-Sperrvertrag." *Europa-Archiv* 24 (Mar. 1969): 209–16.

7499   Brownlie, Ian. "Nuclear Proliferation: Some Problems of Control." *International Affairs* [London] 42 (Oct. 1966): 600–608.

7500   Coffey, Joseph I. "Nuclear Guarantees and Nonproliferation." *International Organization* 25 (Autumn 1971): 836–44.

7501   DeGara, John P. "Security Guarantees and the Non-Proliferation Treaty." Ph.D. diss., Princeton Univ., 1972.

7502   Gilinsky, Victor, and W. Hoehn, Jr. *Nonproliferation Treaty Safeguards and the Spread of Nuclear Technology.* Rpt. R–501. Santa Monica, Ca.: Rand, June 1970.

7503   IAEA. "Belgium-Denmark-Federal Republic of Germany - Ireland - Italy - Luxembourg Netherlands-European Atomic Energy Community-International Atomic Energy

Agency: Agreement on Safeguards under the treaty of the Non-Proliferation of Nuclear Weapons." *International Legal Materials* 12 (May 1973): 469–636.

7504 ———. "Guidelines for Safeguards Agreements under the Non-Proliferation Treaty." *International Legal Materials* 10 (July 1971): 855–72.

7505 ———. *The Structure and Content of Agreements between the Agency and States Required in Connection with the Treaty on the Nonproliferation of Nuclear Weapons.* Pam. INFCIRC 153. Vienna, 1971.

7506 "Inspection Approach for Future Reactors." *Nuclear Engineering International* 21 (Oct. 1976): 68–72.

7507 Korablyov, V. "Non-Proliferation and IAEA." *New Times* [Moscow] (Aug. 14, 1968): 7–9.

7508 Kramish, Arnold. *The Watched and Unwatched: Inspection in the Non-Proliferation Treaty.* Adelphi Paper, no. 36. London: Institute for Strategic Studies, June 1967.

7509 McKnight, Allan D. *Nuclear Non-Proliferation: IAEA and Euratom.* Occasional Paper, no. 7. New York: Carnegie Endowment for International Peace, 1970.

7510 "Measures to Facilitate Adherence to the Nuclear Non-Proliferation Treaty." *International Affairs* [Moscow] 18 (June 1972): 122 ff.

7511 "The Non-Proliferation and the IAEA." *International Atomic Energy Agency Bulletin* 10:4 (1968): 3–9.

7512 "Nuclear Safeguards: Hide and Seek." *Economist* (Sept. 18, 1976): 77–78.

7513 Patijn, S. "Euratom, the Non-Proliferation Treaty, and International Control: The Five and the Five Principles." *Common Market* 8 (Feb. 1968): 40–43.

7514 Quester, George H. "The Nuclear Nonproliferation Treaty and the International Atomic Energy Agency." *International Organization* 23 (Autumn 1969): 163–82.

7515 Rometsch, R. *Development of IAEA Safeguards Systems under NPT.* IAEA A/CONF: 49/P/770. Vienna, 1971.

7516 Rosen, Steven. "Proliferation Treaty Controls and the IAEA." *Journal of Conflict Resolution* 11:2 (1967): 168–75.

7517 Rupprecht, Wilfried. "Die Mitbestimmung der Nichtkernwaffenstaaten in der Internationalen Atomenergie-Organisation. Die Vertretung im Gouverneursrat." *Europa-Archiv* 24 (Apr. 1969): 251 ff.

7518 Scheinman, Lawrence. "Safeguarding Nuclear Materials." *Bulletin of the Atomic Scientists* 30 (Apr. 1974): 32–33.

7519 Schumann, G. "Technical Control and the Non-Proliferation of Nuclear Weapons." *Scientific World* 16:3 (1972): 16–18.

7520 Shapley, Deborah. "Nuclear Explosives: Technology for On-Site Inspection." *Science* (Aug. 27, 1976): 743–44.

7521 Sherman, Michael E. "Guarantees and Nuclear Spread." *International Journal* 21 (Autumn 1966): 484–90.

7522 SIPRI. *Safeguards Against Nuclear Proliferation.* Cambridge: M.I.T. Press, 1975.

7523 Spinrad, Bernard I. "Where Are We? On War and Peace and NPT and Safeguards." *Bulletin of the Atomic Scientists* 30 (Jan. 1974): 34–38.

7524 Sullivan, Michael J., III. "Indian Attitudes on International Atomic Energy Control." *Pacific Affairs* 43 (Fall 1970): 353–69.

7525 Ungerer, Werner, et al. "Safeguards: Five Views." *International Atomic Energy Agency Bulletin* 13:3 (1971): 2–13.

1975 REVIEW CONFERENCE

For text of final declaration, see *Survival* 17 (Nov.–Dec. 1975): 289–95.

7526 Alexander, Tom. "Our Costly Losing Battle Against Nuclear Proliferation." *Fortune* 90 (Dec. 1975): 143–50.

7527 Barnaby, Frank. "Preventing the Spread of Nuclear Weapons." *New Scientist* (May 1, 1975): 243–46.

7528 Carter, Luther J. "Arms Controllers Are Pessimistic on Eve of Non-Proliferation

Treaty Review." *Science* (Apr. 25, 1975): 340–41.

7529   Epstein, William. "Failure at the NPT Review Conference." *Bulletin of the Atomic Scientists* 31 (Sept. 1975): 46–48.

7530   ———. "Nuclear Proliferation: The Failure of the Review Conference." *Survival* 17 (Nov.–Dec. 1975): 262–69.

7531   ———. *Retrospective on the NPT Review Conference: Proposals for the Future.* Occasional paper, no. 9. Muscatine, Ia.: Stanley Foundation, 1975.

7532   Feld, Bernard T. "Making the World Safe for Plutonium." *Bulletin of the Atomic Scientists* 31 (May 1975): 5–6.

7533   Fromm, Joseph. "100 Nations Grapple with a Nightmare: Uncontrolled A-Arms." *U.S. News & World Report* (May 12, 1975): 67–68.

7534   Halsted, Thomas A. "Report From Geneva." *Arms Control Today* 5 (June 1975): 1–4.

7535   ———. "The Spread of Nuclear Weapons: Is the Dam About to Burst?" *Bulletin of the Atomic Scientists* 31 (May 1975): 8–11.

7536   Humphrey, Sen. Hubert H. "Nonproliferation Treaty Conference." *Congressional Record* 121 (June 3, 1975): S9353–54.

7537   Ikle, Fred C. "The Second Nuclear Era." *U.S. Department of State Bulletin* (May 19, 1975): 641–45.

7538   Kalyadin, A. "The Struggle for Disarmament: New Perspectives." *Instant Research on Peace and Violence* 5:1 (1975): 24–34.

7539   Kennedy, Sen. Edward M. "The Nuclear Nonproliferation Treaty." *Congressional Record* 121 (July 30, 1975): S14462–464.

7540   Lodgaard, Sverre. "Review the Non-Proliferation Treaty: Status and Prospects." *Instant Research on Peace and Violence* 5:1 (1975): 7–23.

7541   "The NPT Review Conference and Nuclear Proliferation." *Orbis* 19 (Summer 1975): 316–20.

7542   "Nuclear Non-Proliferation: Final Declaration of the Review Conference, May 30, 1975." *Survival* 17 (Nov.–Dec. 1975): 289–95.

7543   Pastore, Sen. John O. "The Danger of Nuclear Proliferation." *Congressional Record* 121 (June 3, 1975): S9312–27.

7544   Smart, Ian. "Vor der Uberprufungskonferenz fur den Kernwaffen-Sperrvertrag: Probleme und Aussichten." *Europa-Archiv* (Mar. 25, 1975): 201 ff.

7545   "U.S. Reaffirms Support for Non-Proliferation Treaty at Review Conference." *U.S. Department of State Bulletin* (June 30, 1975): 921–29. [Includes text of final declaration.]

7546   Wadlow, Rene V. L. "The Nuclear Non-Proliferation Review Conference: May 1975." *Instant Research on Peace and Violence* 5:1 (1975): 1–6.

Nonnuclear Nations

7547   Alexeyev, A. "Non-Proliferation Treaty and the Non-Nuclear States." *International Affairs* [Moscow] 15 (Mar. 1969): 9–13.

7548   Baker, Steven J. *Italy and the Nuclear Option.* Santa Monica, Ca.: California Arms Control & Foreign Policy Seminar, May 1974.

7549   Bayandor, Darioush. "Maintenance of the NPT in the 1970's: The Asian Dimension." In Andrew W. Cordier, ed., *Columbia Essays in International Affairs.* New York: Columbia Univ. Press, 1971, VI: 198–228.

7550   Beaton, Leonard. "Capabilities of Non-Nuclear Powers." In Alastair Buchan, ed., *A World of Nuclear Powers.* Englewood Cliffs, N.J.: Prentice-Hall, 1966, pp. 13–38.

7551   Bethill, Charles D. "Nonmilitary Incentives for the Acquisition of Nuclear Weapons." In Andrew W. Cordier, ed., *Columbia Essays in International Affairs.* New York: Columbia Univ. Press, 1971, VI: 40–64.

7552   Bloomfield, Lincoln P., and Amelia C. Leiss. "Arms Control and the Developing Countries." *World Politics* 18 (Oct. 1965): 1–19.

7553   Brundtland, Arne O. "The Problems Posed by Nuclear Weapons." In A. Schou and A. O. Brundtland, eds., *Small States in International Relations.* New York : Wiley, 1971, pp. 243–50.

7554 Calder, Ritchie. "The Non-Nuclear Club." *Bulletin of the Atomic Scientists* 16 (Apr. 1960): 123–26.

7555 Coakley, S. "Nuclear Power in Ireland." *Administration* 19 (Summer 1971): 130–36.

7556 Dougherty, James E. "Nuclear Proliferation in Asia." *Orbis* 19 (Fall 1975): 925–57.

7557 ———. "The Treaty and the Nonnuclear States." *Orbis* 11 (Summer 1967): 360–77.

7558 Epstein, William. "Nuclear Proliferation in the Third World." *Journal of International Affairs* 29 (Fall 1975): 185–202.

7559 Fermi, Laura. "Bombs or Reactors?" *Bulletin of the Atomic Scientists* 26 (June 1970): 28–29.

7560 Hoag, Malcolm W. "One American Perspective on Nuclear Guarantees, Proliferation and Related Alliance Diplomacy." In Johan Jorgen Holst, ed., *Security, Order, and the Bomb*. Oslo: Universitetsforlaget, 1972, pp. 152–73.

7561 "IAEA Technical Co-operation Activities: Europe and the Middle East." *International Atomic Energy Agency Bulletin* 17:8 (1975): 38–45.

7562 Khallaf, H. "Guaranty Offered by Nuclear States to Non-Nuclear States." *Revue Egyptienne du Droit International* 30 (1974): 11–43.

7563 Knorr, Klaus E. "Nuclear Weapons: 'Haves and Have-Nots.'" *Foreign Affairs* 36 (Oct. 1957): 167–78.

7564 Larus, Joel, and Robert M. Lawrence, eds. *Nuclear Proliferation: Phase II*. Lawrence: Univ. Press of Kansas, 1974.

7565 Lenefsky, D. "United Nations Security Council Resolution on Security Assurances for Nonnuclear Weapon States." *New York University Journal of International Law and Politics* 3 (Spring 1970): 56 ff.

7566 Marhaw, Onkar, and Ann Schultz, eds. *Nuclear Proliferation and the Near-Nuclear Countries*. Cambridge, Mass.: Ballinger, 1975.

7567 Mazrui, Ali A. "Numerical Strength and Nuclear Status in the Third World." *Journal of Politics* 29 (Nov. 1967): 791–820.

7568 Mueller, John E. "Incentive for Restraint: Canada as a Nonnuclear Power." *Orbis* 11 (Fall 1967): 864–84.

7569 Myrdal, Alva. "The High Price of Nuclear Arms Monopoly." *Foreign Policy* 18 (Spring 1975): 30–43.

7570 Nagchaudhuri, B. D. "Nuclear Treaty May Inhibit Peaceful Uses: Have-Nots Resent Excessive Restrictions." *Indian Marxist* 3 (June 1967): 9–10.

7571 Pfaltzgraff, Robert L., Jr., et al. *The Superpowers in a Multinuclear World*. Lexington, Mass.: Lexington Books, 1974.

7572 Quester, George H. "Paris, Pretoria, Peking . . . Proliferation?" *Bulletin of the Atomic Scientists* 26 (Oct. 1970): 12–16.

7573 "Reflections on the Quarter: The Nonproliferation Treaty and the Nonnuclear Nations." *Orbis* 11 (Spring 1967): 7–11.

7574 Ruehl, Lothar. "Die politische Bedeutung des Besitzes von Kernwaffen: Statusunterschiede zwischen Nuklearmachten und Nichtatomaren." *Europa-Archiv* (Jan. 10, 1973): 17 ff.

7575 Sarabhai, Vikram A., and Karit S. Parikh. "Nuclear Energy in Developing Countries." *Nuclear News* (Oct. 15, 1971): 96–98 ff.

7576 Schelling, Thomas. "Who Will Have the Bomb?" *International Security* 1 (Summer 1976): 77–91.

7577 Schwab, George. "The Swiss Atomic Debate and Its Implications." Ph.D. diss., Columbia Univ., 1968.

7578 ———. "Switzerland's Tactical Nuclear Weapons Policy." *Orbis* (Fall 1969): 900–914.

7579 Schwarz, Urs. "Inhibition through Policy: The Role of the Non-Nuclear Powers." In Alastair Buchan, ed., *A World of Nuclear Powers*. Englewood Cliffs, N.J.: Prentice-Hall, 1966, pp. 143–67.

7580 Showroiski, Andrzej. "Non-Proliferation and Poland." *Polish Perspectives* 11 (July 1968): 11–16.

7581 SIPRI. *The Near Nuclear Countries and the NPT*. New York: Humanities Press, 1972.

7582 U.N. Report: *Effects of the Possible Use of Nuclear Weapons and the Security and*

Economic Implications for States of the Acquisition and Further Development of These Weapons. Report, A/6858. New York, 1968.

7583   U.N. Assoc. of the U.S.A. "Security Assurances for Non-Nuclear Weapon Countries." *Safeguarding the Atom: A Soviet-American Exchange.* New York, 1972, pp. 35–41.

7584   Van Cleave, William R. *Nth Country Threat Analysis: West Germany, Sweden, Canada, Israel, and Selected Other Nations.* AD 848753. Stanford, Ca.: Stanford Research Institute, May 1968.

7585   ———, and Harold R. Rood. "A Technological Comparison of Two Potential Nuclear Powers: India and Japan." *Asian Survey* 6 (July 1967): 482–89.

7586   Viorst, Milton. "The Nuclear Club: Why the Outs Want In." *Nation* (Oct. 18, 1965): 235–39.

7587   Willrich, Mason. "Guarantees to Non-Nuclear Nations." *Foreign Affairs* 44 (July 1966): 683–92.

7588   Zoppo, Ciro E. "Nuclear Technology, Weapons and the Third World." *Annals of the Amer. Acad. of Pol. & Soc. Sci.* 386 (Nov. 1969): 113–25.

CONFERENCE OF NONNUCLEAR STATES (1968)

7589   "Conference of Non-Nuclear Weapons States: Statement Issued." *U.N. Monthly Chronicle* 5 (July 1968): 50–51.

7590   Djerdja, Jasip. "The Nonnuclear Countries and Their Course of Action." *Review of International Affairs* [Belgrade] (Mar. 5, 1968): 1–3.

7591   Schippenkoetter, Swidbert. "Sicherheitsgarantien fur de Nichtnuklearen?" *Aussenpolitik* 19 (Nov. 1968): 645–53.

7592   Shestov, V. "Conference of Non-Nuclear Countries." *International Affairs* [Moscow] 14 (Nov. 1968): 28–30.

7593   U.N. Conference of Non-Nuclear States. *Documents of the Conference.* A/CONF. 35/1–11. Geneva, 1968.

7594   ———. *Provisional Summary Record of the 1st–20th Meeting.* Geneva, 1968.

7595   ———. Committee One. *Documents.* A/CONF. 35/C.1/L. 1–19. Geneva, 1968.

7596   ———. *Provisional Summary Record of the 1st–22d Meeting.* A/CONF. 35/C.1/SR. 1–22. Geneva, 1968.

7597   ———. Committee Two. *Documents.* A/CONF. 35/C.2/1–3; A/CONF. 35/C.2/L. 1–13. Geneva, 1968.

7598   ——— *Provisional Summary Record of the 1st–17th Meeting.* A/CONF. 35/C.2/SR. 1–17. Geneva, 1968.

ARGENTINA

7599   "ACDA Scotches Rumors of Argentine Nuclear Theft." *Science* (Aug. 1, 1975): 360–61.

7600   Guglialmelli, Juan E. "Argentina, Brasil y la Bomba Atomica." *Estrategia* (Sept.–Oct. 1974): 1–15.

7601   Kandell, Jonathan. "Argentines Assay Their Atom Potential." *New York Times,* Apr. 2, 1975.

7602   "Recenti sviluppi nella attività Nucleari in Argentina, Messico e Perù." *Comitato Naz Energia Nucleare Notiz* 20 (Apr. 1974): 94–101.

7603   Redick, John R. "Argentina's Nuclear Connection." *Washington Post,* Sept. 30, 1974.

7604   Sabato, Jorge A. "Atomic Development in Argentina: A Case History." *World Development* 1 (Aug. 1973): 23–38.

AUSTRALIA

7605   Albinski, Henry S. "Australia and Nuclear Affairs." *Pacific Affairs* 38 (Spring 1965): 32–46.

7606   "Australian Doubts on the Treaty." *Quadrant* 12 (May–June 1968): 30–34.

7607   Bellany, Ian. *Australia in the Nuclear Age.* Sydney: Sydney Univ. Press, 1972.

7608   ———. "Australia's Nuclear Policy." *India Quarterly* 25 (Oct.–Dec. 1969): 374–84.

7609   Bull, Hedley. "The Non-Proliferation Treaty and Its Implications for Australia." *Australian Outlook* 22 (Aug. 1968): 162–75.

7610 ———. "In Support of the Non-Proliferation Treaty." *Quadrant* 12 (May–June 1968): 25–29.

7611 Encel, S., and Allan D. McKnight. "Bombs, Power Stations, and Proliferation." *Australian Quarterly* 42 (Mar. 1970): 15–26.

7612 Green, J. H. "The Australian Atom Bomb." *Australian Quarterly* 37 (Dec. 1965): 36–44.

7613 Richardson, James L. *Australia and the Non-Proliferation Treaty.* Canberra: Australian National Univ., Strategic & Defense Studies Centre, 1968.

BRAZIL

7614 "Brazil-Federal Republic of Germany: Agreement on Co-operation in the Field of Peaceful Uses of Nuclear Energy." *International Legal Materials* 15 (May 1976): 485–88.

7615 "Brazil-Federal Republic of Germany—International Atomic Energy Agency: Agreement for the Application of Nuclear Safeguards." *International Legal Materials* 15 (May 1976): 489–98.

7616 Gall, Norman. "Nuclear Proliferation: Atoms for Brazil, Dangers for All." *Foreign Policy,* no. 23 (Summer 1976): 155–201.

7617 Gillette, Robert. "Nuclear Exports: A U.S. Firm's Troublesome Flirtation with Brazil." *Science* (July 25, 1975): 267–69.

7618 Peffau, Louis. "Le Bresil et l'Utilisation Pacifique de l'Energie Nucleaire." *Cahiers des Ameriques Latines* (July–Dec. 1969): 92–111.

7619 Rosenbaum, H. Jon, and Glenn M. Cooper. "Brazil and the Nuclear Non-Proliferation Treaty." *International Affairs* [London] 46 (Jan. 1970): 74–90.

INDIA

7620 Appadorai, A. "India and the Non-Proliferation Treaty." *Essays in Indian Politics and Foreign Policy.* Delhi: Vikas, 1971, pp. 235–40.

7621 Barnaby, Frank. "India's Nuclear Views." *New Scientist* (Feb. 4, 1971): 268–69.

7622 Biswas, S. K. "Nuclear Development in India." *Nuclear Energy* (Mar. 1965): 87–96.

7623 Braun, Dieter, "Wie Friedlich ist Neu-Delhis Atom-programm? Aspekte der Indischen Nuklearpolitik." *Europa-Archiv* (Sept. 25, 1974): 623–32.

7624 Buchan, Alastair. "The Security of India." *World Today* 21 (May 1965): 210–17.

7625 Chopra, Wg. Cmdr. Mahraj K. "India's Nuclear Path in the 1970's." *Military Review* 54 (Oct. 1974): 38–46.

7626 Congdon, Michael B. "Nuclear Weapons and National Influence: International Political Implications of India's Strategic Dilemma." Ph.D. diss., Claremont, 1973.

7627 Couper, Frank E. "The Indian Party Conflict on the Issue of Atomic Weapons." *Journal of Developing Areas* 3 (Jan. 1969): 191–206.

7628 Desai, Manila J. "India and Nuclear Weapons." *Disarmament and Arms Control* 3 (Autumn 1965): 135–42.

7629 Deshingkar, G. D. "China's Earth Satellite: The Case for Indian Bomb." *China Report* 6 (May–June 1970): 28–33.

7630 Doctor, Adi H. "India's Nuclear Policy." *Indian Journal of Political Science* 32 (July–Sept. 1971): 349–56.

7631 Dutt, D. Som. *India and the Bomb.* Adelphi Paper, no. 30. London: Institute for Strategic Studies, 1966.

7632 Edwardes, Michael. "India, Pakistan and Nuclear Weapons: Entanglement Between the Two Countries May Soon Result in Indian Emergence as a Nuclear Power." *International Affairs* [London] 43 (Oct. 1967): 655–63.

7633 Gillette, Robert. "Nuclear Proliferation: India, Germany May Accelerate the Process." *Science* (May 30, 1975): 911–14.

7634 Gonsalves, A. S., and Wayne Wilcox. "The Nonproliferation Treaty: India and American Views." *Asia* 15 (Summer 1969): 72–92.

7635 Grant, N. B. "To Make or Not To Make the Bomb." *United Service Institution of India Journal* 97 (Jan.–Mar. 1967): 1–12.

7636 Gupta, Sisir. "India and the Bomb: Break with the Past." *Survival* 7 (Mar.–Apr. 1965): 63–67.

7637   ———. "The Indian Dilemma." In Alastair Buchan, ed., *A World of Nuclear Powers.* Englewood Cliffs, N.J.: Prentice-Hall, 1966, pp. 55–67.

7638   "India Suggests New Approach for Non-Proliferation of Nuclear Weapons." *Nuclear India* 4 (Oct. 1965): 4–5 ff.

7639   Kapur, Ashok. *India's Nuclear Option: Atomic Diplomacy and Decision-Making.* New York: Praeger, 1976.

7640   ———. "Nuclear Weapons and India Foreign Policy: A Perspective." *World Today* 27 (Sept. 1971): 379–89.

7641   ———. "Peace and Power in India's Nuclear Policy." *Asian Survey* 10 (Sept. 1970): 779–88.

7642   ———. "World Politics and the Security of India." *Journal of the Institute for Defence Studies and Analyses* [New Delhi] 3 (Apr. 1971): 485–509.

7643   Kaul, Lt. Cmdr. Ravi. *India's Strategic Spectrum.* Allahabad: Chanakya Publishing House, 1969.

7644   Kaushik, B. M. "India and the Bomb: Constraints and Political Realities." *South Asian Studies* 5 (Jan. 1970): 79–97.

7645   King, Peter. "How Wide is a Nuclear Threshold? India and the Bomb." *Australian Outlook* 25 (Aug. 1971): 198–212.

7646   Krishna, Raj. "India and the Bomb." *Military Review* 45 (Dec. 1965): 74–78.

7647   Law, R. D. "India's Alternatives." *Military Review* 47 (Apr. 1967): 56–59.

7648   Masters, Roger D. "What About a Nuclear Guarantee for India?" *New Republic* (Dec. 25, 1965): 9–10.

7649   Mirchandani, G. G. *India's Nuclear Dilemma.* New Delhi: Popular Book Services, 1968.

7650   Mishra, Indu Shekhar. "The NPT Is Not Enough for India." *Bulletin of the Atomic Scientists* 24 (June 1968): 4–5.

7651   Mukerjee, Dilip. "Itching for the Bomb." *Far Eastern Economic Review* (July 9, 1970): 83–85.

7652   Nanda, Krish. "Will India Go Nuclear?" *Bulletin of the Atomic Scientists* 27 (Dec. 1971): 39–42.

7653   Nehru, R. K. "The Challenge of the Chinese Bomb." *India Quarterly* 21 (Jan.–Mar. 1965): 3–14.

7654   Noorani, A. G. "India's Quest for a Nuclear Guarantee." *Asian Survey* 7 (July 1967): 490–501.

7655   "Nuclear Weapons for India: Four Views." *Indian and Foreign Review* (June 1, 1970): 9–11, 17–19.

7656   Palsokar, R. D. *Minimum Deterrent: India's Nuclear Answer to China.* Bombay: Thackery, 1969.

7657   Patil, R. L. M. *India: Nuclear Weapons and International Politics.* Delhi: National Publishing House, 1969.

7658   Quester, George H. "India Contemplates the Bomb." *Bulletin of the Atomic Scientists* 26 (Jan. 1970): 13–16 ff.

7659   Rao, R. Rama. "The Non-Proliferation Treaty." *Journal of the Institute for Defence Studies and Analyses* [New Delhi] 1 (July 1968): 12–29.

7660   Rusch, Thomas A. "Indian Socialists and the Nuclear Non-Proliferation Treaty." *Journal of Asian Studies* 28 (Aug. 1969): 755–70.

7661   Schwarz, Urs. "India as a Peaceful Nuclear Power." *Swiss Review of World Affairs* 16 (Jan. 1967): 5–8.

7662   Shastri, Lol B. "India and the Bomb." *Survival* 7 (Mar.–Apr. 1965): 59–61.

7663   Singh, Bishwanath. "National Defense in Nuclear Age: Dilemma of India." *Political Scientist* 2 (Jan.–June 1966): 1–17.

7664   Singh, Sampooran. *India and the Nuclear Bomb.* New Delhi: S. Chand, 1971.

7665   Sinha, K. K. "India's Nuclear Dilemma." *Military Review* 48 (Oct. 1968): 50–55.

7666   *A Strategy for India for a Credible Posture Against a Nuclear Adversary.* New Delhi: Institute for Defence Studies & Analyses, 1968.

7667   Subramanian, R. R. "Nuclear India and the NPT: Prospects for Future?" *Instant Research on Peace and Violence* 5:1 (1975): 35–39.

7668   ———, ed. "Nuclear Weapons and India's Security." *Journal of the Institute for De-*

fence Studies and Analyses [New Delhi] 3 (July 1970): 1–125.

7669   Trivedi, V. C. "India and Nuclear Proliferation." *Disarmament* 11 (Sept. 1966): 1–4.

7670   ———. "Vertical Versus Horizontal Proliferation: An Indian View." In James E. Dougherty and John F. Lehman, Jr., eds., *Arms Control for the Late Sixties.* Princeton: Van Nostrand, 1967, pp. 195–206.

7671   Vas, E. A. "A Nuclear Policy for India." *United Service Institution of India Journal* 99 (Jan.–Mar. 1969): 21–27.

7672   Vohra, H. R. "An Indian View: Cloud Over Geneva." *Progressive* 31 (Jan. 1967): 35–37.

7673   ———. "India's Nuclear Policy of Three Negatives." *Bulletin of the Atomic Scientists* 26 (Apr. 1970): 25–27.

7674   Wasan, R. P. "Nuclear Weapons Debate in India: A Select Bibliography." *Journal of the Institute for Defence Studies and Analyses* 1 (Jan. 1969): 142–61.

7675   Wilcox, Wayne. *Nuclear Weapons Options and the Strategic Environment in South Asia: Arms Control Implications for India.* Santa Monica, Ca.: California Arms Control & Foreign Policy Seminar, June 1971.

7676   Williams, Shelton L. *The U.S., India and the Bomb.* Baltimore: Johns Hopkins Press, 1969.

India—Nuclear Test

7677   "After India's Blast: Fresh Fears of a 'Minor League' A-Bomb Race." *U.S. News & World Report* (June 3, 1974): 45–46.

7678   "The Empress's Bomb: India's Nuclear Device Has Given New Strength to Mrs. Gandhi and to the Argument for an Urgent Reappraisal of . . . Nuclear Proliferation." *Economist* (May 25, 1974): 17–18.

7679   Kapur, Ashok. "India and the Atom." *Bulletin of the Atomic Scientists* 30 (Sept. 1974): 27–29.

7680   ———. "India's Nuclear Presence." *World Today* 30 (Nov. 1974): 459–65.

7681   ———. *India's Nuclear Test: Stretching Out the Options of the First Step towards a Weapons Program.* Los Angeles: California

State Univ., Center for the Study of Armament & Disarmament, 1975.

7682   Lyon, Peter. "The Indian Bomb: Nuclear Tests for 'Peaceful Purposes'?" *Round Table* 64 (Oct. 1974): 403–10.

7683   Misra, K. P., and J. S. Gandhi. "India's Nuclear Explosion: A Study in Perspectives." *International Studies* 14 (July–Sept. 1975): 341–56.

7684   Morrison, Barne, and Donald M. Page. "India's Option: The Nuclear Route to Achieve Goal as World Power." *International Perspectives* (July–Aug. 1974): 23–28.

7685   Nandy, Ashis. "Between Two Gandhis: Psychopolitical Aspects of Nuclearization of India." *Asian Survey* 12 (Nov. 1974): 966–70.

7686   Rajan, M. S. "India: A Case Without Force." *International Journal* 30 (Spring 1975): 299–325.

7687   Ribicoff, Sen. Abraham A. "State Department Position on India's Nuclear Explosion." *Congressional Record* 122 (July 19, 1976): S11790–793.

7688   Shirodkar, V. A. "The Indian Bomb: How It Happened—What Next?" *Canadian Defense Quarterly* 4 (Winter 1974): 26–29.

7689   Tunney, Sen. John V. "Senate Resolution 415—Submission of a Resolution Relating to the Transfer of Nuclear Material to India." *Congressional Record* 122 (Mar. 26, 1976): S4384–85.

7690   Walczak, James R. "Legal Implications of Indian Nuclear Development." *Denver Journal of International Law and Policy* 4 (Fall 1974): 237–56.

Japan

7691   Axelbank, Alexander. "Tokyo Flirts with the Atom." *Nation* (Sept. 11, 1972): 166–67.

7692   Cassuto, Aldo. "Hiroshima's Japan Goes Nuclear." *World Today* 26 (Aug. 1970): 313–16.

7693   Dommen, Arthur J. "Japan, China and the Bomb." *War/Peace Report* 6 (June–July 1966): 17–18.

7694   Dore, Richard P. "Japan's Place in the World." *World Today* 22 (July 1966): 293–306.

7695   Edwards, Catherine. *U.S. Policy and the Japanese Nuclear Option.* Santa Monica, Ca.: California Arms Control & Foreign Policy Seminar, Aug. 1973.

7696   Endicott, John E. *Japan's Nuclear Option: Political, Technical and Strategic Factors.* New York: Praeger, 1975.

7697   Hiroharu, Seki. "Nuclear Proliferation and Our Option." *Japan Quarterly* 22 (Jan.–Mar. 1975): 13–21.

7698   Imai, Ryukichi. "Japan and the Nuclear Age." *Bulletin of the Atomic Scientists* 26 (June 1970): 35–39.

7699   ———. "The Non-Proliferation Treaty and Japan." *Bulletin of the Atomic Scientists* 25 (May 1969): 2–7.

7700   ———. "The Political Outlook for Nuclear Power in Japan." *Atlantic Community Quarterly* 13 (Summer 1975): 226–43.

7701   "Japan Is 94th Nation to Sign Nuclear Nonproliferation Treaty." *U.S. Department of State Bulletin* (Dec. 15, 1969): 544–45.

7702   "JSP-Government Debate on the Question of Nuclear Non-Proliferation in the Diet." *Japan Socialist Review* (June 15, 1967): 37–48.

7703   Kishida, Junnosuke. "Japan's Non-Nuclear Policy." *Survival* 15 (Jan.–Feb. 1973): 15–20.

7704   Langdon, Frank C. "Japanese Reactions to India's Nuclear Explosion." *Pacific Affairs* 48 (Summer 1975): 173–80.

7705   Maeda, H. "The Nuclear Non-Proliferation Treaty." *Japan Quarterly* 15 (Oct.–Dec. 1968): 456–61.

7706   Marks, Thomas A. "The Acquisition of Nuclear Weapons by Japan." *Military Review* 53 (Mar. 1973): 39–48.

7707   Miki, Takeo. "Japan's Reservations." *Survival* 9 (May 1967): 149–50.

7708   Murata, Kiyoaki. "Japan and Non-Proliferation." *Survival* 9 (Aug. 1967): 267–68.

7709   ———. "Japan and Nonproliferation." *Military Review* 48 (Jan. 1968): 86–88.

7710   Niu, Sien-chong. "Will Japan Go Nuclear?" *Ordnance* 56 (Jan.–Feb. 1972): 292–94.

7711   Okimoto, Daniel I. "Japan's Non-Nuclear Policy: The Problem of the NPT." *Asian Survey* 15 (May 1975): 313–27.

7712   "On the Signing of the Nuclear-Proliferation Treaty." *Japan Socialist Review* (Feb. 15, 1970): 8–10.

7713   Pempel, T. J. "Japan's Nuclear Allergy." *Current History* 68 (Apr. 1975): 169–173 ff.

7714   Quester, George H. "Japan and the Non-Proliferation Treaty." *Asian Survey* 10 (Sept. 1970): 765–78.

7715   Schott, David B. "Japan and Nuclear Weapons." *SAIS Review* 16 (Winter 1972): 31–40.

7716   "A Summing Up of the Movement and Organization of the Japan Congress Against Atomic and Hydrogen Bombs." *Japan Socialist Review* (Mar. 1, 1970): 1–15.

7717   Van Edington, Robert. "Japan in the United Nations on the Issues of Nuclear Weapons." Ph.D. diss., Univ. of Washington, 1968.

7718   Wakaizumi, Kei. "Chinese Nuclear Armament and the Security of Japan." *Journal of Social & Political Ideas in Japan* 4 (Dec. 1966): 69–79.

7719   ———. "The Problem of Japan." In Alastair Buchan, ed., *A World of Nuclear Powers.* Englewood Cliffs, N.J.: Prentice-Hall, 1966, pp. 76–88.

7720   Williams, Shelton L. *Nuclear Nonproliferation in International Studies: The Japanese Case.* Monograph Series in World Affairs, 9:3. Denver: Univ. of Denver, 1972.

7721   Yatabe, Atsuhiko. "A Note on the Treaty on the Non-Proliferation of Nuclear Weapons: The Japanese Point of View." *Japanese Annual of International Law* 14 (1970): 17–33.

MIDDLE EAST

7722   "Atomic Danger on the Middle East Horizon." *New Outlook* 8 (Sept. 1965): 54–57.

7723   Beaufre, A. "Les Armes Nucleaires et l'Asie." *Strategie* 19 (July–Sept. 1969): 5–22.

7724 Beres, Louis R. "Terrorism and the Nuclear Threat in the Middle East." *Current History* 71 (Jan. 1976): 27–29.

7725 Flapan, Simha. "Nuclear Power in the Middle East." *New Outlook* 17 (July 1974): 46–54; 17 (Oct. 1974): 34–40.

7726 Green, Harold P. "The Nuclear Proliferation Issue: The Middle East Is One of the Main Locales of a Worldwide Problem." *Issues* 20 (Winter 1966–67): 35–40.

7727 Harkabi, Yehoshafat, et al. *The Bomb in the Middle East.* New York: Friendship Press, 1969.

7728 ———. *Nuclear War and Nuclear Peace.* Jerusalem: Israel Universities Press, 1966.

7729 Lerner, Max. "Nuclear Weapons Over the Middle East?" *Current* 121 (Sept. 1970): 57–58.

7730 Nimrod, Y., and A. Korczyn. "Suggested Patterns for Israeli-Egyptian Agreement to Avoid Nuclear Proliferation." *New Outlook* [Tel Aviv] 10 (Jan. 1967): 9–20.

7731 Oren, Stephen. "The Middle East in the Atomic Age, 1970–1990." *World Affairs* 135 (Winter 1972): 275 ff.

7732 Pranger, Robert J., and Dale R. Tahtinen. *Nuclear Threat in the Middle East.* Washington, D.C.: American Enterprise Institute for Public Policy Research, 1975.

7733 Zoppo, Ciro E. "The Nuclear Genie in the Middle East." *New Outlook* [Tel Aviv] 18 (Fall 1975): 18–21.

Arab States

7734 Evron, Yair. "The Arab Position in the Nuclear Field: A Study of Policies up to 1967." *Cooperation and Conflict* (Nov. 1, 1973): 19–31.

7735 Prittie, Terence. "Bombshop on the Nile: Target Israel." *Atlantic* (Aug. 1964): 37–40.

Israel

7736 Beaton, Leonard. "Why Israel Does Not Need the Bomb." *New Middle East* [London] 7 (Apr. 1969): 7–11.

7737 Bell, J. Bowyer. "Israel's Nuclear Option." *Middle East Journal* 26 (Autumn 1972): 379–88.

7738 Dalma, Alfons. "Israel am Wege zur Atommacht?" *Osterreichische Militarische Zeitschrift* 7 (Mar.–Apr. 1969): 164–65.

7739 Evron, Yair. "Israel and the Atom: The Uses and Misuses of Ambiguity, 1957–1967." *Orbis* 17 (Winter 1974): 1325–43.

7740 Freedman, Lawrence. "Israel's Nuclear Option." *Bulletin of the Atomic Scientists* 30 (Sept. 1974): 30–36.

7741 ———. "Israel's Nuclear Policy." *Survival* 17 (May–June 1975): 114–20.

7742 "How Israel Got the Bomb." *Time* (Apr. 12, 1976): 39–40.

7743 Jabber, Fuad. *Israel and Nuclear Weapons: Present Option and Future Strategies.* London: Chatto & Windus, 1971.

7744 ———. "Israel's Nuclear Options." *Journal of Palestine Studies* 1 (Winter 1971): 21–38.

7745 ———. *Israel's Nuclear Option and U.S. Arms Control Policy.* Santa Monica, Ca.: California Arms Control & Foreign Policy Seminar, Feb. 1972.

7746 Quester, George H. "Israel and the Nuclear Non-Proliferation Treaty." *Bulletin of the Atomic Scientists* 25 (June 1969): 7–9 ff.

7747 Rutherford, Evan. "Israel and the Bomb." *Cambridge Review* 89A (Dec. 2, 1967): 157–60.

7748 Smith, Hendrick. "U.S. Assumes the Israelis Have A-Bomb or Its Parts." *New York Times,* July 18, 1970.

7749 Valery, Nicholas. "Israel's Silent Gamble with the Bomb." *New Scientist* (Dec. 12, 1974): 807–09.

PAKISTAN

7750 Akhund, Iqbal. "Pakistan and the Atom." *New York Times,* Apr. 23, 1976.

7751 Khalilzad, Zalmay. "Pakistan: The Making of a Nuclear Power." *Asia Survey* 16 (June 1976): 580 ff.

SOUTH AFRICA

7752 "Atomic Weapons for West Germany and South Africa." *Atlas* 19 (Fall 1970): 42–43.

7753 Cassuto, Aldo. "Can Uranium Enrichment Enrich South Africa?" *World Today* 26 (Oct. 1970): 419–27.

7754 Gillette, Robert. "With Help, South Africa Is Progressing." *Science* (June 13, 1975): 1090–92.

7755 Krasilnikov, A. "West Germany–South Africa: Nuclear Alliance." *International Affairs* [Moscow] 15 (Aug. 1969): 111.

7756 Limp, W. "South Africa: Soon, the Atomic Bomb?" *Jeune Afrique* (Apr. 27, 1971): 18–19.

7757 Patil, R. L. M. "South Africa's Nuclear Situation." *African Quarterly* 8 (Apr.–July 1968): 44–51.

7758 Quester, George H. "Paris, Pretoria, Peking . . . Proliferation?" *Bulletin of the Atomic Scientists* 26 (Oct. 1970): 12–16.

SWEDEN

7759 Birnbaum, Karl E. "Sweden's Nuclear Policy." *Survival* 7 (Dec. 1965): 314–18.

7760 ———. "The Swedish Experience." In Alastair Buchan, ed., *A World of Nuclear Powers*. Englewood Cliffs, N.J.: Prentice-Hall, 1966, pp. 68–75.

7761 Garris, Jerome. *Sweden and the Spread of Nuclear Weapons: A Study in Restraint.* Santa Monica, Ca.: California Arms Control & Foreign Policy Seminar, 1972.

7762 ———. "Sweden's Debate on the Proliferation of Nuclear Weapons." *Cooperation & Conflict* 8:3–4 (1973): 189–208.

7763 Quester, George H. "Sweden and the Nuclear Non-Proliferation Treaty." *Cooperation and Conflict* 5:1 (1970): 52–60.

7764 Svala, Gertrud. "Sweden's View of the Non-Proliferation Treaty." In Andrew W. Cordier, ed., *Columbia Essays in International Affairs*. New York: Columbia Univ. Press, 1971, VI: 92–115.

WEST GERMANY

7765 Anderson, Edith. "War Games and Neo-Nazis: W. Germany Set for Atomic Arms." *National Guardian* (Nov. 26, 1966): 1 ff.

7766 Bader, William B. "Nuclear Weapons Sharing and the 'German Problem.' " *Foreign Affairs* 44 (July 1966): 693–700.

7767 Brandt, Willy. "Deutschland und der Atomsperrvertrag." *Aussenpolitik* 18 (May 1967): 257–67.

7768 ———. "Non-Proliferation and Equality." *News from Germany* 24 (Jan.–Feb. 1969): 1–7.

7769 Einhorn, Clare. "Non-Proliferation of Nuclear Weapons." *German Foreign Policy* 7:4 (1968): 275–82.

7770 Germany, Federal Republic of. *Treaty on the Non-Proliferation of Nuclear Weapons: German Attitude and Contribution, Documentation.* Bonn: Press & Information Office, Dec. 1969.

7771 Kissinger, Henry A. "Should Germany Be Allowed to Become a Nuclear Power?" *Realities* [London] 189 (Aug. 1966): 13–15.

7772 Klein, Peter. "Bonn's Struggle Against Non-Proliferation of Nuclear Weapons." *German Foreign Policy* 6:5 (1967): 385–93.

7773 Magathan, Wallace G., Jr. "West German Defense Policy." *Orbis* 8 (Summer 1964): 292–315.

7774 Mendershausen, Horst. "Will West Germany Go Nuclear?" *Orbis* 16 (Summer 1972): 411–34.

7775 ———. *Will West Germany Try to Get Nuclear Arms—Somehow?* Rpt. P–4649. Santa Monica, Ca.: Rand, May 1971.

7776 "The Nonproliferation Treaty and Germany." *Central Europe Journal* 16 (Aug.–Sept. 1968): 227–50.

7777 Petri, Alexander. *Die Entstehung des NV-Vertrages: Die Rolle der Bundesrepublik Deutschland.* Tubingen, 1970.

7778 ———. "Germany's Part in the Nonproliferation Treaty." *Aussenpolitik* 21:1 (1970): 14–24.

7779 Roedl, Franz. "Consequences for Germany of the Nonproliferation Treaty." *Central Europe Journal* 17 (Apr. 1969): 122–25.

7780   Rogers, William P. "Federal Republic of Germany Signs Nuclear Nonproliferation Treaty." *U.S. Department of State Bulletin* (Dec. 15, 1969): 545.

7781   Schlosser, Francois. "West Germany's No to Nuclear Non-Proliferation." *Realities* [London] 203 (Oct. 1967): 27–29.

7782   Schmidt, Helmut. *Defense or Retaliation: A German View.* New York: Praeger, 1962.

7783   Somner, Theo. "The Objectives of Germany." In Alastair Buchan, ed., *A World of Nuclear Powers.* Englewood Cliffs, N.J.: Prentice-Hall, 1966, pp. 39–51.

7784   Yuryer, N. "European Security and the German Question." *International Affairs* [Moscow] 11 (Oct. 1965): 56–60.

YUGOSLAVIA

7785   Gedza, Dimitije S. "Yugoslavia and Nuclear Weapons." *Survival* 18 (May–June 1976): 116–17.

7786   Pesic, Milorad. "Yugoslavia and Nuclear Non-Proliferation." *Review of International Affairs* [Belgrade] (Mar. 5, 1970): 6–8.

Continuing Issues
(1969–1976)

7787   Alekseev, A. "Non-Proliferation Talks." *International Affairs* [Moscow] 15 (May 1969): 19–23.

7788   Bader, Thomas M. "Swords and Plowshares." *Naval War College Review* 21 (Oct. 1969): 21–25.

7789   Barnaby, Frank. "Limits on the Nuclear Club." *Survival* 12 (May 1970): 161–63.

7790   Bloomfield, Lincoln P. "Nuclear Spread and World Order." *Foreign Affairs* 53 (July 1975): 743–55.

7791   Bull, Hedley. "Rethinking Non-Proliferation." *International Affairs* 51 (Apr. 1975): 175–89.

7792   Bunn, George. "Horizontal Proliferation of Nuclear Weapons." In Bennett Boskey and Mason Willrich, eds., *Nuclear Proliferation: Prospects for Control.* New York: Dunellen, 1970.

7793   Carter, Gov. Jimmy. "Nuclear Energy and World Order." Address to the U.N., May 13, 1976. Reprinted in *Congressional Record* 122 (June 4, 1976): S8541–44.

7794   Chalfont, Lord Arthur G. J. "The Dangers of a Nuclear Europe." *New Statesman* (Apr. 16, 1971): 52–53.

7795   Clemens, Walter C., Jr. "Controlling Nuclear Spread." *Bulletin of the Atomic Scientists* 30 (Sept. 1974): 63–64.

7796   Coffey, Joseph I. "Threat, Reassurance, and Nuclear Proliferation." In Bennett Boskey and Mason Willrich, eds., *Nuclear Proliferation: Prospects for Control.* New York: Dunellen, 1970.

7797   Cranston, Sen. Alan. "Senate Concurrent Resolution 69: Submission of a Concurrent Resolution Relating to Nuclear Reduction, Testing and Nonproliferation." *Congressional Record* 121 (Oct. 9, 1975): S18090–102.

7798   DeGara, John P. "Nuclear Proliferation and Security." *International Conciliation*, no. 578 (May 1970): 1–53.

7799   Donnelly, Warren H. "Control of Proliferation of Nuclear Weapons." *Congressional Record* 122 (June 18, 1976): E3464–67.

7800   Dunn, Lewis A., and William H. Overholt. "The Next Phase in Nuclear Proliferation Research." *Orbis* 20 (Summer 1976): 467–523.

7801   Epstein, William. "The Proliferation of Nuclear Weapons." *Scientific American* 232 (Apr. 1975): 18–33.

7802   Fisher, Adrian S. "Global Dimensions." In Bennett Boskey and Mason Willrich, eds., *Nuclear Proliferation: Prospects for Control.* New York: Dunellen, 1970.

7803   "Further Activity in Pursuance of the Non-Proliferation Treaty." *International Affairs* [Moscow] 18 (July 1972): 110–12.

7804   Hahn, Walter F. "Nuclear Proliferation." *Strategic Review* 3 (Winter 1975): 16–24.

7805   Hammond, Allen L. "Nuclear Proliferation: Warnings From the Arms Control Community." *Science* (July 9, 1976).

7806   Hoag, Malcolm W. *One American Perspective on Nuclear Guarantees, Proliferation, and Related Alliance Diplomacy.* Paper P–4547. Santa Monica, Ca.: Rand, Feb. 1971.

7807 Humphrey, Sen. Hubert H. "Senator Kennedy's Address on Nuclear Nonproliferation." *Congressional Record* (Apr. 10, 1975): S5831–33.

7808 Kowarski, Lew. "The Spreading Nuclear Wave." *New Scientist* (Aug. 6, 1970): 280–81.

7809 Maddox, John. *Prospects for Nuclear Proliferation.* Adelphi Paper, no. 13. London: Institute for Strategic Studies, Spring 1975.

7810 Miettinen, Jorma K. "Recent Developments in Tactical Nuclear Weapons and Their Bearing on Nuclear Non-Proliferation." *Instant Research on Peace and Violence* 3:4 (1973): 225–30.

7811 Millar, Thomas B. "The Nuclear Non-Proliferation Treaty and Super Power Condominium." In Carsten Holbradd, ed., *Super Powers and World Order.* Canberra: Australian National Univ. Press, 1971, pp. 64–73.

7812 Nelson, Sen. Gaylord. "Nuclear Proliferation: A Growing Danger." *Congressional Record* 121 (Nov. 11, 1975): S19638–641.

7813 Pence, Col. Arthur W. "Controlling the Inevitable: An Alternative to Nonproliferation." *Army Quarterly* 97 (Jan. 1969): 237–46.

7814 Ponte, Lowell. "The Proliferation Non-Treaty." *National Review* (Dec. 15, 1970): 1340–43.

7815 Quester, George H. "Can Proliferation Now Be Stopped?" *Foreign Affairs* 53 (Oct. 1974): 77–97.

7816 ———. "Some Conceptual Problems in Nuclear Proliferation." *American Political Science Review* 66 (June 1972): 490–97.

7817 ———. "Soviet Policy on the Nuclear Non-Proliferation Treaty." *Cornell International Law Journal* 5:1 (1972): 17–34.

7818 Ranger, Robert. "The NPT Two Years On: Lessons for Arms Control." *World Today* 26 (Nov. 1970): 453–57.

7819 Scheinman, Lawrence. "Pandora's Nuclear Box." *International Journal* 25 (Autumn 1970): 779 ff.

7820 Shestov, V. "The Non-Proliferation Treaty in Action." *International Affairs* [Moscow] 19 (Aug. 1973): 33–40.

7821 SIPRI. *The Nuclear Age.* Cambridge: M.I.T. Press, 1974.

7822 ———. *Nuclear Disarmament or Nuclear War?* Stockholm, Jan. 1975.

7823 ———. *Preventing Nuclear-Weapon Proliferation.* Stockholm, Jan. 1975.

7824 Steinfels, Peter. "Non-Proliferation: Two Views. A Nuclear Sarajevo." *Commonweal* (Mar. 14, 1969): 721 ff.

7825 Symington, Sen. Stuart. "Controlling the Cancer of Nuclear Proliferation." *Congressional Record* 121 (Mar. 13, 1975): S3843–44.

7826 Tomilin, Y. "The Non-Proliferation Problem." *International Affairs* [Moscow] 20 (Dec. 1974): 28–36.

7827 U.S. Arms Control & Disarmament Agency. *The Danger of Nuclear Proliferation.* Pub. 75:7. Washington, D.C.: G.P.O., Nov. 1974.

7828 U.S. House. Committee on International Relations. Hearings: *Nuclear Proliferation: Future U.S. Foreign Policy Implications.* 94th Cong., 1st Sess., 1975.

7829 U.S. Senate. Committee on Government Operations. Handbook: *Facts on Nuclear Proliferation.* 94th Cong., 1st Sess., 1975.

7830 Van Doren, Charles N. "U.N. Involvement in Disarmament: The Case of the Non-Proliferation Treaty." *American Journal of International Law* 64 (Sept. 1970): 191–93.

7831 Zablocki, Rep. Clement J. "Nuclear Proliferation: Future U.S. Foreign Policy Implications." *Congressional Record* 122 (May 3, 1976): H3817–20.

NPT & Civilian Nuclear Technology

7832 Baker, Steven J. *Commercial Nuclear Power and Nuclear Proliferation.* Peace Studies Program Occasional Papers, no. 5. Ithaca, N.Y.: Cornell Univ., May 1975.

7833 Beaton, Leonard. "Nuclear Fuel for All." *Foreign Affairs* 45 (July 1967): 662–69.

7834 Delcoigne, G. C., and G. Rubinstein. "Nonproliferation and Control: Peaceful Uses of Atomic Energy." *Bulletin of the Atomic Scientists* 27 (Feb. 1971): 5–7.

7835 Doub, William W., and Joseph M. Dukert. "Making Nuclear Energy Safe and Secure." *Foreign Affairs* 53 (July 1975): 756–72.

7836 Eads, George, and Richard R. Nelson. "Governmental Support of Advanced Civilian Technology: Power Reactors and the Supersonic Transport." *Public Policy* 19 (Summer 1971): 405–28.

7837 Feiveson, Harold A. "Latent Proliferation: The International Security Implications of Civil Nuclear Power." Ph.D. diss., Princeton Univ., 1972.

7838 Gilinsky, Victor. *Fast Breeder Reactors and the Spread of Plutonium.* Santa Monica, Ca.: Rand, Mar. 1967.

7839 ———. "Military Potential of Civilian Nuclear Power." In Bennett Boskey and Mason Willrich, eds., *Nuclear Proliferation: Prospects for Control.* New York: Dunellen, 1970.

7840 ———, and Bruce L. R. Smith. "Civilian Nuclear Power and Foreign Policy." *Orbis* 12 (Fall 1968): 816–30.

7841 ———, and W. Hoehn, Jr. *The Military Significance of Small Uranium Enrichment Facilities Fed with Low-Enrichment Uranium.* Santa Monica, Ca.: Rand, Dec. 1969.

7842 "Mushrooming Spread of Nuclear Power." *Time* (Sept. 9, 1974): 28–30.

7843 Nau, Henry R. "The Practice of Interdependence in the Research and Development Sector: Fast Reactor Cooperation in Western Europe." *International Organization* 26 (Summer 1972): 499–526.

7844 Palfrey, John G. "Atoms for Peace and the Effort to Halt the Spread of Nuclear Weapons." *U.S. Department of State Bulletin* (Sept. 6, 1965): 393–97.

7845 Phillips, James G. "Energy Report/Safeguards, Recycling Broaden Nuclear Power Debate." *National Journal Reports* (Mar. 22, 1975): 419–29.

7846 Plesset, Milton S. "Nuclear Power and Nuclear Proliferation." *Engineering and Science* 31 (Jan. 1968): 15–19.

7847 Richard J. Barber Associates, Inc. *LDC Nuclear Power Prospects, 1975–1990: Commercial Economic & Security Implications.*

ERDA-52. Springfield, Va.: National Technical Information Service, 1975.

7848 Shapley, Deborah. "Plutonium Reactor Proliferation Threatens a Nuclear Black Market." *Science* (Apr. 9, 1971): 143–46.

7849 Stevenson, Sen. Adlai E., III. "Nuclear Reactors: America Must Act." *Foreign Affairs* 53 (Oct. 1974): 64–76.

7850 U.S. Senate. Government Operations Committee. Compendium: *Peaceful Nuclear Exports and Weapons Proliferation.* 94th Cong., 1st Sess. Washington, D.C.: G.P.O., Apr. 1975.

Peaceful Nuclear Explosions (PNE)

7851 *An Analysis of the Economic Feasibility, Technical Significance and Time Scale for Application of Peaceful Nuclear Explosions in the U.S.: With Special Reference to the GURC Report Thereon.* Ithaca, N.Y.: Cornell Univ., Program on Science, Technology & Society, Apr. 1975.

7852 Bechhoefer, Bernhard G. "Plowshare Control." In Bennett Boskey and Mason Willrich, eds., *Nuclear Proliferation: Prospects For Control.* New York: Dunellen, 1970, pp. 103–15.

7853 Beltizky, Boris. "Soviet Science: Atomic Blasts to Save the Caspian?" *New Scientist* (Jan. 15, 1976): 121–22.

7854 Brooks, David B., and John V. Krutilla. *Peaceful Use of Nuclear Explosives: Some Economic Aspects.* Baltimore: Johns Hopkins Press, 1969.

7855 ———; and Henry R. Myers. "Plowshare Evaluation." In Bennett Boskey and Mason Willrich, eds. *Nuclear Proliferation: Prospects for Control.* New York: Dunellen, 1970, pp. 87–101.

7856 Carter, Luther. "Peaceful Nuclear Explosions: Promises, Promises." *Science* (June 6, 1975): 996.

7857 Ehrlich, Thomas. "The Nonproliferation Treaty and Peaceful Uses of Nuclear Explosives." *Virginia Law Review* 56 (May 1970): 587–601.

7858 Emelyanov, V. S. "On the Peaceful Use of Nuclear Explosions." In SIPRI. *Nuclear*

Proliferation Problems. Cambridge: M.I.T., 1974, pp. 215–24.

7859   Ericsson, Ulf. "The Non-Controversial Use of Nuclear Explosions for Peaceful Purposes." *Cooperation and Conflict* 5:1 (1970): 1–19.

7860   IAEA. *Peaceful Uses of Nuclear Explosions.* Bibliographical Series, 38. Vienna, 1970.

7861   Inglis, David R., and Carl L. Sandler. "Prospects and Problems: The Nonmilitary Uses of Nuclear Explosives." *Bulletin of the Atomic Scientists* 23 (Dec. 1967): 46–53.

7862   Johnson, Gerald W. "Plowshare at the Crossroad." *Bulletin of the Atomic Scientists* 26 (June 1970): 83–91.

7863   Koop, Jacob. "Plowshare and the Nonproliferation Treaty." *Orbis* 13 (Fall 1968): 793–815.

7864   Kreith, Frank, and Catherine B. Wrenn. *The Nuclear Impact: A Case Study of the Plowshare Program to Produce Gas by Underground Nuclear Stimulation in the Rocky Mountains.* Boulder, Colo.: Westview Press, 1976.

7865   Long, F. A. "Is There a Future For Peaceful Nuclear Explosions?" *Arms Control Today* 5 (May 1975): 1–2.

7866   ———. "Peaceful Nuclear Explosions." *Bulletin of the Atomic Scientists* 32 (Oct. 1976): 19–28.

7867   Lough, Thomas S. "Peaceful Nuclear Explosions and Disarmament." *Peace Research Review* 2 (June 1968): 1–64.

7868   Myrdal, Alva. " 'Peaceful' Nuclear Explosions." *Bulletin of the Atomic Scientists* 31 (May 1975): 29–33.

7869   ———. *The Right to Conduct Nuclear Explosions: Political Aspects and Policy Proposals.* Stockholm: SIPRI, 1975.

7870   "Nuclear Explosions for Peaceful Purposes." In SIPRI. *The Nuclear Age.* Cambridge: M.I.T. Press, pp. 102–11.

7871   Panofsky, Wolfgang. "Peaceful Uses of Nuclear Explosions." In U.S. House. Committee on Interior and Insular Affairs. Hearings: *Oversight Hearings on Nuclear Energy: Overview of the Major Issues.* 94th Cong., 1st Sess., 1975, pt. 1, pp. 727–39.

7872   *PNE (Peaceful Nuclear Explosion) Activity Projections for Arms Control Planning.* Galveston: Gulf Universities Research Consortium, Apr. 1975.

7873   Roncalio, Rep. Teno. "Plowshare—A Technology in Search of A Use." *Congressional Record* 120 (Feb. 25, 1974): H1090–93.

7874   Scoville, Herbert, Jr. "Peaceful Nuclear Explosions—An Invitation of Proliferation." In Anne Marks, ed., *NPT: Paradoxes and Problems.* Washington, D.C.: Arms Control Assoc., 1975, pp. 47–54.

7875   Teller, Edward, et al. *The Constructive Uses of Nuclear Explosives.* New York: McGraw-Hill, 1968.

7876   U.N. *The Question of Nuclear Explosions for Peaceful Purposes by Non-Nuclear Weapons States and the Possibility of Misuse of Such Technology for the Production of Nuclear Weapons.* Doc. A/CONF 35/Doc. 3. New York, July 3, 1968.

7877   U.S. House. Committee on Interior and Insular Affairs. Hearings: *Oversight Hearings on Nuclear Energy: Overview of the Major Issues.* Pt. 1. 94th Cong., 1st Sess., 1975.

7878   U.S. Joint Committee on Atomic Energy. Hearings: *Commercial Plowshare Services.* 90th Cong., 2d Sess., 1968.

7879   U.S. Senate. Committee on Interior and Insular Affairs. Hearings: *Nuclear Stimulation of Natural Gas.* 93d Cong., 1st Sess., 1973.

7880   Zheleznov, R. "Nuclear Explosions for Peaceful Purposes." *International Affairs* [Moscow] 22 (Aug. 1976): 81–87.

NUCLEAR EXPORT POLICY

7881   Agnew, Harold M. "Atoms For Lease: An Alternative to Assured Nuclear Proliferation." *Bulletin of the Atomic Scientists* 32 (May 1976): 23.

7882   Baker, Steven. "Nuclear Proliferation: Monopoly or Cartel?" *Foreign Policy,* no. 23 (Summer 1976): 202–220.

7883   Boffery, Philip M. "ERDA Gives Boost to Breeder Program." *Science* (Jan. 23, 1976): 269.

7884 Frye, Alton. "How to Ban the Bomb: Sell It." *New York Times Magazine* (Jan. 11, 1976): 11, 76–79.

7885 Glackin, James L. "The Dangerous Drift in Uranium Enrichment." *Bulletin of the Atomic Scientists* 32 (Feb. 1976): 22–29.

7886 Glenn, Sen. John. "The Safety and Security of Our Nuclear Exports." *Congressional Record* 122 (Feb. 18, 1976): S1800–1806.

7887 Joskow, Paul L. "The International Nuclear Industry Today." *Foreign Affairs* 54 (July 1976): 788–803.

7888 Long, Rep. Clarence D. "Congress Must Act Against Nuclear Proliferation." *Congressional Record* 121 (Nov. 19, 1975): E6245–46.

7889 ———. "Strengthening U.S. Nuclear Export Policy." *Congressional Record* 121 (Oct. 23, 1975): H5573–74.

7890 Maxfield, David M. "Legislation to Control Spread of U.S. Nuclear Technology, Weapons Proliferation Dies." *Congressional Quarterly* (Oct. 9, 1976): 2957.

7891 Metz, William D. "European Breeders: France Leads the Way." *Science* (Dec. 26, 1975): 1279–81.

7892 ———. "European Breeders: Fuels and Fuel Cycle Are Keys to Economy." *Science* (Feb. 13, 1976): 551–53.

7893 Mondale, Sen. Walter. "Senate Resolution 199: Submission of a Resolution Relative to Nuclear Weapons Proliferation." *Congressional Record* 121 (June 26, 1975): S11680–681.

7894 Ottinger, Rep. Richard. "Exports of Nuclear Fuel to India Challenged by Environmentalists." *Congressional Record* 122 (Mar. 3, 1976): E1059–60.

7895 Pastore, Sen. John O. "U.S. Export of Nuclear Technology." *Congressional Record* 121 (Apr. 17, 1975): S5989–94.

7896 Phillips, James G. "Energy Report/ Controversy Surrounds Proposed Nuclear Export Policies." *National Journal Reports* (May 10, 1975): 685–89.

7897 Ribicoff, Sen. Abraham A. "A Market-Sharing Approach to the Nuclear Sales Problem." *Foreign Affairs* 54 (July 1976): 763–87.

7898 ———. "NRC's Historic Opinion and Dissent on Nuclear Export Policy." *Congressional Record* 122 (June 21, 1976): S10042–10051.

7899 ———. "West German and French Nuclear Exports Pose a Direct Threat to World Peace." *Congressional Record* 122 (Apr. 26, 1976): S5873–79.

7900 Salaff, Stephen. "Will Trade in Uranium Enrichment Technology Increase Weapons Spread?" *Science Forum* [Canada] (Dec. 1974): 14–17.

7901 Stewart, Walter. "How We Learned to Stop Worrying and Sell the Bomb: All Sales Could Be Final." *Maclean's* 87 (Nov. 1974): 29–33.

7902 U.S. General Accounting Office. *Allocation of Uranium Enrichment Services to Fuel Foreign and Domestic Nuclear Reactors.* Report no. ID–75–45. Washington, D.C.: G.A.O., Mar. 4, 1975.

7903 U.S. House. Committee on International Relations. Hearings: *Resolution of Inquiry Into Proposed Nuclear Agreements With Egypt and Israel.* July 9, 1974. 93d Cong., 2d Sess., 1975.

7904 ———. Report: *Laws and Regulations Governing Nuclear Exports and Domestic and International Nuclear Safeguard,* Doc. no. 94–131. Washington, D.C.: G.P.O., May 6, 1975.

7905 U.S. Senate. Committee on Banking, Housing and Urban Affairs. Hearings: *Exports of Nuclear Materials and Technology* [to Israel & Egypt]. 93d Cong., 2d Sess., 1974.

7906 ———. Committee on Government Operations. Hearings: *Export Reorganization Act of 1976.* 94th Cong., 2d Sess., 1976.

7907 ———. Report: *A Compendium: Peaceful Nuclear Exports and Weapons Proliferation.* 94th Cong., 1st Sess., 1975.

7908 Walsh, John. "Nuclear Exports and Proliferation: The French Think They Have a Case." *Science* (July 30, 1976): 387–89.

7909 Younghusband, Peter. "Nuclear Power Politics." *European Community,* no. 196 (Aug.–Sept. 1976): 22–25.

7910 Zoppo, Ciro E. *Toward a U.S. Policy on Nuclear Technology Transfer to Developing Countries.* Santa Monica: California Arms Control & Foreign Policy Seminar, July 1971.

Thirteen

Rules of War & Stabilizing
the International Environment

THE "RULES OF war" and agreements that "stabilize the international environment" are additional, but frequently overlooked, aspects of arms control. The former topic deals with specific international limitations on military operations once hostilities have begun. The latter category, meanwhile, is a very general catch-all that ranges from politico-military agreements which attempt to stabilize a geographical area to pacts designed to prevent an accidental nuclear war.

Since the "Peace of God" movement in the Middle Ages, the Western world has attempted to reduce the destructiveness of war by developing international rules governing armed conflicts between nations. Two of the many good studies which trace the evolution of these ideas are J. Stone's *Legal Controls of International Conflict* (1954) and S. E. Edmunds' "The Laws of War: Their Rise in the Nineteenth Century and Their Collapse in the Twentieth," *Virginia Law Review* (1929). Also, the impact of 20th century military technology upon these rules has been a matter of frequent concern among international lawyers, as re-

flected in J. L. Kunz's "The Chaotic Status of the Laws of War and the Urgent Necessity for Their Revision," *American Journal of International Law* (1951).

It should be noted that Chapter 10 contains references to related topics—international law and weapons, international law and nuclear weapons, and CBW and international law. The book by S. D. Bailey, *Prohibitions and Restraints in War* (1972), ties the development of the "rules of war" to these related topics.

Of the several issues involved in the "rules of war," noncombatant immunity and military necessity are fundamental. R. S. Hartigan's several essays on noncombatant immunity show its historical origins, while L. Nurick's "The Distinction Between Combatant and Noncombatant in the Law of War," *American Journal of International Law* (1945), reveals the impact of World War II. W. V. O'Brien's "Legitimate Military Necessity in Nuclear War," *World Polity* (1960), grapples with this dilemma.

Efforts to stabilize the international environment, as defined here, include the historical example of the Turkish Straits, efforts aimed at the prevention of accidental war and the protection of the physical environment from the effects of modern weaponry. The Turkish Straits issue is included as an example of an arms control mechanism which allowed a weaker, third power to control a vital waterway and thereby reduce the friction between other major powers. Concern with accidental war has grown as weapons have become so destructive. The "hot line" agreements between the United States and the Soviet Union are often cited as examples of how the possibility of accidental nuclear war may be lessened.

The negotiation of the Nuclear Test Ban Treaty (1963) revealed an appreciation of the dangers that weapons development can hold for mankind. J. M. Fowler's collection of essays, *Fallout: A Study of Superbombs, Strontium 90 and Survival* (1960), and the many essays generated by the debate over the dangers of nuclear testing show the worldwide concern with this new state of affairs.

The Vietnam War directed attention to the possible impact that new weather modification techniques might have on the environment. J. Goldblat's essay, "The Prohibition of Environmental Warfare," *Ambio* (1975), reveals the status of proposals aimed at preventing the use of such techniques as of the end of 1975.

Rules of War

HISTORICAL ASSESSMENTS

7911 Armour, W. S. "The Obstacles of National and Primitive Customs to the Spread of International Law." *Transactions of the Grotius Society* 16 (1934): 1–10.

7912 Bailey, Sidney D. *Prohibitions and Restraints in War.* New York: Oxford Univ. Press, 1972.

7913 Ballis, William. *The Legal Position of War: Changes in its Practice and Theory from Plato to Vattel.* The Hague: Nijhoff, 1937.

7914 Baty, T., and Gen. John H. Morgan. *War: Its Conduct and Legal Results.* London: J. Murray, 1915.

7915 Bohannen, P., ed. *Law and Warfare.* Garden City, N.Y.: Natural History Press, 1967.

7916 Brand, G. "The Development of the International Law of War." *Tulane Law Review* 25 (Feb. 1951): 186–204.

7917 Bühler, G., trans. *The Laws of Manu. Sacred Books of the East,* vol. 25. Oxford: Clarendon Press, 1886 (1969), Bk vii, sec. 90–93.

7918 Coursier, Henri. "Francis Lieber and the Laws of War." *Revue Internationale de la Croix-Rouge* [English Supplement] 6 (Sept. 1953): 156–69.

7919 Decker, Charles L. *Roman Military Law.* Austin: Univ. of Texas Press, 1968.

7920 Edmunds, Sterling E. "The Laws of War: Their Rise in the Nineteenth Century and Their Collapse in the Twentieth." *Virginia Law Review* 15 (Feb. 1929): 321–49.

7921 Edwards, Charles. "The Law of War in the Thought of Hugo Grotius." *Journal of Public Law* 19:2 (1970): 371–98.

7922 France. Foreign Office. *Rapports et Proces-verbaux d'Enquete de la Commission Instituee en Vue Constater les Actes Commis par l'Ennemi en Violation du Droit des Gens (Decret du 23 Septembre 1914).* 9 vols. Paris, 1915.

7923 ———. Ministry of War. *Les Lois de la Guerre Continentale.* 4th ed. Paris, 1919.

7924 Fuller, Gen. J. F. C. *The Conduct of War, 1789–1961.* New Brunswick: Rutgers Univ. Press, 1961.

7925 Garner, James W. *International Law and the World War.* 2 vols. London: Longmans, Green, 1920.

7926   Grotius, Hugo. *The Law of War and Peace.* Trans. by F. W. Kelsey. Indianapolis: Bobbs-Merrill, 1925.

7927   Keen, M. H. *The Laws of War in the Late Middle Ages.* Toronto: Univ. of Toronto Press, 1965.

7928   Korovin, Eugene A. "The Second World War and International Law." *American Journal of International Law* 40 (Oct. 1946): 742–55.

7929   Laurentie, J. *Les Lois de la Guerre.* Paris: Marchal et Godde, 1917.

7930   Marin, Miguel A. "The Evolution and Present Status of the Laws of War." *Recueil de l'Academie de Droit International de La Haye* 92 (1957): 629–754.

7931   Miller, Richard I., ed. *The Law of War.* Lexington, Mass.: Lexington Books, 1975.

7932   Noel-Baker, Philip J. "The League of Nations and the Laws of War." *British Yearbook of International Law* 1 (1920): 109–24.

7933   Phillipson, Coleman. *International Law and the Great War.* London: Unwin, 1915.

7934   Prussia. Great General Staff. Military History Office. *Les Lois de la Guerre Continentale.* Trans. by P. Carpentier. Paris: Librairie Generale de Droit & de Jurisprudence, 1904.

7935   Taylor, Telford. "The Concept of Justice and the Laws of War." *Columbia Journal of Transnational Law* 13:2 (1974): 189–207.

7936   Vanderpol, A. *La Doctrine Scholastique du Droit de Guerre.* Paris: Pedone, 1919.

7937   Vitoria, Franciscus de. *On the Law of War Made by the Spaniards on the Barbarians.* [James Brown Scott, ed. *The Classics of International Law,* no. 7.] Washington, D.C.: Carnegie Endowment for International Peace, 1917.

Contemporary Views

7938   Baxter, Richard R. "The Cambridge Conference on the Revision of the Law of War." *American Journal of International Law* 47 (Oct. 1953): 702–04.

7939   ———. "The Law of War." *Naval War College Review* 5 (Jan. 1957): 39–58.

7940   ———. "The Law of War in the Arab-Israeli Conflict: On Water and on Land." *Towson State Journal of International Affairs* 5 (Spring 1971): 1–17.

7941   ———. "The Role of Law in Modern War." *Proceedings of American Society of International Law* 47 (1953): 90–98.

7942   Bindschedler, Robert D. *A Reconsideration of the Law of Armed Conflict.* New York: Carnegie Endowment for International Peace, 1971.

7943   Bordwell, P. *Law of War.* Chicago: Callaghan, 1908.

7944   Bretton, Philippe. *Le Droit de la Guerre.* Paris: A. Colin, 1970.

7945   Brown, Sidney H. "Les Lois de la Guerre selon la Doctrine du Droit International depuis 1914 (a propos de l'article de M. Jos. L. Kunz)." *Revue Internationale de la Croix-Rouge* 16 (May 1934): 367–87.

7946   Carey, John, ed. *When Battle Rages, How Can Law Protect?* 14th Hammarskjold Forum. Dobbs Ferry, N.Y.: Oceana, 1971.

7947   Chase, Capt. Jack S. "Military Ideals." *Armor* 79 (July–Aug. 1970): 18–20.

7948   Clemens, Rene. *Le Projet de Monaco: Le Droit de la Guerre.* Paris: Librairie du Recueil Sircy, 1938.

7949   Dillard, Hardy C. "Law and Conflict: Some Current Dilemmas." *Washington and Lee Law Review* 24 (Fall 1967): 177–204.

7950   Dunbar, N. C. H. "The Legal Regulation of Modern Warfare." *Transactions of the Grotius Society* 40 (1954): 83–95.

7951   Dupuy, T. N., and Janice B. Fain. "Laws Governing Combat." *National Defense* 60 (Nov.–Dec. 1975): 218–21.

7952   Falk, Richard A. *Law, Morality and War in the Contemporary World.* New York: Praeger, 1963.

7953   Farer, Tom J. "Humanitarian Law and Armed Conflicts: Toward the Definition of 'International Armed Conflict.'" *Columbia Law Review* 71 (Jan. 1971): 37 ff.

7954   ———. "The Law of War 25 Years After Nuremberg." *International Conciliation,* no. 583 (May 1971): 5–54.

7955   Fioravanzo, Giuseppe. "Le Droit de Guerre est-il Mort?" *Revue de Defense Nationale* [Paris] 12 (Feb. 1956): 169–80.

7956 Forman, William H. "Should the Law of War be Changed?" *American Bar Association Journal* 57 (Oct. 1971): 986–89.

7957 Francois, J. P. A. "Reconsideration des Principes du Droit de la Guerre." *Annuaire de l'Institut de Droit International* [Session de Amsterdam] 47:1 (1957): 323 ff.

7958 ———. "Reconsideration des Principes du Droit de la Guerre." *Annuaire de l'Institut de Droit International* [Session de Neuchatel] 48:2 (1959): 178–263.

7959 Frei, Daniel. "The Regulation of Warfare: A Paradigm for the Legal Approach to the Control of International Conflict." *Journal of Conflict Resolution* 18:4 (1974): 620–33.

7960 Giraud, Emile. "Le Respect des Droits de l'Homme dans la Guerre Internationale et dans la Guerre Civile." *Revue du Droit Public et de la Science Politique en France et a l'Etranger* [Paris] 74 (July–Aug. 1958): 613–75.

7961 Goodhart, A. L. *What Acts of War are Justified?* Oxford: Clarendon Press, 1940.

7962 Guelzo, Lt. Col. Carl M. "International Law of War." *Military Review* 50 (Oct. 1970): 47–55.

7963 Hargreaves, Maj. Reginald. "The Rule Book of Warfare." *Marine Corps Gazette* 54 (Aug. 1970): 44–49.

7964 Heydte, Baron F. A. von der. "Grundbegriffe des Modernen Kriegsrechts." *Friedens-Warte* 56:4 (1961): 333–48.

7965 Jessup, Philip C. "Political and Humanitarian Approaches to Limitation of Warfare." *American Journal of International Law* 51 (Oct. 1957): 757–61.

7966 Kelly, Maj. Joseph B. "A Legal Analysis of the Changes in War." *Military Law Review* 13 (July 1961): 89–119.

7967 Kunz, Josef L. "The Chaotic Status of the Laws of War and the Urgent Necessity for Their Revision." *American Journal of International Law* 45 (Jan. 1951): 37–61.

7968 ———. "The Laws of War." *American Journal of International Law* 50 (Apr. 1956): 313–37.

7969 ———. "Plus de Lois de la Guerre?" *Revue Generale de Droit International Public* (Jan.–Feb. 1934): 22–57.

7970 Kunzmann, K. H. "Ein gemeinsames Kriegsrecht der NATO." *Europa-Archiv* (Jan. 10, 1962): 21–26.

7971 Lachs, Manfred. "The Unwritten Laws of Warfare." *Tulane Law Review* 20 (Oct. 1945): 120–28.

7972 Lauterpacht, Sir Hersh. "The Limits of the Operation of the Law of War." *British Yearbook of International Law* 30 (1953): 206–43.

7973 ———. "The Problem of the Revision of the Law of War." *British Yearbook of International Law* 29 (1952): 360–82.

7974 ———. "Rules of Warfare in an Unlawful War." In George A. Lipsky, ed., *Law and Politics in the World Community*. Berkeley: Univ. of California Press, 1953, pp. 89–113.

7975 *The Law of Armed Conflicts: Report of the Conference on Contemporary Problems of the Law of Armed Conflicts, Geneva, Sept. 15–20, 1969.* New York: Carnegie Endowment for International Peace, 1971.

7976 Lukens, E. C. "Public Opinion and the Rules of Civilized Warfare." *Temple Law Quarterly* 21 (Apr. 1948): 376–85.

7977 McNair, Arnold D. *The Legal Effects of War.* New York: Cambridge Univ. Press, 1966.

7978 Moffit, Robert E. *Modern War and the Laws of War.* Res. Ser. no. 17. Tucson: Univ. of Arizona, Institute of Government Research, 1973.

7979 Moritz, Gunther. "The Common Application of the Laws of War Within the NATO Forces." *Military Law Review* 41 (July 1961): 1–33.

7980 Morley, Jeremy D. "Approaches to the Law of Armed Conflict." *Canadian Yearbook of International Law* 9 (1971): 269–75.

7981 Nurick, Lester, and Roger W. Barrett. "Legality of Guerrilla Forces Under the Laws of War." *American Journal of International Law* 40 (July 1946): 563–83.

7982 Pictet, Jean S. "Le Droit de la Guerre." *Revue Internationale de la Croix-Rouge* 43 (Sept. 1961): 417–25.

7983 ———. "The Need to Restore the Laws and Customs Relating to Armed Conflicts." *International Review of the Red Cross* 9 (Sept. 1969): 459–83.

7984 Puttkammer, E. W. *War and the Law.* Chicago: Univ. of Chicago Press, 1944.

7985 Schwarzenberger, George. "From the Laws of War to the Law of Armed Conflict." *Current Legal Problems* 21 (1968): 239 ff.

7986 ———. "Functions and Foundations of the Laws of War." *Archiv fur Rechts- und Sozial-Philosophie* [Berlin] 44:3 (1958): 351–69.

7987 Stone, Julius. *Legal Controls of International Conflict.* New York: Rinehart, 1954.

7988 ———. *Legal Controls of International Conflict: A Treatise on the Dynamics of Disputes and War Law.* 2d rev. ed., with supplement, 1953–1958. New York: Rinehart, 1959.

7989 Suter, Keith D. "Modernizing the Laws of War." *Australian Outlook* 29 (Aug. 1975): 211–19.

7990 Taylor, Telford, et al. "Human Rights and Armed Conflict: Conflicting Views." *American Journal of International Law* 67 (May 1973): 141–68.

7991 Thruiller, Gen. Henry F. "Can Methods of Warfare be Restricted?" *Journal of Royal United Services Institution* 81 (1936): 264–79.

7992 Trainin, I. P. "Questions of Guerrilla Warfare in the Law of War." *American Journal of International Law* 40 (July 1946): 534–62.

7993 Tucker, Robert W. "The Law of War." *Naval War College Review* 7 (May 1955): 25–49.

7994 Wilson, Andrew. "How Relevant are the Rules of War?" *Current* 114 (Jan. 1970): 3–6.

7995 Wright, Quincy. "The Outlawry of War and the Law of War." *American Journal of International Law* 47 (July 1953): 365–76.

Law & Morality

7996 Coursier, Henri. "Définition d'un Droit Humanitaire." *Annuaire Français de Droit International* [Paris] 1 (1955): 223–27.

7997 Derathe, Robert. "Jean-Jacques Rousseau et le Progres des Idees Humanitaires du XVI au XVIII Siecle." *Revue Internationale de la Croix-Rouge* 40 (Oct. 1958): 523–43.

7998 Minguet, Philippe. "Pour un Droit Humanitaire de la Guerre." *Revue de Droit International* [Sottile-Geneva] 34 (Oct.–Dec. 1956): 366–71.

7999 Nagle, William J. *The State of the Question: Morality and Modern Warfare.* Baltimore: Helicon, 1960.

8000 O'Brien, William V. "After Nineteen Years, Let Us Begin." In James Finn, ed., *Peace, the Churches and the Bomb.* New York: Council on Religion & International Affairs, 1965, pp. 26–31.

8001 Plater, Charles D. *A Primer of Peace & War: The Principles of International Morality.* London: P. S. King, 1915.

8002 Rigg, Col. Robert B. "Where Does Killing End and Murder Begin in War?" *Military Review* 51 (Mar. 1971): 3–9.

8003 Ryan, John K. *Modern War and Basic Ethics.* Milwaukee: Bruce, 1940.

8004 Walzer, Michael. "Moral Judgment in Time of War." *Dissent* 14 (May–June 1967): 284–92.

8005 Winters, Francis X. "Morality in the War Room." *America* (Feb. 15, 1975): 106–10.

Implementation

8006 Baxter, Richard R. "Forces for Compliance with the Laws of War." *Proceedings of American Society of International Law* (Apr. 24, 1964): 82–89.

8007 Carnegie, A. R. "Jurisdiction over Violations of the Laws and Customs of War." *British Yearbook of International Law* 39 (1963): 402–24.

8008 Draper, G. I. A. D. "Implementation of International Law in Armed Conflicts." *International Affairs* [London] 48 (Jan. 1972): 46–59.

8009 ———. "The Place of the Laws of War in Military Instruction." *Royal United Services Institution Journal* 3 (Aug. 1966): 189–98.

8010 ———. "Rules Governing the Conduct of Hostilities: The Laws of War and Their Enforcement." *Naval War College Review* 17 (Nov. 1965): 22–44.

8011 Forsythe, David P. "Who Guards the Guardian: Third Parties and the Law of Armed

Conflict." *American Journal of International Law* 70 (Jan. 1976): 41–61.

8012   Ramundo, Bernard A. "Soviet Criminal Legislation in Implementation of the Hague and Geneva Conventions Relating to the Rules of Land Warfare." *American Journal of International Law* 57 (Jan. 1963): 73–84.

8013   Roling, Bernard V. A. "The Law of War and the National Jurisdiction Since 1945." *Hague Academy of International Law* 100 (1952): 323–456.

8014   Van Dyke, Jon M. "The Laws of War: Can They Be Enforced?" *Center Magazine* (July–Aug. 1971): 21–33.

8015   Warnke, Paul C., et al. "Implementing the Rules of War: Training, Command and Enforcement." *American Journal of International Law* 66 (Sept. 1972): 183–205.

8016   Zuckerman, Sir Solly. "Judgment and Control in Modern Warfare." *Foreign Affairs* 40 (Jan. 1962): 196–212.

ARMED FORCES & LAWS OF WAR

8017   Taubenfeld, Howard J. "International Armed Forces and the Rules of War." *American Journal of International Law* 45 (Oct. 1951): 671–79.

Land Warfare

8018   Baldwin, Gordon. "A New Look at the Law of War: Limited War and Field Manual 27–10." *Military Law Review* 4 (Apr. 1959): 1–38.

8019   Clancy, Martin J. "Rules of Land Warfare During the War of the American Revolution." *World Polity* 2 (1960): 203–318.

8020   Darley, Capt. Roger G. "The American Soldier and the Law of War." *Field Artillery Journal* 42 (Jan.–Feb. 1974): 44–45; (Mar.–Apr. 1974): 14–18.

8021   Davis, George B. "Dr. Francis Lieber's Instructions for the Government of Armies in the Field." *American Journal of International Law* 1 (Jan. 1907): 13–25.

8022   Fratcher, William F. "The New Law of Land Warfare." *Missouri Law Review* 22 (Apr. 1971): 143–61.

8023   Garcia-Mora, M. R. "International Law and the Law of Hostile Military Expeditions." *Fordham Law Review* 27 (Aug. 1958): 309–31.

8024   Grabb, Robert F. "The Rule of Land Warfare." *Army* 7:4 (1957): 34–36.

8025   Great Britain. War Office. *Land Warfare: An Exposition of the Laws and Usages of War on Land for the Guidance of Officers of His Majesty's Army.* London: H.M.S.O., 1912.

8026   ———. *Manual of Military Law.* London: H.M.S.O., 1914.

8027   Greenspan, Morris. *The Modern Law of Land Warfare.* Berkeley: Univ. of California Press, 1959.

8028   ———. *The Soldier's Guide to the Laws of War.* Washington, D.C.: Public Affairs Press, 1969.

8029   Holland, Sir Thomas E. *The Laws of War on Land.* Oxford: Clarendon Press, 1908.

8030   Jenkins, Capt. Robert E., and Lt. Martin C. McWilliams. "The Soldier and Law of War." *Infantry* 61 (Nov.–Dec. 1971): 22–25.

8031   Kunz, Josef L. "The New U.S. Army Field Manual on the Law of Land Warfare." *American Journal of International Law* 51 (Apr. 1957): 388–96.

8032   "Ounce of Prevention: Army Course on Laws of Land Warfare." *Newsweek* (Apr. 19, 1971): 30 ff.

8033   "Regulations Respecting the Laws and Custom of War on Land." *American Journal of International Law: Supplement* 2 (1908): 90–116.

8034   Spaight, James M. *War Rights on Land.* London: Macmillan, 1911.

8035   Switzerland. *Manuel des Lois et Coutumes de la Guerre pour l'Armee Suisse.* Geneva, 1963.

8036   U.S. Department of Army. *The Law of Land Warfare.* F.M. 27–10. Washington, D.C.: G.P.O., 1956.

8037   ———. Department of War. *Instructions for the Government of Armies of the United States in the Field* [by Francis Lieber]. Washington, D.C.: General Order 100, Apr. 24, 1863.

8038   ———. *Rules of Land Warfare.* Doc. no. 467, approved Apr. 25, 1914. Washington, D.C.: G.P.O., 1917. [Revised 1940.]

Naval Warfare

For rules governing submarine warfare, see Chapter 7, Limitation of Weapons & Personnel.

8039   Butler, William E. *Soviet Union and the Law of the Sea.* Baltimore: Johns Hopkins Press, 1971.

8040   Carlisle, Geoffrey E. "Aspects of International Law Affecting the Naval Commander." *Naval War College Review* 5 (May 1953): 31–53.

8041   ———. "Interrelationship of International Law and United States Naval Operations in Southeast Asia." *JAG Journal* 22 (July–Aug. 1967): 8–14.

8042   Dean, Arthur H. "The Geneva Conference on the Law of the Sea: What was Accomplished." *American Journal of International Law* 52 (Oct. 1958): 607–28.

8043   Genet, Raoul. *Droit Maritime Pour le Temps de Guerre, 1936–1938.* 2 vols. Paris: E. Muller, 1939–1940.

8044   Hall, J. A. *Law of Naval Warfare.* London: Chapman & Hall, 1914.

8045   Higgins, A. Pearce, and C. J. Colombos. *The International Law of the Sea.* 3d rev. ed. London: Longmans, Green, 1954.

8046   Levie, Howard S. "Mine Warfare and International Law." *Naval War College Review* 24 (Apr. 1972): 27–35.

8047   Miller, Capt. William O. "Law of Naval Warfare." *Naval War College Review* 24 (Feb. 1972): 35–42.

8048   Smith, H. A. *The Law and Custom of the Sea.* 2d ed. London: Stevens, 1950.

8049   Tucker, Robert W. *The Law of War and Neutrality at Sea.* [U.S. Naval War College, *International Law Studies, 1955.*] Washington, D.C.: G.P.O., 1957.

8050   U.S. Department of Navy. *Law of Naval Warfare.* NWIP 10–2. Washington, D.C.: G.P.O., 1955.

8051   Young, Elizabeth. "New Laws for Old Navies: Military Implications of the Law of the Sea." *Survival* 16 (Nov.–Dec. 1974): 262–67.

Military Necessity

8052   Downey, William G., Jr. "The Law of War and Military Necessity." *American Journal of International Law* 47 (Apr. 1953): 251–62.

8053   Dunbar, N. C. H. "Military Necessity in War Crimes Trials." *British Yearbook of International Law* 29 (1952): 442–52.

8054   ———. "The Significance of Military Necessity in the Law of War." *Juridical Review* [Edinburgh] 67 (Aug. 1955): 201–12.

8055   O'Brien, William V. "Legitimate Military Necessity in Nuclear War." *World Polity* 2 (1960): 35–120.

8056   ———. "The Meaning of 'Military Necessity' in International Law." *World Polity* 1 (1957): 109–76.

Reprisals

8057   Albrecht, A. R. "War Reprisals in the War Crimes Trials and the Geneva Conventions of 1949." *American Journal of International Law* 47 (Oct. 1953): 590–614.

8058   Bowett, D. "Reprisals Involving Recourse to Armed Force." *American Journal of International Law* 66 (Jan. 1972): 1–36.

8059   Colbert, Evelyn S. *Retaliation in International Law.* New York: King's Crown Press, 1948.

8060   Higgins, A. Pearce, "Retaliation in Naval Warfare." *British Yearbook of International Law* 8 (1927): 129–46.

8061   Kalshoven, Frits. *Belligerent Reprisals.* Leyden: Sijthoff, 1971.

8062   Kunz, Josef L. "Sanctions in International Law." *American Journal of International Law* 54 (Apr. 1960): 324–47.

8063   McNair, Arnold D. "The Legal Meaning of War and the Relations of War to Reprisals."

Transactions of the Grotius Society 11 (1925): 29–51.

8064 Stowell, Ellery C. "Military Reprisals and the Sanctions of the Laws of War." *American Journal of International Law* 36 (Oct. 1942): 643–50.

NONCOMBATANT IMMUNITY

8065 Adler, Gerald J. "Targets in War." *Houston Law Review* 8 (Sept. 1970): 1–46.

8066 Alexander, Lawrence A. "Self-Defense and the Killing of Non-Combatants: A Reply to Fullinwider." *Philosophy & Public Affairs* 5 (Summer 1976): 408 ff.

8067 Bailey, Sidney D. "Protecting Civilians in War." *Survival* 14 (Nov.–Dec. 1972): 262–67.

8068 Bierzanek, Remigiusz. "Towards More Respect for Human Rights in Armed Conflicts." *Polish Institute of International Affairs* 1 (1973): 75–120.

8069 Bond, J. E. "Protection of Non-Combatants in Guerrilla Wars." *William and Mary Law Review* 12 (Summer 1971): 787 ff.

8070 Farer, Tom J. "Humanitarian Law and Armed Conflicts: Toward the Definition of 'International Armed Conflict.'" *Columbia Law Review* 71 (Jan. 1971): 37 ff.

8071 Ford, John C. "The Hydrogen Bombing of Cities." In William J. Nagle, ed., *Morality and Modern Warfare*. Baltimore: Helicon, 1960, pp. 98–103.

8072 Gottlieb, Gidon. "International Assistance to Civilian Populations in Armed Conflicts." *New York University Journal of International Law and Politics* 4 (Winter 1971): 403 ff.

8073 ———. "Measures to Protect Noncombatants." *American Journal of International Law* 65 (Oct. 1971): 637 ff.

8074 Hartigan, Richard S. "Noncombatant Immunity: Its Scope and Development." *Continuum* 3 (Autumn 1965): 300–314.

8075 ———. "Noncombatant Immunity: Reflections on Its Origins and Present Status." *Review of Politics* 29 (Apr. 1967): 204–20.

8076 ———. "Saint Augustine on War and Killing: The Problem of the Innocent." *Journal of the History of Ideas* 20 (Apr.–June 1960): 195–204.

8077 Hewitt, Warren E. "Recent Developments: Respect for Human Rights in Armed Conflicts." *New York University Journal of International Law and Politics* 4 (Spring 1971): 41–65.

8078 Kalshoven, Frits. "Human Rights, the Law of Armed Conflict, and Reprisals." *International Review of the Red Cross* 11 (Apr. 1971): 183–92.

8079 Kennedy, Sen. Edward M. "Indochina: A Slaughter of Innocents." *Nation* (June 28, 1971): 806–08.

8080 Lifton, Robert J. "Why Civilians are War Victims." *U.S. News & World Report* (Dec. 15, 1969): 25–28.

8081 Nurick, Lester. "The Distinction Between Combatant and Noncombatant in the Law of War." *American Journal of International Law* 39 (Oct. 1945): 680–97.

8082 Pictet, Jean S. *The Principles of International Humanitarian Laws*. Geneva: International Committee of the Red Cross, 1966.

8083 Stillman, Edmund O. "Civilian Sanctuary and Target Avoidance Policy in Thermonuclear War." *Annals of the Amer. Acad. of Pol. & Soc. Sci.* 392 (Nov. 1970): 116–32.

PROTECTION OF CULTURAL TREASURES

8084 League of Nations. "Protection of Monuments and Works of Art in Time of War." *Official Journal* 19 (Nov. 1938), pp. 961–63.

8085 Predome, Gaetano. "Per una migliore protezione del patrimonio artistico monumentale in caso di guerra." *Rivista de Studi Politici Internazionali* [Florence] 17 (1950), pp. 646–650.

8086 Rorimer, James J. *Survival: The Salvage and Protection of Art in War*. New York: Abelard, 1950.

8087 Vedovato, Giuseppe. *Il Patrimonio Storico-Artistico-Culturale e la Guerra Aerea*. Florence: Scuola di Guerra Aerea, 1954.

World War I

8088   France. Foreign Office. *Les Allemands, De-structeurs des Cathedrales et des Tresors du Passe.* Paris, 1915.

8089   Garner, James W. "Destruction of Monuments, Buildings and Institutions Especially Protected by the Law of Nations." *International Law and the World War.* 2 vols. London: Longmans, Green, 1920, I: 434–57.

8090   Letterhove, H. K. *La Guerre et les Oeuvres d'Art en Belgique.* Paris: G. Van Oest, 1917.

8091   Marguiller, Auguste. *La Destruction des Monuments sur le Front Occidental.* Paris: G. Van Oest, 1919.

8092   Michel, G. "Dans les Ruines de nos Monuments Historiques." *Revue des Deux Mondes* (May 1, 1917): 397–416.

8093   Snow, F. H. "Among the Ashes: The Destruction of Art in Northern France and Belgium." *Arts & Decoration* 8 (Apr. 1918): 248–50.

World War II

8094   Control Commission for Germany (British Element). *Works of Art in Germany* [British Zone of Occupation]: *Losses and Survivals in the War.* London: H.M.S.O., 1946.

8095   Hartt, Frederick. *Florentine Art Under Fire.* Princeton: Princeton Univ. Press, 1949.

8096   Kent, William. *The Lost Treasures of London.* London: Phoenix House, 1947.

8097   Lavagnino, Emilio. *Fifty War-Damaged Monuments of Italy.* Rome: Istituto Poligrafico dello Stato, 1946.

8098   Richards, James M., ed. *The Bombed Buildings of Britain: A Record of the Architectural Casualties.* London: Architectural Press, 1947.

8099   Woolley, Sir Charles L. *A Record of the Work Done by the Military Authorities for the Protection of the Treasures of Art and History in War Areas.* London: H.M.S.O., 1947.

Treaties: General

PEACE OF GOD & TRUCE OF GOD (989–1450)

For sample of texts, see Trevor N. Dupuy and Gay M. Hammerman, eds., *A Documentary History of*

Arms Control and Disarmament (New York: Bowker, 1973), pp. 4–10.

General Accounts

8100   Bonnaud-Delamare, Roger. "Fondement des Institutions de Paix au XIe Siècle." In *Mélanges d'Histoire du Moyen Age Dediés à la Memoire de Louis Halphen.* Paris: Presses Universitaires, 1951, pp. 19–26.

8101   ———. *L'idée de Paix à l'Epoque Carolingienne.* Paris: Domat Montchrestien, 1939.

8102   Cowdrey, H. E. J. "The Peace and Truce of God in the Eleventh Century." *Past & Present* 46 (Feb. 1970): 42–67.

8103   Duby, G. "Les Laïcs et la Paix de Dieu." *I Laici Nella "Societas Christiana" Dei Secoli XI e XII.* Miscellanea del contro di Studi Medioevali, 5. Milan, 1968, 448–69.

8104   Ganshof, Francois-Louis. "La 'Paix' au très haut Moyen Âge." [*La Paix*] *Recueil de la Societe Jean Bodin* [Brussels] 14 (1962): 397–414.

8105   Gernhuber, Joachim. "Staat und Landfrieden im Deutschen Reich des Mittelalters." [*La Paix*] *Recueil de la Societe Jean Bodin* [Brussels] 13 (1961) 27–77.

8106   Gorris, Gerhard. *De denkbeelden over oolog en de bemoeeingen voor vrede in de elfde eeuw.* Nijmegen: L. C. G. Malmberg, 1912.

8107   Hoffmann, Hartmut. *Gottesfriede und Treuga Dei.* Schriften der Monumenta Germaniae Historica, 20. Stuttgart: A. Hiersemann, 1964.

8108   Huberti, Ludwig. *Studien zur Rechtsgeschichte der Gottesfrieden und Landfrieden,* Band I: *Die Frieden-Ordnungen in Frankreich.* Ansbach: C. Brugel & Sohn, 1892.

8109   Joris, André. "Observations sur la Proclamation de la Trêve de Dieu a Liège a la Fin du XIe Siecle." [*La Paix*] *Recueil de la Societe Jean Bodin* [Brussels] 14 (1962): 503–45.

8110   Kennelly, Sister Dolorosa. "The Peace and Truce of God: Fact or Fiction?" Ph.D. diss., Univ. of California, Berkeley, 1962.

8111   Kluckhohn, August. *Geschichte des Gottesfriedens.* Leipzig: Neudruck der Ausgabe, 1857. [Aalen: Scientia Verlag, 1966.]

8112   Krey, A. "The International State of the Middle Ages." *American Historical Review* 28 (Oct. 1922): 1–12.

8113   MacKinney, Loren C. "The People and Public Opinion in the Eleventh Century Peace Movement." *Speculum* 5 (Apr. 1930): 181–206.

8114   Semichon, Ernest. *La Paix et la Treve de Dieu: Histoire des Premiers Developpements du Tiers-Etat par l'Eglise et les Associations.* Paris: Didier, 1857.

8115   Töpfer, Bernhard. *Volk und Kirche zur Zeit der gegenden Gottesfriedensbewegung in Frankreich.* Berlin: Rütten & Loening, 1957.

Development of Idea

8116   Bonnaud-Delamare, Roger. "Les Institutions de Paix en Aquitaine au XIe Siècle." [*La Paix*] *Recueil de la Societe Jean Bodin* [Brussels] 14 (1962): 415–88.

8117   ———. "Les Institutions de Paix dans l'Ecclesiastique de Reims au XIe Siècle." *Bulletin Philologique et Historique, Comité des Travaux Historiques et Scientifiques* (1955): 143–200.

8118   ———. "La Paix en Flandres pendant la Premiere Croisade." *Revue du Nord* 39 (1957): 147–52.

8119   Bouard, Michel. "Sur les Origines de lat Treve de Dieu en Normandie." *Annales de Normandie* 9 (1959): 169–89.

8120   Kennelly, Sister Dolorosa. "Medieval Towns and the Peace of God." *Medievalia et Humanistica* 15 (May 1963): 35–53.

8121   Manteyer, Georges de. "La Paix en Viennois, Ans, 1025." *Bulletin de la Société Statistique de l'Isère*, 4e sér., 33 (1904): 91–155.

8122   Molinie, Georges. *L'organisation Judiciaire, Militaire et Financière des Associations de la Paix: Etude sur la Paix et la Trêve de Dieu dans le Midi et le Centre de la France.* Toulouse, 1912.

8123   Prentout, Henri. "La Trêve de Dieu en Normandie." *Mémoires de l'Académie de Caen*, nouv. sér., 6 (1931): 3–25.

8124   Strubbe, Egied I. "La Paix de Dieu dans le Nord de la France." [*La Paix*] *Recueil de la Societe Jean Bodin* [Brussels] 14 (1962): 289–501.

8125   Wohlhaupter, Eugen. *Zur Rechtsgeschichte des Gotts- und Landfriedens in Spanien.* Heidelberg: C. Winter, 1933.

Critiques of Idea

8126   Bonet, Honore. *The Tree of Battles.* G. W. Coopland, ed. & trans. Liverpool: Univ. Press, 1949.

8127   Bury, Richard de. "The Complaint of Books Against War." *The Philobiblon.* Berkeley: Univ. of California Press, 1948, pp. 41–45.

8128   Denifle, Henri. *La Guerre de Cent Ans, La Desolation des Eglises, Monasteres et Hopitaux en France.* 2 Vols. Paris: A. Picard et Fils, 1897–1899.

8129   Keen, M. H. *The Laws of War in the Late Middle Ages.* Toronto: Univ. of Toronto Press, 1965.

8130   Ullmann, Walter. *The Medieval Idea of Law as Represented by Lucas de Penna.* London: Methuen, 1946.

8131   Vitoria, Franciscus de. *De Jure Belli Reflectiones.* Trans. by J. P. Bate. In John Brown Scott. *The Spanish Origin of International Law.* Oxford: Clarendon Press, 1934, Appendix B.

DECLARATION OF ST. PETERSBURG (1868)

For text of declaration, see "Declaration of St. Petersburg, Dec. 11, 1868," *American Journal of International Law: Supplement* I (1907): 95–96.

General Accounts

8132   Garner, James W. *International Law and the World War.* 2 vols. London: Longmans, Green, 1920, I: 14–15.

8133   Meyrowitz, Henri. "Reflections on the Centenary of the Declaration of St. Petersburg." *International Review of the Red Cross* 8 (Dec. 1968): 611–25.

Dum-Dum Bullets

8134   Garner, James W. "Forbidden Weapons and Instrumentalities." *International Law and the World War.* 2 vols. London: Longmans, Green, 1920, I: 262–70.

8135   Greenspan, Morris. *The Modern Law of Land Warfare.* Berkeley: Univ. of California Press, 1959, pp. 315–54.

8136   Lumsden, Malvern. "New Military Technology and the Erosion of International Law: The Case of the Dum-Dum Bullets Today." *Instant Research on Peace and Violence* 4:1 (1974): 15–20.

8137   Stone, Julius. *Legal Controls of International Conflict.* New York: Rinehart, 1954, pp. 350–52.

HAGUE TREATIES (1899, 1907)

For text of treaties, see Trevor N. Dupuy and Gay M. Hammerman, eds., *A Documentary History of Arms Control and Disarmament.* New York: Bowker, 1973, pp. 50–57, 59–71.

Documents

8138   Scott, James Brown, ed. *The Hague Conventions and Declarations of 1899 and 1907, Accompanied by Tables of Signatures, Ratifications and Adhesions of the Various Powers and Texts of Reservations.* 2d ed. New York: Oxford Univ. Press, 1915.

8139   ——. *The Proceedings of the Hague Peace Conferences: Translations of the Official Texts.* 5 vols. New York: Oxford Univ. Press, 1920–1921.

8140   ——. *The Reports of the Hague Conferences of 1899 and 1907. . . .* New York: H. Wilson, 1917.

General Accounts

8141   Choate, Joseph H. *The Two Hague Conferences.* Princeton: Princeton Univ. Press, 1913.

8142   Daehne van Varick, August von. *Documents Relating to the Program of the First Hague Peace Conference, Laid Before the Conference by the Netherlands Government.* Oxford: Clarendon Press, 1921.

8143   Davis, Calvin DeArmond. *The United States and the First Hague Peace Conference.* Ithaca, N.Y.: Cornell Univ. Press, 1962.

8144   ——. *The United States and the Second Hague Peace Conference.* Durham: Duke Univ. Press, 1976.

8145   Ford, Thomas K. "The Genesis of the First Hague Peace Conference." *Political Science Quarterly* 51 (Sept. 1936): 354–82.

8146   Higgins, A. Pearce. *The Hague Conference and Other International Conferences Concerning the Laws and Usages of War.* London: Stevens, 1904.

8147   ——. *The Hague Peace Conferences and Other International Conferences Concerning the Laws and Usages of War.* Cambridge: Univ. Press, 1909.

8148   Holls, Frederick W. *The Peace Conference at the Hague, and Its Bearings on International Law and Policy.* New York: Macmillan, 1914.

8149   Hosono, Gunji. "The Hague Conferences." *International Disarmament.* New York: Columbia Univ., 1926, pp. 85–104.

8150   Huber, Max. "Quelques Considerations sur une Revision Eventuelle des Conventions de La Haye Relatives a la Guerre." *Revue Internationale de la Croix-Rouge* [Geneva] 37 (July 1955): 417–33.

8151   Hudson, Manley O. "Present Status of the Hague Conventions of 1899 and 1907." *American Journal of International Law* 25 (Jan. 1931): 114–17.

8152   Hull, William I. *The Two Hague Conferences and Their Contributions to International Law.* Boston: Ginn, 1908.

8153   Reinsch, Paul S. "Failures and Successes of the Second Hague Conference." *American Political Science Review* 12 (Feb. 1908): 204–20.

8154   Strebel, Helmut. "Die Haager Konvention zum Schutze des Kulturguter im Falle eines bewaffneten Konfliktes vom 14. Mai 1954." *Zeitschrift fur Auslandisches Offentliches Recht und Volkerrecht* [Stuttgart] 16 (Jan. 1955): 35–75.

Hague & Disarmament

8155   Hobson, Richmond P. "Disarmament." *American Journal of International Law* 2 (1908): 743–57.

8156   Mahan, Adm. Alfred T. "The Peace Conference and the Moral Aspects of War." *North American Review* 149 (Oct. 1899): 433–47.

8157   Tate, Merze. *The Disarmament Illusion: The Movement for a Limitation of Armaments to 1907.* New York: Macmillan, 1942, pp. 267–93, 321–46.

Rules of War: Bombardment

See Chapter 10, Regulating & Outlawing Weapons & War, for Hague prohibitions on poison gas and aerial bombardment.

8158   Davis, George B. "The Hague Conventions Concerning Amelioration of the Rules of War on Land." *American Journal of International Law* 2 (Jan. 1908): 63–77.

8159   Garner, James W. "Land and Naval Bombardment." *International Law and the World War.* 2 vols. London: Longmans, Green, 1920, I: 417–33.

8160   Scott, James Brown. "Bombardment by Naval Forces." *American Journal of International Law* 2 (April 1908): 285–94.

ROERICH PACT (1935)

For text of treaty, see League of Nations, *Treaty Series* 167 (London: Harrison, 1936), pp. 290–92.

8161   Burns, Richard Dean, and Charyl L. Smith. "Nicholas Roerich, Henry A. Wallace and the 'Peace Banner': A Study in Idealism, Egocentrism, and Anguish." *Peace and Change* 1 (Spring 1972): 40–47.

8162   "The Centenary of Nicholas Roerich." *International Associations* 26:12 (1974): 588–90.

8163   Hudson, Manley O. *International Legislation.* Washington, D.C.: Carnegie Endowment for International Peace, 1931, VII: 56–59.

8164   "Pan-American: Twenty-One Countries Sign the Roerich Treaty." *Commonweal* (Apr. 26, 1935): 378.

8165   Phelps, G. "Banner to Protect Art in Wartime." *Literary Digest* (Mar. 9, 1935): 26.

8166   Roerich, Nicholas. "Banner of Peace." *Indian Magazine* (Sept. 1933): 315–16.

8167   U.S. Department of State. *Foreign Relations of the United States, 1935.* Washington, D.C.: G.P.O., 1953, I: 502–09.

8168   Wallace, Henry A. "American Treaty on the Roerich Pact." *Science* (Oct. 26, 1934): 375 ff.

HAGUE CONVENTION (1954)

For text of convention to protect cultural properties, see United Nations, *Treaty Series* 249, no. 3511 (New York, 1955), p. 240 ff.

Documents

8169   Netherlands. *Records of the Conference Convened by the United Nations Educational, Scientific and Cultural Organization, Held at The Hague from 21 April to 14 May 1954.* The Hague, 1961.

8170   UNESCO. Paris. *General Conference Records* 8 (1954), IV 24, pp. 37–59; VI 5, pp. 81–82; VI 7, pp. 122–42; VI 8, pp. 1–3; *General Conference Records* 10 (1956), II 19, pp. 11–46; II 20, pp. 1–29.

General Accounts

8171   DeSaussure, Hamilton. "The Laws of Air Warfare: Are There Any?" *Naval War College Review* (Feb. 1971): 35–47.

8172   "The Hague International Convention for the Protection of Cultural Property in the Event of Armed Conflict." *Museum: UNESCO Quarterly Review* 7:3 (1954): 206–07.

8173   Noblecourt, Andre. *Protection of Cultural Property in the Event of Armed Conflict.* Paris: UNESCO, 1958.

8174   "Report by Mr. G. Gariette on his Mission to the Monastery of Saint Catherine, Siena." *UNESCO Chronicle* 3 (Mar. 1957): 51–57.

8175   Wilhelm, Rene-Jean. "The 'Red Cross of Monuments.' " *Revue Internationale de la Croix-Rouge* [English Supplement] 8 (May–June 1955): 76–87, 118–23.

Stabilizing of International Environment

8176   Chalfont, Lord Arthur G. J. "Value of Observation Posts in NATO and Warsaw Pact

Areas." *European Review* 16 (Autumn 1966): 31–33.

8177 Foster, William C. "Possibilities for Reducing the Risks of War Through Accident, Miscalculation, or Failure of Communication." *U.S. Department of State Bulletin* (Jan. 7, 1963): 3–8.

8178 Larus, Joel. "To Reduce the Possibility of Nuclear Catastrophe." *Bulletin of the Atomic Scientists* 21 (Apr. 1965): 33–36.

8179 "Memorandum of the Soviet Government on Measures for the Further Relaxation of International Tension and Restrictions of the Arms Race." *New Times* [Moscow] (Dec. 16, 1964): 37–40.

8180 Osgood, Robert E. "Stabilizing the Military Environment." *American Political Science Review* 55 (Mar. 1961): 24–39.

8181 ———. "Stabilizing the Military Environment." *American Political Science Review* 55 (Dec. 1962): 15–18.

ACCIDENTAL WAR

8182 Eggertsen, Paul F. "The Dilemma of Power: Nuclear Weapons and Human Reliability." *Psychiatry* 27 (Aug. 1964): 211–18.

8183 Halperin, Morton H. *Arms Control and Inadvertent General War.* Study Memo. no 6. Washington, D.C.: Institute for Defense Analyses, 1962.

8184 Hook, Sidney. *The Fail-Safe Fallacy.* New York: Stein & Day, 1963.

8185 Leghorn, Col. Richard S. "The Problem of Accidental War." *Bulletin of the Atomic Scientists* 14 (June 1958).

8186 Phelps, John B., et al. *Accidental War: Some Dangers in the 1960's.* Columbus, Ohio: Mershon National Security Program, 1960.

8187 ———. "Causes of Accidental War." *Survival* 5 (July–Aug. 1963): 176–79.

8188 ———. *Studies on Accidental War.* Research Paper, P–6. Washington, D.C.: Institute for Defense Analyses, 1963.

8189 Wheeler, Harvey, and Eugene Burdick. "The Politics of Destruction." *Saturday Review* (Nov. 9, 1963): 25–27 ff.

8190 Wyden, Peter. "The Chances of Accidental War." *Saturday Evening Post* (June 3, 1961): 17–19.

Treaties: Turkish Straits

A series of agreements were reached between the Ottoman Empire, later Turkey, and the Western Powers, especially Russia. Listed below are the more important general works and treaties.

8191 Ambrosini, Gaspare. *Regime degli Stretti.* Rome: Istituto Nazionale Fascista di Cultura, 1937.

8192 Anchieri, Ettore. *Constantinopli e gli Stretti nella politica Russa ed Europea.* Milan: Guiffre, 1948.

8193 Anderson, M. S. *The Eastern Question, 1774–1923.* London: Macmillan, 1966.

8194 Basgil, Ali F. *La Question des Detroits.* Paris: Paul Geuthner, 1928.

8195 Baxter, Richard R. *The Law of International Waterways.* Cambridge: Harvard Univ. Press, 1964.

8196 Erkin, Feridun C. *Les Relations Turco-Soviétiques et la Question des Detroits.* Ankara: Basnur Matbasi, 1968.

8197 Graves, Phillip P. *The Question of the Straits.* London: E. Benn, 1931.

8198 Grosbois, Jacques. *La Turquie et les Détroits.* Paris: Editions du Chene, 1945.

8199 Herrmann, Gerhard. *Die Dardanellen.* Leipzig: W. Goldmann, 1936.

8200 Howard, Harry N. *The Problem of the Turkish Straits.* Dept. of State Pub. 2752, Near Eastern Series 5. Washington, D.C.: G.P.O., 1947.

8201 Hurewitz, J. C. *Diplomacy in the Near and Middle East.* 2 vols. Princeton: Van Nostrand, 1956.

8202 Lacoste, Raymond. *La Russie Soviétique et la Question d'Orient: La Poussée Soviétique vers les Mers Chaudes, Méditerranée et Golfe Persique.* Paris: Editions Internationales, 1946.

8203 Larew, Karl G. "The Policies of Western Powers Toward the Problem of the Turkish Straits." Ph.D. diss., Yale Univ., 1963.

8204   Mange, Alice E. *The Near Eastern Policy of Emperor Napoleon III.* Urbana: Univ. of Illinois Press, 1940.

8205   Marriott, J. A. R. *The Eastern Question: An Historical Study in European Diplomacy.* 4th ed. Oxford: Clarendon Press, 1947.

8206   Mischef, P. H. *La Mer Noire et les Detroits de Constantinople.* Paris: Arthur Rousseau, 1899.

8207   Papouktchieva, Maria. *La Politique de la Russie a L'Egard des Detroits.* Geneva: Impr. Grivet, 1944.

8208   Phillipson, Coleman, and Noel Buxton. *The Question of the Bosphorus and Dardanelles.* London: Stevens & Haynes, 1917.

8209   Shotwell, James T., and Francis Deak. *Turkey at the Straits: A Short History.* New York: Macmillan, 1940.

8210   Sokolnicki, Michael. *The Turkish Straits.* Beirut: American Press, 1950.

8211   Vali, Ferenc A. *The Turkish Straits and NATO.* Stanford, Ca.: Hoover Institution Press, 1972.

8212   Anthem, T. "Russia and the Dardanelles." *Contemporary Review* 168 (Oct. 1945): 222–26.

8213   Antonoff, Nicolas. "La Bulgarie et les Détroits." *Politique Etrangère* 17 (Nov. 1952): 361–78.

8214   Glasgow, George. "Turkey and the Straits." *Contemporary Review* 149 (June 1936): 740–42.

8215   Graves, Phillip P. "The Question of the Straits." *Royal Central Asian Society Journal* 20 (Jan. 1933): 7–26.

8216   Howard, Harry N. "The United States and Turkey: American Policy in the Straits Question, 1914–1963." *Balkan Studies* 4:4 (1963): 225–50.

8217   Hudson, Geoffrey F. "Guardian of the Straits." *Listener* 21 (Nov. 1939): 1060–63.

8218   Hurewitz, J. C. "Russia and the Turkish Straits: A Reevaluation of the Origins of the Problem." *World Politics* 14 (July 1962): 605–32.

8219   Maclean, Fitzroy. "The Eastern Question in Modern Dress." *Foreign Affairs* 29 (Jan. 1951): 238–47.

8220   Mamopoulos, P. "La Question des Detroits." *Les Balkans* 4 (Mai–Juin 1933): 37–41.

8221   Mandelshtam, Andre N. "La Politique Russe d'Accès à la Méditerranée au XXe Siècle." *Recueil des Cours, 1934* [Hague] 47:1 (1935): 597–802.

8222   Pasvolski, Leo. "Freedom of the Straits: The Emptiest of Phrases." *Advocate of Peace* 85 (Aug. 1923): 293–97.

8223   Pinon, Rene. "L'evolution de la Question des Detroits." *L'Esprit International* 2 (Avril 1928): 184–203.

8224   Roche, Maurice. "Evolution de la Question des Detroits: Bosphore et Dardanelles." *Revue des Sciences Politiques* 56 (Juil. 1933): 429–48.

8225   Thomas, Lewis V. "Turkey: Guardian of the Straits." *Current History* 21 (July 1951): 8–11.

8226   Webb, Sir Richard. "The Problem of the Straits." *Royal Central Asian Society Journal* 18 (July 1931): 307–34.

Turkish Foreign Policy

8227   Campagna, Gerald L. "The Foreign Relations of the Turkish Republic." Ph.D. diss., Boston Univ., 1952.

8228   Fairchild, J. A. "Turkey: Gibraltar of the Middle East: General Progress Since 1923." *U.S. Naval Institute Proceedings* 80 (Feb. 1954): 168–75.

8229   Ireland, Philip W. "Turkish Foreign Policy After Munich." *Political Quarterly* 10 (Apr. 1939): 185–201.

8230   Vali, Ferenc A. *Bridge Across the Bosporus—The Foreign Policy of Turkey.* Baltimore: Johns Hopkins Press, 1971.

RUSSO-OTTOMAN DEFENSIVE ALLIANCE (1805)

See Hurewitz, J. C., *Diplomacy in the Near and Middle East*, 2 vols. (Princeton: Van Nostrand, 1956), pp. 72–77.

8231 Phillipson, Coleman, and Noel Buxton. *The Question of the Bosphorus and Dardanelles.* London: Stevens & Haynes, 1917, pt. 2; ch. 2–4.

8232 Puryear, Vernon J. *Napoleon and the Dardanelles.* Berkeley: Univ. of California Press, 1951, ch. 3–4.

8233 Shupp, Paul F. *European Powers and Near Eastern Question, 1806–1807.* New York: Columbia Univ. Press, 1931, ch. 2–3.

TREATY OF THE DARDANELLES (1809)

For text of treaty, see J. C. Hurewitz, *Diplomacy in the Near and Middle East,* 2 vols. (Princeton: Van Nostrand, 1956), I: 81–84.

8234 Adair, Sir Robert. *The Negotiations for the Peace of the Dardanelles in 1808–9.* 2 vols. London: Longman, Brown, & Green, 1845.

8235 Mischef, P. H. *La Mer Noire et les Detroits de Constantinople.* Paris: Arthur Rousseau, 1899, ch. 3.

8236 Puryear, Vernon J. *Napoleon and the Dardanelles.* Berkeley: Univ. of California Press, 1951, ch. 16.

TREATY OF HUNKIAR-ISKELESI (1833)

For text of treaty, see J. C. Hurewitz, *Diplomacy in the Near and Middle East,* 2 vols. (Princeton: Van Nostrand, 1956), I: 105–06.

8237 Cecil, Algernon. *British Foreign Secretaries, 1807–1916: Studies in Personality and Policy.* New York: Putnam's, 1927, pp. 147–56.

8238 Goriainov, S. M. *Le Bosphore et les Dardanelles.* Paris: Plon-Nourrit, 1910, ch. 8.

8239 Mosely, Philip E. *Russian Diplomacy and the Opening of the Eastern Question in 1838–1839.* Cambridge: Harvard Univ. Press, 1934, ch. 2.

8240 Phillipson, Coleman, and Noel Buxton. *The Question of the Bosphorus and Dardanelles.* London: Stevens & Haynes, 1917, pp. 47–69.

8241 Shotwell, James T., and Francis Deak. *Turkey at the Straits.* New York: Macmillan, 1940, pp. 28–32.

8242 Verete, M. "Palmerston and the Levant Crises, 1832." *Journal of Modern History* 24 (June 1952): 143–51.

8243 Webster, Sir Charles K. *The Foreign Policy of Palmerston, 1830–1841.* 2 vols. London: G. Bell, 1951, I: 301–19.

STRAITS CONVENTIONS (1840–1841)

For text of conventions, see J. C. Hurewitz, *Diplomacy in the Near and Middle East,* 2 vols. (Princeton: Van Nostrand, 1956), I: 116–19, 123.

8244 Anderson, M. S. "2nd Mohemmad Ali Crisis, 1833–41." *The Eastern Question, 1774–1923.* London: Macmillan, 1966, pp. 88–109.

8245 Mosely, Philip E. *Russian Diplomacy and the Opening of the Eastern Question in 1838–1839.* Cambridge: Harvard Univ. Press, 1934.

8246 Phillipson, Coleman, and Noel Buxton. "The Convention of London, 1840, and the Straits Convention, 1841." *The Question of the Bosphorus and Dardanelles.* London: Stevens & Haynes, 1917, pp. 70–80.

8247 Pouthas, C. H. "La Politique de Thiers Pendant la Crise Orientale de 1840." *Revue Historique* 182 (1938): 72–96.

8248 Shotwell, James T., and Francis Deak. "From the Treaty of London [1840] To the Convention of the Straits [1841]." *Turkey at the Straits.* New York: Macmillan, 1940, pp. 33–38.

8249 Webster, Sir Charles K. *The Foreign Policy of Palmerston, 1830–1841.* 2 vols. London: G. Bell, 1951, II: 753–76.

STRAITS CONVENTION (1856)

For text of convention, see J. C. Hurewitz, *Diplomacy in the Near and Middle East,* 2 vols. (Princeton: Van Nostrand, 1956), I: 153–56.

8250 Anderson, M. S. "Anglo-Russian Relations and the Crimean War, 1841–56." *The Eastern Question, 1774–1923.* London: Macmillan, 1966, pp. 110–48.

8251 Henderson, G. B. *Crimean War Diplomacy and other Historical Essays.* Glasgow: Glasgow Univ. Publications, 1947.

8252 Mosse, Werner E. "The Negotiations for a Franco-Russian Convention, 1956." *Cambridge Historical Journal* 10:1 (1950): 59–74.

8253 ———. *The Rise and Fall of the Crimean System, 1855–1871: The Story of a Peace Settlement.* London: Macmillan, 1963.

8254 Temperly, H. W. V. "The Treaty of Paris of 1856 and its Execution." *Journal of Modern History* 4 (Sept. 1932): 387–414, 523–43.

8255 Phillipson, Coleman, and Noel Buxton. "The Treaty of Paris, 1856." *The Question of the Bosphorus and Dardanelles.* London: Stevens & Haynes, 1917, pp. 81–100.

8256 Puryear, Vernon J. *England, Russia and the Straits Question, 1844–1856.* Berkeley: Univ. of California Press, 1931.

8257 Shotwell, James T., and Francis Deak. "The Treaty of Paris, 1856." *Turkey at the Straits.* New York: Macmillan, 1940, pp. 39–43.

PONTUS TREATY (1871)

For text of treaty, see J. C. Hurewitz, *Diplomacy in the Near and Middle East*, 2 vols. (Princeton: Van Nostrand, 1956), I: 173–74.

8258 Anderson, M. S. "From the Treaty of Paris to the Sonian Revolt, 1856–75." *The Eastern Question, 1774–1923.* London: Macmillan, 1966, pp. 149–77.

8259 Marriott, J. A. R. *The Eastern Question.* Oxford: Clarendon Press, 1947, pp. 280–83.

8260 Mischef, P.H. *La Mer Noire et les Detroits de Constantinople.* Paris: Arthur Rousseau, 1899, ch. 7.

8261 Phillipson, Coleman, and Noel Buxton. "Denunciation of the Treaty of Paris—Treaty of London, 1871." *The Question of the Bosphorus and Dardanelles.* London: Stevens & Haynes, 1917, pp. 101–29.

TREATY OF SEVRES (1920)

For text of treaty, see J. C. Hurewitz, *Diplomacy in the Near and Middle East*, 2 vols. (Princeton: Van Nostrand, 1956), II: 81–87.

8262 Shotwell, James T., and Francis Deak, "The Treaty of London, 1871." *Turkey at the Straits.* New York: Macmillan, 1940, pp. 44–54.

8263 Attrep, Abraham M. "The Road to the Empty Peace: Anglo-Turkish Reactions, 1918–1920." Ph.D. diss., Univ. of Georgia, 1972.

8264 "Scrapping the Treaty of Sevres." *Literary Digest* (Aug. 27, 1921): 14–15.

8265 Woods, H. Charles. "Sevres: Before and After." *Fortnightly Review* 118 (Oct. 1922): 545–60.

TREATY OF LAUSANNE (1923)

For text of treaty, see Great Britain, Foreign Office, *Treaty of Peace with Turkey and other Instruments Signed at Lausanne on July 14, 1923,* Cmd. 1923 (London: H.M.S.O., 1923).

Documents

8266 Great Britain. Foreign Office. *Lausanne Conference on Near Eastern Affairs, 1922–1923: Records of Proceedings and Draft Items of Peace.* Cmd. 1814. London: H.M.S.O., 1923.

General Accounts

8267 Afetinan, A. L. *Independence turque et le Traite de Lausanne.* Istanbul: Devlet Basimevi, 1938.

8268 Aras, Tevfik R. *10 Ans sur les Traces de Lausanne.* Istanbul: Aksam Matbassi, 1935.

8269 Burns, Richard Dean, and Donald Urquidi. "The Lausanne Convention: The Straits." *Disarmament In Perspective.* 4 vols. Washington, D.C.: G.P.O., 1968, II: 93–120.

8270 Djonker, Mahumud C. *Le Bosphore et les Dardanelles: Les Conventions des Detroits de Lausanne et Montreux.* Lausanne, 1938.

8271 Mestre, Achille. "L'etranger en Turquie d'apres le Traite de Lausanne." *Revue Politique et Parlementaire* (Aout 10, 1923): 179–206.

8272 Schlesinger, Nathan. *Le Nouveau Regime des Detroits.* Paris: Jouve, 1926.

8273 Schmidt, Nathaniel. "The Peace of Lausanne." *American Review* 2 (Jan. 1924): 55–58.

8274   Strupp, Karl. *Der Vertrag von Lausanne.* Berlin: Emil Roth, 1932.

8275   Toynbee, Arnold J. "East after Lausanne." *Foreign Affairs* (Sept. 15, 1923): 84–99.

8276   Woods, H. Charles. "Lausanne and its Accessories." *Fortnightly Review* 120 (July 1923): 122–33.

8277   ———. "Lausanne and its Antecedents." *Fortnightly Review* 119 (Jan. 1923): 137–52.

8278   ———. "The Straits: Before and After." *Fortnightly Review* 119 (Feb. 1923): 282–92.

Conference

8279   Brown, Philip M. "From Sevres to Lausanne." *American Journal of International Law* 18 (Jan. 1924): 113–16.

8280   ———. "The Lausanne Conference." *American Journal of International Law* 17 (Apr. 1923): 290–96.

8281   Colrat, Raymond, *Lausanne et les Vieillards: Autour d'une Conference.* Paris: Armand Collin, 1923. 821a "The Lausanne Conference." *Round Table* 13 (Mar. 1923): 342–55.

8282   Liais, Michel. "La Conference de Lausanne." *Revue Generale de Droit International Public* 40 (Jan.–Feb. 1933): 71–89.

8283   Rougier, Antoin. "La Question des Detroits et la Convention de Lausanne." *Revue Generale de Droit International Public* 31 (Sept.–Oct. 1924): 309–38.

8284   Stuart, James. "The Failure of the Lausanne Conference." *Fortnightly Review* 120 (Oct. 1923): 574–81.

8285   Turlington, Edgar W. "The Settlement of Lausanne." *American Journal of International Law* 18 (Oct. 1924): 696–706.

British Policies & Attitudes

8286   "Downing Street and the Dardanelles." *Economist* (Sept. 23, 1922): 495–96.

8287   "Lausanne and the Freedom of the Straits." *Economist* (Dec. 9, 1922): 1064–65.

8288   "Lord Curzon and the Turks." *Economist* (Oct. 13, 1923): 548–50.

8289   Nicolson, Harold. *Curzon: The Last Phase, 1919–1925.* Boston: Houghton Mifflin, 1934, chs. 10–11.

8290   Woods, H. Charles. "Lord Curzon and Lausanne." *Fortnightly Review* 119 (Mar. 1923): 491–502.

Turkish Policies

8291   Crouzet, Pierre. "Pourquoi Ismet Pacha a quitte Lausanne." *Revue Hebdomadaire* (Mar. 3, 1923): 90–99.

8292   Davidson, Roderic H. *Turkish Diplomacy from Mudros to Lausanne.* Princeton: Princeton Univ. Press, 1953. [A shorter version appears in Gordon A. Craig and Felix Gilbert, eds., *The Diplomats.* 2 vols. Princeton: Princeton Univ. Press, 1963, I: 172–209.]

8293   Duggan, Stephen P. "Turkish Gains out of Western Discords." *Annals of the Amer. Acad. of Pol. & Soc. Sci.* 108 (July 1923): 148–52.

8294   "Turkey and the Powers." *Quarterly Review* 239 (Jan. 1923): 161–82.

Russian Policies

8295   "How Turkey Failed Russia at Lausanne." *Literary Digest* (Sept. 15, 1923): 22–23.

8296   Jaschke, Gotthard. "Le Role du Communisme dans les Relations Russo-Turques en 1919 a 1922." *Orient* 7:26 (1963): 31–44.

8297   "Plan of Russia and Turkey to Control the Straits." *Literary Digest* (Oct. 21, 1922): 17–19.

U.S. Policy & Attitudes

8298   American Committee Opposed to the Lausanne Treaty. *The Lausanne Treaty, Turkey and Armenia.* New York, 1936.

8299   Daniel, R. L. "The Armenian Question and American-Turkish Relations, 1914–1927." *Mississippi Valley Historical Review* 46 (Sept. 1959): 252–75.

8300   Dennis, Alfred L. P. "The United States and the New Turkey." *North American Review* 217 (June 1923): 721–31.

8301 DeNovo, John A. *American Interests and Policies in the Middle East, 1900–1939*. Minneapolis: Univ. of Minnesota Press, 1963, ch. 4–5.

8302 Earle, Edward M. "Ratify the Turkish Treaty." *Nation* (Jan. 23, 1924): 86–88.

8303 Gerard, J. W. *The Lausanne Treaty: Should the United States Ratify It?* Pamphlet no. 26. New York: Foreign Policy Assoc., 1924.

8304 Gordon, Leland J. "Turkish-American Treaty Relations." *American Political Science Review* 22 (Aug. 1928): 711–21.

8305 Grew, Joseph. "The Peace Conference of Lausanne, 1922–1923." *American Philosophical Society Proceedings* 98 (Feb. 1954): 1–10.

8306 ———. *Turbulent Era: A Diplomatic Record of Forty Years*. 2 vols. Boston: Houghton Mifflin, 1952, chs. 18–20.

8307 Plimpton, George A. "The United States and Lausanne Treaty." *New Orient* 3 (July 1926): 20–24.

8308 Sachar, Howard M. "The United States and Turkey, 1914–1927: The Origins of Near Eastern Policy." Ph.D. diss., Harvard Univ., 1953.

8309 Trask, Roger R. "The 'Terrible Turk' and Turkish-American Relations in the Interwar Period." *Historian* 33 (Nov. 1970): 40–53.

8310 Turlington, Edgar W. *The American Treaty of Lausanne*. World Peace Foundation Pamphlets, no. 7, 1924, pp. 565–603.

8311 "Why the Democrats Defeated the Turkish Treaty." *Literary Digest* (Jan. 29, 1927): 10–11.

International Control of Straits

Summary of annual report of Straits Commission may be found in League of Nations, *Official Journal*, 1924–1936.

8312 Hazleton, Willis B. "The International Administration of the Turkish Straits, 1924–1936." Ph.D. diss., Stanford Univ., 1951.

8313 Schreiner, George A. "The Turkish Straits Under International Control." *Current History* 21 (Oct. 1924): 65–74.

MONTREUX CONVENTION (1936)

For text of convention, see League of Nations, *Treaty Series* (London: Harrison, 1936), vol. 173, pp. 215–41.

Documents

8314 *Actes de la Conférence de Montreux, 22 Juin–20 Juillet 1936. Compte Rendu des Séances Plenieres et Proces-verbaux des Débats du Comité Technique*. Liège: H. Vaillant-Carmanne s.a., 1936.

General Accounts

8315 Baker, Robert L. "Turkey and the Straits." *Current History* 42 (Sept. 1935): 666–67.

8316 Liggett, Michael L. "Turkey and International Cooperation in the League of Nations: Case Studies in Disarmament and Opium Diplomacy, 1928–1938." Ph.D. diss., Univ. of California, Santa Barbara, 1971.

8317 McDowell, Edward C., Jr. "Dardanelles: Explaining their Refortification in the Foreboding Light of History." *Current History* 45 (Nov. 1936): 92–96.

8318 "Money for Guns: Turkey Refortifying Dardanelles." *Literary Digest* (Aug. 1, 1936): 14.

8319 Suche, Joachim. *Der Meerengenvertrag von Montreux vom 20. Juli 1936 und seine Vorgeschichte (Seit 1918)*. Munchen: Duncker, 1936.

Conference

8320 Abrevaya, Juliette. *La Conférence de Montreux et le Régime des Détroits*. Paris: Editions Internationales, 1937.

8321 Bremoy, Guillaume de. *La Conférence de Montreux et le Nouveau Regime des Détroits*. Paris: Les Presses Modernes, 1939.

8322 Colliard, Claude A. "La Convention de Montreux: Nouvelle Solution du Probleme des Détroits." *Revue de Droit International* 10 (July–Sept. 1936): 121–52.

8323 Fenwick, Charles G. "The New Status of the Dardanelles." *American Journal of International Law* 30 (Oct. 1936): 701–06.

8324   Giannini, Amedeo. "Il regime degli Stretti dopo gli atti di Montreux." *Oriente Moderno* 18 (Ott. 1938): 527–36.

8325   Howard, Harry N. "The Straits After the Montreux Conference." *Foreign Affairs* 14 (Oct. 1936): 199–202.

8326   Mousset, Albert. "Montreux et la Question des Detroits." *L'Europe Nouvelle* (Juin 27, 1936): 663–65.

8327   Routh, D. A. "The Montreux Convention Regarding the Regime of the Black Sea Straits." In Royal Institute of International Affairs. *Survey of International Affairs, 1936.* London: Oxford Univ. Press, 1937, pp. 584–651.

8328   Toscano, Mario. *La Conferenza di Montreux e la Nuova Convenzione degli stretti.* Milan: Gontrano Martucci, 1939.

8329   Visscher, Fernand de. "La Nouvelle Convention des Detroits." *Revue de Droit International et de Legislation Comparee* 17:4 (1936): 669–718.

8330   Warsamy, Georges D. *La Convention des Detroits: Montreux 1936.* Paris: Pedone, 1937.

U.S.S.R. Proposal to Revise Montreux Convention (1946)

For text of Soviet note of Aug. 7th, see H. N. Howard, *The Problem of the Turkish Straits* (Washington, D.C.: G.P.O., 1947), pp. 47–49.

8331   Bilsel, Cemil. "The Turkish Straits in the Light of Recent Turkish-Soviet Correspondence." *American Journal of International Law* 41 (Oct. 1947): 727–47.

8332   Black, Cyril E. "The Turkish Straits and the Great Powers." *Foreign Policy Reports* (Oct. 1, 1947): 174–82.

8333   Cramer, A. G. "Turkey in Search of Protectors: An Excursion into the History of a Strategic Area." *Current History* 13 (Oct.–Nov. 1947): 210–16, 280–87.

8334   Dur, Lt. Cmdr. Philip A. "The Montreux Convention: Prospects for an Imminent Change." *U.S. Naval Institute Proceedings* 99 (July, 1973): 110–12.

8335   Esmer, Ahmed Sukru. "The Straits: Crux of World Politics." *Foreign Affairs* 25 (Jan. 1947): 290–302.

8336   Howard, Harry N. "The United States and the Problem of the Turkish Straits: A Reference Article." *Middle East Journal* 1 (Jan. 1947): 59–72.

8337   Padelford, Norman J. "Solutions to the Problem of the Turkish Straits: A Brief Appraisal." *Middle East Journal* 2 (Apr. 1948): 175–90.

8338   Tchirkovitch, Stevan. "La Question de la Revision de la Convention de Montreux concernant la Regime des Detroits Turcs: Bosphore et Dardanelles." *Revue Generale de Droit International Public* 56 (1952): 189–222.

8339   Van Alstyne, Richard W. "The Question of the Turkish Straits." *Current History* 12 (Aug. 1947): 65–70.

Treaties: General, 1963-1975

U.S.-U.S.S.R. Direct Communications Pacts (1963, 1971)

For texts of the "Hot Line" agreements, see "Union of Soviet Socialist Republics Direct Communications Link: Memorandum of Understanding, Geneva, June 20, 1963," *U.S. Treaties and Other International Agreements* 14:1 (Washington, D.C.: G.P.O., 1963), pp. 825–35; "Agreement Between the United States of America and the Union of Soviet Socialist Republics on Measures to Improve the USA-USSR Direct Communications Link, Washington, Sept. 30, 1971," *U.S. Treaties and Other International Agreements* 22:2 (Washington, D.C.: G.P.O., 1971), pp. 1598–1615.

8340   "Dial K for Khrushchev." *Business Week* (Apr. 13, 1963): 36.

8341   "The Establishment of a Direct Communications Link between the Soviet and U.S. Governments." *International Affairs* [Moscow] 9 (Aug. 1963): 140–41.

8342   Foster, William C. "Possibilities for Reducing the Risks of War." *U.S. Department of State Bulletin* (Jan. 7, 1963): 3–8.

1963 Agreement

8343   " 'Hot Line' to Moscow: How it Will Work." *U.S. News & World Report* 55 (July 1963): 8.

8344 Johnson, Lyndon B. *The Vantage Point.* New York: Holt, Rinehart & Winston, 1971, pp. 287–304.

8345 Keesing's Research Report. *Disarmament Negotiations and Treaties, 1946–1971.* New York: Scribner's, 1972, pp. 235–43.

8346 Loomis, Richard T. "The White House Telephone and Crisis Management." *U.S. Naval Institute Proceedings* 95 (Dec. 1969): 63–73.

8347 "Open Wire to Kremlin." *Business Week* (June 29, 1963): 36.

8348 U.S. Arms Control & Disarmament Agency. *Arms Control and Disarmament Agreements: Texts and History of Negotiations.* 2d ed. Washington, D.C.: G.P.O., 1975, pp. 27–29.

8349 "U.S. and U.S.S.R. Sign Agreement for Direct Communication Link." *U.S. Department of State Bulletin* (July 8, 1963): 50.

1971 Agreement

8350 Gorkin, Jess. "A Washington-Peking Hot Line." *Current* 119 (June 1970): 58–59.

8351 SIPRI. *World Armament and Disarmament: SIPRI Yearbook, 1972.* New York: Humanities Press, 1972, pp. 36–37.

8352 U.S. Arms Control & Disarmament Agency. *Arms Control and Disarmament Agreements: Texts and History of Negotiations.* 2d ed. Washington, D.C.: G.P.O., 1975, pp. 107–08.

8353 "U.S. and U.S.S.R. Sign Agreements to Reduce Risk of Nuclear War." *U.S. Department of State Bulletin* (Oct. 18, 1971): 399–403.

WAR RISK REDUCTION AGREEMENT (1971)

For text of the agreement, see "Agreement on Measures to Reduce the Risk of Outbreak of Nuclear War Between the United States of America and the Union of Soviet Socialist Republics," *U.S. Treaties and Other International Agreements* 22:2 (Washington, D.C.: G.P.O., 1971), pp. 1590–97.

8354 SIPRI. *World Armament and Disarmament: SIPRI Yearbook, 1972.* New York: Humanities Press, 1972, pp. 36–37.

8355 "Soviet Union and United States Sign Agreements to Prevent Nuclear War." *Reprints from the Soviet Press* (Oct. 29, 1971): 24–29.

8356 U.S. Arms Control & Disarmament Agency. *Arms Control and Disarmament Agreements: Texts and History of Negotiations.* Washington, D.C.: G.P.O., 1975, pp. 103–04.

8357 "U.S. and U.S.S.R. Sign Agreements to Reduce Risk of Nuclear War." *U.S. Department of State Bulletin* (Oct. 18, 1971): 399–403.

AGREEMENT ON PREVENTION OF INCIDENTS AT SEA (1972)

For text of agreement, see U.S. Department of State, *Treaties and Other International Acts,* no. 7379 (Washington, D.C., 1974).

8358 Harrigan, Anthony. "Brinkmanship at Sea— A Two Way Street?" *Navy* 11 (July 1968): 14–18.

8359 Kidd, Vice Adm. Isaac C. "A Look at U.S.-Soviet Rivalry in the Mediterranean." *U.S. News & World Report* (Nov. 15, 1971): 110–11.

8360 "Ship Anchor Chains Tangle But Not U.S., Soviet Crews." *U.S. Naval Institute Proceedings* 99 (Sept. 1973): 120–21.

PREVENTION OF NUCLEAR WAR, U.S.-U.S.S.R. (1973)

For text of agreement, see *Documents on Disarmament, 1973* (Washington, D.C.: G.P.O., 1975), pp. 283–85.

8361 [Kissinger, Henry A.]. "News Conference Remarks by Presidential Assistant Kissinger on the Agreement on the Prevention of Nuclear War, June 22, 1973." *Documents on Disarmament, 1973.* Washington, D.C.: G.P.O., 1975, pp. 285–94.

8362 Kudrin, M. "Eliminate the Possibility of Nuclear War." *Soviet Military Review* 2 (Feb. 1974): 55–56.

8363 Nerlich, Uwe. "Die Eingehung des Nuklearkrieges: Zur politischen Bedeutung des amerikanisch-sowjetischen Grundsatzabkommens uber die Verhutung von Nuklearkriegen." *Europa-Archiv* (Oct. 10, 1973): 669–78.

8364   York, Herbert F. "Are Nuclear Command and Control Systems Fail-Safe?" *Center Report* (Apr. 1975): 6–7.

WEATHER MODIFICATION PROPOSAL (1972–)

For text of resolution, see U.S. Senate. Resolution [Pell]. "Prohibiting Military Weather Modification," Sen. Res. 281, 92d Cong., 2d Sess., 1972.

Bibliography

8365   Zikeev, Nikolai T. *Weather Modification in the Soviet Union, 1946–1966: A Selected Annotated Bibliography*. Washington, D.C.: Library of Congress, 1967.

Documents

8366   U.S. House. Committee on Foreign Affairs. Hearings: *Prohibition of Weather Modification As a Weapon of War*. 94th Cong., 1st Sess., July 29, 1975.

8367   ———. Hearings: *Weather Modification As a Weapon of War*. 93d Cong., 2d Sess., 1974.

8368   U.S. Senate. Committee on Foreign Relations. Hearings: *Prohibiting Hostile Use of Environmental Modification Techniques*. 94th Cong., 2d Sess., 1976.

8369   ———. Hearings: *Prohibiting Military Weather Modification*. 92d Cong., 2d Sess., July 26, 27, 1972.

8370   ———. Hearings: *Weather Modification*. 93d Cong., 1st Sess., Jan. 25, Mar. 20, 1974.

8371   ———. Report: *Prohibiting Environmental Modification as a Weapon of War*. 93d Cong., 1st Sess., 1973.

General Accounts

8372   Barnaby, Frank. "Environmental Warfare." *Bulletin of the Atomic Scientists* 32 (May 1976): 36–43.

8373   ———. "Towards Environmental Warfare." *New Scientist* (Jan. 1, 1976): 6–8.

8374   Begishev, Valery. "Another Genocide Weapon." *New Times* [Moscow] 32 (Aug. 1972): 26–27.

8375   Dernbach, John. "Tinkering With the Clouds." *Progressive* 40 (Oct. 1976): 44–47.

8376   "Draft Convention on Environment Warfare Tabled in Geneva Disarmament Committee." *U.S. Department of State Bulletin* (Sept. 15, 1975): 417–20.

8377   Goldblat, Jozef. "The Prohibition of Environmental Warfare." *Ambio* 4:5–6 (1975): 186–90.

8378   Gude, Rep. Gilbert. "Weather Modification." *Congressional Record* 121 (Oct. 21, 1975): H5628–30.

8379   ———. "Weather Modification II." *Congressional Record* 121 (Oct. 21, 1975): H10179–180.

8380   Kellogg, W. W., and S. H. Schneider. "Climate Stabilization: For Better or For Worse?" *Science* (Dec. 29, 1974): 1163–72.

8381   Kotsch, W. J. "Forecast: Change." *U.S. Naval Institute Proceedings* 94 (Jan. 1968): 69–77.

8382   MacDonald, Gordon J. F. "Weather Modification as a Weapon." *Technology Review* 78 (Oct.–Nov. 1975): 56–63.

8383   Nelson, Sen. Gaylord. "Weather Modification." *Congressional Record* 118 (July 28, 1972): S25946–956.

8384   Norman, Colin. "Pentagon Admits Viet Nam Rainmaking." *Nature* (May 31, 1974): 402.

8385   Ognibene, Peter J. "Making War With the Weather." *New Republic* (Sept. 30, 1972): 12–14.

8386   Pollack, Herman. "International Aspects of Weather Modification." *U.S. Department of State Bulletin* (Aug. 21, 1972): 212–14.

8387   Rapp, R. R. *Climate Modification and National Security*. P–4476. Santa Monica, Ca.: Rand, Oct. 1972.

8388   Shapley, Deborah. "Arms Control Report Card—Environment Warfare: Needs More Work." *Science* (Sept. 5, 1975): 773.

8389   ———. "Rainmaking: Rumored Use Over Laos Alarms Arms Experts." *Science* (June 16, 1972): 1216–20.

8390 Studer, T. A. "Weather Modification in Support of Military Operations." *Air University Review* 20 (Nov.–Dec. 1969): 44–50.

8391 Sutcliffe, R. C. "Control of Weather and Climate." *Nature* (Apr. 30, 1966): 459–60.

8392 Taubenfeld, Howard J., ed. *Controlling the Weather: A Study of Law and Regulatory Processes.* New York: Dunellen, 1970.

8393 U.S. Central Intelligence Agency. *A Study of Climatological Research as It Pertains to Intelligence Problems.* Washington, D.C.: Library of Congress, 1974.

8394 Weiss, Edith Brown. "International Responses to Weather Modification." *International Organization* 29 (Summer 1975): 805–26.

8395 ———. "Weather Control: An Instrument of War?" *Survival* 17 (Mar.–Apr. 1975): 64–68.

8396 ———. "Weather as a Weapon." *Air, Water, Earth & Fire* [The Impact of the Military on World Environmental Order]. San Francisco: Sierra Club, 1974, pp. 51–62.

Treaties: Nuclear Test Bans

FALLOUT & RADIATION HAZARDS

8397 Arnold, James R. "Effects of the Recent Bomb Tests on Human Beings." *Bulletin of the Atomic Scientists* 10 (Nov. 1954): 352.

8398 Bailey, Sidney D. "U.N. Report on Radiation." *Christian Century* (Aug. 13, 1958): 920–21.

8399 *The Biological Effects of Atomic Radiation.* Washington, D.C.: National Academy of Sciences & National Research Council, 1956.

8400 Bloom, Arthur D., et al. "Chromosome Aberrations and Malignant Disease Among A-Bomb Survivors." *American Journal of Public Health and the Nation's Health* 60 (Apr. 1970): 641–44.

8401 "Brilliant Sunrise?" *Nation* (Mar. 27, 1954): 249.

8402 Carter, J. C. "The Genetic Problem of Irradiated Human Populations." *Bulletin of the Atomic Scientists* 11 (Dec. 1955): 362–63.

8403 Dunning, Gordon M. "Effects of Nuclear Weapons Testing." *Scientific Monthly* 81 (Dec. 1955): 265–70.

8404 Dyer, A. J., and B. B. Hicks. "Radioactive Fallout in Southern Australia During the Years, 1958–1964." *Journal of Geophysical Research* (Aug. 15, 1965): 3879–83.

8405 *Effect of Radiation on Human Heredity.* Geneva: World Health Organization, 1957.

8406 Everett, H., and George E. Pugh. "Distribution and Effects of Fallout in Large Nuclear Weapons Campaigns." *Operations Research* 7 (Mar.–Apr. 1959): 226–48.

8407 "Fall-Out Hazard: An Evaluation." *Bulletin of the Atomic Scientists* 11 (Feb. 1955): 52.

8408 Fowler, John M., ed. *Fallout: A Study of Superbombs, Strontium 90, and Survival.* New York: Basic Books, 1960.

8409 Glass, H. Bentley. "The Hazards of Atomic Radiation to Man: British and American Reports." *Bulletin of the Atomic Scientists* 12 (Oct. 1956): 312–17.

8410 *The Hazards to Man of Nuclear and Allied Radiations.* London: H.M.S.O., 1956.

8411 Hempelmann, Louis H., et al. "The Acute Radiation Syndrome: A Study of Nine Cases and a Review of the Problem." *Annals of Internal Medicine* 36 (Feb. 1952): 279–310.

8412 India, Government of. *Nuclear Explosions and Their Effects.* New Delhi: Publications Division, 1956.

8413 Johnson, Paul. "H-Bomb Over Britain." *Nation* (Mar. 29, 1958): 276–77.

8414 Lapp, Ralph E. "Global Fallout." *Bulletin of the Atomic Scientists* 11 (Nov. 1955): 339–43.

8415 ———. "Radioactive Fallout III." *Bulletin of the Atomic Scientists* 11 (June 1955): 206–09.

8416 Muller, H. J. "The Genetic Damage Produced by Radiation." *Bulletin of the Atomic Scientists* 11 (June 1955): 210–12.

8417 "A Navy Medical Team Studies Fallout Effects." *Bulletin of the Atomic Scientists* 12 (Feb. 1956): 58–59.

8418 Neel, J. V., and W. J. Schull. *The Effect of Exposure to the Atomic Bombs on Pregnancy Termination in Hiroshima and Nagasaki.* Washington, D.C.: National

Academy of Sciences & National Research Council, 1956.

8419   Neuman, W. F. "Uncertainties in Evaluating Effects of Fallout from Weapons Tests." *Bulletin of the Atomic Scientists* 14 (Jan. 1958): 31–34.

8420   Nordheim, L. W. "Tests of Nuclear Weapons." *Bulletin of the Atomic Scientists* 11 (Sept. 1955): 253–55.

8421   Rabinowitch, Eugene. "Genetics in Geneva." *Bulletin of the Atomic Scientists* 11 (Nov. 1955): 314.

8422   "Radiation Exposures in Recent Weapons Tests." *Bulletin of the Atomic Scientists* 10 (Nov. 1954): 352.

8423   "Radiation Hazards from Fallout and X-Rays." *Consumer Reports* 13 (Sept. 1958): 484–88.

8424   Rosenfeld, A. H., et al. "Fallout: Some Measurements and Damage Estimates." *Bulletin of the Atomic Scientists* 11 (June 1955): 213–16.

8425   Schubert, J., and Ralph E. Lapp. *Radiation: What It Is and How It Affects You.* London: Heinemann, 1957.

8426   "Science: Tragic Results of Fallout Among Pacific Victims." *Newsweek* (June 25, 1956): 70.

8427   "Scientists Appraise Atmospheric Tests." *Bulletin of the Atomic Scientists* 18 (Apr. 1962): 33–34.

8428   "Strontium 90 Dosages and Infant Mortality." *Bulletin of the Atomic Scientists* 26 (May 1970): 40–42.

8429   *Summary of the Observation Results for Nuclear Radiation in Japan and Airborne Radioactive Fallout in the World During IGY.* Tokyo: National Committee of the International Geophysical Year, Science Council of Japan, 1960.

8430   "The Truth About Radioactive Fallout." *U.S. News & World Report* (Feb. 25, 1955): 35–36.

8431   "U.N. Finds Fallout Peril Less Than Suspected." *Business Week* (Aug. 16, 1958): 56–58.

8432   U.N. *Report of the United Nations Scientific Committee on the Effects of Atomic Radiation.* New York, 1958.

8433   U.S. Joint Committee on Atomic Energy. Hearings: *Biological and Environmental Effects of Nuclear War.* 86th Cong., 1st Sess., 1959.

8434   ———. Hearings: *Fallout From Nuclear Weapons Tests.* 4 pts. 86th Cong., 1st Sess., 1959, pt. V: Index to Hearings.

8435   ———. Hearings: *Fallout, Radiation Standards and Countermeasures.* 2 pts. 88th Cong., 1st Sess., June 3–6, Aug. 20–22, 27, 1963.

8436   ———. Hearings: *Health and Safety Problems and Weather Effects Associated With Atomic Explosions.* 84th Cong., 1st Sess., Apr. 15, 1955.

8437   ———. Hearings: *The Nature of Radioactive Fallout and Its Effects on Man.* 3 pts. 85th Cong., 1st Sess., 1957.

8438   ———. Report: *Biological and Environmental Effects of Nuclear War.* 86th Cong., 1st Sess., 1959.

8439   ———. Report: *Fallout From Nuclear Weapons Tests.* 86th Cong., 1st Sess., 1959.

8440   ———. Report: *The Nature of Radioactive Fallout and Its Effects on Man.* 85th Cong., 1st Sess., 1957.

"Lucky Dragon" Affair

8441   Deverall, Richard. "H-Bomb Creates Japan-U.S. Fission." *America* (Nov. 6, 1954): 149–51.

8442   Lapp, Ralph E. "The Voyage of the Lucky Dragon." *Harper's* 215 (Dec. 1957): 27–76.

8443   ———. *The Voyage of the Lucky Dragon.* New York: Harper, 1958.

8444   Wilson, E. Raymond. "Japan's Atomic Fears." *Christian Century* (May 1, 1957): 553–54.

U.S. FALLOUT DEBATE

8445   Amrine, Michael. "Disarmament and Defense: The Issue of Fallout." *Current History* 33 (Oct. 1957): 221–26.

8446   "The Atom and the Journalists." *Nation* (Nov. 15, 1958): 358–60.

8447 Bethe. Hans A., and Edward Teller. *The Future of Nuclear Tests.* Headline Series no. 145. New York: Foreign Policy Assoc., Feb. 1961.

8448 "Congress Is Told How Pressures Grew to Ban Tests." *U.S. News & World Report* (June 14, 1957): 75–77.

8449 Cousins, Norman. "The Great Debate Opens." *Saturday Review* (June 15, 1957): 24.

8450 [Eisenhower, Pres. Dwight D.]. "Here Are Eisenhower's Views on the 'Fallout Scare.' " *U.S. News & World Report* (June 14, 1957): 45–46.

8451 Hagan, Roger. "The Atmospheric Tests: Notes From a Vanishing Perspective." *American Scholar* 31 (Autumn 1962): 521–40.

8452 "The H-Bomb and World Opinion." *Bulletin of the Atomic Scientists* 10 (May 1954): 163–67.

8453 Holifield, Rep. Chet. "Congressional Hearings on Radioactive Fallout." *Bulletin of the Atomic Scientists* 14 (Jan. 1958): 52–54.

8454 "Los Alamos Group on Nuclear Tests." *Science* (Aug. 16, 1957): 296.

8455 "Need We Halt Tests?" *America* (Apr. 26, 1958): 131.

8456 "Nuclear Tests: World Debate." *Time* (Apr. 7, 1958): 16.

8457 Rabinowitch, Eugene. "Nuclear Bomb Tests." *Bulletin of the Atomic Scientists* 14 (Oct. 1958): 282–87.

8458 ———. "The People Must Know." *Bulletin of the Atomic Scientists* 10 (Dec. 1954): 370, 398.

8459 Rosi, Eugene J. "Elite Political Communication: Five Washington Columnists on Nuclear Weapons Testing, 1954–1958." *Social Research* 34 (Winter 1967): 703–27.

8460 ———. "How 50 Periodicals and the Times Interpreted the Test Ban Controversy." *Journalism Quarterly* 41 (Autumn 1964): 545–56.

8461 ———. "Mass and Attentive Opinion on Nuclear Weapons Tests and Fallout, 1954–1963." *Public Opinion Quarterly* 29 (Sept. 1965): 280–97.

8462 ———. "Public Opinion and Foreign Policy: Nongovernmental Opinion Concerning the Cessation of Nuclear Weapons Tests, 1954–1958." Ph.D. diss., Columbia Univ., 1967.

8463 Russell, Lord Bertrand. "World Conference of Scientists." *Bulletin of the Atomic Scientists* 12 (Feb. 1956): 41–43.

8464 Schilling, Warner R. "Scientists, Foreign Policy, and Politics." *American Political Science Review* 56 (June 1962): 287–300.

8465 "Should U.S. Stop Nuclear Tests?" *Foreign Policy Bulletin* (May 15, 1958): 132–33.

8466 "Space and the Atom: Tempest Over Tests." *Newsweek* (Mar. 3, 1958): 40.

8467 Stanford, Neal. "H-Bomb Debate Helps Public." *Foreign Policy Bulletin* (Nov. 15, 1956): 35.

8468 ———. "Nuclear Tests: Propaganda or Necessity." *Foreign Affairs Bulletin* (May 1, 1958): 123.

8469 *The Test Ban Debate: Statements of the Governments of the Soviet Union and China on the Treaty on Banning Nuclear Weapons Tests in the Atmosphere, in Outer Space and Under Water.* New Delhi: People's Pub. House, 1963.

8470 U.S. Senate. Committee on the Judiciary. Hearings: *Communist Infiltration in the Nuclear Test Ban Movement.* 2 pts. 86th Cong., 2d Sess., 1960–1961.

8471 "What's All the Talk About Stopping H-Bomb Tests?" *U.S. News & World Report* (Apr. 11, 1958): 41–42.

Test Ban Debate—Pro

8472 "Appeal to Western Evolutionists Against H-Bomb." *Bulletin of the Atomic Scientists* 11 (Jan. 1955): 34.

8473 "Atomic Scientists Warn on More Bomb Tests." *Christian Century* (Nov. 17, 1954): 1390.

8474 "Ban the Bomb Tests." *Nation* (Feb. 11, 1956): 101.

8475 Bethe, Hans A. "The Case for Ending Nuclear Tests." *Atlantic Monthly* 206 (Aug. 1960): 43–51.

8476 "British Scientists Petition Prime Minister." *Science* (July 4, 1958): 18.

8477 Cousins, Norman. "Dr. Teller and the Spirit of Adventure." *Saturday Review* (Mar. 15, 1958): 26.

8478 ———. "An Open Letter to David Lawrence." *Saturday Review* (July 6, 1957): 20–21.

8479 "FAS [Federation of American Scientists] Urges Halt to Test Series." *Science* (Oct. 3, 1958): 761.

8480 "Four Men Challenge Nuclear Tests." *Christian Century* (Feb. 19, 1958): 211.

8481 Inglis, David R. "Ban H-Bomb Test and Favor the Defense." *Bulletin of the Atomic Scientists* 10 (Nov. 1954): 353–56.

8482 "Japanese Protesting British Tests." *Science* (Mar. 22, 1957): 542.

8483 Muller, H. J. "Race Poisoning by Radiation." *Saturday Review* (June 9, 1956): 9–11.

8484 Nishiwaki, Yashuhi. "Death in the Race: Report from Japan." *Nation* (Aug. 6, 1955): 111–14.

8485 Nooh, M. G. "The Danger of Nuclear Tests." *World Marxist Review* 1 (Nov. 1958): 71–72.

8486 Pauling, Linus C. "Genetic Effects of Weapons Test." *Bulletin of the Atomic Scientists* 18 (Dec. 1962): 15–18.

8487 "Petition Urging Agreement to Stop Nuclear Tests." *Science* (Feb. 7, 1958): 277.

8488 Westergaard, Mogens. "Man's Responsibility to His Genetic Heritage." *Bulletin of the Atomic Scientists* 11 (Dec. 1955): 362–63.

Test Ban Debate—Con

8489 "A Ban That Could Cost Us the Arms Race." *U.S. News & World Report* (July 11, 1960): 39–41.

8490 Burnham, James. "We Move Into the Soviet Trap." *National Review* (Oct. 11, 1958): 236.

8491 ———. "Why Moscow Wants to Stop Nuclear Tests." *National Review* (July 19, 1958): 86.

8492 "Can We Stop Testing?" *America* (June 15, 1957): 314.

8493 "H-Bomb Tests: They're Safe." *U.S. News & World Report* (Feb. 25, 1955): 128–30.

8494 Libby, Willard. "Memo from Japan: Crocodile Tears." *U.S. News & World Report* (July 1, 1955): 66–67.

8495 ———. "Radioactive Fallout." *Bulletin of the Atomic Scientists* 11 (Sept. 1955): 256–60.

8496 Murphy, Charles J. V. "The Case for Resuming Nuclear Tests." *Fortune* 61 (Apr. 1960): 148–50 ff.

8497 Murray, Thomas E. "The Case for Resuming Nuclear Tests." *World Affairs* 124 (Spring 1961): 17–20.

8498 ———. "Nuclear Testing and American Security." *Orbis* 4 (Winter 1961): 405–21.

8499 "On the Resumption of Nuclear Testing." *Orbis* 4 (Fall 1961): 259–63.

8500 Pollard, Ernest C. "Fall-Out Fever." *Atlantic Monthly* (Aug. 1957): 27–32.

8501 "Scientists and the Fallout Scare." *U.S. News & World Report* (June 21, 1957): 52.

8502 "A Scientist's View of Sane Nuclear Policy." *National Review* (Aug. 30, 1958): 150.

8503 Strauss, Lewis L. "Why Nuclear Testing Is a Must for Freedom." *Reader's Digest* 79:473 (1961): 54–61.

8504 Teller, Edward. *The Case for Continuing Tests.* Headline Series. New York: Foreign Policy Assoc., Jan.–Feb. 1961.

8505 ———, and Albert L. Latter. "The Compelling Need for Nuclear Tests." *Life* (Feb. 10, 1957): 64–72.

8506 Twining, Gen. Nathan F. "Atomic Tests Are Vital to Safety of U.S. and Allies." *U.S. News & World Report* (Apr. 18, 1958): 66–67.

8507 "The Uproar Over Atom Tests: 'No Dire Things Will Occur.'" *U.S. News & World Report* (May 2, 1958): 66–68.

8508 "We Have Continued Too Long the Ban on Nuclear Tests." *Saturday Evening Post* (July 8, 1961): 10.

8509 "What Scientists 'Agree'?" *National Review* (Apr. 5, 1958): 318.

8510 "Why Nuclear Tests Go On: AEC Gives Official Reasons." *U.S. News & World Report* (June 14, 1957): 136–37.

1956 Presidential Election

8511 Brown, Stuart G. *Conscience in Politics: Adlai Stevenson in the 1950's.* Syracuse: Syracuse Univ. Press, 1961.

8512 "Bulganin Takes a Hand in U.S. Election." *U.S. News & World Report* (Nov. 2, 1956): 140–41.

8513 [Eisenhower, Pres. Dwight D.]. "Ike Says H-Bomb Tests Must Go On." *U.S. News & World Report* (Oct. 12, 1956): 56.

8514 ———. "The Official Story of the H-Bomb Tests." *U.S. News & World Report* (Nov. 2, 1956): 143–51.

8515 ———. "U.S. Policies in Testing of Nuclear Weapons." *U.S. Department of State Bulletin* (Nov. 5, 1956): 704–15.

8516 Frye, William R. "Will Nuclear Weapons Tests Be Curbed?" *Foreign Policy Bulletin* (Oct. 1, 1956): 9–10.

8517 Inglis, David R. "Evasion of the H-Bomb Issue." *New Republic* (Nov. 5, 1956): 7–8.

8518 ———. "Why I Am For Stevenson." *New Republic* (Oct. 22, 1956): 11.

8519 Rabinowitch, Eugene. "Adlai Answers Ike: 'Let's Look at the Facts.'" *U.S. News & World Report* (Oct. 12, 1956): 51.

8520 ———. "The Bomb Test Controversy." *Bulletin of the Atomic Scientists* 12 (Nov. 1956): 322–24.

8521 ———. "Russia's Nuclear Tests." *U.S. News & World Report* (Sept. 7, 1956): 8.

8522 ———. "Survival of Mankind Hinges on H-Bomb Decisions." *U.S. News & World Report* (Nov. 2, 1956): 102–04.

8523 ———. "What the H-Bomb Fuss is all About." *U.S. News & World Report* (Oct. 26, 1956): 126–35.

8524 ———. "Why I Raised the H-Bomb Question." *Look* (Feb. 5, 1957): 23–25.

8525 Strauss, Lewis L. "If the H-Bombs are Banned, Can Russia Be Trusted?" *U.S. News & World Report* (Oct. 19, 1956): 96–98.

8525a ———. "Resumption of Nuclear Tests by Soviet Union." *U.S. Department of State Bulletin* (Sept. 10, 1956): 424–28.

8526 "Test Ban Dialogue Up to October 15." *Bulletin of the Atomic Scientists* 12 (Nov. 1956): 324.

8527 Wadsworth, James J. "Statement on Nuclear Testing." *U.S. Department of State Bulletin* (July 30, 1956): 205–07.

8528 "Why H-Bomb Missed Target." *U.S. News & World Report* (June 29, 1956): 31.

8529 "Why U.S. Must Test More H-Bombs." *U.S. News & World Report* (May 4, 1956): 122.

Schweitzer Declaration (1957)

8530 Cousins, Norman. "The Schweitzer Declaration: Introduction." *Saturday Review* (May 18, 1957): 13–16.

8531 Libby, Willard. "Open Letter to Dr. Schweitzer." *Saturday Review* (May 25, 1957): 8.

8532 Schweitzer, Albert. "Appeal to End Nuclear Tests." *Bulletin of the Atomic Scientists* 13 (June 1957): 204–05.

8533 ———. "An Obligation to Tomorrow." *Saturday Review* (May 24, 1958): 21–28.

The "Clean Bomb"

8534 Cousins, Norman. "Clean Bombs and Dirty Wars." *Saturday Review* (July 13, 1957): 20.

8535 "Has the U.S. Developed Clean Bombs?" *Science Digest* 40 (Oct. 1956): 62.

8536 "Ike Says This About 'Clean Bomb.'" *U.S. News & World Report* (July 5, 1957): 26.

8537 Inglis, David R. "Clean and Dirty Bombs." *New Republic* (June 10, 1957): 10–11.

8538 Lapp, Ralph E. "The Humanitarian Bomb." *Bulletin of the Atomic Scientists* 12 (Sept. 1956): 261–64.

8539 Rabinowitch, Eugene. "H-Bombs Without Fallout." *Bulletin of the Atomic Scientists* 12 (Sept. 1956): 234.

8540 "3 Times at Bat for U.S., 3 Hits: A-Bomb, H-Bomb, 'Clean Bomb.'" *U.S. News & World Report* (July 12, 1957): 86–88.

International Law & Testing

8541   Fliess, P. J. "The Legality of Atmospheric Nuclear Tests." *University of Florida Law Review* 15 (1962): 21–32.

8542   Margolis, Emmanuel. "The Hydrogen Bomb Tests and International Law." *Yale Law Journal* 64 (Apr. 1955): 626–47.

8543   ———. "Legality of Bomb Tests." *Nation* (Dec. 31, 1955): 570–72.

8544   McDougal, Myres S. "The Hydrogen Bomb Tests and the International Law of the Sea." *American Journal of International Law* 49 (July 1955): 356–61.

8545   ———, and Norbert A. Schlei. "The Hydrogen Bomb Tests in Perspective: Lawful Measures for Security." *Yale Law Journal* 44 (Apr. 1955): 648–710.

8546   Taubenfeld, Howard J. "Nuclear Testing and International Law." *Southwest Law Journal* 16 (Spring 1962): 365–408.

NUCLEAR TEST BAN TREATY (1963)

For text of this treaty, see "Multilateral Treaty Banning Nuclear Weapons Tests in the Atmosphere, in Outer Space and Under Water," *U.S. Treaties and Other International Agreements* 14:2 (Washington, D.C.: G.P.O., 1963), pp. 1313–87.

Documents

8547   U.S. Senate. Committee on Armed Services. Hearings: *Military Aspects and Implications of Nuclear Test Ban Proposals and Related Matters.* 2 vols. 88th Cong., 1st Sess., 1963.

8548   ———. Interim Report: *Military Implications of the Proposed Limited Nuclear Test Ban Treaty.* 88th Cong., 1st Sess., 1963.

8549   ———. Committee on Foreign Relations. Hearings: *Nuclear Test Ban Treaty* [on Ex. M]. 88th Cong., 1st Sess., 1963.

8550   ———. Report: *The Nuclear Test Ban Treaty.* Executive Rpt. no. 3. 88th Cong., 1st Sess., 1963.

8551   [U.S.S.R.]. *The Soviet Stand on Disarmament: A Collection of Nineteen Basic Soviet Documents on General and Complete Dis-armament, the Termination of Nuclear Weapons Tests, and the Relaxation of International Tensions.* New York: Crosscurrents Press, 1962, pp. 90–146.

General Accounts

8552   Ahmed, M. Samir. *The Neutrals and the Test Ban Negotiations: An Analysis of the Non-Aligned States' Efforts Between 1962–1963.* Occasional Paper, no. 4. New York: Carnegie Endowment for International Peace, Feb. 1967.

8553   Dean, Arthur H. *Test Ban and Disarmament: The Path of Negotiation.* New York: Harper & Row, 1966.

8554   Huddle, Franklin P. "The Limited Nuclear Test Ban Treaty and the United States Senate." Ph.D. diss., American Univ., 1965.

8555   Jacobson, Harold, and Eric Stein. *Diplomats, Scientists, and Politicians: The United States and the Nuclear Test Ban Negotiations.* Ann Arbor: Univ. of Michigan Press, 1966.

8556   Lepper, Mary M. *Foreign Policy Formulation: A Case Study of the Nuclear Test Ban Treaty of 1963.* Columbus: C. E. Merrill, 1971.

8557   McBride, James H. *The Test Ban Treaty: Military, Technological, and Political Implications.* Chicago: Regnery, 1967.

8558   Mezerik, Avrahm G. *Atom Tests and Radiation Hazards: Test Ban Efforts, UN, Cold War Conferences, Chronology.* New York: International Review Service, 1961.

8559   Sobel, Lester A., ed. *Disarmament & Nuclear Tests, 1960–63: The Search for a Way to Abolish War, End the Costly Burden of Armament and Prevent the Horrors of Radioactive Contamination of the Atmosphere.* New York: Facts on File, 1964.

8560   Terchek, Ronald J. *The Making of the Test Ban Treaty.* The Hague: Nijhoff, 1970.

8561   Voss, Earl H. *Nuclear Ambush: The Test-Ban Trap.* Chicago: Regnery, 1963.

8562   Wilson, Edward D. "The Nuclear Test Ban Treaty, 1963: A Bipartisan Step Toward Detente." Ph.D. diss., Univ. of Oklahoma, 1970.

8563 Zoppo, Ciro E. "The Test Ban: A Study in Arms Control Negotiation." Ph.D. diss., Columbia Univ., 1963.

8564 Ansberry, William F. "The Partial Nuclear Test Ban Treaty: An Example of Limited Success." *Arms Control and Disarmament: Success or Failure?* Berkeley, Ca.: McCutchan, 1969, pp. 38–72.

8565 Bargman, Abraham. "The Study of Test Ban and Disarmament Conferences: A Review. . . ." *Journal of Conflict Resolution* 11:2 (1967): 223–34.

8566 Brennan, Donald G., and Morton H. Halperin. "Policy Considerations of a Nuclear-Test Ban." In Donald G. Brennan, ed., *Arms Control, Disarmament, and National Security*. New York: Braziller, 1961, pp. 234–66.

8567 Goldblat, Jozef. *Ten Years of the Partial Test Ban Treaty, 1963–1973*. SIPRI Research Pamphlet. Stockholm: SIPRI, Aug. 1973.

8568 Hopmann, P. Terrence. "Internal and External Influences on Arms Control Negotiations: The Partial Test Ban." In Bruce M. Russett, ed., *Peace, War, and Numbers*. Beverly Hills, Ca.: Sage, 1972.

8569 ———, and Timothy King. "Interactions and Perceptions in the Test Ban Negotiations." *International Studies Quarterly* 20 (Mar. 1976): 105–42.

8570 Jack, Homer A. "Non-Aligned and a Test Ban Agreement: The Role of Non-Aligned States." *Journal of Conflict Resolution* 7:3 (1963): 542–52.

8571 Medalia, Jonathan E. "Problems in Formulating and Implementing Effective Arms Control Policy: The Nuclear Test Ban Treaty Case." *Stanford Journal of International Studies* [Special Issue on Arms Control] 7 (Spring 1972): 132–61.

8572 Moon, E. "Man-in-the-Street: Test Ban Treaty and Role of Libraries." *Library Journal* (Sept. 1, 1963): 30–35.

8573 Pomerance, Josephine W. "The Cuban Crisis and the Test Ban Negotiations." *Journal of Conflict Resolution* 7:3 (1963): 553–59.

8574 Rao, M. V. Subba. "Diplomatic Background of the Test Ban Treaties." *United Asia* 18:1 (1966): 34–41.

8575 Scott, Richard. "A Ban on Nuclear Tests: The Course of Negotiations, 1958–1962." *International Affairs* [London] 38 (Oct. 1962): 501–10.

8576 Shaker, Mohamed Ibrahim. "The Moscow Test Ban Treaty." *Revue Egyptienne de Droit International* 27 (1971): 41–58.

8577 Stone, I. F. "The Test Ban Comedy." *New York Review of Books* 14 (May 7, 1970): 17.

8578 Wiesner, Jerome B., and Herbert F. York. "National Security and the Nuclear Test Ban." *Scientific American* 211 (Oct. 1964): 27–35.

8579 ———. "The Test Ban and Security." *Survival* 7 (Jan.–Feb. 1965): 13–21.

Negotiations—Documents, 1956–1960

8580 U.N. Conference on the Discontinuance of Nuclear Weapons Tests. *Official Records.* Geneva, 1958–.

8581 U.S. Department of State. *Geneva Conference on the Discontinuance of Nuclear Weapons Tests.* Pub. 7090. Washington, D.C.: G.P.O., 1960.

8582 ———. *Geneva Conference on the Discontinuance of Nuclear Weapons Tests: History and Analysis of Negotiations.* Pub. 7258. Washington, D.C.: G.P.O., 1961.

8583 ———. "United Nations Commission Adopts Three Resolutions on Testing and Surprise Attack." *U.S. Department of State Bulleting* (Nov. 17, 1958): 783–92.

8584 U.S. Senate. Committee on Foreign Relations. Hearings: *Conference on the Discontinuance of Nuclear Weapons Tests: Analysis of Progress and Positions of the Participating Parties October 1958–August 1960.* 86th Cong., 2d Sess., 1960.

8585 ———. Hearings: *Disarmament and Foreign Policy.* 86th Cong., 1st Sess., Jan. 28, 30, Feb. 2, 1959.

8586 ———. Hearings: *Testimony of John A. McCone on Geneva Test Ban Negotiations.* 86th Cong., 1st Sess., June 24, 1959.

8587 ———. Report: *Conference on the Discontinuance of Nuclear Weapons Tests: Analysis of Progress and Positions of the*

Participating Parties, October 1958–August 1960. 86th Cong., 2d Sess., 1960.

Negotiations, 1956–1960

8588   "Ban Nuclear Weapons Tests." *New Times* [Moscow] (May 30, 1957): 3.

8589   Bull, Hedley. "The Arms Race and the Banning of Nuclear Tests." *Political Quarterly* 30 (Oct. 1959): 344–56.

8590   [Eisenhower, Pres. Dwight D.]. "Eisenhower to Khrushchev: The Real Way to End H-tests." *U.S. News & World Report* (Apr. 18, 1958): 78.

8591   ———. "From the President: Terms for Halting Atom Tests." *U.S. News & World Report* (Aug. 29, 1958): 29.

8592   Galay, Nikolai. "The Military Significance of the Soviet's Suspension of Nuclear Tests." *Institute for the Study of the USSR Bulletin* 5 (Apr. 1958): 39–43.

8593   Gamarekian, Edward. "Quarrels Over Underground Testing." *Nation* (Feb. 27, 1960): 179–82.

8594   Gehron, William J. "Geneva Conference on the Discontinuance of Nuclear Weapons Tests: History of Political and Technical Developments of the Negotiations from October 31, 1958 to August 22, 1960." *U.S. Department of State Bulletin* (Sept. 26, 1960): 482–97.

8595   "Halting H-Bomb Tests: What's Involved for the U.S." *U.S. News & World Report* (Aug. 29, 1958): 29.

8596   Humphrey, Sen. Hubert H. "First Step Toward Disarmament." *Nation* (May 24, 1958): 468–70.

8597   "If U.S. Stops H-Bomb Tests: Who Gains, Who Loses." *U.S. News & World Report* (Apr. 25, 1958): 67.

8598   Inglis, David R. "Prospects for Stopping Nuclear Tests." *Bulletin of the Atomic Scientists* 12 (Dec. 1956): 354–55.

8599   ———. *Testing and Taming of Nuclear Weapons.* Pamphlet no. 303. Washington, D.C.: Public Affairs Press, 1960.

8600   "The Inside Story: Why the New Red A-Tests." *Newsweek* (Oct. 20, 1958): 48.

8601   Kirillov, V. "The People Want an End to Nuclear Tests." *International Affairs* [Moscow] 5 (Dec. 1959): 28–31.

8602   ———. "The Western Powers Oppose Discontinuation of Nuclear Tests." *International Affairs* [Moscow] 5 (Mar. 1959): 18–23.

8603   Kissinger, Henry A. "Nuclear Testing and the Problem of Peace." *Foreign Affairs* 37 (Oct. 1958): 1–18.

8604   Lebedinsky, A. V. *The Danger of Nuclear Weapons Tests* [Soviet Scientists Concerning the Dangers of Nuclear Weapons Tests]. OTS: 59–11, 547; JPRS: 719–D. Washington, D.C.: U.S. Department of Commerce, Coordinated & Distributed by Office of Technical Services, May 14, 1959.

8605   ———. "The Harmful Consequences of Nuclear Weapons Tests." *International Affairs* [Moscow] 4 (June 1958): 15–25.

8606   National Planning Assoc. "Establishing International Control of Nuclear Explosions." *Bulletin of the Atomic Scientists* 14 (Sept. 1958): 262–69.

8607   ———. *Establishing International Control of Nuclear Testing.* Special Rep. no. 50. Washington, D.C., 1958.

8608   "The Nuclear Weapons Test Ban." *Bulletin of the Atomic Scientists* 12 (Sept. 1956): 268; 13 (June 1957): 201.

8609   "Proposal for a U.N. Commission to Study Problems of H-Bomb Tests." *Bulletin of the Atomic Scientists* 11 (May 1955): 185–86.

8610   Roberts, Chalmers M. "The Hopes and Fears of an Atomic Test Ban." *Reporter* (Apr. 28, 1960): 20–33.

8611   Semyonov, K. "All Nuclear Tests Must Be Stopped at Once." *International Affairs* [Moscow] 4 (Oct. 1958): 14–19.

8612   Spingarn, Jerome. "Will a Test Ban Treaty Be Signed?" *Bulletin of the Atomic Scientists* 15 (Sept. 1959): 333–36.

8613   Stevenson, Adlai E., et al. "The Nuclear Test Ban." *Bulletin of the Atomic Scientists* 16 (Mar. 1960): 85–92.

8614   "What Soviet Plan Really Means: And U.S. Answer." *U.S. News & World Report* (Apr. 11, 1958): 80–82.

8615 Zoppo, Ciro E. *The Issue of Nuclear Test Cessation at the London Disarmament Conference of 1957: A Study in East-West Negotiations.* RM–2821–ARPA. Santa Monica, Ca.: Rand, Sept. 1961.

8616 ———. *Technical and Political Aspects of Arms Control Negotiation: The 1958 Expert's Conference.* RM–3286–ARPA. Santa Monica, Ca.: Rand, Sept. 1962.

Negotiations—Documents, 1961–1963

8617 U.S. Arms Control & Disarmament Agency. *International Negotiations on Ending Nuclear Weapons Tests, September 1961–September 1962,* ACDA Pub. 9. Washington, D.C.: G.P.O., 1962.

8618 ———. *Review of International Negotiations on the Cessation of Nuclear Weapons Tests, September 1962–September 1965.* Washington, D.C.: G.P.O., 1966.

8619 U.S. Senate. Committee on Foreign Relations. Hearings: *Renewed Geneva Disarmament Negotiations.* 87th Cong., 2d Sess., July 25, Aug. 2, 1962.

8620 ———. Hearings: *Test Ban Negotiations and Disarmament.* 88th Cong., 1st Sess., Mar. 11, 1963.

Negotiations, 1961–1963

8621 "Administration in Center of Test Ban Crossfire." *Congressional Quarterly Weekly Report* (Mar. 1, 1963): 263–72.

8622 Barker, A. J. "The Test Ban and Disarmament." *Army Quarterly* 85 (Oct. 1962): 114–17.

8623 Beam, Jacob D. "A Nuclear Test Ban and Arms Control." *U.S. Department of State Bulletin* (Apr. 1, 1963): 489–93.

8624 "Blasting the Ban." *Time* (Feb. 10, 1961): 16.

8625 "Conversations With the Committee: Excerpts From Hearings Before U.S. Subcommittee on Disarmament." *Bulletin of the Atomic Scientists* 19 (Mar. 1963): 15–18.

8626 Cousins, Norman. "Notes on a 1963 Visit with Khrushchev." *Saturday Review* (Nov. 7, 1964): 16–21, 58–60.

8627 Dean, Arthur H. "United States Considers Question of Suspension of Nuclear and Thermonuclear Tests." *U.S. Department of State Bulletin* (Nov. 26, 1962): 817–24.

8628 "Disarmament and Nuclear Testing." *Current Notes on International Affairs* [Canada] 33 (1962): 5–15.

8629 Foster, William C. "The Nuclear Test Ban Issue." *U.S. Department of State Bulletin* (Mar. 18, 1963): 398–402.

8630 Greenberg, Daniel S. "Test Ban: U.S.S.R., GOP Concur in Opposition to Administration Newest Presented Proposal." *Science* (Aug. 17, 1962): 514–16.

8631 Harriman, W. Averell. "Negotiating a Limited Treaty for Banning Nuclear Tests." *U.S. Department of State Bulletin* (Aug. 19, 1963): 278–83.

8632 Kathinstien, Marion I. "On Atmospheric Testing." *Bulletin of the Atomic Scientists* 18 (Mar. 1962): 34–35.

8633 Kennedy, Pres. John F. "Nuclear Testing and Disarmament." *U.S. Department of State Bulletin* (Mar. 19, 1962): 143–48.

8634 ———. "Report on Progress of Test Ban Talks at Moscow." *U.S. Department of State Bulletin* (Aug. 5, 1963): 198.

8635 Khrushchev, Nikita S. "Khrushchev Speech in East Berlin: Test Ban Proposal." *Current Digest of the Soviet Press* (July 31, 1963): 3–9.

8636 Loosbrock, John F. "What Kind of Test Ban Makes Sense?" *Air Force & Space Digest* 46 (June 1963): 32–33.

8637 McCloy, John J. "Balance Sheet on Disarmament." *Foreign Affairs* 40 (Apr. 1962): 339–59.

8638 Menzies, D. "Soviet Resumption of Nuclear Tests." *Current Notes on International Affairs* [Canada] 32:9 (1961): 32–37.

8639 "The Nuclear Test Ban Issue." *U.S. Department of State Bulletin* (Mar. 18, 1963): 398–402.

8640 Rapoport, Anatol. "New Logic for the Test Ban." *Nation* (Apr. 1, 1961): 280–84.

8641 Rovere, Richard. "Letter From Washington." *New Yorker* (Feb. 4, 1961): 106–12.

8642   Rusk, Dean. "U.S. Efforts to Achieve Safeguarded Test Ban Treaty." *U.S. Department of State Bulletin* (Apr. 1, 1963): 485–89.

8643   ———. "U.S. Urges Soviet Union to Join in Ending Nuclear Weapons Tests." *U.S. Department of State Bulletin* (Apr. 9, 1962): 571–76.

8644   Singer, J. David. "Testing: A Strategic Appraisal." *Nation* (Jan. 13, 1962): 23–27.

8645   Stevenson, Adlai E. "United States Position on Nuclear Testing Explained to the United Nations." *U.S. Department of State Bulletin* (Oct. 29, 1962): 635–41.

8646   "The Suspension of Nuclear Tests." *Current Notes on International Affairs* [Canada] 33:9 (1962): 32–44.

8647   "Test Ban: Choice Between Roles." *Bulletin of the Atomic Scientists* 19 (May 1963): 37–44.

8648   U.S. Department of State. "Draft Treaty on the Discontinuance of Nuclear Weapons Tests Submitted by Western Delegations at Geneva Conference." *U.S. Department of State Bulletin* (June 5, 1961): 870–95.

8649   ———. *The Nuclear Test-Ban Treaty: Gate to Peace.* Pub. 7254. Washington, D.C.: G.P.O., 1961.

8650   ———. "United States and United Kingdom offer New Proposals for Banning Nuclear Tests." *U.S. Department of State Bulletin* (Sept. 17, 1962): 403–16.

8651   Zoppo, Ciro E., and Alice Langley Hsieh. *The Accession of Other Nations to the Nuclear Test Ban.* RM–2730–ARPA. Santa Monica, Ca.: Rand, Mar. 1961.

Inspection & Verification—Documents

8652   U.N. General Assembly. *Report of the Conference of Experts to Study the Possibilities of Detecting Violations of a Possible Agreement on the Suspension of Nuclear Tests.* A/3897. New York, Aug. 28, 1958.

8653   U.S. Department of State. Panel on Seismic Improvement. Report: *The Need for Fundamental Research in Seismology.* Washington, D.C.: G.P.O., July 1959.

8654   U.S. Joint Committee on Atomic Energy. Hearings: *Developments in the Field of Detection and Identification of Nuclear Explosions (Project Vela) and Relationship to Test Ban Negotiations.* 87th Cong., 1st Sess., July 25–27, 1962.

8655   ———. Hearings: *Developments in Technical Capabilities for Detecting and Identifying Nuclear Weapons Tests.* 88th Cong., 1st Sess., Mar. 5–8, 11–12, 1963.

8656   ———. Hearings: *Technical Aspects of Detection and Inspection Controls of a Nuclear Weapons Test Ban.* 2 pts. 86th Cong., 2d Sess., Apr. 18–22, 1960.

8657   ———. Report: *Developments in the Field of Detection and Identification of Nuclear Explosions (Project Vela) and Relationship to Test Ban Negotiations.* 87th Cong., 2d Sess., 1962.

8658   ———. Report: *Technical Aspects of Detection and Inspection Controls of a Nuclear Weapons Test Ban.* 86th Cong., 2d Sess., 1960.

8659   U.S. Senate. Committee on Foreign Relations. Hearings: *Technical Problems and the Geneva Test Ban Negotiations.* 86th Cong., 2d Sess., Feb. 4, 1960.

8660   ———. Staff Study, no. 10: *Control and Reduction of Armaments: Detection of and Inspection for Underground Nuclear Explosions, Replies From Seismologists to Subcommittee Questionnaire.* 85th Cong., 1st Sess., 1958.

Inspection and Verification—General Accounts

8661   "Atomic Detector: How It Would Work." *U.S. News & World Report* (Sept. 5, 1958): 8.

8662   Bohn, Lewis C. "Whose Nuclear Test? Nonphysical Inspection and the Nuclear Test Ban." *Journal of Conflict Resolution* 7:3 (1963): 379–93.

8663   Clemens, Walter C., Jr. *Automated Inspection of Underground Testing.* TAAO 62–5. Santa Barbara, Ca.: General Electric Defense Programs Operation, 1962.

8664   "Detection of Nuclear Explosions." *Science* (Apr. 11, 1958): 805–06.

8665   "Experts' Conclusions on Test Detection." *Bulletin of the Atomic Scientists* 14 (Oct. 1958): 334.

8666   Gauger, Joleroy, et al. *On Detection of an Underground Nuclear Test.* Huntington Beach, Ca.: McDonnell-Douglas Corp., Douglas Advanced Research Laboratories, 1969.

8667   Latter, Albert L. *Concealment of Underground Explosions.* RM–2562–AEC. Santa Monica, Ca.: Rand, Mar. 1960.

8668   ———. *A Method of Concealing Underground Nuclear Explosions.* R–348. Santa Monica, Ca.: Rand, Mar. 1959.

8669   ———. *The Problem of Detecting Nuclear Explosions.* P–2434. Santa Monica, Ca.: Rand, July 1961.

8670   Leet, L. Don. "The Detection of Underground Explosions." *Scientific American* 204 (June 1962): 55–59.

8671   Long, Franklin A. "Impact of VELA Program and Associated Technical Studies of Nuclear Test Ban Proposals." In U.S. Arms Control & Disarmament Agency. *Why a Nuclear Test Ban Treaty?* Washington, D.C.: G.P.O., 1963, pp. 18–38.

8672   Orear, Jay. "Detection of Nuclear Weapons Testing." *Bulletin of the Atomic Scientists* 14 (Mar. 1958): 98–101.

8673   ———. "The Detection of Nuclear Weapons Testing." In Seymour Melman, ed., *Inspection for Disarmament.* New York: Columbia Univ. Press, 1958, pp. 85–99.

8674   ———. "How Feasible is a Test Ban?" *Bulletin of the Atomic Scientists* 15 (Mar. 1959): 99–102.

8675   [Pugwash Committee]. "[Statement on Test Detection]." *Bulletin of the Atomic Scientists* 18 (Nov. 1962): 41.

8676   "Report of the Conference of Experts to Study the Possibility of Detecting Violations of Possible Agreement on the Suspension of Nuclear Tests, August 21, 1958." *U.S. Department of State Bulletin* (Sept. 22, 1958): 453–62.

8677   "Secrecy and Bomb Tests." *New Republic* (Sept. 10, 1956): 8.

8678   "Some Senate Views on Test Ban and Inspection." *Bulletin of the Atomic Scientists* 13 (Sept. 1957): 267.

8679   "Test Bans and the Black Box." *Bulletin of the Atomic Scientists* 19 (Jan. 1963): 34–35.

8680   "U.S. Explores Global Monitoring Methods." *Aviation Week* (May 12, 1958): 26–27.

8681   Wilson, James T. "Underground Shocks." *International Science and Technology* (Jan. 1962): 46–53.

Evaluation of 1963 Treaty

For additional materials on nonsignators, etc., see Nonproliferation Treaty in Chapter 12.

8682   Alsop, Stewart. "Real Meaning of the Test Ban." *Saturday Evening Post* (Sept. 28, 1963): 20.

8683   Americans for National Security. *The Moscow Treaty.* Prepared as a joint project of the research staffs of Americans for National Security and Liberty Lobby. Washington, D.C.: Liberty Lobby, 1963.

8684   Bechhoefer, Bernhard G. "The Test-Ban Treaty: Some Further Considerations." *Bulletin of the Atomic Scientists* 20 (May 1964): 25–27.

8685   Beliaev, K. "The Moscow Treaty: A Real Victory of the Forces For Peace." *Kommunist* 11 (July 1964): 131–39.

8686   "Case For the Test Ban Treaty." *Business Week* (Sept. 7, 1963): 160.

8687   Coffin, Tristram. "The Test Ban." *Correspondent* 28 (July–Aug. 1963): 48–51.

8688   Gottlieb, Sanford. "How Did the Test Ban Happen?" *War/Peace Report* 3 (Nov. 1963): 15–16.

8689   Kennedy, Pres. John F. "The Nuclear Test Ban Treaty: A Step Toward Peace." *U.S. Department of State Bulletin* (Aug. 12, 1963): 234–40.

8690   Kolodziej, Edward A. "What Does the Test Ban Mean?" *Bulletin of the Atomic Scientists* 20 (Mar. 1964): 22–23.

8691   Lippmann, Walter. "Hard Treaty." *Newsweek* (Aug. 19, 1963): 15.

8692   Meany, George. "Test-Ban Treaty: Address, Sept. 2, 1963." *Vital Speeches* (Sept. 15, 1963): 710–12.

8693   Meyer, F. S. "Khrushchev-Kennedy Treaty." *National Review* (Aug. 13, 1963): 107.

8694   "Nonsigners." *Time* (Aug. 23, 1963): 22.

8695   Preston, Richard S. "The Nuclear Test Ban Treaty." *Current History* 46 (June 1964): 341–45.

8696   "Pro and Con of the Test-Ban Treaty: Symposium." *U.S. News & World Report* (Aug. 26, 1963): 54–67.

8697   "Realities of the Test Ban." *Nation* (Sept. 7, 1963): 101.

8698   Rusk, Dean. "The Nuclear Test Ban Treaty: Symbol of a New Course." *U.S. Department of State Bulletin* (Sept. 2, 1963): 350–56.

8699   ———. "Test Ban Treaty: National Security Will be Fully Maintained." *Vital Speeches* (Sept. 1, 1963): 674–77.

8700   "Three Years After Test Ban—Nuclear Race Speeds Up." *U.S. News & World Report* (July 18, 1966): 50–52.

8701   "Toward Peace: Away from War: Test Ban Treaty Initialed." *Newsweek* (Aug. 5, 1963): 15–16.

8702   U.S. Arms Control & Disarmament Agency. *Test Ban Treaty: Questions and Answers.* ACDA Pub. 18. Washington, D.C.: G.P.O., 1965.

8703   ———. *Why a Nuclear Test Ban Treaty?* ACDA Pub. 15. Washington, D.C.: G.P.O., 1963.

8704   "Who Gains in a Test-Ban Treaty?" *U.S. News & World Report* (Aug. 5, 1963): 35–36.

8705   Williams, David C. "Lessons of the Test Ban." *War/Peace Report* 3 (Oct. 1963): 7–8.

8706   Yudin, Y. "The American Business Community and the Treaty." *New Times* [Moscow] (Sept. 4, 1963): 7–9.

U.S. & Ratification

8707   "Big Guns Speak on the Test Ban: Questions and Answer." *Newsweek* (Aug. 26, 1963): 17–18.

8708   "Both Sides of the Test Ban Debate in the Senate." *U.S. News & World Report* (Sept. 30, 1963): 74–75.

8709   Breasted, D. C. "Teller Broadens Attack on Test Ban Agreement." *Missiles and Rockets* (Aug. 26, 1963): 18.

8710   "Bumps on the Ratification Road." *Time* (Aug. 9, 1963): 13–14.

8711   "Bumpy Road in the Senate for Test-Ban Treaty." *U.S. News & World Report* (Sept. 4, 1963): 8.

8712   "Foreign Relations Committee Approves Test Ban Treaty." *Congressional Quarterly Weekly Report* (Aug. 31, 1963): 1516–17.

8713   "From Former President Eisenhower: An O.K. For Test-Ban Treaty, If." *U.S. News & World Report* (Sept. 9, 1963): 24.

8714   "From Washington Straight Senate Ratification." *National Review* (Aug. 27, 1963): 22–28.

8715   Goldwater, Sen. Barry. "Test Ban Treaty." *Vital Speeches* (Oct. 1, 1963): 767–68.

8716   Greenfield, Meg. "Ping Pong on the Potomac." *Reporter* (Sept. 12, 1963): 27–29.

8717   Hosmer, Rep. Craig. "Speaking Out: Beware of the Test Ban." *Saturday Evening Post* (Sept. 7, 1963): 10 ff.

8718   Jackson, Sen. Henry M. "Test Ban: Summing Up." *Reporter* (Sept. 26, 1963): 18.

8719   Johnsen, Katherine. "Power, Senate Unit Voice Test Ban Fears." *Aviation Week* (Sept. 16, 1963): 30–31.

8720   ———. "Senate Committee Calls Test-Ban Small Firm Step to Arms Control." *Aviation Week* (Sept. 16, 1963): 9 ff.

8721   ———. "York, Kistiakowsky Back Test Ban Treaty." *Aviation Week* (Sept. 2, 1963): 22–23.

8722   [Kennedy, Pres. John F.]. "Remarks of the President at the Signing of the Nuclear Test Ban Treaty." *Congressional Quarterly Weekly Report* (Oct. 11, 1963): 178 ff.

8723   "Man Who Challenges the President: Chief Opponent of Test-Ban Treaty." *U.S. News & World Report* (Sept. 2, 1963): 12 ff.

8724   McNamara, Robert S. "Test Ban: The Military Argument." *Bulletin of the Atomic Scientists* 19 (Oct. 1963): 42–43.

8725   "Military Chiefs Give Views on Treaty." *Aviation Week* (Aug. 26, 1963): 29 ff.

8726   "Nuclear Test Ban Treaty Endorsed by Science Advisory Committee." *U.S. Department of State Bulletin* (Sept. 23, 1963): 430–31.

8727 "Nuclear Test Ban Treaty Signed at Moscow: Transmitted to Senate for Advice and Consent to Ratification." *U.S. Department of State Bulletin* (Aug. 26, 1963): 314–19.

8728 "Nuclear Treaty Nears Senate Vote." *Business Week* (Aug. 17, 1963): 26–27.

8729 "Of Treaties and Togas: Concerning Testimony Before the Senate Preparedness Investigating Subcommittee." *Time* (Aug. 30, 1963): 15.

8730 "Ratify the Test Ban Pact!" *Christian Century* (Aug. 14, 1963): 995.

8731 Rovere, Richard. "Letter From Washington: Senate Ratification." *New Yorker* (Oct. 5, 1963): 149–56.

8732 Saltonstall, Sen. Leverett. "Test Ban Treaty: The Military Considerations." *Vital Speeches* (Oct. 1, 1963): 149–56.

8733 "Senate Consents." *Time* (Oct. 4, 1963): 32.

8734 "Senate Roll Call on Test-Ban Treaty." *U.S. News & World Report* (Oct. 7, 1963): 12.

8735 "Senator Dirksen: Vandenberg of the 1960's? Role in Test-Ban Treaty Debate." *U.S. News & World Report* (Sept. 23, 1963): 24.

8736 "Test Ban: Testimony on Technical Aspects to Help Senators Decide If Treaty is a Boon or a Bane." *Science* (Aug. 14, 1963): 618–20.

8737 "Test Ban Treaty: After Signing, a Senate Fight." *Business Week* (July 27, 1963): 17–18.

8738 "Trading Blows on the Test Ban." *Business Week* (Aug. 24, 1963): 27–28.

8739 "Why the Fears Over a Nuclear Test Ban?" *U.S. News & World Report* (Sept. 23, 1963): 39–41.

8740 "Wisdom of Test Ban: McNamara and the Joint Chiefs Differ." *U.S. News & World Report* (Aug. 5, 1963): 36 ff.

Sino-Soviet Conflict & Test Ban

8741 Chiu, Hungdah. "Communist China's Attitude Toward Nuclear Tests." *China Quarterly* 21 (Jan.–Mar. 1965): 96–107.

8742 Clemens, Walter C., Jr. "The Nuclear Test Ban and Sino-Soviet Relations." In Morton H. Halperin, ed., *Sino-Soviet Relations and Arms Control.* Cambridge: M.I.T. Press, 1967, pp. 145–67. See *Orbis* 10 (Spring 1966): 152–83.

8743 Halperin, Morton H. "Sino-Soviet Nuclear Relations, 1957–1960." *Sino-Soviet Relations and Arms Control.* Cambridge: M.I.T. Press, 1967, pp. 117–43.

8744 Hsieh, Alice Langley. *The Chinese Genie: Peking's Role in the Nuclear Test Ban Negotiations.* P–2022. Santa Monica, Ca.: Rand, June 1960.

8745 ———. "The Sino-Soviet Nuclear Dialogue, 1963." *Journal of Conflict Resolution* 8:2 (1964): 99–115.

8746 "Soviet Government Answers Statement by the Chinese Government on Nuclear Test Ban [August 3, 1963]." *Current Digest of the Soviet Press* (Aug. 4, 1963): 4–8.

8747 "Soviet Government Statement [August 21, 1963]." *Current Digest of the Soviet Press* (Aug. 21–22, 1963): 8–13.

8748 "Soviet Government Statement—Reply to Statement Made by the Chinese Government [Sept. 21, 1963]." *Current Digest of the Soviet Press* (Sept. 21, 1963): 3–15.

8749 "Statement by the Spokesman of the Chinese Government: A Comment on the Soviet Government's Statement of August 3." *Peking Review* (Aug. 16, 1963): 16–19.

8750 "Statement by the Spokesman of the Chinese Government: A Comment on the Soviet Government's Statement of August 21." *Peking Review* (Sept. 6, 1963): 7–16.

Test Ban: Next Step

8751 "Beyond the Test Ban." *Commonweal* (Aug. 23, 1963): 491–92.

8752 Brzezinski, Z. "After the Test Ban the United States Must Take the Initiative." *New Republic* (Aug. 31, 1963): 18–21.

8753 Cockcroft, Sir John D. "Extending the Nuclear Test Ban." *Disarmament and Arms Control* 2 (Winter 1963–64): 16–22.

8754 "Cold Peace: The Test Ban and After." *Round Table* 53 (Sept. 1963): 319–21.

8755 "First Step to Where?" *Bulletin of the Atomic Scientists* 19 (Oct. 1963): 2–3.

8756 Healey, Denis. "After the Test Ban Treaty." *New Leader* (Aug. 19, 1963): 6–7.

8757 Inglis, David R. "The Rest of the Test Ban." *Bulletin of the Atomic Scientists* 19 (Dec. 1963): 39–40.

8758 Jacobson, Harold K. "The Test Ban Negotiations: Implications for the Future." *Annals of the Amer. Acad. of Pol. & Soc. Sci.* 351 (Jan. 1964): 92–101.

8759 Meyer, K. E. "After the Test Ban Treaty." *New Statesman* (Aug. 2, 1963): 134 ff.

8760 Walsh, John B. "United Nations, Space Committee Sees Test Ban, U.S.-Soviet Accord as New Footing for Negotiation." *Science* (Sept. 20, 1963): 1164–65.

COMPREHENSIVE NUCLEAR TEST BAN (1974–)

U.S.-U.S.S.R. agreed to a "threshhold" ban on tests of more than 150 kilotons; see U.N., Conference of Committee on Disarmament, Document CCD/431, July 3, 1974.

Documents

8761 U.S. Arms Control & Disarmament Agency. *Treaties on the Limitation of Underground Nuclear Weapon Tests and on Underground Nuclear Explosions For Peaceful Purposes.* Pub. 87. Washington, D.C.: G.P.O., May 1976.

8762 U.S. Senate. Committee on Foreign Relations. Hearings: *Prospects for a Comprehensive Nuclear Test Ban Treaty.* 92d Cong., 1st Sess., July 22–23, 1971.

8763 ———. Hearings: *To Promote Negotiations for a Comprehensive Test Ban Treaty.* 93d Cong., 1st Sess., 1973.

8764 ———. Hearings: *Toward a Comprehensive Nuclear Test Ban Treaty.* 92d Cong., 2d Sess., 1972.

General Accounts

8765 Bazell, Robert J. "Nuclear Tests: Big Amchitka Shot Target of Mounting Opposition." *Science* (June 18, 1971): 1219–21.

8766 Brennan, Donald G. "A Comprehensive Test Ban: Everybody or Nobody." *International Security* 1 (Summer 1976): 92–117.

8767 Buckley, Sen. James L. "Comprehensive Test Ban on Nuclear Tests." *Congressional Record* 118 (May 16, 1972): S7903–04.

8768 Buckley, William F., and James Burnham. "Under the Sign of the Umbrella." *National Review* (Sept. 10, 1973): 180–81.

8769 Carlin, Capt. Robert J. "A 400-Megaton Misunderstanding." *Military Review* (Nov. 1974): 3–12.

8770 "Chen Chu Reaffirms China's Principled Stand on Complete Prohibition, Through Destruction of Nuclear Weapons [and opposes 'test ban']." *Survey of China Mainland Press* (Dec. 21, 1971): 85–86.

8771 "Chinese Representative Speaks on Preservation of Marine Environment, Prohibition of Nuclear Testing." *Survey of China Mainland Press* (Aug. 15, 1972): 93–95.

8772 Federation of American Scientists. "Test Ban: Presuppositions of Successful Negotiation." *F.A.S. Public Interest Report* (June 1976): 1–6.

8773 Finney, John W. "Experimental Moratorium on Underground Tests?" *New Republic* (July 16, 1966): 10–11.

8774 Foster, William C. "Ban All Nuclear Testing." *Atlantic Community Quarterly* 9 (Summer 1971): 174–83.

8775 Gillette, Robert. "Arms Control: U.S., Soviets Revive Threshold Test Ban Talks." *Science* (May 17, 1974): 774–76.

8776 Halsted, Thomas A. "Why Not a Real Nuclear Test Ban?" *Arms Control Today* 6 (June 1976): 1–2.

8777 Hosmer, Rep. Craig. "On Comprehensive Test Bans." *Congressional Record* 117 (June 30, 1971): H23107–109.

8778 Ignatieff, George. "How Much is Enough? A Report on Nuclear Testing?" *Vista* 7:4 (1972): 14–20.

8779 Kennedy, Sen. Edward M. "Senate Resolution 163: Submission of a Resolution Calling on the President to Promote Negotiations For a Test Ban Treaty." *Congressional Record* 121 (May 20, 1975): S8679–80.

8780 Lall, Betty G. "A Comprehensive Nuclear Test Ban Treaty." *International Conciliation*, no. 587 (Mar. 1972): 17–38.

8781 Leary, Frank. "Underground Nuclear Testing: Is It Getting Too Dangerous?" *Armed Forces Management* 16 (Mar. 1970): 32–36.

8782 Mastny, Vojtech, ed. *Disarmament & Nuclear Tests, 1964–1967.* New York: Facts on File, 1970.

8783 Myers, Henry R. "Comprehensive Test Ban Treaty: Grounds For Objection Diminish." *Science* (Jan. 21, 1972): 283–86.

8784 ———. "Extending the Nuclear-Test Ban." *Scientific American* 226 (Jan. 1972): 12–23.

8785 Neild, Robert. *The Test Ban.* Stockholm: SIPRI, Nov. 1971.

8786 ———, and J. D. Ruina. "A Comprehensive Ban on Nuclear Testing." *Science* (Jan. 14, 1972): 140–46.

8787 "Nuclear Test Offer." *Aviation Week & Space Technology* (Mar. 22, 1976): 13.

8788 "Nuclear Test Suspension." *U.N. Monthly Chronicle* 2 (Dec. 1965): 46–52.

8789 "Playing With Dice on Amchitka." *Nature* [London] (Oct. 11, 1969): 98–99.

8790 Scoville, Herbert, Jr. "A New Look at a Comprehensive Nuclear Test Ban." *Stanford Journal of International Studies* 7 (Spring 1972): 45–63.

8791 Shestov, V. "For a Total End to Nuclear Weapons Tests." *International Affairs* [Moscow] 20 (Dec. 1974): 33–40.

8792 Siegal, Charles D. "Proposals for a True Comprehensive Nuclear Test Ban Treaty." *Stanford Law Review* 27 (Jan. 1975): 387–418.

8793 "That Nuclear Explosion Treaty." *NATO's Fifteen Nations* 21 (Aug.–Sept. 1976): 17–18.

8794 Tomilin, Y. "On Banning Underground Nuclear Tests." *International Affairs* [Moscow] 18 (Mar. 1972): 73–77.

8795 Viktorov, V. "Ten Years of the Moscow Treaty." *International Affairs* [Moscow] 19 (Sept. 1973): 32–37.

8796 Willis, Paul. "New Hope for an Underground Test Ban." *War/Peace Report* 6 (June–July 1966): 20.

8797 York, Herbert F. "The Great Test-Ban Debate." *Scientific American* 227 (Nov. 1972): 15–23.

Threshold Treaty Assessed

8798 Barnaby, Frank. "Nuclear Test Ban's Last Chance?" *New Scientist* (Apr. 1, 1976): 11–12.

8799 Carter, Luther J. "Nuclear Testing: U.S.-Soviet Treaties Viewed With Doubts and Misgivings." *Science* (June 18, 1976): 1217–18.

8800 Chayes, Abram, et al. "Threshold Treaty: A Step Backward." *Bulletin of the Atomic Scientists* 31 (Jan. 1975): 16.

8801 Drummond, Roscoe. "A Plea for Nuclear Disarmament." *Saturday Review* (Apr. 17, 1976): 11–12.

8802 Gillette, Robert. "Arms Control Report Card Nuclear Treaty: Fatal Flaw." *Science* (Sept. 5, 1975): 772.

8803 Thorsson, Inga. ["Analysis of Threshold Test Ban"]. *Bulletin of Peace Proposals* 4:4 (1974): 296–97 ff.

8804 "Time to Speak Out Against Cosy Bilateralism." *Nature* [London] (Jan. 15, 1976): 71.

Inspection & Verification

8805 Bolt, Bruce A. *Nuclear Explosions and Earthquakes: The Parted Veil.* San Francisco: Freeman, 1976.

8806 Farley, Philip J. "The Advantages of a Comprehensive Nuclear Test Ban and the Question of Verification." *U.S. Department of State Bulletin* (Aug. 16, 1971): 182–85.

8807 Gillette, Robert. "Nuclear Testing Violations: Keeping It All in the Family." *Science* (Aug. 9, 1974): 506–10.

8808 "Hosmer Warns of 'Cheat' Testing Peril." *Technology Week* (Jan. 9, 1967): 16.

8809 Lgaard, P. L. "Verifying a Comprehensive Test Ban." *Survival* 14 (July–Aug. 1972): 162–68.

8810 "New Violations of Soviet Nuclear Test Limit?" *Science* (Oct. 8, 1976): 168.

8811 "Nuclear Explosion Treaties Jeopardized by Loophole." *Aviation Week & Space Technology* (June 8, 1976): 21–22.

8812 Prawitz, Jan, and Ulf Ericsson. "A Test Detection Club." *Disarmament and Arms Control* 3 (Autumn 1965): 184–87.

8813 SIPRI. "The Test Ban." *SIPRI Yearbook 1972: World Armament and Disarmament.* New York: Humanities Press, 1972, pp. 389–436.

8814 U.S. Congress. Joint Committee on Atomic Energy. Hearings: *Request for Supplemental Fiscal Year 1975 Funds for AEC Nuclear Weapons Testing.* 93d Cong., 2d Sess., 1974.

8815 ———. Hearings: *Status of Current Technology to Identify Seismic Events as Natural or Man-Made.* 92d Cong., 1st Sess., Oct. 27–28, 1971.

8816 ———. Report: *Status of Current Technology to Identify Seismic Events as Natural or Man-Made.* 92d Cong., 1st Sess., 1971.

8817 "USSR Nuclear Blasts Labeled Violation." *Aviation Week & Space Technology* (Oct. 18, 1976): 24.

8818 Wade, Nicholas. "Earthquake Accord and the Test Ban." *Science* (Oct. 6, 1972): 38.

Detecting Underground Explosions

Items listed below represent only a fraction of those published; see indexes to technical journals and *Arms Control & Disarmament: A Quarterly Bibliography.*

8819 Basham, P. W., et al. "An Analysis of the 'Banham' Aftershock Sequence Using Canadian Recordings." *Journal of Geophysical Research* (Mar. 10, 1970): 1545–56.

8820 "Breakthrough in Test Detection." *Scientific American* 212 (Mar. 1965): 54.

8821 Bullard, Sir Edward. "Detecting Underground Explosions." *Survival* 9 (Feb. 1967): 38–46.

8822 ———. "The Detection of Underground Explosions." *Scientific American* 215 (July 1966): 19–29.

8823 Carter, Luther J. "Test Detection: Decoupling Theory Verified, But Does it Matter?" *Science* (Jan. 27, 1967): 438–40.

8824 Davies, David. *Seismic Methods for Monitoring Underground Explosions.* New York: Humanities Press, 1971.

8825 "Detecting Underground Nuclear Explosions at Last?" *Nature* [London] (Sept. 3, 1971): 8.

8826 "The Limits of Seismology." *Nature* [London] (Nov. 5, 1971): 6–7.

8827 Molnar, Peter, et al. "Small Earthquakes and Explosions in Western North America Recorded by New High Gain, Long Period Seismographs." *Nature* [London] (Dec. 27, 1969): 1268–73.

8828 "Nuclear Test Blast Under Grand Tatum Salt Dome Proves that Some Explosions can be Muffled." *Business Week* (Jan. 7, 1967): 100.

8829 Sisemore, Clyde J., et al. "Project Sterling: Subsurface Phenomenology Measurements Near a Decoupled Nuclear Event." *Journal of Geophysical Research* (Dec. 15, 1969): 6623–37.

8830 Verguese, Dominique. "Detection of Underground Nuclear Explosions." *Disarmament* 15 (Sept. 1967): 9–11 ff.

Special Issues: French Testing

8831 Barrera, V. Humberto. "Detonacion de Bombas Nucleares en el Pacifico Sur." *R. Chilena de Historia* 139 (1971): 190–98.

8832 D'Amato, Anthony A. "Legal Aspects of the French Nuclear Tests." *American Journal of International Law* 61 (Jan. 1967): 66–77.

8833 Dyer, Colin. "French Attitudes to Nuclear Experiments in the South Pacific, 1971–1973." *Australian Outlook* 27 (Aug. 1973): 172–78.

8834 Evans, Alona E. "Judicial Decisions: Nuclear Test Case [Australia v. France]." *American Journal of International Law* 69 (July 1975): 558–683.

8835 Franck, Thomas M. "Word Made Law: The Decision of the International Court of Justice in the Nuclear Test Cases." *American Journal of International Law* 69 (July 1975): 612–20.

8836 Higgins, Rosalyn. "French Tests and the International Court." *World Today* 29 (July 1973): 277–80.

8837 Holyoake, Keith. "French Nuclear Tests H-Bomb Explosion." *External Affairs Review* [New Zealand] 18 (Aug. 1968): 48–49.

8838 "International Court of Justice: Resolution Concerning the Nuclear Test Cases." *International Legal Materials* 13 (May 1974): 613–14.

8839 Mercer, A. G. "International Law and the French Nuclear Weapons Tests." *Pacific View-Point* 9 (May 1968): 51–68.

8840 "Nuclear Test Case [Australia v. France]: Order Concerning Interim Measures." *International Legal Materials* 12 (July 1973): 749–73.

Special Issues: Radiation Problems

8841 Brown, Bruce. "Atmospheric Nuclear Testing: A Survey of Medical Statistics in Australia." *Bulletin of the Atomic Scientists* 30 (Feb. 1974): 13–15.

8842 "A Government Survey of Atom-Bomb Survivors." *Japan Quarterly* 14 (July–Sept. 1967): 278–83.

8843 Hamilton, L. D. "On Radiation Standards." *Bulletin of the Atomic Scientists* 28 (Mar. 1972): 30–33.

8844 Sagan, Leonard A. "Nuclear Testing and Infant Deaths." *Current* 113 (Dec. 1969): 62 ff.

8845 Shimizu, Kiyoshi. "Little-Known Effects of the Bomb." *Japan Quarterly* 14 (Jan.–Mar. 1967): 93–98.

8846 Sternglass, E. J. "Nuclear Testing and Infant Deaths." *Current* 110 (Sept. 1969): 12–15.

8847 "Underground Nuclear Testing." *Environment* 11 (July–Aug. 1969): 2–13 ff.

Indexes

*Prepared by Frances R. Burns and Richard Dean Burns III

*Prepared by Frances R. Burns and Richard Dean Burns III

Arms Control and Disarmament was prepared for composition
and copy edited by Paulette Wamego;
typographical design by Shelly Lowenkopf; proofreading by Barbara Phillips;
cover design by Jack Swartz.
Composition by Graphic Typesetting Service, Los Angeles;
Printing and binding by R. R. Donnelley and Sons Co.,
Crawfordsville, Ind.